Reference Library of
BLACK
AMERICA

Reference Library of

BLACK AMERICA

VOLUME

Edited by
L. Mpho Mabunda

Multiculture In Print

Reference Library of Black America is based upon the seventh edition of *The African American Almanac,* published by Gale Research. It has been published in this 5-volume set to facilitate wider usage among students.

Linda Hubbard, *Managing Editor*
L. Mpho Mabunda, *Editor*
David G. Oblender, *Associate Editor*
Beth Baker, Craig Barth, Dawn Berry, Gene Brady, Carol Brennan, Melissa Walsh Doig, DeWitt S. Dykes, Jr., Kimberly Burton Faulkner, Simon Glickman, Joyce Harrison, Bob Jacobson, Carmen Johnson, Michael Knes, Jeffrey Lehman, Sipho C. Mabunda, William J. Moses, Anna Sheets, David Sprinkle, Stephen Stratton, Chris Tower, Aaron Turley, *Contributing Editors*

George Hobart, *Photo Researcher*

Marlene Hurst, *Permissions Manager*
Margaret McAvoy-Amato,*Permissions Assistant*

Victoria B. Cariappa, *Research Manager*
Barbara McNeil, Andrew Guy Malonis, Gary J. Oudersluys, *Research Specialists*
Norma Sawaya, Cheryl L. Warnock, *Research Associates*
Laura C. Bissey, *Research Assistant*

Mary Beth Trimper, *Production Director*
Evi Seoud, *Assistant Production Manager*
Shanna Heilveil, *Production Assistant*

Cynthia Baldwin, *Art Director*
Barbara J. Yarrow, *Graphic Services Supervisor*
Mark C. Howell, *Cover Designer*
Arthur Chartow, *Page Designer*
C.J. Jonik, *Desktop Publisher*
Randy Bassett, *Image Database Supervisor*
Robert Duncan, Mikal Ansari, *Imaging Specialists*
Pamela Hayes, *Photographic Coordinator*

Benita L. Spight, *Data Entry Supervisor*
Gwendolyn S. Tucker, *Data Entry Group Leader*
Beverly Jendrowski, *Senior Data Entry Associate*

The paper used in this publication meets the minimum requirements of American National Standard for Information Sciences—Permanence Paper for Printed Library Materials, ANSI Z 39.48-1984.

ISBN 0-7876-1536-6 (Vol. 2)

Printed in the United States of America

Advisory Board

Contributors

Stephen W. Angell
Associate Professor of Religion, Florida A&M University

Robin Armstrong
Adjunct Lecturer, University of Michigan, Dearborn

Claudette Bennett
Bureau of the Census, United States Department of Commerce

Allen G. Harris
President, Air Force Association, General Daniel James Chapter

Hayward Derrick Horton
Assistant Professor of Sociology, Iowa State University

George Johnson
Professor of Law, Howard University School of Law

Faustine C. Jones-Wilson
Professor of Education, Howard University; Editor, *The Journal of Negro Education*

Donald Franklin Joyce
Director, Felix G. Woodward Library, Austin Peay State University

Mark Kram
Sportswriter, *Philadelphia Daily News*

Robyn M. Lupa
Assistant Branch Manager, Middle Village, Queens Borough Public Library

Doris H. Mabunda
Director of Youth Programs, YWCA-Grand Rapids, MI

Ionis Bracy Martin
Lecturer, Central Connecticut State University

Marilyn Hortense Mackel
Associate Professor, Western State University College of Law,
Judge Pro Tempore, Los Angeles County Superior Court, Juvenile Department

Dan Morgenstern
Director, Institute for Jazz Studies, Rutgers University

Wilson J. Moses
Professor of History, Pennsylvania State University

Richard Prince
National Association of Black Journalists

Floyd Thomas, Jr.
Curator of Fine Art and Military History, National Afro-American Museum and Cultural Center

Michael D. Woodard
Director, Los Angeles Institute for Multicultural Training;
Visiting Scholar, UCLA Center for Afro-American Studies

Contents

Volume 3

Volume 4

Volume 5

Introduction

The Reference Library of Black America is based on the seventh edition of *The African American Almanac*, first published in 1967 as *The Negro Almanac* and since cited by *Library Journal* as an outstanding reference work.

New Features in This Edition

All material was extensively reviewed by the editor and a board of prominent advisors, and, where appropriate, updated and/or expanded. In many instances, completely new topics were added to existing essays. Some chapters were totally rewritten to focus on issues facing contemporary African Americans. The most significant changes include the expansion of chapters three ("Significant Documents"), five ("Africa and the Black Diaspora"), 15 ("The Family"), and 19 ("Media"); and the revision of key essays within chapter ten ("Law"), chapter 11 ("Politics"), chapter 16 ("Education"), chapter 22 ("Blues and Jazz"), chapter 23 ("Popular Music"), chapter 24 ("Fine and Applied Arts"), chapter 25 ("Science and Medicine"); chapter 26 ("Sports"), and chapter 27 ("Military"). All 27 chapters were also made as current as possible, including chapter one ("Chronology") and chapter 2 ("African American Firsts").

Anyone familiar with earlier editions will be excited to find such new features such as a chronology current to April of 1996; coverage of newly anointed African American pioneers from 1994 and 1995; inclusion of "The Million Man March Mission Statement;" more and more useful information regarding the black diaspora; more extensive information regarding the origins of those enslaved in America; an essay on the history of federal judges in the United States; a brief history of African American involvement in the political system along with a list of addresses for current Congressional Black Caucus members; more profiles of trailblazing entrepreneurs both current and historical; coverage of more topics related to health and increased discussion of such issues related to family as marriage; a complete listing of African American chaired professors and endowed university chairs; summarization of the rash of black church fires; an accounting of black involvement on the information superhighway, including a list of more than 30 World Wide Web sites of interest to African Americans; new information on African American craft art, the Black Arts movement, and the role of historically black learning institutions in the preservation and presentation of African American art; more about black contributions to science and technology; more dynamic discussion of African American military participation in the Revolutionary War as well as the wars in Vietnam and the Persian Gulf; and better coverage of the blues, popular music, and sports.

Content and Arrangement

Information in this edition appears in 27 subject chapters. Many chapters open with an essay focusing on historical developments or the contributions of African Americans to the subject area, followed by concise biographical profiles on selected individuals. Although the listees featured in this set represent only a small portion of the African American community, they embody excellence and diversity in their respective fields of endeavor. Where an individual has made a significant contribution in more than one area, his or her biographical profile appears in the subject area for which he or she is best known.

In order to facilitate further research, a bibliography is provided at the end of each volume of *The Reference Library of Black America*. The bibliography has been divided into two major divisions: "Africana" and "African Americana." Within these two divisions titles are arranged alphabetically by author under categories indicative of their subject matter.

Three appendixes provide timely information of special interest to students. The first lists African American winners of many popular and professional awards. The second identifies all the medalists at the centennial Olympic Games celebrated in Atlanta in 1996. The final one guides students in selecting a suitable college or university from among the many historically black institutions profiled in the same section.

More than five hundred maps and illustrations aid the reader in understanding the topics and people covered in the work. A name and keyword index provides access to the contents of the entire set.

Africa and the Black Diaspora

5

Africa and the Black Diaspora

◆ A Brief History of Africa ◆ The Modern Day People of Africa ◆ Blacks in the Western Hemisphere ◆ Country Profiles

by Kenneth Estell, Doris H. Mabunda, and Lorna M. Mabunda

According to renowned Kenyan scholar Dr. Ali Mazrui, modern Africa has been heavily influenced by three main forces—indigenous traditions, the tenants of Islam, and Western culture, including Christianity—with both positive and negative results. Among the benefits are a strong sense of continuity and regard for heritage, moral order, and membership in the global village. However, the mingling of such dynamic and divergent threads has caused a clash of cultures, with an aftermath of "inefficiency, mismanagement, corruption, and decay of the infrastructure." (Ali Mazrui, The Africans: A Triple Heritage, *1986, p. 12.)*

◆ A BRIEF HISTORY OF AFRICA

Archeologists have come to believe that early humans, *Hominidea*, originated in Africa some two to three million years and migrated to other continents. By the Middle Stone Age, three distinct groups had evolved—Bushmanoid, Pygmoid, and Negroid. Only a few Bushmen, and related Hottentot people, are still found in parts of the south-west portion of the continent, while a few isloated Pygmy groups have survived, mainly in the Congo forests. However, it was the Negroid group which became dominant on the continent.

Sophisticated societies developed in early Africa, among them the Kush, between 700 B.C. and A.D. 200 and the ancient Ghana, Kanen, Mali Songhai, and the Haissa states. In the Congo, the Kingdoms of Lunda, Lula, Bushong, and Kongo were founded, probably between the sixteenth and eighteenth centuries. On the Guinea Coast, the city states of Benin, Ite, Oyo, Ashanti, and Yoruba date back to the fifteenth century. These states traded extensively in gold, ivory, salt, and livestock.

Trade with Europe began around the fifteenth century, with the slave trade an important part; an estimated ten to 30 million people were sold into slavery by the mid-nineteenth century. The interior of Africa was first exposed to Europeans in the eighteenth century by missionaries, traders, and adventurers. Reports of the continent's resources eventually spurred European conquest and direct control of virtually all of Africa. By 1900 only Ethiopia and Liberia, remained free of European control.

In 1910 the British granted dominion status to the Union of South Africa. However, independence for the black-dominated regions of Africa, did not come until some 40 years later. In 1957, independence movements started with a rush in Kenya, Ghana, and Guinea. By the late 1960s most of Africa had achieved independence.

◆ THE MODERN DAY PEOPLE OF AFRICA

Geography

The second largest continent on the globe, Africa is bisected by the equator and bordered to the west by the Atlantic Ocean and to the east by the Indian Ocean. Roughly the shape of an inverted triangle—with a large bulge on its northwestern end and a small horn on its eastern tip—it contains 52 countries and six islands that, together, make up about 20 percent of the world's land mass, or 11.5 million square miles.

Africa is essentially a huge plateau divided naturally into two sections. Northern Africa, a culturally and historically Mediterranean region, includes the Sahara desert—the world's largest expanse of desert, coming close to the size of the United States. Sub-Saharan, or so-called "Black Africa," also contains some desert

Cyrille Adoula, Jomo Kenyatta, and other members of the Pan-African Movement for East and Central Africa meet, 1962.

land, but is mainly tropical, with rain forests clustered around the equator; vast savanna grasslands covering more than 30 percent of continent and surrounding the rain forests on the north, east, and south; some mountainous regions; and rivers and lakes that formed from the natural uplifting of the plateau's surface.

Notable geographical marvels in Africa include Mts. Kenya and Kilamanjaro (the latter of whose highest peak is one of the tallest in the world); the rivers Niger, Senegal, Congo, Zambezi (home of the mile-wide Victoria Falls, one of the world's seven natural wonders), Orange, Limpopo, Malawi, and Nile (the longest river in the world); Tanganyika, Albert, Rudolf, and Victoria (the second largest freshwater body in the world) lakes; and the Libyan, Nubian, and Kalahari deserts.

Economics/Natural Resources

A mineral rich continent, Africa is the pristine source of copper, diamonds, gold, manganese, oil, uranium, zinc, and several other deposits. The equatorial forests produce ebony, teak, and rosewood, while cash crops like bananas, cocoa, coffee, cloves, cotton, sisal, sugar cane, tobacco, yams, and all kinds of nuts, including cashews and groundnuts. In fact, agriculture has formed the basis of most African economies for centuries. Despite such a wealth of resources, many African nations rank amongst the poorest in the world. Tribal and political wars, illiteracy, droughts, lack of technological prowess, and the commonality of corruption among government officials all contribute to the weak economy encountered in much of the continent.

Though Africa does have booming urban and industrial centers—for example, Johannesburg, South Africa; Lagos, Nigeria; Dakar, Senegal; Harare, Zimbabwe—the continent is better known to visitors for the national parks and reserves of East and Southern Africa. Wildlife concentrations in these locations vary but include antelope, impala, Thompson's gazelles, and wildebeests; buffalo, hippos, and rhinos; elephants; giraffes; zebras; crocodiles; a variety of bird species; hyenas, jackels, and wild dogs; and "big cats," i.e. cheetahs, jaguars, leopards, lions, and tigers.

Kenya, located in East Africa, is one of the oldest and most popular game-viewing destinations for safari-seeking tourists. The Samburu National Reserve, Lake Nakuru (also known as the "pink lake" because of an abundance of flamingos), Masai Mara National Re-

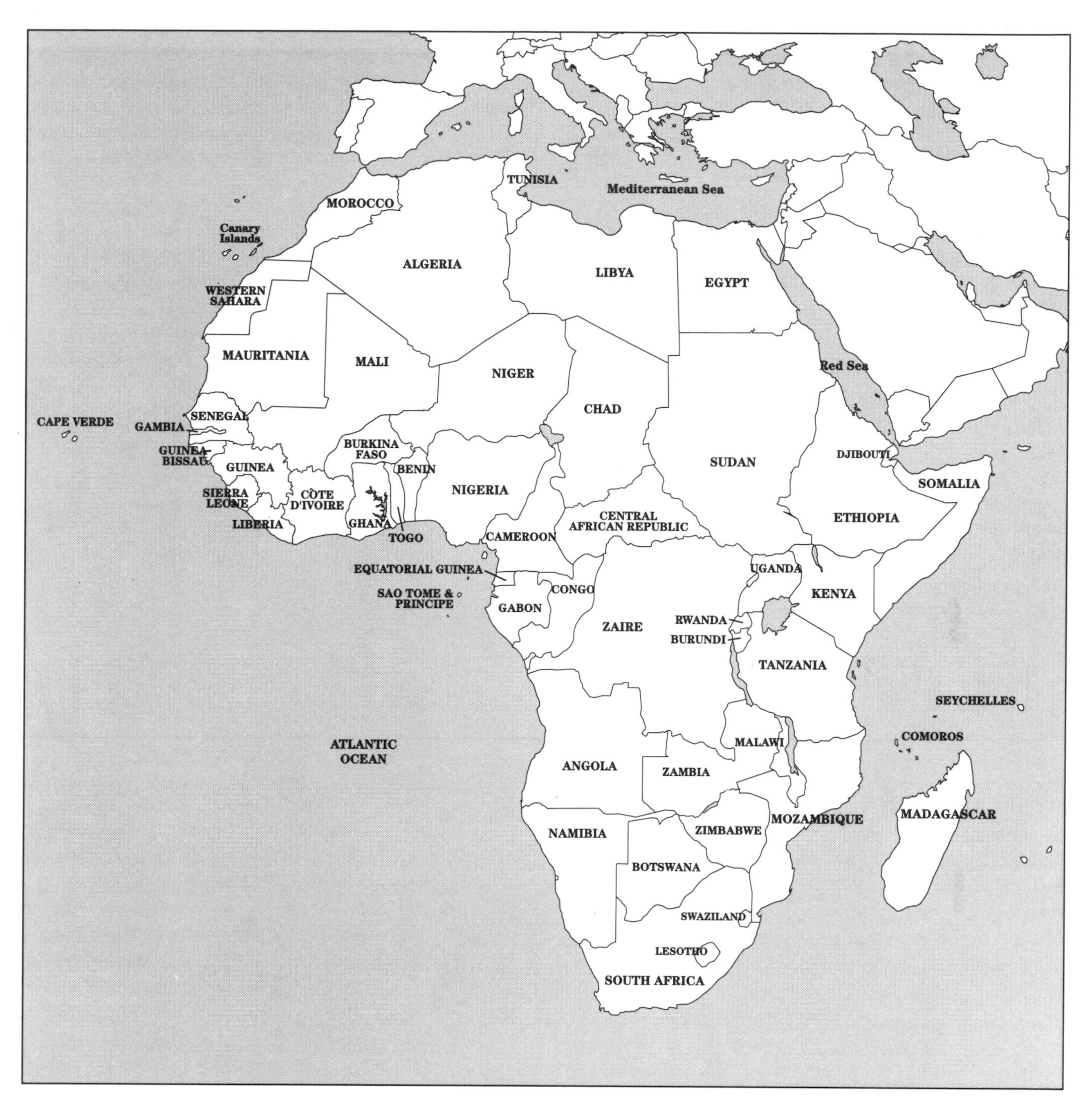

Africa.

serve, and Amboseli, are all favored spots. Nearby, Tanzania offers Lake Manyara National Park, Serengeti National Park, and Ngorongoro Crater (a natural amphitheatre that formed by the collapse of a volcano). Uganda features Bwindi Forest, home of the Buhoma Gorilla Camp. In the southern region of Africa, South Africa contains ostrich farms; Kruger National Park, one of the continent's largest reserves; Cango Caves; and Kirstenbosch Botanical Gardens. Zimbabwe contributes man-made Lake Kariba, a permanent water source for monkeys, warthogs, waterbuck, and other species, including birds; Hwange, a game reserve filled with more than 107 species; and the Zambezi Nature Sanctuary and Crocodile Farm.

Population

The African population is most heavily concentrated in Nigeria, southern Ghana, along the Gulf of Guinea, Benin and Togo, the Nile Valley, in northern Sudan, the East Africa highlands of Ethiopia, Kenya, and Tanzania, eastern Zaire, the eastern and southern coasts, and the inland High Veld of South Africa. The desert and mountain regions are largely uninhabited.

In recent years the population of Africa has grown rapidly. In 1950 the total population was estimated at 281 million; by 1990 the population had reached 817 million, making it the third most populous continent on the planet. No African nation has developed an effective population control program, and such practices as having multiple wives and early marriages continue. By the year 2020, the population of Sub-Sharan Africa alone is expected to reach 1.2 billion.

Until recently, almost 90 percent of Africa's population lived in rural areas. African cities with populations exceeding one million include Accra, Ghana; Addis Ababa, Ethiopia; Cape Town and Johannesburg, South Africa; Cairo, Egypt; Maputo, Mozambique; Ibadan and Lagos, Nigeria; and Kinshasa, Zaire. In addition to indigenous Africans, about 5 million people are of predominantly European descent, and 1 million are of Asian descent.

During a 1959 archaeological expedition in Olduvai Gorge, Tanzania, Kenyan-born anthropologist L. S. B. Leakey and his wife Mary discovered a skull of a species thought to date back more than 2 million years called Australopithecus boisei, Zinjanthropus, *or "Nutcracker Man" in popular vernacular. Within the next ten years they unearthed* Homo habilis, *also estimated to date between 1.5 to 2 million years ago, and* Kenyapithecus africanus. *Fossils of early hominoids resembling man have been found in Ethiopia, Kenya, and South Africa by other scientists. The remains are believed to be predecessors of our own human species,* Homo sapiens.

A Malian woman pounding grain.

Language

The diversity of Africa's people is underscored by the existence of more than 2,000 languages and dialects, including africanized forms of English, French, and Portugues. Some 50 major languages are spoken by groups of one million or more people. The major language groups include Arabic (spoken mainly in north Africa), Fula, Hausa, Lingala, Malinke, Nguni (which includes SiNdebele, Xhosa, and Zulu), SeTwana-SeSotho, Swahili, and Yoruba.

"African-language" names are often derived from the names of the ethnic tribes that speak them. For example, Zulu is spoken primarily by Zulus and Kibondi is the language of the Bondi tribe. Swahili, the most widely spoken language on the continent, is the only one that breaks the pattern. A commercial language originally used among traders and business people, it evolved from Portuguese, Arabic, and Bantu.

As many languages were never translated into written form, Africa acquired a very long and rich oral tradition—in many cases, the only method of passing literature and history from generation to generation in ancient times. After the fourteenth century, the use of Arabic by educated Muslim blacks was extensive, and some oral literature was subsequently reduced to a more permanent written form. But, in spite of the Arab influence, the oral heritage of Africans remained strong, serving not only as an educational device, but as a guide for the administration of government and the conduct of religious ceremonies.

A wealth of proverbs from African culture have survived through the generations. Some of the more popular ones are: If you want to know the end, look at the beginning; When one door closes, another one opens; If we stand tall it is because we stand on the backs of those who came before us; Two men in a burning house must not stop to argue; Where you sit when you are old shows where you stood in youth; You must live within your sacred truth; The one who asks questions doesn't lose his way; If you plant turnips you will not harvest grapes; God makes three requests of his children: Do the best you can, where you are, with what you have now; You must act as if it impossible to fail; Some would be great drinkers but they haven't got the wine; some great eaters but they haven't got the food.

Some of Africa's best known authors include Cameroon's Mongo Beti; Ghana's Ayi Kwei Armah and J. E. Casely-Hayford; Kenya's Ngugi wa Thiong'o; Lesoto's Thomas Mofolo; Nigeria's Chinua Achebe, Wole Soyinka, Amos Tutuola, and Ken Saro-Wiwa; Senegal's Sembène Ousmane and Léopold Sédar Senghor; Somali's Nuruddin Farah; South Africa's Bessie Head, Ezekiel Mphahlele, and Lewis Nkosi; Uganda's Okot p'Bitek; and Zimbabwe's Dennis Brutus.

Unfortunately for prose writers, freedom of the press is a scarce commodity in much of Africa, with many of those who dare to report the truth about government corruption or abuse of human rights being forced into exile or constantly threatened and harrassed if they stay. For that reason, many Africans learn more about their neighbors—both locally and continentally—through Western media. But among Africa's most courageous and well-respected journalists are Liberia's Kenneth Y. Best and Issac Bantu, Ghana's Ben Ephson, and South Africa's Percy Qoboza.

Music

Despite the Western stereotype that associates the beating of tribal drums with the whole of "traditional" music, African music is incredibly diverse and reflective of the vast array of peoples, cultures, and traditions. Confined to localities, some of the world's greatest and most unheralded musicians—many self-taught—play to crowds in Africa. In the past few decades, "cross-over" artists have breached the boundaries of their homeland to win acclaim and fans in the United States and Europe. The irony is that these so-called "African superstars" may not even be stars in their own countries, let alone on the rest of the continent.

Nonetheless, many contemporary American forms such as blues and jazz have been heavily influenced by African styles and polyrhythms carried over by slaves. In fact the African lute evolved into the modern day guitar. Guitars form the basis of *benga* music (popular in Kenya); *juju* (a Nigerian music replete with talking drums and vocal call and response); palm wine music (an acoustic form popular in regions of West Africa, where palm wine is a favorite elixir); highlife (a jazzy, complex West African dance music punctuated by horns); and *soukous* (derived by the French word for "shake," a peppy dance form originating mainly in Zaire and the Congo). Percussion-based music includes *apala* (a street-form emergent from Islamic music); *mbalax* (a modern dance style popularized in Senegal); and *jit* (a Zimbabwean hybrid of traditional *chimurenga* guitar, disco-style drum beats, highlife, and *soukous*). *Kora* features a 21-string harp, *kwela* incorporates a penny whistle, and *mbira* got its moniker from the Zimbabwean name for a finger piano. Cameroonians may jive to *makossa* while those in Sierre Leone pop their fingers to milo jazz and Cape Verdeans release their troubles with the deep blues of *morna*. South Africans may party to *mbaquanga* on one night and get spiritual with the choral vocals of *mbube* the next. Permutations of once solely African music include *salsa* (Spanish folk music combined with African drums and Cuban rhythms), *soca* (African music with a heady dose of English and Latin folk music), and *zouk* (a mix of French, African, and Guadeloupian music).

Some of Africa's biggest artists, "cross-over" or otherwise include Angola's Kuenda Bonga (a political-minded singer-songwriter); Burkino Faso's Farafina (a group led by balafon *virtuoso Mahama Konaté); Cape Verde's Cesaria Evora ("The Barefoot Diva"); Gabon's Pierre Akendengue (a blind singer, guitarist, poet, and playwright); Guinea's Bembeya Jazz National (featuring Sekou "Diamond Fingers" Diabate); Mali's Toumani Diabate (considered the world's greatest* kora *player), Oumou Sangare (the country's favorite female "praise singer") and Ali Farka Toure ("The Bluesman of Mali"); Nigeria's King Sunny Ade ("The King of* Juju *") and Fela Anikulapo Kuti (an outspoken social critic, pianist, saxophonist, and singer), Sierre Leone's Abdul Tee-Jay (a London-based studio guitarist adept at several forms, including highlife,* soukous, makossa, *and* soca*); South Africa's Ladysmith Black Mambazo (an* a capella *group led by tenor vocalist Joseph Shabalala), Mahlathini (legendary, deep voiced "King of the Groaners"), the Mahotella Queens (*mbaqanga *mavens), Miriam Makeba ("The Empress of African Song"), Hugh Masekela (trumpet– and flugelhorn–playing jazz legend), West Nkosi (multi-talented musician, arranger, producer, and bandleader), and The*

Soul Brothers (one of the nation's biggest selling groups); Tanzania's Zuhura Swaleh (a female taarab *singer); Zaire/Congo's 4 Etoiles (featuring* soukous *guitarist Syran Mbenza), Les Bantous (a* rhumba *band), Mbilia Bel (one of Africa's most successful female singers), Tshala Muana ("Queen of* Mutuashi,*" a dance form), Tabu Ley (a* soukous *master), Papa Wemba (one of the world's greatest singers), and Zap Mama (an all-female group led by poet Marie Daulne); and Zimbabwe's Thomas Mapfumo (credited with having created* chimurenga, *or liberation music) and Stella Chiweshe ("The Queen of* Mbira*").*

Family

Family is the social backbone of Africa. Within most African cultures, family impacts all realms of day to day living, both politically and economically. Familial obligations are not restricted just to immediate family; tribal conflict notwithstanding, in Africa each individual is regarded as a dear cousin. In fact, the Western method of breaking familial relationships down to degree's—e.g. first cousin, second aunt, great-great grandfather twice removed—is virtually nonexistent. Either two people are related or not—and more often then not, without even looking, those individuals will find ties. This unique kinship is inclusive of ancestors. The dead are forever remembered among the living, and the elderly are held with a special regard. Rather than being hidden away or considered burdens, older Africans are viewed as storehouses of wisdom and are a welcome part of society. Women, too, are highly-esteemed in much of African tradition, particularly in the agri-based cultures. Often women, not men, are heads of households.

Among Africans, marriage represents a union of two families, not just a bride and groom. Parents and extended family members offer emotional support to a couple throughout their marriage. The bonding of families begins when a man obtains formal permission to marry a prospective bride. In true oral tradition, Africans often deliver the news of their upcoming nuptials by word of mouth. Any offspring are extremely valued. Additions to the family are cause for celebration.

In some cultures bride prices or dowries are still negotiated as are pre-arranged marriages.

Health

Diseases that have been successfully monitored and controlled in Western nations—diphtheria, measles, pertussis, poliomyelitis, tetanus, and tuberculosis—continue to be a problem in many parts of Africa. Diarrhea and tuberculosis account for one-half of all deaths in children. The emergence of Acquired Immune Deficiency Syndrome (AIDS) has had a devastating effect on the continent. In 1990, an estimated 1.2 million AIDS cases surfaced, including some 400,000 cases in children under the age of five.

In the mid-1990s, Ebola outbreaks have wreaked havoc in Zaire, Liberia, Gabon, and the Ivory Coast. Spread through contact with bodily fluids, the virus is hardy and can survive on moist surfaces such as bodies or food for long periods. The deadly Ebola virus disinigrates the mebranous linings of blood vessels and organs, usually leading to heart and other organ failure. Each erruption of the modern day plague has warranted strict quarantines. One of most contagious and lethal viruses known to mankind, the international scientific community has come together in trying to locate the sources of contamination, in hopes of bringing an end to a virus whose newer strains have increased the fatality rate of the afflicated from 80 percent to 97 percent since earlier Sudanese and Zairean outbreaks in the mid-to-late 1970s.

Food shortages caused by drought and civil conflicts continue to cause mass starvation and malnutrition in Ethiopia, Somalia, and Mozambique, as well as in parts of Western Africa. In the late 1980s and into the 1990s, the international community has joined forces to try to alleviate the situation by sending food and aid to the needy and even resorting to peace-keeping military personnel in situations caused by on-going civil disturbances.

The practice of female circumcision or genital mutilation—one of many varying rites of passage performed in parts of Africa—has been denounced by Western society as the harbinger of medical problems for women later in life, including the inability to walk, chronic infections, and difficult childbirth. While an African and Western effort to stamp out the sometimes fatal ritual is growing, many others decry what they deem to be cultural interference. Tradition holds that the surgery preserves the chastity of those upon whom it is performed.

Medicine and medical advice are often dispensed by traditional healers in Africa, often referred to as "witch doctors" by skeptical Westerners. Diviners and healers treat mental disorders as well as physical ones. They also provide advice for resolving social disputes.

Senegalese microbiologist Soulyemane Mboup and other African researchers have made significant contributions to the fight against AIDS. While Mboup is credited as one of the discoverers of the HIV-2 virus, other African scientists seem to have developed a method of using interferon, an immune system-enhancing protein, to alleviate the symptoms of both Ebola and AIDS. In some cases researchers have claimed to completely eradicate the presence of these diseases in affected patients.

Cuisine

Food plays a large role in African traditions, customs, and beliefs. Africans make liberal use of fresh, locally grown foods in their cooking. Papayas, coconuts, avocados, mangos, guavas, and other "exotic" fruits are abundant and along with other fruits and vegetables are eaten much more liberally than in the United States; many such as yams and cassava root are used as staples. For example maize, cassava, and plaintains are often dried and ground into flour. Legumes are also prevalent in African meals. Particularly in the coastal nations, seafood and fish, including shark, is frequently eaten fresh, dried, or smoked. Bat, beef, chicken, goat, monkey, pigeons, and pork are just some of the meats that can be found in different regions. Most Africans enjoy very spicy-hot food. An African pepper that goes by many names—*pilli-pilli, piri-piri, beri-beri*—is frequently used. Much hotter than cayenne pepper, *pilli-pilli* does more than increase the palatability of meal. Like garlic, pepper is thought to enhance the body's immune system. Coconut flesh is incorporated into many dishes as is coconut milk, which is also imbibed as a refreshing beverage. African beer, wine, and liquor—both homemade and commercial—also provide good libations.

In many African cultures, food is served in one large common bowl; diners then eat with their hands, thus re-enforcing the idea of community.

◆ BLACKS IN THE WESTERN HEMISPHERE

The black population of the Caribbean and much of South America, like that in North America, is decended from African slaves who were transported to the New World to work on European settlements. On many islands of the Caribbean persons of African descent make up the majority of the population; on Barbados and Jamaica, blacks are the overwhelming majority. In other areas, notably on the continental mainland from Mexico south to Argentina, Africans have been largely absorbed into the mainstream of the population. In South America, the black population consists of a mixture of Africans and Indians, known as Zambos. Those who are primarily a mixture of Caucasian and American Indian are known as mestizos, and those who are a mixture of Caucasian and black are, as in the United States, referred to as mulattoes.

In recent years, the Caribbean basin has been a source of black immigration, with immigrants primarily from Jamaica and Haiti entering the United States in search of work. In 1980, the *Mariel* boatlift was successful in bring Cuban refugees to the United States. More recently, thousands of Haitians have attempted, with little success, to emigrate to the United States, since the September of 1991 coup that ousted President Jean-Bertrand Aristide, later reinstated with the aid of the U.S. government.

◆ COUNTRY PROFILES

Africa

Algeria

Official name: Democratic and Popular Republic of Algeria
Independence: July 5, 1962
Capital: Algiers
Currency: Dinar
Income: (per capita US$) 2,060 (1991)
Area: 918,497 sq. mi.
Population: (1991 estimate) 23 million
Illiteracy: 42.5% (1991)
Ethnic divisions: Arab and Berber
Religious groups: Sunni Islam
Languages spoken: Arabic (official), Berber dialects, French
International relations: UN, OAU, Arab League

Since the fifth century BC, the area that makes up what is now Algeria has been populated by indigenous tribes who have been progressively pushed back from the coast by invaders. As a result, the country boundaries have shifted during various stages of the conquests. Nearly all Algerians are Muslim, of Arab, Berber, or mixed Arab-Berber stock.

French colonization began in 1830 and continued until 1954, when the indigenous population staged a revolt on November 1. The revolution was launched by a small group of nationalists who called themselves the National Liberation Front. Negotiations led to a cease-fire signed by France and the National Liberation Front on March 18, 1962; France declared Algeria independent on July 3.

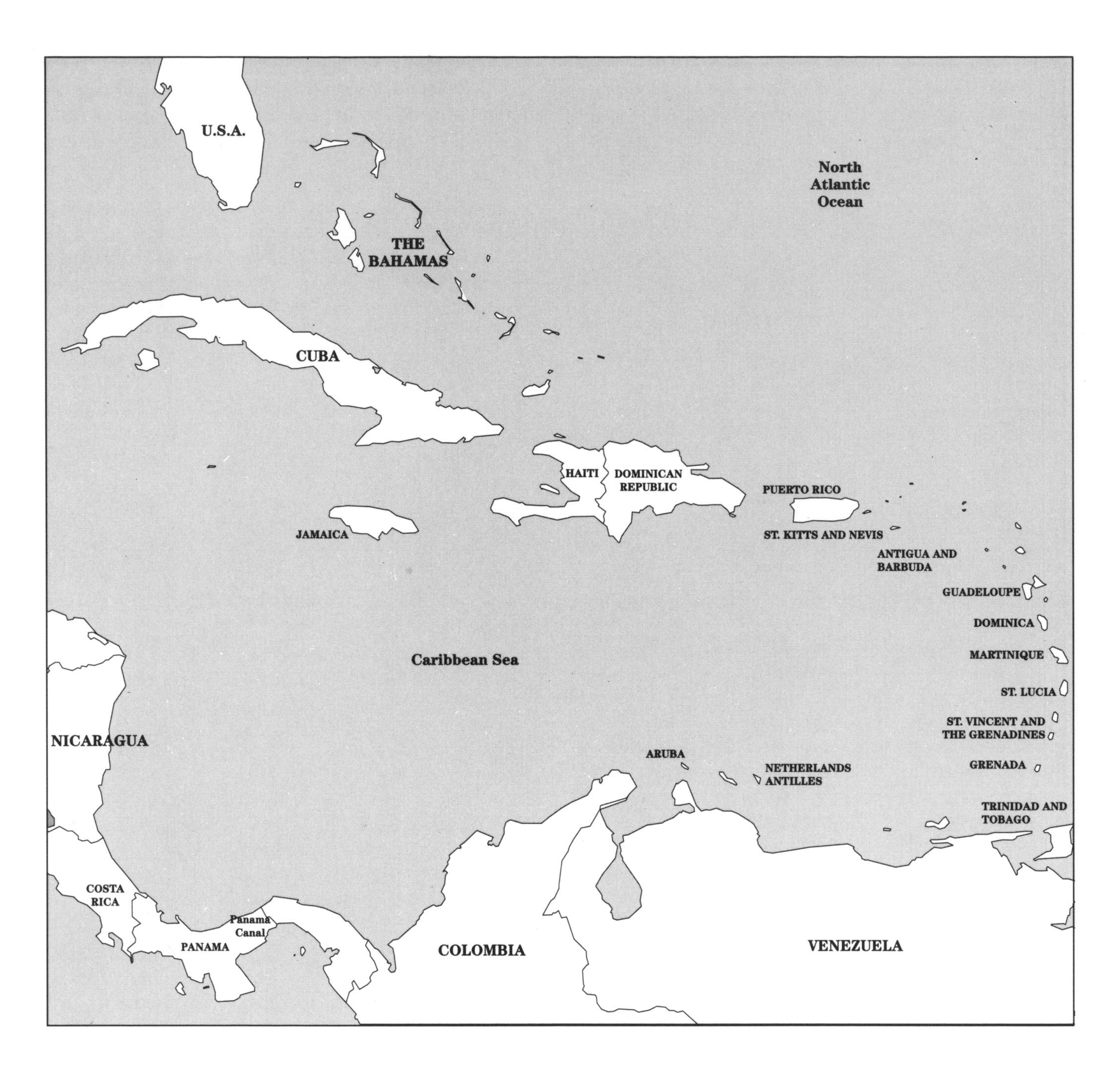

The Caribbean

Mohammed Ben Bella became Algeria's first post-independence president only to be ousted three years later. In 1965, Col. Boume'dienne lead a successful *coup de' etat.* After he died, Chadi Benjadid became the head of state. In 1991, Algeria held its first free election after 30 years of a one-party system, and the National Liberation Front was defeated by the Islamic Salvation Front.

Angola

Official name: People's Republic of Angola

Independence: November 11, 1975

Capital: Luanda

Currency: Kwanza

Income (per capita US$) 750 (1990)

Area: 481,351 sq. mi.

Population: (1991 estimate) 8.6 million

Illiteracy: 72% (1991)

Ethnic divisions: Ovimbundu 37%, Kimbundu 25%, Bakongo 15%, Lunda-Chokwe 8%, Nganguela 6%, Haneca and Humbe 3%, Ovambo 2%, mestico and European 2%, other 2%

South America

Religious groups: Roman Catholic, Protestant, traditional belief
Languages spoken: Portuguese (official), tribal languages and dialects
International relations: UN, OAU, EC
Form of Government: Multi-party
Exports: Crude oil, petroleum-based products, coffee, diamonds

Angola's boundaries were formally established by the Berlin West Africa Congress of 1884 to 1885. Following World War II, Portuguese interest in colonizing Angola increased. Here, the Portuguese established a slave trade and a strict and harsh colonial rule.

Discontent over Portuguese unwillingness to concede eventual independence led to the formation of the Popular Movement for the Liberation of Angola (MPLA), the National Front for the Liberation of Angola (FNLA) and the National Union for the Total Independence of Angola (UNITA). In January 1975, the Portuguese and the three liberation movements worked out a complicated agreement—the Alvor Accord—which provided for a transitional government composed of all three groups and for elections in preparation for independence in November of 1975. Since 1976, Angola has been politically unstable because of civil war and repeated incursions by South African forces operating from Namibia. The United States does not maintain diplomatic relations with Angola, but since 1978 the two countries have had frequent contacts to discuss regional and bilateral matters.

The MPLA party's Augustinho became the first president of the newly independent People's Republic of Angola. Upon his death in 1979, José Eduardo Dos Santos became the head of state. UNITA, led by Jonas Savimbi and supported by South Africa, continued to wage a war against MPLA, which was back by Cuba. An agreement withdrawing foreign troops was signed in 1988. Following a cease fire, a national election was scheduled to be held under the watching eyes of the United Nations.

Angolans are almost entirely Bantu of various ethnic subgroupings. The Ovimbundu, in central and southeastern Angola are the largest group, consisting of about 37 percent of the population. The Bakongo, concentrated in the northwest but also living in areas adjacent to the Congo and Zaire as well as Cabinda, constitute about 15 percent. The Kimbundu, about 25 percent of the population, are concentrated in the area around Luanda and out toward the east.

Angolans celebrating independence from Portugal.

Benin
Official name: People's Republic of Benin
Independence: August 1, 1960
Capital: Cotonou
Currency: CFA franc
Income (per capita US$) 421 (1990)
Area: 43,483 sq. mi.
Population: (1991 estimate) 4.8 million
Illiteracy: 73% (1991)
Ethnic divisions: Fon, Adja, Bariba, Yoruba
Religious groups: traditional belief 61%, Christian 17%, Muslim 12%
Languages spoken: French (official)
International relations: UN, OAU, EC
Form of government: Multi-party
Exports: Coffee, cocoa beans, cotton, palm products

During the precolonial era, Benin was a collection of small principalities, the most powerful of which was the Fon Kingdom of Dahomey. By the seventeenth and eighteenth centuries, first the Portuguese and later other Europeans established trading posts along the coast. From there thousands of slaves were shipped to the New World, primarily to Brazil and the Caribbean—this part of West Africa became known as the Slave Coast.

In 1892, the King of Dahomey was subjugated and the country organized as the French protectorate of Dahomey. It remained a French colony until independence in 1960, when the name was changed to the Republic of Dahomey,

The Bakongo people of Angola are concentrated in the northwest part of the country, adjacent to the Congo and Zaire.

and Hubert Maga became president. Three years later, he was overthrown by military commanders. Mathieu Ke're'kou took over the military regime in 1972. In 1975, the name was finally changed to the People's Republic of Benin. When the government reverted to civilian control in 1980, Ke're'kou was re-elected president of the republic.

The population of Benin comprises about 20 socio-cultural groups. Four groups—the Fon, Aja (who are related), Bariba, and Yoruba—account for more than half of the population.

Botswana
Official name: Republic of Botswana
Independence: September 30, 1966
Capital: Gaberoni
Currency: Pula
Income (per capita US$) 2,200 (1990)
Area: 224,710 sq. mi.
Population: (1991 estimate) 1.3 million
Illiteracy: 29.2% (1991)
Ethnic divisions: Tswana 55%-60%, Kalanga 25%-20%, Kgalagadi, Yei, Herero, Mbukushu, Basarwa (Bushmen), Khoi (Hottentots), whites about 1%
Religious groups: Traditional belief 50%, Christianity 50%
Languages spoken: English (official), SeTswana
International relations: UN, OAC, Commonwealth, EC
Form of government: Multi-party
Exports: Meat, diamonds, copper, nickel

Europeans made first contact with the area in the early ninteenth century. In the last quarter of the century, hostilities broke out between the Botswana and the Afrikaners from South Africa (Transvaal). Following appeals by the Botswana for assistance, the British government in 1885 proclaimed "Bechuanaland" to be under British protection. In 1909, despite South African pressure, inhabitants of Bechuanaland, Basutoland (now Lesotho), and Swaziland demanded and received British agreement that they not be included in the proposed Union of South Africa.

In June 1964, the British government accepted proposals for a form of self-government for Botswana that would lead to independence. Botswana became independent on September 30, 1966, and Seretse Khama was installed as the prime minister after the Bechuanaland Democratic Party won majority votes. The country was later named Botswana, and upon Khama's death in 1980, Quett Masire became the president.

In 1977, the Botswana Defense Force was formed, largely in response to the Rhodesian conflict, which was affecting Botswana. Facing a threat of overt or covert military raids from South Africa directed against believed African National Congress targets, Botswana has embarked on modernization and expansion of the BDF. The nation remains opposed to South Africa's policy of apartheid and maintains no formal diplomatic relations with that country. In part because of its geographic location and reliance on South African transportation systems and goods, Botswana, nevertheless, maintains a pragmatic working relationship and close economic ties with South Africa. Large deposits of diamonds have been discovered in Botswana in recent years, making the country one of the world's major producers of the valuable gemstone.

Some 50 to 60 percent of the country's population is made up of the Tswana tribe (Botswana), which is divided into eight subgroups: Bamangwate, Bakwena, Batawana, Bangwaketse, Bakgatla, Bamalete, Barolong, and Batlokwa. The Kalanga, Herero, Bushmen (Basarwa), Yei, and Kgalagadi are minorities.

Burkina Faso (formerly Upper Volta)
Independence: August 5, 1960
Capital: Ouagadougou
Currency: CFA franc

The Fon constitute one of the largest groups in Benin.

Income (per capita US$): 370 (1990)
Area: 106,000 sq. mi.
Population: (1991 estimate) 9.3 million
Illiteracy: 81.8% (1991)
Ethnic divisions: Mossi, Bobo, Mande, Fulani
Religious groups: Traditional belief 45%, Muslim 40%, Christian 15%
Languages spoken: French (official), More, other tribal languages
International relations: UN, OAU, EC
Form of government: M.ulti-party
Exports: Cotton, petroleum, live animals

Until the end of the ninteenth century, the history of Burkina Faso was dominated by the Mossi, who are believed to have come from central or eastern Africa in the eleventh century. When the French arrived and claimed the area in 1896, the Mossi resisted but were defeated when their capital at Ouagadougou was captured. After World War II, the Mossi renewed their pressure for separate territorial status; Upper Volta became an autonomous republic in the French Community on December 11, 1958, and achieved independence on August 5, 1960. The country became known as Burkino Faso in 1984.

The majority of the population belong to two major West African cultural groups, the Voltaic and the Mande. The Voltaic are far more numerous and include the Mossi, which make up about one-half of the population. The Mossi are still bound by the traditions of the emperor, the Mogho Naba, who holds court in Ouagadougou. One of the poorest nation's in the world, most inhabitants subsist on agriculture and animal husbandry.

Burundi
Official name: Republic of Burundi
Independence: July 1, 1962
Capital: Bujumbura
Currency: Burundi franc
Income (per capita US$) 210 (1990)
Area: 10,747 sq. mi.
Population: (1991 estimate) 5.8 million
Illiteracy: 50% (1991)
Ethnic divisions: Hutu 85%, Utusi 14%, Twa 1%
Religious groups: Roman Catholic 62%, traditional belief 32%, Protestant 5%, Muslim 1%
Languages spoken: Kirundi and French (both official), Swahili
International relations: UN, OAU, EC

Form of government: Military
Exports: Coffee, cotton, animal hides

Prior to the arrival of Europeans, Burundi was a kingdom with a highly stratified, feudal social structure. Rulers were drawn from princely dynastic families *(ganwa)*, from whom a king or *mwami* was chosen. A *mwami* continued to rule even after independence was granted.

European explorers and missionaries began making brief visits to the area as early as 1858; however, Burundi did not come under European administration until the 1890s, when it became part of German East Africa. In 1916 Belgian troops occupied the country; the League of Nations mandated it to Belgium in 1923 as part of the Territory of Ruanda-Urundi, now the nations of Rwanda and Burundi. Burundi became independent on July 1, 1962.

Burundi's population is made up of three ethnic groups—Hutu, Tutsi, and Twa. Hutus, who make up 85 percent of the population, are primarily farmers whose Bantu-speaking ancestors migrated into Burundi 800 to 1,000 years ago. The Tutsi, who make up 14 percent of the population, are a pastoral people who apparently migrated from Ethiopia several hundred years later. Years of dispute with neighboring Rwanda has continued into the 1990s. Ethnic conflict between the Hutus and Tutsis has led to many attrocities.

Cameroon
Official name: Republic of Cameroon
Independence: January 1, 1960
Capital: Yaoundé
Currency: CFA franc
Income (per capita US$): 1090 (1990)
Area: 183,568 sq. mi.
Illiteracy: 43% (1991)
Population: (1991 estimate) 11.7 million
Ethnic divisions: More than 200 groups
Religious groups: Christian, Muslim, traditional belief
Languages spoken: English and French (official), more than 200 tribal languages
International Relations: EC, OAU, UN
Form of government: Multi-party
Exports: Bananas, cocoa, coffee, cotton

The earliest inhabitants of Cameroon were probably Pygmies, who still inhabit the southern forests. However, Bantu-speaking people were among the first to invade Cameroon from equatorial Africa, settling in the south and later in the west. The Muslim Fulani from the Niger basin arrived in the eleventh and ninetenth centuries and settled in the north.

Europeans first made contact with the area in the 1500s. For the next three centuries, Spanish, Dutch, and British traders visited the area.

In July of 1884, Germany, the United Kingdom, and France each attempted to annex the area. A 1919 declaration divided Cameroon between the United Kingdom and France, with the larger, eastern area under France. In December of 1958, the French trusteeship was ended; French Cameroon became the Republic of Cameroon on January 1, 1960.

The Republic of Cameroon is made up of a federal system integrating the French controlled south and the British controlled north under the leadership of president Ahmadou Ahidjo. The country heavily depends on foreign capital and has been faced with internal problems both ethnic and social under the leadership of Ahidjo's successor, Paul Biya.

Cameroon has about 200 tribal groups and clans, speaking at least as many languages and dialects.

Cape Verde
Official name: Republic of Cape Verde
Independence: July 5, 1975
Capital: Praia
Currency: Escudo
Income (per capita US$): 890 (1990)
Area: 1,557 sq. mi.
Population: (1991 estimate) 386,000
Illiteracy: 53% (1991)
Ethnic divisions: Creole (mixed African and Portuguese), African, European
Religious groups: Roman Catholic, Protestant
Languages spoken: Portuguese (official), Crioulo (national)
Form of government: Multi-party
Exports: Animal products, vegetable products

Located in the north Atlantic Ocean, the Cape Verde archipelago remained uninhabited until the Portuguese visited it in 1456, and African slaves were brought to the islands to work on Portuguese plantations. As a result, Cape Verdeans have mixed African and Portuguese origins.

In 1951, Portugal changed Cape Verde's status from a colony to an overseas province. In 1956, the African Party for the Independence of Guinea-Bissau and Cape Verde (PAIGC) was organized to bring about improvement in economic, social, and political conditions in Cape Verde and Portuguese Guinea. The PAIGC began an armed rebellion against Portugal in 1961. Acts of sabotage eventually grew into a war in Portuguese Guinea that pitted 10,000 Soviet bloc-supported PAIGC soldiers against 35,000 Portuguese and African troops.

In December of 1974, the PAIGC and Portugal signed an agreement providing for a transitional government

Cameroonian women husking corn.

composed of Portuguese and Cape Verdeans. On June 30, 1975, Cape Verdeans elected a National Assembly, which received the instruments of independence from Portugal on July 5, 1975. After winning independence, the country voted for a union with Guinea-Bissau. In 1980, the link ended when Joao Vieira seized power in Guinea-Bissau. The PAIGC was dissolved and replaced by PAICV (African Party for the Independence of Cape Verde). Aristides Pereira was elected head of state in 1986.

The official language is Portuguese. However, most Cape Verdeans speak a Creole dialect, Crioulo, which consists of archaic Portuguese modified through contact with African and other European languages.

Central African Republic
Independence: August 13, 1960
Area: 242,000 sq. mi.
Capital: Bangui
Currency: CFA franc
Income: (per capita US$) 440 (1990)
Population: (1991 estimate) 2.9 million
Illiteracy: 62% (1991)
Ethnic divisions: More than 80 groupos, including Baya 34%, Banda 28%, Sara 10%, Mandja 9%, Mboum 9%, M'Baka 7%
Religious groups: Traditional belief 35%, Protestant 25%, Roman Catholic 25%, Muslim 15%
Languages spoken: French (official), Sangho (national)
International relations: EC, OAU, UN
Form of government: One-party system (1996)
Exports: Coffee, cotton, diamonds

The first Europeans to settle in the area that is now the Central African Republic were the French. In 1889, the French established an outpost at Bangu. United with Chad in 1906, the outpost formed the Oubangui-Chari-Chad colony.

In 1910, it became one of the four territories of the Federation of French Equatorial Africa, along with Chad, Congo (Brazzaville), and Gabon. However, a constitutional referendum of September 1958 dissolved the federation. The nation became an autonomous republic within the newly established French Community on December 1, 1958, and acceded to complete independence as the Central African Republic on August 13, 1960. The first president, revered as the founder of the Central African Republic, was Bathelemy Boganda.

Boganda's successor, David Dacko, was overthrown in 1966 by Gen. Jean-Badel Bokassa, who embarked on a reign of terror, proclaiming himself "emperor." A 1981 *coup d'e'tat* put Dacko back in power. Gen. André Kolingba succeeded Dacko and a multi-party state was established in 1991.

Central African woman preparing a meal.

The Central African Republic is made up of more than 80 ethnic groups, each with its own language. About 70 percent of the population comprises Baya-Mandjia and Banda, with approxiamtely seven percent M'Baka. Sangho, the language of a small group along the Oubangui River, is the national language spoken by the majority of Central Africans. The country is one of the poorest nations in Afrcia, with a high mortality rate and widespread malnutrition and illiteracy.

Chad
Official name: Republic of Chad
Independence: August 11, 1960
Capital: N'Djamena.
Currency: CFA franc
Income: (per capita US$) 207 (1990)
Area: 496,000 sq. mi.
Population: (1991 estimate) 5.8 million
Illiteracy: 82.% (1991)
Ethnic divisions: More than 200 groups including, Toubou (Gourane), Arabs, Fulbe, Kotoko, Hausa, Kanembou, Bagirmi, Boulala, Zaghawa, Hadjerai, and Maba; about 2,500 French citizens live in Chad
Religious groups: Muslim, Christian, traditional beliefs
Languages spoken: French and Arabic (official); 200 tribal languages
International relations: EC, OAU, UN
Form of government: One-party
Exports: Cotton, diamonds, petroleum products, wood

The region that is now Chad was known to Middle Eastern traders and geographers as far back the late

Middle Ages. Since then, Chad has served as a crossroads for the Muslim peoples of the desert and savanna regions and the animist Bantu tribes of the tropical forests.

The Sao people populated the Chari River basin for thousands of years, but their relatively weak chiefdoms were overtaken by the powerful chiefs of what were to become the Kanem-Bornu and Baguirmi kingdoms. At their peak, these two kingdoms and the kingdom of Ouaddai controlled a good part of what is now Chad, as well as parts of Nigeria and Sudan.

The French first made contact with the region in 1891. The first major colonial battle for Chad was fought in 1900 between the French major Lamy and the African leader Rabah. Although the French won that battle, they did not declare the territory until 1911; armed clashes between colonial troops and local bands continued for many years thereafter. Although Chad joined the French colonies of Gabon, Oubangui-Charo, and Moyen Congo to form the Federation of French Equatorial Africa in 1910, Chad did not have colonial status until 1920.

In 1959, the territory of French Equatorial Africa was dissolved, and four states—Gabon, the Central African Republic, Congo (Brazzaville), and Chad—became autonomous members of the French Community. In 1960, Chad became an independent nation under its first president, Francois Tombalbaye. He was faced with the pressure of resolving the on-going conflict between the Muslim north and the black south and responded by instituting authoritarian rule. Backed by Libya, FRONAT (Front de Libération Nationale) guerillas of the north gained power, naming Goukouni Oueddei as head of state. In 1982, he was succeeded by Hisséne Habré, but civil war broke out one year later. In the 1990s, Chad remains impoverished, having faced long periods of drought and civil strife.

Chad is made up of more than 200 ethnic groups. Those in the north and east are generally Muslim; most southerners are animists and Christians.

Rural farmers in Chad.

Comoros
Official name: Comoros Federal Islamic Republic
Independence: July 6, 1975
Capital: Moroni
Currency: CFA franc
Income: (per capita US$) 480 (1990)
Area: 838 sq. mi.
Population: (1991 estimate): 476,000
Illiteracy: 46% (1991)
Ethnic divisions: Antalote, Cafre, Makoa, Oimatsaha, Sakalava
Religious groups: Sunni Muslim 98%, Roman Catholic 2%
Languages spoken: Shikomoro (a Swahili-Arab dialect), Malagasy, French
International relations: EC, OAU, UN
Form of government: One-party
Exports: Cloves, vanilla, ylang ylang

Located off the northwestern coast of Madagascar, Portuguese explorers visited the archipelago in 1505. In 1843, the sultan of Mayotte was persuaded to relinquish the island of Mayotte to the French. By 1912, France had established colonial rule over the islands of Grande Comore, Anjouan, and Hoheli and placed the islands under the administration of the governor general of Madagascar. After World War II, the islands became a French overseas territory and were represented in France's National Assembly. On July 6, 1975, the Comorian Parliament passed a resolution declaring unilateral independence. However, the deputies of Mayotte abstained; as a result, the Comorian government has effective control over only Grande Comore, Anjouan, and Moheli—Mayotte remains under French administration. After gaining independence, the country faced an enormous economical crisis.

The Comorians inhabiting the islands of Grande Comore, Anjouan, and Moheli (about 86 percent of the population) share African-Arab origins. Islam is the dominant religion, but a substantial minority of the citizens of Mayotte (the Mahorais) are Catholic and have been influenced strongly by French culture. The most common language is Shikomoro, a Swahili dialect. French and Malagasy are also spoken.

Congo
Official name: People's Republic of the Congo
Independence: August 15, 1960
Capital: Brazzaville
Currency: CFA franc
Income: (per capita US$) 1010 (1991)
Area: 132,000 sq. mi.

Children studying at a Koranic school in Chad.

Population: (1991) 2.4 million
Illiteracy: 43.% (1991)
Ethnic divisions: 15 main groups, 75 subgroups; largest groups are Bacongo, Bateke, M'Bochi, Sangha
Religious groups: Traditional belief 48%, Christian 47%, Muslim 2%
Languages spoken: French (official), Lingala, Kikongo
International relation: Member EC, OAU, UN
Form of government: Multi-party
Exports: Crude petroleum, diamonds, wood

The early history of the Congo is believed to have focused on three tribal kingdoms—the Kongo, the Loango, and the Teke. Established in the fourth century AD, the Kongo was a highly centralized kingdom that later developed a close commercial relationship with the Portuguese, the first Europeans to explore the area.

With the development of the slave trade, the Portuguese turned their attention from the Kongo Kingdom to the Loango. By the time the slave trade was abolished in the 1800s, the Loango Kingdom had been reduced to many small, independent groups. The Teke Kingdom of the interior, which had sold slaves to the Loango Kingdom, ended its independence in 1883, when the Teke king concluded a treaty with Pierre Savorgnan de Brazza, placing Teke lands and people under French protection. Under the French, the area became known as Middle Congo.

In 1910, Middle Congo became part of French Equatorial Africa, which also included Gabon, the Central African Republic, and Chad.

A constitutional referendum in September 1958 replaced the Federation of French Equatorial Africa with the French Community. Middle Congo, under the name Republic of the Congo, and the three other territories of French Equatorial Africa became fully autonomous members within the French Community. On April 15, 1960, it became an independent nation but retained close, formal bonds with the community. President Fulbert Youlou instituted a dictatorship for the first three years following independence,then was succeeded by a revolutionary government headed by Alphonse Massamba Debat. The military imposed themselves as head of the nation under Gen. Marien Ngouabi, who declared the Congo a republic to be governed under a one-party system.

Cote d' Ivoire (Ivory Coast)
Independence: August 7, 1960
Capital: Abidjan
Currency: CFA franc
Income: (per capita US$) 730 (1990)
Area: 124,500 sq. mi.
Population: (1991 estimate): 12.9 million
Illiteracy: 46% (1991)
Ethnic divisions: More than 60 groups
Religious groups: Muslim 55%, Traditional belief 25%, Christian 20%
Languages spoken: French (official), tribal dialects
International relations: EC, OAU, UN
Form of government: Multi-party
Exports: Cocoa, cocoa butter, coffee, petroleum products, wood

The first Europeans, the French, made its initial contact with Cote d'Ivoire in 1637, when missionaries landed at Assinie near the Gold Coast (now Ghana) border. However, these early contacts were limited. In 1843 and 1844, France signed treaties with the kings of the Grand Bassam and Assinie regions, placing their territories under a French protectorate. French explorers, missionaries, trading companies, and soldiers gradually extended the area under French control, until 1893 when Cote d'Ivoire was officially made a French colony.

In December of 1958, Cote d'Ivoire became an autonomous republic within the French community. Cote d'Ivoire became independent on August 7, 1960. Felix Houphouët-Boigny led the country under a one-party system. He maintained ties with Europe, which helped bring about rapid development and economic stability.

Cote d'Ivoire's more than 60 ethnic groups usually are classified into seven principal divisions—Akan, Krou, Lagoon, Nuclear Mande, Peripheral Mande, Senoufo, and Lobi. The Baoule, in the Akan division, is probably the largest single subgroup, with perhaps 20 percent of the overall population. The Bete, in the Krou division, and the Senoufo in the north are the second and third largest groups, with roughly 18 and 15 percent of the national population, respectively.

Djibouti
Official name: Republic of Djibouti
Independence: June 27, 1977
Capital: Djibouti
Currency: Djibouti franc
Income: (per capita US$) 1250 (1990)
Area: 9,000 sq. mi.
Population: (1991 estimate) 541,000
Illiteracy: 41% (1987)
Ethnic divisions: Somalis (Issas), Afars, French, Arab, Ethiopian, Italian
Religious groups: Muslim 94%, Christian 6%
Languages spoken: French (official) Somali, Afar, Arabic
International relations: Arab League, EC, OAU, UN
Form of government: One-party.
Exports: Cereals, coffee, leather and skins, tea

The region, which now makes up the Republic of Djibouti, was first settled by the French in 1862, as a result of growing French interest in British activity in Egypt. In 1884, France expanded its protectorate to include the shores of the Gulf of Tadjourah and the hinterland, designating the area French Somaliland. The boundaries of the protectorate, marked out in 1897 by France and Emperor Manelik II of Ethiopia, were affirmed further by agreements with Emperor Haile Selassie I in 1945 and 1954.

A July of 1967 directive from Paris formally changed the name of the territory to the French Territory of Afars and Issas. In 1975, the French Government began to accommodate increasingly insistent demands for independence. In June of 1976, the territory's citizenship law, which had favored the Afar minority, was revised to reflect more closely the weight of the Issa Somali. In a May of 1977 referendum, the electorate voted for independence, and the Republic of Djibouti was inaugurated on June 27, 1977. Independence was followed by a republican form of government.

The indigenous population of the Republic of Djibouti is divided between the majority Somalis (predominantly of the Issa tribe with minority Ishaak and Gadaboursi representation) and the Afars and Danakils.

Egypt
Official name: Republic of Egypt
Independence: February 28, 1922
Capital: Cairo
Currency: Egyptian pound
Income: (per capita US$) 600 (1990)
Area: 386,650 sq. mi
Population: (1991 estimate) 54.8 million
Illiteracy: 52% (1991)
Ethnic divisions: Egyptian, Bedouin Arab, Nubian
Religious groups: Sunni Muslim 90%, Coptic Christian
Languages spoken: Arabic (official), English
International relations: Arab League, OAU, UN
Form of government: Presidential republic

Egypt has endured as a unified state for more than 5,000 years, and archeological evidence indicates that a developed Egyptian society has existed much longer. In about 3100 BC, Egypt was united under a ruler known as Mena, or Menes, who inaugurated the thirty pharaonic dynasties into which Egypt's ancient history is divided—the Old and Middle Kingdoms and the New Empire.

In 525 BC, Persians dethroned the last pharaoh of the 26th dynasty. The country remained a Persian province until the conquest of Alexander the Great in 332 BC. After Alexander's death in 323 BC, the Macedonian commander, Ptolemy, established personal control over Egypt, assuming the title of pharaoh in 304 BC. The Ptolemaic line ended in 30 BC with the suicide of Queen Cleopatra. The Emperor Augustus then established direct Roman control over Egypt, initiating almost seven centuries of Roman and Byzantine rule.

Egypt was invaded and conquered by Arab forces in AD 642; a process of Arabization and Islamization ensued. The French arrived in Egypt in 1798. An Anglo-Ottoman invasion force drove out the French in 1801, and following a period of chaos, the Albanian Muhammad Ali obtained control of the country.

In 1882, the British occupies Egypt and declared a formal protectorate over Egypt on December 18, 1914. In deference to growing nationalist feelings, Britain unilaterally declared Egyptian independence on February 28, 1922. King Faud I ruled after independence until 1952, when he was overthrown and Gamal Abdel Nasser was elected president of the republic a few years later. Upon his death, Anwar el-Sadat took over the leadership until he was brutally assassinated in 1981 and succeeded by Hosni Mubarak.

The Egyptian population is fairly homogenous—Mediterranean and Arab influences appear in the north, as well as some mixing in the south with the Nubians of northern Sudan. Ethnic minorities include a small number of Bedouin Arab nomads dispersed in the eastern and western deserts and in the Sinai, as well as some 50,000 to 200,000 Nubians clustered along the Nile in Upper Egypt.

Eritrea
Official name: Eritrea
Independence: May 25, 1993
Capital: Asmara
Currency: Ethiopian birr
Area: 46,761 sq. mi.
Population: (1996 estimate) 3.1 million
Religious groups: Muslim 50%, Monophysite Christian 35%, Animist 15%

Eritrea was an integral part of the kingdom of Aksum and has shared its destiny with Ethiopia. Islamic colonists became established in the coastal area. Consequently, the Arab domination of the region lasted until the later half of the nineteenth century, when Egyptians settled in the area. Founded in 1890 by the Italians, the colony of Eritrea was annexed by Ethiopia after World War II. For years the Eritrian People's Liberation Forum waged a struggle for independence that was eventually won on May 25, 1993.

Once a marvel, Asmara, the capital city was built by Italians in the 1920s. During conflicts between Soviet-backed Ethiopian troops and Eritrean rebels, Asmara's railway system was destroyed. Upon gaining independence, the former rebels, along with hundreds of other local workers, discovered all the missing parts in order to reassemble the crucial rail link and repair the vintage steam locomotives. The system was to by readied by 1997. Meanwhile, hundreds of exiles returned, bringing with them necessary capital and technological expertise. The ruling party, People's Front for Democracy and Justice and the country's president, Isais Afewerki, have promoted privitization and encouraged foreign investors to do business in Eritrea. These events have led many to consider the new nation one of Africa's greatest successes.

Equatorial Guinea
Official name: Republic of Equatorial Guinea
Independence: October 12, 1968
Capital: Malabo
Currency: CFA franc
Income: (per capita US$) 310 (1990)
Area: 10,820 sq. mi.
Population: (1991 estimate) 360,000
Illiteracy: 69% (1991)
Ethnic divisions: Fang 80%, Bubi 15%, other 5%
Religious groups: Roman Catholic 83%, Protestant, traditional belief
Languages spoken: Spanish (official), Fang, Bubi, pidgin, English, French, other tribal languages
International relations: EC, OAU, UN
Form of government: One-party

Equatoguinean children.

Exports: Cocoa, coffee

The first inhabitants of the region that is now Equatorial Guinea are believed to have been Pygmies, of whom only isolated pockets remain in northern Rio Muni. Bantu migrations between the seventeenth and ninteenth centuries brought the coastal tribes and later the Fang people to the area.

The Portuguese, seeking a route to India, landed on the island of Bioko in 1471. The Portuguese retained control until 1778, when the island and adjacent islets, were ceded to Spain. From 1827 to 1843, Britain established a base on the island to combat the slave trade. Conflicting claims to the mainland were settled in 1900 by the Treaty of Paris.

In 1959, the Spanish territory of the Gulf of Guinea was established. In 1963, the name of the country was changed to Equatorial Guinea. In March 1968, under pressure from Equatoguinean nationalists and the United Nations, Spain announced that it would grant independence to Equatorial Guinea. In September 1968, Francisco Macias Nguema was elected first president of Equatorial Guinea, and independence was granted in October with Francisco Macias Nguema as the head of state. A military coup occurred in 1979, deposing Nguema, who was put to death for "crimes against humanity."

The majority of the Equatoguinean people are of Bantu origin. The largest tribe, the Fang, constitute 80 percent of the population and are divided into about 67 clans. Those to the north of Rio Benito on Rio Muni speak Fang-Ntumu, and those to the south speak Fang-Okak, two mutually intelligible dialects. The Bubi, who form 15 percent of the population, are indigenous to Bioko Island. In addition, several coastal tribes exist, who are sometimes referred to as "Playeros," and include the Ndowes, Bujebas, Balengues, and Bengas on the mainland and small islands, and Fernandinos, a Creole community, on Bioko. These groups comprise five percent of the population.

Ethiopia

Official name: People's Democratic Republic of Ethiopia
Capital: Addis Ababa
Income: (per capita US$) 120 (1990)
Area: 472,000 sq. mi.
Population: (1990 estimate) 51.3 million
Illiteracy: 95% (1991)
Ethnic divisions: Oromo 40%, Amhara 25%, Tigre 12%, Sidama 9%
Religious groups: Muslim 40%-45%, Ethiopian Orthodox Christian 35%-40%, traditional beliefs 15%-25%
Languages spoken: Amharic (official), Tigrinya, Orominga, Arabic, English
International relations: EC, OAU, UN
Form of government: Multi-party
Exports: Coffee, hides and skins, live animals

Ethiopia is the oldest independent country in Africa and one of the oldest in the world. Herodotus, the Greek historian of the fifth century BC, describes ancient Ethiopia in his writings; the Old Testament of the Bible records the Queen of Sheba's visit to Jerusalem. Missionaries from Egypt and Syria introduced Christianity in the fourth century AD. The Portuguese established contact with Ethiopia in 1493.

In 1930 Haile Selassie, was crowned emperor. His reign was interrupted in 1936 when Italian fascist forces invaded and occupied Ethiopia. The emperor was eventually forced into exile in England despite his plea to the League of Nations for intervention. Five years later, the Italians were defeated by British and Ethiopian forces, and the emperor returned to the throne. After a period of civil unrest, which began in February 1974, the aging Haile Selassie I was deposed on September 13, 1974. After deposing Selasie, the military, led by Col. Mariam Haile Mengistu, took over the government and nationalized nearly all the country's economic institutions.

Haile Selassie

Discontent had been spreading throughout Ethiopian urban elites, and an escalating series of mutinies in the armed forced, demonstrations, and strikes led to the seizure of state power by the armed forces coordinating committee, which later became the Provisional Military Administrative Council (PMAC). The PMAC formally declared its intent to remake Ethiopia into a socialist state. It finally destroyed its opposition in a program of mass arrests and executions known as the "red terror," which lasted from November of 1977 to March of 1978. An estimated 10,000 people, mostly in Addis Ababa, were killed by government forces. Mengistu's failure to respond to growing national problems—compounded by droughts, an armed struggle by Eritre and Tigre, and declining Soviet aid—brought him down. Early in 1991, he was forced into exile in Zimbabwe.

Ethiopia's population is highly diverse. Most of its people speak a Semitic or Cushitic language. The Amhara, Tigreans, and Oromo make up more than three-fourths of the population, but there are more than 40 different ethnic groups within Ethiopia.

Gabon
Official name: Gabonese Republic
Independence: August 17, 1960
Capital: Libreville
Currency: CFA franc
Income: (per capita US$) 3450 (1990)
Area: 102,317 sq. mi.
Population: (1990 estimate): 1.2 million
Illiteracy: 39% (1991)
Ethnic divisions: Fang, Myene, Bapounou, Eschira, Bandjabi, Beteke/Obamba
Religious groups: Christian, Muslim, traditional belief
Languages spoken: French (official), Fang, Myene, Bateke, Bapounou/Eschira, Bandjabi
International relations: EC, OAU, UN
Form of government: Multi-party
Exports: Crude petroleum, manganese, uranium

Gabon's first European visitors were Portuguese traders who arrived in the 15th century. The coast became a center of the slave trade. Dutch, British, and French traders came in the 16th century. France assumed the status of protector by signing treaties with Gabonese coastal chiefs in 1839 and 1841. In 1910, Gabon became one of the four territories of French Equatorial Africa, a federation that survived until 1959. The territories became independent in 1960 as the Central African Republic, Chad, Congo (Brazzaville), and Gabon, which, Léon M'ba led the government after independence. Upon his death in 1967, Albert Bongo took over has head of state.

Almost all Gabonese are of Bantu origin. Gabon has at least forty tribal groups, with separate languages and cultures; the largest group is the Fang. Other tribes include the Myene, Bandjabi, Eshira, Bapounou, Bateke/Obamba, and Okande.

Gambia
Official name: Republic of The Gambia
Independence: February 18, 1965
Capital: Banjul
Currency: Dalasi
Income: (per capita US$) 260 (1990)
Area; 4,361 sq. mi.
Population: (1991 estimate) 874,000
Illiteracy: 73% (1991)
Ethnic divisions: Mandinka 36.1%, Fula 16.8%, Wolof 13.4%, Jola 9.2%, Serahuli 7.3%, other 1.4%
Religious groups: Muslim 95%, Christian traditional belief
Languages spoken: English (official), Mandinka, Wolof, Fula, other traibal languages
International relations: Commonwealth, EC, OAU, UN
Form of government: Multi-party
Exports: Groundnuts

Gambia was once part of the Empire of Ghana and the Kingdom of Songhai. When the Portuguese visited in the fifteenth century, it was part of the Kingdom of Mali.

By the sixteenth century, Portuguese slave traders and gold seekers had settled. In 1588, the Portuguese sold exclusive trade rights on the Gambia River to English merchants. During the late seventeenth century

An Ethiopian market

and throughout the eighteenth, England and France struggled continuously for political and commercial supremacy in the regions of the Senegal and Gambia Rivers.

In 1807, slave trading was abolished throughout the British Empire, and the British tried unsuccessfully to end the slave traffic in Gambia. An 1889 agreement with France established the present boundaries, and Gambia became a British Crown Colony. Gambia achieved independence on February 18, 1965, as a constitutional monarchy within the British Commonwealth. In 1970, Gambia became a republic. Several attempts were made to establish a post-independence union with Senegal. A contingent of Senegalese soldiers were stationed in Gambia, but the arrangement soured. Coupled with mounting economic problems, the confederation ended.

Ghana
Official name: Republic of Ghana
Independence: March 6, 1957

Cattleherders in rural Gambia.

Capital: Accra
Currency: Cedi
Income: (per capita US$) 390 (1990)
Area: 92,100 sq. mi.
Population: (1991 estimate): 15,6 million
Illiteracy: 40% (1991)
Ethnic divisions: Akan, Ewe, Ga
Religious groups: Christian 42%, traditional belief 38%, Muslim 12%, other 7%
Languages spoken: English (official), Akan 44%, Mole-Dagbani 16%, Ewe 13%, Ga-Adangbe 8%
International relations: Commonwealth, EC, OAU, UN
Form of government: Provisions for multi-party has been set
Exports: Cocoa, diamonds, gold, manganese ore, wood

The first contact between Europe and the Gold Coast dates from 1470, when a party of Portuguese landed. For the next three centuries, the English, Danes, Dutch, Germans, and Portuguese controlled various parts of the coastal areas. In 1821, the British government took control of the British trading forts on the Gold Coast. In 1844, Fanti chiefs in the area signed an agreement with the British. Between 1826 and 1900, the British fought a series of campaigns against the Ashantis, whose kingdom was located inland. By 1902, the British had succeeded in colonizing the Ashanti region.

On March 6, 1957, the United Kingdom relinquished its control over the Colony of the Gold Coast and Ashanti, the Northern Territories Protectorate, and British Togoland. The Gold Coast and the former British Togoland merged to form what is now Ghana. Focusing on anti-imperialism and pan-Africanism, Ghana became a model for the whole continent. Though he had idolized throughout the diaspora, Nkruma was overthrown in 1966, subjecting the nation to military and dictatorial regimes. When Jerry Rawlings, who had masterminded two successfuly coups in 1979 and 1981, became head of state in 1982, he promised to return the country to pluralism. In 1992, he was elected to the presidency in a multi-party election.

Most Ghanaians descended from migrating tribes that probably came down the Volta River valley in the thirteenth century. Ethnically, Ghana is divided into small groups speaking more than 50 languages and dialects. Among the more important linguistic groups are the Akans, which include the Fantis along the coast and the Ashantis in the forest region north of the coast; the Guans, on the plains of the Volta River; the Ga- and Ewe-speaking peoples of the south and southeast; and the Moshi-Dagomba-speaking tribes of the northern and upper regions.

Guinea
Official name: Republic of Guinea
Independence: October 2, 1958
Capital: Conakry
Currency: Guinea franc
Income: (per capita US$) 480 (1990)
Area: 95,000 sq. mi.
Population: (1991 estimate) 7.4 million
Illiteracy: 72% (1991)
Ethnic divisions: Foulah, Malinke, Soussou, 15 smaller groups
Religious groups: Muslim 85%, Christian 10%, traditional belief 5%
Languages spoken: French (official), tribal languages
International relations: EC, OAU, UN
Form of government: Military
Exports: Agricultural products, minerals

The empires of Ghana, Mali, and Songhai spanned the period from about the tenth to the fifteenth centuries. French military penetration into the area began in the mid-nineteenth century. By signing treaties with the French in the 1880s, Guinea's Malinke leader, Samory Toure, secured a free hand to expand eastward. In 1890, he allied himself with the Toucouleur Empire and Kingdom of Sikasso and tried to expel the French from the area. However, he was defeated in 1898, and France

Gambian President, Dauda Jawara addresses local authorities.

gained control of Guinea and the Ivory Coast (now Cote d'Ivoire).

Guinea became an independent republic in 1958, and voted against entering the French community. Se'kou Touré was the first president until his death in 1984. The country then heavily relied upon aid from the Soviet bloc and attempts were made to insitute socialism. A military committee for national redressment (CMRN) lead a coup and later dissolved the one-party system with promises to restore democracy.

Guinea consists of four main ethnic groups—Peuls (Foulah or Foulani), who inhabit the mountainous Fouta Djallon; Malinkes (or Mandingos), in the savannah regions; Soussous in the coastal areas; and Forestal tribes in the forest regions.

Guinea-Bissau
Official name: Republic of Guinea-Bissau
Independence: September 24, 1973
Capital: Bissau
Currency: Guinea peso
Income: (per capita US$) 155 (1990)
Area: 14,000 sq. mi.
Population: (1991 estimate) 1 million
Illiteracy: 64% (1991)
Ethnic divisions: Balanta 27%, Fula 23%, Mandinka 12%, Manjaco 11%, Papel 10%, Biafada 3%, Mancanha 3%, Bijagos 3%
Religious groups: Traditional belief 65%, Muslim 30%, Christian 5%
Languages spoken: Portuguese (official); Criolo, tribal languages
International relations: EC, OAU, UN
Form of government: Pluralism
Exports: Coconuts, fish, groundnuts

The rivers of Guinea and the islands of Cape Verde were one of the first areas in Africa explored by the Portuguese in the fifteenth century. Portugal claimed Portuguese Guinea in 1446. In 1630, a "captaincy-general" of Portuguese Guinea was established to administer the territory. With the assistance of local tribes, the Portuguese entered the slave trade, exporting large numbers of Africans to the New World via Cape Verde. The slave trade declined in the ninteenth century and Bissau, originally founded as a fort in 1765, became the major commercial center.

In 1956, the African Party for the Independence of Guinea and Cape Verde (PAIGC) was organized by

Amilcar Cabral and Raphael Barbosa. Despite the presence of more than 30,000 Portuguese troops, the PAIGC exercised influence over much of the country; the Portuguese were increasingly confined to their garrisons and larger towns. The PAIGC National Assembly declared the independence of Guinea-Bissau on December 24, 1973, the same year that PAIGC leader Amilcar Cabral was assassinated by the Portuguese secret police; Portugal granted *de jure* independence on September 19, 1974, when the United States recognized the new nation. Luis Cabral, Amilcar's brother, became president of Guinea-Bissau and Cape Verde. In 1980 Cape Verde established its independence from Guinea-Bissau and its leader, Joao Bernado Vieira.

The population of Guinea-Bissau comprises several diverse tribal groups, each with its own language, customs, and social organization. The Fula and Mandinka tribes, in the north and northeast of the country, are mostly Muslim. Other important tribal groups are the Balanta and Papel, living in the southern coastal regions, and the Manjaco and Mancanha, occupying the central and northern coastal areas.

Kenya
Official name: Republic of Kenya
Independence: December 12, 1963
Capital: Nairobi
Currency: Kenyan shilling
Income:(per capita 370 (1990)
Area: 224,960 sq. mi.
Population: (1991 estimate) 25.2 million
Illiteracy: 41% (1991)
Ethnic divisions: Kikuyu 21%, Luhya 14%, Luo 13%, Kalenjin 11%, Kamba 11%, Kisii 6%, Meru 5%. Non-Africans 1%
Religious groups: Traditional belief 26%, Protestant 38%, Roman Catholic 28%, Muslim 6%
Languages spoken: Swahili (official), English, tribal languages
International relations: Commonwealth, EC, OAU, UN
Form of government: Multi-party
Exports: Coffee, hides and skins, petroleum products, soda ash, tea

The Cushitic-speaking people, who occupied the area that is now Kenya around 1000 BC, were known to have maintained contact with Arab traders during the first century AD; Arab and Persian settlements were founded along the coast as early as the eighth century AD. By then, Bantu and Nilotic peoples also had moved into the area. The Arabs were followed by the Portuguese in 1498, by Islamic control under the Imam of Oman in the 1600s, and by British influence in the ninteenth century. In 1885, European powers first partitioned east Africa into spheres of influence. In 1895, the British government established the East African Protectorate.

Nairobi, Kenya.

From October 1952 to December 1959, Kenya was under a state of emergency, arising from the Mau Mau rebellion against British colonial rule. The first direct elections for Africans to the legislative council took place in 1957. Kenya became fully independent on December 12, 1963. Jomo Kenyatta, a member of the predominant Kikuyu tribe and head of the Kenya African National Union, became Kenya's first president. He adopted a moderate, pro-Western policy and persued capitalism internally, allowing Kenya to achieve a higher level of economic prosperity than its neighbors. Kenyatta died in 1978, and was succeeded by Daniel Arap Moi, who insisted on persuing a one-party system until recently.

Lesotho
Official name: Kingdom of Lesotho
Independence: October 4, 1966
Capital: Maseru
Currency: Loti

A Masai tribesman.

Income: (per capita US$) 485 (1990)
Area: 11,718 sq. mi.
Population: (1991): 1.8 million
Illiteracy: 26% (1991)
Ethnic divisions: Basotho
Religious groups: Roman Catholic, Lesotho Evangelical, Anglican
Languages spoken: English, Sesotho
International relations: Commonwealth, EC, OAU, UN
Form of government: Constitutional monarchy
Exports: Diamonds, live animals, mohair, wool

Until the end of the sixteenth century, Basutoland, now Lesotho, was sparsely populated by bushmen (Qhuaique). Between the sixteenth and ninteenth centuries, refugees from surrounding areas gradually formed the Basotho ethnic group. In 1818, Moshoeshoe I, consolidated various Basotho groupings and became king. During his reign from 1823 to 1870, a series of wars with South Africa resulted in the loss of extensive lands, now known as the "Lost Territory." Moshoeshoe appealed to Queen Victoria for assistance, and in 1868 the country was placed under British protection.

In 1955, the Basutoland Council asked that it be empowered to legislate on internal affairs, and in 1959 a new constitution gave Basutoland its first elected legislature. On October 4, 1966, the new Kingdom of Lesotho attained full independence. Three years later, Leabua Jonathan became the head of state and embarked on repressing internal opposition. Years later, when he appeared to be losing the presidental elections, he seized pwoer in order to retain his leadership. Soon after, he was overthrown by the military.

Liberia
Official name: Republic of Liberia
Capital: Monrovia
Currency: Liberian dollar
Income: (per capita US$) 250 (1990)
Area: 43,000 sq. mi.
Population: (1991 estimate) 2.7 million
Illiteracy: 78% (1991)
Ethnic divisions: 5% descendants of freed American slaves, 95% indigenous tribes (the largest of which are Kpelle, Bassa, Gio, Kru, Grebo, Mano, Krahn, Gola, Gbandi, Loma, Kissi, Vai, Mandingo, and Belle)
Religious groups: Traditional belief 65%, Muslim 20%, Christian 15%
Languages spoken: English (official), more than 20 tribal languages of the Niger-Congo language group
International relations: EC, OAU, UN
Exports: Cocoa, coffee, diamonds, iron ore, rubber, wood

It is believed that the forebears of many present-day Liberians migrated into the area from the north and east between the twelfth and seventeenth centuries. Portuguese explorers visited Liberia's coast in 1461, and during the next 300 years, European merchants and coastal Africans engaged in trade.

The history of modern Liberia dates from 1816, when the American Colonization Society, a private organization, was given a charter by the United States Congress to send freed slaves to the west coast of Africa. The United States government, under President James Monroe, provided funds and assisted in negotiations with native chiefs for the ceding of land for this purpose. The first settlers landed at the site of Monrovia in 1822. In 1838, the settlers united to form the Commonwealth of Liberia, under a governor appointed by the American Colonization Society.

In 1847, Liberia became Africa's first independent republic. The republic's first 100 years have been described as a "century of survival" due to attempts by neighboring colonial powers (France and Britain) to encroach on Liberia. Independence gave power to the black elite of American origin and technically excluded the indigenous population, creating social tension. In 1980, Sargent Samuel Doe and his Council of Popular Redemption came to power in a bloody coup. Doe leaned on the Soviet Union and established himself as a dictator. He was killed, however, during an insurrection led by the National Patriotic Front. The nation continues to be in turmoil.

Libya
Official name: Socialist People's Libyan Arab Jamahiriya
Independence: December 24, 1951
Capital: Tripoli
Currency: Dinar
Income: (per capita US$) 6,060 (1990)
Area: 679,536 sq.mi.
Population: (1991 estimate) 4.3 million
Illiteracy: 36% (1991)
Ethnic divisions: Arab and Arab/Berber 80%, Berber 15%, Touareg and Tebous Arab
Religious groups: Sunni Muslim 97%
Languages spoken: Arabic
International relations: Arab League, OAU, UN
Form of government: Military

In the seventh century AD, Arabs conquered the area that is now Libya. In the following centuries, most of the inhabitants adopted Islam and the Arabic language and culture. The Ottoman Turks conquered the country in the sixteenth century. Libya remained part of their empire—although at times virtually autonomous—until Italy invaded in 1911 and, after years of resistance, incorporated Libya as its colony.

King Idris I, Emir of Cyrenaica, led a Libyan resistance to Italian occupation between the two World Wars. Under the terms of the 1947 peace treaty with the allies, Italy relinquished all claims to Libya. On November 21, 1949, the United Nations General Assembly passed a resolution stating that Libya should become independent before January 1, 1952. Libya declared its independence on December 24, 1951.

In a military coup of 1969, King Idris was overthrown by Muammar al-Qaddafi, who, nationalized all the petroleum resources and embarked on supporting international terrorism against the Western countries Some of Qaddafi's activities have also created friction with some of the neighboring countries, and, in 1986, the United States bombed Tripoli and Benghazi.

Madagascar
Official name: Democratic Republic of Madagascar
Independence: June 26, 1960
Capital: Antananarivo
Currency: Malagasy franc
Income:(per capita US$) 230 (1990)
Area: 228,880 sq. mi.
Population (1991 estimate) 12.1 million

Illiteracy: 20% (1991)
Ethnic divisions: 18 Malagasy tribes, small groups of Comorians, French, Indians, and Chinese
Religious groups: Traditional belief 55%, Christian 40%, Muslim 5%
Languages spoken: Malagasy (official), French
International relations: EC, OAU, UN
Form of government: Multiparty
Exports: Coffee, cloves, crude petroleum, sugar, vanilla

Located east of the African mainland in the Indian Ocean, Madagascar is home to people who arrived from Africa and Asia during the first five centuries AD. Three major kingdoms ruled the island—Betsimisaraka, Merina, and Sakalava. In the seventh century AD, Arabs established trading posts in the coastal areas of what is now Madagascar. Portuguese sighted the island in the sixteenth century, and in the late seventeenth century, the French established trading posts along the east coast.

In the 1790s, the Merina rulers succeeded in establishing hegemony over the major part of the island including the coast. The Merina ruler and the British governor of Mauritius concluded a treaty abolishing the slave trade, which had been important in Madagascar's economy, and in return the island received British military assistance. British influence remained strong for several decades. The British accepted the imposition of a French protectorate over Madagascar in 1885. France established control by military force in 1895, and the Merina monarchy was abolished. The Malagasy Republic was proclaimed on October 14, 1958, as an autonomous state within the French community. A period of provisional government ended with the adoption of a constitution in 1959 and full independence in 1960.

Madagascar persued a moderate policy after independence and collaboration with France continued until 1972 when a military coup took over and launched a socialist policy aligning itself with the eastern block. Malagasy as the country is know today, has suffered a severe economic crisis after having nationalized all the French property and having very little foreign investment.

Madagascar's population is predominantly of mixed Asian and African origin. The largest groups are the Betsimisaraka (one million), the Tsimihety (500,000), and the Sakalava (500,000).

Malawi
Official name: Republic of Malawi
Independence: July 6, 1964
Capital: Lilongwe
Currency: Kwacha
Income: (per capita US$) 212 (1990)
Area: 45,747 sq. mi.
Population: (1991 estimate) 9.4 million
Illiteracy: 59% (1991)
Ethnic divisions: Chewa, Nyanja, Tumbuka, Yao, Lomwe, Sena, Tonga, Ngoni Asians
Religious groups: Protestant 55%, Roman Catholic 20%, Muslim 20%, traditional belief
Languages spoken: Chicewa and English (official), tribal languages
International relations: EC, OAU, UN
Form of government: Multi-party
Exports: Cotton, groundnuts, sugar, tea, tobacco

Hominid remains and stone implements, dating back more than 1 million years, have been identified in Malawi; early humans are belived to have inhabited the area surrounding Lake Malawi 50,000 to 60,000 years ago.

Malawi derives its name from the Maravi, a Bantu people who came from the southern Congo about six hundred years ago. By the sixteenth century, the two divisions of the tribe had established a kingdom stretching from north of today's Nkhotakota to the Zambezi River in the south and from Lake Malawi in the east to the Luangwa River in Zambia in the west.

The Portuguese first reached the area in the sixteenth century. David Livingston reached the shore of Lake Malawi in 1859. By 1878 a number of traders, mostly from Scotland, formed the African Lakes Company to supply goods and services to the missionaries. In 1891, the British established the Nyasaland Protectorate. Nyasaland joined with Northern and Southern Rhodesia in 1953 to form the Federation of Rhodesia and Nyasaland.

Throughout the 1950s, pressures were exerted within Nykasaland for independence. In July 1958, Dr. H. Kamazu Banda returned to the country after a long stay in the United States (where he had obtained his medical degree at Meharry Medical College in 1937), the United Kingdom, and Ghana. He assumed leadership of the Nyasaland African Congress, which later became the Malawi Congress Party (MCP). In 1959, Banda was sent to Gwele Prison for his political activities but was released in 1960.

On April 15, 1961, the MCP won an overwhelming victory in elections for a new Legislative Council. In a second constitutional conference in London in November of 1962, the British government agreed to give Nyasaland self-governing status the following year. Dr. Banda became prime minister on February 1, 1963, although the British still controlled Malawi's financial security and judicial systems. The Federation of Rhodesia and Nyasaland was dissolved on December 31, 1963, and Malawi became fully independent on July 6, 1964. Two years later, Malawi adopted a new constitution and became a republic with Dr. Banda as its first president. In 1996, Bakili Mluzi, a woman, was elected to the presidency.

The Chewas constitute 90 percent of the population of the central region; the Nyanja tribe predominates in the south and the Tumbuka in the north. In addition, significant numbers of the Tongas live in the north; Ngonis—an offshoot of the Zulus who came from South Africa in the early 1800s—live in the lower northern and lower central regions; and the Yao, who are mostly Muslim, live along the southeastern border with Mozambique.

Mali
Official name: Republic of Mali
Independence: September 22, 1960
Capital: Bamako
Currency: CFA franc
Area: 474,764 sq. mi.
Population: (1991 estimate) 8.3 million
Illiteracy: 90% (1991)
Ethnic divisions: Mande (Bambara or Bamana, Malinke, Sarakole) 50%, Peul 17% Voltaic 12%, Songhai 6%, Tuareg and Moor 5%
Religious groups: Islam 90%, traditional belief 9%, Christian 1%
Languages spoken: French (official) and Bambara (spoken by about 80% of the population)
International relations: EC, OAU, UN
Exports: Cotton, groundnuts, live animals

Mali is the cultural heir to the succession of ancient African empires—Ghana, Malinke, and Songhai—that occupied the West African savanna. The Ghana empire, dominated by the Soninke people and centered in the area along the Malian-Mauritanian frontier, was a powerful trading state from about 700 to 1075 AD. The Malinke kingdom of Mali, from which the republic takes its name, had its origins on the upper Niger River in the eleventh century. Expanding rapidly in the thirteenth century under the leadership of Soundiata Keita, it reached its height about 1325, when it conquered Timbuktu and Gao. The Songhai empire expanded its power from its center in Gao during the period 1465 to 1530. At its peak under Askia Mohammad I, it encompassed the Hausa states as far as Kano (in present-day Nigeria) and much of the territory that had belonged to the Mali Empire in the west. It was destroyed by a Moroccan invasion in 1591.

French military penetration of the area began around 1880. A French civilian governor of Soudan (the French name for the area) was appointed in 1893, but resistance to French control was not abrogated until 1898 when the Malinke warrior, Samory Toure, was defeated after seven years of war. In January 1959, Soudan joined Senegal to form the Mali Federation, which became fully independent within the French Community on June 20, 1960. The federation collapsed on August 20, 1960, when Senegal seceded. On September 22, Soudan proclaimed itself the Republic of Mali and withdrew from the French Community.

The first head of state—Modibo Keita followed a socialist orientation but gradually increased his authoritarian leadership. In 1968, Military Committee of National Liberation coup overthrew Keita's government. Mali remains a poor country, compounded by the fact that more than half of its territory is a desert.

Mali's population consists of diverse sub-Saharan ethnic groups, sharing similar historic, cultural, and religious traditions. Exceptions are the Tuaregs and Moors, desert nomads, who are related to the North African Berbers.

Mauritania
Official name: Islamic Republic of Mauritania
Independence: November 28, 1960
Capital: Nouakchott
Currency: Ouguiya
Income (per capita US$) 500 (1990)
Area: 419,229 sq. mi.
Population: (1991 estimate) 1.9 million
Illiteracy: 72% (1991)
Ethnic divisions: Arab-Berber, Arab-Berber-Negroid, Negroid
Religious groups: Moslem
Languages spoken: Hassaniya Arabic (national), French (official), Pular, Wolof, and Soninke
International relations: Arab League, EC, OAU, UN
Form of government: Military
Exports: Fish, gypsum, iron ore

Archeological evidence suggests that Berber and Negroid Mauritanians lived beside one another before the spread of the desert drove them southward. Migration of these people increased during the third and fourth centuries AD, when Berber groups arrived seeking pasture for their herds and safety from political unrest and war in the north. The Berbers established a loose confederation, called the Sanhadja. Trading towns were established to facilitate the trade of gold, ivory, and slaves.

In the tenth century, conquests by warriors of the Soudanese Kingdom of Ghana broke up the Berber confederation. In the eleventh century, the conquest of the Western Sahara regions by a Berber tribe, decimated the Ghanaian kingdom and firmly established Islam throughout Mauritania. However, these people were defeated by Arab invaders in the sixteenth century.

French military penetration of Mauritania began early in the twentieth century. However, the area come

Malian men on camels.

under French control until about 1934. Until independence, the French governed the country largely by relying on the authority of the tribal chiefs, some of whom, such as the Emirs of Trarza and Adrar, had considerable authority. Under French occupation, slavery was legally abolished.

Mauritania became a French colony in 1920. The Islamic Republic of Mauritania was proclaimed in November 1958. Mauritania became independent on November 28, 1960 and withdrew from the French Community in 1966.

Mokhtar Ould Daddah, leader of the Mauritian People's Party was the first head of state, but a series of coups took place: the first, in 1978, replaced Daddah with Col. Moustabpha Ould Mohammed Salek, who was then replaced by Prime Minister Mohammed Khouma Ould Haidalla. In 1984, another coup, this one led by Maawiya Ould Sid'Ahmed Taya took place.

Moors, heterogeneous groups of Arab-Berber people who speak Hassaniya dialects, make up an estimated three-quarters of the population and are traditionally nomadic pastoralists. The country's black population—the Toucouleur, Soninke, Bambara, and Wolof—are mainly cultivators and are concentrated along the Senegal River.

Mauritius

Independence: March 12, 1968
Capital: Port Louis
Currency: Rupee
Income: (per capita US$) 2300 (1990)
Area: 720 sq. mi.
Population: (1991 estimate) 1 million
Illiteracy: 17% (1991)
Ethnic divisions: Indo-Mauritians 68%, Creoles 27%, Sino-Mauritians 3%, Franco-Mauritians 2%
Religious groups: Hindo, Muslim, Roman Catholic
Languages spoken: English (official), Creole, French, Hindi, Urdu, Hakka, Bhojpuri
International relations: Commonwealth, EC, OAU, UN
Form of government: Multi-party
Exports: Garments, molasses, sugar, tea, textiles

Portuguese sailors first visited Mauritius in the early sixteenth century, although the island has been known to Arabs and Malays much earlier. Dutch sailors, who named the island in honor of Prince Maurice of Nassau, established a small colony in 1638, but abandoned it in

A Bamana artistian.

1710. The French claimed Mauritius in 1715, renaming it Ile de France. In 1810, Mauritius was captured by the British, whose possession of the island was confirmed four years later by the Treaty of Paris. After slavery was abolished in 1835, indentured laborers from India brought an additional cultural influence to the island. Mauritius achieved independence on March 12, 1968. After independence Mauritius continued to face not only severe economic problems but also ethnic diversity crisis between the French cultural influence and English.

27 percent of Mauritians are of mixed European and African descent, tracing their origins to the plantation owners and slaves who were the first to exploit the island's potential for growing sugar. Descendants of the Indian immigrants constitute 68 percent of the population and are the principal laborers in the sugar industry.

Mayotte (Mahoré)
Independence: n/a (overseas territory of France)
Capital: Dziaodzi
Area: 375 sq.km.
Population: (1992 estimate) 86,628
Religious groups: Muslim 99%; remainder Christian (mostly Roman Catholic)
Languages spoken: Mahorian (a Swahili dialect), French
Exports: Coconut, sugar cane, vanilla, ylang-ylang

Part of the Comoros archipelago, Mayotte shares its history with the Comoros Federal Islamic Republic. When Comoros declared independence in 1975, Mayotte voted to remain an overseas territory of France. Although Comoros has since claimed Mayotte, the French have promised the islanders that they may remain French citizens for as long as they wish.

Morocco
Official name: Kingdom of Morocco
Independence: March 2, 1956
Capital: Rabat
Currency: Dirham
Income: (per capita US$) 950 (1990)
Area: 173,413 sq. mi.
Population (1991 estimate) 26.1 million
Ethnic divisions: Arab-Berber
Religious groups: Sunni Muslim
Languages spoken: Arabic (official), French, Berber dialects
International relations: Arab League, UN
Form of government: Mornachy

Arab forces began occupying Morocco in the seventh century AD, bringing with them Arab civilization and Islam. Morocco's location and resources led to early competition among Europeans in Africa, beginning with successful Portuguese efforts to control the Atlantic coast in the fifteenth century. France showed a strong interest in Morocco as early as 1830. The Treaty of Fez (1912) made Morocco a protectorate of France. By the same treaty, Spain assumed the role of protecting power over the northern and southern (Saharan) zones. The Kingdom of Morocco recovered its political independence from France on March 2, 1956. By agreements with Spain in 1956 and 1958.

From 1904 until 1975, Spain occupied the entire territory, which is divided into a northern portion, the Saguia el Hamra, and the southern two-thirds, known as Rio de Oro. Calls for the decolonization of these territories began in the 1960s, first from the surrounding nations and then from the United Nations.

Morocco's claim to sovereignty over the Western Sahara is based largely on the historical argument of traditional loyalty of the Saharan tribal leaders to the Moroccan sultan as spiritual leader and ruler. The International Court of Justice, to which the issue was referred, delivered its opinion in 1975 that while historical ties exist between the inhabitants of the Western Sahara and Morocco, they are insufficient to establish Moroccan sovereignty.

Dancers from Morocco.

The monarchy has been under King Hassan II since the death of Mohammed V who tends to be authoritarian. Moroccan economy has had a boost from the discovery of phosphate and increased tourism, but the gross domestic product is low and the populations subsist on farming and livestock.

Mozambique
Official name: People's Republic of Mozambique
Independence: June 25, 1975
Capital: Maputo
Currency: Metical
Income: (per capita US$) 85 (1990)
Area: 303,769 sq. mi.
Population (1991) 15.1 million
Illiteracy: 83% (1991)
Ethnic divisions: Makua, Tsonga, Makonde, and other tribal groups
Religious groups: Traditional belief 50%, Muslim 30% Christian 15%
Languages spoken: Portuguese (official), tribal languages
International relations: EC, OAU, UN
Form of government: Multi-party
Exports: Cotton, molasses, nuts, sugar, tea

Mozambique's first inhabitants were Bushmanoid hunters and gatherers, ancestors of the Khoisani peoples. During the first four centuries AD, waves of Bantu-speaking peoples migrated from the north through the Zambezi River Valley and then gradually into the plateau and coastal areas. When Portuguese explorers reached Mozambique in 1498, Arab trading settlements had existed along the coast for several centuries. Later, traders and prospectors penetrated the hinterland seeking gold and slaves.

After World War II, while many European nations were granting independence to their colonies, Portugal clung to the concept that Mozambique and other Portuguese possessions were "overseas provinces." In 1962, several Mozambican anti-Portuguese political groups formed the Front for Liberation of Mozambique (FRELIMO) which in September 1964 initiated and armed campaign against Portuguese colonial rule. After ten years of sporadic warfare and major political changes in Portugal, Mozambique became independent on June 25, 1975.

Samora Machel led Frelimo to independence in 1975, and immediately faced civil war with RENAMO (Mozambique National Resistance). More than 600,000 were killed; farms, roads, railways were destroyed; and half of the population was dislocated. After Samora was killed in air crash, Joaquim Chissano became head of state. A cease fire was entered with RENAMO in 1992, and multi-party elections were scheduled.

The ten major ethnic groups living in Mozambique are divided into subgroups with diverse languages, dialects, cultures, and history; the largest are the Majua and Tsonga.

Namibia (Formerly South West Africa)
Official name: Republic of Namibia
Capital: Windhoek
Currency: South African rand
Income: per capita 1342 (1990)
Area: 320,827 sq. mi.
Population (1991 estimate) 1.5 million
Illiteracy: 28% (1991)
Ethnic divisions: Black 87%; White 6%; mixed race 7%
Religious groups: Predominantly Christian, traditional belief
Languages spoken: English (official), Afrikaans, German, tribal languages
International relations: OAU, UN
Form of government: Multi-party

In 1878, the United Kingdom annexed Walvis Bay on behalf of Cape Colony, and the area was incorporated into the Cape of Good Hope in 1884. In 1883, a German trader, Adolf Luderitz, claimed the remainder of the coastal region after negotiations with a local chief. German administration ended during World War I, when the territory was occupied by South African forces in 1915.

On December 17, 1920, South Africa undertook the administration of South West Africa under the terms of Article 22 of the Covenant of the League of Nations and a mandate agreement confirmed by the League Council. The mandate agreement gave South Africa full power of administration and legislation over the territory as an integral part of South Africa. During the 1960s, as other Afican nations gained independence, pressure mounted on South Africa to do so in South West Africa.

In 1966, the United Nations General Assembly revoked South Africa's mandate. Also in 1966, the South

West Africa People's Organization (SWAPO) began guerrilla attacks on Namibia, infiltrating the territory from bases in Zambia. In a 1971 advisory opinion, the International Court of Justice upheld United Nation authority over Namibia, determining that the South African presence in Namibia was illegal and that South Africa therefore was obligated to withdraw its administration from Namibia immediately. In 1977, the United Nations approved as Security Council Resolution 435, calling for, among other things, the holding of elections in Namibia under United Nations supervision and control the cessation of hostile acts by all parties. South Africa agreed to cooperate in achieving implementation of Resolution 435. Nevertheless, in December 1978, in defiance of the United Nations proposal, it unilaterally held elections in Namibia which were boycotted by SWAPO and other political parties.

Intense discussions between the concerned parties continued during the 1978–1988 period. In May 1988, an American mediation team brought negotiators from Angola, Cuba, and South Africa and observers from the Soviet Union together in London. On April 1, the Republic of South Africa agreed to withdraw its troops. Implementation of Resolution 435 officially began on April 1, 1989. The elections held November 7–11, 1989, were certified as free and fair by the special representative, with SWAPO taking 57 percent of the vote; the Democratic Turnhalle Alliance, the principal opposition party, received 29 percent of the vote. By February 9, 1990, the constituent assembly had drafted and adopted a constitution. March 21 was set as the date for independence. SWAPO's Sam Nujoma won elections, and he became the first head of state in 1990.

Namibia is one of the least populated country in Africa. Namibia's indigenous Africans are of diverse linguistic and ethnic origins. The principal groups are the Ovambo, Kavango, Herero/Himba, Damara, mixed race ("Colored" and Rehoboth Baster), white (Afrikaner, German and Portuguese), Nama, Caprivian (Lozi), Bushman, and Tswana. The minority white population is primarily of South African, British, and German descent. Approximately 60 percent of the white population speaks Afrikaans (a variation of Dutch), 30 percent German, and ten percent English.

Niger

Official name: Republic of Niger
Independence: August 3, 1960
Capital: Niamey
Currency: CFA franc
Income: (per capita US$) 300 (1990)
Area: 490,000 sq. mi.
Population (1991) 8.1 million
Illiteracy: 86% (1991)
Ethnic divisions: Hausa 56%, Djerma 22%, Fulani 8.5% Tuareg 8%, Beri Beri (Kanouri) 4.3% Arab, Toubou, and Gourmantche 1.2%
Religious groups: Muslim, traditional belief, and Christians
Languages spoken: French (official), Hausa, Djerma
International relations: Ec, OAU, UN
Form of government: Multi-party
Exports: Crude materials, live animals, uranium

Considerable evidence indicates that about 600,000 years ago, humans inhabited what has since become the desolate Sahara of northern Niger. Niger was an important economic crossroads, and the empires of Songhei, Mali, Gao, Kanem, and Bornu, as well as a number of Hausa states, claimed control over portions of the area.

During recent centuries, the nomadic Taureg formed large confederations, pushed southward, and siding with various Hausa states, clashed with the Fulani empire of Sokoto, which had gained control of much of the Hausa territory in the late eighteenth century. In the ninteenth century, the first European explorers reached the area searching for the mouth of the Niger River.

Although French efforts at colonization began before 1900, dissident ethnic groups, especially the desert Taureg, were not defeated until 1922. On December 4, 1958, after the establishment of the Fifth French Republic, Niger became an autonomous state within the French Community. Following full independence on August 3, 1960, however, membership was allowed to lapse. Hamani Diori was overthrown in a military coup and replaced by Col. Seyni Kountche as president. 13 years later Ali Saibou succeeded him.

The two largest ethnic groups in Niger are the Hausa, who also constitute the major ethnic group in northern Nigeria, and the Djerma-Songhai. Both groups are farmers who live in the arable, southern tier. The rest of the population consists of nomadic or seminomadic livestock-raising peoples, which include the Fulani, Tuareg, Kanouri, and Toubou.

Nigeria

Official name: Federal Republic of Nigeria
Independence: October 1, 1960
Capital: Abuja
Currency: Naira
Income (per capita US$) 270 (1990)
Area: 356,700 sq. mi.
Population (1991): 88.5 million
Illiteracy: 58% (1991)
Ethnic divisions: 250 tribal groups, the largest are Hausa-Fulani, Ibo, and Yoruba
Religious groups: Muslim, Christian, traditional belief
Languages spoken: English (official), Hausa, Ibo, Yoruba
International relations: Commonwealth, EC, OAU, UN

Hausa men on horseback.

Form of government: Military

Evidence shows that more than 2,000 years ago, the Nok people who lived in what is now the Plateau state worked iron and produced sophisticated terra cotta sculpture. In the centuries that followed, the Hausa kingdom and the Bornu empire, near Lake Chad, prospered as important terminals of north-south trade between North African Berbers and forest people who exchanged slaves, ivory, and kola nuts for salt, glass beads, coral, cloth, weapons, brass rods, and cowrie shells used a currency. In the southwest, the Uoruba kingdom of Oyo, which was founded about 1400 and reached its height between the seventeenth and ninteenth centuries, attained a high level of political organization and extended as far as modern Togo. In the south-central part of present-day Nigeria, as early as the fifteenth century, the kingdom of Benin had developed an efficient army, an elaborate ceremonial court, and artisans whose works in ivory, wood, bronze, and brass are prized throughout the world today.

Between the seventeenth and ninteenth centuries, European traders established coastal ports for the increasing traffic in slaves destined for the Americas. In 1855, British claims to a sphere of influence in that area received international recognition, and, in the following year, the Royal Niger Company was chartered. In 1900, the company's territory came under the control of the British government. In 1914, the area was formally united as the "Colony and Protectorate of Nigeria." Nigeria was granted full independence on October 1, 1960, as a federation of three regions.

Since independence, Nigeria has faced numerous coups. The Ibos tried to cesede and tension between various ethnic groups increased, while the country began a rapid economic development based on oil production. Yakubu Gowon who had managed to stay in power was overthrown in 1976 by Mohammed Murtala, followed by Ge. Olusegun Obasanjo. A return to civilian rule came in 1979, under Shehu Shagari, however the military returned in 1984 under Mohammed Buhari and then again under Maj. Gen. Ibrahim Babangida. Sani Abacha ascended to power on November 17, 1993. His government has been internationally announced for hurman rights abuses, including executions.

The most populous country in Africa, Nigeria accounts for one quarter of Sub-Saharan Africa's people. The dominant ethnic group in the northern two-thirds of the country is the Hausa-Fulani, most of whom are

A minaret in Agadez, Niger.

Tomi of Ede John Adetoyese with a boy drummer.

Muslims. Other major ethnic groups of the north are the Nupe, Tiv, and Kanuri. The Yoruba people are predominant in the southwest. About half of the Yorubas are Christian and half Muslim. The predominately Catholic Ibos are the largest ethnic group in the southeast, with the Efik, Ibibio, and Ijaw comprising a substantial segment of the population in that area as well.

Réunion

Independence: n/a (overseas department of France)
Area: 2,510 sq. km.
Population: (1992 estimate) 626,414
Ethnic divisions: Intermixed African, French, Malagasy, Chinese, Pakistani, and Indian ancestry
Religious groups: Roman Catholic 94%
Languages spoken: French (official), Creole

The island of Réunion, located in the Indian Ocean, remained uninhabited until 1654, when the French East India Company established bases and brought in slaves from Africa and Madagascar. France governed the island as a colony until 1946, when it was granted department status.

The population of Réunion is of mixed African, French, Indian, and Chinese origin.

Rwanda

Official name: Republic of Rwanda
Independence: July 1, 1962
Capital: Kigali
Currency: Rwandan franc
Income (per capita US$) 310 (1990)
Area: 10,169 sq. mi.
Population: (1991 estimate): 7.9 million
Ethnic divisions: Hutu 85%, Tutsi 14%, Twa 1%
Religious groups: Christian 74%, traditional belief 25%, Muslim 1%
Languages spoken: French, Kinyarwanda
Exports: Coffee, tea, tin

For centuries Hutu farmers farmed the area that is now Rwanda; in the fifteenth century Tutsi herders settled in the area. In 1899, the court of Mwami submitted to a German protectorate with resistance. Belgian troops from Zaire occupied Rwanda in 1916; after World War I, the League of National mandated Rwanda and its southern neighbor, Burundi, to Belgium as the Territory of Ruanda-Urundi. Following World War II, Ruanda-Urundi became a United Nations trust territory with Belgium as the administering authority. The Party of the Hutu Emancipation Movement (PARMEHUTU) won an overwhelming victory in a United Nations-supervised referendum.

The PARMEHUTU government, formed as a result of the September 1961 election, was granted internal autonomony by Belgium on January 1, 1962. A June of 1962 United Nations General Assembly resolution terminated the Belgian trusteeship and granted full independence to Rwanda (and Burundi) effective July 1, 1962. Gregiore Kayibanda, leader of the PARMEHUTU Party, became Rwanda's first elected president.

Ethnic clashes continued with neighboring Burundi. Gen. Juve'nal Habyarimana, who had been a military head of state, returned to power in the presidential elections of 1978 and 1983 (both having been the only candidate). In 1990 the BaTutsi launched an armed struggle. The ethnic crisis was still continuing in the mid-1990s.

The indigenous population consists of three ethnic groups. The Tutsi (14 percent) are a pastoral people of Nilotic origin. The Hutus, who comprise the majority of the population (85 percent), are farmers of Bantu origin. The Twa pygmies (1 percent) are thought to be the remnants of the earliest settlers of the region.

Saint Helena

Independence: n/a (dependent territory of the United Kingdom)
Area: 410 sq. km.
Population: (1992 estimate) 6,698
Religious groups: Anglican majority, Baptist, Seventh-Day Adventist, and Roman Catholic
Languages spoken: English
Exports: Fish, livestock

The islands of Saint Helena, Ascension, and Tristan da Cunha lie about one-thirds of the way between Africa and South America in the South Atlantic Ocean. The islands remained uninhabited, until they were visited by the Portuguese in 1502. In 1659, the British East India Company established a settlement on Saint Helena and in 1673 was granted a charter to govern the island. These islands represent the last of what was once the British Empire.

Sao Tome and Principe

Official name: Democratic Republic of Sao Tome and Principe
Independence: July 12, 1975
Capital: Sao Tomé
Currency: Dobra
Income: (per capita US$) 380 (1990)
Area: 372 sq. mi.
Population: (1991 estimate) 128,000
Ethnic divisions: Mixed African, Portuguese-African
Religious groups: Christian 80%
Languages spoken: Portuguese
International relations: EC, OAU, UN
Form of government: Multi-party
Exports: Cocoa, coffee, cinchona bark, copra, palm kernels

These uninhabited islands were first visited by Portuguese navigators between 1469 and 1472. The first successful settlement of Sao Tome was established in 1493. Principe was settled in 1500. By the mid-1500s, with the help of slave labor, the Portuguese settlers had turned the islands into Africa's foremost exporter of sugar. Sao Tome and Principe were taken over and administered by the Portuguese crown in 1522 and 1573 respectively. By 1908, Sao Tome had become the world's largest producer of cocoa, still the country's most important crop.

The rocas system, which gave the plantation managers a high degree of authority, led to abuses against the African farm workers. Although Portugal officially abolished slavery in 1876, the practice of forced paid labor continued. Sporadic labor unrest and dissatisfaction continued well into the twentieth century, culminating in an outbreak of riots in 1953 in which several hundred African laborers were killed.

By the late 1950s, a small group of Sao Tomeans had formed the Movement for the Liberation of Sao Tome and Principe (MLSTP). In 1974, Portuguese representatives met with the MLSTP in Algiers and worked out an agreement for the transfer of sovereignty. After a period of transition, Sao Tome and Principe achieved independence on July 12, 1975, choosing as its first president the MLSTP Secretary General Manuel Pinto da Costa. Four years after independence, da Costa consolidated his power by eliminating the position of prime minister and assuming those duties himself.

Sao Tome and Principe's population, consists of people descended from groups that have migrated to the islands since 1485. Six groups are identifiable: Mestico, of mixed-blood, descendants of African slaves brought to the islands during the early years of settlement from Benin, Gabon, Congo, and Angola. Anglares, reputedly descendants of Angolan slaves who survived on a 1540 shipwreck and now earn their livelihood fishing; Forros, descendants of freed slaves; Servicais, contract laborers from Angola, Mozambique, and Cape Verde, living temporarily on the islands; Tongas, children of servicais born on the islands; and Europeans, primarily Portuguese.

Senegal

Official name: Republic of Senegal
Independence: April 4, 1960
Capital: Dakar
Currency: CFA franc
Income: (per capita US$) 658 (1988)

Area: 76,000 sq. mi.
Population: (1991 estimate): 7.9 million
Illiteracy: 62% (1990)
Ethnic divisions: Wolof 43%, Fulani (Peulh) and Toucouleur 23%, Serer 15%, Diola, Mandingo, others 22%
Religious groups: Muslim 94%, Christian 5%, traditional belief 1%
Languages spoken: French (official), Solof, Pulaar, Diola, Mandingo
International relations: EC, OAU, UN
Form of government: Multi-party
Exports: Fish, groundnuts, petroleum, phosphates

Archaeological findings throughout the area indicate that Senegal was inhabited in prehistoric times. Islam established itself in the Senegal River valley during the eleventh century. In the thirteenth and fourteenth centuries, the area came under the influence of the great Mandingo empires to the east, during which the Jolof empire of Senegal was founded. The empire comprised the states of Cayor, Baol, Oualo, Sine, and Soloum until the sixteenth century, when they revolted for independence.

The Portuguese were the first Europeans to trade in Senegal, arriving in the fiteenth century. They were soon followed by the Dutch and French. During the ninteenth century, the French gradually established control over the interior regions and administered them as a protectorate until 1920, and as a colony thereafter.

In January of 1959, Senegal and the French Soudan merged to form the Mali Federation, which became fully independent on June 20, 1960. Due to internal political difficulties, the federation broke up on August 20, 1960; Senegal and Soudan (renamed the Republic of Mali) each proclaimed separate independence. Leopold Sedar Senghor, internationally renowned poet, politician, and statesman, was elected Senegal's first president in August of 1960. Senghor guided the nation and instituted a multi-party state by 1978. He resigned three years later (an unheard of action in Africa) and Abdou Dious became the head of state. In the summer of 1995, Dakar hosted the African–African American Summit.

Seychelles
Official name: Republic of Seychelles
Independence: June 29, 1976
Capital: Victoria
Currency: Rupee
Income: (per capita US$) 4670 (1990)
Area: 171 sq. mi.
Population (1991 estimate): 68,000
Illiteracy: 43% (1991)
Ethnic divisions: Creole (mixture of Asians, Africans, and Europeans)
Religious groups: Roman Catholic 90%, Anglican 8%, other 2%
Languages spoken: Creole, English, and French
International relations: Commonwealth, EC, OAU, UN
Form of government: One-party
Exports: Cinnamon bark, copra, fish

In 1742, the French governor of Mauritius, sent an expedition to the islands. A second expedition in 1756 reasserted formal possession by France. The Seychelles islands were captured and freed several times during the French Revolution and the Napoleonic wars, then passed officially to the British under the Treaty of Paris in 1814. Negotiations with the British resulted in an agreement by which Seychelles became a sovereign republic on June 29, 1976. After independence Seychelles had a multi-party government but one year later Albert René instituted his People's Progressive Front as the only party. He was overthrown in a coup in 1981.

Most Seychellois are descendants of early French settlers and the African slaves brought to the Seychelles in the nineteenth century by the British, who freed them from slave ships on the East African coast. Indians and Chinese (1.1 percent of the population) account for the other permanent inhabitants.

Sierra Leone
Official name: Republic of Sierra Leone
Independence: April 27, 1961
Capital: Freetown
Currency: Leone
Income (per capita US$) 160 (1990)
Area: 27,925 sq. mi.
Population: (1991 estimate) 4.2 million
Illiteracy: 79% (1991)
Ethnic divisions: Temne 30%, Mende 29%, Creole 2%
Religious groups: Muslim 60%, Animist 30%, Christian 10%
Languages spoken: English (official), Krio (lingua franca), Temne, Mende, other tribal languages
International relations: Commonwealth, EC, OAU, UN
Exports: Bauxite, cocoa, coffee, diamonds, rutile

Sierra Leone was one of the first West African British colonies. Foreign settlement did not occur for another two centuries, when the British laid plans for a refuge within the British Empire for freed slaves. In 1787, the site of Freetown received the first four-hundred freedmen from Great Britain. Disease and hostility from the indigenous people almost eliminated this first group. Five years later, however, another group of settlers, 1,000 freed slaves who had fled from the United States to Nova Scotia during the American Revolution, arrived under the auspices of the newly formed British Sierra

Leone Company. In 1800, about 550 blacks arrived from Jamaica via Nova Scotia; these were the Maroons, escaped slaves who maintained their independence in the mountains of Jamaica.

The 1951 constitution provided the framework for decolonization. Independence came in April 1961, and Sierra Leone became a parliamentary system within the British Commonwealth. In April 1971, it adopted a republican constitution, cutting the link to the British monarchy but remaining with the Commonwealth. Siaka Steven who fought for government control of the country's major resources, namely—iron and diamonds—eventually held the power. In 1984 countrywide disturbances spread and several attempted coups have took place.

18 ethnic groups make up the indigenous population of Sierra Leone. The Temne in the north and the Mende in the south are the largest. About 60,000 are Creoles, descendants of black settlers from Great Britain or North America.

Somalia
Official name: Somalia Democratic Republic
Independence: July 1, 1960
Capital: Mogadoshu
Currency: Somalian shilling
Income:(per capita US$) 150 (1990)
Area: 246,000 sq. mi.
Population: (1991 esttimate): 6.7 million
Illiteracy: 45% (1991)
Ethnic divisions: Somali 98.8%, Arab and Asian 1.2%
Religious groups: Muslim
Languages spoken: Somali
Exports: Bananas, fish, hides, live animals

The British East India Company's desire for unrestricted harbor facilities led to the conclusion of treaties with the sultan of Tajura as early as 1840. It was not until 1886, however, that the British gained control over northern Somalia through treaties with various Somali chiefs. The boundary between Ethiopia and British Somaliland was established in 1897 through treaty negotiations between British negotiators and King Menellik.

In 1855, Italy obtained commercial advantages in the area from the sultan of Zanzibar and in 1889 concluded agreements with the sultans of Obbia and Caluula, who placed their territories under Italy's protection. Between 1897 and 1908, Italy made agreements with the Ethiopians and the British that marked out the boundaries of Italian Somaliland. In June 1940, Italian troops overran British Somaliland and drove out the British garrison. In 1941, British forces began operations against the Italian East African Empire and quickly brought the greater part of the Italian Somaliland under British control.

From 1941 to 1950, while Somalia was under British military administration, transition toward self-government had begun. Elections for the Legislative Assembly were held in February 1960. The protectorate became independent on June 26, 1960; five days later, on July 1, it joined Italian Somaliland to form the Somali Republic. Gen. Mohammed Siad Barre led a military coup in 1969, and established a Marxist political system. Years later Barre concentrated power in his own family and clan. In 1991, he was toppled, but opposing factions have continued fighting for power. After years of civil war, and severe drought, the United States and the international community gave aid to starving Somalians. It was not clear whether any true government existed.

The Somali people are herders and farmers. The largest group in the country is the Somali, who are nomadic or seminomadic herders. The remaining population consists of Jiiddu, Tunni, and Maay.

South Africa
Official name: Republic of South Africa
Capital: Pretoria
Currency: Rand
Income: (per capita US$) 2680 (1990)
Area: 472,359 sq. mi.
Population: (1991 estimate) 40.6 million
Illiteracy: 21% (1991)
Ethnic divisions: Black 75%; white 14%; "colored" (mixed-race) 8%; Asian (Indian) 3%.
Religious groups: Christian, traditional belief, Hindu, Muslim, Jewish
Languages spoken: English and Afrikaans (official), Zulu, Xhosa, Luvenda, North and South SeSotho, SeTswana, other tribal languages.
Form of government: Multi-party
Exports: Diamonds, gold

Of the present inhabitants of South Africa, the earliest are Bushmen and Hottentots—members of the Khoisan language group, of whom only a few survive. The Portuguese were, in 1988, the first Europeans to reach the Cape of Good Hope. Permanent white settlement began when the Dutch East India Company established a provisioning station there in 1652. In subsequent decades, French Huguenot refugees, Dutch, and Germans settled in the Cape area to form the Afrikaner segment of the modern population.

Britain seized the Cape of Good Hope at the end of the eighteenth century. Partly to escape British political rule and cultural hegemony, many Afrikaner farmers (Boers) undertook a northern migration (the "Great Trek") beginning in 1836. This movement brought them into contact with several African groups, the most formidable of which were the Zulu. Under their powerful leader, Shaka (1787–1828), the Zulu conquered most of

Two black South African youth.

the territory between the Drakensberg Mountains and the sea (now Natal). The Zulu were defeated at the Battle of Blood River in 1838.

The independent Boer republics of the Transvaal (the South African Republic) and the Orange Free State were created in 1852 and 1854. Following the two Boer wars from 1880 to 1881 and 1899 to 1902, British forces conquered the Boer republics and incorporated them into the British Empire. A strong resurgence of Afrikaner nationalism in the 1940s and 1950s led to a decision, through a 1960 referendum among whites, to give up dominion status and establish a republic. The republic was established on May 31, 1961.

South African laws are based on the doctrine of apartheid, which prescribes basic rights and obligations according to racial or ethnic origin. The country's black majority continues to suffer from pervasive, legally sanctioned discrimination based on race in political, economic, and social aspects of life. The "colored" and Asian minorities also suffer from discrimination, although to a somewhat lesser degree than blacks. Political rights of the black majority are confined to participation in tightly controlled urban councils in the country's black residential areas (townships) and in the ten so-called homelands. The National Party extended racial segregation through passage of a number of legislative acts.

In 1950, the white parliament passed the Group Areas Act, which established residential and business sections in urban areas for each race and strengthened existing "pass laws," which require blacks to carry documents authorizing their presence in restricted areas. In the 1960s and the 1970s, other laws were passed to restrict every black African, irrespective of actual residence. Other laws were enacted to forbid most social contacts between the races, mandate segregated public facilities, establish separate educational standards, restrict each race to certain kinds of jobs, curtail black labor unions, and abolish nonwhite participation (through white representatives) in the national government.

The African National Congress (ANC), a predominantly black South African political and paramilitary organization founded in 1912, is the oldest organization opposing legalized racism and white rule in South Africa. It was banned by the South African government from 1960 to 1990, operating underground and in exile. The ANC was founded with the objectives of eliminating all restrictions based on color and obtaining black representation in Parliament. The long-term aims of the ANC were set forth in the "Freedom Charter," which was adopted in 1955. This document states that the ANC's ultimate goal is a liberated, nonracial South Africa in which individual rights would be guaranteed and nationalization of certain industries would occur within a basically mixed economy.

The government released two elderly long-term prisoners in 1988, Zeph Mothopeng, President of the Pan African Congress, and Henry Gwala, an ANC leader. In December 1988, under great international pressure, the government commuted the death sentences of the Sharpeville Six, who were convicted of murder for their presence in a crowd that killed a black township official. President F. W. DeKlerk took several steps in 1989 and 1990 to demonstrate his commitment to ending apartheid, including the release of ANC leader Nelson Mandela, imprisoned in 1962 and sentenced to life in 1964 for treason and sabotage, and other political prisoners and detainees; and unbanning the ANC and 32 other antiaparthied organizations. The tide of social and political changes instigated by De Klerk led to a new constitution and eventually a multi-party election that put Mandela in power as the first black African president of the nation. With Mandela's rise has come a new middle class among blacks, comprising nearly eight percent of the economically active citizenship.

South African law divides the population into four major racial categories—Africans (blacks), whites, "coloreds," and Asians. The Africans, who comprise 72

South African children behind a fence that separates them from a white community near Johannesburg.

percent of the population, are mainly descendants of the Sotho and Nguni peoples, who migrated southward centuries ago. The largest African ethnic groups are the Zulu (nearly six million) and Xhosa (nearly 5.8 million).

Africans are officially subdivided into ten groups corresponding to the ten ethnically based, government-created "homelands"—Bophuthatswana, Ciskei, Lebowa, Gazankulu, KaNgwane, KwaNdebele, KwaZaulu, Qwaqwa, Transkei, and Venda. The so-called homelands have been granted various degrees of automony (four have been granted independence) but none have been recognized by any other government. The four independent homelands are: Bophuthatswana, which is made-up of mostly SeTswana-speaking people; Ciskei and Transkei, which consists of mainly Xhosa; and Venda, which is composed largely of Luvenda-speaking peoples.

The white population consists primarily of descendants of Dutch, French, English, and German settlers, with smaller admixtures of other European peoples, and constitutes about 14 percent of the total population.

Johannesburg, South Africa.

"Coloreds" are mostly descendants of indigenous peoples and the earliest European and Malay settlers in the area. "Coloreds" comprise nine percent of the population and live primarily in Cape Province. Asians, mainly descendants of the Indian workers brought to South Africa in the mid-nineteenth century to work as indentured laborers on sugar estates in Natal, constitute about three percent of the population.

Sudan
Official name: Republic of the Sudan
Independence: January 1, 1956
Capital: Khartoum
Currency: Sudanese pound
Income(per capita US$) 150 (1990)
Area: 967,500 sq. mi.
Population (1991 estimate): 27.2 million
Illiteracy: 78% (1991)
Ethnic divisions: Arab, black
Religious groups: Islam, traditional belief (southern Sudan), Christian
Languages spoken: Arabic (official), English, tribal languages
International relations: Arab Leageu, EC, OAU, UN
Form of government: Military
Exports: Cotton, groundnuts, sorghum

From the beginning of the Christian era until 1820, Sudan existed as a collection of small, independent states. In 1881, a religious leader named Mohammed Ahmed Ibn Abdalla proclaimed himself the Mahdi, or "expected one," and began to unify tribes in western and central Sudan. The Mahdi led a nationalist revolt culminating in the fall of Khartoum in 1855. He died shortly thereafter, but his state survived until overwhelmed by Anglo-Egyptian forces in 1898; in 1899, Sudan was proclaimed a condominium under British-Egyptian administration. In February 1953, the United Kingdom and Egypt concluded an agreement providing for Sudanese self-government. Col. Nimeiry reintroduced the law of Koran in 1983. Another military coup led by Omar Hasan el-Bashir seized power in 1989. Sudan achieved independence on January 1, 1956. Clashes have continued for years between the Arab north and black south made up of non-Muslims.

Swaziland
Official name: Kingdom of Swaziland

The Black South African village of Cross Roads.

Independence: September 6, 1968
Capital: Mbabane
Currency: Lilangeni
Income: (per capita US$) 789(1990)
Area: 6,704 sq. mi.
Population (1991 estimate): 859,000
Illiteracy: 32% (1991)
Ethnic divisions: Swazi, some Zulu
Religious groups: Christian and indigenous belief
Languages spoken: English, SiSwazi (both official)
International relations: Commonwealth, EC, OAU, UN
Form of government: Monarchy
Exports: Asbestos, citrus, sugar, wood pulp

The people of the present Swazi nation migrated south sometime before the sixteenth century to what is now Mozambique. After a series of conflicts with people living in the area that is now Maputo, the Swazi settled in northern Zululand in about 1750. Unable to match the growing Zulu strength there, the Swazis moved gradually northward in the early 1800s and established themselves in the area of modern Swaziland. The Swazi consolidated their hold in this area under several able leaders. The most important of these was Mswati, from whom the Swazi derive their name. Under his leadership in the 1840s, the Swazi expanded their territory to the northwest and stabilized the southern frontier with the Zulus.

The first Swazi contact with the British came early in Mswati's reign when he asked the British agent general in South Africa for assistance against Zulu raids into Swaziland. Agreements made between the British and the Transvaal (South Africa) governments in 1881 and 1884 provided that Swaziland should be independent. In 1903, Britain formally took over the administration of Swaziland.

Sobhuza II became head of the Swazi Nation in 1921. By the 1960s, political activity intensified, partly in response to events elsewhere in Africa. Several political parties were formed that agitated for independence. The traditional Swazi leaders, including King Sobhuza and his council, formed the Imbokodvo National Movement. In 1966, the British agreed to hold talks on a new constitution. The constitutional committee, consisting of representatives of the king and of the Swazi National Council, other political parties, and the British government agreed on a constitutional monarchy for Swaziland, with self-government to follow parliamentary elections in 1967. Swaziland became independent on September

6, 1968. In 1973, Sobhuza II repealed the constitution and dissolved the political parties and assumed full power and died in 1982. Mswati III became king in 1986.

Tanzania

Official name: United Republic of Tanzania
Independence: December 9, 1961
Capital: Dodoma
Currency: Tanzanian shilling
Income:(per capita US$) 120 (1991)
Area: 363,950 sq. mi.
Population: (1991 estimate) 26.8 million
Illiteracy: 15% (1991)
Ethnic divisions: More than 130 groups
Religious groups: Muslim 35%, traditional belief 35%, Christian 30%
Languages spoken: Swahili (official), English
International relations: Commonwealth, EC, OAU, UN
Form of government: Multi-party
Exports: Cashews, coffee, cloves, cotton, diamonds, sisal, tea

The area, that is now Tanzania, is believed to have been inhabited originally by ethnic groups using a click-tongue language similar to that of southern Africa's Bushmen and Hottentots. Although remnants of these early tribes still exist, most were gradually displaced by Bantu farmers migrating form the west and south and by Nilotes and related northern peoples.

A Swazis woman.

The coastal area first felt the impact of foreign influence as early as the eighth century. By the twelfth century, traders and immigrants came from as far away as Persia (now Iran) and India. The Portuguese navigator, Vasco da Gama, first visted the East African coast in 1498 on his voyage to India; by 1506, the Portuguese claimed control over the entire coast. This control was nominal, however, for the Portuguese did not attempt to colonize the area or explore the interior. By the early eighteenth century, Arabs from Oman had assisted the indigenous coastal dwellers in driving out the Portuguese from the area north of the Ruvuma River. They established their own garrisons at Zanzibar, Pemba, and Kilwa and carried on a lucrative trade in slaves and ivory.

German colonial interests were first advanced in 1884. Karl Peters, who formed the Society for German Colonization, concluded a series of treaties by which tribal chiefs in the interior accepted German protection. In 1886 and 1890, Anglo-German agreements were negotiated that delineated the British and German spheres of influence in the interior of East Africa. In 1891, the German government took over direct administration of the territory from the German East Africa Company and appointed a governor with headquarters at Dar es Salaam. German colonial administration provided African resistance, culminating in the Maji Maji rebellion of 1905 to 1907. German colonial domination of Tanganyika ended with World War I. Control of most of the territory passed to the United Kingdom under a League of Nations mandate.

In the following years, Tanganyika moved gradually toward self-government and independence. In 1954, Julius K. Nyerere, a schoolteacher educated abroad, organized the Tanganyika African Union (UANU). In May 1961, Tanganyika became autonomous, and Nyerere became prime minister under a new constitution. Full independence was achieved on December 9, 1961. On April 26, 1964, Tanganyika united with Zanzibar to form the United Republic of Tanganyika and Zanzibar, renamed the United Republic of Tanzania on October 29, 1964. Julius Nyerere became one of the few leaders on the continent to retire peacefully. Multi-parties were allowed to organize and participate in a national election in 1995. Chama cha Mapinduzi (Revolutionary Party) won the last election, and Ben Mkapa became the new head of state.

Tanzania's population consists of more than 130 ethnic groups, of which only the Sukuma has more than

Tanga, Tanzania

one million members. The majority of Tanzanians, including such large tribes as the Sukuma and the Nyamwezi, are of Bantu stock. Groups of Nilotic or related origin include the nomadic Masai and the Luo, both of which are found in greater numbers in neighboring Kenya. Two small groups speak languages of the Khoisan family peculiar to the Bushman and Hottentot peoples. Cushitic-speaking peoples, originally from the Ethiopian highlands, reside in a few areas of Tanzania.

Togo
Official name: Republic of Togo
Independence: April 27, 1960
Capital: Lomé
Currency: CFA franc
Income:(per capita US$) 390 (1989)
Area: 21,853 sq. mi.
Population: (1991 estimate) 3.8 million
Illiteracy: 57% (1991)
Ethnic divisions: Ewe, Mina, Kabye, Cotocoli, Moba
Religious groups: Animist 50%, Christian 30%, Muslim 20%
Languages spoken: French (official), Ewe, Mina, Kabye
International relations: EC, OAU, UN
Exports: Cocoa, coffee, phosphates

The Ewe people first moved into the area that is now Togo from the Niger River Valley, sometime between the twelfth and fourteenth centuries. During the fifteenth and sixteenth centuries, Portuguese explorers and traders visited the coast. For the next two hundred years, the coastal region was a major raiding center for Europeans in search of slaves, earning Togo and the surrounding region the name "the Slave Coast."

In a 1884 treaty signed at Togoville, Germany declared a protectorate over the area. In 1914, Togoland was invaded by French and British forces and fell after a brief resistance. Following the war, Togoland became a League of Nations mandate divided for administrative purposes between France and the United Kingdom. By statute in 1955, French Togo became an autonomous republic within the French Union. In 1957, the residents of British Togoland voted to join the Gold Coast as part of the new independent nation of Ghana. On April 27, 1960, Togo severed its juridical ties with France, shed its United Nations trusteeship status, and became fully independent. The first president— Sylvanus Olympia was overthrown three years after independence in 1963. Nicholas Grunitzky headed the government for short period; in 1976 Col. Gnassingbé Eyadema sized power and instituted a one- party state He was elected president in 1979 and 1986 and was deposed in 1991. Since then, a multi-party system has existed.

Togo's population is composed of about 21 ethnic groups. The two major ones are the Ewe in the south and the Kabye in the north.

Tunisia
Official name: Republic of Tunisia
Capital: Tunis
Currency: Dinar
Income: (per capita US$) 1560 (1991)
Area: 63,378 sq. mi.
Population (1991 estimate) 8.2 million
Illiteracy: 35% (1991)
Ethnic divisions: Arab 98%, Berber 1%, European 1%
Religious groups: Muslim 99%, Christian and Jewish less than 1%
Languages spoken: Arabic (official), French

Tunisians are descended mainly from indigenous Berber tribes and from Arab tribes which migrated to North Africa during the seventh century AD. Recorded history in Tunisia begins with the arrival of Phoenicians, who founded Carthage and other North African settlements. In the seventh century, the Muslim conquest transformed North Africa, and Tunisia became a center of Arab culture until its assimilation in the Turkish Ottoman Empire in the sixteenth century. In 1881, France established a protectorate there, only to see a rise of nationalism lead to Tunisia's independence in 1956.

One year after independence, Habib Bourguiba deposed the president and instituted a socialist system, later declaring himself president for life. He was later removed and his position was assumed by Gen. Al Ben Ali, who promoted democratization.

Uganda
Official name: Republic of Uganda
Independence: October 9, 1962
Capital: Kampala

Magila Mission, Tanzania

Currency: Ugandan shilling
Income: (per capita US$) 220 (1990)
Area: 93,354 sq. mi.
Population: (1991 estimate) 18.6 million
Illiteracy: 52% (1991)
Ethnic divisions: Baganda, Iteso, Basoga, Banyaruanda, Bakiga, Bagisu
Religious groups: Christian (majority), Muslim, traditional belief
Languages spoken: English (official), Luganda, Swahili, other Bantu and Nilotic languages
International relations: Commonwealth, EC, OAU, UN
Exports: Coffee, copper, cotton, tea

Arab traders moving inland from Indian Ocean coastal enclaves reached the interior of Uganda in the 1830s and found several African kingdoms, one of which was the Buganda kingdom, that had well-developed political institutions dating back several centuries.

In 1888, control of the emerging British sphere of interest in East Africa was assigned by royal charter to the Imperial British East Africa Company, an arrangement strengthened in 1890 by an Anglo-German agreement confirming British dominance over Kenya and Uganda. In 1894, the Kingdom of Uganda was placed under a formal British protectorate. The British protectorate period began to change formally in 1955, when constitutional changes leading to Uganda's independence were adopted. The first general elections in Uganda were held in 1961, and the British government granted internal self-government to Uganda on March 1, 1962, with Benedicto Kiwanuka as the first prime minister.

In February of 1966, Prime Minister Milton Obote suspended the constitution, assumed all government powers, and removed the president and vice president. On January 25, 1971, Obote's government was ousted in a military coup led by armed forces commander Idi Amin Dada. Amin declared himself president, dissolved the parliament, and amended the constitution to give himself absolute power. Idi Amin's eight-year rule produced economic decline, social disintegration, and massive human rights violations. In 1978, Tanzanian forces pushed back an incursion by Amin's troops. Backed by Ugandan exiles, Tanzanian forces waged a war of liberation against Amin. On April 11, 1979, the Ugandan capital was captured, and Amin and his remaining forces fled.

Milton Obote, the first president, was overthrown in 1971 by Gen. Idi Amin who led the country through a

A Togolese woman making pottery.

reign of terror and violence. In 1973, Amin was toppled and during that year with the aide of neighboring country Tanzania. A chaotic year followed when three presidents attempted to lead the government and failed. Eventually Yuveri Museveni assumed power, bringing some stability to the country.

Bantu, Nilotic, and Nilo-Hamitic peoples constitute most of Uganda's population. The Bantu are the most numerous and include the Baganda, with more than one million members. The Nilo-Hamitic Iteso is the second largest group, followed by the Banyankole and Basoga, both of Bantu extraction.

Zaire

Official name: Republic of Zaire
Independence: June 30, 1960
Capital: Kinshasa
Currency: Zaire
Income (per capita US$) 230 (1990)
Area: 905,063 sq. mi.
Population: (1991 estimate) 37.8 million
Illiteracy: 39% (1991)
Ethnic divisions: 250 tribal groups
Religious groups: Roman Catholic 50%, Protestant 20%, Muslim 10%, Kimbanguist 10%, other syncretic sects and traditional belief 10%
Languages spoken: French, Lingala, Swahili, Kingwana (a variant), Kikongo, Tshiluba

The area that is now Zaire is believed to have been populated as early as 10,000 years ago. An influx of peoples occurred in the seventh and eighth centuries AD, when Bantu people from present-day Nigeria settled, bringing with them knowledge of the manufacture and use of metals. In 1482, the Portuguese arrived at the mouth of the Congo River. They found an organized society—the Bakongo Kingdom—which included parts of present-day Congo, Zaire, and Angola. The Portuguese named the area Congo. At the Berlin Conference of 1885, King Leopold's claim to the greater part of the Zaire River basin was recognized. The Congo Free State remained his personal possession until he ceded it to the Belgian State in 1907, when it was renamed the Belgian Congo.

Following riots in Leopoldville in 1958, Belgian King Bedouin announced that the colony could look forward to independence. Roundtable conferences were convened at Brussels in January 1960, and Belgium granted independence on June 30, 1960. Parliamentary elections

Tutsi dancers form Zaire.

were held in April of 1960. The Congolese National Movement (MNC) obtained a majority of the seats, and Patrice Lumumba was named prime minister. After much maneuvering, the leader of the Alliance of the Bakongo (ABAKO) Party, Joseph Kasavubu, was named president.

Chaos started right after independence. Moise Tshombe declared Katanga (a copper-rich province) independent. Belgian military intervened and soon after UN troops arrived to help normalize the situation. Meanwhile, Lumumba got assassinated. Tshombe served as prime minister until 1965, when Joseph Désiré Mobutu organized a coup. Still at the helm in the early 1990s, opposition to his regime and attempts are regular. The country has been rumored to be on the verge of bankruptcy while Mobutu has amassed huge fortunes abroad.

As many as 250 ethnic groups in Zaire have been distinguished and named. The largest group, the Kongo, may include as many as 2.5 million persons. Other socially and numerically important groups are the Luba, Lunda, Bashi, and Mongo. Some groups, including the aboriginal Pygmies, occupy isolated ecological niches and number only a few thousand.

Approximately 700 local languages and dialects are spoken; four serve as official languages. Lingala developed along the Congo River in the 1880s in response to the need for a common commercial language. Swahili, introduced into the country by Arabs and especially the Zanzibari Swahilis during the ninteenth century slaving operations, is spoken extensively in the eastern half of the country. Kikongo is used primarily in the area between Kinshasa and the Atlantic Ocean, as well as in parts of Congo and Angola. Tshiluba is spoken primarily by the tribal groups of south-central Zaire.

Zambia

Official name: Republic of Zambia
Independence: October 24, 1964
Area: 290,585 sq. mi.
Population: (1991 estimate) 8.4 million
Ethnic divisions: More than 70 tribal groups
Religious groups: Christian, indigenous belief
Languages spoken: English (official), about 70 local languages and dialects, including Bemba, Tonga, Nyanja, Lozi, Luvale, Ndembu (Lundu), and Kaonde

About 2,000 years ago, the indigenous hunter-gatherer occupants of Zambia began to be displaced or absorbed by more advanced migrating tribes. By the fifteenth century, the major waves of Bantu-speaking immigrants began, with the greatest influx occuring between the late seventeenth and early ninteenthth centuries. These groups came primarily from the Luba and Lunda tribes of southern Zaire and northern Angola but were joined in the ninteenth century by Ngoni peoples from the south. By the latter part of that century, the various peoples of Zambia were largely established in the areas they currently occupy.

Except for an occasional Portuguese explorer, the area lay untouched by Europeans for centuries, until the mid-nineteenth century, when it was penetrated by European explorers, missionaries, and traders. In 1888, Northern and Southern Rhodesia (now Zambia and Zimbabwe) were proclaimed a British sphere of influence. In 1953, both Rhodesias were joined with Nyasaland (now Malawi) to form the Federation of Rhodesia and Nyasaland.

Northern Rhodesia was the center of much of the turmoil and crises that characterized the federation in its last years. At the core of the controversy were insistent African demands for greater participation in government and the Europeans' fear. A two-stage election held in October and December 1962 resulted in an African majority in the Legislative Council. The council passed resolutions calling for Northern Rhodesia's secession from the federation and demanding full internal self-government. On December 31, 1963, the federation was dissolved, and Northern Rhodesia became the Republic of Zambia on October 24, 1964. Robert Mugabe continues to serve as the head of state since independence, and has managed-to get himself re-elected several times. The government is multi-party, including ZAPU officials. A cautious land reform has been institut-

Mbuti people of the Ituri forest in Zaire.

ed giving land to black farmers. Frederick Chiluba was ruler of the nation in 1996.

Zambia's population comprises more than 70 Bantu-speaking tribes. Some tribes are small, and only two have enough people to constitute at least ten percent of the population.

Zimbabwe
Independence: April 18, 1980
Area: 151,000 sq. mi.
Population: (1991 estimate)
Ethnic divisions: Shona 80%, Ndebele 19%
Religious groups: 50% syncretic (part Christian, part traditional belief), Christian 25%, traditional beliefs 24%, Hindu and Muslim less than 1%
Languages spoken: English (official), Shona, SiNdebele

Archaeologists have found Stone Age implements and pebble tools in several areas of Zimbabwe, suggesting human habitation for many centuries, and the ruins of stone buildings provide evidence of early civilization.

In the sixteenth century, the Portuguese were the first Europeans to attempt colonization of south-central Africa, but the hinterland lay virtually untouched by Europeans until the arrival of explorers, missionaries, and traders some three hundred years later. In 1888, the area that became Southern and Northern Rhodesia was proclaimed a British sphere of influence. The British South Africa Company was chartered in 1889, and the settlement of Salisbury (now Harare, the capital) was established in 1890.

In 1895, the territory was formally named Rhodesia. In 1923, Southern Rhodesia's white settlers were given the choice of being incorporated into the Union of South Africa or becoming a separate entity within the British Empire. The settlers rejected incorporation, and Southern Rhodesia was formally annexed by the United Kingdom. In September 1953, Southern Rhodesia was joined with the British protectorates of Northern Rhodesia and Nyasaland. The federation was dissolved at the end of 1963 after much crisis and turmoil, and Northern Rhodesia and Nyasaland became the independent states of Zambia and Malawi in 1964.

Although prepared to grant independence to Rhodesia, the United Kingdom insisted that the authorities at Salisbury first demonstrate their intention to move toward eventual majority rule. Desiring to keep their dominant position, the white Rhodesians refused to give such assurance. On November 11, 1965, after lengthy and unsuccessful negotiations with the British government, Prime Minister Ian Smith issued a Unilateral Declaration of Independence (UDI) from the United Kingdom. The British government considered the UDI unconstitutional and illegal but made clear that it would not use force to end the rebellion. The British government imposed unilateral economic sanctions on Rhodesia and requested other nations to do the same. On December 16, 1966, the United Nations Security Council, for the first time in its history, imposed mandatory economic sanctions on a state.

In the early 1970s, informal attempts at settlement were renewed between the United Kingdom and the Rhodesia administration. In 1974, the major African nationalist groups—the Zimbabwe African People's Union (ZAPU) and the Zimbabwe African National Union (ZANU), which split away from ZAPU in 1963—were united into the "Patriotic Front" and combined their military forces. In 1976, the Smith government agreed in principle to majority rule and to a meeting in Geneva with black nationalist leaders. Blacks represented at the Geneva meeting included ZAPU leader Joshua Nkomo, ZANU leader Robert Mugabe, UANC chairman Bishop Abel Muzorewa, and former ZANU leader, the Reverend Ndabaningi Sithole. The meeting failed.

On March 3, 1978, the Smith administration signed the "internal settlement" agreement in Salisbury with Bishop Muzorewa, Reverend Sithole, and Chief Jeremiah Chirau. The agreement provided for qualified majority rule and elections with universal suffrage. Following elections in April 1979, in which his UANC part won a majority, Bishop Muzorewa assumed office on June 1, becoming Zimbabwe's first black prime minister. However, the installation of the new black majority government did not end the guerrilla conflict that had claimed more than 20,000 lives.

The British and the African parties began deliberations on a Rhodesian settlement in London on September 10, 1979. On December 21, the parties signed an agreement calling for a cease-fire, new elections, a transition period under British rule, and a new constitution implementing majority rule while protecting minority rights. The elections were supervised by the British government and monitored. Robert Mugabe's ZANU Party won an absolute majority and was asked to form Zimbabwe's first government. The British government formally granted independence to Zimbabwe on April 18, 1980. Most nations recognized Zimbabwe following independence. The 6th annual All Africa Games were held in Harawe in September of 1995. Athletes from more than 30 nations participated.

Zimbabwe's population is divided into two major language groups, which are subdivided into several tribal groups. The Mashona (Shona speakers), who constitute about eighty percent of the population, have lived in the area the longest and are the majority language groups. The Matabele (Sindebele speakers), representing about nineteen percent of the population and centered in the southwest near Bulawayo, arrived within the last 150 years. An offshoot of the South African Zulu group, they had maintained control over the Mashona until the white occupation of Rhodesia.

Western Hemisphere

Anguilla

Independence: n/a (dependent territory of the United Kingdom)
Area: 91 sq. km.
Population: (1992 estimate) 6,963
Ethnic divisions: Black Africans
Religious groups: Anglican 40%, Methodist 33%, Seventh-Day Adventist 7%, Baptist 5%, Roman Catholic 3%, other 12%
Languages spoken: English
Exports: Fish, lobster

Beginning in 1816, the islands of Anguilla, the (British) Virgin Islands, Saint Christopher (Saint Kitts) and Nevis were governered by the British as a single colony. However, when Saint Christopher was granted statehood in 1967, Anguilla unilaterally declared independence from Saint Christopher. Anguilla has remained an economically dependent territory of the United Kingdom.

Antigua and Barbuda

Independence: November 1, 1981
Capital: St. John's
Currency: East Caribbean dollar
Income (per capita US$): 4600 (1990)
Area: 108 sq. mi.
Population: (1991 estimate) 64,400
Illiteracy: 10% (1991)
Ethnic divisions: Black Africans, some British and Portuguese
Religious groups: Principally Anglican, with evangelical Protestant and Roman Catholic minorities.
Languages spoken: English (official), regional dialects

Christopher Columbus first visited the islands of Antigua and Barbuda in 1493. Missionaries attempted to settle on the island but were hindered by the Carib Indians, who inhabited the islands, and the absence of natural freshwater springs. In 1632, the British successfully established a colony; Sir Christopher Codrington established the first large sugar estate in Antigua in 1674, bringing slaves from Africa's west coast to work the plantations. Although Antiguan slaves were emancipated in 1834, they remained bound to their plantation owners. Economic opportunities for the new freemen

A Zimbabwean man with ox-drawn cart.

were limited by a lack of surplus farming land, no access to credit, and an economy built on agriculture rather than manufacturing. The Labor Party retained power after the 1989 elections.

Argentina
Official Name: Republic of Argentina
Capital: Buenos Aires
Currency: Austral
Income (per capita US$) 2370 (1990)
Area: 1,072,156 sq. mi.
Population: (1980 estimate) 27,947,446
Illiteracy: 5% (1991)
Form of government: Presidential republic
Exports: Iron ore, livestock, petroleum

Blacks consistute a very small percentage of the population of Argentina.

Aruba
Independence: (Autonomous part of the Kingdom of the Netherlands)
Population: 60,000
Ethnic divisions: Mixed European and Carib Indian 85%, black Africans
Religious groups: Roman Catholic, Protestant, Jewish
Languages spoken: Papiamento, English, Dutch, Spanish

The Spanish landed in Curacao (now the Netherlands Antilles) in 1499 and in 1527 took possession of Curacao, Bonaire, and Aruba. In 1634, the three islands passed to the Netherlands, where they have remained, except for two short periods of British rule during the Napoleonic Wars. Before the war, the Dutch Caribbean islands were administered as Dutch colonies; afterward, negotiations to confer a greater measure of self-government began. On December 15, 1954, the Netherlands Antilles became an autonomous part of the kingdom. In 1983, Aruba sought autonomy from the Netherlands Antilles; on January 1, 1986, it achieved separate status equal to that of the Antilles and is slated to become fully independent in 1996.

Some 40 nationalities are represented in the Netherlands Antilles and Aruba; Arubans mostly are a mixture of European and Caribbean Indian.

Bahamas
Official Name: Commonwealth of The Bahamas
Independence: July 10, 1973
Capital: Nassau

Currency: Bahamian dollar
Income (per capita US$) 11,400 (1990)
Area: 5,380 sq. mi
Population: (1991 estimate) 251,000
Illiteracy: 5% (1991)
Ethnic divisions: Black African 85%, European 15%
Religious groups: Baptist, Anglican, Roman Catholic, Methodist
Languages spoken: English, Creole
International relations: CARICOM, EC, OAS, UN
Exports: Shellfish, sugar, timber, turtles

Christopher Columbus first visited the islands of the Bahamas in 1492, when he first landed in the Western Hemisphere, either on Samana Cay or San Salvador Island. In 1647, the first permanent European settlement was founded. In 1717, the islands became a British crown colony. The Bahamas were granted self-government through a series of constitutional and political steps, culminating in independence on July 10, 1973. The Progressive Liberal Party led the Bahamas to independence and remain in power in the 1990s.

85 percent of Bahamians are of African descent. Many of their ancestors arrived in the Bahamas when it was a staging area for the slave trade, or were brought there by the thousands of British loyalists who fled the American colonies during the Revolutionary War.

Barbados
Independence: November 30, 1966
Capital: Bridgetown
Currency: Barbados dollar
Income (per capita US$) 6,745 (1990)
Area: 166 sq. mi.
Population: (1991 estimate) 254,000
Illiteracy: 2% (1991)
Ethnic divisions: African 80%, mixed 16%, European 4%
Religious groups: Anglican 70%, Roman Catholic, Methodist, Baptist and Moravian
Languages spoken: English
International relations: CARICOM, EC, OAS, UN
Form of government: Independenct state under British sovereignty
Exports: Fish, sugar

From the arrival of the first British settlers in 1627 until independence in 1966, Barbados had been under uninterrupted British control. As the sugar industry developed into the main commercial enterprise, Barbados was divided into large plantation estates. Slaves were brought from Africa to work on these plantations until slavery was abolished throughout the British Empire in 1834. From 1958 to 1962, Barbados was one of ten members of the West Indies Federation. Barbados negotiated its own independence at a constitutional conference with the United Kingdom in June 1966. The country attained self-rule on November 30, 1966.

Nassau Police Band.

Ethnically, the population of Barbados is 80 percent African, 16 percent mixed, and four percent European.

Belize
Independence: September 21, 1981
Capital: Belmopan
Currency: Belize dollar
Income (per capita US$) 1,975 (1990)
Area: 8,866 sq. mi.
Population: (1991 estimate): 228,000
Illiteracy: 7% (1991)
Ethnic divisions: Creole, African, mestizo, Amerindian
Religious groups: Roman Catholic, Anglican, Methodist, Muslim, Buddhist
Languages spoken: English (official), Spanish, Mayan
International relations: CARICOM, EC, UN
Exports: Bananas, citrus fruit, sugar, wood

The Mayan civilization spread into the area of Belize between 1500 BC and AD 300 and flourished until about AD 1000. European contact began in 1502 when Columbus sailed along the coast; the first recorded European settlement was 1638. During the next 105 years, more English settlements were established. Belize was named the Colony of British Honduras in 1840; it became a crown colony in 1862. Self-government was granted in January 1964. The official name of the territory was changed from British Honduras to Belize in June of 1973, and full independence was granted on September 21, 1981, with George C. Price of the People's United Party installed as the head of government.

Most Belizeans are of multiracial descent. Nearly 40 to 45 percent of the population is of African ancestry; more than 25 percent is of mixed local Indian and European descent (mestizo). Another one-fifth of the population is composed of Carib, Mayan, or other Amerindian ethnic groups.

Bermuda
Independence: n/a (parliamentary British colony with internal government since 1620)
Capital: Hamilton
Income (per capita US$) 17,000 (1987)
Area: 20.6 sq. mi.
Population (1987 est.): 57,619
Ethnic divisions: Black Africans 61%, white and others 39%
Religious groups: Anglican 37%, Protestant 21%, Roman Catholic 14%, other 28%
Languages spoken: English
Form of government: Semi-autonomous British colony
Exports: Bananas, coffee, cotton, tobacco

Located in the Atlantic Ocean about 650 miles east of North Carolina, Bermuda is relatively isolated.

The first Europeans to visit Bermuda were Spanish explorers in 1503. In 1609, a group of British explorers became stranded on the islands, and their reports aroused great interest about the islands in England. In 1612, British colonists arrived and founded the town of Saint George, the oldest, continuously inhabited English-speaking settlement in the Western Hemisphere.

Slaves from Africa were brought to Bermuda soon after the colony began. When the slave trade was outlawed in Bermuda in 1807, all slaves were freed in 1834. Although Bermuda is a British colony, it has a great degree of internal autonomy, based on the June 8, 1968 constitution.

Nearly two-thirds of the Bermudians are of African descent. An estimated 7,000 U.S. citizens live on the island; approximately 2,800 of them are military personnel and their dependents.

Bolivia
Official Name: Republic of Bolivia
Capital: La Paz
Currency: Boliviano
Income (per capita US$) 590 (1990)
Area: 424,162 sq. mi.
Population: 4,613,486 (c.1976)
Illiteracy: 22% (1990)
International relations: LAIA, OAS, UN
Form of government: Presidential republic
Exports: Copper, gold, zinc

Military regimes and authoritarian governments ruled Bolivia for years, until 1989, when Jaime Paz Zamora, representing Movimiento de la Izquierda Revolucionaria (MIR) was elected president. Blacks comprise a very small percentage of Bolivia's population.

Brazil
Official Name: Federative Republic of Brazil
Independence: September 7, 1822
Capital: Brasilia
Currency: Cruzado
Income (per capita US$: 2680 (1990)
Area: 3,290,000 sq. mi.
Population: (1991 estimate) 150.1 million
Illiteracy: 19% (1991)
Ethnic divisions: Portuguese, black Africans, Indians (principally Tupi and Guarani linguistic stock), Italian, German, Japanese
Religious groups: Roman Catholic 89%
Form of government: Presidential republic
Exports: Coffee, iron ore, soybean, steel, sugar

Brazil was formally claimed in 1500 by the Portuguese and was ruled from Lisbon as a colony until 1808. Brazil successfully declared independence on September 7, 1922. Four major groups make up the Brazilian population: indigenous Indians of Tupi and Guarani language stock; the Portuguese; Africans brought to Brazil as slaves; and various European and Asian immigrant groups that have settled in Brazil since the mid-ninteenth century.

Slavery was introduced into Brazil in the 1530s, expanded greatly after 1540, when sugar became important, and grew most rapidly between 1580 and 1640, when Spain controlled the country. Estimates of the total number of slaves brought to Brazil varies from six to 20 million. Slavery did not finally end in Brazil until 1888. Though slavery in Brazil was often extremely brutal, and the death rate of blacks on sugar, coffee and cotton plantations was enormous, large numbers of Africans achieved freedom. About 25 percent of Brazil's blacks were free during slavery.

During the nineteenth century, free blacks intermarried so rapidly their numbers fell from about 400,000 in 1800 to 20,000 by 1888 when slavery was finally abolished. Free blacks enjoyed full legal equality during both the period of slavery and after it was abolished.

In Brazil, slaves who served masters in cities were often allowed to seek part-time and temporary employment elsewhere. They were able to read and write and develop employable skills. Blacks became important to the development and economy of the country and some became prominent in public life. Black Brazilian Nilo Pecanha served as vice-president and briefly as president of Brazil in the first decade of this century. Blacks also achieved fame in Brazil's intellectual and artistic life.

After the oppressive military regimes of the 1960s, José Sarney was elected in 1985.

Canada
Capital: Ottawa

Currency: Canadian dollar
Income (per capita US$) 22,040 (1990)
Illiteracy: 4% (1991)
International relations: Commonwealth, NATO, OECD, UN
Form of government: Independent state with British sovereignty
Exports: manufactured goods, minerals

Blacks comprise a very small portion of Canada's population—less than 25,000, or 0.1 percent of the total population. Canada's major race problem reflects in its treatment of the Indians and Eskimos, who total about 200,000.

Blacks were prominent in the early seventeenth-century explorations and development of Canada by French explorers and Jesuit missionaries. The first black slave is believed to have been a native of Madagascar (Malagasy) and to have been sold to a French resident of Quebec in 1628. As French Canada expanded, slaves were purchased in the United States.

In 1749, the British brought slaves to Halifax, and slavery was legalized in British Canada in 1762. Slavery increased shortly thereafter, when the British took all of Canada in the French and Indian Wars. Many British fleeing from the revolutionary colonies to the south after 1775 brought slaves with them.

British slave codes were more severe than the French, under whom slaves could marry, own property, and maintain parental rights. However, the British were not to sustain slavery for long. London had divided Canada into two governments, Upper Canada and Lower Canada. The governor of Upper Canada, Colonel James Simcoe, an ardent abolitionist, induced the area's legislature to pass laws forbidding importation of slaves and freeing every slave born in the area by the age of 25. As a result, slavery in Upper Canada soon collapsed.

Similar legislation was not enacted in Lower Canada. However, by 1800 the courts, through complex legal decisions, established the principle that a slave could leave his master whenever he wished. In the Maritime Provinces, courts also acted so as to eliminate slavery in fact if not in theory. Slavery was formally abolished in Canada in 1833.

Meanwhile, starting slowly in the eighteenth century, Canada was becoming a haven for slaves fleeing across her southern borders. Slaves who had served with the British in the American War for Independence came to Halifax from New York in large numbers in 1782 and 1783. Though many were to migrate to Freetown on the West Coast of Africa, others stayed. In 1826, Canada defied the United States and formally refused to return fugitive slaves. In 1829, the legislature of Lower Canada announced that every slave that entered the Province was immediately free, a declaration that gave impetus to the underground railroad and stimulated moves for resettlement by blacks in Canada.

The passage of the Fugitive Slave Act in 1850 meant that any escaped slave who remained in the United States was to be returned to his owner. Within a year after passage of the law, some ten thousand slaves arrived in Canada, welcomed by a majority of Canadians who provided communities and services for them.

African Americans were accepted into the mainstream of Canadian life, were allowed to choose separate or integrated schools, were elected to local office and served as officers in the Canadian Army. Black laborers contributed substantially to the expansion of the Canadian Pacific Railroad, as immigrants from Eastern and Southern Europe were to contribute to the development of railroads in the United States. Black skilled laborers were much in demand. By 1861, at the outbreak of the Civil War in the United States, there were 50,000 blacks in Canada. However, after the Civil War, feelings of fear among white Canadians led to discrimination in employment and schools. Many African Americans re-emigrate to the United States, feeling that, with slavery outlawed there, a bright future awaited them. By 1871, the black population of Canada dipped to about 20,000.

Canada, the most sparsely populated country in the world with 1.5 persons per square mile, has become a haven for so many refugees that it has earned awards for outstanding achievement from human rights organizations. In fact, so many immigrants from Asia, Africa, the Caribbean and elsewhere have moved to Canada, that the established British-Caucasian population has expressed fears it will become extinct (assimilated) within 100 years. Toronto alone has become one of the world's most cosmopolitan cities with more than 100 cultural or ethnic groups. Canada maintains close ties with both the United Kingdom and the United States, and plays a major role in world peace and aid to poor nations. The movement of independence of Quebec Province continues to grow.

Cayman Islands
Independence: n/a (dependent territory of the United Kingdom)
Capital: Georgetown
Currency: Dollar
Income (per capita US$) 11,000
Area: 260 sq. km.
Population: (1992 estimate) 29,139
Ethnic divisions: 40% mixed, 20% white, 20% black
Religious groups: United Church (Presbyterian and Congregational), Anglican, Baptist, Roman Catholic, Church of God, other Protestant denominations

Languages spoken: English
Form of government: British colony
Exports: Farm products, wood

Chile
Capital: Santiago
Currency: Peso
Income (per capita US$) 2010 (1990)
Area: 292,257 sq. mi.
Population: 11, 568,000 (1982)
International relations: LAIA, OAS, UN
Form of government: Presidential republic
Exports: Almonds, copper, gold, grapes, nitrate, silver, sulfur

Blacks comprise a very small percentage of Chile's population. After the coalition government of president Salvador Allende ended in a coup of 1973, Gen. Augusto Pinichet Ugarte became a dictator for 14 years. A civilian government was established in 1990, when the Christian Democrat Patricio Aylwin was elected president.

Colombia
Official Name: Republic of Colombia
Independence: July 20, 1810
Capital: Bogota
Currency: Columbian peso
Income (per capita US$) 1200 (1990)
Area: 440,000 sq. mi.
Population: (1991 estimate) 33.7 million
Illiteracy: 14% (1990)
Ethnic divisions: Mestizo 589%, white 20%, Mulatto 14%, black 4%, mixed black-Indian 3%, Indian 1%
Religious groups: Roman Catholic 95%
Languages spoken: Spanish
International relations: LAIA, OAS, UN
Form of government: Presidential republic
Exports: Coffee, emeralds, petroleum, silver

The diversity of ethnic origins results from the intermixture of indigenous Indians, Spanish colonists, and African slaves. In 1549, the area was established as a Spanish colony with the capital at Bogota. In 1717, Bogota became the capital of the viceroyalty of New Granada, which included what is now Venezuela, Ecuador, and Panama. On July 20, 1810, the citizens of Bogota created the first representative council to defy Spanish authority. Total independence was proclaimed in 1813, and in 1819 the Republic of Greater Colombia was formed.

Blacks comprise a small part of Colombia's population. Pledad Corboda de Castro became the first black woman to be elected to the Senate in the 1990s. In 1993, she wrote a law instituting equal rights for black Colombians.

Costa Rica
Official Name: Republic of Costa Rica
Independence: September 15, 1821
Capital: San José
Currency: Colon
Income (per capita US$: 1759 (1990)
Area 51,032 sq. km.
Population: (1991 estimate) 3.1 million
Illiteracy: 7% (1991)
Ethnic divisions: European (including a few mestizos), 96%, black 3%, indigenous 1%
Languages spoken: Spanish, Jamaican dialect of English spoken around Puerto Limon
International relations: CACMO, OAS, UN
Form of government: Presidential republic
Exports: Bananas, cocoa, sugar, timber

In 1502, on his fourth and last voyage to the New World, Christopher Columbus made the first European landfall in the area. Settlement of Costa Rica began in 1522. In 1821, Costa Rica joined other Central American provinces in a joint declaration of independence from Spain. Unlike most of their Central American neighbors, Costa Ricans are largely of European rather than mestizo descent, and Spain is the primary country of origin. The indigenous population today numbers no more than 25,000. Blacks, descendants of nineteenth-century Jamaican immigrant workers, constitute a significant English-speaking minority of about 30,000, concentrated around the Caribbean port city of Limon.

Cuba
Official name: Republic of Cuba
Independence: May 20, 1902
Capital: Havana
Currency: Cuban peso
Income (per capita US$): 1000 (1990)
Area: 44,200 sq. mi.
Population: (1991 estimate) 10.7 million
Illiteracy: 6% (1991)
Ethnic divisions: Spanish-African mixture
Languages spoken: Spanish
International relations: CELA, UN
Form of government: Socialist Military
Exports: Chromium, nickel, sugar

Cuba is a multi-racial society with a population of mainly Spanish and African origins. Before the arrival of Columbus in 1492, Cuba was inhabited by three groups—Cyboneys, Guanahabibes, and Tainos. As Spain developed its colonial empire in the Western Hemisphere, Havana became an important commercial seaport. Settlers eventually moved inland, devoting themselves mainly to sugarcane and tobacco farming. As the native Indian population died out, African slaves were imported to work on the plantations. A 1774 census counted 96,000 whites, 31,000 free blacks, and 44,000 slaves in Cuba. Slavery was abolished in 1886.

Fidel Casro, who seized power in 1959, transformed Cuba into a socialist nation with the aid of the Soviet Union. Castro became a champion of anti-colonialism, which made him popular in "third world" countries struggling for independence. Soviet ties have created difficulties in Cuba, and many Cubas are still trying to leave the island.

Dominica
Official name: Commonwealth of Dominica
Independence: November 3, 1978
Capital: Roseau
Currency: Eastern Caribbean Dollar
Income (per capita US$: 1940 (1990)
Area: 290 sq. mi.
Population: (1991 estimate) 86,000
Illiteracy: 6% (1991)
Ethnic divisions: Black African, Carib Indians
Religious groups: Roman Catholic 80%, Church of England, other Protestant denominations
Languages spoken: English (official), a French patois is widely spoken
International relations: CARICOM, Commonwealth, OAS, UN
Form of government: Parliamentary republic
Exports: Citrus fruit, cocoa, coconuts

Dominica was first visited by Europeans on Columbus's second voyage in 1493. Spanish ships frequently landed on Dominica during the sixteenth century, but toiled at establishing settlements. In 1635, France claimed Dominica. As part of the 1763 Treaty of Paris that ended the Seven Years' War being fought in Europe, North America, and India, the island became a British possession.

In 1763, the British established a legislative assembly, representing only the white population. In 1831, reflecting a liberalization of official British racial attitudes, the "Brown Privelege Bill" conferred political and social rights on nonwhites. Three blacks were elected to the Legislative Assembly the following year, and by 1838 the recently enfranchised blacks dominated that body. Most black legislators were smallholders or merchants, who held economic and social views diametrically opposed to the interests of the small, wealthy English planter class. Reacting to a perceived threat, the planters lobbied for more direct British rule. In 1865, after much agitation and tension, the colonial office replaced the elective assembly with one of half of the members appointed.

The power of the black population progressively eroded until all political rights for the vast majority of the population were effectively curtailed. On November 3, 1978, the Commonwealth of Dominica was granted independence by the United Kingdom. Almost all 81,000 Dominicans are descendants of African slaves imported by planters in the eighteenth century.

In 1980, Mary Eugenia Charles became the first woman to come to power in the Carribbean as well as the only black woman to lead an independent nation. Her longevity and determination earned her the nickname "The Iron Lady of the Caribbean." Trained as a lawyer, Charles rose through the ranks of government, spending most of her career in politics. She was elected to the prime ministership for three terms; in 1996, she was thinking of retiring.

Dominican Republic
Independence: February 27, 1844
Capital: Santo Domingo
Currency: Dominican peso
Income (per capita US$: 820 (1990)
Area: 18,704 sq. mi.
Population: (1991 estimate) 7.3 million
Illiteracy: 18% (1991)
Ethnic divisions: Mixed 73%, black African 11%
Religious groups: Roman Catholic 95%
Languages spoken: Spanish
International relations: OAS, UN
Form of govt: Presidential republic
Exports: Gold, silver, sugar cane

The island of Hispaniola, of which the Dominican Republic forms the eastern two-thirds and Haiti the remainder, was originally occupied by members of the Taino tribe when Columbus and his companions landed there in 1492. Brutal colonial conditions reduced the Taino population from an estimated one million to about five hundred in only fifty years. To assure adequate labor for plantations, the Spanish began bringing African slaves to the island in 1503.

In the next century, French settlers occupied the western end of the island, which Spain ceded to France in 1697. In 1804, this became the Republic of Haiti. The Haitians conquered the whole island in 1822 and held it until 1844, when forces led by Juan Pablo Duarte, the hero of Dominican independence, drove the Haitians out and established the Dominican Republic as an independent state. In 1861, the Dominicans voluntarily returned to the Spanish Empire; in 1865, independence was restored.

After Rafael Trujillo's dictatorship ended in a 1961 assassination, Joaquín Balaguer became president and instituted a police state. He was however reelected

Improvised housing in Santo Domingo, Dominican Republic.

between 1966 and 1990. Pro- Cuban groups have been active in the nation.

Ecuador
Official name: Republic of Ecuador
Capital: Quito
Currency: Sucre
Income (per capita US$): 940 (1990)
Area: 109,483 sq. mi.
Population (1974 estimate) 6,521,710
Illiteracy: 14% (1991)
International relations: LAIA, OAS, UN
Form of government: Presidential republic
Exports: Coffee, cocoa, gold, petroleum

Blacks comprise a very small percentage of Ecuador's population.

•

El Salvador
Official name: Republic of El Salvador
Capital: San Salvador
Currency: Colon
Income (per capita US$): 1040 (1990)
Area: 8260 sq. mi.
Population (1980 estimate) 4,748,000
Illiteracy: 30 (1991)
International relations: CACM, OAS, UN
Form of government: Presidential republic
Exports: Coffee

Blacks comprises a very small percentage of El Salvador's population. After a long period of military dictatorships and conservative regimes, Napoléon Duarte of the Christian Democratic Party became president in 1980. In 1989, he was succeeded by Alfredo Cristiani leader of ARENA party.

French Guiana
Capital: Cayenne
Area: 43,740 sq. mi.
Population: (1988 estimate) 90,240
Ethnic divisions: African and Afro-European 66%, European 18%, East Asian, Chinese, Amerindian, Brazilian 16%
Religious groups: Roman Catholic, Protestant sects, Hindu, traditional African belief
Languages spoken: French

Stevedores transferring bananas in the Caribbean.

Exports: Cocoa, coffee, gold, sugar cane

The first French settlement in French Guiana was established in 1604. The first permanent settlement began in 1634, and in 1664, the town of Cayenne was established. Following the abolition of slavery in 1848, the fragile plantation economy declined precipitously. French Guiana as an overseas department of France since 1946, is an integral part of the French Republic. About two-thirds of the population of French Guiana are Afro-European Creoles or Guianese. The remainder include French serving in military or administrative positions.

Grenada
Independence: February 7, 1974
Capital: Saint George
Currency: East Caribbean dollar
Income (per capita US$): 2120 (1990)
Area: 133 sq. mi.
Population (1991 estimate) 84,000

Illiteracy: 15% (1991)
Ethnic divisions: Black African descent, some East Indian, European, Arawak/Carib Indian
Religious groups: Roman Catholic 63%, Church of England, other Protestant denominations
Languages spoken: English (official), some vestigial French patois
International relations: CARICOM, EC, OAS, UN
Form of government: Independent within British sovereignty
Exports: Banana, cocoa, coffee, coconuts

Like the rest of the West Indies, Grenada was originally settled to cultivate sugar, which was grown on estates using slave labor. Most of Grenada's population is of African descent; little trace of the early Arawak and Carib Indians remains.

Columbus first visited Grenada in 1498. Grenada remained uncolonized for more than one hundred years after the first visit by Europeans; British efforts to settle the island were unsuccessful. In 1650, a French company purchased Grenada from the British and established a small settlement. The island remained under French control until captured by the British a century later during the Seven Year's War. Slavery was outlawed in 1833, the same year Grenada was made part of the British Windward Islands Administration. In 1958, the Windward Islands Administration dissolved. Grenada became an associated state on March 3, 1967, but sought full independence, which the British government granted on February 7, 1974.

The New Jewel Movement led by Maurice Bishop assumed power in 1979. He was overthrown and killed in 1983 when Bernard Coard took over. The United States, along with forces from the other Caribbean countries intervened.

Guadeloupe
Independence: n/a (overseas department of France)
Capital: Point-à-Pitre
Area: 660 sq. mi.
Population: (1988 estimate) 337,524
Ethnic divisions: Afro-European, European, Afro-East Asian, East Asian
Religious groups: Roman Catholic, Hindu, and traditional African belief
Languages spoken: French, creole
Exports: Bananas, rum, sugar cane

Columbus sighted Guadeloupe in 1493. The area was permanently settled by the French in the seventeenth century. The first slaves were brought from Africa to work the plantations around 1650, and the first slave rebellion occurred in 1656. Guadeloupe was poorly administered in its early days and was a dependency of Martinique until 1775.

An open-air market in Guadeloupe.

Most Guadeloupeans are of mixed Afro-European and Afro-Indian ancestry (descendants of laborers brought over from India during the ninteenth century). Several thousand metropolitan French reside there; most are civil servants, business people, and their dependents.

Guatemala
Capital: Guatemala City
Currency: Quetzal
Income (per capita US$) 900 (1990)
Area: 42,042 sq. mi.
Population: (1981 estimate) 6,043,559
Illiteracy: 53% (1991)
International relations: CACM, OAS, UN
Form of government: Presidential republic

Blacks comprise a very small percentage of Guatemala's population.

Guyana
Official name: Co-operative Republic of Guyana
Independence: May 26, 1966
Capital: Georgetown
Currency: Guyana dollar
Income (per capita US$): 370 (1990)
Illiteracy: 4% (1991)
Area: 83,000 sq. mi.
Population (1991 estimate): 748,000
International relations: CARICOM, Commonwealth, EC, UN

Ethnic divisions: East Indian 49.6%, African 30.4%, mixed 14.1%, European and Chinese 0.5%
Religious groups: Christian 46%, Hindu 37%, Muslim 9%, other 8%
Languages spoken: English, Guyanese Creole, Amerindian dialects
Form of government: Multi-party
Exports: Bauxite, gold, sugar

Guiana was the name given the area sighted by Columbus in 1498, comprising modern Guyana, Suriname, French Guiana, and parts of Brazil and Venezuela. The Dutch settled in Guyana in the late sixteenth century. Dutch control ended when the British became the de facto rulers in 1796. In 1815, the colonies of Essequibo, Demerara, and Berbice were officially ceded to the British by the Congress of Vienna and, in 1831, were consolidated as British Guiana.

Slave revolts, such as the one in 1763 led by Guyana's national hero, Cuffy, stressed the desire to obtain basic rights and were underscored by a willingness to compromise. Following the abolition of slavery in 1834, indentured workers were brought primarily from India but also from Portugal and China. A scheme in 1862 to bring black workers from the United States was unsuccessful.

Independence was achieved in 1966, and Guyana became a republic on February 23, 1970, the anniversary of the Cuffy slave rebellion. Between 1968 and 1972 Guyana was ruled by the PNC party. In 1975. Guyana gained unfortuante international recognition after a religious cult in Jonestown was led into mass suicide by its leader, Jim Jones.

Political conflict with opposing parties resulted in the assassination of the nations leader, Dr. Walter Roberts, in 1980. Human rights were continually being violated under the Forbes Burnham government (1980-85). Upon his death he was succeeded by Desmond Hoyte. Cheddi Jagan who had been a prominent political figure of Peoples's Progressive Party many years ago was elected president in 1992.

Haiti
Official name: Republic of Haiti
Independence: 1804
Capital: Port-au-Prince
International relations: EC, OAS, UN
Currency: Gourde
Income (per capita US$): 400 (1989)
Area: 10,714 sq. mi.
Population: (1991 estimate): 6.2 million
Illiteracy: 53% (1991)
Ethnic Group: Black African 95%, mulatto and European 5%
Religious groups: Roman Catholic 80%, Protestant 10%, traditional (voodoo) practices 10%
Languages spoken: French (official), Creole
Form of government: Multi-party
Exports: Coffee, cotton, sugar

Columbus first visited the Island of Hispaniola in 1492. In 1697, Spain ceded the western third of Hispaniola to France. During this period, slaves were brought from Africa to work the sugarcane and coffee plantations. In 1791, the slave population, led by Toussaint L'Ouverture, Jean Jacques Dessalines, and Henri Christophe, revolted and gained control of the northern part of Saint-Domingue. The French were unable to regain control. In 1804, the slaves established an independent nation, renaming the area Haiti.

Haiti is the world's oldest black republic and the second oldest republic in the Western Hemisphere, after the United States. In September 1991, the newly elected President Jean-Bertrand Aristide was ousted in a coup leading by Brigadier General Raoul Cedras. Since Aristide's ouster, thousands of Haitians have attempted to immigrate to the United States, with no success. In 1994, U.S. forces took control and Aristide was returned to power, only to lose in the following years elections. The U.S. government has also forcibly returned Haitian refugees illegally attempting to emigrate, maintaining that the majority have been economic, and not political, refugees.

Almost 95 percent of the Haitians are of black African descent; the rest of the population are mostly of mixed African-Caucasian ancestry (mulattoes).

Honduras
Official name: Republic of Honduras

Blacks comprise a very small percentage of Honduras' population.

Jamaica
Independence: August 6, 1962
Capital: Kingston
Currency: Jamaican dollar
Income (per capita US$): 1510 (1990)
Area: 4,244 sq.mi.
Population: (1991 estimate) 2.4 million.
Illiteracy: 18% (1990)
Ethnic divisions: African 76.3%, Afro-European 15.1%, Chinese and Afro-Chinese 1.2%, East Indian and Afro-East Indian 3.4%, European 3.2%
Religious groups: Anglican, Baptist and other Protestant denominations, Roman Catholic
Languages spoken: English, Creole
International relations: CAROCOM, EC, OAS, UN
Form of government: Independent under British sovereignty
Exports: Bauxite

Workers on a banana plantation in Central America.

Jamaica was first visited in 1494 by Christopher Columbus and settled by the Spanish during the early sixteenth century. In 1655, British forces seized the island, and in 1670 gained formal possession through the Treaty of Madrid.

In 1958, Jamaica joined nine other British territories in the West Indies Federation but withdrew when, in a 1961 referendum, Jamaican voters rejected membership. Jamaica gained independence from the United Kingdom in 1962 but has remained a member of the Commonwealth. Sugar and slavery, were important elements in Jamaica's history and development. With the abolition of slavery in 1834, the settlers were forced to recruit other sources of cheap labor, resorting to the importation of East Indian and Chinese farm hands. As a result, Jamaica is a multi-racial society.

Extreme povery is a distinguishing factor of all the lesser developed nations, and Jamaica is no exception. A new phenomenon has became particularly apparent in Jamaica, a country that has lost nearly 30 percent of its population to the United States. Though prevalent in all countries that experience heavy emigration, tens of thousands of Jamaican parents have gone abroad, leaving behind children whom they hope to one day be able to summon. The youngsters have acquired the nickname "barrel children" from the barrels filled with goodies—food, clothing, photographs—the parents send back whenever possible. Though these children have not actually been abandoned, they are often passed from relative to relative or to friends or strangers. Highly at risk, the children are often susceptible to abuse from their supposed benfactors, many drop out of school, some get into trouble with the law.

After years under the Jamaican Labor party, the 1972 elections put Michael Norman Manley in power and reelected in 1989. His regime ended when Perciaval Patter was elected in 1992.

Martinique
Independence: n/a (overseas region of France)
Capital: Fort-de-France
Area: 425 sq. mi.
Population: (1988 estimate): 351,105
Ethnic divisions: Afro-European, Afro-Indian, European
Religious groups: Roman Catholic 95%, Baptist, Seventh-day Adventist, Jehovah Witness, Pentecostal, Hindu, traditional African belief 5%
Languages spoken: French

Linstead market, Jamaica.

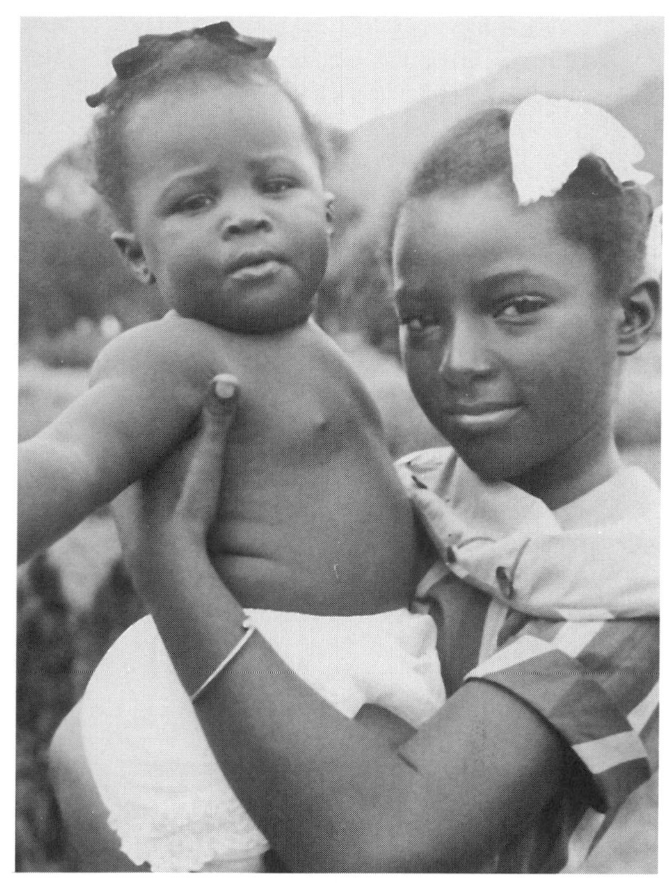

Two Jamaican children.

Exports: Bananas, pineapples, sugar cane

Columbus sighted Martinique in 1493 or 1502. The area was permanently settled by the French in the seventeenth century. Except for three short periods of British occupation, Martinique has been a French possession since 1635.

About 95 percent of the people of Martinique are of Afro-European or Afro-European-Indian descent. The rest are traditional white planter families, commonly referred to as bekes or creoles, and a sizable number of metropolitan French work in administration and business.

Mexico
Official name: The United Mexican States
Capital: Mexico City
Currency: Mexican peso
Income (per capita US$: 2604 (1992)
International relations: LAIA, SELA, UN
Form of government: Federal republic
Exports: Coffee, copper, cotton, petroleum, silver, sugar, sulfur

Blacks accompanied the Spanish as conquerors to Mexico in the sixteenth century, and later were brought in large numbers as slaves. It is estimated that there were 150,000 black slaves in Mexico in the sixteenth century. One of the earlier slaves, Estevanico, is credited with opening up the northern interior lands of what is now New Mexico and Arizona, to Spanish conquest.

The use of slavery dropped sharply in the eighteenth and early nineteenth centuries. In 1829, Mexico abolished slavery in all its states except Texas, allowing it to remain there to pacify the United States. As slavery in the United States moved westward into Texas, Mexico became a haven for escaped slaves who slipped into the heart of the country and blended with the population.

Since the sixteenth century, Mexico's blacks have intermarried with Indians and whites so that their African heritage is no longer clearly identifiable. Some 100,000 blacks, about 0.5 percent of the population, do live in Mexico, mostly in the port cities of Vera Cruz and Acapulco. Blacks in lesser density live in Mexico City and in border cities across the Rio Grande River from Texas.

In 1988, a 39-year-old economist, Carlos Salinas de Gortari was elected to the presidency. The North American Free Trade Agreement (NAFTA) was concluded in

1992, and Mexico became a member of this fair trade agreement. 1994 brought an uprising by the Zapatista Army of National Liberation.

Montserrat

Independence: n/a (dependent territory of the United Kingdom)
Capital: Plymouth
Population: (1992 estimate) 12,617
Ethnic divisions: Black African, European
Religious groups: Anglican, Methodist, Roman Catholic, Pentecostal, Seventh-Day Adventist, other Christian denominations
Languages spoken: English

When the Leeward Islands (Antigua, Anguilla, Barbuda, Montsarrat, Nevis, and Saint Kitts) were first visited by Christopher Columbus in 1493, they were inhabited by Carib Indians. Montserrat was first colonized in 1632. The French captured some of the islands in 1666 and again in 1782, but the islands were returned to the British under the Treaty of Versailles in 1783. Most of the population is an intermixture of European settlers and the descendants of West African slaves.

Netherlands Antilles

Independence: n/a (Autonomous part of the Kingdom of the Netherlands)
Currency: Guilder or florin
Area: 324 sq. mi.
Population: 187,500
Ethnic divisions:Black African 85%, European, Carib Indian
Religious groups: Roman Catholic, Protestant
Languages spoken: Papiamento, English, Dutch, Spanish
Form of government: Dutch colony

The Spanish first landed in Curacao in 1499, and in 1527 they took possession of Curacao, Bonaire, and Aruba. In 1634, the three islands were passed to the Netherlands, where they have remained except for two short periods of British rule during the Napoleonic Wars.

Curacao was the center of the Caribbean slave trade until emancipation in 1863. Before the war, the Dutch Caribbean islands were administered as Dutch colonies; afterward, negotiations to confer a greater measure of self-government began. On December 15, 1954, the Netherlands Antilles became an autonomous part of the kingdom.

Some 40 nationalities are represented in the Netherlands Antilles and Aruba. The people of the Netherlands Antilles primarily are of African or mixed African and European descent.

Nicaragua

Official name: Republic of Nicaragua
Independence: 1821
Capital: Managua
Currency: Cordoba
Income (per capita US$): 434 (1991)
Area: 57,000 sq. mi.
Population: 3.3 million
Illiteracy: 13% (1991)
Ethnic divisions: Mestizo (mixed) 69%, white 17%, black African 9%, Indian 5%
Religious groups: Roman Catholic 85%
Languages spoken: Spanish
International relations: CACM, OAS, UN
Form of government: Presidential republic
Exports: Bananas, coffee, gold

Columbus sailed along the Nicaraguan coast on his last voyage in 1502. Wars between the Spanish on the Pacific and Indians and British on the Caribbean (the British presence did not end until 1905) marked the colonial period. Guatemala declared its independence from Spain in 1821, but Nicaragua did not become an independent republic until 1838.

In 1974, Anastasio Somoza Garcia won elections and immediately faced opposition by the Sandinist National Liberation front. After 13 politicians were kidnaped, martial law was instituted which eventually led Somoza to lose all support. He left the country in 1980, and was later assassinated. More than 30,000 people lost their lives during that time. A peace accord was finally reached between the Sandinistas and the Contras (anti-Sandinistas). Leading a 10-party alliance, Violetta Chamorro was elected president in 1990.

Most Nicaraguans are a mix of European and Indian. Only the Indians of the Caribbean coast remain ethnically distinct and retain tribal customs and dialects. A large black minority (of Jamaican origin) is concentrated on the Caribbean coast.

Panama

Official name: Republic of Panama
Independence: November 3, 1903
Capital: Panama City
Currency: Balboa
Income (per capita US$): 1790 (1990)
Area: 29,762 sq. mi.
Population: (1991 estimate) 2.4 million
Illiteracy: 12% (1991)
Ethnic divisions: Mestizo 70%, West Indian 14%, white 10%, Indian 6%
Religious groups: Roman Catholic 93%, Protestant (Evangelical) 6%

A market at Managua, Nicaragua.

Languages spoken: Spanish (official), English, Indian languages
International relations: OAU, UN
Form of government: Presidential republic
Exports: Cocoa, coffee

Prior to the arrival of Europeans, Panama was inhabited by Amerindian groups. By 1519 the Spanish had established settlements, killing or enslaving much of the indigenous Indian population. Africans were brought in to replace the Indian slave population. Today, most Panamanians are of mixed parentage—Spanish, Indian, or black.

The most importance source of income is the operation of the Panama Canal, which the United States, under the Carter administration agreed to return to the Panamian sovereignty by 1999. During the 1980s, the political scene was dominated by Gen. Manuel Antonio Noriega, who was accused of trafficking drugs. A U.S. military attack forced him to surrender his leadership in 1989, after he was incarcerated in a U.S. jail.

Paraguay
Official name: Republic of Paraguay

Blacks comprise a very small percentage of Paraguay's population.

Peru
Official name: Republic of Peru

Blacks comprise a small percentage of Peru's population.

A Panamanian craftsman.

Puerto Rico
Independence: n/a (commonwealth associated with the United States)
Capital: San Juan
Income (per capita US$): 5,000
Area: 9,104 sq. km.
Population: (1992 estimate) 3,776,654
Illiteracy: 10%
Ethnic division: Mixed, black, indian, whites
Religious groups: Roman Catholic 85%, Protestant denominations and other 15%
Languages spoken: Spanish (official), English

First visited by Columbus in 1493 on his second voyage to the New World, Puerto Rico was soon conquered by the Spaniard Ponce de Leon, who was appointed governor of the island in 1509. The indigenous Carib Indians, almost all of whom were utilized by the Spaniards as plantation laborers, were eventually wiped out—to be replaced in 1513 by African slaves. Puerto Rico was held by the English in 1598 and San Juan was besieged by the Dutch in 1625. Otherwise, Spanish control remained unchallenged until the Spanish-American War.

The island was captured by United States forces during this conflict and ceded outright to the United States under the Treaty of Paris (1898). In 1900, Congress established a local administration, with a governor appointed by the American president, an executive council, and an elected house of delegates. Puerto Ricans were granted United States citizenship in 1917. After World War II, Congress provided that the governor of the island be an elected official. In 1950, a further act of Congress enabled Puerto Rico to draft its own constitution and, in three years, it became a U.S. Commonwealth; Puerto Ricans are considered U.S. citizens, but they do not have the right to vote. Unemployment has been on the rise precipitating two thirds of families to depend of government aid.

Many Puerto Ricans today are of mixed black and Spanish ancestry. Africans were slaves in Puerto Rico until 1873, when slavery was abolished. The United States acquired the island in 1898, and Puerto Ricans have been U.S. citizens since the 1917 passage of the Jones Act. Sexual relations between the descendants of the African slaves and the Spanish colonizers resulted in a multiracial population. For the most part, the original Indian inhabitants of the island were exterminated in the sixteenth century.

Saint Kitts and Nevis
Official name: Federation of Saint Kitts and Nevis
Independence: September 19, 1983
Captial: Basseterre
Currency: Eastern Caribbean dollar
Income (per capita US$): 1610 (1990)
Form of govt: Independent within British Commonwealth
Area: Saint Kitts, (68 sq. mi.); Nevis, (36 sq. mi.)
Population: (1991 estimate) 40,293
Illiteracy: 15% (1989)
Ethnic divisions: Black Africans, some British
Religious groups: Principally Anglican, with evangelical Protestant and Roman Catholic minorities
Languages spoken: English
International relations: EC, OAS, UN
Exports: Sugar cane

Christopher Columbus first visited the islands in 1493 on his second voyage to the area, naming the larger Saint Christopher, after his patron saint. In 1624, Saint Christopher became the first English settlement in the West Indies, and it was from here that colonists spread to other islands in the region. In 1624, the French colonized part of the island. However, it was ceded entirely to Britain by the Treaty of Utrecht in 1713. The Federation of Saint Kitts and Nevis attained full independence on September 19, 1983.

Saint Lucia
Independence: February 22, 1979
Capital: Castries
Currency: East Caribbean dollar
Income (per capita US$): 1950 (1990)
Area: 238 sq. mi.
Population: (1991 estimate) 163,075.
Illiteracy: 10% (1991)
Ethnic divisions: Black African 90.3%, mixed 5.5%, East Indian 3.2%, Caucasian 0.8%
Religious groups: Roman Catholic 90%, Church of England 3%
Languages spoken: English (official), French patois
International relations: CARICOM, EC, OAS, UN
Form of government: Independent state within British Commonwealth
Exports: Bananas, coconuts

Europeans first visited the island in either 1492 or 1502. In the seventeenth century, the Dutch, English, and French all tried to establish trading outposts on Saint Lucia but faced opposition from Carib Indians, who inhabited the island. The French, who had claimed the island, established a successful settlement in 1651 as an offshoot of the colony in neighboring Martinique; for the next century and a half, ownership was disputed hotly between France and England.

The English, with their headquarters in Barbados, and the French, centered on Martinique, found Saint Lucia even more attractive when the sugar industry developed in 1765. By 1780, nearly 50 sugarcane estates had been established on the island; heavy labor needs of the estates led to large scale importation of slaves from West Africa.

A 1924 constitution gave the island its first form of representative government. As an associated state of the United Kingdom from 1967 to 1979, Saint Lucia had full responsibility for internal self-government, but left its external affairs and defense responsibilities to Great Britain. This interim arrangement ended on February 22, 1979, when Saint Lucia achieved full independence. John Compton, leader of the United Workers' Party, became the prime minister at independence. In the 1992 elections the UWP won again.

Saint Lucia is now inhabited mainly by people of African and mixed African-European descent, with small Caucasian and East Indian minorities.

Saint Vincent and the Grenadines
Independence: October 27, 1979
Capital: Kingstown
Currency: East Caribbean dollar
Income (per capita US$): 1610 (1990)
Population: (1992 estimate) 115,339
Illiteracy: 15% (1989)
Ethnic division: Black African, white, East Indian, Carib Indian
Religious groups: Anglican, Methodist, Roman Catholic, Seventh-Day Adventist
Languages spoken: English, French patois
International relations: CARICOM, EC, OAS, UN
Form of government: Independent within British Commonwealth
Exports: Bananas, coconuts, cotton

Saint Vincent and the Grenadine islands began as a British territory during the eighteenth century. The islands were granted full autonomy in 1969 and attained full independence in 1979. Following independence, St.

Vincent was faced with a rebellion when the Union Island attempted to secede. The New Democratic Party led by James FitzAllen Mitchel won at the 1989 elections.

Suriname
Official name: Republic of Suriname
Independence: November 25, 1975
Capital: Paramaribo
Currency: Surinam guilder
Income (per capita US$): 3050 (1990)
Area: 63,037 sq. mi.
Population: (1991 estimate) 402,000
Illiteracy: 5% (1990)
Ethnic divisions: Hindustani (East Indian) 37%, Creole 31%, Javanese 15%, Bush Negro 10%, Amerindians 3%, Chinese 1.7%
Religious groups: Hindu, Muslim, Roman Catholic, Dutch Reformed, Moravian and several other Christian groups
Languages spoken: Dutch (official) English, Sranang Tongo (a Creole language), Hindustani, Javanese
International relations: EC, OAS, UN
Form of government: Constitutional republic
Exports: Bananas, bauxite, citrus, coffee, cocoa, sugar cane

Columbus first sighted the Suriname coast in 1498; Spain claimed the area in 1593. Suriname became a Dutch colony in 1667. However, the new colony, Dutch Guiana did not thrive. The colony experienced frequent uprisings by the slave population, which was often treated with extraordinary cruelty. Many of the slaves fled to the interior, where they resumed a West African culture and established the five major Bush Negro tribes in existence today: the Djuka, Saramaccaner, Matuwari, Paramaccaner, and Quinti.

Beginning in 1951, Suriname began to acquire an increasing measure of autonomy from the Netherlands. On December 15, 1954, Suriname became an autonomous part of the Kingdom of the Netherlands and gained independence on November 25, 1975. Désiré Bourtese led a military coup in 1980, and instituted a socialist state. Political upheaval continued in spite of the elections held in 1987. International pressure prevailed and the military relinquished. Ronald Venetiaan was elected in 1991.

Trinidad and Tobago
Official name: Republic of Trinidad and Tobago
Independence: August 31, 1962.
Capital: Port of Spain
Currency: Trinidad/Tobago dollar
Income (per capita US$): 3470 (1990)

A statue of former Surinamese President John Adolf Pengel.

Area: 1,980 sq. mi.
Population: (1988) 1,279,920
Ethnic divisions: (1988): African 43%, East Indian 40%, mixed 14%
Religious groups: Roman Catholic 32,9%, Hindu 25.0%, Anglican 14.7%, other Christian denominations 14.3%, Muslim 5.9%
Languages spoken: English
International relations: CARICOM, Commonwealth, EC, OAS, UN
Form of government: Constitutional republic
Exports: Natural asphault, petroleum

The island of Trinidad was first visited by Columbus in 1498 on his third voyage to the Western Hemisphere. The Spanish made the first successful attempt to colonize Trinidad in 1592. Trinidad continued under Spanish rule until it was captured by the British in 1797. Africans were brought to the islands during the eighteenth century to provide labor on the sugar cane plantations. Following the abolition of slavery, Indian and Chinese labour was brought in.

Trinidad was ceded formally to the United Kingdom in 1802; the island of Tobago was ceded to the United Kingdom in 1814. In 1888, Trinidad and Tobago merged to form a single colony. In 1958, the United Kingdom established the autonomous Federation of the West Indies. Jamaica withdrew in 1961, and when Trinidad and Tobago followed, the federation collapsed. Trinidad and Tobago obtained full independence and joined the Commonwealth in 1962.

Eric Williams became prime minister a independence and held that position until he died in 1981. During the 1991 elections Patric Augustus Mervyn Manning was elected prime minister. Black-led since 1956, the two-island nation elected its first Indian prime minister, Basdeo Panday, in 1996.

Turks and Caicos Islands
Independence: n/a (dependent territory of the United Kingdom)
Capital: Grand Turk
Currency: US dollar
Area: 430 sq. km.
Population: (1992 estimate) 12,697
Ethnic divisions: Black African
Religious groups: Baptist 41.2%, Methodist 18.9%, Anglican 18.3%, Seventh-Day Adventist 1.7%
Languages spoken: English (official)
Exports: Conch, lobster

Between 1874 and 1959, the Turks and Caicos islands were administered as a dependency of Jamaica. In 1962, the islands became a separate colony. In 1985, Norman B. Saunders, the chief minister and two other ministers caused a scandal when they were arrested in Florida on drug charges and later charged, convicted, and jailed. One year later the ministerial government ended when other ministers were found guilty of "unconstitutional behavior." The islands remain a crown colony.

Venezuela
Official name: Republic of Venezuela
Independence: July 5, 1821
Capital: Caracas
Currency: Bolivar
Income (per capita US$) 2560 (1990)
Area: 352,143 sq. mi.
Population: (1991 estimate) 20.1 million.
Illiteracy: 12%
Ethnic divisions: Spanish, Italian, Portuguese, Amerindian, black African
Religious groups: Roman Catholic 96%
Languages spoken: Spanish (official), Indian dialects
International relations: LAIA, OAS, UN
Form of government: Presidential republic
Exports: Coffee, cocoa, cotton, sugar cane, tobacco

About 900,000 of Venezuela's 17 million people are black and another 500,000 are Zambos. In the sixteenth and seventeenth centuries, Caracas was a major center for the import of slaves. In the early nineteenth century, blacks and mulattoes comprised more than half of the population of The Captaincy General of Caracas, as Venezuela was known then. Blacks remain a significant part of the country because of its proximity to the Caribbean and employment opportunities that have been available in this oil-rich nation.

Carlos Andrés Pérez, who had been president 15 years earlier was elected again in 1988. He immediately imposed austerity measures, removing governemnt subsidies on consumer goods. This resulted in mass riots that had to be quelled by the military. In 1992, two coups were unsuccessful. Pérez was eventually suspended from office for allegations of embezzlement and theft. In the 1993 elections, Rafael Caldera became the head of state.

Uruguay
Official name: Oriental Republic of Uruguay

Blacks comprise a very small percentage of Uruguay's population.

Virgin Islands, British
Independence: n/a (dependent territory of United Kingdom)
Capital: Road Town
Area: 150 sq. km.
Population: (1992 estimate) 12,555
Ethnic divisions: Black African 90%, remainder white and Asian
Religious groups: Protestant 86% Methodist 45%, Anglican 21%, Church of God 7%, Roman Catholic 6%, Seventh-Day Adventist 5%, Baptist 4%, Jehovah's Witnesses 2%, other 6%
Languages spoken: English (official)
Exports: Bananas, citrus fruit, coconut, sugar

First visited by Christopher Columbus in 1493, the Virgin Islands (an archipelago of 74 islands) is now divided into two distinct clusters—the British Virgin Islands (six main islands, nearly forty islets) and the U.S. Virgin Islands (three main islands, 65 islets). Great Britain obtained title to the islands and islets in 1666 and, until 1960, administered them as part of the Leeward Islands. At present, the government is headed by a Crown-appointed administrator who is assisted by both executive and legislative councils. Almost the entire population is of African descent. Recreational boating accounts for nearly 55 percent of the nation's gross national product and employs one third of the population.

Virgin Islands, United States
Independence: n/a (territory of the United States)
Area: 352 sq. km.

Population: (1992 estimate) 98,942
Ethnic divisions: Black African
Religious groups: Baptist, 42%, Roman Catholic 34%, Episcopalian 17%, other 7%
Languages spoken: English (official), Spanish, Creole

The U.S. Virgin Islands—the largest of which are the islands of Saint Croix, Saint John, and Saint Thomas—were originally settled by the Danish West India Company. Saint Thomas was the first to be colonized in 1672; in 1683 Saint John was colonized; and by 1733, Saint Croix had been acquired from France. Some twenty years later, the holdings of this company were taken over by the Danish crown, which then reconstituted them as the Danish West Indies.

The United States bought the territory from Denmark in 1917 for some $25 million and granted citizenship to its inhabitants ten years later. In 1931, its administration was transferred from the United States Navy to the Department of the Interior. The first black governor, William H. Hastie, was appointed in 1946.

Under the terms of the constitution, the United States retains the authority to introduce and enact legislation to govern the territory. The courts are also controlled by the United States, with an American district judge serving as the territory's highest judicial officer. Pursuant to a bill passed by Congress in 1968, the governor of the island is elected, rather than appointed. In 1972, the Virgin Islands were granted the right to send one nonvoting delegate to the House of Representatives. Island residents enjoy the same rights as mainlanders with the exception that they may not vote in a presidential election.

Africans in America: 1600 to 1900

6

Africans in America: 1600 to 1900

◆ Exploration and the First Settlements in the Americas ◆ Slavery in Colonial America: 1619-1787
◆ African American Status in the New Republic ◆ Expansion of Slavery ◆ Anti-Slavery Movements
◆ The Compromise of 1850 ◆ Civil War ◆ Reconstruction
◆ African American Status after Reconstruction ◆ Early African American Gatekeepers

◆ EXPLORATION AND THE FIRST SETTLEMENTS IN THE AMERICAS

The presence of the first African Americans in the Americas is a point of contention among historians. Some scholars assert that Africans established contact with the Americas prior to the Europeans, arguing from archeological, anthropological, botanical, and linguistic evidence that Africans were present in pre-Columbian America; the work of Ivan Van Sertima is notable in this regard. Others mark the advent of the African presence as coinciding with the presence of the Europeans. Pedro Alonzo Niño, an explorer and companion to Christopher Columbus on his exploratory journey of 1492, appears to have been African; and it is known that an African named Estevanico accompanied the Spanish explorers Panfilo de Narvaez and Alvar Nuñez Cabeza de Vaca on trips throughout the American southwest during the 1500s. Several other European explorers, including Vasco Nuñez de Balboa and Hernán Cortés, also had African members in their parties.

In 1496 Santo Domingo was established as the first permanent European settlement in the Americas. Indigenous Carib Indians were at first used as laborers; however, they were ill suited to the rigors of the European system of slavery and died in large numbers from either disease or the constant pressure of forced labor. Portuguese explorers first visited the west coast of Africa in the fifteenth century and found that slave trading was an established institution. West Africans had for some time sold each other to Arabic traders from North Africa. By the early sixteenth century the Portuguese and Spanish were supplying newly established colonies in the Americas with African slave labor, and by the seventeenth century several other European nations had entered the trade. African slaves proved to be a relatively cheap and inexhaustible source of labor, and from about 1501 they were increasingly used as slaves, replacing the dwindling Native American labor pool.

Clearly, relations between African Americans and Native Americans were extensive. Occasionally, African Americans made slaves of Native Americans—sometimes with the same harshness that whites showed black slaves—but most scenarios involved African American slaves running away, finding sanctuary with Native American tribes, and eventually being assimilating into the tribe. Most notable were African American contacts with the Seminoles in Florida, and the Cherokee, Creeks, Choctaws, Chickasaws, and others in North Carolina, Tennessee, Georgia, Alabama, Mississippi, and Oklahoma. (The most extensive data available to trace and document family ties of African Americans and Native Americans was collected by the U.S. government, starting in the late nineteenth century, to determine all individuals who were tribal members and thus eligible for benefits from the federal government.)

◆ SLAVERY IN COLONIAL AMERICA: 1619-1787

The Emergence of Slave Status

Twenty Africans accompanied the Europeans who landed at Jamestown, Virginia, in 1619. These people were not slaves but indentured servants, and upon completing their contracts they were free to enjoy the liberties and privileges of the "free laboring class." By 1650 there were about three hundred Africans in the American colonies, most of whom were indentured servants and some of whom eventually became property holders and active citizens. The first African American born in the colonies, William Tucker, shared with the other settlers the common birthright of freedom. The slave Anthony Johnson apparently became free about 1622 and had by 1651 amassed enough wealth to import five servants of his own, for which he obtained two hundred and fifty acres from the colonial government. The African American carpenter Richard Johnson imported two white servants in 1654 and received one hundred acres.

It is unclear when the first African slaves arrived in the North American colonies. From the 1640s Africans were increasingly regarded as chattel (or persons regarded as fixed items of personal property). In 1641 Massachusetts became the first state to make perpetual bondage legal, and the institution gradually spread among the original thirteen colonies. Rhode Island had an antislavery ordinance, but this was openly violated, and only Pennsylvania maintained a sustained opposition to slavery. By the 1650s Africans were commonly sold for life, and in 1661 the Virginia House of Burgesses formally recognized the institution of black slavery. The erosion of African indentured servitude in Maryland was finalized with the slave law of 1663, which stated specifically that "All negroes or other slaves within the province, [and] all negroes to be hereafter imported, shall serve *durante vita.*"

As white indentured servitude gradually disappeared from the colonial labor market, the flow of African labor into the colonies was accelerated, and planters rigidly institutionalized the perpetual servitude of Africans. One practical reason for this system was that slaves of African origin could be more easily detected than whites should they escape. And among the common rationalizations for the enslavement of Africans was reference to their non-Christian status; it was asserted that Africans were primitive and savage, and fit for nothing better than a life of unbroken labor. Even after African Americans became Christianized, their slave status was not altered; in 1667 the Virginia legislature enacted a statute which proclaimed that "baptism doth not alter the condition of the person as to his bondage or freedom."

The Trans-Atlantic Slave Trade

The Dutch West Indies Company began to provide slave labor to the American colonies in 1621. By the late seventeenth century the Royal African Company, an English company whose most profitable commodity was slaves, began to exert powerful influence within the English court and parliament. The British government in turn exerted great pressure upon the American colonies to develop attitudes and laws which would support a slave economy. The influence of the Royal African Company contributed to William Penn's decision to overrule the objections of fellow Quakers and permit slavery in Pennsylvania. The company also drew the shipping industry of New England into the slave trade. By the time the Royal African Company lost its monopoly on the West African slave trade in 1696, the sea captains of New England were participating in the massive slave incursions into Africa.

According to Donald Wright in *African Americans in the Colonial Era*, most slaves brought to the North American English colonies by English and colonial American traders came from a 3,500-mile area of west and west-central Africa, stretching from "the mouth of the Senegal River to Benguela on the Angola coast" (p. 25). Most of these slaves came from the following areas: Congo-Angola (25 percent, including the Mbundu peoples), an area within 500 miles north or south of the Zaire (formerly the Congo) River; the coast of Nigeria (25 percent, including the Ibo and Ibibio), known in slave trade times as the "Bight of Benin" and the "Bight of Biafra "; Senegambia (15 percent, including the Mandinka, Fulbe, Serer, Wolof, Bambara, and Jola tribes), from the land between and around the Senegal and Gambia rivers; the Gold Coast (15 percent, including the Ashanti, Fanti, and Akan), present-day Togo, Benin, and Ghana; the Sierre Leone-Ivory Coast area (15 percent, including the Vai, Mende, Kpelle, and Kru peoples); and the Malagasy Republic (formerly Madagascar) and coast of Mozambique (1.6 percent). The number of Africans who reached the Americas is estimated at between ten and twenty million. About six hundred thousand Africans were brought during the sixteenth century, two million in the seventeenth century, five million in the eighteenth century; and three million in the nineteenth century. In addition to those who reached the Americas must be added the enormous number who died in passage. It is estimated that 15 percent of those who were shipped to the Americas died of disease on the overcrowded boats of the "Middle Passage," and that another 30 percent died during the brutal training period faced in the West Indies before shipment to the American mainland.

Slavery Expansion in Colonial America

The colonies of New England played a principal role in the slave trade, despite their having little local need for slave labor. By 1700 African Americans of New England numbered only one thousand among a population of ninety thousand. In the mid-Atlantic colonies the

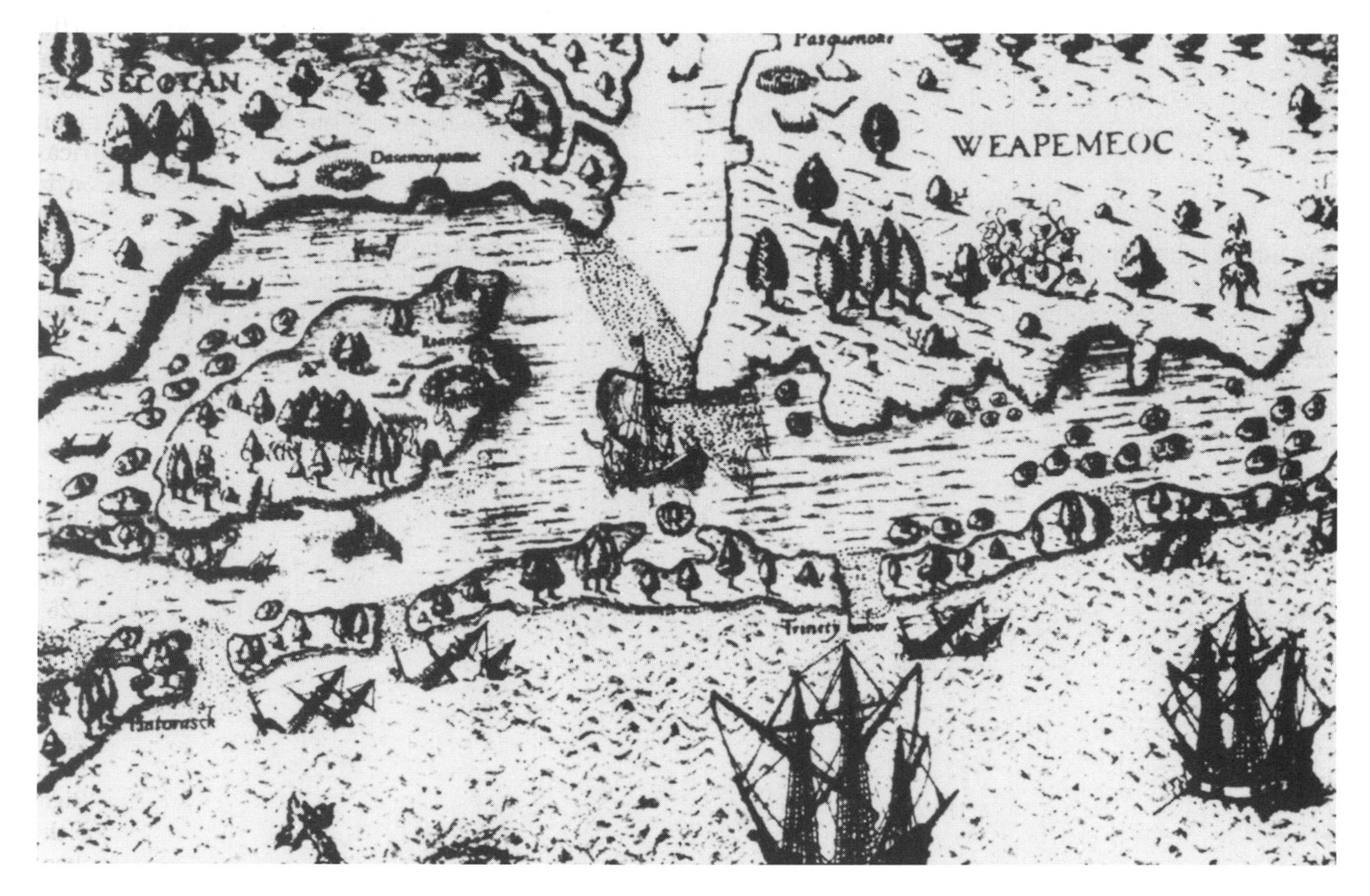

Early map of Virginia.

population comprised a larger percentage, as small slaveholdings employed slaves as farm laborers, domestics, and craftsmen. In New York slaves comprised 12 percent of the population during the mid-eighteenth century. The Quakers of Pennsylvania protested that slavery violated the principles of Christianity and the rights of man, and passed laws prohibiting the slave trade in 1688, 1693, and 1696, but the British parliament overruled these statutes in 1712. Most slaves lived in the South. The southern colonies were divided between the tobacco producing provinces of Virginia, Maryland, and North Carolina, and the huge rice and indigo plantations now comprising Carolina and Georgia. Tobacco tended to be grown on family farms around the Chesapeake Bay area, and because of this the slave population was not as concentrated as it was on the plantations further to the south.

The growth of a plantation economy and the concentration of a large number of African Americans in the southern states led first Virginia (1636) and then the other states to form all white militias. The terror of slave uprisings led the slaveholders to institute ever harsher slave codes. Ultimately, a slave could not own anything, carry a weapon, or even leave his plantation without a written pass. Murder, rape, arson, and even lesser offenses were punishable by death; small offenses were commonly punished by whipping, maiming, and branding. In the area where 90 percent of colonial African Americans lived, a slave had no rights to defend himself against a white, and as far north as Virginia it was impossible for a white to be convicted for the murder of a slave.

The Maiden Lane slave revolt in New York City in 1712 and the public paranoia over the alleged slave conspiracy of 1741 led to the development of slave codes which were in some cases as severe as those in the South, but in general the North was a relatively less oppressive environment. In Pennsylvania the Quakers allowed African Americans a relative degree of freedom, and in New England the slave codes tended to reflect Old Testament law, maintaining the legal status of slaves as persons with certain limited rights.

Military Service before and during the Revolutionary War

Records of King William's War (1689-1697) relate that the first to fall in Massachusetts was "an Naygro of Colo. Tyng," slain at Falmouth. During Queen Anne's

A group of African slaves disembark in America.

War (1702-1713), African Americans were drafted and sent to fight the French and the Indians when white colonists failed to provide the number of requisitioned men. Many armed African Americans fought at Fort William Henry in New York. Slaves sought freedom as their payment for fighting, and those who were already free sought the wider benefits of land and cash payments. The colony of Virginia ended its policy of excluding African Americans from the militia by 1723, and in 1747 the South Carolina Company made slaves eligible for enlistment in the territorial militia according to a quota system in which a 3:1 ratio was maintained between whites and blacks, thus abating the white's fears of insurrection. African Americans also fought for the British in the French and Indian War.

African American Patriots

In the years leading up to the Revolutionary War it became apparent that, despite the growth of slavery, at least some African Americans were willing to fight alongside white Americans. On March 5, 1770, an African American named Crispus Attucks was one of the first men killed in the Revolutionary War, when British troops fired on a crowd of protesters in the Boston Massacre. Many African-American Minutemen fought at the defense of Concord Bridge: among them were Lemuel Haynes, a gifted speaker and later a prominent Congregationalist minister; and Peter Salem, who had received his freedom to enlist. Other figures of the Revolutionary War include Pomp Blackman, Caesar Ferrit and his son John, Prince Estabrook (who was wounded at Lexington), Samuel Craft, and Primas Black and Epheram Blackman (who were members of Ethan Allen's Green Mountain Boys).

The Move to Disarm African Americans

A major issue during the Revolutionary War was whether African-American slaves, and even freemen, should be permitted to bear arms. On May 29, 1775, the Massachusetts Committee of Safety, in a move which reflected their desire to strengthen ties with southern states, proclaimed that the enlistment of slaves "was inconsistent with the principles that are to be supported, and reflect[ed] dishonor on the colony." On July 9, 1775, Horatio Gates, the adjutant general of the Continental Army, issued from General Washington's headquarters the order that recruiting officers should not accept "any stroller, Negro, or vagabond."

The enormous slave populations of certain southern states meant that many whites lived in perpetual fear of slave uprisings. In South Carolina slaves outnumbered whites, and in Georgia the population was above 40 percent slaves. To minimize the risk of slaves arming themselves, Edward Rutledge of South Carolina introduced a measure in Congress to discharge all African Americans (whether free or enslaved) from the Continental Army. Although the proposal was rejected, General George Washington's own council of war decided to terminate all African-American enlistment two weeks later, and on October 13, 1775, Congress passed the law. Colonial generals like John Thomas argued that African Americans soldiered as well as whites and had already "proved themselves brave" in action, but their protests went unheeded. At the close of 1775 it was extremely difficult for African Americans to join the revolutionary forces at any level.

As the leaders of the Revolution realized that there were inadequate numbers of white troops, they brought an end to their racially exclusionary policy. Local militias which were unable to fill their muster rolls won the quiet agreement of recruiting boards and the reluctant acceptance of slave owners as slaves were substituted for those white men who bought their way out of service. As the war progressed slaveowners were compensated for the enlistment of slaves who were then made free. During the course of the Revolution many colonies granted freedom to slaves in return for military service. Rhode Island passed the first slave enlistment act on

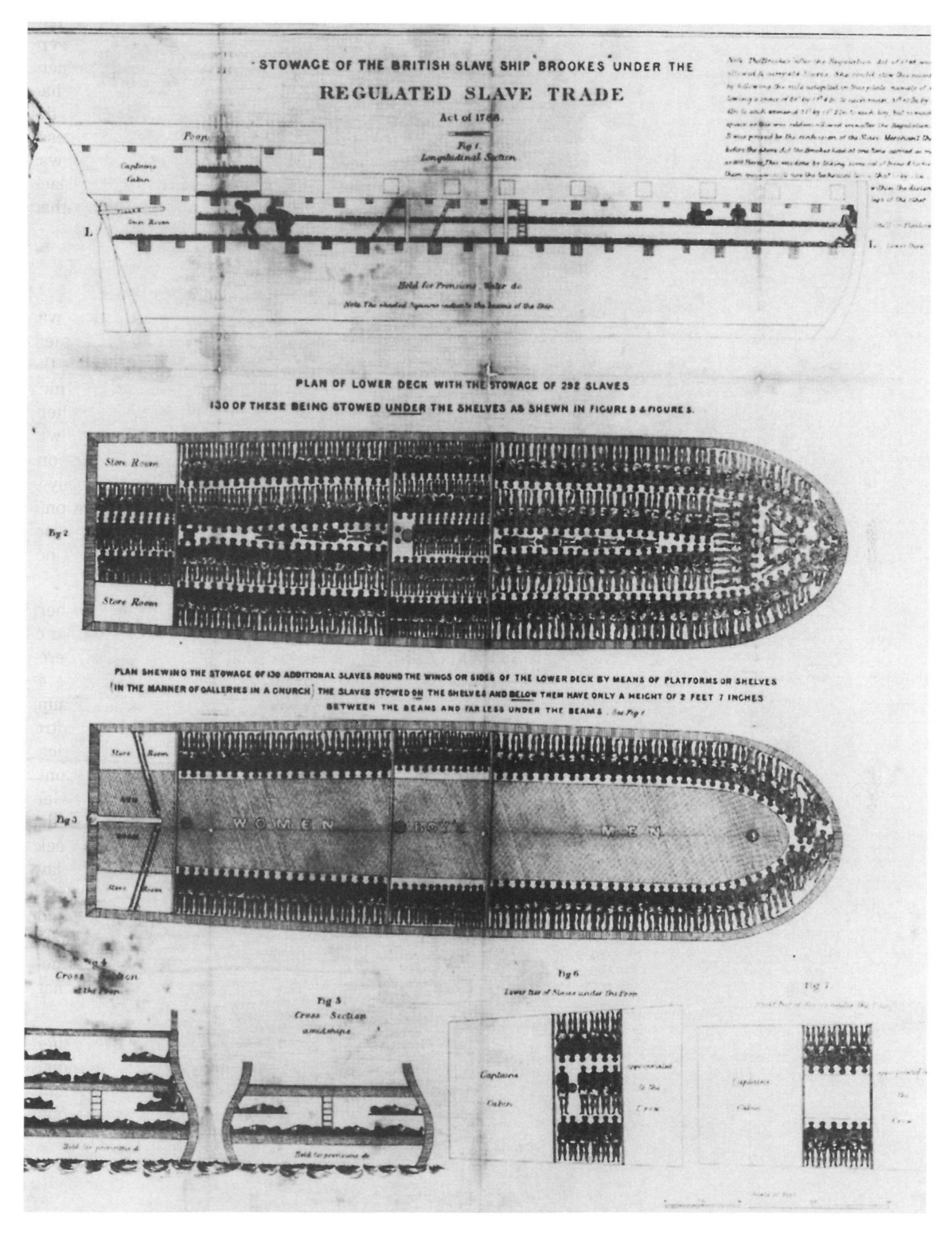

Diagram illustrating the layout of a slave ship.

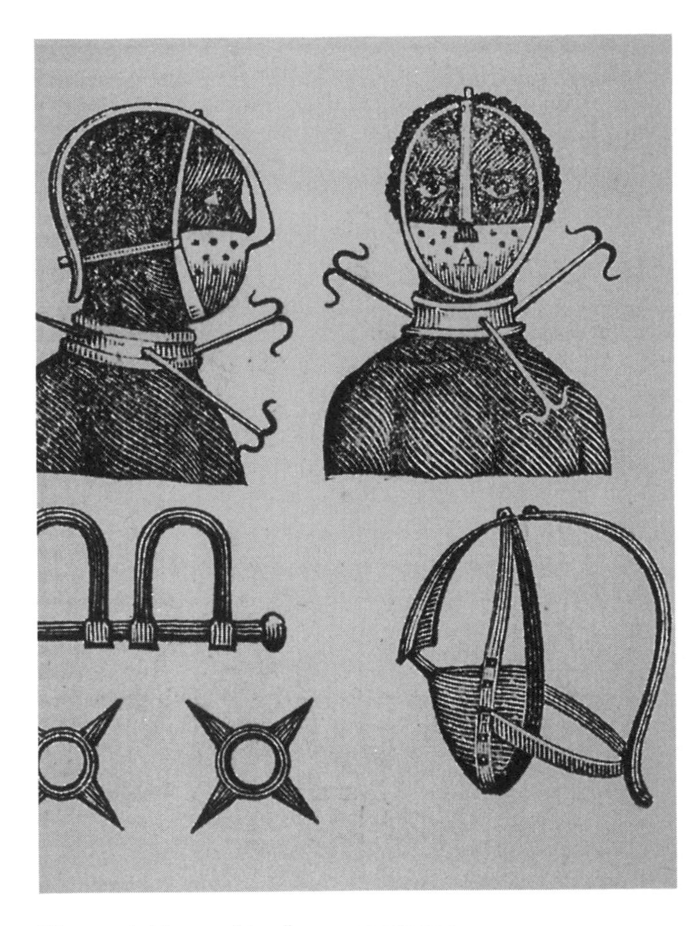

Slave catching and trading apparatuses.

TO BE SOLD, on WEDNESDAY 3d AUGUST next,
By COWPER & TELFAIRS,
A CARGO
Of 170 prime young likely healthy
GUINEA SLAVES,
Just imported, in the Bark Friends, William Ross Master, directly from Angola. Savannah, July 25, 1774.

To be Sold at Private Sale, any Time before the 18th of next Month,

THE PLANTATION, containing one hundred acres, on which the subscriber lives, very pleasantly situated on Savannah River in sight of town. The terms of sale may be known by applying to
July 21, 1774 RICHARD WYLLY.

WANTED,

AN OVERSEER thoroughly qualified to undertake the settlement of a River Swamp Plantation on the Alatamaha River. Any such person, who can bring proper recommendations, may hear of great encouragement by applying to NATHANIEL HALL.

THE subscriber being under an absolute necessity of closing his concerns without delay, gives this last publick notice, that all persons indebted to him by bond, note or otherwise, who do not discharge the same by the first day of October next, will find their respective obligations, &c in the hands of an Attorney to be sued for without distinction. It is hoped those concerned will avail themselves of this notice.
PHILIP BOX

RUN AWAY the 20th of May last from John Forbes, Esq.'s plantation in St. John's parish, TWO NEGROES, named BILLY and QUAMINA, of the Guiney Country, and speak good English. Billy is lusty and well made, about 5 feet 10 or 11 inches high, of a black complection, has lost some of his upper teeth, and had on when he went away a white negroe cloth jacket and trowsers of the same. Quamina is stout and well made, about 5 feet 10 or 11 inches high, very black, has his country marks on his face, had on when he went away a jacket, trowsers and robbin, of white negroe cloth. Whoever takes up said Negroes, and deliver them to me at the above plantation, or to the Warden of the Work-House in Savannah, shall receive a reward of 20s. besides what the law allows.
DAVIS AUSTIN.

Poster advertising a slave sale.

February 2, 1778, raising a regiment that participated gallantly in many important battles. In 1780 Maryland became the only southern state to enroll slave troops, while South Carolina and Georgia refused altogether to even arm their slaves. While slave conscripts were at first assigned to combat support, in the heat of battle they were often armed. African Americans were often enlisted for longer terms than whites, and by the latter years of the war many of the most seasoned veterans were African American troops.

◆ AFRICAN AMERICAN STATUS IN THE NEW REPUBLIC

Slaves and Freemen after the Revolution

At the end of the war about five thousand African Americans had been emancipated through military service. In the following years the northern states abolished slavery: Vermont in 1777, Massachusetts in 1783, Connecticut and Rhode Island in 1784, New York in 1785, New Jersey in 1786, and Pennsylvania in 1789. In the mid-Atlantic state of Virginia, Thomas Jefferson convinced the state legislature to allow slaveowners to manumit their slaves in 1783. In 1790 there were 757,208 African Americans comprising 19 percent of the population of the United States: 697,681 were slave, and 59,527 were free. During this time the free population faced many of the same restrictions as the slave population: they could not walk on the streets after dark, travel between towns without a pass, or own weapons. There was also the danger of being captured and enslaved, whether one was free or not.

The United States Constitution

The U.S. Constitution, drafted in 1787 and ratified in 1788, provided fundamental political principles for the nation. Key among these principles were the belief that all people share a fundamental equality, that they possess certain unalienable rights, and that government derives its power from the people. But African Americans were not afforded the rights and privileges of the Constitution. At the time, it was generally believed by

Crispus Attucks

whites that people of African descent were racially inferior and incapable of being assimilated into society. It was also widely believed that they were not citizens of the new republic. Article I, Section 2 of the Constitution specifies that all persons who are not free shall be counted as three-fifths a person for the sake of tax purposes, and Article I, Section 9 authorizes the continued importation of slaves until 1808.

Slavery in the New Nation

In 1793 Eli Whitney invented the cotton gin, which separated cotton from cotton fiber, led to a subsequent increase in the consumption of cotton, and heightened the demand for slaves in the cotton-producing states. In 1800 there were more than 893,600 African slaves in the United States; by 1810 there were 1,191,300. Although the slave trade was technically discontinued in 1808, it is estimated that from that date until 1860 more than 250,000 slaves were illegally imported; furthermore, nothing prohibited slaves from being bartered, and the breeding of slaves for sale became a specialized business. Some of the largest slave trading firms in the nation were located in Maryland, Virginia, and the District of Columbia. Such was the expansion of slavery that, between 1800 and 1859, the population of Mississippi grew from 3489 slaves and 5179 whites to 309,878 slaves and 295,718 whites.

By the mid-eighteenth century, three-fourths of the cotton produced in the world came from the United States, and profits from cotton were so great that vast plantations were hacked from the wilderness, allowing armies of slaves to work the fields. By mid-century the states of Georgia, Alabama, Mississippi, and Louisiana annually produced 1,726,349 bales of cotton, forty-eight million pounds of rice, and 226,098,000 pounds of sugar. With the outbreak of the Civil War there were nearly four million slaves in the United States, and nearly three-fourths of them worked in cotton agriculture.

Slave Life

Slavery was by its very nature a brutal and exploitative business, and the average slave lived a terribly grim life. The more fortunate slaves tended to work on family sized farms or had positions as house servants. Whatever one's surroundings, much of one's fortune depended on the kindness of the master. On the larger plantations slaves were divided between house and field hands. The former group was charged with such assorted tasks as caring for the grounds and garden of the house, maintenance of the rigs and appliances, house cleaning, and caring for the master's children. House servants were frequently allowed to practice trades such as smithery, masonry, and tailoring; some even became skilled musicians and doctors. Body slaves served their masters as valets and personal messengers, and from this intimacy real friendships sometimes developed.

But house servants were in a sense aristocrats among slaves. Their daily lives had little in common with those of the faceless masses of field hands who confronted the brutal monotony of sowing and reaping without respite or prospect of change. On larger plantations with 25 or more slaves, the only contact between field hands and whites occurred through the overseer, who often employed cruel and vicious brutality to maintain control. Many planters felt that the largest profits were made by working a slave to death in eight or ten years and then buying a new one. Even tenderhearted masters often had little contact with their field workers, and so long as the overseer returned a profit no questions were asked. In many places slaves were given no free time at all, but were forced to work fourteen or fifteen hours a day. Louisiana was the only state with a law regarding

Engraving depicting slaves cultivating cotton.

the amount of work that could be demanded of a slave; the law permitted a slave to be worked 21 hours every day.

Most slaves could only expect to live with the bare necessities of shelter, clothing, and food. Shelter often consisted of a cramped, windowless, mud-floored shack in which a large family was expected to live; clothing was basic in design and made of course materials; and food was often limited to a bucket of rice or corn per week with no meat. The only break in the routine occurred on holidays such as Christmas, though in some cases slaves were able to hunt, fish, or garden in the hours after work.

Slave Naming Practices

Slaves had purposeful naming practices that were distinctively different from those of their masters. Most slaves were able to choose the names of their children, usually naming sons after fathers and daughters after female relatives other than the mother, in order to help identify kin relationships and keep track of which cousins one should not marry. (Slaves following marriage rules that prohibited marrying one's cousin, even though many planters and free blacks did.)

Generally, many slaves used English or European names for themselves and their children to satisfy the preferences of masters. Yet many Africans kept alive their sense of cultural independence and roots by choosing English equivalents of African names or English names that sounded similar to African names. Still, some African slaves used African names all their lives.

In addition to given or first names, slaves could also have surnames distinctive from those of their owners, although owners were usually unaware of the surnames. Normally, slaves chose a surname that represented or identified the first slave owner of the earliest born-in-Africa ancestor who came to North America as a slave. The surname would then be handed down over the generations to help track relations and lineage. Though many slaves had their own surnames, or "titles" many did not. After the end of slavery, those who already possessed surnames revealed them, while others chose one for the first time. During and immediately after the Civil War, government agencies often insisted that slaves have surnames to enroll in their programs or receive government benefits. Those whose family had been owned by members of the same family for several generations might have the same last name as the last owner although the name was originally chosen to identify a more distant owner within the same family. Those who were aware of a slave family surname extending over two or more generations were likely to keep it in order to feel connected with ancestors even if the name was one associated with a disliked master. Some persons changed names several times to avoid the possibility of re-enslavement. Even after a name was chosen, it was often recorded differently at various times due to the low level of literacy and variations in spelling.

The Denmark Vesey Conspiracy

The mistreatment of slaves in the years after the Revolution led to an atmosphere of suspicion and terror. Masters lived in constant fear of uprisings, and much time was given over to surveillance. Although organized rebellions were rare, there were many instances of angry slaves burning dwellings and murdering their masters. Slave codes became increasingly strict, but no amount of regulation could dissipate the anger of the slaves, nor the guilt and unease which many slave owners experienced.

In 1800 an African American named Denmark Vesey purchased his freedom and from about 1817 planned a slave revolt in Charleston, South Carolina. The revolt was scheduled to begin on July 14, 1822. With the help of five other African Americans as many as nine thousand slaves were recruited before their plans were uncovered. As word of the revolt began to leak out, Vesey was forced to move the date forward to June 16; again word was leaked. The state militia was mustered, and an intense investigation of the plot was begun. 135 slaves were arrested during the course of the investigation; 97 were bound over for trial; 45 were transported out of the country; and Vesey and 34 others were hanged. As news of the conspiracy spread, southern states further tightened their slave codes.

Slaves outside their quarters.

◆ EXPANSION OF SLAVERY

Slavery in the Northwest Territory

In the early seventeenth century the French began to settle in what comprises present-day Illinois, Indiana, Michigan, Ohio, and Wisconsin, and part of Minnesota. The British began to settle in the area during the mid-eighteenth century; and, in July of 1787, Congress passed the Northwest Ordinance, which established a government for the Northwest Territory and provided terms under which states could be formed for entrance into the Union. The ordinance also contained controversial provisions: one prohibited slavery and involuntary servitude in the territory, and the other provided for the return of fugitive slaves to the states from which they had escaped. The European farmers who had brought slaves into the territory were angered by the clause prohibiting slavery and Congress was petitioned for its repeal. The prohibition against slavery was practically circumvented when the Illinois and Indiana territories

Fieldworkers returning from the fields.

established a system of indentured servitude under which any person owning slaves could bring them into the region and place them under lifetime indenture. The restrictions placed on these servants were much like the slave codes of the southern colonies—indentured servants could not travel alone without a pass or attend public gatherings independently.

The Missouri Compromise

In April of 1803 the United States paid $15 million for the Louisiana Territory, an area comprising the entire Mississippi drainage basin, which had been settled by the French in the late seventeenth century. Many southerners hoped to extend slavery into the vast new territory, and it was widely expected that Missouri would be admitted to the Union as a slave state. A series of heated debates erupted over the extension of slavery in the region, and in 1819 the House of Representatives introduced legislation authorizing statehood for Missouri while prohibiting the further introduction of slavery into the new state. This drew angry protest from proslavery supporters. The controversy was further escalated by two events: Alabama was admitted to the Union as a slave state in 1819, making the total number of slave and free states equal, and Maine applied for statehood in 1820. In 1820-1821 the Missouri Compromise was reached, admitting Missouri to the Union as a slave state with a slave population of almost 10,000, and Maine as a free state, with the understanding that the future expansion of slavery would be prohibited above the latitude of 36 degrees 33'N.

Slaves working on a cotton plantation.

Texas and the Mexican-American War

The territory comprising Texas was part of the Louisiana Territory when the United States purchased it in 1803, but, by 1819, it had become part of Mexico. Mexico provided land grants to American settlers (many of whom brought their slaves with them), and soon Americans outnumbered the Mexicans of the region. In 1836, Texas declared its independence from Mexico and requested annexation to the United States. The possibility of another slave state entering the Union stirred fresh debate. On March 1, 1845, President John Tyler signed the joint resolution of Congress to admit Texas as a slave state; the voters of Texas supported the action, and Texas became a slave state on December 29, 1845. In 1846, Mexican and American troops clashed in Texas, and the United States declared war on the Republic of Mexico. The war ended in 1848 with the Treaty of Guadalupe Hidalgo, whereby Mexico relinquished its claims to Texas and the United States acquired all of the land extending to the Pacific Ocean.

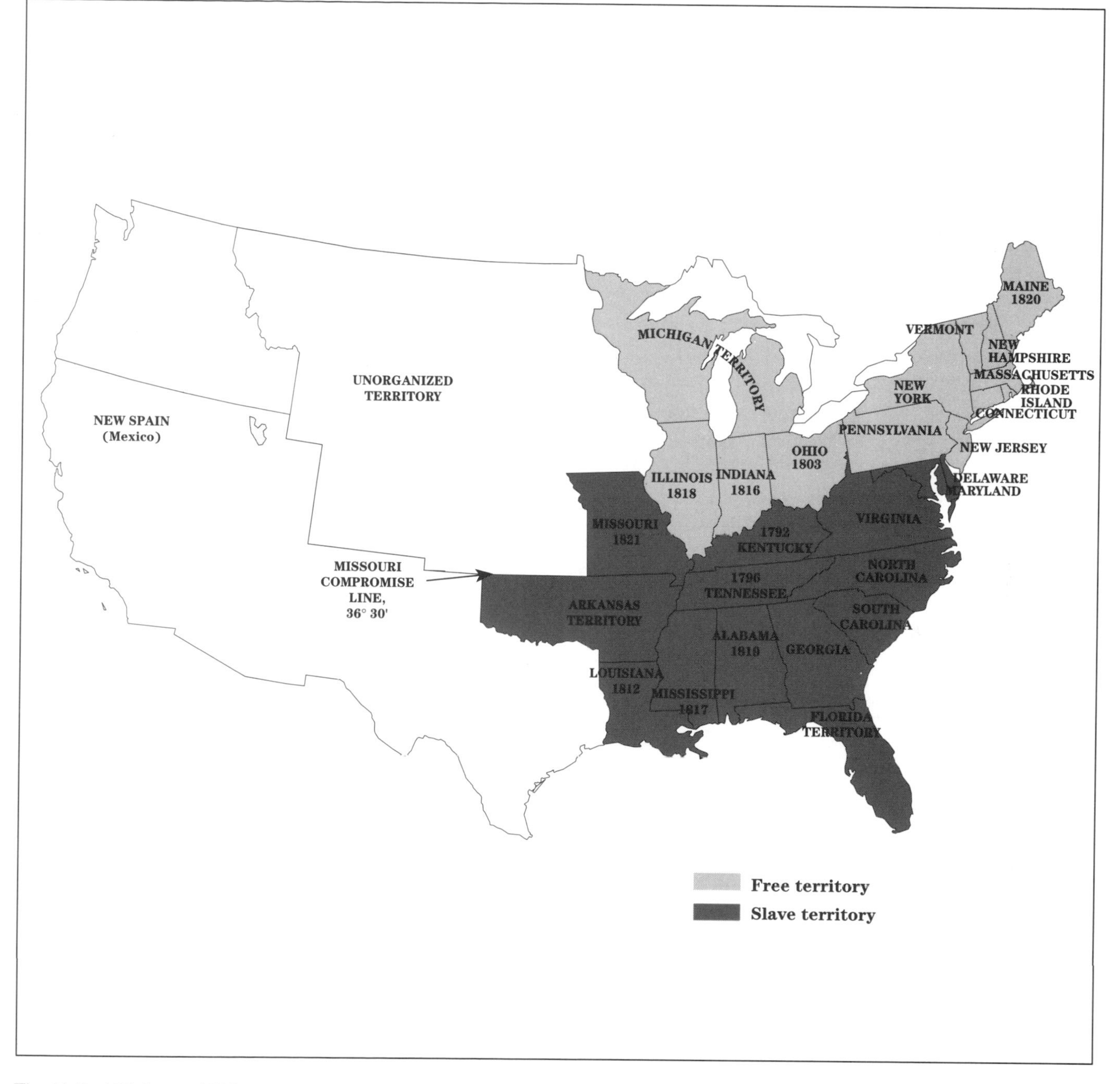

The United States c. 1821.

The Wilmot Proviso

In 1846 David Wilmot, a Democrat from Pennsylvania, introduced an amendment to a bill appropriating $2 million for President James Polk to use in negotiating a territorial settlement with Mexico; the amendment stipulated that none of the newly acquired land would be open to slavery. Although the amendment received strong support from northern Democrats and was passed by the House of Representatives, the Senate adjourned without voting on it. During the next session of Congress a new bill providing $3 million for territorial settlement was introduced. Wilmot again proposed an amendment prohibiting the expansion of slavery into the newly acquired territory. The bill was passed by the House of Representatives, but the Senate drew up a new bill excluding the Wilmot Proviso.

Fugitive Slave Laws

Tensions between northern and southern politicians continued to mount over the issue of fugitive slaves.

Article IV, Section 2 of the Constitution authorized the return of fugitive slaves and provided procedures for recovery, and in 1793 the Fugitive Slave Act was passed. In northern states that strongly opposed slavery, "personal liberty" laws were passed in order to undermine federal law; liberty laws placed the burden of proof on masters in cases concerning alleged fugitive slaves. Such a law was enacted in Pennsylvania in 1826, requiring state certification before alleged fugitives could be returned. When Edward Prigg, a professional slave catcher, attempted to capture a fugitive slave residing in the state, he was arrested on kidnapping charges for failing to acquire necessary certification. The Supreme Court ruled in *Prigg v. Pennsylvania* (1842) that the state's law could not interfere with federal action regarding fugitives and the right of slaveholders to recover property; it also found that states would not be obligated to enforce federal fugitive slave statutes. This led abolitionists to seize upon the idea of not enforcing federal statutes. Following the court's decision several northern states enacted even more radical personal liberty laws prohibiting the enforcement of the Fugitive Slave Act.

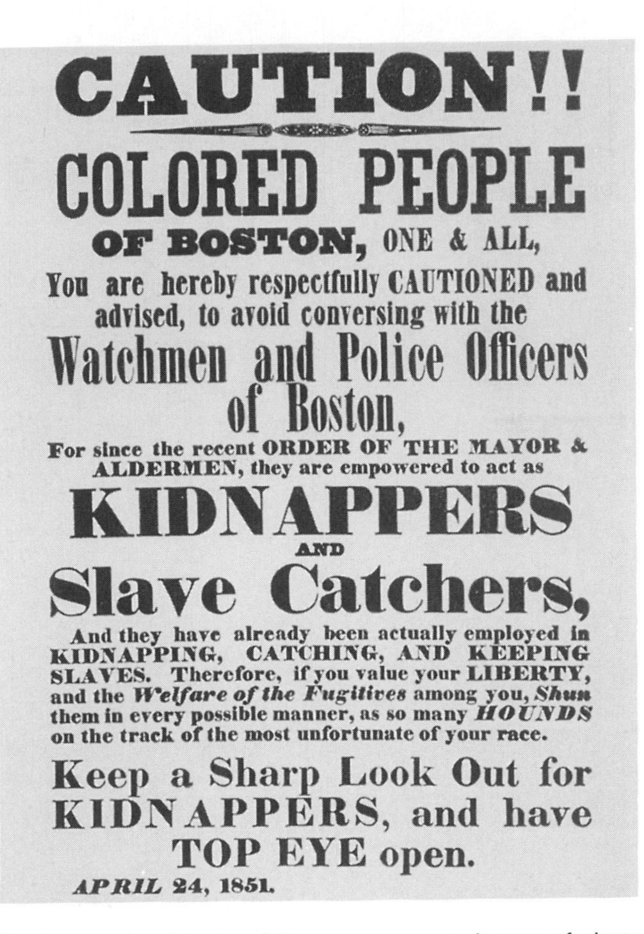

Poster warning blacks of the ever present danger of slave catchers.

◆ ANTI-SLAVERY MOVEMENTS

Quakers and Mennonites

The early opposition to slavery was generally based on religious beliefs; Christian ethics were seen as incompatible with slavery. Quakers (or the Society of Friends) and Mennonites were two of first groups to oppose the practice in the United States. Quakers and Mennonites settled mainly in Pennsylvania, though also in the South, and advocated simple living, modest dress, and nonviolence. In 1652 the Quakers passed a resolution against lifetime indenture, and in 1688 the Mennonites did the same. With the continued rise of slavery in the South, many Quakers protested and moved north into Indiana and Ohio.

The Free African Society

In 1787 the Free African Society was organized in Philadelphia by two African Americans, the Reverend Richard Allen and Absalom Jones; Adams later founded the Bethel African Methodist Church, and Jones became the rector of a Protestant Episcopal Church. The society was an important model for political consciousness and economic organization for African Americans throughout the country. It provided economic and medical aid, advocated abolition, and maintained channels of communication with African Americans in the South. Like the many other African American organizations that followed, the society was rooted in religious principles. Throughout the nineteenth century a number of mutual aid societies also sprung up in African American communities of the eastern seaboard, providing loans, insurance, and various other economic and social services to their members and the larger community.

American Colonization Society

In 1816 the American Colonization Society was organized in Washington, DC, with the objective of encouraging the repatriation of African Americans to Africa. While the idea of returning free African Americans was motivated in part by humanitarian intent, the society was rather moderate in its opposition to slavery. Support for the society came in part from those who feared the possibility of a large free African American population in the United States.

Congress issued a charter to the society for the transportation of freed slaves to the west coast of Africa, provided funds, and assisted in negotiations with African chiefs who ceded the land that comprised what

A photograph of the Pennsylvania Abolition Society.

became Liberia. While northerners contributed support and donations to the society, southern patrols threatened freedmen into emigrating. In 1822 the first settlers landed at the site on the western coast of Africa which was later named Monrovia after President James Monroe. In 1838 the Commonwealth of Liberia was formed and placed under the administration of a governor appointed by the society.

Abolition Societies Formed in Philadelphia and New York

The earliest abolition societies were the Pennsylvania Society for Promoting the Abolition of Slavery, formed in Philadelphia in 1775, and the New York Manumission Society, formed in the city in 1785. Prior to the 1830s a number of anti-slavery societies arose in both the North and the South, and during the 1830s and 1840s numerous abolitionist organizations arose alongside the women's rights organizations as part of the general social reform movement. The American Anti-Slavery Society was formed in Philadelphia in 1833, and after attending one of its meetings, the Quaker abolitionist Lucretia Coffin Mott formed the Philadelphia Female Anti-Slavery Society with the assistance of Elizabeth Cady Stanton. Mott and her husband, James, were active in the underground railroad and various other anti-slavery activities, and James served as a delegate to the World Anti-Slavery Convention.

The press served as the primary tool of the anti-slavery movement. In 1827, the journalists Samuel Cornish and John Russwurm launched *Freedom's Journal*, the first African American owned and edited newspaper; in 1831, William Lloyd Garrison published the first issue of *Liberator;* and other anti-slavery papers followed, including *Anti-Slavery Record;* the *Emancipator; Human Rights;* and the *North Star*, launched by Frederick Douglass.

While many of the anti-slavery organizations were dominated by whites, African American leaders played an important role in the abolition movement. Some of the most notable leaders were Alexander Crummell, Frederick Douglass, Sarah Mapp Douglass, Charlotte Forten, Henry Highland Garnet, Sojourner Truth, and David Walker. Most of these leaders were committed to cooperative relations with whites and opposed separatist doctrines, while some of the more militant abolition-

A page from the *American Anti-Slavery Almanac,* 1840.

ists (like Garnet and Walker) stressed the conditional necessity of violence in the struggle against slavery.

In the South the activities of the abolition movement only hardened the resolve of the slaveholding class to maintain the system of slavery. Depending on the circumstances, southern justification of slavery continued along several lines: it was an economic necessity, a means of converting African pagans to Christianity, and a means of controlling an inferior race.

The Underground Railroad Transports Slaves to Freedom

A vast network of individuals and groups developed throughout the country to assist African Americans in escaping from slavery, reaching their height between 1835 and 1865. Abolitionists provided "stations," food, shelter, and financial assistance, while experienced "conductors," who were often themselves runaway slaves, led thousands of "passengers" to freedom in the North, Canada, and the Caribbean. Most of the movement occurred at night, with passengers hiding in the barns and homes of sympathetic whites and African Americans during the day. Two of the most famous conductors were Josiah Henson and Harriet Tubman.

Nat Turner

In February of 1831, Nat Turner, a slave in Southampton County, Virginia, began to plan a slave revolt, and on August 22, Turner and his co-conspirators killed Turner's master and family. Within 24 hours about 60 whites in the county had been killed. Turner was captured on October 30 and hung on November 11. The incident contributed to the increasing paranoia of southern society.

Free Labor and Free Soil Movements

Radical Democrats and members of the Whig party who opposed slavery united to form a new political party in Buffalo, New York, in 1848. The party adopted a platform supporting free labor and free soil in response to feelings among northerners that slavery restricted the freedom of northern workers to contract for work and should therefore be excluded from the developing regions of the West. Southerners wanted the freedom to expand westward and take their slaves with them. Senator John C. Calhoun of South Carolina and other southern delegates maintained that both Congress and the territorial legislatures lacked the authority to restrict the expansion of slavery into the territories. The control of northern states over the national government led these men to consider secession from the Union.

◆ THE COMPROMISE OF 1850

As the debate over the admission of new western states continued, southerners argued that the South should be given guarantees of equal positioning in the territories. In 1850 Senator Henry Clay proposed a compromise in which California would be admitted as a free state, the new territories of New Mexico and Utah would be organized, slavery would be abolished in the District of Columbia, more forceful fugitive slave legislation would be enacted, and the Texas war debt would be resolved. At the time the compromise was hailed by many as the solution to the debate over slavery.

Dred Scott v. Sandford

The slavery debate presented supporters and opponents of the institution with two very important questions: how should fugitives from slavery be treated in jurisdictions where slavery was illegal, and should a slave brought into a free state by his master be viewed as free? The first question was partially addressed by Article IV, Section 2 of the Constitution and by the Fugitive Slave Acts of 1793 and 1850; however the second question had not as yet been addressed. During

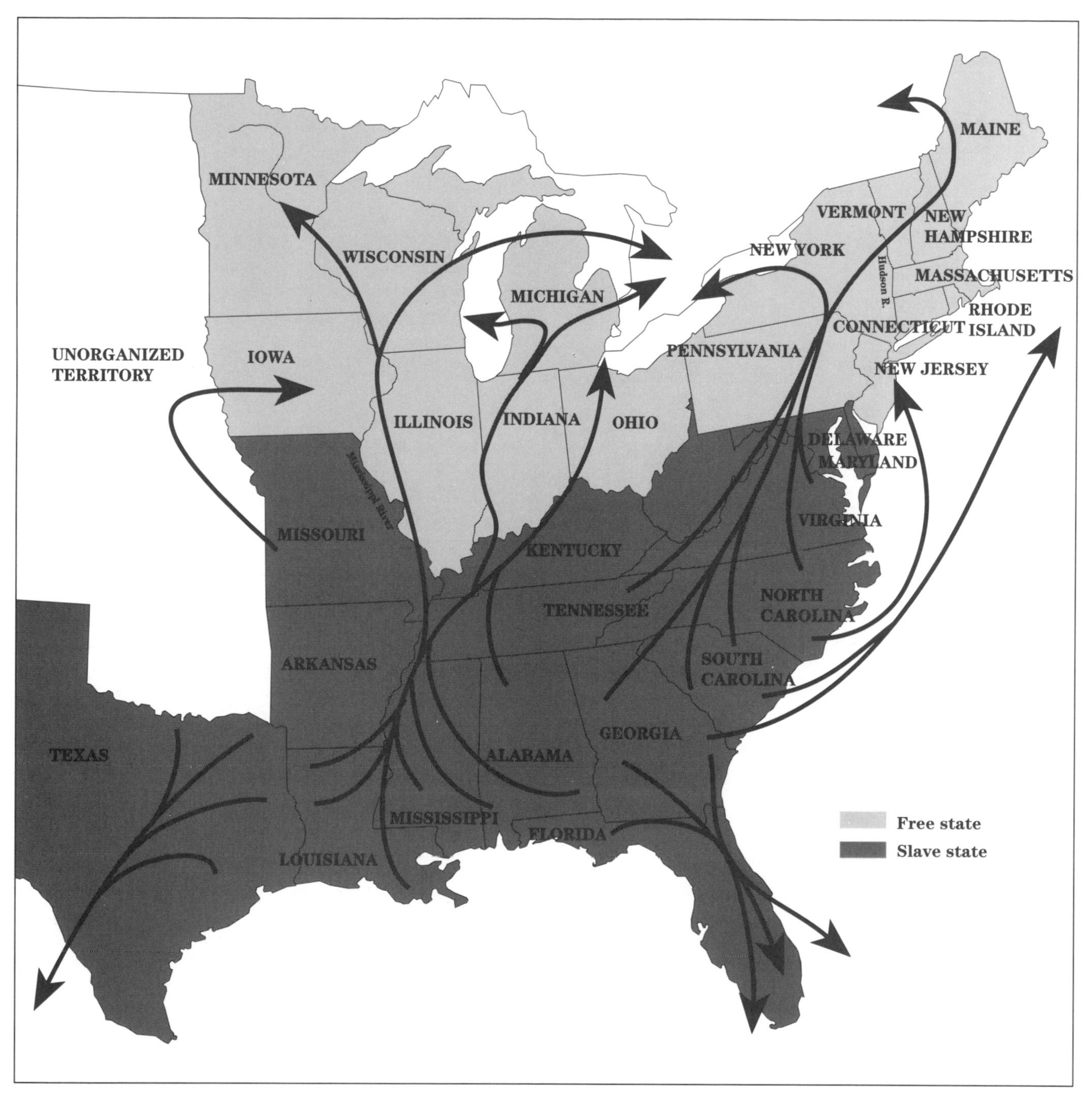

Underground Railroad Routes.

the 1830s and 1840s a slave by the name of Dred Scott accompanied his master, a surgeon in the U.S. Army on numerous trips to military posts around the country, including the free states of Illinois and the territory of Wisconsin. In 1846 Scott sued his master for his freedom, asserting that his sojourns in free jurisdictions made him free. After numerous delays, trials, and retrials, the case reached the Supreme Court in 1856. The court responded with nine separate opinions, and Chief Justice Roger Brook Taney delivered the deciding opinion. The ruling was both complex and controversial: the Missouri Compromise of 1820 was ruled unconstitutional on the grounds that Congress did not have authority to limit the expansion of slavery; slavery was found to be legal in the territories until the citizens voted for or against it; and Africans and their descendants were found to be ineligible for citizenship in the United States as the framers of the Constitution had not viewed Africans as citizens. Since African Americans were not viewed by the court as citizens, they could not file suit. Despite the finality of the court's decision, the issue of slavery remained unresolved.

Slaves believed to have used the Underground Railroad to escape the South.

John Brown and Harpers Ferry

On October 16, 1859, a white, visionary abolitionist named John Brown led a band of 21 men (five of whom were African Americans) in the seizure of the federal arsenal at Harpers Ferry. After holding the site for several hours, Brown and his followers were captured by federal troops under the command of Robert E. Lee. Southerners were outraged by Brown's actions, interpreting them as symptomatic of a willingness among northerners to attempt the forcible overthrow of slavery. In December of 1859, Brown was hanged alongside Dangerfield Newby, a runaway slave; John A. Copeland of Carolina; Sheridan Leary, a harness maker and freedman; and Shields Gree, a sailor from South Carolina.

◆ CIVIL WAR

In 1860 Abraham Lincoln, a northern Republican, was elected president amid continuing polarization over the issue of slavery. Lincoln had voiced opposition to the expansion of slavery in the past, and with his election southerners became even more fearful of an ideological assault on state's rights and the abolition of slavery nationwide. In 1860 a delegation from South Carolina voted unanimously for the repeal of the state's 1788 ratification of the Constitution and the severing of all relations with the Union; Georgia, Florida, Alabama, Mississippi, Louisiana, and Texas soon followed. In February of 1861, the seven states drew up a constitution and elected Jefferson Davis as president of the Confederate States of America. As northern leaders sought a means of preserving the nation, southern troops seized federal installations, post offices, and customs houses, and in April of 1861 Confederate forces took one of the last Union holds in the south, Fort Sumter in Charleston Harbor, South Carolina. Lincoln was forced to retaliate.

African American Soldiers in the Civil War

From the beginning of the war African Americans engaged in the fighting, although Lincoln at first refused to officially employ them in the Union army. By 1862 Lincoln concluded that the use of African American

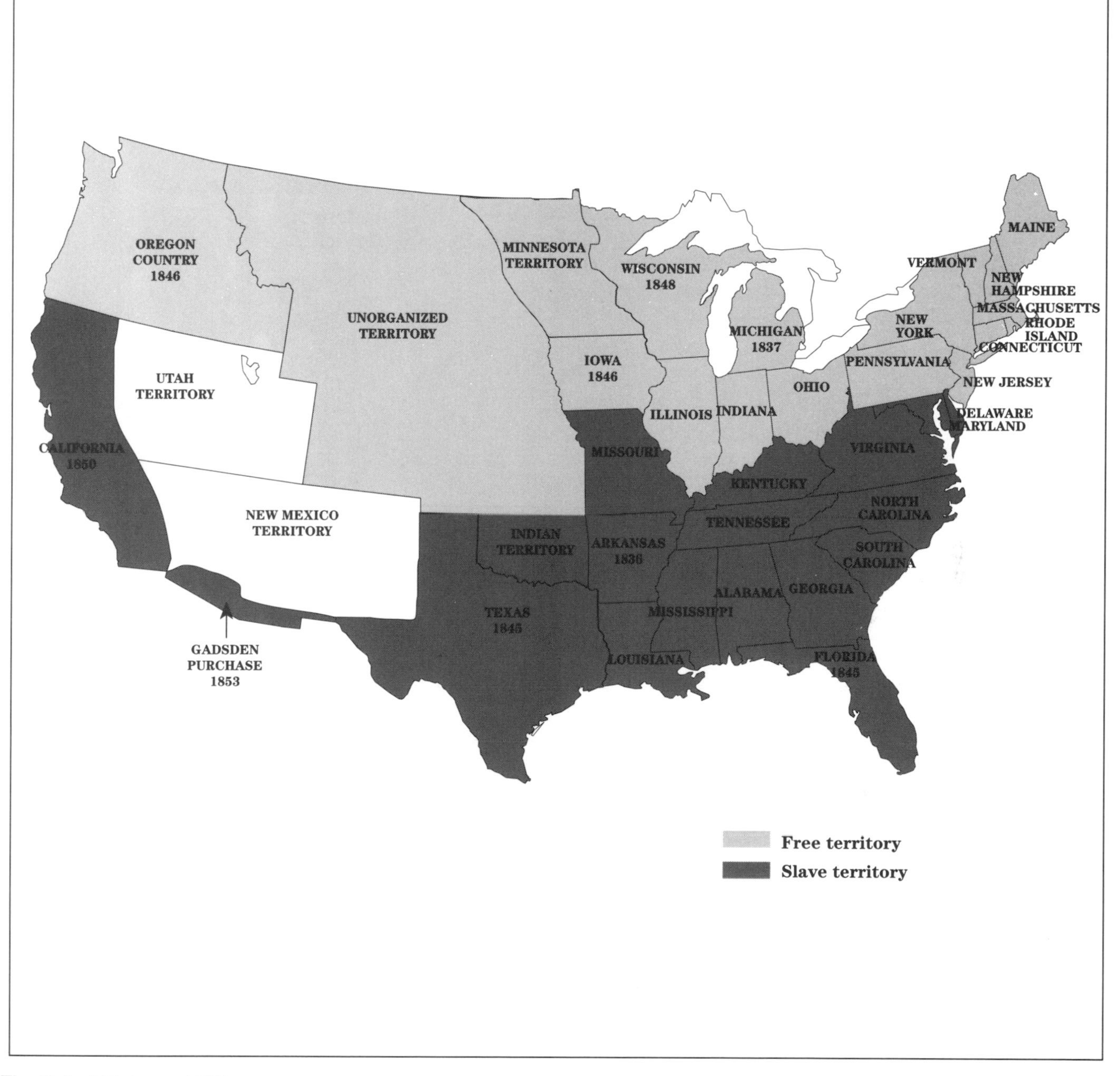

The United States c. 1850.

soldiers was a necessity. An estimated 180,000 black soldiers served in the Union army and another 20,000 served in its navy; however, not all of those African Americans who participated in the war fought on the Union side. There are no accurate records of how many black soldiers fought for the south, but their numbers grew as white southerners became more desperate.

Lincoln faced a dilemma in that if he issued an order of universal emancipation, as the abolitionists encouraged him to do, he risked alienating the border states that remained supportive of the Union: these were Delaware, Maryland, Kentucky, and Missouri. In a letter to Horace Greeley, Lincoln stated:

> "If I could save the Union without freeing any slave, I would do it; if I could save it by freeing all the slaves, I would do it; and if I could save it by freeing some and leaving others alone, I would also do that. What I do about slavery and the colored race, I do because I believe it helps save the Union...."

Abraham Lincoln

During the summer of 1862, Lincoln began to feel that the emancipation of the slaves would be necessary to realizing victory over the South, and on January 1, 1863, he issued the Emancipation Proclamation, freeing slaves in those states that had seceded from the Union. Because the proclamation did not apply to the areas under occupation by Union forces, 800,000 slaves remained unaffected by its provisions. He dared not alienate the slave owning states on the Union side, especially in light of the growing antipathy toward African Americans in many northern cities. In the Draft Riots of July 13-16, 1863, huge mobs of whites in New York City (angry over the provisions of the Conscription Act) attacked blacks and abolitionists, destroying property and viciously beating many to death.

The Civil War lasted from April 1861 to April 1865, and at the end more than 360,000 Union soldiers and 258,000 Confederate solders were dead. By the end of the war twenty-one African Americans had received the Medal of Honor, and indeterminate numbers of others had made sacrifices for the cause. On December 18, 1865, the Thirteenth Amendment of the Constitution was ratified, formally abolishing slavery in the United States.

Freed black migrants leaving the South.

◆ RECONSTRUCTION

Civil Rights and Reconstruction Acts

On March 3, 1865, Congress enacted the first of several acts, which set up and empowered the Bureau of Refugees, Freedmen and Abandoned Lands (or the Freedmen's Bureau). The organization provided former slaves with basic health and educational services, and administered land that had been abandoned during the war. In 1866 Congress passed the Civil Rights Act, in which a number of personal liberties were outlined, including the right to make contracts, sue or be sued, own and sell property, and receive the equal benefit of the law. The Reconstruction Act of March 2, 1867, outlined the terms under which the southern states might re-enter the Union; one of these terms required the drafting of a new state constitution with the guarantee of voting rights for all races. President Andrew Johnson vetoed this bill, but radical Republicans in Congress were able to muster the necessary two-thirds majority needed to override the veto.

◆ AFRICAN AMERICAN STATUS AFTER RECONSTRUCTION

The Fourteenth and Fifteenth Amendments

On July 23, 1868, the Fourteenth Amendment was ratified, providing definitions of national and state citizenship, effectively overriding the Supreme Court's de-

Engraving depicting freed blacks in North Carolina.

cision in Dred Scott v. Sandford, and providing for equal privileges of citizenship and protection of the law. On March 30, 1870, the Fifteenth Amendment was ratified to ensure the right to vote. But the amendment proved unsuccessful in its aims, as many state and local governments created voting regulations that ensured African Americans would not vote; these included grandfather clauses, requiring that one's grandfather had voted; literacy tests; poll taxes; and "white primaries," which were held prior to general elections and permitted only whites to vote. In addition, southern states enacted many laws (known as black codes) that curbed the new rights of the freed slaves: South Carolina made it illegal for African Americans to possess firearms, and other states restricted their right to make and enforce contracts; to marry and intermarry; and even to assemble, "wander," or be "idle."

The Civil Rights Act of 1875

In 1875, Congress attempted to establish a semblance of racial equality by enacting a law that made it illegal to deprive another person of the "full and equal enjoyment of the accommodations, advantages, facilities, and privileges of inns, public conveyance, ... and other places of public amusement" on account of race. In a number of cases (known as the Civil Rights Cases) the Supreme Court ruled that the Fourteenth Amendment did not authorize Congress to legislate against discriminatory state action, while disregarding discrimination by private individuals, including the owners of hotels, theaters, and restaurants. This point led to an end of federal efforts to protect the civil rights of African Americans until the mid-twentieth century.

Plessy v. Ferguson

In *Hall v. DeCuir* (1878) the Supreme Court decided that states could not outlaw segregation on common carriers such as streetcars and railroads, and in 1896 the Court again faced the issue of segregation on public transportation in the case of *Plessy v. Ferguson.* The case concerned Homer Adolph Plessy, an African American who was arrested for refusing to ride in the "colored" railway coach while traveling by train from New Orleans to Covington, Louisiana. The law in Louisiana required that "equal but separate" accommodations for blacks and whites be maintained in public facilities, but Plessy challenged this. Justice Billings Brown delivered the majority opinion that separate but equal accommo-

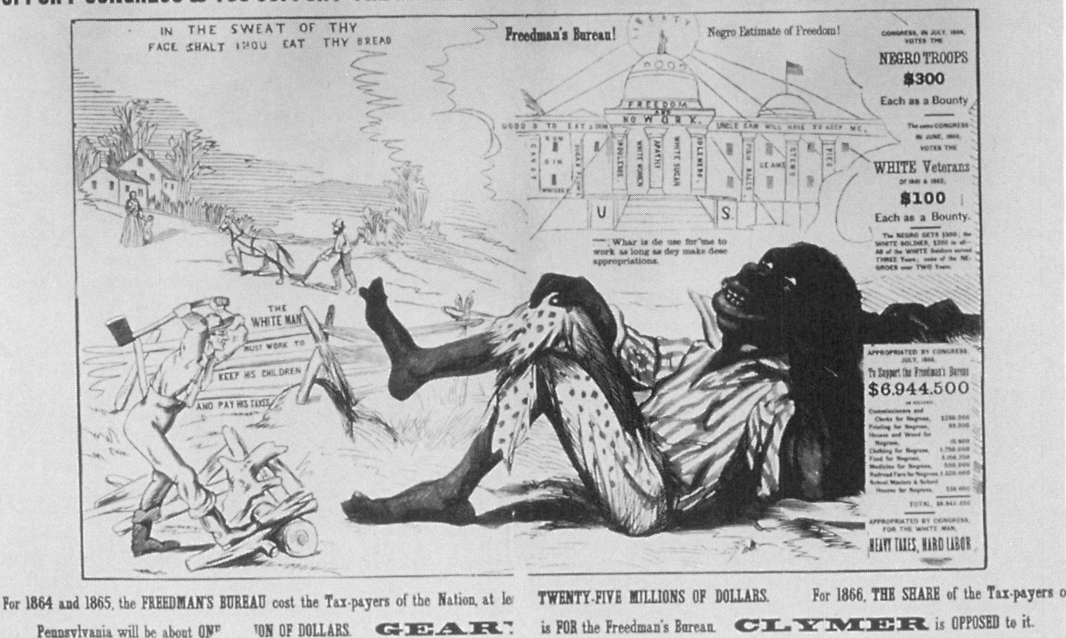

Poster mocking the Freedman's Bureau.

dations constituted a reasonable use of state police power and that the Fourteenth Amendment could not have been an effort to abolish social or racial distinctions or to force a co-mingling of the races. In his dissenting opinion, Justice John Marshall Harlen remarked that, "The judgement this day rendered will, in time, prove to be quite as pernicious as the decision made by this tribunal in the *Dred Scott v. Sandford* case. The thin disguise of equal accommodation for passengers in railroad coaches will not mislead anyone nor atone for the wrong this day done."

The ruling paved the way for the doctrine of separate but equal in all walks of life, and not until the case of *Brown v. Board of Education of Topeka* (1954) would the constitutionality of segregation be seriously challenged.

◆ EARLY AFRICAN AMERICAN GATEKEEPERS

Crispus Attucks 1723?-1770
Revolutionary Patriot

A runaway slave who lived in Boston, he was the first of five men killed on March 5, 1770, when British troops fired on a crowd of colonial protesters in the Boston Massacre. The most widely accepted account of the incident is that of John Adams, who said at the subsequent trial of the British soldiers that Attucks undertook "to be the hero of the night; and to lead this army with banners, to form them in the first place in Dock Square, and march them up to King Street with their clubs." When the crowd reached the soldiers it was Attucks who "had hardiness enough to fall in upon them, and with one hand took hold of a bayonet, and with the other knocked the man down." At that point the panicked soldiers fired, and in the echoes of their volley, five men lay dying; the seeds of the Revolution were sown. Attucks is remembered as "the first to defy, the first to die."

Joseph Cinque 1811-1912
Insurrectionist

Born in 1811 and purchased by Spaniards in Havana, Cuba, in 1838, Cinque was placed aboard the *Amistad* bound for Puerto Principe. When the crew became exhausted from battling a storm, Cinque led the slaves in seizing the ship and killing all but two of the crew, who were kept alive to navigate a course back to Africa. The captive pilots headed north, against the slaves'

A typical rural residence.

knowledge, and when the ship was sighted off the coast of Long Island the slaves were taken to Connecticut and placed in prison. Abolitionists took up the cause of the men and enabled Cinque to raise funds for judicial appeals by speaking on their lecture circuit; his words were translated from Mendi, and he became known as an excellent speaker. In 1841, John Quincy Adams won the slaves' case, and they were released.

Frederick Douglass 1817-1895

Lecturer, Abolitionist, Editor, Diplomat, Federal Government Official, Federal Legislator, Municipal Government Official, Marshall

Born in Talbot County, Maryland, on February 14, 1817, Frederick Douglass was sent to Baltimore as a house servant at the age of eight, where his mistress taught him to read and write. Upon the death of his master, he was sent to the country to work as a field hand. During his time in the South, he was severely flogged for his resistance to slavery. In his early teens he began to teach in a Sunday school which was later forcibly shut down by hostile whites. After an unsuccessful attempt to escape from slavery, he succeeded in making his way to New York disguised as a sailor in 1838. He found work as a day laborer in New Bedford, Massachusetts, and after an extemporaneous speech before the Massachusetts Anti-Slavery Society, he became one of its agents.

Douglass quickly became a nationally recognized figure among abolitionists. In 1845 he bravely published his *Narrative of the Life of Frederick Douglass*, which related his experiences as a slave, revealed his fugitive status, and further exposed him to the danger of reenslavement. In the same year, he went to England and Ireland, where he remained until 1847, speaking on slavery and women's rights, and ultimately raising sufficient funds to purchase his freedom. Upon returning to the United States, he founded the *North Star*. In the tense years before the Civil War he was forced to flee to Canada when the governor of Virginia swore out a warrant for his arrest.

Douglass returned to the United States before the beginning of the Civil War and, after meeting with President Abraham Lincoln, he assisted in the formation of the 54th and 55th Negro regiments of Massachusetts. During Reconstruction, he became deeply involved in

Joseph Cinque

the civil rights movement, and, in 1871, he was appointed to the territorial legislature of the District of Columbia. He served as one of the presidential electors-at-large for New York in 1872 and, shortly thereafter, became the secretary of the Santo Domingo Commission. After serving for a short time as the police commissioner of the District of Columbia, he was appointed marshall in 1871, and held the post until he was appointed the recorder of deeds in 1881. In 1890, his support of the presidential campaign of Benjamin Harrison won him his most important federal post: he became minister resident and consul general to the Republic of Haiti and, later, the charge d'affaires of Santo Domingo. In 1891, he resigned the position in protest of the unscrupulous business practices of American businessmen. Douglass died at home in Washington, DC, on February 20, 1895.

Lemuel Haynes 1753-1833
Religious Leader

The son of a black father and white mother, and born in 1753, he was deserted and brought up by Deacon David Rose of Granville, Massachusetts. He was a precocious child and began writing mature sermons while still a boy. His preparation for the ministry was interrupted by the American Revolution. On April 19, 1775, he fought in the first battle of the war at Lexington, Massachusetts; he then joined the regular forces and served with Ethan Allen's Green Mountain Boys at the capture of Fort Ticonderoga.

Frederick Douglass

Josiah Henson 1789-1883
Educational Administrator, Abolitionist, Religious Leader

Born a slave in a log cabin in Charles County (near Rockville), Maryland, on June 15, 1789, Josiah Henson grew up with the experience of his family being cruelly treated by his master. By the time he was 18, Henson was supervising the master's farm. In 1825 he and his wife and children were moved to Kentucky, where conditions were greatly improved, and in 1828 he became a preacher in a Methodist Episcopal Church. Under the threat of being sold, he and his family escaped to Ohio in 1830, and in the following year entered Canada by way of Buffalo, New York. In Canada he learned to read and write from one of his sons, and he soon began preaching in Dresden, Ontario.

While in Canada he became active in the underground railroad, helping nearly two hundred slaves to escape to freedom. In 1842 he and several others attempted to start the British-American Manual Labor Institute, but the industrial school proved unsuccessful. Henson related his story to Harriet Beecher Stowe (the author of Uncle Tom's Cabin), and it has been disputed whether or not her story is based in part on aspects of

Lemuel Haynes

his life. He traveled to England three times, where he met distinguished people, was honored for his abolitionist activities and personal escape from slavery, and was offered a number of positions which he turned down in order to return to Canada. He published his autobiography in 1849 and rewrote and reissued it in 1858 and 1879. Henson died in Ontario.

James Armistead Lafayette 17??-?

Spy

Born a slave, he risked his life behind enemy lines collecting information for the Continental Army. He furnished valuable information to the Marquis de Lafayette and enabled the French commander to check the troop advances of British General Cornwallis; this set the stage for General George Washington's victory at Yorktown in 1781 and for the end of the Revolutionary War. In recognition of his services, he was granted his freedom by the Virginia legislature in 1786, although it was not until 1819 that Virginia awarded him a pension of $40 a year and a grant of $100. He adopted the surname "Lafayette" in honor of his former commander, who visited him during a trip to the United States in 1824.

Toussaint L'Ouverture 1743-1803

Insurrectionist

Born Francois Dominique Toussaint L'Ouverture, a slave on the island of Hispaniola (now Haiti and the Dominican Republic) in 1743, he learned to read and write under a benevolent master. When he was 50 a violent revolt erupted on the island. White French planters, African slaves, and free mulattoes (some of whom owned slaves) clashed over issues of rights, land, and labor, as the forces of France, Britain, and Spain manipulated the conflict. At first the slaves and mulattoes shared the goals of the French revolution in opposition to the royalist French planters, but with time a coalition of planters and mulattoes arose in opposition to the slaves.

L'Ouverture became the leader of the revolutionary slave forces, which by 1794 consisted of a disciplined group of four thousand mostly ex-slaves. He successfully waged various campaigns first against the British, and was at the height of his power and influence, when, in 1796, General Rigaud (who led the mulatto forces) sought to re-impose slavery on the black islanders. He quickly achieved victory, captured Santo Domingo, and by 1801 had virtual control of the Spanish part of the island. In 1802, a French expeditionary force was sent to re-establish French control of the island. L'Ouverture was tricked, captured, and sent to France where he died on April 7, 1803, under inhumane conditions.

Gabriel Prosser 1775-1800

Insurrectionist

Gabriel Prosser was born around 1775. He became the coachman of Thomas Prosser of Henrico County, Virginia, and planned a large, highly organized revolt to take place on the last night of August of 1800 around Richmond, Virginia. About 32,000 slaves and only eight thousand whites were in the area, and it was his intention to kill all of the whites except for the French, Quakers, elderly women, and children. The ultimate goal was that the remaining 300,000 slaves in the state would follow his lead and seize the entire state. The revolt was set to coincide with the harvest so that his followers would be spared any shortage of food, and it was decided that the conspirators would meet at the Old Brook Swamp outside of Richmond and marshal forces to attack the city.

The insurrection fell apart when a severe rainstorm made it impossible for many of the slaves to assemble and a pair of house slaves who did not wish their master killed revealed the plot. Panic swept through the city, martial law was declared, and those suspected of involvement were rounded up and hanged; when it became clear that the slave population would be decimated if all of those implicated were dealt with in like fashion, the courts began to mete out less severe sen-

James Armistead Lafayette

tences. Prosser was apprehended in the hold of a schooner that docked in Norfolk, Virginia. Brought back in chains, he was interrogated by the governor. When he refused to divulge details of the conspiracy, he was hanged.

Dred Scott 1795-1858
Negotiator

Born in Southhampton, Virginia, in 1795, his first name was simply "Sam." He worked as a farmhand, handyman, and stevedore, and moved with his master to Huntsville, Alabama, and later to St. Louis, Missouri. In 1831 his owner, Peter Blow, died, and he was bought by John Emerson, a surgeon in the U.S. Army. Sam accompanied his new master to Illinois (a free state) and Wisconsin (a territory). Sometime after 1836 he received permission to marry, and by 1848 he had changed his name to Dred Scott. At various times he attempted to buy his freedom or escape but was unsuccessful. In 1843, Emerson died and left his estate to his widow Irene Emerson, who also refused Scott his freedom. He then obtained the assistance of two attorneys who helped him to sue for his freedom in county court.

Scott lost this case, but the verdict was set aside, and in 1847 he won a second trial on the grounds that his slave status had been nullified upon entering into a free state. Scott received financial backing and legal representation through the sons of Peter Blow, Irene Emerson's brother John Sanford, and her second husband Dr. C. C. Chaffee, all of whom apparently saw the case as an important challenge to slavery. In 1857, the U.S. Supreme Court ruled against Scott, stating that slaves were not legally citizens of the United States and therefore had no standing in the courts. Shortly after the decision was handed down, Mrs. Emerson freed Scott. The case led to the nullification of the Missouri Compromise of 1820, allowing the expansion of slavery into formerly free territories, and strengthening the abolition movement.

Sojourner Truth 1797-1883
Lecturer, Abolitionist

Born Isabella Baumfree in Ulster County, New York, around 1797, she was freed by the New York State Emancipation Act of 1827 and lived in New York City for a time. After taking the name Sojourner Truth, which she felt God had given her, she assumed the "mission" of spreading "the Truth" across the country. She became famous as an itinerant preacher, drawing huge crowds with her oratory (and some said "mystical gifts") wherever she appeared. She became one of an active group of black women abolitionists, lectured before numerous abolitionist audiences, and was friends with such leading white abolitionists as James and Lucretia Mott and Harriet Beecher Stowe. With the outbreak of the Civil War she raised money to purchase gifts for the soldiers, distributing them herself in the camps. She also helped African Americans who had escaped to the North to find habitation and shelter. Age and ill health caused her to retire from the lecture circuit, and she spent her last days in a sanatorium in Battle Creek, Michigan.

Harriet (Ross) Tubman 1826-1913
Lecturer, Abolitionist, Nurse

Born in 1826 in Dorchester County, Maryland, she had the hard childhood of a slave: much work, little schooling, and severe punishment. In 1848 she escaped, leaving behind her husband John Tubman, who threatened to report her to their master. As a free woman, she began to devise practical ways of helping other slaves escape. Over the following ten years she made about twenty trips from the North into the South and rescued more than three hundred slaves. Her reputation spread

Sojourner Truth

Harriet Tubman

rapidly, and she won the admiration of leading abolitionists (some of whom sheltered her passengers). Eventually a reward of $40,000 was posted for her capture.

Tubman met and aided John Brown in recruiting soldiers for his raid on Harpers Ferry—Brown referred to her as "General Tubman." One of her major disappointments was the failure of the raid, and she is said to have regarded Brown as the true emancipator of her people, not Lincoln. In 1860 she began to canvass the nation, appearing at anti-slavery meetings and speaking on women's rights. Shortly before the outbreak of the Civil War she was forced to leave for Canada, but she returned to the United States and served the Union as a nurse, soldier, and spy; she was particularly valuable to the army as a scout because of the knowledge of the terrain she had gained as a conductor on the Underground Railroad.

Tubman's biography (from which she received the proceeds) was written by Sarah Bradford in 1868. Tubman's husband, John, died two years after the end of the war, and in 1869 she married the war veteran Nelson Davis. Despite receiving many honors and tributes (including a medal from Queen Victoria), she spent her last days in poverty, not receiving a pension until thirty years after the Civil War. With the $20 dollars a month that she finally received, she helped to found a home for the aged and needy, which was later renamed the Harriet Tubman Home. She died in Auburn, New York.

Nat Turner 1800-1831
Insurrectionist

Born a slave in Southampton County, Virginia, on October 2, 1800, he was an avid reader of the Bible who prayed, fasted, and experienced "voices," ultimately becoming a visionary mystic with a belief that God had given him the special destiny of conquering Southampton County. After recruiting a handful of conspirators, he struck at isolated homes in his immediate area, and within 48 hours the band of insurrectionists had reached 60 armed men. They killed 55 whites before deciding to attack the county seat in Jerusalem, but while en route they were overtaken by a posse and dispersed. Turner took refuge in the Dismal Swamp and remained there for six weeks before he was captured, brought to trial, and hanged along with 16 other African Americans.

Denmark Vesey 1767-1822
Religious Leader

Born in 1767, Vesey was sold by his master at an early age and later bought back because of epilepsy. He sailed with his master, Captain Vesey, to the Virgin Islands and Haiti for twenty years. He enjoyed a considerable degree of mobility in his home port of Charleston, South Carolina, and eventually purchased his freedom from his master for $600—he had won $1500 in a lottery. He became a Methodist minister and used his church as a base to recruit supporters to take over Charleston. The revolt was planned for the second Sunday in July of 1822.

Vesey's plans were betrayed when a slave alerted the white authorities of the city. Hundreds of African Americans were rounded up, though some of Vesey's collaborators most likely escaped to the Carolinas where they fought as maroons. After a twenty-two day search, Vesey was apprehended and stood trial. During the trial he adeptly cross-examined witnesses, but ultimately could not deny his intention to overthrow the city, and he was hanged along with several collaborators.

The Slave Population: 1630 to 1780

Year	Total	North	South
1630	60	10	50
1640	597	427	170
1650	1,600	880	720
1660	2,920	1,162	1,758
1670	4,535	1,125	3,410
1680	6,971	1,895	5,076
1690	16,729	3,340	13,389
1700	27,817	5,206	22,611
1710	44,866	8,303	36,563
1720	68,839	14,091	54,748
1730	91,021	17,323	73,698
1740	150,024	23,958	126,066
1750	236,420	30,222	206,198
1760	325,806	40,033	285,773
1770	459,822	48,460	411,362
1780	575,420	56,796	518,624

Civil Rights

Civil Rights

◆ Early Rights Movements ◆ Civil Rights at the End of the Civil War
◆ Civil Rights in the Twentieth Century ◆ Civil Rights Gatekeepers
◆ Federal and State Civil Rights Agencies

Throughout the history of the United States, African Americans have struggled to obtain basic civil rights. It is a stuggle that has spanned several centuries—from the mutinies by Africans during the Atlantic crossing, to the insurrections organized by slaves in the New World, to the founding of such organizations as the Free African Society, the abolition movement, and to the civil rights marches and demonstrations of the twentieth century.

◆ EARLY RIGHTS MOVEMENTS

The Free African Society

In 1787, as a result of segregation and discriminatory practices within the Methodist church, the Reverends Richard Allen and Absalom Jones formed the Free African Society in Philadelphia. Adams later founded the Bethel African Methodist Church, and Jones became the rector of a Protestant Episcopal Church. The society was an important model for political consciousness and economic organization for African Americans throughout the country. It provided spiritual guidance and religious instruction; economic aid, burial assistance, and relief to widows; and medical and financial assistance to orphans. The society also advocated abolition and maintained channels of communication with African Americans in the South. Like the many other African American organizations that followed, the society was rooted in religious principles. Throughout the nineteenth century a number of mutual aid societies sprung up in African American communities in eastern cities such as New York, Newport, and Boston, providing loans, insurance, and various other economic and social services to their members and the larger community. The society also helped to faciliate communications between free blacks throughout the country.

The Abolition Movement

The press and the pulpit served as important tools in the anti-slavery movement. In 1827 in New York, Samuel Cornish and John Russwurm founded Freedom's Journal, the first black owned and operated newspaper in the United States. *Freedom's Journal*, which ceased publication after only three years, was concerned not only with eradicating slavery but also with the growing discrimination and cruelty against free blacks in both the South and North.

In 1847 abolitionist Frederick Douglass published the first edition of the *North Star*, which eventually became one of the most successful black newspapers in America prior to the outbreak of the Civil War. Douglass, an escaped slave from Maryland, became one of the best known black abolitionists in the country. He lectured extensively throughout the United States and England. In 1845 he published his autobiography, *Narrative of the Life of Frederick Douglass.*

Although the abolition movement was dominated by whites, numerous black leaders played a major role in the movement, including such figures as Henry Highland Garnet, Harriet Tubman, and Sojourner Truth.

◆ CIVIL RIGHTS AT THE END OF THE CIVIL WAR

Following the war, Republicans, who controlled the U.S. Congress, took up the cause of the newly freed

Richard Allen

Frederick Douglass

African Americans. Between 1865 and 1875, three amendments to the Constitution and a string of civil rights and Reconstruction legislation was passed by Congress. The Thirteenth Amendment, ratified December 18, 1865, abolished slavery and involuntary servitude. The Fourteenth Amendment, ratified July 28, 1868, guaranteed citizenship and provided equal protection under the laws. Ratified March 30, 1870, the Fifteenth Amendment was designed to protect the right of all citizens to vote. In 1866, 1870, 1871, and 1875 Congress passed civil rights legislation outlining and protecting basic rights, including the right to purchase and sell property and access to public accommodations. The Reconstruction acts, passed between 1867 and 1869, called for new state constitutional conventions in those states that had seceded from the Union prior to the Civil War.

Reconstruction eventually produced a wave of anti-African sentiment. White organizations, like the Ku Klux Klan, aimed at intimidating blacks and preventing them from taking their place in society, sprang up throughout the North and the South. In 1871 Congress enacted the Ku Klux Klan Act as an effort to end intimidation and violence directed at blacks. However the act failed to exterminate the Klan and other terrorist organizations.

The civil rights and Reconstruction legislation were difficult for many whites to accept and did little to change their attitudes. The last of the civil rights acts, passed by Congress in 1875, prohibited discrimination in public accommodations. However, by the 1880s the debate as to the constitutionality of such legislation had reached the U.S. Supreme Court. Ruling in a group of five cases in 1883, which became known as the *Civil Rights Cases*, the U.S. Supreme Court concluded that the 1875 Civil Rights Act was unconstitutional on the grounds that the Fourteenth Amendment authorized Congress to legislate only against discriminatory state action, and not discrimination by private individuals. The Court's ruling brought about an end to federal efforts to protect the civil rights of African Americans until the mid-twentieth century.

Anti-lynching Efforts

By the late nineteenth and early twentieth century, lynching had become a weapon used by whites against blacks throughout the country. Between 1882 and 1990, approximately 1,750 African Americans were lynched in the United States. Victims, who included women, had been accused of a variety of "offenses" ranging from testifying in court against a white man to failing to use the word "mister" when addressing a white person. Ida B. Wells Barnett, a journalist and social activist, became one of the leading voices in the anti-lynching crusade by writing and lecturing throughout the United States against the practice of lynching.

Institutionalized Segregation

In 1896, the U.S. Supreme Court was faced with the issue of segregation on public transportation. At the time, as was the case in many parts of the South, a Louisiana state law was enacted requiring that "equal but separate" accommodations for blacks and whites be maintained in all public facilities. When Homer Adolph Plessy, a black man traveling by train from New Orleans to Covington, Louisiana, refused to ride in the "colored" railway coach, he was arrested.

Prior to the case of *Plessy v. Ferguson*, the court had started to build a platform upon which the doctrine of separate but equal would be based. In 1878, ruling in the case *Hall v. DeCuir* the court declared that states could not outlaw segregation on common carriers, such as streetcars and railroads. Segregation laws sprung up throughout the South.

With Justice Billings Brown delivering the majority opinion in the *Plessy* case, the Court declared that "separate but equal" accommodations constituted a reasonable use of state police power and that the Fourteenth Amendment of the Constitution could not be used to abolish social or racial distinctions or to force a co-mingling of the two races. The Supreme Court had effectively reduced the significance of the Fourteenth Amendment, which was designed to give blacks specific rights and protections. The ruling, in the *Plessy* case, which was termed the "separate but equal" doctrine, paved the way for the segregation of African Americans in all walks of life.

Ida B. Wells Barnett

◆ CIVIL RIGHTS IN THE TWENTIETH CENTURY

Booker T. Washington and W. E. B. Du Bois

During the late nineteenth and early twentieth centuries, two figures— Booker T. Washington and William Edward Burghardt Du Bois—emerged as leaders in the struggle for black political and civil rights. Washington, an educator and founder of the Tuskegee Normal and Industrial Institute, was a strong advocate of practical, utilitarian education and manual training as a means for developing African Americans. Tuskegee Normal and Industrial Institute, which was founded in 1881 and based on a program at Hampton Institute, provided vocational training and prepared its students to survive economically in a segregated society. In Washington's opinion, education was to provide African Americans with the means to become economically self-supporting. Speaking at the Cotton States International Exposition in Atlanta in 1895, Washington outlined his philosophy of self-help and cooperation between blacks and whites:

> "To those of my race who depend on bettering their condition in a foreign land, or who underestimate the importance of cultivating friendly relations with the Southern white man, who is their next door neighbor, I would say: 'Cast down your bucket where you are'—cast it down in making friends in every manly way of the people of all races by whom we are surrounded."

W. E. B. Du Bois, a young historian and Harvard graduate, challenged Washington's passive policies in a

A Colored drinking fountain in North Carolina.

series of stinging essays and speeches. Du Bois advocated the uplifting of African Americans through an educated black elite, which he referred to as the "Talented Tenth", or roughly a tenth of the African American population. He believed that these African Americans must become proficient in education and culture, which would eventually benefit all. In 1905 Du Bois, along with a group of other black intellectuals, formed the Niagara Movement. The group drew up a platform which called for full citizenship rights for blacks and public recognition of their contributions to America's stability and progress. The movement eventually evolved into what became known as the National Association for the Advancement of Colored People (NAACP).

Civil Rights in the Mid-to Late-Twentieth Century

The civil rights movement suffered many defeats in the first half of the twentieth century. Repeated efforts to obtain passage of federal anti- lynching bills failed.

Booker T. Washington

W. E. B. Du Bois

The all-white primary system, which effectively disenfranchised southern blacks, resisted numerous court challenges. The Depression worsened conditions on farms and in ghettos. On the positive side, the growing political power of blacks in northern cities and an increasing liberal trend in the Supreme Court portended the legal and legislative victories of the 1950s and 1960s.

Brown v. Board of Education of Topeka

A great deal of the civil rights struggle throughout this period was carried on by the NAACP, which had begun chipping away at the roots of legalized segregation in a series of successful lawsuits. A major breakthrough for the NAACP came in 1954, when the U.S. Supreme Court ruled in *Brown v. Board of Education of Topeka* that discrimination in education was unconstitutional. This decision was as momentous as the Supreme Court's ruling in *Plessy v. Ferguson* in 1896, which legalized the doctrine of "separate but equal" treatment for blacks.

The *Brown* case involved the practice of denying black children equal access to state public schools due to state laws requiring or permitting racial segregation. The U.S. Supreme Court unanimously held that segregation deprived the children of equal protection under the Fourteenth Amendment to the U.S. Constitution, overturning the "separate but equal" doctrine established in *Plessy*.

A. Philip Randolph

In 1941, A. Philip Randolph, organizer of an employment bureau for untrained blacks and founder the Brotherhood of Sleeping Car Porters, came up with the idea of leading a protest march of blacks in Washington, DC to protest discrimination. On July 25, less than a week before the scheduled demonstration, President Franklin D. Roosevelt issued Executive Order No. 8802, which banned discrimination in the defense industry and led to the creation of the Fair Employment Practices Committee.

Civil Rights in the 1960s

Rosa Parks was one of the major catalysts of the 1960s civil rights movement. When on December 1,

Police officers using police dogs to break up a demonstration in Birmingham, Alabama, 1963.

1955, Parks refused to give up her seat on a Montgomery bus to a white man, as the law required, she was arrested and sent to jail. As a result of Parks' arrest, blacks throughout Montgomery refused to ride city buses. The Montgomery Bus Boycott led by Martin Luther King, Jr. was highly successful and ultimately led to the integration of all Montgomery city buses.

The eventual success of the Montgomery Bus Boycott encouraged a wave of massive demonstrations that swept across the South. In 1960 a group of students denied service at a Greensboro, North Carolina lunch counter started the sit-in movement. That same year, the Student Non-Violent Coordinating Committee was created and would include among its members Julian Bond, H. Rap Brown, Stokely Carmichael, and John Lewis.

The civil rights movement of the 1960s galvanized blacks and sympathetic whites as nothing had ever done before, but was not without cost. Thousands of people were jailed because they defied Jim Crow laws. Others were murdered and homes and churches were bombed. People lost their jobs and their homes because they supported the movement.

On August 28, 1963, nearly 250,000 people marched in Washington, DC to awaken the nation's consciousness regarding civil rights and to encourage the passage of civil rights legislation pending in Congress. The march was a cooperative effort of several civil rights organizations, including the Southern Christian Leadership Conference, the Congress of Racial Equality, the National Association for the Advancement of Colored People, the Negro American Labor Council, and the National Urban League. It was during this demonstration that Dr. Martin Luther King, Jr., in the shadow of the Lincoln Memorial, gave his "I Have a Dream" speech.

At its zenith, the civil rights movement was the most important event taking place in America. Through demonstrations, "sit-ins," marches, and soaring rhetoric, the movement aroused widespread public indignation, thus creating an atmosphere in which it was possible to make positive changes in American society.

Civil Rights Legislation in the 1990s

Although the civil rights movement of the 1950s and 1960s produced significant gains for African Americans, progress continues today. This progress is evident in the passage of the most recent civil rights legislation. In June of 1989, the U.S. Supreme Court delivered opinions in several cases dealing with seniority systems and racial discrimination in employment. Ruling in the cases *Lorance v. AT&T Technologies Inc.*, *Martin v. Wilks*, *Patterson v. McLean Credit Union*, and *Wards Cove Packing Co. v. Antonio* the Court appeared to reverse earlier civil rights rulings.

Prior to the Court's ruling in *Wards Cove*, the burden of proof in job discrimination suits had been placed on employers, requiring businesses to prove that there was a legitimate business reason for alleged discriminatory practices. With the *Wards Cove* decision, the Court made it more difficult for groups to win such suits by requiring workers to prove that no clear business reason existed for an employer's use of practices that result in discrimination. Civil rights organizations were quick to protest the rulings; opponents of the ruling, including the NAACP Legal Defense and Educational Fund and the Leadership Conference on Civil Rights argued that the Court had undermined the protection granted by federal civil rights and equal employment legislation.

On October 16 and 17, 1990, both houses of Congress approved a bill designed to reverse the Court's ruling. The proposed legislation, not only reversed the Court's ruling in *Wards Cove*, but strengthened provisions of the 1964 Civil Rights Act. On October 22, President George

Bayard Rustin (left) and A. Philip Randolph at a news conference, 1963.

Bush vetoed the bill, claiming that the bill's provisions would encourage employers to establish hiring quotas.

This was not the first time that Congress moved to reverse a Court action in the area of civil rights—in 1987 Congress passed the Civil Rights Restoration Act of 1988 which reversed the Court's ruling in *Grove City College v. Bell* (1984). In the *Grove City College* case, the U.S. Supreme Court ruled that not all programs and activities of an institution were covered by Title IX of the Education Amendments of 1972 (Public Law 89-10, 79 Stat. 27), prohibiting discrimination in educational programs receiving federal financial assistance.

After vetoing Congress' 1990 civil rights legislation, the Bush administration joined both houses of Congress in working on alternative bills. On October 30, following months of negotiation, the Senate passed a bill, designed to provide additional remedies to deter harassment and intentional discrimination in the workplace, provide guidelines for the adjudication of cases arising under Title VII of the Civil Rights Act of 1964, and expand the scope of civil rights legislation weakened by Supreme Court decisions 1745. The House of Representatives passed the bill on November 7, and on November 21, President George Bush signed the Civil Rights Act of 1991

◆ CIVIL RIGHTS GATEKEEPERS

Ralph D. Abernathy 1926-1990
religious leader, Civil Rights/Human Rights Activist, Organization Executive/Founder

Born March 11, 1926, in Linden, Alabama, the Reverend Ralph David Abernathy was ordained a minister in 1948. He received his bachelor's degree from Alabama State College (now Alabama State University) in 1950 and his master's degree from Atlanta University in 1951. The alliance between Abernathy and Martin Luther King, Jr. stretched back to the mid-1950s. While attending Atlanta University, Abernathy had the opportunity to hear King preach at Ebenezer Baptist Church.

After obtaining his master's degree, Abernathy returned to Alabama to serve as a part-time minister at the Eastern Star Baptist Church in Demoplis. In 1951 Abernathy moved to First Baptist Church in Montgomery. Around this time King accepted a position at Montgomery's Dexter Avenue Baptist Church; Abernathy and King became close friends. In 1955, the two organized

High pressure hoses are turned on demonstrators in Birmingham, Alabama, 1963.

the Montgomery Improvement Association to coordinate a citywide bus boycott. The success of the Montgomery Bus Boycott led to the creation of the Southern Negro Leaders Conference; the organization's name was later changed to the Southern Leadership Conference and finally the Southern Christian Leadership Conference (SCLC). In January of 1957, Dr. King was elected the organization's first president.

From the time of Martin Luther King's death in 1968 until 1977, Abernathy served as president of the Southern Christian Leadership Conference. Abernathy continued as a leading figure in the movement until his resignation in 1977, when he made an unsuccessful bid for a U.S. Congressional seat. In 1989, he published his autobiography, *And The Walls Came Tumbling Down*, which was criticized by some black leaders for Abernathy's inclusion of details regarding King's extramarital affairs. Abernathy died of cardiac arrest on April 17, 1990.

Ella Josephine Baker 1903-1986
Community Activist, Civil Rights/Human Rights Activist, Executive/General Manager

In 1903, Ella Baker was in Norfolk, Virginia, to Blake and Georgiana Ross Baker, both educated people who worked hard to educate their children. The family and community in which she grew up instilled in her a sense of sharing and community cooperation; neighbors shared food from their gardens and gave a helping hand when needed. Her family instilled in her a sense of racial pride and resistance to any form of oppression. Her grandfather, a minister and community leader, was an ardent proponent of civil rights and universal suffrage, and passed his beliefs on to her.

When she was 15, Baker was sent to the Shaw Boarding School in Raleigh. The Shaw school was both a high school and college, and she graduated with a bachelor's degree as valedictorian in 1927. After graduation, she moved to New York City. She quickly became involved in progressive politics and attended as many meetings and discussions as she could find. During the Depression, she was outraged at the poverty she saw in the black areas of the city. Believing in the power of community and group action, she became involved with the Young Negroes Cooperative League, a buying cooperative that bought food in bulk to distribute at low prices to members; in 1931, she became the national director of the League. When President Franklin Roosevelt's Works Progress Administration started, she be-

Nearly 250,000 gather in Washington, DC, August 1963.

came involved with their literacy program. Throughout these years she worked closely with other politically aware and motivated people, discussing and evolving a political philosophy of cooperation, equality, and justice.

In the 1940s, Baker began to work for the NAACP. Between 1940 and 1943, she was a field secretary, traveling all over the country setting up branch offices and teaching people to fight for their own rights; her traveling gave her the opportunity to develop a vast network of contacts in the south that she later relied on when working for the Student Non-Violent Coordinating Committee and Southern Christian Leadership Conference. In 1943, she became the director of branches for the NAACP. During the 1950s, she started fund raising activities in New York for the civil-rights struggles in the south, and in 1958, moved to Atlanta to work with the SCLC.

Working for the Southern Christian Leadership Conference, Baker became disillusioned with the top-heavy, male-dominated organizational structure of the group.

Ralph Abernathy

In 1960 she quit the SCLC and took a job with the Young Women's Christian Association instead. When students began leading sit-ins, she shifted her focus to the development of the Student Non-Violent Coordinating Committee. She acted as an unofficial advisor for the group, counseling them to set up their own student-run organization rather than be subsumed under the SCLC or the NAACP. She helped launch the Mississippi Freedom Democratic Party that challenged the all-white Democratic delegation at the 1964 presidential convention. She also acted as staff consultant for the interracial SCLC educational fund.

Baker returned to New York City in 1965, but kept working with national and international civil rights organizations. Among her other activities, she raised money to send to the freedom fighters in Rhodesia and South Africa. She remained an active organizer and speaker as long as her health allowed. Baker's belief in the power of communal action and reliance on the workers rather than the leaders had an enormous impact. She worked for all of the major civil-rights organizations at their time of greatest need. By the time the SCLC and the SNCC were formed, she had almost 30 years of civil-rights and community organizing experience to offer. She continually strove to keep the movement people oriented, and she succeeded in helping the SNCC remain a student group. Through her philosophy and actions, she motivated hundreds to act, to help themselves, and their neighbors as she had learned to do as a child.

Daisy Lee Gatson Bates 1920-

Publisher, Civil Rights/Human Rights Activist, Executive/General Manager

After attending segregated schools where all of the new equipment and up-to-date texts were reserved for whites only, Daisy Bates spent much of her energy as an adult successfully integrating the schools of Little Rock, Arkansas.

Shortly after their marriage in 1941, Daisy and her husband Lucius Christopher Bates, a journalist, started to publish a newspaper, the Arkansas *State Press.* They made it a point in their paper to keep track and report incidents of police brutality and other racially-motivated violence; their paper became known throughout the state for its campaign to improve the social and economic circumstances of African Americans. Because of their work, the city of Little Rock began to hire black police officers, and the number of racial incidents lessened.

In 1952, Daisy Bates became the Arkansas president of the NAACP; after the 1954 court decision in the *Brown v. Board of Education* case, she became very active in school desegregation. She began taking black children to white schools to be registered. If the school refused to register the children, she would report it in her paper. In 1957, the superintendent of schools in Little Rock decided to try to integrate the schools and chose nine students, now called the Little Rock Nine, to be the first black children to attend Central High, a white school. Most white citizens of Little Rock objected. Bates organized the Little Rock Nine, accompanied them to Central High, and stood with them against the state troopers that Governor Orval Faubus had sent in to prevent the integration. For days she escorted the children to school, only to be turned away by an angry mob. On September 25, 1957, Daisy Bates entered Central High in Little Rock with the nine children, escorted by 1000 paratroopers President Dwight Eisenhower had sent in; the first steps towards integration were successful. For the rest of their years at Central High, Bates kept track of the students and acted as their advocate when problems arose, frequently accompanying them and their parents to meetings with school officials.

Ralph Abernathy (left) and Martin Luther King, Jr. (rear) were active in the boycott of segregated buses in Montgomery, Alabama.

In October of 1957, one month after she marched into Central High, Daisy Bates was arrested on charges of failing to provide membership information on the NAACP to city officials. The charges were later overturned. Two years later, the Arkansas *State Press* folded, but Bates kept active in the civil-rights fight, touring and speaking, and working with the Student Non-Violent Coordinating Committee to register voters. In 1985, the *State Press* began to publish again, and it has continued to serve the needs of the African-American community in Little Rock.

Stokely Carmichael (Kwame Toure) 1941-
Civil Rights/Human Rights Activist, Nationalist/Repatriationist, Executive/General Manager

If, during the 1960s, one individual stood at the forefront of the Black Power movement, Stokely Carmichael was that person. He soared to fame as popularizer of the dynamic phrase "Black Power" and as one of the most powerful and influential leaders of the Student Non-Violent Coordinating Committee (SNCC).

Daisy Bates leaving Little Rock Police headquarters, 1957.

Stokely Carmichael

Carmichael was born in Trinidad, on June 29, 1941, and moved to the United States with his family when he was 11. As a teenager, Carmichael was jolted by ghetto life in which "black" and "impotent" seemed to be synonymous terms. He was not reassured later when he was admitted to the Bronx High School of Science, encountered white liberals, and felt he had been adopted by them as a mascot. Although he was offered good scholarships to white universities, Carmichael opted to attend Howard University. During his first year there, 1960, he joined the Congress of Racial Equality (CORE) in its efforts to integrate public accommodations in the South. After graduation in 1964, he rejected scholarship opportunities for graduate school, and went south to join the SNCC. As one of their finest organizers, he worked ceaselessly, registering and educating voters in the south. In 1966, he was elected chairman of the SNCC, but as the youngest chair the group had, his views were considered too radical by some members.

Carmichael's cry for "black power" thrilled many disenfranchised young African Americans, but troubled others, who thought it sounded too violent. He was labeled as potentially violent by the media and the legal authorities. Disagreement with SNCC members arose over the issues of self-defense versus nonviolence, and the participation of whites in black grass-roots organizations. In 1967, he resigned as chairperson, and was later expelled from the SNCC.

Carmichael spent much of 1968 traveling around the world, speaking to many organizations, including some in communist countries. His travels included Ghana, where he joined the Pan-African movement. After returning to the United States, he went to work for the Black Panther party. In this country, however, he was subject to almost constant harassment from the FBI because of his connection with the Panthers, and because he had visited communist countries while traveling. In 1969, he resigned from the Black Panthers, and moved to Guinea, where he had been offered political asylum.

In Guinea, Carmichael turned his efforts to supporting Pan-Africanism; he has organized many local chapters through the world of the All African Peoples Revolutionary Party. In 1978, to honor the two men who most influenced his Pan-African philosophical education, SeKou Toure and Kwame Nkrumah, he changed his name to Kwame Toure. Toure continues to live in

Guinea and travel throughout the world, working toward a united African people.

Mandy Carter 1946-
Civil Rights/Human Rights Activist

Carter was born in Albany, New York, in the late 1940s and spent her childhood in orphanages. She attended community college for a time in Troy, New York—and lived at the downtown YWCA—but moved to New York City in 1967 with a savings of $100. There she slept in Central Park before taking a job at drug guru Timothy Leary's League for Spiritual Discovery; she moved to San Francisco later that year and soon became active in protests against the war in Vietnam. For several years Carter was involved with the War Resister's League, and it was to her colleagues there that she first admitted her sexual orientation. She worked for the group's San Francisco offices for a number of years, and it was during this time, the late 1970s, that she first became active in gay and lesbian politics.

In 1982, Carter moved to North Carolina, where she continued her work with the War Resister's League, and also became involved on a national level with gay and lesbian organizations; one of her accomplishments was helping coordinate the 1987 lesbian and gay march on the nation's capital, a role she reprised in 1993. In addition to co-producing an annual festival of women's music and art, Carter has also been instrumental (but ultimately unsuccessful) in campaigns to unseat North Carolina's right-wing Republican senator Jesse Helms. She has also worked to combat the Christian Right's attempts to infiltrate African American churches in efforts to stymie support of gay and lesbian rights among the congregations; she has done this work in her role as liaison of the Human Rights Campaign Fund to the National Black and Gay Lesbian Leadership Forum. Carter has spoken of her political activism in the 1994 volume *Uncommon Heroes: A Celebration of Heroes and Role Models for Gay and Lesbian Americans.*

Angela Yvonne Davis 1944-
Women's Rights Activist, Civil Rights/Human Rights Activist, Professor, Lecturer, Author/Poet

Angela Davis was born on January 26, 1944, in Birmingham, Alabama, to middle class parents who stressed both academic excellence and political awareness and activism. Her mother, Sallye E. Davis, had been politically active since her college days, and Angela participated in demonstrations with her mother from the time she was in elementary school. To insure her a better education than she would be able to receive in the segregated schools of the south, her parents sent her to Elizabeth Irwin High School, a private progressive school in New York. The school had many radical teachers and students, and Angela soon joined a Marxist study group.

Angela Davis

After graduation, Davis continued to seek high quality education. She majored in French at Brandeis College, studying at the Sorbonne in Paris her junior year. She then pursued graduate studies in philosophy at the Goethe University in Frankfurt, and in 1967 she returned to the United States to study with the well known philosopher, Herbert Marcuse, at the University of California at San Diego. When she was almost done with her degree, she took a teaching job at the University of California at Los Angeles.

In 1969, Davis joined the communist party; the regents of UCLA tried to fire her, but she fought them in court. The following year she became involved with the Black Panther Party. Guns she had bought for self defense were used by a member of the Black Panthers in a courtroom shooting. Believing she was involved, the Federal Bureau of Investigation (FBI) sought her arrest, so she went underground to avoid them. She was put on the FBI's ten most wanted list, and later arrested. In 1972, she was acquitted of all charges, but was not hired back by the university. Then-California governor Ronald Reagan and the Regents of the University decreed that she would never teach in California again.

Following her trial, Davis founded the National Alliance against Racism and Political Repression, a legal group providing defense of minority prisoners. In 1980 and 1984, she ran for vice president of the United States on the Communist Party ticket. A writer and philosopher, Davis has written several books, including *If They Come in the Morning* (1971), *Women, Race and Class* (1983), *Angela Davis: An Autobiography* (1988), and *Women, Culture and Politics* (1989).

In the 1990s, politically active Davis has remained a popular yet controversial figure. Davis's 1995 appointment as presidential chair in charge of developing new ethnic studies courses at University of California-Santa Cruz was heavily opposed by state Republican legislators concerned with her Communist Party affiliation. A much sought after though often protested against Davis has lectured around the country about "envisioning a new movement" set apart from the radicalism of the 1960s. Meanwhile, Davis continues to write and to support such causes as women's rights, workers' rights, health care, and nuclear disarmament.

W. E. B. Du Bois

William Edward Burghardt Du Bois 1868-1963

Organization Executive/Founder, Civil Rights/Human Rights Activist, Professor, Lecturer, Author/Poet, Editor, Critic, Women's Rights Activist, Sociologist, Executive Director, Political Scientist, Correspondent/Reporter

An outstanding critic, editor, scholar, author, and civil rights leader, W. E. B. Du Bois is certainly among the most influential blacks of the twentieth century. Born in Great Barrington, Massachusetts on February 23, 1868, Du Bois received a bachelors degree from Fisk University and went on to win a second bachelors, as well as a Ph.D., from Harvard. He was for a time professor of Latin and Greek at Wilberforce and the University of Pennsylvania, and also served as a professor of economics and history at Atlanta University.

One of the founders of the National Association for the Advancement of Colored People (NAACP) in 1909, Du Bois served as that organization's director of publications and editor of *Crisis* magazine until 1934. In 1944, he returned from Atlanta University to become head of the NAACP's special research department, a post he held until 1948. Dr. Du Bois emigrated to Africa in 1961, and became editor-in-chief of the *Encyclopedia Africana*, an enormous publishing venture which had been planned by Kwame Nkrumah, since then deposed as president of Ghana. Du Bois died in Ghana on August 27, 1963, at the age of 95.

Du Bois's numerous books include *The Suppression of the Slave Trade* (1896), *The Philadelphia Negro* (1899), *The Souls of Black Folk* (1903), *John Brown* (1909), *Quest of the Silver Fleece* (1911), *The Negro* (1915), *Darkwater* (1920), *The Gift of Black Folk* (1924), *Dark Princess* (1928), *Black Folk: Then and Now* (1939), *Dusk of Dawn* (1940), *Color and Democracy* (1945), *The World and Africa* (1947), *In Battle for Peace* (1952), and a trilogy, *Black Flame* (1957-1961). It is this enormous literary output on such a wide variety of themes which offers the most convincing testimony to Du Bois's lifetime position that it was vital for blacks to cultivate their own aesthetic and cultural values even as they made valuable strides toward social emancipation. In this he was opposed by Booker T. Washington, who felt that the black should concentrate on developing technical and mechanical skills before all else.

Du Bois was one of the first male civil rights leaders to recognize the problems of gender discrimination. He was among the first men to understand the unique problems of black women, and to value their contributions. He supported the women's suffrage movement and strove to integrate this mostly white struggle. He encouraged many black female writers, artists, poets, and novelists, featuring their works in *Crisis* and sometimes providing personal financial assistance to them. Several of his novels feature women as prominently as men, an unusual approach for any author of his day. Du Bois spent his life working not just for the equality of all men, but for the equality of all people.

Medgar Evers 1925-1963
Civil Rights/Human Rights Activist

Medgar Evers was one of the first martyrs of the civil-rights movement. He was born in 1925 in Decatur, Mississippi to James and Jessie Evers. After a short stint in the army, he enrolled in Alcorn A&M College, graduating in 1952. His first job out of college was traveling around rural Mississippi selling insurance. He soon grew enraged at the despicable conditions of poor black families in his state, and joined the NAACP. In 1954, he was appointed Mississippi's first field secretary.

Medgar Evers

Evers was outspoken, and his demands were radical for his rigidly segregated state. He fought for the enforcement of the 1954 court decision of *Brown v. Board of Education of Topeka* which outlawed school segregation; he fought for the right to vote, and he advocated boycotting merchants who discriminated. He worked unceasingly despite the threats of violence that his speeches engendered. He gave much of himself to this struggle, and in 1963, he gave his life. On June 13, 1963, he drove home from a meeting, stepped out of his car, and was shot in the back.

Immediately after Evers's death, the shotgun that was used to kill him was found in bushes nearby, with the owner's fingerprints still fresh. Byron de la Beckwith, a vocal member of a local white-supremacist group, was arrested. Despite the evidence against him, which included an earlier statement that he wanted to kill Evers, two trials with all-white juries ended in deadlock decisions, and Beckwith walked free. 20 years later, in 1989, information surfaced that suggested the jury in both trials had been tampered with. The assistant District Attorney, with the help of Evers's widow, began putting together a new case. In 1990, Beckwith was arrested one more time; on February 5, 1994, Beckwith was convicted of murder and sentenced to life in prison.

While knowing that Evers did not die in vain is small comfort, it is nevertheless true. His death changed the tenor of the civil-rights struggle. Anger replaced fear in the south, as hundreds of demonstrators marched in protect. His death prompted President John Kennedy to ask Congress for a comprehensive civil-rights bill, which President Lyndon Johnson signed into law the following year. Evers death, as his life had, contributed much to the struggle for equality.

Fannie Lou Townsend Hamer 1917-1977
Lecturer, Civil Rights/Human Rights Activist, Organization Executive/Founder

As a poor sharecropper she had only an elementary education, yet Fannie Lou Hamer was one of the most eloquent speakers for the civil rights movement in the south. She worked for political, social and economic equality for herself and all African Americans; she fought to integrate the national Democratic party, and became one of its first black delegates to a presidential convention.

The youngest of 20 siblings, Hamer was born in 1917 to Jim and Ella Townsend in Montgomery County, Mississippi. She began picking cotton at the age of six; she attended school until she had to drop out in the sixth grade to work full time. She worked first as a share-

Fannie Lou Hamer

cropper and then as a time keeper on the same plantation in Mississippi for almost forty years. In 1962, because she tried to exercise her right to vote, she lost her job and, frightened by threats of violent reprisals, was forced to move away from her home and her family. Angered into action, she went to work for the Student Non-Violent Coordinating Committee (SNCC), helping many blacks register to vote.

Because the Democratic party refused to send blacks as delegates to the national presidential convention, in 1964, Hamer and others formed the Mississippi Freedom Democratic party to send black delegates to the convention. They challenged the Democratic delegates from Mississippi for their seats at the convention, arguing that the all-white delegation could not adequately represent their state which had a large black population. Hamer's own speech on their behalf frightened the incumbent President Lyndon Johnson so much so that he tried to block the televised coverage of her. The MFDP lost its bid that year, but their actions did result in a pledge from the national party not to seat delegations excluding blacks in the 1968 convention. In 1968, Fannie Lou Hamer was among the first black delegates to the Democratic National Convention.

For the next decade, Hamer remained active in the struggle for civil and economic rights. In 1969, she founded the Freedom Farms Corporation to help needy families raise food and livestock. They also provided basic social services, scholarships and grants for education, and helped fund minority business opportunities. She became a sought-after speaker, and in the 1970s, even as her health was failing from cancer, she still toured the country speaking about civil rights for all.

Jesse Jackson 1941-
Religious Leader, Civil Rights/Human Rights Activist, and *Organization Executive/Founder*

Jesse Louis Jackson was born October 8, 1941, in Greenville, South Carolina. In 1959 Jackson left South Carolina to attend the University of Illinois. Dissatisfied with his treatment on campus, he decided to transfer to North Carolina Agricultural and Technical College. After receiving his B.A. in sociology, Jackson attended the Chicago Theological Seminary. He was ordained a Baptist minister in 1968.

Jackson joined the Southern Christian Leadership Conference (SCLC) in 1965. In 1966 Jackson became involved with the SCLC's Operation Breadbasket, and from 1967 to 1971, he served as the program's executive director. Jackson resigned from the SCLC in 1971 to found his own organization, Operation PUSH (People United to Save Humanity). Through PUSH Jackson continued to pursue the economic objectives of Operation Breadbasket and expanded into areas of social and political development.

Jackson soon became the most visible and sought-after civil rights leader in the country. His magnetic personality came across as appealing on television, and while he described himself as "a country preacher," his command of issues and his ability to reach the heart of matters marked him as an individual of intellectual depth. Of all the civil rights leaders, Jackson was the one who could relate best to the young. He was possessed with a gift of being able to summon out the best in them, in a phrase that became his trademark, "I am somebody."

Out of this came Jackson's program, PUSH-EXCEL, which sought to motivate young school children to do better academically. In 1981, *Newsweek* magazine credited Jackson with building a struggling community improvement organization into a nationwide campaign to revive pride, discipline, and the work ethic in inner-city schools. With funding from the Carter administration, the PUSH-EXCEL program was placed in five other cities.

The Jesse Jackson of the 1980s will be best remembered for his two runs for the Democratic nomination for President of the United States. In 1983, many, but not all, black political leaders endorsed the idea of a black presidential candidate to create a "people's" platform, increase voter registration and have a power base from which there could be greater input into the political process. His 1984 campaign was launched under the aegis of the National Rainbow Coalition, Inc., an umbrella organization of minority groups. Black support was divided, however, between Jackson and former Vice President Walter Mondale. During this campaign, Jackson attracted considerable media coverage with controversial remarks and actions, demonstrating a lack of familiarity with national politics.

The 1988 campaign of Jackson showed enormous personal and political growth; his candidacy was no longer a symbolic gesture but was a real and compelling demonstration of his effectiveness as a candidate. By the time the Democratic convention rolled around, media pundits were seriously discussing the likelihood of Jackson's nomination as the Democratic presidential candidate, and "what to do about Jesse" became the focus of the entire Democratic leadership. At the end of the primary campaign, Jackson had finished a strong second to Massachusetts Governor Michael Dukakis, and changed forever the notion that a black President in America was inconceivable. Jackson took his defeat in stride and continued to campaign for the Democratic ticket until the November election.

Since the 1988 election, Jackson has worked less publicly, but no less energetically. In 1989 he moved with his Rainbow Coalition from Chicago to Washington, DC; he believed that the coalition could be more effective in the nation's capital. Jackson continues to write, speak, and lead protests for social change. His primary concerns include crime, violence, drug use, and teenage pregnancy in inner-city neighborhoods; voter registration; health care; affirmative action; and baseball hiring practices. In 1993 Jackson was awarded the Martin Luther King, Jr. Nonviolent Peace Prize.

Jackson has been active in foreign affairs as well. In 1991, he traveled to Iraq, and convinced Saddam Hussein to begin releasing Americans held hostage after Hussein's invasion of Kuwait. In 1994, Jackson met with Fidel Castro in Cuba and, later that year, President Clinton sent him on a peace mission to Nigeria. Although many expected him to run for president again in 1992 or 1996, Jackson decided against it, saying that he was too tired, and the strain on his family too severe. He did support his son, Jesse Jackson, Jr., who was elected to the House of Representatives (Chicago's 2nd Congressional District) on December 12, 1995.

Coretta Scott King 1927-

Organization Executive/Founder, Civil Rights/Human Rights Activist, Women's Rights Activist, Lecturer, National/International Diplomat, Educator, Community Activist

As the wife of civil-rights leader Martin Luther King, Jr., Coretta Scott King was ready to continue his work and perpetuate his ideals after his 1968 assassination. While her primary role in the early years of marriage was to raise her four children, she became increasingly involved in the struggle for civil rights through her husband's activities. After his death, she quickly became a dynamic activist and peace crusader.

Born one of three children on April 27, 1927, King is a native of Heilberger, Alabama. During the Depression she was forced to contribute to the family income by hoeing and picking cotton, but she resolved early to overcome adversity, seek treatment as an equal, and struggle to achieve a sound education. After graduating from the private Lincoln High School in 1945, she entered Antioch College in Yellow Springs, Ohio, on a scholarship, majoring in education and music. A teaching career appealed to her, but she became badly disillusioned when she was not allowed to do her practice teaching in the public schools of the town. No black had ever taught there, and she was not destined to be the first to break the tradition.

Musical training in voice and piano absorbed much of her time, with the result that, upon graduation, she decided to continue her studies at the New England Conservatory of Music in Boston, attending on a modest fellowship which covered tuition but made part-time work a necessity. Her meeting with Martin Luther King thrust her into a whirlwind romance, and also presented her with the opportunity to marry an exceptional young minister whose intense convictions and concern for humanity brought her a measure of rare self-realization early in life. Sensing his incredible dynamism, she suffered no regrets at the prospect of relinquishing her own possible career.

Completing her studies in 1954, King moved back south with her husband, who became pastor of Dexter Avenue Baptist Church in Montgomery, Alabama. Within a year, King had led the Montgomery bus boycott, and given birth to a new era of civil rights agitation. Two years later, he was the head of the Southern Christian Leadership Conference (SCLC).

Over the years King gradually became more involved in her husband's work. She would occasionally perform at his lectures, raising her voice in song as he did in speech. She became involved in separate activities as well. In 1962, she served as a Woman's Strike for Peace delegate to the 17-nation Disarmament Conference in Geneva, Switzerland. In the mid 1960s, she sang in the multi-arts Freedom Concerts that raised money for the SCLC. As demands on Martin became too much, she began to fill the speaking engagements he could not. After his assassination, she filled many of the commitments his death left empty, but soon became sought-after in her own right.

King's speech on Solidarity Day, June 19, 1968, is often identified as a prime example of her emergence

Coretta Scott King

from the shadow of her husband's memory. In it, she called upon American women to "unite and form a solid block of women power" to fight the three great evils of racism, poverty, and war. Much of her subsequent activity revolved around building plans for the creation of a Martin Luther King, Jr. Memorial in Atlanta, which she began to work on in 1969, and which was established under the care of the National Park Service in 1980. She also published *My Life with Martin Luther King, Jr.*, a book of reminiscences.

King's activism has extended beyond U.S. borders. For example, in the mid-1980s, she and two of her children were arrested for demonstrating against apartheid outside of the South African embassy in Washington, DC. The following year, in 1986, she visited South Africa for eight days, meeting with businessmen and anti-apartheid leaders. King has also decried the human rights violations of the Haitian military regime against Haitian citizens. In 1993, she implored the United Nations to reimpose an embargo against the nation.

Meanwhile, the well-respected Martin Luther King Jr. Center for Non-Violent Social Change became involved in an ugly scuffle with the National Park Service over the issue of how best to utilize some of the historic Atlanta district in which the King memorial are located. As CEO, King was forced to mediate between the family's desire for an interactive museum with exhibitions and programs for youngsters and the National Park Service's plan for a visitor's center on the same site. The dispute was not resolved until April of 1995, a few months after King had officially stepped down, handing the reigns over to her son Dexter, who was unanimously voted the center's director and CEO.

Controversy continued brewing. In 1964, Martin Luther King, Jr. had given nearly 83,000 documents, including correspondence and other manuscripts to Boston University. Mrs. King had hoped to regain control of that legacy, but in April of 1995, the Massachusetts Supreme Judicial Court ruled in favor of the university, leaving King, and many other Atlantans displeased.

On a brighter note, King remains an eloquent and respected spokesperson on behalf of black causes and nonviolent philosophy. She is often recognized for keeping her husband's dream alive. In September of 1995, King, along with two other famous civil rights widows—Myrlie Evers-Williams and Betty Shabazz—were honored for their influence by the National Political Congress of Black Women.

Martin Luther King Jr. 1929-1968.
Religious Leader, Civil Rights/Human Rights Activist, Author/Poet, Labor Activist, Organization Executive/Founder, Minister, Antiwar Activist

Any number of historic moments in the civil rights struggle have been used to identify Martin Luther King Jr.—prime mover of the Montgomery bus boycott (1956), keynote speaker at the March on Washington (1963), youngest Nobel Peace Prize laureate (1964). But in retrospect, single events are less important than the fact that King, and his policy of nonviolent protest, was the dominant force in the civil rights movement during its decade of greatest achievement, from 1957 to 1968.

King was born Michael Luther King in Atlanta on January 15, 1929—one of the three children of Martin Luther King, Sr., pastor of Ebenezer Baptist Church, and Alberta (Williams) King, a former schoolteacher. (He did not receive the name of "Martin" until he was about six years of age.) After attending grammar and high schools locally, King enrolled in Morehouse College (also in Atlanta) in 1944. At this time he was not inclined to enter the ministry, but while there he came under the influence of Dr. Benjamin Mays, a scholar whose manner and bearing convinced him that a religious career could have its intellectual satisfactions as well. After receiving his B.A. in 1948, King attended Crozer Theological Seminary in Chester, Pennsylvania, winning the Plafker Award as the outstanding student of the graduating class, and the J. Lewis Crozer Fellowship as well. King completed the course work for his doctorate in 1953, and was granted the degree two years later upon completion of his dissertation.

Married by then, King returned South, accepting the pastorate of the Dexter Avenue Baptist Church in Mont-

Coretta Scott King (left), Dr. Martin Luther King, Jr. (center) and Floyd McKissick attend a rally in Chicago, 1966.

gomery, Alabama. It was here that he made his first mark on the civil rights movement, by mobilizing the black community during a 382-day boycott of the city's bus lines.Working through the Montgomery Improvement Association, King overcame arrest and other violent harassment, including the bombing of his home. Ultimately, the U.S. Supreme Court declared the Alabama laws requiring bus segregation unconstitutional, with the result that blacks were allowed to ride Montgomery buses on equal footing with whites.

A national hero and a civil rights figure of growing importance, King summoned together a number of black leaders in 1957 and laid the groundwork for the organization now known as the Southern Christian Leadership Conference (SCLC). Elected its president, he soon sought to assist other communities in the organization of protest campaigns against discrimination, and in voter-registration activities as well.

After completing his first book and making a trip to India, King returned to the United States in 1960 to become co-pastor, with his father, of Ebenezer Baptist Church. Three years later, in 1963, King's nonviolent tactics were put to their most severe test in Birmingham, Alabama during a mass protest for fair hiring practices, the establishment of a biracial committee, and the desegregation of department-store facilities. Police brutality used against the marchers dramatized the plight of blacks to the nation at large with enormous impact. King was arrested, but his voice was not silenced as he issued his classic "Letter from a Birmingham Jail" to refute his critics.

Later that year King was a principal speaker at the historic March on Washington, where he delivered one of the most passionate addresses of his career. At the beginning of the next year *Time* magazine designated him as its Man of the Year for 1963. A few months later he was named recipient of the 1964 Nobel Peace Prize. Upon his return from Oslo, where he had gone to accept the award, King entered a new battle, in Selma, Alabama, where he led a voter-registration campaign which culminated in the Selma-to-Montgomery Freedom March. King next brought his crusade to Chicago where he launched a slum-rehabilitation and open-housing program.

In the North, however, King soon discovered that young and angry blacks cared little for his pulpit oratory and even less for his solemn pleas for peaceful protest. Their disenchantment was clearly one of the factors

Dr. King joins other civil rights leaders at a rally in Selma, Alabama, 1965.

influencing his decision to rally behind a new cause and stake out a fresh battleground: the war in Vietnam. Although his aim was to fuse a new coalition of dissent based on equal support for the peace crusade and the civil rights movement, King antagonized many civil rights leaders by declaring the United States to be "the greatest purveyor of violence in the world."

The rift was immediate. The National Association for the Advancement of Colored People (NAACP) saw King's shift of emphasis as "a serious tactical mistake"; the Urban League warned that the "limited resources" of the civil rights movement would be spread too thin; Bayard Rustin claimed black support of the peace movement would be negligible; Ralph Bunche felt King was undertaking an impossible mission in trying to bring the campaign for peace in step with the goals of the civil rights movement.

From the vantage point of history, King's timing could only be regarded as superb. In announcing his opposition to the war, and in characterizing it as a "tragic adventure" which was playing "havoc with the destiny of the entire world," King again forced the white middle class to concede that no movement could dramatically affect the course of government in the United States unless it involved deliberate and restrained aggressiveness, persistent dissent, and even militant confrontation. These were precisely the ingredients of the civil rights struggle in the South in the early 1960s.

As students, professors, intellectuals, clergymen and reformers of every stripe rushed into the movement (in a sense forcing fiery black militants like Stokely Carmichael and Floyd McKissick to surrender their control over antiwar polemics), King turned his attention to the domestic issue which, in his view, was directly related to the Vietnam struggle: the War on Poverty. At one point, he called for a guaranteed family income, he threatened national boycotts, and spoke of disrupting entire cities by nonviolent "camp-ins." With this in mind, he began to draw up plans for a massive march of the poor on Washington, DC itself, envisioning a popular demonstration of unsurpassed intensity and magnitude designed to force Congress and the political parties to recognize and deal with the unseen and ignored masses of desperate and downtrodden Americans.

King's decision to interrupt these plans to lend his support to the Memphis sanitation men's strike was

Dr. Martin Luther King, Jr.

based in part on his desire to discourage violence, as well as to focus national attention on the plight of the poor, unorganized workers of the city. The men were bargaining for little else beyond basic union representation and long-overdue salary considerations. Though he was unable to eliminate the violence which had resulted in the summoning and subsequent departure of the National Guard, King stayed on in Memphis and was in the process of planning for a march which he vowed to carry out in defiance of a federal court injunction if necessary.

Death came for King on the balcony of the black-owned Lorraine Hotel just off Beale Street on the evening of April 4. While standing outside with Jesse Jackson and Ralph Abernathy, a shot rang out. King fell over, struck in the neck by a rifle bullet which left him moribund. At 7:05 P.M. he was pronounced dead at St. Joseph's Hospital. His death caused a wave of violence in major cities across the country. However, King's legacy has lasted much longer than the memories of those post-assassination riots. In 1969, his widow, Coretta Scott King, organized the Martin Luther King Jr. Center for Non-Violent Social Change. Today it stands next to his beloved Ebenezer Baptist Church in Atlanta, and with the surrounding buildings is a national historic landmark under the administration of the National Park Service. His birthday, January 15, is a national holiday, celebrated each year with educational programs, artistic displays, and concerts throughout the United States. The Lorraine Hotel where he was shot is now the National Civil Rights Museum.

Rosa Louise McCauley Parks 1913-

Aide, Civil Rights/Human Rights Activist

Rosa Parks has been called the spark that lit the fire, and the mother of the movement. Her courage to defy custom and law to uphold her personal rights and dignity inspired the African Americans in Montgomery, Alabama, to fight for their rights by staging one of the longest boycotts in history.

Born Rosa Louise McCauley on February 4, 1913, in Tuskegee, Alabama, she was raised by her mother and grandparents in Tuskegee and Montgomery. After attending segregated schools, she went to the all-black Alabama State College. In 1932, she married Raymond Parks, a barber. Both of them worked for the local National Association for the Advancement of Colored People (NAACP) chapter, and Rosa became local NAACP secretary in the 1950s.

On December 1, 1955, as Parks was riding home from work, she was ordered by the bus driver to give up her seat so that a white man might sit. She refused. She was arrested and fined $14. Her case was the last straw for the blacks of Montgomery, as tired of being underclass citizens as Parks was. A city-wide boycott was organized to force the city to desegregate public transportation. A young, unknown minister by the name of Martin Luther King, Jr. became involved, and lectured the nation on the injustice of it all. Blacks, and a few whites, organized peacefully together to transport boycotters to and from work, and they continued, despite opposition from the city and state governments, for 382 days.

When the boycott ended on December 21, 1956, both Parks and King were national heroes, and the Supreme Court had ruled that segregation on city buses was unconstitutional. The mass movement of non-violent social change that was started would last over a decade, and would culminate in the Civil Rights Act of 1964 and the Voting Rights Act of 1965. Because of the harassment Rosa Parks and her family received during and after the boycott, they moved to Detroit, Michigan, in 1957. She found a job with Congressman John Conyers, but continued to be involved in the civil rights struggle. She gave speeches and attended marches and demonstrations. She marched on Washington in 1963, and into

Dr. King addressing a crowd of protestors.

Montgomery in 1965. Even as her life has quieted down, she has received tributes for her dedication and inspiration; in 1980, she received the Martin Luther King, Jr. Nonviolent Peace Prize. As she headed towards retirement from John Conyers office in 1988, she became involved in other activities, like the Rosa and Raymond Parks Institute of Self Development in Detroit, founded in 1987.

Al Sharpton 1954-
Religious Leader, Community Activist, Sports Manager, Marketing, Advertising, Public Relations Manager, Organization Executive/Founder

While being shunned by many middle class African Americans, Al Sharpton draws support from the ranks of the youth and the disenfranchised. Sharpton was born in 1954 in Brooklyn, New York. He went to public schools, graduated from Tilden High School and briefly attended Brooklyn College. At the early age of four, Sharpton began delivering sermons and at the age of 13 he was ordained a Pentecostal minister. During and after high school Sharpton preached in neighborhood churches and went on national religious tours, often with prominent entertainers. Sharpton was soon befriended by a number of well known and influential African Americans including Congressman Adam Clayton Powell, Jr., Jesse Jackson, and singer James Brown.

In 1969, Jackson appointed Sharpton youth director of Operation Breadbasket. Around this same time James Brown made Sharpton one of his bodyguards and soon he was doing promotions for the singer. In 1983, Sharpton married singer Kathy Jordan and soon became involved with fight promoter Don King. Even though Sharpton was promoting boxers and entertainers he had long before put himself in the public spotlight in the role of social activist. In 1971 he founded the National Youth Movement (later called the United African Movement) ostensibly to combat drug use. The movement however soon became a vehicle for Sharpton to draw attention to himself. He urged children to forsake Christmas in favor of a Kwanza celebration and the elderly to protest New York City police tactics.

Sharpton made himself part of the publicity surrounding the Bernard Goetz murder trial (1984), the Howard Beach racial killing (1986), the Twana Brawley debacle (1987) and the Yusef Hawkins-Bensonhurst

Outside of Ebenezer Baptist Church in Atlanta, while King's body had been lying in state.

killing (1989). In 1988, Sharpton was accused of being an FBI informant and passing on information about Don King, reputed organized crime figures and various African American leaders. In 1989 and 1990, he was acquitted on charges of income tax evasion and embezzling National Youth Movement funds. In 1991, Sharpton was briefly hospitalized after being stabbed by a man wielding a pocket knife.

On August 2, 1994, Sharpton announced the formation of a new political party. He aimed at countering the Liberal Party and at reaching black voters that traditional, mainstream parties have ignored. Sharpton unsuccessfully ran for the U.S. Senate as a candidate of his own Freedom Party, even participating in that year's New York Democratic primary.

Leon Howard Sullivan 1922-
Civil Rights/Human Rights Activist

Sullivan was born October 16, 1922, in Charlestown, West Virginia. After being ordained a Baptist minister at the age of 17, Sullivan earned a B.A. from West Virginia State College (1943) and an M.A. from Columbia University (1947). Sullivan also attended the Union Theological Seminary (1945) and earned a D.D. from Virginia Union University.

From 1950 to 1988 Sullivan was the pastor of the Zion Baptist Church in Philadelphia. While there he entered into a lifelong crusade to provide better and expanding job opportunities for African Americans. Sullivan fought racist hiring practices by protest and economic boycott. He provided job training through the Opportunities Industrialization Center. Opening in 1964 with money from a Ford Foundation grant, the Center offered training in electronics, cooking, power-sewing and drafting. Sullivan also founded Zion Investment Associates, which makes available seed money for new African American business ventures. Sullivan has also been associated with Progress Aerospace Inc., General Motors, Mellon Bank, and he is a cofounder of Self-Help.

Sullivan is a recipient of the Russwurm Award (National Publisher's Association, 1963), American Exemplar Medal (1969), Philadelphia Book Award (1966), Philadelphia Fellowship Community Award (1964) and the Franklin D. Roosevelt Four Freedoms Medal (1987).

Al Sharpton (center) leads a demonstration in New York City, 1992.

Upon retiring from the Zion Baptist Church in 1988, Sullivan was made Pastor Emeritus.

William Monroe Trotter 1872-1934

Organization Executive/Founder, Civil Rights/Human Rights Activist

Born in 1872, Trotter became an honor student and Phi Beta Kappa at Harvard and founded the militant newspaper, *Boston Guardian*, in 1901, for the purpose of "propaganda against discrimination." In 1905, Trotter joined W. E. B. Du Bois in founding the Niagara Movement but refused to move with him into the National Association for the Advancement of Colored People because he felt it would be too moderate. Instead, Trotter formed the National Equal Rights League. In 1919 Trotter appeared at the Paris Peace Conference in an unsuccessful effort to have it outlaw racial discrimination. The State Department had denied him a passport to attend, but he had reached Paris nonetheless, by having himself hired as a cook on a ship.

Because of his strident unwillingness to work with established groups, the civil rights movement has been slow to recognize Trotter. But many of his methods were to be adopted in the 1950s, notably his use of nonviolent protest. In 1903, Trotter deliberately disrupted a meeting in Boston at which Booker T. Washington was preaching support of segregation; Trotter's purpose was to be arrested to gain publicity for his militant position. Trotter also led demonstrations against plays and films that glorified the Ku Klux Klan.

Booker Taliafero Washington 1856-1915

Lecturer, Civil Rights/Human Rights Activist, Educational Administrator, Professor, Organization Executive/Founder, Author/Poet

Booker T. Washington was born a slave in Hale's Ford, Virginia, reportedly on April 5, 1856. After emancipation, his family was so poverty stricken that he worked in salt furnaces and coal mines from age nine. Always an intelligent and curious child, he yearned for an education and was frustrated when he could not receive good schooling locally. When he was 16 his parents allowed him to quit work to go to school. They had no money to help him, so he walked 200 miles to attend the Hampton Institute in Virginia and paid his tuition and board there by working as the janitor.

Booker T. Washington

Dedicating himself to the idea that education would raise his people to equality in this country, Washington became a teacher. He first taught in his home town, then at the Hampton Institute, and then in 1881, he founded the Tuskegee Normal and Industrial Institute in Tuskegee, Alabama. As head of the Institute, he traveled the country unceasingly to raise funds from blacks and whites both; soon he became a well-known speaker.

In 1895, Washington was asked to speak at the opening of the Cotton States Exposition, an unprecedented honor for a black man. His Atlanta Compromise speech explained his major thesis, that blacks could secure their constitutional rights through their own economic and moral advancement rather than through legal and political changes. Although his conciliatory stand angered some blacks who feared it would encourage the foes of equal rights, whites approved of his views. Thus his major achievement was to win over diverse elements among southern whites, without whose support the programs he envisioned and brought into being would have been impossible.

In addition to Tuskegee Institute, which still educates many today, Washington instituted a variety of programs for rural extension work, and helped to establish the National Negro Business League. Shortly after the election of President William McKinley in 1896, a movement was set in motion that Washington be named to a cabinet post, but he withdrew his name from consideration, preferring to work outside the political arena. He died on November 14, 1915.

◆ FEDERAL AND STATE CIVIL RIGHTS AGENCIES

Equal Employment Opportunity Commission
1801 L St., NW
Washington, DC 20507
(202)663-4900

United States Commission on Civil Rights
1121 Vermont Ave. NW
Washington, DC 20425
(800)552-6843

Alabama Attorney General's Office
State House
Montgomery, AL 36130
(205)242-7300)

Alaska Human Rights Commission
800 A St., Ste. 202
Anchorage, AK 99501-3669
(907)276-7474

Arizona Attorney General's Office
1275 W. Washington
Phoenix, AZ 85007
(602)542-5025

Arkansas Attorney General's Office
200 Tower Bldg.
323 Center St.
Little Rock, AR 72201-2610
(501)682-2007

California Attorney General
Public Rights Div.
1515 K. Street Suite 511
PO Box 944255
(916)445-9555

California Fair Employment and Housing Department
2014 T. St., Ste. 210
Sacramento, CA 95814-6835
(916)739-4600

Colorado Attorney General's Office
1525 Sherman St., 5th Fl.
Denver, CO 80203
(303)866-3611

Connecticut Attorney General's Office
55 Elm St.
Hartford, CT 06106
(203)566-2026

Delaware Attorney General's Office
Carvel State Office Bldg.
820 N. French St.
Wilmington, DE 19801
(302)577-3047

Florida Attorney General's Office, Legal Affairs Dept.
The Capitol
Tallahassee, FL 32399-1050
(904)488-2526

Georgia Equal Opportunity Commission
710 Cain Tower, Peachtree Ctr.
229 Peachtree St. NE
Atlanta, GA 30303
(404)656-1736

Hawaii Attorney General's Office
425 Queen St.
Honolulu, HI 96813
(808)586-1500

Idaho Human Rights Commission
450 W. State St.
1st Fl. West
Boise, ID 83720
(208)334-2873

Illinois Human Rights Department
100 W. Randolph St.
Ste. 10-100
Chicago, IL 60601
(312)814-6200

Indiana Civil Rights Commission
Indiana Government Ctr. North
100 N. Senate Ave., Rm. N-103
Indianapolis, IN 46204
(317)232-2600

Iowa Human Rights Department
Lucas Bldg
Des Moines, IA 50319
(515)281-5960

Kansas Human Rights Commission
851-S. Landon State Office Bldg.
900 SW Jackson St.
Topeka, KS 66612-1252
(913)296-3206

Kentucky Human Rights Commission
The Heyburn Bldg., 7th Fl.
PO Box 69
Louisville, KY 40202-0069
(502)588-4024

Louisiana Attorney General's Office
Justice Dept.
PO Box 94005
(504)342-7013

Maine Human Rights Commission
State House Sta. 51
Augusta, ME 04333-0051
(207)624-6050

Maryland Human Relations Commission
20 E. Franklin St.
Baltimore, MD 21202-2274
(410)333-1700

Massachusetts Attorney General's Office
1 Ashburton Pl., Rm. 2010
Boston, MA 02108
(617)727-2200

Michigan Attorney General's Office
Law Bldg.
PO Box 30212
Lansing, MI 48909
(517)373-1100

Michigan Civil Rights Department
303 W. Kalamazoo, 4th Fl.
Lansing, MI 48913
(517)335-3165

Minnesota Human Rights Department
500 Bremer Tower
St. Paul, MN 55101
(612)296-5663

Missouri Human Rights Commission
3315 W. Truman Blvd.
PO Box 504
Jefferson City, MO 65102
(314)751-3325

Montana Attorney General's Office
Justice Bldg.
215 N. Sanders
Helena, MT 59620
(406)444-2026

Nebraska Equal Opportunity Commission
PO Box 94934
Lincoln, NE 68509-4934
(402)471-2024

Nevada Equal Rights Commission
1515 E. Tropicana Ave., Ste. 590
Las Vegas, NV 89158
(702)486-7161

New Hampshire Human Rights Commission
163 Loudon Rd.
Concord, NH 03301
(603)271-2767

New Jersey Attorney General's Office
Civil Rights Division
383 W. State St.
CN 089
Trenton, NJ 08625
(609)984-3100

New Mexico Labor Department
Human Rights Division
Aspen Plaza
1596 Pacheco St.
Santa Fe, NM 87502
(505)827-6838

New York Human Rights Division
55 W. 125th St.
New York, NY 10027
(212)870-8400

North Carolina Human Relations Commission
Elks Bldg.
121 W. Jones St.
Raleigh, NC 27603-1368
(919)733-7996

North Dakota Attorney General's Office
State Capitol, 1st Fl.
600 E. Boulevard Ave.
Bismarck, ND 58505
(701)224-2210

Ohio Civil Rights Commission
220 Parsons Ave.
Columbus, OH 43266-0543
(614)466-2785

Oklahoma Human Rights Commission
2101 N. Lincoln Blvd., Rm. 480
Oklahoma City, OK 73105
(405)521-3441

Oregon Attorney General's Office
Justice Department
100 Justice Bldg.
Salem, OR 97310
(503)378-4400

Pennsylvania Human Relations Commission
101 2nd St., Ste. 300
Box 3145
Harrisburg, PA 17015-3145
(717)787-4410

Rhode Island Human Rights Commission
10 Abbott Park Pl.
Providence, RI 02903-3768
(401)277-2661

South Carolina Human Affairs Commission
PO Box 4490
Columbia, SC 29240
(803)253-6336

South Dakota Attorney General's Office
State Capitol
500 E. Capitol Ave.
Pierre, SD 57501-5070
(605)773-3215

Tennessee Human Rights Commission
400 Cornerstone Square Bldg.
530 Church St.
Nashville, TN 37243-0745
(615)7411-5825

Texas Attorney General's Office
Price Daniel, Sr. Bldg.
PO Box 12548
Austin, TX 78711-2548
(512)463-2100

Utah Attorney General's Office
236 State Capitol
Salt Lake City, UT 84114
(801)538-1015

Vermont Attorney General's Office
Pavilion Office Bldg.
109 State St.
Montpelier, VT 05609-1001
(802)828-3171

Virginia Human Rights Council
PO Box 717
Richmond, VA 23206
(804)225-2292

Washington Human Rights Commission
711 S. Capitol Way, Ste. 402
PO Box 42490
Olympia, WA 98504-2490
(206)753-4840

West Virginia Human Rights Commission
1321 Plaza East
Charleston, WV 25301
(304)558-2616

Wisconsin Attorney General's Office
PO Box 7857
Madison, WI 53707-7857
(608)266-1221

Wyoming Attorney General's Office
123 State Capitol
Cheyenne, WY 82002
(307)777-7841

Black Nationalism

Black Nationalism

◆ The Ideology of Black Nationalism ◆ Early Black Nationalism in the United States
◆ Black Nationalism in the Twentieth Century ◆ Black Nationalist and Pan-African Gatekeepers

by William Jeremiah Moses

Black nationalism, in its classic nineteenth-century form, consisted of efforts by African-American groups and individuals to create a sovereign nation-state. The quest for a national homeland expressed a perceived need to demonstrate the capacity of black people for self-government. In its more inclusive form, black nationalism has been indistinguishable from such movements as African Civilizationism, Pan-Negro Nationalism, and Pan-Africanism. Sometimes it has advocated a "back-to-Africa movement," but often it has simply implied moral support for decolonizing Africa and advancing the material and spiritual interests of African peoples everywhere.

◆ THE IDEOLOGY OF BLACK NATIONALISM

The back-to-Africa movement went through several phases of rise and decline, from its resurgence in the 1850s to its apex in the Garvey movement, to its denouement thereafter. The major proponents of classical black nationalism invariably placed religious historicism and teleology at the center of their ideological conceptions or utopian visions. While their goals were political and economic, they usually included a cultural agenda as well—though the cultural concerns of nineteenth-century nationalists were often Eurocentric and are not to be confused with the Negritude movement or the cultural nationalism of the late twentieth century. Black nationalism met the psychological need for a response to the slavery, colonialism, and racism imposed by Europeans and white Americans. In the minds of its adherents, it was the only sensible reaction to the almost universal military, technological, and economic domination of blacks by whites.

Documents expressing the ideology of black nationalism began to appear during the late eighteenth century. As Elie Kedourie has argued, nationalism, the idea that peoples are naturally divided into nations, is European in its origins. The American and French revolutions, and conceptions of the nation-state arising with them, came to dominate political thought, not only in the North Atlantic but also among African and Asian peoples. The 1804 slave revolt and seizure of the state in Haiti, as W. E. B. Du Bois and Eugene Genovese have argued, was both a cause and an effect of rising conceptions of nationalism and manifest destiny in the United States. It was also an inspiration to black nationalism among both the slaves and the free African Americans of the black population in the United States. Literary documents of black nationalism in England and the United States coincided with the revolutions in France or Haiti. Immanuel Geiss has referred to these expressions, typified by *The Interesting Narrative of the Life of Olaudah Equiano or Gustavus Vassa, the African, Written by Himself* (1787), as "proto Pan-Africanism." (For a time Gustavus Vassa believed that the African condition could be improved by repatriating Afro-Europeans in Africa. Although he was to abandon that plan, he remained committed to the destruction of African slavery through the agencies of Christian missionary activity and free trade.)

◆ EARLY BLACK NATIONALISM IN THE UNITED STATES

Early black nationalism in the United States is associated with the activities of two enterprising capitalists in the maritime industries, Paul Cuffe, a New Bedford sea captain, and James Forten, a Philadelphia sail-maker. These two figures combined a bourgeois economic nationalism with a Christian thrust, and hoped to develop Christianity, commerce, and civilization in Africa while providing a homeland for African Americans. Their repatriationist activities were brought to a halt in 1817, when Henry Clay, Andrew Jackson, and other white Americans formed the American Society for Colonizing the Free People of Color in the United States, usually called the American Colonization Society. The American Colonization Society had other prominent slave holders among its leadership, and expressly denied any sympathy for abolition; large numbers of blacks reacted by demonstrating a marked hostility to the society and its aims. Cuffe died shortly after the society's founding, and Forten felt constrained to silence, although he continued to believe that black Americans would "never become a people until they come out from amongst the white people." Those who continued to support repatriation, or who migrated under the auspices of the American Colonization Society, became the objects of extreme vituperation.

Black nationalism and repatriationism were not the same thing, however, and hostility to the American Colonization Society did not always lead to the abandonment of nationalist rhetoric. Maria Stewart referred to herself as an African, but was hostile to the colonization movement. She insisted on her rights as an American, but at the same time denounced the United States with strident jeremiadic rhetoric. Stewart clearly viewed black America as a captive nation, existing in a type of Babylonian captivity, and conceived of African Americans as a people with a national destiny without advocating political separatism or the desire to form a nation-state. In a similar vein, David Walker denounced colonization and emigration with the religious fervor of an Old Testament prophet. Curiously, he insisted on the separate mission and destiny of African Americans as colored citizens of the world, while simultaneously maintaining that black and white Americans could be "a united and happy people."

Early black nationalism in the United States has been associated with Paul Cuffe.

Black nationalist motivations have been attributed to the major slave conspiracies of Gabriel Prosser and Denmark Vesey, who were inspired by the Haitian revolt, and both seem to have had as their goal the creation of a black nation with ties to the Caribbean. For the most part, however, evidence of black nationalism in the United States is found among the free black population of the North. It was in the so-called Free African Societies, which sprang up in the black communities of New York, Boston, and Philadelphia, that a conception of black historical identity and destiny was strongest. During the 1830s and 1840s, black nationalist thinking was associated with religious leadership such as that provided by the bishop of the African Methodist Episcopal Church, Richard Allen, who believed in a special God-given mission for black Americans as a people, but steadfastly opposed the American Colonization Society. Peter Williams, leader of the Afro-American Group of the Episcopal Church in New York, took a more tolerant view of colonization. He eulogized Paul Cuffe and remained friendly with John Russwurm, even after the latter emigrated to Liberia and was burned in effigy by anti-colonization activists.

The flourishing of black nationalism occurred during the 1850s and 1860s. To some degree, the movement owed its rebirth to the passage of the Fugitive Slave Act (1850) and the *Dred Scott v. Sandford* decision (1858). Emigration sentiment, which had been quiescent since the death of Cuffe, experienced a resurgence marked by the calling of several colonization conventions. The leaders of the movement were Henry Highland Garnet and Martin R. Delany, who founded the African Civilization Society in 1858. Edward Wilmot Blyden, the principal nineteenth-century Pan-African theorist, migrated to Liberia in 1850. Alexander Crummell emigrated to Liberia under the auspices of the Domestic and Foreign Missionary Society of the Protestant Episcopal Church in 1853, but eventually became involved with the American Colonization Society. During the early years of the

Civil War, *The Weekly Anglo-African* became the principal journal of the emigration movement.

Emigrationism died out during the peak years of Reconstruction that followed the Civil War, as the black American population strove to take advantage of opportunities presented by emancipation. During the years from 1876 to 1914, a number of back-to-Africa movements were organized. Most prominent among these were the movements under the leadership of Rev. Henry McNeal Turner, an AME Bishop, Rev. Orishatukeh Faduma, a Yoruba man from Barbados, and Chief Alfred C. Sam, a Twi speaker from the Gold Coast. Some scholars have detected black nationalist elements in the Kansas Exodus of the 1870s and the Oklahoma movement that established all-black towns during the 1890s. Fadumah had been a missionary in Oklahoma, which proved an important recruiting ground for Alfred C. Sam.

◆ BLACK NATIONALISM IN THE TWENTIETH CENTURY

Marcus Garvey's revitalization of the emigration movement came at an opportune moment. He arrived in the United States in 1916, shortly after Alfred C. Sam's voyage to the Gold Coast and a few months after the death of Bishop Henry McNeal Turner. His Universal Negro Improvement Association was, according to some speculations, the largest mass movement ever to occur among black Americans. Although Garvey was less successful as a repatriationist than some of his predecessors, he enjoyed tremendous success as a journalist and community organizer. His reputation became a source of great inspiration to many black leaders, and spread among the masses of people in Africa and the Americas.

Martin R. Delany

Cultural nationalism, the exaltation of the "African personality" and the celebration of the contributions of black people to world history, made its appearance in the mid-nineteenth century. Cultural nationalist rhetoric occasionally has been adopted even by persons who have strongly opposed political nationalism. Frederick Douglass shared with Edward Wilmot Blyden an admiration for the ancient Egyptians, whom he believed to be of exactly the same racial type as African Americans. Towards the end of the century, younger scholars, such as W. E. B. Du Bois, were to make much of Egypt, Ethiopia, and Meroe as black contributors to world civilization. Writers such as William H. Ferris and John E. Bruce, who, like Du Bois, were proteges of Alexander Crummell, sought to vindicate the black race and to popularize the notion that black peoples of the upper Nile were the progenitors of civilization. The height of the vindicationist school was reached in the writings of Joel Augustus Rogers, sometime contributor to Marcus Garvey's paper, the *Negro World*.

During the 1930s, new versions of cultural nationalism began to focus on the importance of West Africa, in addition to that of ancient Egypt. This development was partially due to the Negritude movement among Francophone intellectuals, but also due to the "Jazz Age" interest in Africa among white artists and social scientists. The researches of Leo Frobenius, the German scholar, kindled the interest of Du Bois, Aime Cesaire, and Leopold Senghor in the cultures of "tribal" Africa. The growing interest of European artists such as Picasso and Modigliani in primitivism and African cultural expression led black Americans to a revaluation of their folk heritage and its African roots. The new-found respectability of jazz after its acceptance in continental Europe was another factor in the rise of black cultural nationalism. The ideology of scientific relativism in the writings of Franz Boas and Melville Herskovits, which stressed cultural relativism and a respect for "primitive" cultures also helped to make an interest in sub-Saharan Africa fashionable.

After the deportation of Marcus Garvey in 1925, black nationalism went into decline, as John Henrik Clarke

Although Garvey was less successful as a repatriationist than some of his predecessors, he enjoyed tremendous success as a journalist and community organizer.

and other scholars have noted. The search for a black nationality was kept alive by such religious groups as the Black Jews of Harlem, the Moorish Science Temple, and the Nation of Islam, which was under the leadership of the Honorable Elijah Muhammad. The rise of Malcolm X, a follower of Elijah Muhammad, did much to popularize black nationalism with young radical intellectuals during the early 1960s. After his split with Elijah Muhammad, Malcolm X seemed to abandon traditional black nationalist separatism as well, embracing socialism and, at the same time, his white Muslim brethren. Black nationalist attitudes persisted in some radical groups during the late 1960s, but seldom showed any relationship to or awareness of the black nationalist traditions of the nineteenth century. In recent years, cultural black nationalists such as Molefi K. Asante have shown a renewed interest in black nationalist intellectual history, especially as it relates to figures like Edward Wilmot Blyden and Marcus Garvey.

In the twentieth century, the search for a black nationality was kept alive by such religious groups as the Nation of Islam.

◆ BLACK NATIONALIST AND PAN-AFRICAN GATEKEEPERS

Edward Wilmot Blyden (1832-1912)
Black Nationalist, Repatriationist

Although he was not an American, Edward Blyden had a great influence on American Pan-African philosophy. As a scholar he wrote at great length about blacks in Africa and America, and about Christianity and Islam. He also held many different political and diplomatic offices in Liberia where he tried to put his beliefs into action.

Blyden was born in St. Thomas in the West Indies in 1832. When he was twelve, a white pastor undertook his education, encouraging him to become a minister. When he was eighteen he went to America, but was unable to find a seminary that would accept a black student. Instead, under the sponsorship of the New York Colonization Society, he went to Liberia to study at the new Alexander High School in Monrovia. Seven years later, he became the principal of the school.

Throughout his adult life, Blyden had two concurrent careers. He was a teacher and scholar. As a writer and editor, he constantly defended his race, championed the achievements of other blacks, attacked slavery, and advocated the repatriation of blacks in Africa. As a teacher, he held many prominent posts, including professor of classics (1862-1871) and president of Liberia College (1880-1884). At the same time, Blyden was also a politician and diplomat in Liberia, holding many different offices. He was secretary of state from 1864 to 1866, minister of the interior from 1880 to 1882, minister to Britain from 1877 to 1878 and again in 1892, and minister plenipotentiary to London and Paris in 1905.

Blyden traveled to America eight times. In 1861, he was commissioned by the Liberian government to interest Americans in a Liberian education. He returned again the following year to recruit African-American immigrants to Africa. His last visit in 1895 was in hopes of furthering racial accommodation in the south so that racial problems in America would not travel to Africa with new emigrants.

Because of his own religious training, Blyden was interested in Islam as a religion for Africans. Between 1901 and 1906, he was director of education in Sierra Leone. He studied both Christianity and Islam extensively, and summed up his views in an influential book,

Elijah Muhammad being interviewed by Buzz Anderson.

Christianity, Islam and the Negro Race. After his death in 1912, his funeral was attended by large numbers of both Christians and Muslims.

Elaine Brown (1943-)
Political Activist, Author

When Huey Newton, the founder of the Black Panther Party, fled the country in 1974 on a murder charge, he appointed Brown as his successor. In the mid-1960s, Brown became involved with the Black Congress, a group of African American organizations in the Los Angeles area that served the needs of black people. By 1967, Brown had become acquainted with the Black Panther Party, and in 1968, joined the Southern California chapter, agreeing to live by the strict Black Panther code.

The Black Panther program combined revolutionary rhetoric, violent actions in the name of self-defense and a strong commitment to building and strengthening black communities. The last tenet particularly appealed to Brown, who saw the party as a way of unifying the African American community. But the support of violent actions drew the attention of the FBI.

By the early 1970s, much of the party leadership had been killed or jailed in police battles. In 1974, with the expulsion of cofounder Bobby Seale, Brown became chairperson of the Black Panther Party. Later that same year, she was appointed the minister of defense by Huey Newton after he fled to Cuba to escape criminal prosecution.

During Brown's tenure as head of the party, she sought legitimate channels of power. She guided the Black Panther Party's efforts to electing an African American mayor in the city of Oakland, California. The party registered 90,000 black Democrats and secured the endorsement of California Governor Jerry Brown for Black Panther candidate Lionel Wilson. Wilson won, becoming the first black mayor of Oakland in 1976.

With Wilson in as mayor, Newton, who was acquitted of his crime, was allowed to come home. All the progress Brown had made, in the area of women's rights in the Black Panther Party and in the political arena, had become inconsequential as Newton focused on supporting the brothers in the party. The brothers quickly withdrew their support of Brown, ending their years of frustration at having been led by a progressive woman. For her safety, and the safety of her daughter, Brown

Black Muslim rally, 1961.

Edward Wilmont Blyden

left Oakland and immigrated to France in 1977, where she now lives just outside of Paris. In 1992 she penned the autobiography, *A Taste of Power: A Black Woman's Story.*

Alexander Crummell (1819-1898)
Black Nationalist, Repatriationist, Minister

Crummell was born in New York City on March 3, 1819. He was descended from African royalty, as his paternal grandfather was the son of a West African ruler. Crummell began his schooling at the Mulberry Street School in New York City. In 1831 he began attending high school but in 1835 transferred to a school founded by abolitionists in Canaan, New Hampshire. The school however was destroyed by a mob of angry townspeople and Crummell began attending the Oneida Institute in Whitesboro, New York, where he stayed for three years. He later studied in Boston and was ordained into the Episcopal Church in 1844. In 1847 he went to England and studied at Queens College, Cambridge, from 1851 to 1853 where he was awarded an A.B. degree.

Crummell then spent twenty years in Liberia and Sierra Leone where he served as professor of Mental and Moral Science at the College of Liberia. In 1873 he returned to St. Mary's Mission in Washington, DC and soon founded St. Luke's Protestant Episcopal Church where he spent his last twenty-two years. In 1897 he was instrumental in the founding of the American Negro Academy.

Crummell published many collections of his essays and sermons including *Future of Africa* (1862), *Greatness of Christ* (1882), and *Africa and America* (1892). Crummell died on September 10, 1898, at Point Pleasant, New York.

Paul Cuffe (1759-1817)
Black Nationalist, Repatriationist, Entrepreneur

Cuffe was born January 17, 1759, on Cuttyhunk Island near New Bedford, Massachusetts. He was the son of Cuffe Slocum, a freed slave and Ruth Moses, a Wampanoag Indian.

By the time Cuffe was sixteen he was earning a living as a sailor on a whaling vessel. After making numerous voyages he was captured by the British but later released. He studied arithmetic and navigation but soon returned to the sea. In 1795 he had his own ship, *Ranger*, and in eleven years he had become a landholder and owner of numerous other sailing vessels.

Besides being a merchant seaman, Cuffe was also a civil rights activist. He discarded his father's slave surname and took his father's Christian first name in its place. He filed suffrage complaints in the Massachusetts' court and although unsuccessful, his court actions laid the groundwork for later civil rights legislation.

Cuffe was also a believer in free blacks voluntarily returning to Africa. In 1811 aboard his ship *Traveller* he sailed to Sierra Leone where he founded the Friendly Society which helped blacks return to Africa. In 1815 he sailed with thirty-eight colonists for Africa. It was to be his last voyage however, for he died September 9, 1817.

Martin Robins Delany (1812-1885)

Black Nationalist, Repatriationist

Born in Charles Town, West Virginia, in 1812, editor, author, physician, abolitionist and black nationalist Martin Delany received his first education from a book peddler who also served as an itinerant teacher. Since blacks in the south were forbidden to learn to read, when others found out he could read, the family was forced to flee north to Pennsylvania so that their children could continue to study. At the age of nineteen, he left home to seek further education. He studied with a young divinity student and a white doctor for a time.

As an adult, he became involved in anti-slavery reform, and the literacy movement. He began to publish *The Mystery*, a weekly newspaper devoted to news of the anti-slavery movement. When it folded after only a year of publication, Delany became co-editor of the *North Star*, a newspaper started by Frederick Douglass.

In 1848, Delany quit the *North Star* to pursue his medical studies. After being rejected on account of his race from several prominent Pennsylvania medical schools, he was able to attend the Harvard Medical School for a year before he was expelled from there due to his race. While he did not receive his degree, he did learn enough to practice medicine the rest of his life. In the 1850s, he became something of a local legend when he saved many lives during a fierce cholera epidemic in Pittsburgh.

The years following medical school were a grave disappointment to Delany, for blacks in America continued to be treated inhumanely no matter how hard he worked against slavery. He became an ardent black nationalist and recommended emigration to establish an independent colony for African Americans in South America or Africa. He wrote prolifically on the subject, held several national conventions, and set out on an exploratory expedition to Africa.

After the Emancipation Proclamation of 1863, Delany met with President Abraham Lincoln to discuss the establishment of black regiments in the army. Lincoln commissioned him as the first black major in the United States Army.

After the Civil War, Delany continued to work with reconstructionists trying to get fair treatment for newly freed slaves, still advocating emigration. He continued to pursue his scholarship, and in 1879 published his *Principal of Ethnology: The Origin of Races and Color* in which he discussed the role of black people in the world's civilization. He died in 1885, before he was able to actually move to Africa himself.

Louis Farrakhan (1933-)

Black Nationalist, Nation of Islam National Minister

Born in New York City in 1933, Louis Farrakhan (then known as Louis Eugene Walcott) was an outstanding student at Boston English High School and then attended (but did not earn a degree at) Winston-Salem Teacher's College. Farrakhan was an excellent musician; he played the violin and was a calypso singer. It was as a singer that he earned his livelihood prior to converting to Elijah Muhammad's Nation of Islam in the 1950s. He quickly worked his way up to a leadership position, becoming the minister of the Boston mosque. He loudly denounced Malcolm X after the latter split with Elijah Muhammad in 1963. He soon assumed leadership of the Harlem mosque which Malcolm had previously led. After Elijah Muhammad's death in 1975, he briefly supported Muhammad's son and designated successor, Warith Muhammad, as leader of the Nation of Islam. Shortly after Warith Muhammad began accepting whites as members within the Nation of Islam, now renamed the World Community of Al-Islam in the West, Farrakhan split from him and established a rival organization with about 10,000 members.

Farrakhan's vigorous support for Jesse Jackson's presidential candidacy in 1984 quickly became an issue after Farrakhan made several controversial statements, most notably calling Judaism a "gutter religion." Overshadowed in the controversy was the involvement of Nation of Islam leaders in American electoral politics for the first time. Previously, Black Muslims had generally followed Elijah Muhammad's counsel not to vote or to take part in political campaigns.

In January 1995 Qubilah Bahiyah Shabazz, daughter of slain black nationalist leader Malcolm X, was arrested and charged with trying to hire an FBI informant to kill Farrakhan, who some believe was involved in the 1965 assassination of her father. Farrakhan publicly defended Shabazz, claiming that the charges were an

Louis Farrakhan

FBI attempt to entrap her. On May 1, 1995, Shabazz avoided a trial and possible prison sentence by accepting responsibility for the plot. The court ordered her to seek psychiatric counseling, enter a drug and alcohol treatment program, and to obtain a steady job.

On October 16, 1995, African American men from across the United States convened in Washington D.C. for the Million Man March, which was organized by Farrakhan. Billed as a "holy day of atonement and reconciliation," marchers were urged to make a commitment to improve themselves, their families, and their communities. Those who could not attend the march were urged to stay home from work and avoid spending money at businesses as a show of solidarity with the marchers. Farrakhan closed the march with a two-hour speech in which he condemned the doctrine of white supremacy and claimed that there are still "two Americas, one black, one white, separate and unequal." He also challenged the marchers to return home and work to make their communities "safe and decent places to live."

Farrakhan embarked on a controversial 18-nation tour of Africa and the Middle East in early 1996. During the tour, he visited Iran and Libya, nations which the United States government believes support international terrorism. Although he claimed that the trip was designed to promote peace and reconciliation, Farrakhan was widely criticized by U.S. officials for several anti-American statements he made while overseas.

James Forten (1766-1842)
Black Nationalist, Entrepreneur

Forten was born of free African-American parents in Philadelphia on September 2, 1766. He studied at a Quaker school, but at the age of fifteen, he quit to serve as a powder boy aboard the privateer *Royal Louis* during the American Revolution. He was captured by the British and held prisoner for seven months. He eventually spent a year in England where he was introduced to abolitionist philosophy.

Upon returning to America he was apprenticed to a sailmaker, but by 1786 he was foreman, and, in 1798, he became owner of the company. The business prospered and in 1832 employed forty white and African American workers.

By the 1830s Forten had become active in the abolitionist movement and was a strong opponent of African colonization. He became a noted pamphleteer, a nineteenth century form of social activism and was an early fund-raiser for William Lloyd Garrison's *The Liberator.*

Forten was president and founder of the American Moral Reform Society and was active in the American Anti-Slavery Society. He was a vigorous opponent of northern implementation of the Fugitive Slave Act of 1793. Forten died in Philadelphia on March 4, 1842.

Marcus Garvey (1887-1940)
Black Nationalist, Pan-African Theorist

Born in St. Ann's Bay, Jamaica, on August 17, 1887, Garvey was the youngest of eleven children. Garvey moved to Kingston at the age of fourteen, found work in a printshop, and became acquainted with the abysmal living conditions of the laboring class. He quickly involved himself in social reform, participating in the first Printers' Union strike in Jamaica in 1907 and in setting up the newspaper *The Watchman*. Leaving the island to earn money to finance his projects, he visited Central and South America, amassing evidence that black people everywhere were victims of discrimination.

Garvey returned to Jamaica in 1911 and began to lay the groundwork of the Universal Negro Improvement Association, to which he was to devote his life. Undaunted by lack of enthusiasm for his plans, Garvey left for England in 1912 in search of additional financial backing. While there, he met a Sudanese-Egyptian journalist, Duse Mohammed Ali. While working for Ali's publication *African Times and Oriental Review*, Garvey began to study the history of Africa—particularly, the exploitation of black peoples by colonial powers. He read Booker T. Washington's *Up From Slavery*, which advocated black self-help.

In 1914 Garvey organized the Universal Negro Improvement Association and its coordinating body, the African Communities League. In 1920 the organization held its first convention in New York. The convention opened with a parade down Harlem's Lenox Avenue. That evening, before a crowd of 25,000, Garvey outlined his plan to build an African nation-state. In New York City his ideas attracted popular support, and thousands enrolled in the UNIA. He began publishing the newspaper *The Negro World* and toured the United States preaching black nationalism to popular audiences. In a matter of months, he had founded over thirty UNIA branches and launched some ambitious business ventures, notably the Black Star Shipping Line.

In the years following the organization's first convention, the UNIA began to decline in popularity. With the Black Star Line in serious financial difficulties, Garvey promoted two new business organizations—the African Communities League and the Negro Factories Corporation. He also tried to salvage his colonization scheme by sending a delegation to appeal to the League of Nations for transfer to the UNIA of the African colonies taken from Germany during World War I.

Financial betrayal by trusted aides and a host of legal entanglements (based on charges that he had used the U.S. mail to defraud prospective investors) eventually led to Garvey's imprisonment in Atlanta Federal Penitentiary for a five-year term. In 1927 his half-served sentence was commuted, and he was deported to Jamaica by order of President Calvin Coolidge.

Garvey then turned his energies to Jamaican politics, campaigning on a platform of self-government, minimum wage laws, and land and judicial reform. He was soundly defeated at the polls, however, because most of his followers did not have the necessary voting qualifications.

In 1935 Garvey left for England where, in near obscurity, he died on June 10, 1940, in a cottage in West Kensington.

Malcolm X (El-Hajj Malik El-Shabazz) (1925-1965)
Black Nationalist

Malcolm X was one of the most fiery and controversial blacks of the twentieth century.

Born Malcolm Little in Omaha, Nebraska on May 19, 1925, Malcolm was the son of a Baptist minister, who was an avid supporter of Marcus Garvey's Universal Negro Improvement Association. While living in Omaha, the family was often harassed—at one point the family's house was set afire. In 1929 the family moved to Lansing, Michigan. While in Michigan, Malcolm's father was killed; his body severed in two by a streetcar and his head smashed. In his autobiography, written with Alex Haley, Malcolm asserted that his father may have been killed by members of the Ku Klux Klan. His mother, stricken by the death of her husband and the demands of providing for the family, was committed to a mental institution.

Leaving school after the eighth grade, Malcolm made his way to New York, working for a time as a waiter at Smalls Paradise in Harlem. Malcolm began selling and using drugs, turned to burglary, and, in 1946, was sentenced to a ten-year prison term on burglary charges.

While in prison Malcolm became acquainted with the Black Muslim sect, headed by Elijah Muhammad, and was quickly converted. Following his parole in 1952, he soon became an outspoken defender of black Muslim doctrines, accepting the basic argument that evil was an inherent characteristic of the "white man's Christian world."

Unlike Muhammad, Malcolm sought publicity, making provocative and inflammatory statements to predominantly white civic groups and college campus audiences. Branding white people "devils," he spoke bitterly of a philosophy of vengeance and "an eye for an eye." When, in 1963, he characterized the Kennedy assassination as a case of "chickens coming home to roost," he was suspended from the Black Muslim movement by Elijah Muhammad.

Disillusioned with Elijah Muhammad's teachings, Malcolm formed his own organizations, the Organization of Afro-American Unity and the Muslim Mosque Inc. In 1964 he made a pilgrimage to Islam's holy city, Mecca, and adopted the name El-Hajj Malik El Shabazz. He also adopted views that were not popular with other black nationalists, including the idea that not all whites were evil and that blacks could make gains by working through established channels.

As a result of Malcolm's new views, he became the victim of death threats. On February 14, 1965, his home was firebombed; his wife and children escaped unharmed.

Malcolm X

A week later, on the 21st, Malcolm was shot and killed at the Audubon Ballroom in Harlem, while preparing to speak. Three of the men arrested were later identified as members of the Nation of Islam.

Malcolm X had a profound influence on both blacks and whites. Many blacks responded to a feeling that he was a man of the people, experienced in the ways of the street rather than the pulpit or the college campus, which traditionally had provided the preponderance of black leaders. Many young whites responded to Malcolm's blunt, colorful language and unwillingness to retreat in the face of hostility.

The memory and image of Malcolm X has changed as much after his death as his own philosophies changed during his life. At first thought to be a violent fanatic, he is now understood as an advocate of self-help, self-defense, and education; as a philosopher and pedagogue, he succeeded in integrating history, religion, and mythology to establish a framework for his ultimate belief in world brotherhood and in human justice. Faith, in his view, was a prelude to action; ideas were feckless without policy. At least three books published since his death effectively present his most enduring thoughts. In 1992, a monumental film by Spike Lee, based on Malcolm's autobiography, renewed interest and understanding in the meaning of the life and death of Malcolm X.

Elijah Muhammad (1897-1975)
Black Nationalist, Nation of Islam Spiritual Leader

Elijah Muhammad was born Elijah Poole in Sandersville, Georgia, on October 10, 1897. His father, a Baptist preacher, had been a slave.

As a boy, Elijah worked at various jobs involving manual labor. At the age of twenty-six, he moved with his wife and two children (he was to have eight children in all) to Detroit. There in 1930, Poole met Fard Muhammad, also known as W.D. Fard, who had founded the Lost-Found Nation of Islam. Poole soon became Fard's chief assistant and in 1932 went to Chicago where he established the Nation of Islam's Temple, Number Two, which soon became the largest. In 1934, he returned to Detroit. When Fard disappeared in that year, political and theological rivals accused Poole of foul play. He returned to Chicago where he organized his own movement, in which Fard was deified as Allah and Elijah (Poole) Muhammad became known as Allah's Messenger. This movement soon became known as the Black Muslims.

During World War II, Elijah Muhammad expressed support for Japan, on the basis of its being a nonwhite

Elijah Muhammad

country, and was jailed for sedition. The time Muhammad served in prison was probably significant in his later, successful attempts to convert large numbers of black prison inmates, including Malcolm X, to the Nation of Islam. During the 1950s and 1960s, the Nation grew under Muhammad's leadership. Internal differences between Muhammad and Malcolm X, followed by the break between the two men and Malcolm's assassination, for which three Black Muslim gunmen were convicted, provided a great deal of unfavorable media coverage, but this did not slow the growth of the movement. In the late 1960s and early 1970s, Elijah Muhammad moderated the Nation's criticism of whites without compromising its message of black integrity. When Muhammad died on February 25, 1975, the Nation was an important religious, political, and economic force among America's blacks, especially in this country's major cities.

Elijah Muhammad was not original in his rejection of Christianity as the religion of the oppressor. Noble Drew Ali and the Black Jews had arrived at this conclusion well before him. But Muhammad was the most successful salesman for this brand of African American religion. Thus he was able to build the first strong black religious group in the United States that appealed primarily to the unemployed and underemployed city dweller, and ultimately to some in the black middle class. In addition, his message on the virtues of being black was explicit and uncompromising, and he sought with at least a little success to bolster the economic independence of African Americans by establishing schools and businesses under the auspices of the Nation of Islam.

Khalid Abdul Muhammad (1951?-)
Nation of Islam Spokesperson

Muhammad was born Harold Moore Vann in Houston, Texas, in the early 1950s. Raised by an aunt, he excelled in academics and athletics as a youth and graduated from high school in 1966. He spent then four years at Dillard University, where his attendance at a speech given by Nation of Islam figure Louis Farrakhan in 1967 changed his life. He became one of Farrakhan's original security personnel and soon changed his name to Khalid Abdul Muhammad as he immersed himself in the tenets of the faith.

After the death of longtime Nation of Islam leader Elijah Muhammad, the organization fell into disarray and Khalid Muhammad relocated to Uganda to work with black nationalist leader Idi Amin. He returned to the United States upon learning that Farrakhan was reviving the Nation of Islam, and by the late 1970s was a minister of the group's Los Angeles mosque. He later headed congregations in New York City and Atlanta, while continuing to play an important role in the Fruit of Islam, the security team assigned to protect the outspoken Farrakhan. In 1988 Muhammad was charged with the fraudulent use of a Social Security number to obtain a mortgage and spent nine months in prison, despite Farrakhan's appeal to the judicial authorities for leniency.

After his release, Muhammad became supreme captain of the Fruits of Islam and in 1991 became Farrakhan's national assistant, a position of public prominence once held by Farrakhan himself as well as Malcolm X. Muhammad's speeches soon attracted renewed interest in the Nation of Islam, especially from among prominent figures in rap music. His discourses often promote an independent nation for people of African descent, one free from what he sees as dead-end dreams of integration with the white community; he also points out that millions of blacks have died over the centuries at the hands of white oppression, a trend which continues to modern times in the worst sectors of urban America. A 1993 oration given in Union, New Jersey, however, landed Muhammad in trouble with the Nation of Islam for his fiery pronouncements on black-white relations and what Jewish leaders later denounced as anti-Semitic remarks. Muhammad was demoted shortly after by

Farrakhan, but still continues his work as a lecturer and activist.

Henry McNeal Turner (1834-1915)
Black Nationalist, Repatriationist, Minister

Henry McNeal Turner was born on February 1, 1834, near Abbeville, South Carolina, of free parents. He was ordained a minister in the African Methodist Episcopal Church in 1853 and bishop in 1880. In 1863 Turner became the first African-American Army chaplain. He was also president of Morris Brown College for twelve years.

Turner was a leading advocate of repatriation. In 1876 he was elected vice president of the American Colonization Society. He made several trips to Africa and lectured throughout world.

Turner was convinced that blacks had no future in America. Instead, he felt that God had brought blacks to the New World as a means of spreading Christianity and preparing them to redeem Africa. Turner edited and published several papers, including *Voice of Missions* and *Voice of the People*, in which he advocated black colonization of Africa. Turner died on May 8, 1915.

Robert F. Williams (1925–)
Civil Rights and Political Activist

When Robert F. Williams was ten years old, he saw a grinning policeman drag a black woman by her heels down the street, her dress over her hips, her back scraping the pavement. The impression this must have made on the young boy stayed with him into his adult years, adding fuel to his lifelong political activism.

Henry McNeal Turner

In 1956, in Williams's hometown of Monroe, North Carolina, he was elected president of the Monroe NAACP. The organization's membership had dwindled to six. Williams went out and recruited working class people and the unemployed to become members, as opposed to the NAACP's practice of appealing to middle and upper-class professionals. The membership grew to become more militant than past groups had been.

Williams then targeted institutions in Monroe for desegregation, first being the County Library. It was desegregated without protest. Williams then tried to desegregate Monroe's municipal swimming pool, which didn't happen. In response, Williams led groups of black youths on sit-ins and other organized protests.

The Ku Klux Klan retaliated against Williams and the activities of Monroe's NAACP by holding rallies attended by several thousand members. When Monroe's police refused to quell the sometimes violent rallies, Williams encouraged a program of armed self-defense by Monroe's black community, which proved effective in reducing the number of midnight rides by the Klan.

In 1959, responding to the unjust acquittal in Monroe of the attempted rape by a white man on a pregnant black woman, Williams exhorted the black men and women on the courthouse steps with his legendary statement: "Since the federal government will not bring a halt to lynching in the South, and since the so-called courts lynch our people legally, if it's necessary to stop lynching with lynching, then we must be willing to resort to that method. We must meet violence with violence." The next day the national office of the NAACP suspended Williams from office for six months. Later in 1959, through a grave misunderstanding, Williams was indicted for kidnapping. He became a fugitive by the FBI, fleeing to Cuba with his family.

Bringing the Monroe chapter into the center of a national controversy did not hurt Williams's local popularity in the African American community, as he was reelected president of Monroe's NAACP chapter in 1960. From Cuba, Williams produced a revolutionary radio program, *Radio Free Dixie*, and produced a Cuba edition of the *Crusader*. In 1966, Williams sought refuge in the People's Republic of China. In 1968, Williams published a pamphlet, "Listen Brother!" hoping to dissuade African American servicemen to stop fighting against their Asiatic "dark-skinned brothers."

In 1968, a group of African Americans, dedicated to establishing a separate black nation within the United States, formed the revolutionary Marxist–Leninist Republic of New Africa (RNA). The RNA elected Williams as its president in exile. In 1969, the U.S. embassy granted Williams a passport to return to the United States, which he did later that year. Disillusioned with the RNA's prevalent internal struggles, he resigned as its president in December of 1969.

National Organizations

9

National Organizations

◆ A Brief History ◆ Organization Leaders ◆ National Organizations

In a dispute between the National Association for the Advancement of Colored People and the state of Alabama, Justice Harlen of the United States Supreme Court, pointed out the significance of association membership, claiming that it is through associations that individuals have sought "to make more effective the expression of their own views." Associations are one of the largest and most influential forces in the United States and have played an important part in the economic, social, and educational development of African Americans; organizations have been crucial in developing and disseminating information, ensuring representation for private interests, and promoting social and policy objectives.

◆ A BRIEF HISTORY

Early Black Organizations

Due to restrictive ordinances and limited tolerance by whites, prior to the eighteenth century only the most informal and limited assembling of blacks was permitted. Most often meeting as religious assemblies, African Americans were forced to meet secretly, in small numbers. Thus the very first black organizations to exist in the United States cannot definitively be identified.

The Free African Society , organized in Philadelphia in 1787, has been generally accepted as the first African American organization in the United States. Founded by Methodist ministers Richard Allen and Absalom Jones, the Free African Society served as an important source of political consciousness and welfare for blacks throughout the country, combining economic and medical aid for poor blacks with support of abolition and sub rosa communication with blacks in the South.

The abolitionist movement of the nineteenth century, produced numerous organizations concerned with issues of importance to African Americans, including the American Colonization Society (founded in 1816), the New England Anti-Slavery Society (founded in 1832), and the American Anti-Slavery Society (founded in 1833). Although most of these organizations were dominated by whites, black leaders, including Paul Cuffe and Frederick Douglass played an active role in the movement and in anti-slavery organizations of the time.

During the late nineteenth and early twentieth centuries a great many black organizations came into existence; the thrust of most of these groups was toward education, betterment, and religious training. In 1895 the National Medical Association was founded to further the interests of black physicians, pharmacists, and nurses; Mary McLeod Bethune organized the National Association of Colored Women in 1896; and in 1900 the National Negro Business League was formed to promote commercial development.

The Niagara Movement

The Niagara Movement of 1905, marked a turning point in African American history. This new organization, founded by a group of black intellectuals—headed by W. E. B. Du Bois.

The Niagara Movement, however, suffered from weak finances and a policy which restricted membership to black intellectuals. In 1909 the Niagara Movement was succeeded by a new organization—one which would later become the National Association for the Advancement of Colored People.

National Association for the Advancement of Colored People

The new organization was largely the brainchild of three people: William English Walling, a white Southerner who feared that racists would soon carry "the race war to the North"; Mary White Ovington, a wealthy young white woman who had attended the 1905 meeting

W. E. B. Dubois

of the Niagara group as a reporter for the *New York Evening Post* and had experience with conditions in the black ghettos of New York City; and Dr. Henry Moskowitz, a New York social worker. The trio proposed that a conference be called "for the discussion of present evils, the voicing of protests, and the renewal of the struggle for civil and political liberty." The three-day conference, held May 30 through June 1, was followed by four meetings, the results of which were an increase in membership and the selection of an official name—the National Negro Committee. In 1910 the organization adopted its present name and was incorporated in New York state; by 1914 the association had established some 50 branches throughout the country.

Over the years, the organization has attempted to better the condition of African Americans through litigation, legislation, and education; *Crisis* magazine, edited by W. E. B. Du Bois, became its chief vehicle for the dissemination of information. Perhaps its most significant victory was won in 1954 when the historic *Brown v. Board of Education of Topeka* case threw out the "separate but equal" doctrine established by the Supreme Court in *Plessy v. Ferguson* in 1896 and eliminated segregation in public education.

NAACP Legal Defense and Educational Fund, Inc.

Established in 1939 by the National Association for the Advancement of Colored People, the NAACP Legal Defense and Educational Fund maintained its own board, program, staff, office, and budget for some 20 years. It has served in the forefront of legal assaults against discrimination and segregation and has an outstanding record of victories. In addition to its litigation, the Legal Defense Fund provides scholarships and training for young lawyers, advises lawyers on legal trends and decisions, and monitors federal programs.

Originally for tax purposes, the NAACP Legal Defense Fund had been maintained as a separate arm of the NAACP, until it officially was divorced from its parent organization in 1959. Following the separation of the organizations, a dispute over identity and the use of the parent organization's name erupted. The National Association for the Advancement of Colored People sued the NAACP Legal Defense Fund for name infringement. However, after several months of legal wrangling, a federal court ruled that the LDF could keep NAACP in its name, since the NAACP was its parent organization.

Organizations Concerned with Urban Problems

During the early part of the twentieth century several organizations concerned with the plight of urban blacks emerged. In 1906, at the urging of William H. Baldwin, president of the Long Island Railroad, a group of blacks and whites met for the purpose of studying the employment needs of African Americans. This group, known as the Committee for the Improvement of Industrial Conditions Among Negroes in New York, studied the racial aspects of the labor market (particularly the attitudes and policies of employers and unions) and sought to find openings for qualified African Americans.

At the same time, the League for the Protection of Colored Women was established to provide similar services for black women in New York and Philadelphia arriving from various parts of the South. These women, who often had no friends or relatives in the North, often fell prey to unscrupulous employment agencies which led them into low wage jobs.

A third organization, the Committee on Urban Conditions Among Negroes, appeared in 1910. It was organized by Ruth Standish Baldwin, widow of the former Long Island Railroad president, and Dr. George Edmond Haynes, one of only three trained black social workers in the country and the first black person to receive a doctorate from Columbia University. Haynes was named as the first executive secretary of the new agency. A year later the organization merged with the Committee for the Improvement of Industrial Conditions Among

An early NAACP office.

Negroes in New York and the National League for the Protection of Colored Women to form the National League on Urban Conditions Among Negroes. That name was later shortened to the now-familiar National Urban League.

From the outset, the organization focused on the social and economic needs of blacks, seeking training, improved housing, health, recreation, and job assistance for blacks. The organizational model that the League had established in New York City attracted attention and soon affiliates were formed in various cities across the country.

A major goal of the National Urban League and its affiliates was to broaden economic opportunities for African Americans. It was not until the 1960s when Whitney M. Young, Jr. became its new leader that the League began to emerge as a force in the civil rights struggle.

Leadership Conference on Civil Rights

The Leadership Conference on Civil Rights was organized in 1950 by A. Philip Randolph, Roy Wilkins, and Arnold Aronson to implement the historic report of President Harry S. Truman's Committee on Civil Rights, *"To Secure These Rights."* Beginning with only 30 organizations, the conference has grown in numbers, scope, and effectiveness, and has been responsible for coordinating the campaigns that have resulted in the passage of the civil rights legislation of the 1950s and 1960s, including the Civil Rights Act of 1957, the Civil Rights Act of 1960, and the Civil Rights Act of 1964, the Voting Rights Act of 1965, and the Fair Housing Act of 1968 (also known as the Civil Rights Act of 1968).

The Leadership Conference on Civil Rights currently consists of approximately 157 national organizations representing minorities, women, major religious groups, the handicapped, the aged, labor, and minority businesses and professions. These organizations speak for a substantial portion of the population and together comprise one of the most broad based coalition in the nation.

Southern Christian Leadership Conference

Following the arrest of Rosa Parks, who had refused to give up her seat on a public bus, the Reverends Dr. Martin Luther King, Jr. and Ralph Abernathy organized the Montgomery Improvement Association in 1955 to

Black women looking for work in Northern cities often fell prey to unscrupulous employment practices and to low wage jobs.

coordinate a citywide bus boycott. The success of the boycott led to the creation of a new organization.

This new organization, consisting mainly of black ministers, met at the Ebenezer Baptist Church in January 1957 and elected Dr. King as its first president. Initially called the Southern Negro Leaders Conference, and later the Southern Leadership Conference, the Southern Christian Leadership Conference grew to become one of the most influential and effective of all the civil rights organizations.

Organizations and the Court

Although public and private associations of all kinds have traditionally flourished in this country, it has not always been an easy road for organizations for blacks and other minorities. The freedom of association—the freedom to assemble, immunity from state scrutiny—like the First Amendment freedoms of speech and press, has from time to time been questioned and challenged.

Since the founding of the National Association for the Advancement of Colored People and similar organizations, state and local governments have attempted to prevent the operation of such groups. During the late 1950s the state of Alabama set out to ban the NAACP from conducting activities with the state, claiming that the association had failed to comply with statutes governing corporations operating within the state. The dispute, *NAACP v. Alabama*, was finally resolved by the United States Supreme Court in 1958 in favor of the association. However, the association was met with other interferences—some of the most notable disputes include, *Bates v. Little Rock* (1960), Louisiana ex rel. Gremillion v. NAACP (1961), and *Gibson v. Florida Legislative Investigating Committee* (1963).

Congress of Racial Equality

The Congress of Racial Equality (CORE), an interracial organization organized to confront racism and discrimination, was founded in 1942 by James Farmer, as the result of a campaign protesting discrimination at a Chicago restaurant. From Chicago, the organization spread to other cities and other causes, organizing sit-ins and Freedom Rides throughout the South.

By the mid-1960s, CORE had changed directions, and Farmer turned leadership of the organization over to Floyd McKissick, a North Carolina lawyer. With McKissick

A. Philip Randolph

Dr. Martin Luther King, Jr.

as national director, the organization moved toward an all-black membership and staff. (In 1967 CORE, at its convention, eliminated the word "multiracial" from its constitution). McKissick left the organization in 1968 and was replaced by the present national director, Roy Innis, former chairman of the Harlem chapter.

Student Non-Violent Coordinating Committee

In 1960 a group of black college students founded the Student Non-Violent Coordinating Committee (SNCC) to coordinate the activities of students engaged in direct action protest. SNCC achieved enormous results in the desegregation of public facilities and earned respect from the country for its determination to act peacefully, no matter how violent or demeaning the provocation.

However, by 1964 the organization's leader, Stokely Carmichael, had become convinced that the American system could not be turned around without the threat of wholesale violence. In 1967 Carmichael left the organization to join the more militant Black Panther Party. H. Rap Brown, the former minister of justice in the old organization, took over leadership, renaming the organization the Student National Coordinating Committee and promoting violent retaliation when situations so demanded. The organization gradually declined in membership and is now essentially defunct.

Black Panther Party

From its founding by Huey P. Newton and Bobby Seale in 1966, the Black Panther Party departed from the platform and tactics of other civil rights organizations. It rejected the institutional structure which, in its view, made American society corrupt; it rejected established channels of authority which oppressed the black community; it rejected middle-class values, which it felt contributed to indifference toward, and contempt for, the disinherited black urban youth.

The party imposed strict discipline on its members, denouncing the use of intoxicants, drugs, and artificial stimulants "while doing party work." The intellectual fare of every party member is the ten-point program (supplemented by daily reading of political developments), which every member is obliged to know and understand, presumably even to commit to memory.

However, by 1970 most of the organization's leadership was either jailed, in exile, or dead—Newton was

Benjamin Chavis speaks at a commission meeting in Los Angeles, 1993.

jailed in 1968 on manslaughter changes; Seale had been jailed on charges stemming from the 1968 Chicago convention riot; minister of information, Eldridge Cleaver, in 1969 fled to Algeria to avoid a prison sentence; in 1970 Mark Clark and Fred Hampton were killed during a police raid.

Organizations Providing Community Support

In 1967 the National Urban Coalition was founded to improve the quality of life for the disadvantaged in urban areas through the combined efforts of business, labor, government, and community leaders. Another organization, the National Black United Fund, which provides financial and technical support to projects serving the critical needs of black communities nationwide, was founded in 1972.

The Reverend Jesse Jackson, in 1971, organized Operation PUSH (People United to Save Humanity). The organization has pursued its economic objectives through its Operation Breadbasket program. It also has worked to motivate young people through its PUSH-EXCEL program, which is designed to instill pride and build confidence in young people. Jackson left Operation PUSH to organize another group, the National Rainbow Coalition, Inc., in 1984.

Organizations Responding to Africa and the Caribbean

During the nineteenth and early part of the twentieth century, a number of individuals and organizations arose to unite Africans throughout the world. Most notable was Marcus Garvey, black nationalist and advocate of repatriation of blacks to Africa, who founded the Universal Negro Improvement Association in 1914. Garvey's organization, whose goal was to instill pride, gain economic and political power for blacks in the United States, and to establish an independent black colony in Africa, and to promote unity between African throughout the world, attracted millions worldwide. On February 19 1918, under the leadership of W. E. B. Du Bois, the first Pan-African Congress was held in Paris. The meeting was attending by blacks from around the world and focused on the problems facing Africans worldwide.

More recently new organizations have formed to address the concerns of Africans around the world. Founded in 1977 by Randall Robinson, TransAfrica has

Stokely Carmichael at a rally at the University of California, 1966.

worked to influence American foreign policy regarding political and human rights in African and the Caribbean by informing the public of violations of social, political, and civil rights. Responding to the policy of apartheid in South Africa, TransAfrica supported sanctions against South Africa and organized demonstrations in front of the South African embassy in Washington, D.C. During one such demonstration, Robinson and numerous others were arrested. Other organizations have also taken a stand on policies affecting Africans around the world. In 1986 leaders representing major black organizations united to press for passage of the more stringent legislation regarding sanctions against South Africa.

◆ ORGANIZATION LEADERS

H(ubert) Rap Brown (Jamil Abdullah Al-Amin) (1943-)

Student National Coordinating Committee Chairman

H. Rap Brown was born on October 4, 1943, in Baton Rouge, Louisiana. In 1967 he took over leadership of the Student Non-Violent Coordinating Committee renaming the organization the Student National Coordinating Committee. During his leadership of the Student National Coordinating Committee, Brown was an advocate of violence against the white establishment and used fiery rhetoric in many of his speeches, often saying that "violence is as American as cherry pie." Since the late 1960s the organization has gradually declined in membership and is now essentially defunct.

In 1968 Brown was charged with inciting a riot in Cambridge, Maryland, and was convicted in New Orleans on a federal charge of carrying a gun between states. In 1969 Brown published the book *Die Nigger Die*. Brown disappeared in 1970, after being slated for trial in Maryland, and in 1972 he was shot, arrested, and eventually convicted for a bar holdup in New York City.

While in prison, Brown converted to the Islamic faith and took the name of Jamil Abdullah Al-Amin. On his release, he founded a community grocery store in Atlanta. He is currently leader of the Community Mosque in Atlanta.

In August 1994, Al-Amin was arraigned on weapons possession and assault charges stemming from a shooting in an Atlanta city park. Al-Amin claimed that the charges were the result of harrassment by federal agents

Bobby Seale (left) and Huey Newton, 1969.

who targeted him because of his radical past and Muslim beliefs.

Benjamin Franklin Chavis, Jr. (1948-)
Former National Association for the Advancement of Colored People Executive Director

Benjamin Chavis was born on January 22, 1948 in Oxford, North Carolina. He received a B.A. from the University of North Carolina in 1969. Chavis went on to earn an M.A. from the Duke University Divinity School and a Ph.D. in theology from Howard University in Washington D.C.

He came to national attention in 1971, when as a civil rights organizer for the United Church of Christ he was indicted along with nine other people for the fire-bombing of a grocery store in Wilmington, Delaware, during a period of racial unrest. In the controversial trial that followed all of the "Wilmington 10" were found guilty. Chavis was sentenced to a prison term of 29 to 34 years. Chavis was granted parole and in 1980 his conviction

Randall Robinson meets with African National Congress President, Nelson Mandela, 1991.

H. Rap Brown

was reversed amidst conflicting testimony by various witnesses.

Prior to becoming active in the civil rights movement, Chavis taught chemistry at the high school level. He also worked as an AFSCME labor organizer (1969), a civil rights organizer for the Southern Christian Leadership Council (1967–1969), as a minister for the United Church of Christ, and as director of their Commission for Racial Justice in Washington, D.C. (1972). In 1985 he was appointed executive director of the Commission for Racial Justice. Chavis has also served as co-chairman of the National Alliance Against Racism and Political Repression (1977) and as co-chairman of the Organizing Committee for Economic and Social Justice.

In 1977 Chavis wrote *Let My People Go: Psalms From Prison.* He also received the George Collins Service Award (1977), given by the Congressional Black Caucus, the William L. Patterson award given by the Patterson Foundation, and the Shalom award presented by the Eden Theological Seminary. He is also a recipient of the Gertrude E. Rush Distinguished Service Award, J. E. Walker Humanitarian Award, and the Martin Luther King Jr. Freedom Award. Chavis has since become active in the South African civil rights struggle and continues his position with the United Church of Christ.

On April 9, 1993, the NAACP board of directors elected Chavis to succeed retiring executive director, Benjamin Hooks. Chavis assumed leadership of the NAACP with an agenda designed to increase the membership of young African Americans and revitalize an organization that some people viewed as stagnant. However, Chavis's early initiatives, which included defending "gangsta rap" music, meetings with street gang leaders, and seeking closer ties with controversial Nation of Islam leader Louis Farrakhan, angered many of the NAACP's more traditional members. By the time the NAACP met for its 85th annual convention in July 1994, the NAACP had been split into two factions, one supporting Chavis and the other which believed the organization was being overrun by radical and extremist elements.

In August 1994, it was disclosed that Chavis committed hundreds of thousands of dollars of NAACP money in November 1993 to settle a sexual harassment suit against him. On the weekend of August 20, 1994, the NAACP board of directors met and voted to oust Chavis as executive director. Chavis sued the NAACP, claiming that he had been wrongfully terminated. The NAACP settled out of court with Chavis, but he was not reinstated as executive director.

Following his dismissal from the NAACP, Chavis formed a new civil rights organization, the National

Benjamin Chavis

African American Leadership Summit. He continued his close association with Louis Farrakhan and together they organized the Million Man March, which convened on October 16, 1995 in Washington D.C. Chavis also serves as a talk show host on Washington D.C.'s WOL-AM.

Ramona Hoage Edelin (1945-)
National Urban Coalition President and Chief Executive

Born in Los Angeles, California, on September 4, 1945, Ramona Hoage Edelin received her B.A. (magna cum laude) from Fisk University, her M.A. from the University of East Anglia, in Norwich, England, and her Ph.D. from Boston University. She has been a lecturer at the University of Maryland and a visiting professor at Brandeis University; she has also served as chair of Afro-American studies at Emerson College.

In 1977 Edelin joined the National Urban Coalition as an executive assistant to the president. The National Urban Coalition, an organization to improve the quality of life for the disadvantaged in urban areas, has been active in advocating initiatives designed to encourage youth and promote leadership. Between 1979 and 1982 she moved from director of operations, to vice president of operations, then to senior vice president of program and policy, during which time she directed programs in housing, health, education, and advocacy. In 1982 Edelin became the organization's chief executive.

Marian Wright Edelman (1939-)
Children's Defense Fund President

Born in Bennettsville, South Carolina, on June 6, 1939, Marian Wright Edelman received her undergraduate degree from Spelman College and her law degree from Yale. In 1963 she joined the NAACP Legal Defense and Education Fund as staff attorney. A year later she organized the Jackson, Mississippi, branch of the NAACP Legal Defense and Education Fund, serving as its director until 1968. In 1968 she founded the Washington Research Project of the Southern Center for Public Policy which later developed into the Children's Defense Fund.

Wright has served as director of the Harvard University Center for Law and Education, chairman of the Spelman College board of trustees, a member of the Yale University Corporation, the National Commission on Children, and on the boards of the Center on Budget and Policy Priorities, the US Committee for UNICEF, and the Joint Center for Political and Economic Studies.

As Children's Defense Fund president, Edelman has become the nation's most effective lobbyist on behalf of children. Even while social spending was being cut, she has managed to score some victories. In 1986, nine federal programs known as "the Children's Initiative" received a $500 million increase in their $36 billion budget for families and children's health care, nutrition, and early education.

The most visible focus of CDF is its teen pregnancy prevention program. Through Edelman's efforts, Medicaid coverage for expectant mothers and children was boosted in 1984. In 1985, Edelman began holding an annual Pregnancy Prevention Conference, bringing thousands of religious leaders, social and health workers and community organizations to Washington to discuss ways of dealing with the problem. In 1996, Edelman and the CDF staged the well-attended "Stand for Children" rally in Washington, DC.

In her 1987 book, *Families in Peril: An Agenda for Social Change*, Edelman wrote, "As adults, we are responsible for meeting the needs of children. It is our moral obligation. We brought about their births and their lives, and they cannot fend for themselves." Her other books include, *Children Out of School in America*, *School Suspensions: Are They Helping Children?*, *Portrait of Inequality: Black and White Children in America*, *Families in Peril: An Agenda for Social Change*, *The Measure of Our Success: A Letter to My Children*, and *Guide My Feet: Prayers and Meditations on Loving and Working for Children.*

James Farmer (1920-)
Congress of Racial Equality Founder and Former National Director

Born in Marshall, Texas, on January 12, 1920, Farmer attended public schools throughout the South. He earned his B.S. degree in chemistry from Wiley College in 1938 and his B.D. degree from Howard University in 1941. Active in the Christian Youth Movement, and once vice-chairman of the National Council of Methodist Youth and the Christian Youth Council of America, Farmer refused ordination when confronted with the realization that he would have to practice in a segregated ministry.

In 1941 Farmer accepted a post as race relations secretary for the Fellowship of Reconciliation. The following year he and a group of University of Chicago students organized the Congress of Racial Equality (CORE), the first protest organization in the United States to utilize the techniques of nonviolence and passive resistance advocated by the Indian nationalist Mohandas Karamchand Gandhi.

In June 1943 CORE staged the first successful sit-in demonstration at a restaurant in the Chicago Loop. The organization soon supplemented this maneuver with what came to be known as the standing-line, which involved the persistent waiting in line by CORE members at places of public accommodation where blacks had been denied admission.

In 1961 CORE introduced the Freedom Ride into the vocabulary and methodology of civil rights protest, dispatching bus riders throughout the South for the purpose of testing the desegregation of terminal facilities. Attacked in Alabama and later arrested in Mississippi, the Freedom Riders eventually succeeded in securing the court ordered desegregation of bus terminals, with the United States Supreme Court decision of 1960 which outlawed segregation in interstate transportation.

Farmer left the organization in 1966. In 1969, President Richard Nixon appointed Farmer to the post of assistant secretary of Health, Education and Welfare. The appointment created a furor in some black circles, where it was felt that it was inappropriate for a former civil rights leader to serve in such an administration; in other circles, the appointment was praised by those who thought it necessary for African Americans to be represented in all areas. However, Farmer found that there was little of substance in the position and resigned.

Farmer began to give lectures, and for a while headed a think tank at Howard University. In 1976 he broke all ties with CORE, criticizing its leader, Roy Innis, for such things as attempting to recruit black Vietnam veterans as mercenaries in Angola's civil war. Disturbed over the course that the organization had taken, Farmer and a score of former CORE members attempted to create a

James Farmer, 1965.

new racially mixed civil rights organization in 1980. Farmer, along with Floyd McKissick, attempted to meet with Innis to reach an agreement on the future of the organization, but nothing developed.

Farmer has written several books, including *Freedom When?* and *Lay Bare the Heart.*

Prince Hall (1735?-1807)
Founder of Black Freemasonry in the United States

Prince Hall is believed to have been born in Bridge Town, Barbados, around 1735. Historians contend that he migrated to the United States in 1765; others claim that during the late 1740s he had been a slave to William Hall of Boston, Massachusetts, and freed by William Hall on April 9, 1770.

In March 1775 Hall along with 15 other blacks were initiated into a lodge of British army Freemasons stationed in Boston. The group of black masons was issued a permit to meet at a lodge on March 17, 1775, and on July 3, 1775, they organized the African Lodge No. 1, with Hall as master of the lodge. The lodge received official recognition from England as a regular Lodge of Free and Accepted Masons in 1784 and was designated the African Lodge 459.

Hall, in addition to leading the organization of black Freemasonry, was active as an abolitionist. In January 1777, he was the prime force behind a black petition sent to the Massachusetts state legislature requesting the abolition of slavery in the state. Another important petition, drawn up under his leadership in 1788, called

Grand Lodge No. 1, Greensville, Mississippi, 1887.

for an end to the kidnapping and sale of free blacks into slavery. He also actively lobbied for the organization of schools for black children in Boston. Prince Hall died on December 4, 1807, in Boston.

Dorothy I. Height (1912–)

National Council of Negro Women President

Born in 1912 in Richmond, Virginia, Dorothy Height holds a masters degree from New York University and has studied at the New York School of Social Work. In the fall of 1952, she served as a visiting professor at the Delhi School of Social Work in New Delhi, India. Six years later, she was appointed to the Social Welfare Board of New York by Governor Averell Harriman, and was reappointed by Governor Nelson Rockefeller in 1961. Since 1957 she has been president of the National Council of Negro Women, an organization founded by Mary McLeod Bethune in 1935.

Before becoming the fourth president of the National Council of Negro Women, Height had served on the organization's board of directors. She has also served as associate director for leadership training services for the Young Women's Christian Association, as a member of the Defense Advisory Committee on Women in the Services, as president of Delta Sigma Theta sorority, as vice president of the National Council of Women, as president of Women in Community Services, Inc., as well as in numerous other organizations. Height is also the founder of the Black Family Reunion, which she created in the 1980s to combat negative media stereotypes of African Americans.

In 1994, President Bill Clinton presented Height and nine other distinguished Americans with the Medal of Freedom, America's highest civilian honor. She was also awarded the Salute to Greatness Award.

Benjamin L. Hooks (1925–)

Former National Association for the Advancement of Colored People Former Executive Director

Hooks was born in Memphis, Tennessee, on January 31, 1925, and attended LeMoyne College and Howard University. He received his J.D. degree from DePaul University College of Law in 1948. During World War II he served in the 92nd Infantry Division in Italy. From 1949 to 1965, and again from 1968 to 1972, Hooks worked as a lawyer in Memphis. In 1966 Hooks became the first black judge to serve in the Shelby County

Dorothy Height

Benjamin Hooks

(Tennessee) criminal court. As an ordained minister, he preached at Middle Baptist Church in Memphis and the Greater New Mount Moriah Baptist Church in Detroit. As a prominent local businessman, he was the co-founder and vice president of the Mutual Federal Savings and Loan Association in Memphis.

On January 10, 1977, Hooks was unanimously elected executive director of the National Association for the Advancement of Colored People by the NAACP board of directors, succeeding the retiring Roy Wilkins.

Under his progressive leadership, the association took an aggressive posture on United States policy toward African nations. Among his many battles on Capitol Hill, Hooks led the historical prayer vigil in Washington, D.C., in 1979 against the Mott anti-busing amendment, which was eventually defeated in Congress; led in the fight for passage of the District of Columbia Home Rule bill; and was instrumental in gathering important Senate and House votes on the Humphrey-Hawkins Full Employment Bill.

At the NAACP's national convention in 1986, Hooks was awarded the association's highest honor, the Spingarn Medal. In March 1993, Hooks retired as executive director of the NAACP and was replaced by Benjamin Chavis.

Following his retirement, Hooks became senior vice president of Chapman Co., a minority brokerage firm. He was also installed as professor of social justice at Fisk University.

Roy Emile Alfredo Innis (1934–)

Congress of Racial Equality National Chairman

Born June 6, 1934, in St. Croix, Virgin Islands, Roy Emile Alfredo Innis has lived in the United States since the age of twelve. He attended Stuyvesant High School in New York City and majored in chemistry at City College of New York.

In 1963 Innis joined the Congress of Racial Equality (CORE). In 1965 Innis was elected chairman of the Harlem branch and went on to become associate national director three years later. In 1968 Innis became national director of the organization. Innis founded the Harlem Commonwealth Council, an agency designed to promote the development of black-owned businesses and economic institutions in Harlem. He also took a plunge into journalism, serving with William Haddad as

Roy Innus, 1976.

co-editor of the *Manhattan Tribune*, a weekly featuring news from Harlem and the upper West Side.

Innis' leadership of CORE, however, has been marked with controversy. Numerous members have left the organization, charging that Innis has run the organization as a one-man show. CORE was also the target of a three-year investigation by the New York state attorney general's office into allegations that it had misused charitable contributions. (An agreement was reached in 1981 that did not require CORE to admit to any wrong doing in its handling of funds, but stipulated that Innis would have to contribute $35,000 to the organization over the next three years.) Innis was challenged by a group of former CORE members, headed by James Farmer, the founder and former chairman of organization; the effort was unsuccessful and Innis continued as head of the organization. In 1981 Innis became national chairman of the organization.

While remaining president of the largely inactive CORE, Innis has sought to build a political base in Brooklyn. He has run for public office on several occasions. In 1986, Innis was a Republican candidate for Brooklyn's twelfth Congressional district, but lost the election. He also ran unsuccessfully for the Democratic mayoral nomination in New York City in 1993 against David Dinkins. In 1994, Innis unsuccessfully challenged Mario Cuomo for the governorship of New York.

John Edward Jacob (1934-)

Former National Urban League President

Born in Trout, Louisiana, on December 16, 1934, John Edward Jacob grew up in Houston, Texas. He received his bachelor's and master's degrees in social work from Howard University. During the early 1960s Jacob worked for the Baltimore Department of Public Welfare, first as a caseworker, then later as a child welfare supervisor. In 1965 he joined the Washington Urban League as director of education and youth incentives.

During his early career with the organization he held a number of increasingly important positions, serving as director of its Northern Virginia Branch in 1966, associate director for administration of the affiliate in 1967, and as its acting executive director from 1968 until 1970. He also spent several months as director of community organization training in the Eastern Regional Office of the NUL.

Jacob left the Washington Urban League in 1970 to serve as executive director for the San Diego Urban League, a post he held until his return to the Washington Urban League in 1975. In 1982 Jacob replaced Vernon E. Jordan, Jr. as the organization's president, when Jordan retired after ten years as Urban League president.

Jacob has also served on the Howard University board of trustees, the Board of the Local Initiatives Support Corporation, the board of A Better Chance, Inc., the community Advisory Board of New York Hospital, and the National Advertising Review Board, among others.

In 1994, Jacob retired as president of the National Urban League and was succeeded by Hugh P. Price. Jacob is currently an executive vice president for Anheuser-Busch Inc.

Vernon Eulion Jordan, Jr. (1935-)

Former National Urban League President

Vernon Eulion Jordan, Jr. was born in Atlanta on August 15, 1935. After graduating from DePauw University in 1957 and from Howard Law School in 1960, he returned to Georgia.

From 1962 to 1964 Jordan served as field secretary for the Georgia branch of the NAACP. Between 1964 and 1968 Jordan served as director of the Voter Education Project of the Southern Regional Council and led its successful drives that registered nearly two million blacks in the South. In 1970 Jordan moved to New York to become executive director of the United Negro College Fund, helping to raise record sums for its member

John Jacob

colleges, until he was tapped by the Urban League to become the successor to the late Whitney Young.

Taking over as National Urban League executive director in January 1972, Jordan moved the organization into new areas, including voter registration in northern and western cities, while continuing and strengthening the League's traditional social service programs. An outspoken advocate of the cause of the black and the poor, Jordan has taken strong stands in favor of busing, an income maintenance system that ends poverty, scatter-site housing, and a federally financed and administered national health system. Maintaining that the "issues have changed," since the 1960s, Jordan has called for "equal access and employment up to and including top policy-making jobs."

The nation was stunned on May 29, 1980 when Jordan, who had just delivered an address to the Fort Wayne Urban League, was shot by a sniper as he returned to his motel; Jordan was confined to the hospital, first in Fort Wayne and later in New York City, for 90 days.

On September 9, 1981, Jordan announced his retirement, after ten years as head of the National Urban League. During Jordan's tenure, the League increased its number of affiliates from 99 to 118, its staff from 2,100 to 4,200, and its overall budget, from $40 million annually to $150 million.

In January 1993, Jordan served as a member of President Bill Clinton's transition team. President Clinton appointed Jordan to his Foreign Intelligence Advisory Board in April 1993. He is also senior partner at the Washington D.C. law firm of Akin, Gump, Strauss, Hauer & Feld.

Joseph E. Lowery (1924-)

Southern Christian Leadership Conference President

The Reverend Joseph E. Lowery was born in Huntsville, Alabama, on October 6, 1924. He holds a doctor of divinity degree, among others, and has attended numerous educational institutions, including Clark College, the Chicago Ecumenical Institute, Garrett Theological Seminary, Payne College and Theological Seminary, and Morehouse University. Reverend Lowery's ministry began in 1952 at the Warren Street Church in Birmingham, where he served until 1961. From there he moved on to become pastor of St. Paul Church from 1964 to 1968.

Vernon Jordan

Since 1986, Lowery has served as pastor of the Cascade United Methodist Church in Atlanta, Georgia.

Lowery was one of the co-founders of the Southern Negro Leaders Conference (which later became the Southern Christian Leadership Conference); the Reverend Dr. Martin Luther King, Jr. served as the organizations' first president, with Lowery serving as vice-president.

In 1977, Lowery succeeded Reverend Ralph David Abernathy, as president of the SCLC. Under his leadership, SCLC has broadened its activities to include the reinstitution of its Operation Breadbasket to encourage businesses that earn substantial profits in the black community to reinvest equitably and employ blacks in equitable numbers; involvement in the plight of Haitian refugees jailed by the American government; and a march from Selma to Washington, D.C., in connection with the renewal of the Voting Rights Act of 1982.

Jewell Jackson McCabe (1945-)

Chairperson of the National Coalition of 100 Black Women

Jewell Jackson was born in Washington D.C. on August 2, 1945. She later kept her married name from her second marriage becoming Jewell Jackson McCabe. McCabe studied at New York City's High School for the Performing Arts as a teen, and after graduating, she studied dance at Bard College from 1963 to 1966. She married Frederick Ward, who worked in advertising, while at Bard, whom she later divorced. Her marriage to Eugene McCabe, president of North General Hospital in New York City, also ended in divorce, but McCabe chose to keep his name.

After studying at Bard, it was a few years before McCabe took a job as director of public affairs for the New York Urban Coalition in 1970, and concurrently, she joined an organization called the New York Coalition of 100 Black Women, founded by her mother, business woman Julia Jackson. At that time, the group was about 75 women shy of the 100 mark. The group reached this goal by the mid-1970s. During this time, McCabe tried to find her niche. She left the Urban Coalition in 1973 to become the public relations officer for Special Services for Children in New York City. In 1975, she took a post as associate director of public information in the Women's Division of the Office of the Governor in New York City and from there to become director of government and community affairs at WNET-TV in 1977.

From 1975 to 1977, she published *Women In New York* through the state office as well as donating her time to the United Way, the NAACP, the United Hospital Fund, and the Association for the Betterment of New York. In 1977, because of her good work, she was named president of the, soon to be, National Coalition of 100 Black Women, a post she held until 1991, when she became chair of the board of directors. By 1981, McCabe had established the organization nationally with chapters in 22 states, attracting the most well-known black women in the country.

Within two years, McCabe received several prestigious awards, including an Eastern Region Urban League Guild Award in 1979 and a Seagrams Civic Award, a Links Civic Award, and an outstanding community leadership award from Malcolm/King College all in 1980. Also, in 1980, she served as deputy grand marshal of the annual Martin Luther King Jr. parade in New York City. In addition to her chairman of the board duties for the Coalition, McCabe is president of her own Jewell Jackson McCabe Associates, a firm that does consulting work on government relations, marketing, and events dealing with minority issues.

Floyd Bixler McKissick (1922-1981)

Congress of Racial Equality Former National Director

Born in Asheville, North Carolina on March 9, 1922, Floyd Bixler McKissick did his undergraduate work at Morehouse and North Carolina colleges. Having determined that he wanted to become a lawyer, McKissick

Reverend Joseph Lowery, 1988.

applied to the University of North Carolina at Chapel Hill Law School. Since the school was not integrated at that time, he was denied admission. With the help of NAACP lawyer Thurgood Marshall, McKissick sued the university and became the first African American to earn an LL.B. degree there.

While still in school, McKissick had become an active member of the Congress of Racial Equality (CORE). When McKissick replaced James Farmer as head of CORE on January 3, 1966, he quickly made a name for himself. Under McKissick's direction, the organization moved more firmly into the Black Power movement, refusing to support Martin Luther King's call for massive nonviolent civil disobedience in northern cities, concentrating instead on programs aimed at increasing the political power and improving the economic position of African Americans. In 1967 the organization moved to eliminate the word "multiracial" from its constitution.

McKissick resigned as national director of CORE in 1968. After leaving CORE, he launched a plan to establish a new community, Soul City, in Warren County, North Carolina. McKissick saw Soul City as community with sufficient industry to support a population of 50,000. For his venture, he received a $14 million bond issue guarantee from the Department of Housing and Urban Development and a loan of $500,000 from the First Pennsylvania Bank.

Soul City, however, ran into difficulties and despite the best efforts of McKissick, the project never developed as planned. In June 1980 the Soul City Corporation and the federal government reached an agreement that would allow the government to assume control of the project. Under the agreement, the company retained 88 acres of the project, including the site of a mobile home park and a 60,000 square foot building that had served as the project's headquarters.

McKissick died on April 28, 1991, of lung cancer and was buried at Soul City.

Huey P. Newton (1942-1989)

Black Panther Party Cofounder

The youngest of seven children, Huey Newton was born in Monroe, Louisiana on February 17, 1942. He attended Oakland City College, where he founded the Afro-American Society, and later studied at San Francisco Law School. In 1966, Newton joined forces with Bobby Seale and established the Black Panther Party for Self-Defense.

Newton and his partner almost immediately became targets of sharp police resentment and uneasiness. The hostility came to a climax in 1967, when Newton allegedly killed an Oakland police officer. His eight-week trial was a cause celebre in which more than 2,500 demonstrators surrounded the courthouse chanting Panther slogans and demanding his release. Newton was convicted of voluntary manslaughter and sent to the California Men's Colony. His conviction was later overturned by the California court of appeals.

By the 1970s the Black Panther Party became a potent political force in California. Co-leader Bobby Seale made an almost-successful bid for the mayorship of Oakland in 1973. In 1977, the Panthers helped to elect the city's first black mayor, Lionel Wilson. Meanwhile, Newton continued to have problems with the law. He was charged with shooting a prostitute, but after two hung juries, the charges were dropped. He was retried and convicted for the 1969 death of the police officer; however, the conviction was reversed.

In 1980, he earned his Ph.D. in philosophy from the University of California; his doctoral thesis was "War Against the Panthers: Study of Repression in America." However, this achievement was followed by further problems. He was charged with embezzling state and federal funds from an educational and nutritional program he headed in 1985 and in 1987, he was convicted of illegal possession of guns. In 1989, he was fatally shot by a small-time drug dealer.

Huey Newton

Hugh B. Price (1941-)

National Urban League President and CEO

When Hugh Price was named president and CEO of the National Urban League in 1994, he inherited an organization with financial problems and a lack of visibility. But he was just the person to address and eradicate those problems. Price graduated from Amherst in 1963, then received his law degree from Yale in 1966. Immediately going to work in the inner city, Price worked first as an attorney for the New Haven Legal Assistance Association, than as executive director of the Black Coalition of New Haven.

Price continued his focus on the inner city by joining, in 1970, the urban affairs consulting firm of Cogen, Holt & Associates in New Haven, specializing in the analysis of municipal government. After serving as Human Resources Administration director for the city of New Haven, Price was offered the opportunity to express his opinions to a much larger audience: he was named to the editorial board of the *New York Times*. Price primarily concentrated on writing about domestic policy issues.

After spending six years working at WNET-TV, New York City's public television station, Price became vice president of the Rockefeller Foundation, helping minorities get more opportunities in groups served by the organization. With his background of serving the inner city community, speaking out on urban concerns, supervising large programs and being able to get funding for them, Price caught the attention of the people responsible for choosing a new president in 1994 for the National Urban League.

Price continued to focus on poor schools, inner city youngsters with time on their hands, and high unemployment. But he vowed that the Urban League would not be race–specific in its help—it would be need–specific. Price felt that a better approach the Urban League could take would be to focus on helping entire urban neighborhoods, instead of singling out a particular race in that neighborhood. This approach has gained Hugh Price the deserved attention in the media for his worthwhile efforts.

Asa Philip Randolph (1889-1979)

Brotherhood of Sleeping Car Porters and A. Philip Randolph Institute Founder

Asa Philip Randolph was born in Crescent City, Florida on April 15, 1889. He attended Cookman Insti-

A. Philip Randolph Institute, Cincinnati, Ohio.

tute in Jacksonville, Florida, before moving to New York City.

In New York Randolph worked as a porter, railroad waiter, and an elevator operator. While attending the College of the City of New York, he was exposed to the socialist movement, and in 1917 he organized *The Messenger*, a socialist newspaper. In 1925 Randolph founded the Brotherhood of Sleeping Car Porters to help black railway car attendants working for the Pullman Palace Car Company. After a ten year struggle, in 1935, Randolph and the union negotiated a contract with Pullman.

Randolph served as a member of New York City's Commission on Race and as president of the National Negro Congress. In 1941 Randolph organized a march on Washington, D.C., to bring attention to discrimination in employment. In 1942 he was appointed to the New York Housing Authority and in 1955 was appointed to the AFL-CIO executive council.

In 1960 Randolph organized the Negro American Labor Council. He was also one of the organizers of the 1963 march on Washington. In 1964 he founded the A. Philip Randolph Institute in New York City to eradicate discrimination and to defend human and civil rights. He died on May 16, 1979.

Randall S. Robinson (1942-)
TransAfrica Founder and Director

Randall Robinson, brother to the late news anchor Max Robinson, was born in Richmond, Virginia, in the early 1940s and is a graduate of Virginia Union University and Harvard Law School. In 1977 Robinson founded TransAfrica to lobby Congress and the White House on foreign policy matters involving Africa and the Caribbean. Since its creation, the organization has grown from two to over 15,000 members.

In 1984 and 1985, in protest to the policy of apartheid in South Africa, TransAfrica organized demonstrations in front of the South African embassy in Washington, D.C.; Robinson along with other protesters, including singer Stevie Wonder, were arrested. In addition to its opposition to apartheid, the organization was active in the Free South Africa Movement and is an advocate for the cessation of aid to countries with human rights problems. In 1981 TransAfrica Forum, an educational and research arm of TransAfrica, was organized to

Randall Robinson

collect and disseminate information on foreign policy affecting Africa and the Caribbean and to encourage public participation in policy debates.

In 1994, the United States was beseiged by scores of refugees seeking to escape Haiti's brutal military dictatorship. Many of these refugees, upon reaching the United States or the American military base in Guantanamo, Cuba, were often sent back to Haiti without receiving asylum hearings. On April 12, 1994, Robinson began a liquid-fast diet in an attempt to increase awareness of the plight of Haitian refugees and to pressure the Clinton administration to change its refugee policy. On May 8, Robinson ended his fast after the Clinton administration announced that it would grant Haitian refugees asylum hearings.

On March 16, 1995, Robinson announced that TransAfrica would lead a group of prominent African Americans to pressure Nigeria's brutal military leaders to step down from power. Along with other demonstrators, Robinson was arrested during protests in front of the Nigerian Embassy in Washington D.C. on April 21, 1995 and Aug. 31, 1995. On November 10, 1995, Robinson, along with notable South African Archbishop Desmond Tutu, announced that they would seek economic sanctions or an oil embargo against Nigeria after its military regime executed a prominent Nigerian writer and eight other minority rights activists.

Bayard Rustin (1910-1987)
A. Philip Randolph Institute Former Executive Director

Bayard Rustin was born in West Chester, Pennsylvania, on March 17, 1910. While in school, he was an honor student and star athlete, experiencing his first act of discrimination when he was refused restaurant service in Pennsylvania while on tour with the football team. He attended Wilberforce University, Cheyney State Normal School (now Cheyney State College) and the City College of New York.

Rustin was active in various peace organizations, efforts to restrict nuclear armaments, and movements toward African independence. Between 1936 and 1941, Rustin worked as an organizer of the Young Communist League. In 1941 he joined the Fellowship of Reconciliation, a nonviolent antiwar group, and later served as its director of race relations. In 1942 Rustin, along with James Farmer, became active in the Chicago Committee of Racial Equality, out of which the Congress of Racial Equality grew.

Rustin was one of the founding members of the Southern Christian Leadership Conference (SCLC). In 1963 he was named chief logistics expert and organizational coordinator of the March on Washington. From 1964 to 1979, Rustin served as executive director of the A. Philip Randolph Institute in New York City. In 1975 he founded the Organization for Black Americans to Support Israel.

Throughout the 1960s Rustin was hard pressed to maintain support for the nonviolent philosophy to which he had dedicated his life. Nonviolence, he argued, was not outdated; it was a necessary and inexorable plan called for by the black's condition in the United States. Guerrilla warfare and armed insurrection, Rustin explained, required friendly border sanctuaries, a steady source of arms and equipment, and the support of the majority of a country's inhabitants. Rustin continued to be active in the civil rights movement until his death on August 24, 1987, at the age of 77.

Bobby Seale (1936-)
Black Panther Party Co-Founder

Born Robert George Seale in Dallas, Texas on October 20, 1936, Bobby Seale, along with Huey P. Newton and Bobby Hutton, was one of the founding members of the Black Panther Party for Self-Defense. His family, poverty-stricken, moved from Dallas to Port Arthur, Texas, before settling in Oakland, California.

Seale joined the United States Air Force and trained as a sheet-metal mechanic, after leaving high school. However, he was discharged for disobeying an officer. Returning home, he found sporadic work as a sheet-metal mechanic. In 1959 Seale enrolled at Merritt College in engineering drafting. While attending Merritt, Seale joined the Afro-American Association, a campus organization that stressed black separatism and self-improvement. It was through this organization that Seale met Panther co-founder Huey Newton.

Seale and Newton soon became disenchanted with the association. In 1966 Seale and Newton formed the Black Panther Party for Self-Defense. One of their objectives was to form armed patrols to protect citizens from what they considered racist police abuse.

In March of 1971, Seale was charged with kidnapping and killing Panther Alex Rackley, a suspected police informant. However, a mistrial was declared, and the charges dismissed. Seale began to steer the Panthers away from its revolutionary agenda and toward one of creating community action programs. In 1974 Seale left the party to form Advocates Scene, an organization aimed at helping the underprivileged from grass-root political coalitions.

More recently Seale has served as a community liaison for Temple University's African American Studies department. He has lectured throughout the country and has written several books—*Seize the Time: The Story of the Black Panther Party* (1970), *A Lonely Rage: The Autobiography of Bobby Seale* (1978), and *Barbeque'n with Bobby Seale* (1987).

Bobby Seale

Roy Wilkins (1901-1981)
National Association for the Advancement of Colored People Former Executive Director

Born in St. Louis, Missouri on August 30, 1901, Wilkins was reared in St. Paul, Minnesota. He attended the University of Minnesota, where he majored in sociology and minored in journalism. He served as night editor of the *Minnesota Daily* (the school paper) and edited a black weekly, the St. Paul *Appeal.* After receiving his B.A. in 1923, he joined the staff of the Kansas City *Call*, a leading black weekly.

In 1931 Wilkins left the *Call* to serve under Walter White as assistant executive secretary of the NAACP. In 1934 he succeeded W. E. B. Du Bois as editor of *Crisis* magazine. Wilkins was named acting executive secretary of the NAACP in 1949, when White took a year's leave of absence from the organization. Wilkins assumed the position as executive secretary of the NAACP in 1955. He quickly established himself as one of the most articulate spokesmen in the civil rights movement. He testified before innumerable Congressional hearings, conferred with United States Presidents, and wrote extensively.

For several years, Wilkins served as chairman of the Leadership Conference on Civil Rights, an organization of more than 100 national civic, labor, fraternal, and religious organizations. He was a trustee of the Eleanor Roosevelt Foundation, the Kennedy Memorial Library Foundation, and the Estes Kefauver Memorial Foundation. He was also a member of the Board of Directors of the Riverdale Children's Association, the John LaFarge Institute, and the Stockbridge School, as well as the international organization Peace with Freedom. Wilkins died on September 8, 1981.

Whitney Moore Young, Jr. (1922-1971)
National Urban League Former Director

Whitney Moore Young, Jr., was born in Lincoln Ridge, Kentucky, on July 31, 1922. He received his B.A. degree

Roy Wilkins

Whitney Young, Jr.

from Kentucky State College in 1941. He went on to attend the Massachusetts Institute of Technology, and in 1947 he earned an M.A. degree in social work from the University of Minnesota.

In 1947 Young was made director of industrial relations and vocational guidance for the St. Paul, Minnesota, Urban League. In 1950 he moved on to become executive secretary at the St. Paul chapter. Between 1954 and 1961 Young served as dean of the Atlanta University School of Social Work. He also served as a visiting scholar at Harvard University under a Rockefeller Foundation grant.

In 1961 the National Urban League's board of directors elected Young as president of the organization. Young instituted new programs like the National Skills Bank, the Broadcast Skills Bank, the Secretarial Training Project and an on-the-job training program with the United States Department of Labor. Between 1961 and 1971, the organization grew from 63 to 98 affiliates.

In addition to his work with the National Urban League, Young served as president of the National Association of Social Workers and the National Conference on Social Welfare, and on the boards and advisory committees of the Rockefeller Foundation, Urban Coalition, and Urban Institute, and on seven presidential commissions. In 1969 Young was selected by President Johnson to receive the Medal of Freedom, the nation's highest civilian award. Young authored two books, *To Be Equal* (1964) and *Beyond Racism: Building an Open Society* (1969), and coauthored *A Second Look* (1958).

Young died on March 11, 1971, while attending a conference in Africa.

◆ NATIONAL ORGANIZATIONS

A. Philip Randolph Educational Fund
1444 I Street, NW, No. 300
Washington, DC 20005
(202) 289-2774

Founded in 1964. Seeks to eliminate prejudice and discrimination from all areas of life; educate individuals and groups on their rights and responsibilities; defend human and civil rights; assist in the employment and education of the underprivileged; combat community deterioration, delinquency, and crime.

Africa Faith and Justice Network
401 Michigan Ave
PO Box 29378
Washington, DC 20017
(202) 832-3412

Founded in 1983. Purpose is to examine the role the network believes Europe, America, and other northern countries play in causing injustices in Africa. Challenges national policies found to be detrimental to the interest of African peoples. Gathers information on issues and policies that adversely affect Africa, analyzes the data, and makes recommendations for advocacy or action. Consults with churches of Africa, field missionaries, and other African individuals and groups.

The Africa Fund
17 John St
New York, NY 10038
(212) 962-1210

Founded in 1966. Established by the American Committee on Africa. Works to: defend human and civil rights of needy Africans by providing or financing legal assistance; provide medical relief to Africans, particularly refugees; render aid to indigent Africans in the United States, Africa, or elsewhere who are suffering economic, legal, or social injustices; provide educational aid or grants to Africans, particularly refugees; inform the American public about the needs of Africans; engage in study, research, and analysis of questions relating to Africa. Encourages divestment by U.S. corporations in South Africa; seeks to increase public support for U.S. economic sanctions against South Africa; has supported legislation which prevents U.S. corporations operating in South Africa from claiming U.S. tax credits for taxes paid to the South African government. Operates Unlock Apartheid's Jails Project, which seeks to inform the U.S. public about the plight of political prisoners in South Africa; disseminates information on the activities of South African puppet forces, including those in other areas of southern Africa.

Africa News Service
PO Box 3851
Durham, NC 27702
(919) 286-0747

Founded in 1973. News agency whose purpose is to supply material on Africa for broadcast and print media. Covers African politics, economy and culture, and U.S. policy and international issues affecting Africa. Obtains news by monitoring African radio stations on shortwave equipment, by subscribing to African publications, and through a network of reporters based in Africa. Also produces investigative stories on U.S. policy and its implications. Provides audio news and programming for radio, articles and graphics for newspapers and magazines, and prints for libraries and institutions. Carries out research for feature articles, news programs, and individuals.

Africa Travel Association
347 Fifth Avenue, Suite 610
New York, NY 10016
(212) 447-1926

Founded in 1975. Conducts regional seminars and trade show exhibitions. Sponsors Africa Guild (see separate entry) to help develop a general interest in Africa.

Africa Watch
485 Fifth Avenue
New York, NY 10017
(212) 972-8400

Founded in 1988. Monitors and promotes internationally recognized human rights in Africa.

Africa World Press
PO Box 1892
Trenton, NJ 08607
(609) 771-1666

Founded in 1979. Scholar activists and members of the African intellectual community. Promotes and maintains the development of an independent, democratic, and critical thinking African intellectual community. Utilizes the scientific knowledge and skills of the community to give service to African peoples and social movements. Conducts seminars on subjects such as the energy crisis, human rights, political repression, and food.

African-American Institute
833 United Nations Plaza
New York, NY 10017
(212) 949-5666

Founded in 1953. Works to further development in Africa, improve African American understanding, and inform Americans about Africa. Engages in training, development assistance, and informational activities. Sponsors African American conferences, media and congressional workshops, and regional seminars.

African-American Labor Center
1925 K Street, NW, Suite 300
Washington, DC 20006
(202) 778-4600

Founded in 1964. Assists, strengthens, and encourages free and democratic trade unions in Africa. Has undertaken projects in 43 countries in partnership with African trade unions. Programs are developed upon request and advice of African unions with knowledge of host government. Projects are geared to eventual assumption of complete managerial and financial responsibility by African labor movements. Objective is to help build sound national labor organizations that will be of lasting value to workers and the community, institutions that contribute to the economic and social development of their countries and to Africa's total political and economic independence. Major areas of activity are workers' education and leadership training, vocational training, cooperatives and credit unions, union medical and social service programs, administrative support for unions, and communication and information. Sponsors study tours and visitor programs to permit African and American trade unionists to become familiar with each other's politics, economies, and trade union movements; Africans are exposed to technical training not available in their homeland.

Africare
440 R Street, NW
Washington, DC 20001
(202) 462-3614

Founded in 1971. Seeks to improve the quality of life in rural Africa. Provides health and environmental protection services in rural areas of Africa; works to improve African water and agricultural resources; conducts public education programs in the United States on African development.

Alcoholism in the Black Community
ABC Addiction Services
East Orange General Hospital
East Orange, NJ 07019

All-African People's Revolutionary Party
1738 A Street, SE
Washington, DC 20003

Founded in 1971. Africans and persons of African descent who support Pan-Africanism, "the total liberation and unification of Africa under an all-African socialist government."

Alliance of Minority Women for Business and Political Development
PO Box 13858
Silver Spring, MD 20911-3858
(301) 230-5583

Founded in 1982. Objectives are to unite Minority women entrepreneurs and to encourage joint ventures and information exchange.

Alliance to End Repression
523 South Plymouth Ct., Suite 800
Chicago, IL 60605
(312) 427-4064

Founded in 1970. Religious, community, and human relations organizations united to safeguard the Bill of Rights and constitutional freedoms and to ensure the just application of state and local laws. Has initiated and developed three organizations: Citizens Alert (deals with police and community problems); Illinois Gay and Lesbian Task Force; and Illinois Prisons and Jails Project (monitoring county and state prisons). Other areas of activity include media accountability, cable television license ordinances, rights of minors, juvenile justice, national and state legislation, and rights of immigrants.

Alpha Kappa Alpha
5656 South Stony Island Avenue
Chicago, IL 60637
(317) 684-1282

Founded in 1908. Social and service sorority.

Alpha Phi Alpha
2313 St. Paul Street
Baltimore, MD 21218
(410) 554-0040

Founded in 1906. Service fraternity.

Alpha Pi Chi
PO Box 255
Kensington, MD 20895
(301) 559-4330

Founded in 1963. Service sorority.

American-African Affairs Association
1001 Connecticut Avenue, NW, Suite 1135
Washington, DC 20036
(202) 223-5110

Founded in 1965. Educational organization designed to circulate information about African countries to the people of the United States, especially with respect to "the cause of freedom in its struggle against world Communism and the best interests of the United States of America." Distributes literature to opinion molders, political leaders, university personnel, and business leaders, both here and in other countries.

American Association of Blacks in Energy
927 15th Street, NW, Suite 200
Washington, DC 20005
(202) 371-9530

Founded in 1977. Blacks in energy-related professions, including engineers, scientists, consultants, academicians, and entrepreneurs; government officials and public policymakers; interested students. Represents blacks and other minorities in matters involving energy use and research, the formulation of energy policy, the ownership of energy resources, and the development of energy technologies. Seeks to increase the knowledge, understanding, and awareness of the minority community in energy issues by serving as an energy information source for policymakers, recommending blacks and other minorities to appropriate energy officials and executives, encouraging students to pursue professional careers in the energy industry, and advocating the participation of blacks and other minorities in energy programs and policymaking activities. Updates members on key legislation and regulations being developed by the Department of Energy, the Department of Interior, the Department of Commerce, the Small Business Administration, and other federal and state agencies.

American Baptist Black Caucus
Beth Eden Baptist Church
Tenth and Adeline Streets
Oakland, CA 94607
(510) 444-1625

Founded in 1968. Concerned with reforming the American Baptist Convention in terms of bridging the gap between whites and minority members. Seeks to develop convention support for: scholarship aid for disadvantaged students; resources for business and religious projects in the inner city; adequate representation of minorities in the convention structure; support for black colleges and universities; open hiring policies on local, state, and national levels.

American Black Book Writers Association
PO Box 10548
Marina Del Rey, CA 90295
(213) 822-5195

Founded in 1980. Represents African Americans in the United States publishing industry. Encourages development of black authors; works to preserve and advance black literature. Promotes and gives market support to members' works; holds mutual promotions and tours; sponsors cooperative advertising in black-oriented media. Conducts research on problems affecting black authors and their works in the United States.

American Black Chiropractors Association
1918 East Grand Boulevard
St. Louis, MO 63107
(314) 531-0615

Founded in 1980. Objectives are to: educate the public, health care institutions, and health care providers about chiropractic and promote black chiropractic in the community; develop career orientation programs for high school and college students and sponsor scholarship funds; study history of chiropractic; sponsor publicity programs, public forums, counseling services, research, and establishment of free chiropractic clinics; provide for exchange of information, techniques, and reports of researchers and clinicians.

American Committee on Africa
198 Broadway
New York, NY 10038
(212) 962-1210

Founded in 1953. Devoted to supporting African people in their struggle for freedom and independence. Focuses on southern Africa and the Western Sahara and support for African liberation movements. Works with legislators, churches, trade unions, and interested students to help stop what the group feels is U.S. collaboration with racism in South Africa. Arranges speaking tours for African leaders; publicizes conditions and developments in Africa; sponsors research, rallies, and demonstrations.

Anti-Repression Resource Team
PO Box 8040
State College, PA 16803-8040
(814) 237-3095

Founded in 1979. Combats all forms of political repression including: police violence and misconduct; Ku Klux Klan and Nazi terrorism; spying and covert action by secret police and intelligence agencies. Focuses on research, writing, lecturing, organizing, and publishing. Conducts training workshops for church, labor, and community organizations.

Association of African American People's Legal Council
c/o William Bert Johnson
13902 Robson Street
Detroit, MI 48227
(313) 837-0627

Founded in 1959. Seeks to achieve equal justice under the law for African Americans and to provide free legal counsel to people of African American descent. Compiles statistics and reports on cases of international inequality. Obtains research from public systems on education and its effect on discrimination.

Association of Black Admissions and Financial Aid Officers of the Ivy League and Sister Schools
Admissions Office
PO Box 208234
Yale University
New Haven, CT 06520-8234
(203) 432-9316

Founded in 1970. Present and former minority admissions and financial aid officers employed at Ivy League or sister schools. These schools include: Brown, Columbia, Cornell, Dartmouth, Harvard/Radcliffe, Massachusetts Institute of Technology, University of Pennsylvania, Princeton, Yale, Barnard, Bryn Mawr, Mount Holyoke, Smith, and Wellesley. Aids minority students who wish to pursue a college education. Seeks to improve methods of recruitment, admittance, and financial services that support the growth and maintenance of the minority student population at these institutions. Encourages Ivy League and sister schools to respond to the needs of minority students and admissions and financial aid officers.

Association of Black Anthropologists
4350 North Fairfax Drive, Suite 640
Arlington, VA 22203
(703) 528-1902

Founded in 1970. Works to: formulate conceptual and methodological frameworks to advance understanding of all forms of human diversity and commonality; advance theoretical efforts to explain the conditions that produce social inequalities based on race, ethnicity, class, or gender; develop research methods that involve the peoples studied and local scholars in all stages of investigation and dissemination of findings.

Association of Black Cardiologists
13404 Southwest 128th Street, No. A
Miami, FL 33186-5800
(305) 641-2224

Founded in 1974. Seeks to improve prevention and treatment of cardiovascular diseases.

Association of Black Foundation Executives
1828 L Street, NW
Washington, DC 20036
(202) 466-6512

Founded in 1971. Encourages increased recognition of economic, educational, and social issues facing blacks in the grantmaking field. Promotes support of blacks and their status as grantmaking professionals. Seeks an increase in the number of blacks entering the grantmaking field; helps members improve their job effectiveness. Though involved with grantmaking organizations, the ABFE itself does not award grants.

Association of Black Nursing Faculty
5823 Queens Cove
Lisle, IL 60532
(708) 969-3809

Founded in 1987. Works to promote health-related issues and educational concerns of interest to the black community and ABNF. Serves as a forum for communication and the exchange of information among members; develops strategies for expressing concerns to other individuals, institutions, and communities. Assists members in professional development; develops and sponsors continuing education activities; fosters networking and guidance in employment and recruitment activities. Promotes health-related issues of legislation, government programs, and community activities.

Association of Black Psychologists
PO Box 55999
Washington, DC 20040-5999
(202) 722-0808

Founded in 1968. Aims to: enhance the psychological well-being of black people in America; define mental health in consonance with newly established psychological concepts and standards; develop policies for local, state, and national decision-making which have impact on the mental health of the black community; support established black sister organizations and aid in the development of new, independent black institutions to enhance the psychological, educational, cultural, and economic situation.

Association of Black Sociologists
Dept. of Sociology
Central Michigan University
Mt. Pleasant, MI 48859
(517) 774-3160

Founded in 1968. Purposes are to: promote the professional interests of black sociologists; promote an increase in the number of professionally trained sociologists; help stimulate and improve the quality of research and the teaching of sociology; provide perspectives regarding black experiences as well as expertise for understanding and dealing with problems confronting black people; protect professional rights and safeguard the civil rights stemming from executing the above objectives.

Association of Black Women in Higher Education
234 Hudson Avenue
Albany, NY 12210
(516) 572-7141

Founded in 1979. Objectives are to nurture the role of black women in higher education, and to provide support for the professional development goals of black women.

Association of Concerned African Scholars
PO Box 11694
Berkeley, CA 94701-2694

Founded in 1977. Facilitates scholarly analysis and opinion in order to impact U.S. policy toward Africa; formulates alternative government policy toward Africa and disseminates it to the public; works to develop a communication and action network among African scholars. Mobilizes support on current issues; participates in local public education programs; stimulates research on policy-oriented issues and disseminates findings; informs and updates members on international policy developments.

A Better Chance
419 Boylston Street
Boston, MA 02116
(617) 421-0950

Founded in 1963. Identifies, recruits, and places academically talented and motivated minority students into leading independent and selected public secondary schools. Prepares students to attend selective colleges and universities and encourages their aspirations to assume positions of responsibility and leadership in American society.

Big Eight Council on Black Student Government
Minority Student Services
Hester Hall, Room 213
731 Elm Avenue
University of Oklahoma
Norman, OK 73019

Founded in 1978. Black student unions and other groups at Big Eight Athletic Conference universities. Seeks to represent the concerns of black collegians at universities where the majority of students are white. Encourages the genesis of all black student organizations and lends support to them. Seeks to effect changes in curricula and to help legitimize and develop black studies departments as accredited degree programs. Functions as a communications medium among member schools and assists in efforts to reduce the attrition rate of black students. Promotes the placement of students and the hiring of black faculty and staff.

Black Affairs Center for Training and Organizational Development
c/o Margaret V. Wright
10918 Jarboe Court
Silver Spring, MD 20901
(301) 681-9827

Founded in 1970. Multidisciplinary management research organization which promotes social change, educational improvement, organization renewal and goal achievement, systematic problem solving, and multicultural skills development through custom-designed training programs and consultation services. Individuals, groups, educational systems, and governmental and community agencies use programs such as Equal Employment Opportunity Training; Employee Motivation, Productivity and Improvement Training; Career Education and Development Training. Programs are continually being developed in areas including women's concerns, single parents, youth and sex, drugs and alcoholism, the aging, day-care, sexual harassment, and stress management.

Black American Cinema Society
3617 Monclair Street
Los Angeles, CA 90018
(213) 737-3292

Founded in 1975. Works to bring about an awareness of the contributions made by blacks to the motion picture industry in silent films, early talkies, and short and feature films. Feels that by viewing these films black children can see the sacrifice and humiliation endured by black actors and actresses, directors, film writers, and producers while making films. Maintains collection of early black films owned by the Western States Black Research Center. Conducts research projects, film shows, and Black History Month seminars. Provides financial support to independent black filmmakers.

Black American Response to the African Community
127 North Madison Avenue, Suite 400
Pasadena, CA 91101
(818) 584-0303

Founded in 1984. A grass roots organization of entertainers, journalists, clergy, and business, health, and community leaders working to assist the victims of drought and famine in Africa. Focuses on emergency efforts involving medical needs, water irrigation, housing, and food supplies. Provides relief for orphans through its Family Network Program. Disseminates current information on drought-stricken areas in Africa; assists in the development of regeneration projects in affected areas. Maintains the National Education Task Force to educate Americans on the African crisis; sponsors media updates.

Black Americans for Life
419 Seventh Street, NW, Suite 500
Washington, DC 20004
(202) 626-8800

Promotes alternatives to abortion for women with crisis pregnancies; strives to be a visible presence defending the rights of the unborn in the black community. Asserts that black women are twice as likely as white women to have abortions; believes that abortions are counterproductive to advances made through civil rights efforts.

Black and Indian Mission Office
2021 H Street, NW
Washington, DC 20006
(202) 331-8542

Founded in 1884. Coordinates the distribution of funds from the annual Black and Indian Mission Collection in Catholic churches across the United States; these funds go to support priests, nuns, and other religious workers at black and Indian missions and schools.

Black Awareness in Television
13217 Livernois
Detroit, MI 48238-3162
(313) 931-3427

Founded in 1970. Produces black media programs for television, video, radio, film, and theater. Trains individuals in the media and conducts research projects including surveys. Produces public affairs, cultural arts, soap opera, and exercise programs; sponsors theater companies. Seeks television exposure for black-produced products and black performing artists. Promotes "September is Black Reading Month" program.

Black Business Alliance
PO Box 26443
Baltimore, MD 21207
(410) 467-7427

Founded in 1979. Acts as a national and international support system for black businesses, providing assistance in organizational management and resource development. Provides children's services; sponsors fundraising events; offers placement services.

Black Caucus of Health Workers
353 Lewis
Carbondale, IL 62901

Black Caucus of the American Library Association
Newark Public Library
5 Washington Street
Newark, NJ 07101
(718) 522-4827

Founded in 1970. Promotes librarianship; encourages active participation of blacks in library associations and boards and all levels of the profession. Monitors activities of the American Library Association with regard to its policies and programs and how they affect black librarians and library users. Reviews, analyzes, evaluates, and recommends to the ALA actions that influence the recruitment, development, advancement, and general working conditions of black librarians. Facilitates library services that meet the informational needs of black people including increased availability of materials related to social and economic concerns. Encourages development of authoritative information resources concerning black people and dissemination of this information to the public.

Black Citizens for a Fair Media
156-20 Riverside Drive, No. 13L
New York, NY 10032
(212) 568-3168

Founded in 1971. Community organizations concerned with employment practices in the television industry, images of black people projected by television, and how those images affect viewers. Works to improve programming, employment practices, and training of blacks; evaluates compliance with the Federal Communication Commission's equal opportunity rules for the electronic media. Believes that the airways belong to the people and seeks to prevent any change in that ownership.

Black Coaches Association
PO Box J
Des Moines, IA 50311
(515) 271-3010

Founded in 1986. Promotes the creation of a positive environment in which issues such as stereotyping, lack of significant media coverage, and discrimination can be exposed, discussed, and resolved. Provides member services. Petitions the NCAA legislative bodies to design, enact, and enforce diligent guidelines and policies to improve professional mobility for minorities.

Black Data Processing Associates
PO Box 7466
Philadelphia, PA 19101
(215) 843-9120

Founded in 1975. Seeks to accumulate and share information processing knowledge and business expertise in order to increase the career and business potential of minorities in the information processing field.

Black Entertainment and Sports Lawyers Association
3432 West Vollmer Road, Suite 314
Olympia Fields, IL 60461
(708) 798-3798

Founded in 1979. Purpose is to provide more efficient and effective legal representation to African American entertainers and athletes. Offers referral system for legal representation and a resource bank for providing information to students, groups, and nonprofit and civic organizations involved in the entertainment industry; and serves as an industry watchdog in protecting the rights of blacks within the entertainment community.

Black Filmmaker Foundation
Tribeca Film Center
375 Greenwich, Suite 600
New York, NY 10013
(212) 941-3944
Susan Christian, Exec. Dir.

Founded in 1978. Fosters audience development by programming local, national, and international film festivals. Maintains video library. Conducts seminars and workshops.

Black Filmmakers Hall of Fame, Inc.
405 14th Street, Suite 515
Oakland, CA 94612
(510) 465-0804

Founded in 1973. Seeks to study, teach, and preserve the contributions of black filmmakers to American cinema. Fosters cultural awareness through educational, research, and public service programs in the film arts. Holds film-lecture series, Black Filmworks Festival, and annual International Film Competition.

Black Health Research Foundation
14 East 60th Street, Suite 307
New York, NY 10022
(212) 408-3485

Founded in 1988. Voluntary health agency devoted to reducing preventable causes of premature death among African Americans. Funds scientific research in areas including AIDS, alcoholism, infant mortality, sickle cell disease, substance abuse, and other diseases that have a disproportionate impact on African Americans. Seeks recognition as the foremost authority on health and science regarding African Americans. Promotes professional and community education; recruits and trains volunteers. Seeks to influence public policy on crucial issues.

Black Methodists for Church Renewal
601 West Riverview Avenue
Dayton, OH 45406
(513) 227-9460

Founded in 1968. Serves as platform from which blacks can express concerns to the general church on issues such as: revival and survival of the black church; involvement of blacks within the structure of the church; the conduct of the church as it relates to investment policies and social issues; economic support in the black community; and the support of the 12 black colleges. Encourages black Methodists to work for economic and social justice. Works to expose racism in agencies and institutions of the United Methodist church. Seeks improvement of educational opportunities for blacks, the strengthening of black churches, and an increase in the number of black persons in Christian-related vocations. Advocates liberation, peace, justice, and freedom for all people. Supports programs that alleviate suffering in third world countries.

Black Military History Institute of America
PO Box 1134
Fort Meade, MD 20755
(410) 757-4250

Founded in 1987. Seeks to: provide archival facilities to collect, preserve, and exhibit materials pertaining to military history; motivate and support underprivileged youths by using military role models as a source of inspiration; foster a spirit of camaraderie and goodwill among all persons sharing an interest in community involvement programs for the underprivileged.

Black Psychiatrists of America
c/o Dr. Isaac Slaughter
2730 Adeline Street Oakland, CA 94607
(510) 465-1800

Founded in 1968. Black psychiatrists, either in practice or training, united to promote black behavioral science and foster high quality psychiatric care for blacks and minority group members. Sponsors public information service.

Black Resources Information Coordinating Services
614 Howard Avenue
Tallahassee, FL 32304
(904) 576-7522

Founded in 1972. Designed to solidify the various sources of information and research by and about minority groups in America and convert them into a coordinated information system by using bibliographic control, storage, retrieval, transfer, and dissemination. Focuses on information by and about African Americans, but also includes other minorities. Acts as referral and consulting service; aids in genealogical research and archival management and organization. Offers bibliographic services and lecture demonstrations on African American culture. Sponsors seminars, workshops, and institutes.

Black Revolutionary War Patriots Foundation
1612 K Street, NW, Suite 1104
Washington, DC 20006
(202) 452-1776

Founded in 1985. Raises private funds for the establishment of a memorial, in Washington, DC, to commemorate black patriots of the American Revolutionary War.

Black Rock Coalition
PO Box 1054, Cooper Station
New York, NY 10276
(212) 713-5097

Founded in 1985. Promotes, produces, and distributes alternative/black music and provides information, technical expertise, and performance and recording opportunities for "musically and politically progressive musicians." Also works to increase the visibility of black rock artists in music media and on college radio stations.

Black Silent Majority Committee of the U.S.A.
Box 5519
San Antonio, TX 78201
(210) 340-2424

Founded in 1970. Seeks to show the people of America and the world that there is a black majority in the United States which is patriotic and believes in saluting the flag, going to church, and paying taxes. Organizes Americans who do not want to be identified with black "radicals" and emphasizes the positive gains that blacks have made. Works throughout the United States and the world for better race relations. Opposes forced busing and supports prayer in public schools.

Black Student Leadership Network
25 East Street, N.W.
Washington, DC 20001
(202) 662-3515

Black Stuntmen's Association
8949 West 24th Street
Los Angeles, CA 90034
(213) 870-9020

Founded in 1966. Serves as an agency for stuntpeople in motion pictures and television. Plans to operate school for black stuntpeople.

Black Tennis and Sports Foundation
1893 Amsterdam Avenue
New York, NY 10032

Founded in 1977. Participants include members of the business community involved in sports who are dedicated to helping black and minority inner-city youths and developing athletes interested in tennis or other individual sports such as skating and gymnastics. Acts as a source of support and resources for black and minority youth. Organizes tennis teams and sponsors these teams and their coaches on trips and games overseas. Sponsors the Annual Arthur Ashe/Althea Gibson Tennis Classic in New York City.

Black Veterans for Social Justice
686 Fulton Street
Brooklyn, NY 11217
(718) 935-1116

Founded in 1979. Seeks to aid black veterans in obtaining information concerning their rights, ways to upgrade a less-than-honorable discharge, and Veterans Administration benefits due them and their families. Seeks to prohibit discrimination against black veterans. Provides educational programs; facilitates veterans' sharing of skills acquired while in service. Services include counseling and community workshops on veteran issues and a program to provide services to veterans in local prisons. Assists veterans who have suffered from the effects of Agent Orange, an herbicide containing dioxin, used as a defoliant in Vietnam until 1969.

Black Women in Church and Society
c/o Interdenominational Theological Center
671 Beckwith Street, SW
Atlanta, GA 30314
(404) 527-7740

Founded in 1982. Seeks to provide: structured activities and support systems for black women whose goals include participating in leadership roles in church and society; a platform for communication between laywomen and clergywomen. Conducts research into questions and issues pivotal to black women in church and society. Maintains a research/resource center and a library with subject matter pertaining to liberation and black theology, feminism, and womanist movements.

Black Women in Publishing
10 East 87th Street
New York, NY 10128
(212) 427-8100

Founded in 1979. A networking and support group whose purpose is to encourage minorities interested in all sectors of the print industry, including book, newspaper, and magazine publishing. Promotes the image of minorities working in all phases of the book, newspaper, and magazine industries; recognizes achievements of minorities in the media. Works for a free and responsible press. Facilitates the exchange of ideas and information among members, especially regarding career planning and job security. Keeps members informed about the publishing industry and their impact on it. Encourages and works to maintain high professional standards in publishing. Collaborates with other organizations in striving to improve the status of women and minorities.

Black Women Organized for Educational Development
518 17th Street, Suite 202
Oakland, CA 94612
(510) 763-9501

Founded in 1984. Fosters self-sufficiency in and encourages empowerment of low-income and socially disadvantaged women by establishing and maintaining programs that improve their social and economic well-being. Sponsors mentor program for junior high-aged young women in low-income urban areas; offers support groups, workshops, and seminars. Maintains Black Women's Resource Center, an information and referral service for African American women and youth.

Black Women's Agenda
208 Auburn Avenue, NE
Atlanta, GA 30303
(404) 524-8279

Founded in 1977. Works to educate the public about the economic, social, and political issues relevant to African American women. Recommends public policy that will benefit women and their families. Conducts workshops.

Black Women's Educational Alliance
6625 Greene Street
Philadelphia, PA 19119

Founded in 1976. Active and retired women in the field of education. Seeks a strong union among members in order to foster their intellectual and professional growth. Conducts public awareness programs to improve educational standards and delivery of educational services; works for equal opportunities for women.

Black Women's Network
PO Box 12072
Milwaukee, WI 53212
(414) 562-4500

Founded in 1979. Black professional women organized to improve the political, economic, and educational conditions of minority women. Offers support services and networking opportunities to address issues affecting African American women.

Black Women's Roundtable on Voter Participation
1629 K Street, NW, Suite 801
Washington, DC 20006
(202) 659-4929

Founded in 1983. A program of the National Coalition on Black Voter Participation (see separate entry). Black women's organizations committed to social justice and economic equity through increased participation in the political process. Organizes voter registration, education, and empowerment programs in the black community; emphasizes the importance of the women's vote. Seeks to: develop women's leadership skills through nonpartisan political participation; encourage black women's involvement in discussions concerning the influence of the women's vote in elections. Supports volunteer coalitions that work on voter registration, voter education, and get-out-the-vote efforts.

Black World Foundation
PO Box 2869
Oakland, CA 94609
(510) 547-6633

Founded in 1969. Black persons united to develop and distribute black educational materials and to develop black cultural and political thought. Offers books in the areas of black literature, history, fiction, essays, political analysis, social science, poetry, and art. Maintains library.

Blacks in Government
1820 Eleventh Street, NW
Washington, DC 20001-5015
(202) 667-3280

Founded in 1975. Federal, state, or local government employees or retirees concerned with the present and future status of blacks in government. Develops training and other programs to enhance the liberty and sense of well-being of blacks in government.

Blacks in Law Enforcement
256 East McLemore Avenue
Memphis, TN 38106
(901) 774-1118

Founded in 1986. Seeks to educate the public concerning the contributions made by blacks in the field of law enforcement. Documents the lives and achievements of the first blacks to participate in law enforcement in the United States. Develops programs to improve the public image of law enforcement officers; has established a short-term training program for law enforcement officers.

Catholic Interracial Council of New York
899 Tenth Avenue
New York, NY 10019
(212) 237-8255

Founded in 1934. Works in cooperation with local parishes and governmental and voluntary groups to combat bigotry and discrimination and to promote social justice for all racial, religious, and ethnic groups.

Sponsors research, educational forums, workshops, and community action programs. Presents annual John LaFarge Memorial Award for Interracial Justice to community leaders and annual Hoey Award to community leaders who have worked to promote objectives of the council.

Center for Constitutional Rights
666 Broadway, Seventh Floor
New York, NY 10012
(212) 614-6464

Founded in 1966. Works in areas such as abuse of the grand jury process, women's rights, civil rights, freedom of the press, racism, electronic surveillance, criminal trials, and affirmative action. Conducts the Ella Baker Student Program, the Movement Support Network, and in Mississippi, The Voting Rights Project.

Center for Third World Organizing
1218 East 21st Street
Oakland, CA 94606-3132
(510) 533-7583

Founded in 1980. Provides training, issue analyses, and research to low-income minority organizations including welfare, immigrant, and Native American rights groups. Monitors and reports on incidents of discrimination against people of color. Sponsors Minority Activist Apprenticeship Program, which works to develop minority organizers and leaders for minority communities.

Center for Urban Black Studies
Graduate Theological Union
2465 LeConte Avenue
Berkeley, CA 94709
(415) 841-8401

Founded in 1969. Provides seminarians and laypersons with resources "to respond to life in the urban community and to represent its oppressed minority people." Develops and offers courses, seminars, and other training programs dealing with issues of race, social justice, urban life, and the black religious experience. Initiates new ministries; develops and implements community service programs; counsels and assists black seminarians in placement and in obtaining and developing employment. Conducts workshops and seminars addressing racial justice, church and race, and urban ministry.

Chi Eta Phi
3029 13th Street, NW
Washington, DC 20009
(202) 232-3858

Founded in 1932. Registered and student nurses. Objectives are to: encourage continuing education; stimulate friendship among members; develop working relationships with other professional groups for the improvement and delivery of health care services. Sponsors leadership training seminars. Offers educational programs for entrance into nursing and allied health fields. Presents scholarships and other financial awards to assist students. Sponsors recruitment and retention programs for minority students. Operates speakers' bureau on health education and biographical archives on African American nurses.

Christians Concerned for Racial Equality
PO Box 1643
Oroville, WA 98844
(604) 498-3895

Citizens for a Better America
PO Box 356
Halifax, VA 24558
(804) 476-7757

Founded in 1975. Churches and individuals united to create a better America by strengthening individual rights in the United States. Serves as a public advocacy organization that lobbies for civil rights and environmental legislation. Conducts legal research in civil rights cases; provides research services to communities investigating issues such as fair housing and toxic waste disposal.

Coalition of Black Trade Unionists
PO Box 66268
Washington, DC 20035
(202) 429-1203

Founded in 1972. Members of 76 labor unions united to maximize the strength and influence of black and minority workers in organized labor. Activities include voter registration and education, improvement of economic development, and employment opportunities for minority and poor workers. Sponsors regional seminars.

Co-ette Club
2020 West Chicago Boulevard
Detroit, MI 48206
(313) 867-0880

Founded in 1941. Teenage high school girls "outstanding in one or all of the following categories—Academic Scholarship, School and Community, Extra-Curricular, Community Volunteer Service, and Leadership." Helps members channel interests and become leaders in educational, cultural, and artistic activities on local and national levels. Raises funds for the United Negro College Fund and contributes to local charity and social service groups in each community.

Commission for Racial Justice
475 Riverside Drive, 16th Floor
New York, NY 10115
(212) 870-2077

Founded in 1963. A racial justice agency representing the 1.7 million members of the United Church of Christ. Promotes human rights programs and strategies to foster racial justice in black, Third World, and other minority communities.

Community Access Producers and Viewers Association
PO Box 68002
Jackson, MS 39286-8002
(601) 352-3398

Founded in 1965. Researches activities of workers, blacks, and grass roots organizations through the FIS Deep South People's History Project. Maintains extensive Mississippi-centered library and archives. Distributes press releases on current southern news; reprints items on women's liberation and political education.

Conference of Minority Public Administrators
1120 G Street, NW, Suite 700
Washington, DC 20005
(202) 393-7878

Founded in 1971. Members of the American Society of Public Administration who belong to a minority group or are interested in the promotion of minorities within public administration.

Conference of Prince Hall Grand Masters
Fourth and State Streets
Pine Bluff, AR 71601

Congress of National Black Churches
1225 I Street, NW, Suite 750
Washington, DC 20005-3914
(202) 371-1091

Founded in 1978. Seeks to find answers to problems that confront blacks in the United States and Africa, including economic development, family and social support, housing, unemployment, education, and foreign relations. Focus is on religious education and evangelism.

Congressional Black Associates
1504 Longworth
Washington, DC 20515
(202) 225-5865

Founded in 1979. Provides information on the operations of the federal government to members and the black community; fosters contacts among members and the community. Works to enhance the social, political, and economic status of all people, but concentrates on the black experience in America.

Congressional Black Caucus
2244 Rayburn
Washington, DC 20515
(202) 225-3121

Founded in 1971. Black members of the U.S. House of Representatives. Seeks to address the legislative concerns of black and other underrepresented citizens and to formalize and strengthen the efforts of its members. Establishes a yearly legislative agenda setting forth the key issues which it supports: full employment, national health care, education, minority business assistance, urban revitalization, rural development, welfare reform, and international affairs. Works to implement these objectives through personal contact with other House members, through the dissemination of information to individual black constituents, and by working closely with black elected officials in other levels of government. Operates the Congressional Black Caucus Foundation.

Delta Sigma Theta
1707 New Hampshire Avenue, NW
Washington, DC 20009
(202) 986-2400

Founded in 1913. Service sorority.

Educational Equity Concepts
114 East 32nd Street, Suite 701
New York, NY 10016
(212) 725-1803

Founded in 1982. Organized to create educational programs and materials that are free of sex, race, and disability bias. Offers training programs for parents, teachers, and students; conducts seminars, symposia, and workshops. Provides conference planning, consulting, and materials development services. Conducts Women and Disability Awareness Project, which discusses and writes on matters concerning disabled women, feminism, and the links between the disability rights and women's movements.

Episcopal Commission for Black Ministries
815 Second Avenue
New York, NY 10017
(212) 867-8400

Founded in 1973. Works to strengthen the witness of black Episcopalians in the church through programs that include parish and clergy development, scholarships and grants, and international relations. Provides financial assistance and consultations to parishes and church organizations.

Eta Phi Beta
c/o Elizabeth Anderson
1724 Mohawk Boulevard
Tulsa, OK 74110
(918) 425-8612

Founded in 1942. Professional business sorority.

Institute for the Advanced Study of Black Family Life and Culture
175 Filbert Street, Suite 202
Oakland, CA 94607
(510) 836-3245

Seeks to reunify African American families and to revitalize the black community. Advocates the reclamation of what the group considers traditional African American culture. Conducts research on issues impacting the black community such as teenage pregnancy, child-rearing practices, mental health support systems, and the effects of alcohol and drugs. Maintains HAWK Federation (High Achievement, Wisdom, and Knowledge Federation), a training program employed in school systems to aid in the character development of young black males. Sponsors in-service training for agencies, school systems, and the juvenile justice system. Develops training curricula for teen parents.

International Association of African and American Black Business People
18900 Schoolcraft
Detroit, MI 48223

Founded in 1965. Establishes, operates, and fosters business education and related activities among African American and African members of the business community worldwide.

International Association of Black Professional Fire Fighters
8700 Central Avenue, Suite 206
Landover, MD 20785
(301) 808-0804

Founded in 1970. Strives to: promote interracial communication and understanding; recruit blacks for the fire services; improve working conditions for blacks in the fire services; assist blacks in career advancement; promote professionalism; represent black fire fighters before the community.

International Black Toy Manufacturers Association
PO Box 348
Springfield Gardens, NY 11413

Founded in 1987. Works to provide shelf space and distribution opportunities commensurate with the spending power of the black community. Promotes black toy manufacturers.

International Black Women's Congress
1081 Bergen Street
Newark, NJ 07112
(201) 926-0570

Founded in 1983. Objective is to unite members for mutual support and socioeconomic development through: annual networking tours to Africa; establishing support groups; assisting women in starting their own businesses; assisting members in developing resumes and other educational needs; offering to answer or discuss individual questions and concerns.

International Black Writers
PO Box 1030
Chicago, IL 60690
(708) 331-6421

Founded in 1970. Seeks to discover and support new black writers. Conducts research and monthly seminars in poetry, fiction, nonfiction, music, and jazz. Operates library of 500 volumes on black history. Provides writing services and children's services. Plans to establish hall of fame, biographical archives, and museum.

International Black Writers and Artists
PO Box 43576
Los Angeles, CA 90043
(213) 964-3721

Founded in 1974. Black writers and artists in the United States and West Indies. Provides encouragement and support to members.

International Committee Against Racism
231 West 29th Street
Brooklyn, NY 10001
(212) 629-0003

Founded in 1973. Is dedicated to fighting all forms of racism and to building a multi-racial society. Opposes racism in all its economic, social, institutional, and cultural forms. Believes racism destroys not only those minorities that are its victims, but all people.

International Council of African Women
PO Box 91812
Washington, DC 20090
(202) 546-8459

Founded in 1982. Promotes worldwide networking between African American women. Addresses such issues as: employment, poverty and welfare, health, child care, housing. Disseminates information to disadvantaged women on developments and events of interest to women. Conducts self-help programs.

Iota Phi Lamba
503 Patterson Street
Tuskegee, AL 36088
(205) 727-5210

Founded in 1929. Business and professional civic sorority. Seeks to develop leadership expertise among business and professional women. Promotes increased interest in business education among high school and college women through planned programs and scholarships.

John Brown Anti-Klan Committee
PO Box 14422
San Francisco, CA 94114
(415) 567-9699

Activists fighting racism and sexism; advocates of freedom for political prisoners. (Abolitionist John Brown is best known for his command of the "raiders", a group of men who burned a U.S. armory at Harpers Ferry in 1859 in order to further the fight against slavery.) Offers educational programs. Disseminates information.

Kappa Alpha Psi
2322-24 North Broad Street
Philadelphia, PA 19132
(215) 228-7184

Founded in 1911. Social fraternity.

Leadership Conference on Civil Rights
1629 K Street, NW, Suite 1010
Washington, DC 20006
(202) 466-3311

Founded in 1950. Coalition of national organizations working to promote passage of civil rights, social and economic legislation, and enforcement of laws already on the books. Has released studies examining former President Ronald Reagan's tax and budget programs in areas including housing, elementary and secondary education, social welfare, Indian affairs, and tax cuts. Has evaluated the enforcement of activities in civil rights by the U.S. Department of Justice; has also reviewed civil rights activities of the U.S. Department of Education.

Minorities in Media
PO Box 9198
Petersburg, VA 23806
(804) 524-5902

Founded in 1975. Works to facilitate communication and convey ideas in the area of educational communications and technology.

Minority Business Enterprise Legal Defense and Education Fund
900 Second Street, Suite 8
Washington, DC 20002
(202) 289-1700

Founded in 1980. Serves as an advocate and legal representative for the minority business community.

Most Worshipful National Grand Lodge Free and Accepted Ancient York Masons
PO Box 2789
Orangeburg, SC 29116-2789
(803) 531-1985

Founded in 1847. Also known as the Most Worshipful National Grand Lodge Free and Accepted Ancient York Masons Prince Hall Origin National Compact U.S.A.

NAACP Legal Defense and Educational Fund
99 Hudson Street, 16th Floor
New York, NY 10013
(212) 219-1900

Founded in 1940. Legal arm of the civil rights movement, functioning independently of the National Association for the Advancement of Colored People since the mid-1950s. Works to provide and support litigation in behalf of blacks, other racial minorities, and women defending their legal and constitutional rights against discrimination in employment, education, housing, and other areas. Represents civil rights groups as well as individual citizens who have bona fide civil rights claims. Contributed funds are used to finance court actions for equality in schools, jobs, voting, housing, municipal services, land use, and delivery of health care services. Has organized litigation campaign for prison reform and the abolition of capital punishment. Hosts annual institute to develop public awareness of new problems being faced by minorities. Maintains Herbert Lehman Education Fund, through which scholarships are awarded to black students attending state universities; sponsors Earl Warren Legal Training Program, which provides scholarships to black law students.

National Action Council for Minorities in Engineering
3 West 35th Street
New York, NY 10001
(212) 279-2626

Founded in 1980. Seeks to increase the number of minority students enrolled in and graduating from engineering schools. Works with support organizations to motivate and encourage pre-college students to engage in engineering careers. Operates project to assist engineering schools in improving the retention and graduation rates of minority students.

National Alliance Against Racist and Political Repression
11 John Street, Room 702
New York, NY 10038
(212) 406-3330

Founded in 1973. Coalition of political, labor, church, civic, student, and community organizations; individuals dedicated to protecting people's right to organize. Seeks to mobilize millions of people to unite in word and action against many forms of repression of human rights in the United States including: persecution and jailing of political activists; attempts to suppress prisoners' rights movements and use of behavior control against prisoners and the poor; assaults on labor's right to organize, strike, and act effectively; police crimes against the people, especially nonwhites; legislation and court decisions repressing basic rights; the death penalty.

National Alliance of Black Interpreters
PO Box 70322
New Orleans, LA 70172-0322
(504) 943-6597

National Alliance of Black Organizations
3724 Airport Boulevard
Austin, TX 78722
(512) 478-9802

Founded in 1976. Presidents of black organizations and associations. Coordinates and encourages voter registration efforts among member organizations. Serves as a forum for the exchange of ideas and experiences.

National Alliance of Black School Educators
2816 Georgia Avenue, NW
Washington, DC 20001
(202) 483-1549

Founded in 1970. Purpose is to promote awareness, professional expertise, and commitment among black educators. Goals are to: eliminate and rectify the results of racism in education; work with state, local, and national leaders to raise the academic achievement level of all black students; increase members' involvement in legislative activities; facilitate the introduction of a curriculum that more completely embraces black America; improve the ability of black educators to promote problem resolution; create a meaningful and effective network of strength, talent, and professional support. Plans to establish a National Black Educators Data Bank and offer placement service.

National Alumni Council of the United Negro College Fund
8260 Willow Oaks Corporate Drive
PO Box 10444
Fairfax, VA 22031
(703) 205-3463

Founded in 1946. Provides a structure for cooperation among black college alumni groups and friends of black colleges. Works to acquaint the public with the value of black colleges and black higher education. Informs students and the public about contributions of black college alumni to civic betterment and community progress. Recruits students for United Negro College Fund member colleges.

National Association for Black Veterans
PO Box 11432
Milwaukee, WI 53211
(414) 265-8940

Founded in 1970. Represents the interests of minority veterans before the Veterans Administration. Operates Metropolitan Veterans Service to obtain honorable discharges for minority and low-income veterans who in the organization's opinion unjustly received a less than honorable discharge. Defends incarcerated veterans through its Readjustment Counseling Program; operates job creation program; offers services to geriatric and homeless veterans.

National Association for Equal Educational Opportunities
2181 Brigden Road
Pasadena, CA 91104
(714) 856-6362

Founded in 1975. College and university professionals concerned with the development and operation of secondary school and collegiate programs to serve the needs of low-income and disadvantaged students.

National Association for the Advancement of Black Americans in Vocational Education
PO Box 04437
Detroit, MI 48204
(313) 494-1660

Founded in 1977. Goal is to generate national leadership and increase the impact of blacks in the field of vocational/technical education by: assuring opportunities and promoting recruitment and the retention of black Americans in all areas and levels; utilizing research discoveries as a basis for influencing key funding sources at the national, state, and local levels; providing a career information exchange system. Develops training models for marketable skills; links black talent with vocational/technical employment opportunities in the public and private sectors at the federal, state, and local levels; identifies, assesses, and evaluates critical issues that affect the extent of participation of blacks and offers recommendations for improvement.

National Association for the Advancement of Colored People
4805 Mt. Hope Drive
Baltimore, MD 21215
(410) 358-8900

Founded in 1909. Persons "of all races and religions" who believe in the objectives and methods of the NAACP. To achieve equal rights through the democratic process and eliminate racial prejudice by removing racial discrimination in housing, employment, voting, schools, the courts, transportation, recreation, prisons, and business enterprises. Offers referral services, tutorials, job referrals, and day care. Sponsors seminars; maintains law library. Awards Spingarn Medal annually to a black American for distinguished achievement. Sponsors the NAACP National Housing Corporation to assist in the development of low and moderate income housing for families.

National Association of Black Accountants
7249A Hanover Parkway
Greenbelt, MD 20770
(301) 474-6222

Founded in 1969. Works to unite accountants and accounting students who have similar interests and ideals, who are committed to professional and academic excellence, who possess a sense of professional and civic responsibility, and who are concerned with enhancing opportunities for minorities in the accounting profession.

National Association of Black and White Men Together
1747 Connecticut Ave. NW
Washington, DC 20009-1108
(800) NA4-BWMT, (202) 462-3599
Fax: (202) 462-3690

National Association of Black Catholic Administrators
1531 West Ninth Street
Los Angeles, CA 90015-1194
(213) 251-3435

Founded in 1976. Assists the church in its role of evangelization and in defining its mission to the black community. Seeks to provide an inner resource for the social and spiritual needs and concerns of Catholics of African ancestry.

National Association of Black Consulting Engineers
1979 Beaumont Drive
Baton Rouge, LA 70806
(504) 927-7240

Founded in 1975. Purpose is to gain recognition and increase professional opportunities for black consulting engineers. Lobbies the federal government.

National Black Deaf Advocates
c/o Arkansas Rehabilitation Services
PO Box 3781
1616 Brookwood
Little Rock, AR 72203
(501) 296-1635
TDD: (501) 296-1670
Fax: (501) 296-1675

National Association of Black Geologists and Geophysicists
PO Box 720157
Houston, TX 77272

Founded in 1981. Assists minority geologists and geophysicists in establishing professional and business relationships. Informs minority students of career opportunities in geology and geophysics. Seeks to motivate minority students to utilize existing programs, grants, and loans. Provides scholarships and oversees the educational careers of scholarship recipients.

National Association of Black Hospitality Professionals
PO Box 8132
Columbus, GA 31908-8132
(706) 569-6105

Founded in 1985. Works to develop global educational and economic opportunities for the hospitality industry through the expansion and diversification of minority involvement in the industry. Encourages professional development and opportunity in the industry through the design and implementation of workshops and seminars. Seeks to increase the number, size, and capability of minority-owned businesses within the hospitality and tourism industries.

National Association of Black Journalists
PO Box 17212
Washington, DC 20041
(703) 648-1270

Founded in 1975. Aims are to: strengthen the ties between blacks in the black media and blacks in the white media; sensitize the white media to the "institutional racism in its coverage"; expand the white media's coverage and "balanced reporting" of the black community; become an exemplary group of professionals that honors excellence and outstanding achievement among black journalists. Works with high schools to identify potential journalists; awards scholarships to journalism programs that especially support minorities.

National Association of Black Owned Broadcasters
1333 New Hampshire Avenue, NW, Suite 1000
Washington, DC 20036
(202) 463-8970

Founded in 1976. Represents the interests of existing and potential black radio and television stations. Is currently working with the Office of Federal Procurement Policy to determine which government contracting major advertisers and advertising agencies are complying with government initiatives to increase the amount of advertising dollars received by minority-owned firms. Conducts lobbying activities; provides legal representation for the protection of minority ownership policies.

National Association of Black Professors
PO Box 526
Crisfield, MD 21817
(410) 968-2393

Founded in 1974. Goals are to: provide a forum for the exchange of information among college professors; enhance education for black people and enrich the educational process in general; support and promote intellectual interests of black students.

National Association of Black Real Estate Professionals
PO Box 21421
Alexandria, VA 22320
(703) 920-7661

Founded in 1984. Provides a forum for the discussion of information related to the industry. Offers career development and networking opportunities.

National Association of Black Social Workers
271 West 125th, Room 317
New York, NY 10027
(212) 348-0035

Founded in 1968. Seeks to support, develop, and sponsor community welfare projects and programs which will serve the interest of the black community and aid it in controlling its social institutions. Assists with adoption referrals.

National Association of Black Storytellers
PO Box 67722
Baltimore, MD 21215
(410) 947-1117

Founded in 1984. Seeks to establish a forum to promote the black oral tradition and to attract an audience. Works for the reissue of out-of-print story collections.

National Association of Black Women Attorneys
724 Ninth Street, NW, Suite 206
Washington, DC 20001
(202) 637-3570

Founded in 1972. Seeks to: advance jurisprudence and the administration of justice by increasing the opportunities of black and non-black women at all levels; aid in protecting the civil and human rights of all citizens and residents of the United States; expand opportunities for women lawyers through education; promote fellowship among women lawyers.

National Association of Black Women Entrepreneurs
PO Box 1375
Detroit, MI 48231
(313) 559-9255

Founded in 1979. Black women who own and operate their own businesses; black women interested in starting businesses; organizations and companies desiring mailing lists. Acts as a national support system for black businesswomen in the United States and focuses on the unique problems they face. Objective is to enhance business, professional, and technical development of both present and future black businesswomen.

National Association of Blacks in Criminal Justice
Criminal Justice Building, Room 106
PO Box 19788
Durham, NC 27707
(919) 683-1801

Founded in 1972. Criminal justice professionals concerned with the impact of criminal justice policies and practices on the minority community. Advocates with local, state, and federal criminal justice agencies for the improvement of minority recruitment practices and for the advancement of minority career mobility within those agencies. Sponsors regional conferences, career development seminars, and annual training institutes; maintains speakers' bureau. Provides financial and in-kind services to community groups.

National Association of Blacks Within Government
1820 Eleventh Street, NW
Washington, DC 20001-5015
(202) 667-3280

Founded in 1982. Purpose is to enhance and increase the employability of black officials within government and to prepare black youths for government and private sector careers. Sponsors yearly seminar to help young people develop management, learning, interpersonal, and specialized skills.

National Association of Colored Women's Clubs
5808 16th Street, NW
Washington, DC 20011
(202) 726-2044

Founded in 1896. Federation of black women's clubs. Carries on civic service, education, social service, and philanthropy programs.

National Association of Investment Companies
1111 14th Street, NW, Suite 700
Washington, DC 20005
(202) 289-4336

Founded in 1971. Represents the minority small business investment company industry. Monitors regulatory action. Collects and disseminates trade and business information.

National Association of Minority Automobile Dealers
1250 Connecticut Avenue, NW
Washington, DC 20036
(202) 637-9095

Founded in 1980. Serves as a liaison between automobile dealers, the government, the community, and industry representatives.

National Association of Minority Contractors
1333 F Street, NW, Suite 500
Washington, DC 20004
(202) 347-8259

Founded in 1969. Minority construction contractors and companies interested in doing business with minority contractors. Identifies procurement opportunities. Provides specialized training. Serves as a national advocate for minority construction contractors.

National Association of Minority Political Women
6120 Oregon Avenue, NW
Washington, DC 20015
(202) 686-1216

Founded in 1983. Professional women interested in the American political process. Conducts research and educational programs.

National Association of Minority Women in Business
906 Grand Avenue, Suite 200
Kansas City, MO 64106
(816) 421-3335

Founded in 1972. Serves as a network for the exchange of ideas and information on business opportunities for minority women.

National Association of Negro Business and Professional Women's Clubs
1806 New Hampshire Avenue, NW
Washington, DC 20009
(202) 483-4206

Founded in 1935. Women actively engaged in a business or a profession and who are committed to rendering service through club programs and activities.

National Association of Negro Musicians
11551 South Laflin Street
Chicago, IL 60643
(312) 568-3818

Founded in 1919. Promotes the advancement of all types of music, especially among young black musicians. Sponsors annual competitions in which winners compete for scholarships.

National Association of Urban Bankers
1010 Wayne Avenue, Suite 1210
Silver Spring, MD 20910
(301) 589-2141

Founded in 1975. Minority professionals in the financial services industry.

National Bankers Association
1802 T. Street, NW
Washington, DC 20009
(202) 588-5432

Founded in 1927. Minority banking institutions. Serves as an advocate for the minority banking industry.

National Bar Association
1225 Eleventh Street, NW
Washington, DC 20001
(202) 842-3900

Founded in 1925. Minority attorneys, members of the judiciary, law students, and law faculty. Sponsors educational and research programs.

National Black Alcoholism Council
1629 K Street, NW, Suite 802
Washington, DC 20006
(202) 296-2696

Founded in 1978. Works to support and initiate activities that will improve alcoholism treatment services and lead to the prevention of alcoholism in the black community. Provides training on how to treat black alcoholics from a cultural perspective. Compiles statistics concerning alcoholism among blacks.

National Black Catholic Clergy Caucus
343 North Walnut Street
PO Box 1088
Opelousas, LA 70571
(318) 942-2392

Founded in 1968. Black priests, brothers, seminarians, and deacons. Purpose is to support the spiritual, theological, educational, and ministerial growth of the black Catholic community within the church. Serves as a vehicle to bring contributions of the black community to the church. Advances the fight against racism within the Catholic church and society.

National Black Catholic Seminarians Association
780 Porter Street
Beaumont, TX 77701

Founded in 1969. Black Catholic seminarians united for the growth and development of each member as a person, Christian, and potential priest or religious brother. "Attempts to reflect both the heritage of the church and black people in terms of the richness of their spirituality." Stresses the importance of individual contribution and total involvement of each black seminarian to the organization.

National Black Caucus of Local Elected Officials
1301 Pennsylvania Avenue, NW, Suite 600
Washington, DC 20004
(202) 626-3000

Founded in 1970. Elected black municipal and county officials united to recognize and deal with problems of members. Attempts to provide the organizational structure required to better present and respond to issues affecting constituents. Seeks to influence the National League of Cities in the development of policies affecting black Americans; promotes legislative and economic development initiatives directed toward the needs of the black community.

National Black Caucus of State Legislators
Hall of States
444 North Capitol Street, NW, Suite 622
Washington, DC 20001
(202) 624-5457

Founded in 1977. Organized to provide more political networking to black legislators from the federal and state levels. Goals are to: provide a network through which state legislators can exchange information and ideas on state and national legislation; provide a unified front or platform; serve as a focal point for involvement of black legislators in the "new federalism." Activities include arranging meetings between all governmental groups representing black elected officials and analyzing and forming a position on the "new federalism." Conducts seminars. Maintains speakers' bureau and biographical archives; compiles statistics.

National Black Chamber of Commerce
117 Broadway
Oakland, CA 94609-1709
(510) 215-5410

Founded in 1983. Black chambers of commerce organized to create a strategy for members of local chambers to share in the collective buying power of black minority communities. Primary focus is on the tourism industry, because, according to the association, blacks spend approximately $25 billion in the tourism market each year, but black-owned businesses net very little from this industry. Conducts training sessions to acquaint black businesspeople with the tourism market and marketing strategies.

National Black Child Development Institute
1023 15th Street, NW, Suite 600
Washington, DC 20005
(202) 387-1281

Founded in 1970. Conducts direct services and advocacy campaigns aimed at both national and local public policies focusing on issues of health, child welfare, education, and child care. Organizes and trains network of members in a volunteer grassroots affiliate system to voice concerns regarding policies that affect black children and their families. Stimulates communication between black community groups, through conferences and seminars, to discuss and make recommendations that will be advantageous to the development of black children. Analyzes selected policy decisions and legislative and administrative regulations to determine their impact on black children and youth. Informs national policymakers of issues critical to black children.

National Black Coalition of Federal Aviation Employees
Washington Headquarters
PO Box 44392
Washington, DC 20026-4392
(202) 267-7911

Founded in 1976. Purposes are to: promote professionalism and equal opportunity in the workplace; locate and train qualified minorities for FAA positions; help the FAA meet its affirmative action goals; monitor black, female, and minority trainees; educate members and the public about their rights and FAA personnel and promotion qualifications; develop a voice for black, female, and minority FAA employees.

National Black Gay and Lesbian Leadership Forum (BGLLF)
1219 S. La Brea Ave.
Los Angeles, CA 90019
(213) 964-7820
Fax: (213) 964-7830

The nation's leading organization addressing the leadership and skill development needs of the black lesbian and gay communities relative to social, legal, economic, and health issues. BGLLF maintains the AIDS Prevention Team, an innovative national AIDS education and prevention model. Other major BGLLF programming includes the Womyns Caucus and sponsorship of the 1995 "Black Lesbian and Gay Leadership Summit: Our Families, Our Communities, Our Lives." Held in Los Angeles, sessions included symposiums, on AIDS/health care and public policy; workshops on community organizing and outreach; and an awards ceremony.

National Black Law Student Association
1225 Eleventh Street, NW
Washington, DC 20001

Founded in 1967. Black law students united to meet the needs of black people within the legal profession and to work for the benefit of the black community. Objectives are to: articulate and promote professional competence, needs, and goals of black law students; focus on the relationship between black students and attorneys and the American legal system; instill in black law students and attorneys a greater commitment to the black community; encourage the legal community to bring about change to meet the needs of the black community.

National Black Leadership Roundtable
1424 Longworth House Building
Washington, DC 20515

Founded in 1983. Goals are to: provide a forum for leaders of national black organizations to discuss and exchange ideas on issues critical to black Americans; aid in the development of political, economic, and networking strategies that are advantageous to the needs of the black community; ensure that elected and appointed officials represent and are accountable to the black community.

National Black MBA Association
180 North Michigan Avenue, Suite 1515
Chicago, IL 60601
(312) 236-2622

Founded in 1971. Business professionals, lawyers, accountants, and engineers concerned with the role of blacks who hold Master of Business Administration degrees. Encourages blacks to pursue continuing business education; assists students preparing to enter the business world. Provides programs for minority youths, students, and professionals, including workshops, panel discussions, and Destination MBA seminar. Works with graduate schools; grants scholarships to graduate business students.

National Black McDonald's Operators Association
6363 West Sunset Boulevard, Suite 809
PO Box 8204
Los Angeles, CA 90008
(213) 296-5495

Founded in 1972. Provides a forum for the exchange of ideas on the improvement of community relations and on the operation and management of restaurants. Seeks to build and improve the McDonald's restaurant image throughout the community. Sponsors training seminars on marketing, better sales practices, labor relations, and profit sharing.

National Black Media Coalition
38 New York Avenue, NE
Washington, DC 20002
(202) 387-8155

Founded in 1973. Black media advocacy group seeking to maximize media access for blacks and other minorities in the communications industry through employment, ownership, and programming. Has been recognized by the FCC, Congress, and trade organizations concerned with blacks and other minorities in the media. Past activities include participating in FCC rulemaking proceedings, speaking before university and professional audiences, conducting classes, and negotiating affirmative action plans with large media corporations.

National Black Music Caucus of the Music Educators National Conference
University of Michigan School of Music
Ann Arbor, MI 48109
(313) 764-0586

Founded in 1972. Purpose is to foster the creation, study, and promotion of black-derived music in education. Seeks to heighten public awareness of the problems faced by black music educators and students and to increase public understanding of those problems. Provides a forum for the discussion of concerns. Coordinates and disseminates materials concerning black-derived music in order to assist music teachers in teaching black music and students. Encourages blacks to aspire to leadership positions and to demand inclusion in the development and presentation of Music Educators National Conference activities, including participation in MENC's regional conferences.

National Black Nurses Association
1511 K Street, NW., Suite 415
Washington, DC 20005
(202) 393-6870

Founded in 1971. Functions as a professional support group and as an advocacy group for the black community and their health care. Recruits and assists blacks interested in pursuing nursing as a career.

National Black on Black Love Campaign
1000 East 87th Street
Chicago, IL 60619
(312) 978-0868

Founded in 1983. Individuals and businesses united to promote the motto, "Replace Black on Black crime with Black on Black love" and foster love and respect in all communities where people are, the group believes, inordinately affected by crime. Organizes No Crime Day in various communities and Adopt A Building Program for businesses. Sponsors youth organizations and seminars in schools and communities to educate the public in ways of dealing with crime.

National Black Police Association
3251 Mt. Pleasant Street, NW
Washington, DC 20010-2103
(202) 986-2070

Founded in 1972. Seeks to: improve relationships between police departments and the black community; recruit minority police officers on a national scale; eliminate police corruption, brutality, and racial discrimination.

National Black Programming Consortium
929 Harrison Avenue, Suite 101
Columbus, OH 43215
(614) 299-5355

Founded in 1979. Objectives are to: assist the public broadcasting system in supplying programming that serves the needs of all population segments of the United States; serve as a collection, distribution, and archival center for black-oriented television programming; coproduce black programming; serve as a liaison between the black community and telecommunications systems with regard to black programming; provide funds for and encourage more and better black productions. Participates in the acquisition and distribution of programs for the cable and international markets.

National Black Republican Council
375 South End Avenue, Plaza 400-84
New York, NY 10280
(212) 662-1335

Founded in 1972. Black Republicans in the United States. Works to elect more black Republicans to national, state, and local offices. Maintains speakers' bureau.

National Black Sisters' Conference
3027 Fourth Street, NE
Washington, DC 20017
(202) 529-9250

Founded in 1968. Seeks to develop the personal resources of black women; challenges society, especially the church, to address issues of racism in the U.S. Activities include: retreats; consulting, leadership, and cultural understanding; formation workshops for personnel. Maintains educational programs for facilitating change and community involvement in inner-city parochial schools and parishes. Operates Sojourner House to provide spiritual affirmation for black religious and laywomen.

National Black Survival Fund
PO Box 3885
Lafayette, LA 70502-3885
(318) 232-7672

Founded in 1982. A project of the Southern Development Foundation. Objective is to improve the ability of black and other minority poor to achieve economic progress through their own effort and initiative. Believes that the economic, cultural, and physical survival of the nation's black community is endangered due to the recession, discrimination, and government cutbacks in social assistance programs. Seeks to maintain and increase support for programs that can avert the economic and human catastrophe the fund says will result if the opportunities offered to blacks are undermined by current assistance cutbacks. Maintains: Food for Survival Program in which landowners and sharecroppers in Mississippi volunteer land, equipment, and labor to provide food and employment for needy families; Health Care for Survival Program, a cooperative low-cost health center in Mississippi; Jobs for Survival Program, which has assisted in providing jobs for black workers in Alabama in construction, farming, and community service.

National Black United Front
PO Box 470665
Brooklyn, NY 11247

Founded in 1980. Purpose is to unite black people of diverse political ideologies, age groups, socioeconomic backgrounds, and religious beliefs in order to build "a viable force for social transformation." Goals are: the elimination of racism, sexism, bigotry, and racial violence; redistribution of the resources and wealth of the nation to provide abundantly for all citizens; elimination of the "genocidal mis-education system," police brutality, and denial of human rights nationally and internationally. Believes that current conditions in the United States threaten the survival of black people as a whole, and urges blacks to overlook individual differences by working together for common goals. Addresses such issues as unemployment, police brutality, budget cuts harmful to black communities, and the resurgence of the Ku Klux Klan. Conducts seminars and forums; maintains speakers' bureau; offers charitable program; sponsors competitions. Plans to organize boycotts, hold demonstrations, engage in electoral politics, and seek new vehicles for change.

National Black United Fund
50 Park Pl., Suite 1538
Newark, NJ 07102
(201) 643-5122

Founded in 1972. Provides financial and technical support to projects serving the critical needs of black communities nationwide. Local affiliates solicit funds through payroll deduction to support projects in the areas of education, health and human services, economic development, social justice, arts and culture, and emergency needs. Programs supported by NBUF emphasize self-help, volunteerism, and mutual aid. Maintains Walter Bremond Memorial Fund campaign.

National Black Women's Consciousness Raising Association
1906 North Charles Street
Baltimore, MD 21218
(410) 727-8900

Founded in 1975. Acts as a support group for women. Provides educational and informational workshops and seminars on subjects of concern to black women and women in general.

National Black Women's Health Project
1237 Ralph David Abernathy Boulevard, SW
Atlanta, GA 30310
(404) 758-9590

Founded in 1981. Encourages mutual and self-help advocacy among women to bring about a reduction in health care problems prevalent among black women. Urges women to communicate with health care providers, seek out available health care resources, become aware of self-help approaches, and communicate with other black women to minimize feelings of powerlessness and isolation, and thus realize they have some control over their physical and mental health. Points out the higher incidence of high blood pressure, obesity, breast and cervical cancers, diabetes, kidney disease, arteriosclerosis, and teenage pregnancy among black women than among other racial or socioeconomic groups. Also notes that black infant mortality is twice that of whites and that black women are often victims of family violence. Offers seminars outlining demographic information, chronic conditions, the need for health information and access to services, and possible methods of improving the health status of black women. Sponsors Center for Black Women's Wellness.

National Black Women's Political Leadership Caucus
3005 Bladensburg Road, NE, No. 217
Washington, DC 20018
(202) 529-2806

Founded in 1971. Women interested in understanding their political role and the need for females to work toward equality; auxiliary membership includes men, senior citizens, and youths. Works to educate and incorporate all black women and youth in the political and economic process through participation. Encourages women to familiarize themselves with the role of city, state, and federal governments. Presents awards for humanitarianism; trains speakers and conducts research on the black family and on topics concerning politics and economics; compiles statistics.

National Black Youth Leadership Council
250 West 54th Street, Suite 800
New York, NY 10019
(212) 541-7600

Founded in 1983. Conducts workshops for groups involved with black youth and minority student academic and leadership development; works to reduce the number of minority students that do not finish high school. Provides resources, information, skills, and strategies for fostering such development. Advises educators and parents on their role and responsibility to display leadership and success skills to youths they come in contact with; makes available to educational institutions training and expertise on cultural diversity, multiculturalism, and problems of bigotry and racism. Sponsors drug abuse awareness programs.

National Brotherhood of Black Skiers
National Headquarters
1525 East 53rd Street, Ste. 408
Chicago, IL 60615
(312) 955-4100

Founded in 1975. Bringing together African American ski clubs throughout the United States. A primary focus of the group is sponsoring black youth in hopes of placing an African American on the U.S. Ski Team and eventually getting a black skier into the Olympics.

National Business League
1511 K. Street, NW, Suite 432
Washington, DC 20005
(202) 737-4430

Founded in 1900. Encourages minority ownership and management of small businesses and supports full minority participation in the free enterprise system.

National Catholic Conference for Interracial Justice
3033 Fourth Street, NE
Washington, DC 20017-1102
(202) 529-6480

Founded in 1959. Catholic organization working for interracial justice and social concerns in America. Initiates programs within and outside the Catholic church to end discrimination in community development, education, and employment.

National Caucus and Center on Black Aged
1424 K Street, NW, Suite 500
Washington, DC 20005
(202) 637-8400

Founded in 1970. Seeks to improve living conditions for low-income elderly Americans, particularly blacks. Advocates changes in federal and state laws in improving the economic, health, and social status of low-income senior citizens. Promotes community awareness of problems and issues effecting low-income aging population. Operates an employment program involving 2000 older persons in 14 states. Sponsors, owns, and manages rental housing for the elderly. Conducts training and intern programs in nursing home administration, long-term care, housing management, and commercial property maintenance.

National Center for the Advancement of Blacks in the Health Professions
PO Box 21121
Detroit, MI 48221
(313) 345-4480

Founded in 1988. Participants belong to organizations including the American Public Health Association, National Urban League, National Black Nurses Association, and the American Hospital Association. Promotes the advancement of blacks in the health professions. Publicizes the disparity between the health of black and white Americans and its relationship to the underrepresentation of blacks in the health professions. (According to the National Center for Health Statistics, blacks have a higher death rate from cancer, heart disease, stroke, and diabetes than whites; blacks also have a higher infant mortality rate.) Acts as clearinghouse.

National Coalition for Quality Integrated Education
1201 16th Street, NW
Washington, DC 20036
(202) 822-7708

Founded in 1975. National organizations committed to desegregating and improving the quality of elementary and secondary schools in the United States. Serves as a forum for issues and developments pertaining to quality integrated education; encourages and coordinates citizen involvement in legislative developments.

National Coalition of Black Lesbians and Gays
New York, NY
(718) 622-3576

National Coalition of Black Meeting Planners
8630 Fenton Street, Suite 328
Silver Spring, MD 20910
(202) 628-3952

Founded in 1983. Purposes are to: act as liaison with hotels, airlines, convention centers, and bureaus in an effort to assess the impact of minorities in these fields; assess the needs of the convention industry and how best to meet these needs; enhance members' sophistication in planning meetings; maximize employment of minorities in the convention industry.

National Coalition of 100 Black Women
38 West 32nd Street, 16th Floor
New York, NY 10001-3816
(212) 974-6140

Founded in 1981. African American women actively involved with issues such as economic development, health, employment, education, voting, housing, criminal justice, the status of black families, and the arts. Seeks to provide networking and career opportunities for African American women in the process of establishing links between the organization and the corporate and political arenas. Encourages leadership development; sponsors role-model and mentor programs to provide guidance to teenage mothers and young women in high school or who have graduated from college and are striving for career advancement.

National Coalition on Black Voter Participation
1629 K Street, NW, Suite 801
Washington, DC 20006
(202) 659-4929

Founded in 1976. Seeks to: increase black voter registration and participation in electoral voting; develop and fund local independent coalitions that will conduct campaigns to increase nonpartisan voter participation and citizenship empowerment programs. Conducts training programs. Collects and analyzes data; disseminates information on voter education including data on the black voting age population. Sponsors Operation Big Vote and Black Women's Roundtable on Voter Participation.

National Conference of Black Lawyers
2 West 125th Street
New York, NY 10027
(212) 864-4000

Founded in 1968. Maintains projects in legal services to community organizations, voting rights, and international affairs; provides public education on legal issues affecting blacks and poor people. Researches racism in law schools and bar admissions. Conducts programs of continuing legal education for member attorneys. Maintains general law library. Compiles statistics; maintains lawyer referral and placement services.

National Conference of Black Mayors
1422 West Peachtree Street, NW, Suite 800
Atlanta, GA 30309
(404) 892-0127

Founded in 1974. Objectives are to: improve the executive management capacity and efficiency of member municipalities in the delivery of municipal services; create viable communities within which normal government functions can be performed efficiently; provide the basis upon which new social overhead investments in the infrastructure of municipalities can utilize federal, state, local, and private resources to encourage new industry and increase employment; assist municipalities in stabilizing their population through improvements of the quality of life for residents and, concurrently, create alternatives to outward migration. Facilitates small town growth and development through energy conservation.

National Conference of Black Political Scientists
c/o Franklin D. Jones
Dept. of Public Affairs
Texas Southern University
Houston, TX 77045
(404) 656-0763

Founded in 1969. Political and social science faculty, lawyers, and related professionals interested in black politics and related fields. Seeks to encourage research, publication, and scholarship by black Americans in political science; and to improve the political life of black Americans.

National Conference of Black Student Retention
PO Box 10121
Tallahassee, FL 32302-2121
(904) 599-3466

Founded in 1985. Members share programs, research, and strategies to reduce the dropout rate of minority students in colleges and universities.

National Consortium for Black Professional Development
PO Box 18308
Louisville, KY 40218-0308
(502) 896-2838

Founded in 1974. Goal is to increase substantially, by the year 2000, the number of black professionals in business administration, communications, applied and natural sciences, engineering, and law. Sponsors a science and engineering competition for black students and Ph.D. programs in the agricultural sciences and business administration. Maintains clearinghouse and placement bureau for black professionals seeking employment. Provides recruitment service for universities seeking qualified black faculty and students.

National Consortium of Arts and Letters for Historically Black Colleges and Universities
c/o Dr. Walter Anderson
The Westbridge, Suite 818
2555 Pennsylvania Avenue, NW
Washington, DC 20037
(202) 833-1327

Founded in 1984. Encourages academic excellence with an emphasis on cultural growth. Promotes study of African American history and culture in the context of the scholarly study of world cultures. Offers no grants, but helps sponsor programs through fundraising efforts.

National Council for Black Studies
Ohio State University
208 Mount Hall
1050 Carmack Road
Columbus, OH 43210
(614) 292-1035

Founded in 1975. Faculty members, students, and institutions united to promote and strengthen academic and community programs in black and/or African American studies. Bestows awards for scholarly contributions; sponsors undergraduate and graduate student essay contests. Offers professional opportunities referral service; compiles statistics on black studies activities including information on students, faculty, research, and curricula.

National Council of Negro Women
1001 G Street, NW, Suite 800
Washington, DC 20006
(202) 628-0015

Founded in 1935 by Mary McLeod Bethune. Assists in the development and utilization of the leadership of women in community, national, and international life. Maintains the Women's Center for Education and Career Advancement, which offers programs designed to aid minority women in pursuing nontraditional careers; also maintains the Bethune Museum and Archives for Black Women's History.

National Council on Black Aging
Box 51275
Durham, NC 27717
(919) 493-4858

Founded in 1975. Persons interested in research and policies affecting older blacks and other minorities and in the dissemination of research findings. Maintains speakers' bureau. Conducts lectures on minority aging.

National Emergency Civil Liberties Committee
175 Fifth Avenue, Room 814
New York, NY 10010
(212) 673-2040

Founded in 1951. To reestablish in full the traditional freedoms guaranteed under the Constitution and Bill of Rights. Committee "stands uncompromisingly for civil liberties for everyone and every variety of dissent." Legal staff handles test cases in the courts, without charge to the clients. Also functions as information service.

National Forum for Black Public Administrators
777 North Capitol Street, NE, Suite 807
Washington, DC 20002
(202) 408-9300

Founded in 1983. Works to promote, strengthen, and expand the role of blacks in public administration. Seeks to focus the influence of black administrators toward building and maintaining viable communities. Develops specialized training programs for managers and executives. Provides national public administrative leadership resource and skills bank. Works to further communication among black public, private, and academic institutions. Addresses issues that affect the administrative capacity of black managers. Maintains Executive Leadership Institute which grooms mid-level executives for higher positions in government, the Mentor Program which matches aspiring black managers with seasoned executives over an 8-month period, and the Leadership Institute for Small Municipalities, which provides intensive training for elected and appointed officials from small communities. Offers training programs for black South Africans intent on achieving public administrative positions in the post-apartheid era. Sponsors the National Minority Business Development Forum to increase the participation of small and minority businesses in local government procurement and contracting programs.

National Hook-Up of Black Women
c/o Wynetta Frazier
5117 South University Avenue
Chicago, IL 60615
(312) 643-5866

Founded in 1975. Purpose is to provide a communications network in support of black women who serve in organizational leadership positions, especially those elected or appointed to office and those wishing to elevate their status through educational and career ventures. Works to form and implement a Black Women's Agenda that would provide representation for women, families, and communities and that would help surmount economic, educational, and social barriers. Supports efforts of the Congressional Black Caucus in utilizing the legislative process to work toward total equality of opportunity in society. Seeks to highlight the achievements and contributions of black women.

National Institute Against Prejudice and Violence
Towson State University
Stephens Hall Annex
Towson, MD 21204-7097
(410) 830-2435

Founded in 1984. Purpose is to study and respond to the problem of violence and intimidation motivated by racial, religious, ethnic, or anti-gay prejudice. Collects, analyzes, produces, and disseminates information and materials on programs of prevention and response. Conducts research on the causes and prevalence of prejudice and violence and their effects on victims and society; provides technical assistance to public agencies, voluntary organizations, schools, and communities in conflict; analyzes and drafts model legislation; conducts educational and training programs; sponsors conferences, symposia, and other forums for information exchange among experts.

National Minority AIDS Council
300 I St. NE, #400
Washington, DC 20012
(202) 544-1076

National Minority Health Association
PO Box 11876
Harrisburg, PA 17108
(717) 763-1323

Founded in 1987. Health care providers and associations, consumers, executives and administrators, educators, pharmaceutical and health insurance companies, and other organizations with an interest in health. Seeks to focus attention on the health needs of minorities.

National Office for Black Catholics
3025 Fourth Street, NE
Washington, DC 20017
(202) 635-1778

Founded in 1970. Participating organizations include National Black Sisters' Conference; National Black Catholic Clergy Caucus. Serves as a "foundation for the renewal of the credibility of the church in the black community." Works to coordinate actions designed "to liberate black people and to serve as a unifying strength." Plans to: have specialists and technicians working within the black community to coordinate community organization and development; provide leadership training for youth; attack problems of poverty and deprivation; sensitize blacks to their heritage through historical, cultural, and liturgical experience. Seeks cooperation with groups working toward black liberation. Concerns include: training black and white clergy and religious, Catholic, and non-Catholic laity; influencing decisions involving race and the church; monitoring, in order to prevent, manifestations of racism. Sponsors Pastoral Ministry Institute and Afro-American Culture and Worship Workshop; provides workshops and leadership training for parish councils and parochial schools.

National Organization for the Professional Advancement of Black Chemists and Chemical Engineers
525 College Street, NW
Washington, DC 20059
(202) 667-1699

Founded in 1972. Seeks to aid black scientists and chemists in reaching their full professional potential; encourages black students to pursue scientific studies and employment; promotes participation of blacks in scientific research. Provides volunteers to teach science courses in selected elementary schools; sponsors scientific field trips for students; maintains speakers' bureau for schools; provides summer school for students of the U.S. Naval Academy. Conducts technical seminars in Africa.

National Organization of Black College Alumni
PO Box 729
Bluefield, WV 24701
(304) 325-6869

Founded in 1982. Works to ensure the survival of black colleges by addressing their concerns and needs and providing resources to meet these needs. Coordinates and focuses alumni support for black colleges; strengthens existing alumni associations; urges black youth to obtain a college education.

National Organization of Black County Officials
440 First Street, NW, Suite 500
Washington, DC 20001
(202) 347-6953

Founded in 1982. Black county officials organized to provide program planning and management assistance to selected counties in the United States. Acts as a technical information exchange to develop resolutions to problems on the local and national levels. Promotes the sharing of knowledge and methods of improving resource utilization and government operations. Conducts seminars and training sessions. Plans to maintain resource file on the achievements and history of black county officials.

National Organization of Black Law Enforcement Executives
4609 Pinecrest Office Park Drive, Suite 2-F
Alexandria, VA 22312
(703) 658-1529

Founded in 1976. Goals are: to provide a platform from which the concerns and opinions of minority law enforcement executives and command-level officers can be expressed; to facilitate the exchange of programmatic information among minority law enforcement executives; to increase minority participation at all levels of law enforcement; to eliminate racism in the field of criminal justice; to secure increased cooperation from criminal justice agencies; to reduce urban crime and violence. Seeks to develop and maintain channels of communication between law enforcement agencies and the community; encourages coordinated community efforts to prevent and abate crime and its causes.

National Rainbow Coalition, Inc.
1700 K Street, NW, Suite 800
Washington, DC 20006
(202) 728-1192

Founded in 1984 by the Reverend Jesse L. Jackson. Works to build a consensus in the area of civil rights, government, politics, labor, education, and business. Provides a platform for debate; encourages the development of a new political leadership committed to progressive domestic and international policies and programs.

National Society of Black Engineers
1454 Duke Street
Alexandria, VA 22313-5588
(703) 549-2207

Founded in 1975. Seeks to increase the number of minority graduates in engineering and technology.

National Society of Black Physicists
1601 East Market Street
101 Martena Hall
Greensboro, NC 27411
(919) 334-7646

Addresses the needs of black physicists; works to create opportunities for minorities in the field. Sponsors mentor program and lectures on research findings.

National Urban Coalition
8601 Georgia Avenue, Suite 500
Silver Spring, MD 20910
(301) 495-4999

Founded in 1967. The National Urban Coalition seeks to improve the quality of life for the disadvantaged in urban areas through the combined efforts of business, labor, government, and community leaders. Operates programs which work to increase the participation by minority students in science, math, and computer education; operates the Say Yes to a Younger's Future program.

National Urban League
500 East 62nd Street
New York, NY 10021
(212) 310-9000

Founded in 1910. Aims to eliminate racial segregation and discrimination in the United States and to achieve parity for blacks and other minorities in every phase of American life. Works to eliminate institutional racism and to provide direct service to minorities in the areas of employment, housing, education, social welfare, health, family planning, mental retardation, law and consumer affairs, youth and student affairs, labor affairs, veterans' affairs, and community and minority business development.

Negro Airmen International
PO Box 1340
Tuskegee, AL 36087
(205) 727-0721

Founded in 1967. Seeks greater participation of blacks in the field of aviation through the encouragement of broader job opportunities. Encourages black youth to remain in school and enter the field. Maintains a Summer Flight Academy for teenagers at Tuskegee Institute in Alabama.

Office for Advancement of Public Black Colleges of the National Association of State Universities and Land Grant Colleges
1 Dupont Circle NW, Suite 710
Washington, DC 20036-1191
(202) 778-0818

Founded in 1968. Collects, organizes, interprets, and disseminates data on 35 predominantly black public colleges. The colleges, located in 18 states, enroll over 135,000 students.

Omega Psi Phi
2714 Georgia Avenue, NW
Washington, DC 20001
(202) 667-7158

Founded in 1911. Social fraternity.

Operation Crossroads Africa
475 Riverside Drive, Room 830
New York, NY 10115
(212) 870-2106

Founded in 1958. Students and professionals, mostly from the United States, who live and work with African counterparts during July and August on self-help community development projects in Africa. Opportunities are provided for interaction with village elders, educators, and political and other community leaders. Emphasizes community growth from within a "Third World" structure. Before departure, participants make an intensive study of Africa; after their return, they give speeches about their experiences. Participants pay part of the cost of the project. Organizes workcamp projects for U.S. high school students in the Caribbean and programs the visits of African and Caribbean leaders to the United States. Sponsors training and exchange programs.

Operation PUSH (People United to Save Humanity)
930 East 50th Street
Chicago, IL 60615
(312) 373-3366

Founded in 1971 by the Reverend Jesse Jackson. National and international human rights organization directed toward education and economic equity and parity for all, particularly black, Hispanic, and poor people. Seeks to create an ethical atmosphere; encourages self and community motivation and social responsibility. Sponsors PUSH for Education Program to aid the nation's public schools and restore academic excellence and discipline.

Organization of Black Airline Pilots
PO Box 5793
Englewood, NJ 07631
(201) 568-8145

Founded in 1976. Seeks to enhance minority participation in the aerospace industry. Maintains liaison with airline presidents and minority and pilot associations. Conducts lobbying efforts, including congressional examinations into airline recruitment practices. Provides scholarships; cosponsors Summer Flight Academy for Youth at Tuskegee Institute in Alabama.

Phi Beta Sigma
145 Kennedy Street, NW
Washington, DC 20011-5294
(202) 726-5424

Founded in 1914. Service fraternity. Sponsors the Sigma Beta Club for high school aged males.

Phylaxis Society
PO Box 75680
Washington, DC 20013

Founded in 1973. Prince Hall Masonic writers and editors of Masonic publications.

Planning and the Black Community
Department of the Army
PO Box C-3755
Seattle, WA 98124-2255
(206) 764-3614

Founded in 1980. Members of the American Planning Association interested in issues related to planning in the black community. Objectives are to: formulate and articulate positions on national, regional, and statewide policy issues related to blacks for presentation to the APA and the public; provide a forum for exchange of practical experience and knowledge among black planners; establish and strengthen liaison with black professionals and groups such as social workers, economists, lawyers, public administrators, International City Management Association, National Association for the Advancement of Colored People, and National League of Cities.

Project Equality
1020 East 63rd Street, Suite 102
Kansas City, MO 64110
(816) 361-9222

Founded in 1965. A nationwide interfaith program enabling religious organizations, institutions, and others to support equal opportunity employers with their purchasing power. Services include: validation of hotels for conventions and meetings of organizations, validations of suppliers to member organizations and institutions, and consultant and educational services to assist employers in affirmative action and equal employment opportunity programs.

Quality Education for Minorities Network
1818 N Street, NW, Suite 350
Washington, DC 20036
(202) 659-1818

Founded in 1987. Created to implement the plan developed by the Quality Education for Minorities Project. Believes that minorities are underserved by the educational system and thus disproportionately lack the skill needed to participate effectively in a society increasingly based on high technology. Plans to work with school systems, communities, universities, and public and private sector institutions to ensure that minority students have equal access to educational opportunities.

Sigma Pi Phi
920 Broadway, Suite 703
New York, NY 10010
(212) 477-5550

Founded in 1904. Social fraternity. Maintains the Boule Foundation. Sigma Pi Phi is the oldest black Greek letter society in the United States.

Southern Christian Leadership Conference
334 Auburn Avenue, NE
Atlanta, GA 30303
(404) 522-1420

Founded in 1957. Nonsectarian coordinating and service agency for local organizations seeking full citizenship rights, equality, and the integration of African Americans in all aspects of life in the United States and subscribing to the Ghandian philosophy of nonviolence. Works primarily in 16 southern and border states to improve civic, religious, economic, and cultural conditions. Fosters nonviolent resistance to all forms of racial injustice, including state and local laws and practices. Conducts leadership training program embracing such subjects as registration and voting, social protest, use of the boycott, picketing, nature of prejudice, and understanding politics. Sponsors citizenship education schools to teach reading and writing, help persons pass literacy tests for voting, and provide information about income tax forms, tax-supported resources, aid to handicapped children, public health facilities, how government is run, and social security. Conducts Crusade for the Ballot, which aims to double the black vote in the South through increased voter registrations.

Southern Coalition for Educational Equity
PO Box 22904
Jackson, MS 39225-2904
(601) 362-6774

Founded in 1978. Coalition of parents, students, teachers, and administrators that operates in Alabama, Georgia, Louisiana, Mississippi, and North Carolina, with plans to include eight additional states. Works toward developing more efficient educational programs and eliminating racism and sexism within southern schools. Has organized projects including: Arkansas Career Resources Project, which provides minorities and single heads of households with marketable skills and jobs; New Orleans Effective Schools Project, which attempts to increase school effectiveness through high expectations, stressing academic achievement, and quality instruction; Project MiCRO, which seeks to provide computer access for, and sharpen analytical skills of, minority students; Summer Program, which focuses on students' reading comprehension skills.

Southern Poverty Law Center
PO Box 2087
Montgomery, AL 36102
(205) 264-0286

Founded in 1971. Seeks to protect and advance the legal and civil rights of poor people, regardless of race, through education and litigation. Does not accept fees from clients. The center is currently involved in several lawsuits representing individuals injured or threatened by activities of the Ku Klux Klan and related groups. Attempts to develop techniques and strategies that can be used by private attorneys. Operates Klanwatch.

Southern Regional Council
1900 Rhodes Haverty Building
134 Peachtree Street, NW
Atlanta, GA 30303-1825
(404) 522-8764

Founded in 1944. Leaders in education, religion, business, labor, the community, and the professions interested in improving race relations and combatting poverty in the South. Comprises an interracial research and technical assistance center that addresses issues of social justice and political and economic democracy. Seeks to engage public policy as well as personal conscience in pursuit of equality. Develops educational programs; provides community relations consultation and field services when requested by official and private agencies. Distributes pamphlets pertaining to desegregation of various public facilities and fosters elimination of barriers to black voting registration. Acts as official sponsor of overseas government officials, leaders, and other visitors who wish to view race relations in the South.

Special Committee on the Situation With Regard to the Implementation of the Declaration on the Granting of Independence to Colonies
United Nations, Room S-3341
New York, NY 10017
(212) 963-5515

Founded in 1961. United Nations committee comprising representatives of 25 nations concerned with the progress of people under colonial rule toward self-determination and independence. Considers situations in 18 territories based on information received from administering powers or local governments, nongovernmental organizations, published sources, and observations of the committee's visiting missions. Reviews military activities and activities of foreign economic interests in colonial territories; enlists support of United Nations specialized agencies and international institutions to assist decolonization efforts, especially through aid to colonial people; seeks to mobilize public opinion in support of decolonization by disseminating information.

369th Veteran's Association
369th Regiment Armory
1 369th Plaza
New York, NY 10037
(212) 281-3308

Founded in 1953. Seeks to support all patriotic endeavors of the United States, and to assist members and their families through charitable programs and community activities. Donates funds, equipment, and other supplies to children's camps, needy families, religious institutions, Veterans Administration Hospitals, and community and senior citizen centers. Conducts seminar and counseling sessions to assist unemployed veterans, and offers study classes to adults for preparation in Civil Service examinations.

Trade Union Leadership Council
8670 Grand River Avenue
Detroit, MI 48204
(313) 894-0303

Founded in 1957. Seeks to eradicate injustices perpetrated upon people because of race, religion, sex, or national origin. Seeks increased leadership and job opportunities for blacks.

TransAfrica
1744 R Street, NW
Washington, DC 20009
(202) 797-2301

Founded in 1977. Concerned with the political and human rights of people in Africa and the Caribbean, and those of African descent throughout the world. Attempts to influence U.S. foreign policy in these areas by informing the public of violations of social, political, and civil rights, and by advocating a more progressive attitude in the U.S. policy stance. Supports the work of the United Nations in Africa. Sponsors TransAfrica Action Alert to mobilize black opinion nationally on foreign policy issues by contacting influential policymakers.

TransAfrica Forum
1744 R Street, NW
Washington, DC 20009
(202) 797-2301

Founded in 1981. Research and education arm of TransAfrica. Seeks to provide an independent review of differing perspectives on political, economic, and cultural issues affecting black communities globally through its publications. Conducts seminars with scholars and government officials.

Try Us Resources
2105 Central Avenue, NE
Minneapolis, MN 55418
(612) 781-6819

Founded in 1968. Compiles and publishes minority business directories. Sponsors minority purchasing seminars.

Tuskegee Airmen, Inc.
2643 Jackson Street
Denver, CO 80205
(313) 965-8858

Founded in 1972. Former airmen who flew in the segregated U.S. Army Air Corps during World War II, men and women involved in military aviation, service academies, and ROTC units. Seeks to maintain a relationship among those who fought and served in World War II. Provides information about the contributions black Americans have made to aviation history. Operates a museum at Historic Fort Wayne in Detroit, MI.

Unitarian Universalist Association Black Concerns Working Group
25 Beacon Street
Boston, MA 02108
(617) 742-2100

Founded in 1985. Attempts to raise denominational public awareness of racism as a current justice issue. Works to implement recommendations regarding racial justice that were adopted by the Unitarian Universalist General Assembly in 1985. Conducts local and regional workshops in an effort to coordinate racial justice work among Unitarian Universalist congregations.

United Black Christians
1380 East Hyde Park Boulevard, No. 815
Chicago, IL 60615

Founded in 1970. Seeks to increase the relevance of United Church of Christ in the struggle for liberation and justice.

United Black Church Appeal
c/o Christ Church
860 Forest Avenue
Bronx, NY 10456
(718) 665-6688

Founded in 1980. Objective is to awaken the power of the black clergy and the black church to provide leadership for the liberation of the black community. Is concerned with black economic development and political power, and the strengthening of black families and churches. Believes pastors in black churches should reestablish legitimate leadership roles within the black community. Works with troubled black youths in the community; rallies against drugs in urban areas. Supports community betterment projects including surplus food programs and distribution of food to needy families.

United Black Fund of America
1101 14th Street, NW, Suite 601
Washington, DC 20005
(202) 783-0430

Founded in 1969. Nonprofit agencies that provide human care services to low-income or disabled blacks and other minorities. Assists disadvantaged blacks and other minorities in becoming self-sufficient by providing funding to member agencies for the establishment of health and welfare programs.

United Church of Christ Commission for Racial Justice
c/o United Church of Christ
700 Prospect Avenue, East
Cleveland, OH 44115-1110
(216) 736-2161

Founded in 1965. Works to ensure racial justice and social equality for ethnic and racial minorities worldwide. Maintains higher education program to provide scholarships to minority college students.

United Negro College Fund
8260 Willow Oak Corporation Drive
Fairfax, VA 22031
(703) 205-3432

Founded in 1944. Fundraising agency for historically black colleges and universities which are private and fully accredited. Provides information on educational programs. Sponsors college fairs for high school and community college students. Administers scholarship awards and corporate and foundation programs.

Universal Masonic Brotherhood
PO Box 1067
South Orange, NJ 07079
(201) 763-1780

Universal Masonic Order of the Eastern Star
PO Box 1067
South Orange, NJ 07079
(201) 763-1780

Universal Negro Improvement Association and African Communities League of the World
1611 West Columbia Avenue
Philadelphia, PA 19151
(215) 236-6063

Washington Office on Africa
110 Maryland Avenue, NE, Suite 112
Washington, DC 20002
(202) 546-7961

Founded in 1972. Established to monitor and analyze developments in U.S. policy toward southern Africa and work with national and local groups which support the attainment of majority rule. Lobbies on congressional legislation affecting southern Africa.

World Africa Chamber of Commerce
PO Box 33144
Washington, DC 20033

Founded in 1973. Sponsors trade missions to Africa and seminars to assist members with personal contacts and in gaining knowledge in the market and the needs of the countries they service. Conducts research and development studies on the changing economic developments and attitudes in specific countries and on the continent as a whole. Provides professional consulting in areas including market development, export promotion, joint venture projects, trade finance counseling, and market research studies. Operates trade center to provide facilities for exhibits, meetings, and other activities. Additional services include: assistance with visas and business trip planning; job referrals; clearinghouse on business, political, and cultural information; office and secretarial aid for businessmen and dignitaries traveling abroad. Maintains the Continental Africa Chamber Foundation.

Young Black Programmers Coalition
PO Box 1051
Vicksburg, MS 39181
(601) 631-7191

Founded in 1976. Provides professional training and offers technical assistance to black entrepreneurs in the broadcast and music industries. Conducts lobbying activities pertaining to legislation affecting the music industry. Provides scholarships to attend black colleges and universities.

Zeta Phi Beta
1734 New Hampshire Avenue, NW
Washington, DC 20009
(202) 387-3103

Founded in 1920. Service and social sorority. Maintains the Zeta Phi Beta Sorority Educational Foundation.

Law

Law

◆ The Legal Status of African Americans: 1790-1883
◆ African Americans and the Criminal Justice System
◆ African Americans in the Federal Courts ◆ African Americans on the U.S. Supreme Court
◆ Major Federal Legislation ◆ Major U.S. Supreme Court Decisions ◆ Legal Gatekeepers

by George R. Johnson, Jr., Marilyn Hortense Mackel, and Lorna M. Mabunda

◆ THE LEGAL STATUS OF AFRICAN AMERICANS: 1790-1883

by George R. Johnson, Jr.

The legal treatment of African Americans during the period 1790 to 1883, like their treatment in most other periods in American history, was one of decided ambivalence. Consequently, no useful discussion of the Supreme Court's treatment of African Americans can begin in 1790. An understanding of the period must begin with 1787 and the adoption of the American Constitution. Moreover, the Supreme Court's treatment of African Americans during this period in the nation's history must be viewed in context—in the context of the history and of the events which gave shape to the period.

In 1776, the nation began with a declaration of universal equality. But that promise ended at the color line. The ringing testimony to equality in the Declaration of Independence had its limits: it did not include the African American. In short, America began with a contradiction that centered on race. The constitutional debates of the 1780s highlight the nation's contradictory, confusing positions on race questions: this was a nation founded on the principle of individual liberty, but that liberty did not extend to the African slaves and their progeny. In the 1790s, as in the 1990s, the ambivalence persisted: Should the slaves be counted for purposes of representation? Should Congress be empowered to prohibit slavery and the slave trade? Should an escaped slave be "free" to live among the rest of us? These were some of the issues that dominated much of the discussion among the framers of the new constitution.

Perhaps one should not be surprised by this ambivalence on matters of race and equality in this country. It always has been present. The history of Constitution and the Supreme Court reveals dramatic instances of the nation's tortuous history on matters of racial equality. The "race" problem has a long history in the United States, a history as long as the history of the nation itself. This country's inability squarely to face the "race" question can trace its origins to the institution of African slavery. That blot on the national history still clouds the country's ability to discuss issues of race with candor. It cannot be surprising: slavery itself was never discussed with candor, either in the Constitution or in the country. As far as the Constitution was concerned, slavery was the shame "that dare not speak its name."

At the outset, the United States was mired in a debate over the question of slavery. While the debates about the composition of the national legislature were openly about the number of representatives to be accorded each state, the institution of human slavery and what to do about it clearly were major subtexts. Underneath those lofty discussions, however, lay the real issue: how to count the black slaves, who were to be found largely in the planting regions of the South? The problem of race predated the Constitution, and it would persist into the 1790s and beyond.

Even though the institution of human slavery vexed members of the constitutional convention, not once was the word itself used in the document that they submitted to the convention for ratification. Perhaps in their own minds they recognized that their championing of equality was vitiated and debased by the specter of slavery that they silently tolerated. Even though their document alluded to slavery's existence, it failed to acknowledge its presence.

In setting forth the number of representatives to be accorded each state in the lower house of Congress, the Constitution originally counted the African slaves as "three-fifths of all other persons." The "three-fifths" clause augured the history of the African American in the United States: the black American would share less in the promise of the new nation. That clause, though no longer effective, proved to be prophetic.

The original Constitution also forbade the new federal government from abolishing the slave trade or otherwise affecting matters of race before the year 1808. Again, however, the language is so abstract: "The Migration or Importation of such Persons as any of the States now existing shall think proper to admit, shall not be prohibited by the Congress prior to the Year one thousand eight hundred and eight..." (Art. 1, section 9, part. 1).

Runaway slaves were referred to as "person[s] held to service or labour in one state...escaping into another...." This fugitive-slave clause sought to ensure that the slaveowners' "escaped" property, when found, would be returned to him. Despite these deliberately neutral and innocuous-sounding provisions, there was no mistaking their purpose: to enshrine and ensure by law the political superiority of white Americans over the African slaves and their progeny. At the time of the Constitution's framing, one thing was certain: the African slaves and their descendants would be politically inferior to white people.

Even though the framers of the Constitution recognized the peculiar dilemma of racial discrimination as it then existed, they nonetheless decided that they could postpone a decision on the "race question," that its resolution could wait. So may have developed the recurrent American idea that matters of racial justice and racial equality can always be put off, postponed, to be decided at some other time. With such constitutional antecedents, it is not surprising that the Supreme Court has been enormously conflicted on matters of race. The Court takes its cases as it finds them, and cases on race have never been easily or calmly settled in this country. They are not now. They were not in the period 1790-1883.

The Early Days: *Prigg v. Pennsylvania*

Before the 1800s the Court had very few opportunities to render a decision directly on the question of slavery, so accepted was the institution as a feature of American life. Not that it was universally supported, but the law clearly recognized slaves as species of property and therefore subject to regulation as other real property might be. This regulation was often justified by citing the fugitive-slave clause of the Constitution (Art. 4, section 2). One of the few pre-Civil War cases to address the slavery question and state regulatory powers in any degree was *Prigg v. Pennsylvania* (41 US [16 Peters] 539, 1842).

Pennsylvania had enacted a statute prohibiting any person from removing blacks from the state by force or violence with the intention of detaining them as slaves. The Court explained that the fugitive-slave clause "contemplates the existence of a positive, unqualified right on the part of the owner of the slave, which no state law or regulation can in any way qualify, regulate, control, or restrain." The statute was declared invalid with respect to an escaped slave because, in the words of the Court, "any state law which interrupts, limits, delays, or postpones the right of the owner to the immediate possession of the slave, and the immediate command of his service and labor, operates pro tanto, a discharge of the slave therefrom." The Court further held that the clause implicitly vested Congress with the power to assist owners in securing the return of escaped slaves, that Congress had exercised that power by enacting the Fugitive Slave Act of 1793, that this national power was exclusive, and that any state laws regulating the means by which slaves were to be delivered up were unconstitutional.

Prigg announced no landmark policy in 1842. It simply affirmed the social and political realities of its time. However, during the period 1790 to 1883, two major cases involving African Americans and the issues of race did reach the Supreme Court. These two cases—*Dred Scott v. Sandford* (60 US [19 Howard] 393, 1856), *The Civil Rights Cases* (109 US 18, 1883), and the relatively minor case *Strauder v. West Virginia* (100 US 303, 1880) reveal the abiding ambivalence that consistently has characterized American racial relations.

Dred Scott v. Sandford

The 1800s were consumed with sectional strife, primarily strife about race. And that period gave the nation *Dred Scott* and an irreversible impetus toward civil war. No other case in judicial American history has achieved as much notoriety as has *Dred Scott*. The case continues to symbolize the marginal status in which African Americans often have been held in the nation's social and political order.

Dred Scott declared that no African American, whether free or slave, could claim U.S. citizenship. It also held that Congress could not prohibit slavery in the U.S.

territories. In addition, the decision also includes what is undoubtedly the most infamous line in American constitutional history. In his opinion, Chief Justice Roger Brook Taney wrote that African Americans had "no rights which any white man was bound to respect."

This decision—only the second in the nation's history in which the Supreme Court declared an act of Congress unconstitutional—was a clear victory for the political interests that supported slavery, particularly the South. Southerners long had argued that neither Congress nor the territorial legislature had the power to exclude slavery from a territory. Only a state could exclude slavery, they maintained.

Of course, the ruling in *Dred Scott* aroused angry resentment in the North and other parts of the country and launched the nation further along the course to civil war. It also influenced the introduction and the adoption of the Fourteenth Amendment to the Constitution after the Civil War. The 1868 Amendment, which explicitly overruled *Dred Scott*, extended citizenship to former slaves and sought to give them full civil rights.

Dred Scott was the slave of a U.S. Army surgeon, John Emerson of Missouri, a state that permitted slavery. In 1834, Scott traveled with Emerson to live in Illinois, where slavery was prohibited. They later lived in the Wisconsin Territory, where slavery was prohibited by the Missouri Compromise. In 1838, Scott returned to Missouri with Emerson. Emerson later died there in 1843, and three years later Scott sued Emerson's widow for his freedom.

Dred Scott

Scott's claim was based on the argument that his former residence in a free state and a free territory—Illinois and Wisconsin, respectively—made him a free man. A Missouri state circuit court ruled in Scott's favor, but the Missouri Supreme Court later reversed that decision. Meanwhile, Scott had become legally regarded as the property of John F.A. Sanford of New York. Because Sanford did not live in Missouri, Scott's lawyers were able invoke the diversity of citizenship jurisdiction to transfer the case to a federal court. The lower federal court ruled against Scott, and his lawyers appealed to the Supreme Court of the United States. By a vote of seven to two, the Supreme Court ruled that Scott could not bring a suit in federal court. The decision was announced on March 6, 1857, two days after the inauguration of President James Buchanan.

Each justice in the majority wrote a separate opinion. However, Chief Justice Taney's opinion is most often cited because of its far-reaching implications for sectional crisis and for the monumentally horrible view of the rights of African Americans that it announced. Speaking for the majority, Chief Justice Taney declared that Scott was not entitled to rights such as the right to vote or to sue in a federal court, because, as an African American, he was not a citizen of the United States (60 US 393, 1856).

The Court did not dismiss the case after ruling on Scott's citizenship, as it could easily have done. Because there was a growing national desire for a ruling on the constitutionality of such laws as the Missouri Compromise of 1820, the Taney court seized the opportunity to express its views on both congressional power and the legal status of African Americans (Catton. p. 86).

The Missouri Compromise had forbidden slavery in that part of the Louisiana Territory north of the latitude 36 degrees 30', except for Missouri. Instead of dismissing the suit, the Court discussed this issue as a part of its decision in *Dred Scott*. By the same seven to two margin, it ruled that the Missouri Compromise, which had been repealed in 1854, was unconstitutional. Taney argued that because slaves were property, Congress could not forbid slavery in territories without violating a slaveowner's right to own property under the fifth Amendment. As for Scott's temporary residence in the free state of Illinois, the majority ruled that Scott then had still been subject to Missouri law. Dred Scott was sold shortly afterward, and his new owner gave him his freedom two months after the decision.

The *Dred Scott* decision could have been a mortal blow to the newly created Republican Party, which had been formed to curb the expansion of slavery into the western territories. The decision forced Stephen A. Douglas, an advocate of popular sovereignty to devise a system that would enable settlers to ban slavery in their jurisdictions. President Buchanan, the South, and a majority of the Supreme Court had hoped that the decision would end the antislavery agitation that consumed the country. Instead, the decision increased antislavery sentiment in the North, strengthened the Republican Party, and fed the sectional antagonisms that finally exploded into war in 1861.

Strauder v. West Virginia and the *Civil Rights Cases*

Between the time of the Civil War and the *Civil Rights Cases*, one exception to the otherwise bleak and ambivalent record of the U.S. Supreme Court existed in the civil-rights area. That was in the case of *Stauder v. West Virginia* (100 US 303, 1880). The state of West Virginia permitted only "white male persons who are 21 years of age" to serve on juries in the state. This, of course, meant that it was impossible for African Americans brought before West Virginia courts ever to have another African American serve on a jury deliberating in their cases. The Supreme Court invalidated this provision as a violation of the Fourteenth Amendment's guarantee of equal protection.

Ironically, the Civil War, caused in part by Justice Taney's dictum in *Dred Scott* that Congress could not bar slavery in the territories, actually resulted in the destruction of slavery. Moreover, the war also resulted in a completely new balance of power between the national and the state governments. Federalism, unlike it had been understood prior to the Civil War, now would function with a totally new calculus, a calculus in which the federal government was the defining constant.

The years following the war produced the Civil War amendments—the Thirteenth Amendment, the Fourteenth Amendment, and the Fifteenth Amendment to the Constitution—with their concerted purpose completely to emancipate and empower the former slaves. These three amendments are compelling evidence of the new calculus that operated on federalism. In fact, the text of the Fourteenth Amendment, overturning *Dred Scott*, emphasized the significance of this new relationship and the new power realignments that now obtained: "All persons born or naturalized in the United States and subject to the jurisdiction thereof are citizens of the United States and of the state wherein they reside..." (United States Constitution, Amendment 14, section 1).

Now no dispute that citizenship in the United States was defined and protected by the national constitution and that state citizenship derived from national citizenship and was not independent of it could be had. Augmented by Congress' enforcement powers, these amendments were the constitutional foundations that supported reconstruction, where the recently freed slaves were affirmatively supported and protected by the federal government. A principal legislative result of this period was the passage of the Civil Rights Act of 1875 (18 Stat. 335). According to the statute, its purpose was "to protect all citizens in their civil and legal rights." Even though couched in disarmingly general terms, it was clear that the statute was designed with particular solicitude for the recently emancipated slaves, whose fate otherwise might largely have remained in the hands of people who generally were not favorably disposed to them and their new status.

The 1870s became unique years for testing race relations in the United States. Interestingly, during this period, no state had laws requiring the separation of the races in places of public accommodation. Whatever the practice in a particular establishment or a particular jurisdiction, it was a matter of local custom, individual choice, or personal preference. An earlier statute, the Civil Rights Act of 1866, and the ratification of the Fourteenth Amendment in 1868 had spawned several test suits throughout the country—among them suits for denying sleeper accommodations to African Americans on a Washington-to-New York train, for refusing to sell theater tickets to blacks in Boston, for restricting blacks to front platforms in Baltimore streetcars, and for barring African-American women from the waiting rooms and parlor cars of railroads in Virginia, Illinois, and California. There also had been massive resistance on the part of whites to the social integration of the races.

Faced with these challenges, Congress, controlled by the republicans, enacted a new civil-rights act in 1875. The 1875 statute sought to invalidate all racially motivated interference by individuals with other individuals' exercise of the right to make use of "the accommodations, advantages, facilities, and privileges of inns, public conveyances and theatres..." (109 US 9-10). In short, the statute sought to provide legislative specificity to the constitutional norms embodied in the Thirteenth and Fourteenth amendments.

The *Civil Rights Cases* (109 US 3, 1883) were actually six different cases: *United States v. Singleton*, *United States v. Stanley*, *United States v. Nichols*, *United States v. Ryan*, *United States v. Hamilton*, and *Robinson v. Memphis & Charleston Railroad.* Five of these cases were criminal prosecutions, which directly challenged the constitutionality of the 1875 statute. The first of these cases, *United States v. Singleton*, involved the refusal of Samuel Singleton, doorkeeper of New York's Grand Opera House to honor the tickets of William R. Davis, Jr. and his fiance.

On November 22, 1879, the pair had attempted to see a matinee performance of Victor Hugo's *Ruy Blas*, starring Edwin Boothe. Davis, business agent of the African American newspaper, *The Progressive-American*, was obviously black. However, Davis's fiance, who without incident, had purchased the tickets earlier that day was described as "a bright octoroon, almost white" (Allan F. Westin. 1964. "The Case of the Prejudiced Doorkeeper," p. 129). When the couple returned for the performance, they were told by Singleton that "these tickets are no good."

Stanley presented the refusal of hotelier, Murray Stanley, to serve a meal to Bird Gee, an African American, in Murray's Topeka, Kansas, hotel. *Nichols* involved the refusal of owner of Nichols House in Jefferson City, Missouri, to accept an African American as a guest. In *Ryan*, the doorkeeper at Maguire's Theater in San Francisco denied a black man named George M. Tyler entry to the dress circle at Maguire's. In *Hamilton*, the conductor of the Nashville Chattanooga & St. Louis Railroad denied an African American woman with a first-class ticket access to the ladies' car. Instead, she was relegated to "a dirty, disagreeable coach known as a smoking car."

The sixth of these cases, *Robinson v. Memphis & Charleston Railroad*, was different. This case involved travel on the Memphis & Charleston Railroad by a young African American woman, Mrs. Sallie Robinson, and her nephew, Joseph C. Robinson. Mr. Robinson was described as a young African American "of light complexion, light hair, and light blue eyes." The train's conductor attempted forcibly to refuse the two passengers entry to the first-class parlor car for which they had purchased tickets. The conductor mistook the pair for a white man and his paramour, whose association he had thought to be for "illicit purposes." In fact, he testified at trial that these couples usually "talked, drank, smoked and acted disorderly, and were objectionable to the other passengers" in the first-class section."

The railroad conceded the constitutionality of the 1875 statute, but argued that it did not apply to the conductor's actions. The trial judge ruled that motive was dispositive under the act. So, if the conductor believed Mrs. Robinson to be a prostitute, whether reasonable or not in that assumption, the exclusion was not based on race and, therefore, the railroad was not liable. The jury found for the railroad and the Robinsons appealed.

The United States, represented before the Supreme Court by Solicitor General Samuel F. Phillips, argued strongly that the act should be upheld in all these cases. In addition, the government's brief discussed the history of the American race relations and the genesis of the Civil War amendments and their statutory descendants. The government stressed particularly the importance of equal access to public accommodations. The Solicitor General emphasized that this act was one of several enacted by "a Congress led by men who had fought in the Civil War and had framed the war amendments." Implicit in the Solicitor General's position was the idea that Congress understood, as clearly as anyone could, that it was not sufficient to outlaw slavery and to declare equal protection to be the law of the land. More was needed: specific statutory protection was necessary to ensure that every vestige of slavery and every reminder of its stigma were eliminated from public life.

The government's arguments, however, did not persuade the high court. The Court announced its decision on October 15, 1883. The Court ruled against the United States, dashing the hopes of these African American petitioners and other citizens who believed the Civil War had eliminated racial discrimination in the United States. The vote in the *Civil Rights Cases* was eight to one. The majority included Chief Justice Waite and Associate Justices Blatchford, Bradley, Fields, Gray, Matthews, Miller, and Woods. Justice Bradley wrote the opinion of the court, which asserted two simplistically devastating conclusions: (1) the Fourteenth Amendment is prohibitory upon the states only (101 US at 11), and (2) the Thirteenth Amendment relates only to slavery and involuntary servitude (101 US at 21).

Bradley and his colleagues maintained that the Fourteenth Amendment operated only as a prohibition and restriction against the states. Because the Civil Rights Act of 1875 sought to outlaw acts of private individuals, shopkeepers, and other businesses, it violated the constitution. This "state action" doctrine holds that, because the government was not the actor in these cases, the Fourteenth Amendment did not empower Congress to outlaw these practices. Also, Bradley's opinion held that, while Congress was empowered by the Thirteenth Amendment to eliminate slavery and all its vestiges, the denial of access to accommodations in commercial establishments, public conveyances, and public amusements was not a "badge or incident of slavery" (109 US at 21). Bradley's opinion effectively halted the progress of civil rights and limited the ability of the federal government, acting through its legislature, to eliminate and eradicate racial discrimination in this country for almost 90 years.

A single justice on the Court dissented—John Marshall Harlan. At the time, Harlan was the court's only southerner and a former slaveholder himself. Ironically, he had also been a bitter critic of the civil war amendments during the 1860s. Between that time and the time of the decision in the case, Harlan had undergone a radical transformation. (His transformation was to achieve its fullest development 13 years later, when he dissented again in another famous civil-rights case, *Plessy v. Ferguson).*

Justice Harlan's dissent was not announced on the day of the majority's decision. In fact, the dissent probably was not written until early November of 1883. His dissent proceeds directly to attack the central failing of the majority's assertions: the grounds for the decision were "too narrow and artificial" (109 US at 26). According to Harlan, the majority have refused to embrace both "the substance and the spirit" of the Civil Rights Act. "It is not the words of the law but the internal sense of it that makes the law. The letter of the law is the body; the sense and reason of the law is the soul." And, in Justice Harlan's view, the purpose of the act "was to prevent *race* [emphasis in original] discrimination." The majority, as Harlan develops the dissent, betrayed this purpose "by a subtle and ingenious verbal criticism."

Justice Harlan's voice was eloquent, but it was a lone one, crying in the wilderness. Neither the majority of the Supreme Court nor the nation it represented cared to do much else to promote the civil rights of its new black citizens. Harlan's dissent in the *Civil Rights Cases* forecasted his more famous one in *Plessy v. Ferguson* (163 US 537, 1896), because the decision in the *Civil Rights Cases* led inexorably to the black codes, Jim Crow, and other examples of *de jure* segregation that came to define race relations in the United States.

The *Civil Rights Cases* starkly revealed the nation's ambivalence on the questions of race. On the one hand, Congress had sought to guarantee the rights of the recently freed slaves by proposing constitutional amendments that were ultimately ratified, even if some coercion was necessary. Congress went further and augmented the constitutional guarantees with additional legislative protections and safeguards. The Supreme Court, however, frustrated these constitutional and legislative initiatives with a cold and constricted reading of the Thirteenth and the Fourteenth amendments. An ancient pattern had reasserted itself.

◆ AFRICAN AMERICANS AND THE CRIMINAL JUSTICE SYSTEM

by Marilyn Hortense Mackel

Criminal justice in the United States consists of three major components, law enforcement, judicial and legal services, and corrections. In the past 25 years, African Americans have assumed significant leadership roles in both law enforcement and correctional services as evidenced by the rising number of African American judges, prosecutors, and defense attorneys. However, since 1970, employment of African Americans as judges and prosecutors has not increased at the rate necessary to give a formidible presence blacks working in the system. As a result, courts in large metropolitan areas have begun a critical examination of the impact of low numbers of African American judges on the perpetuation of racism in the court system—particularly on the disproportionate arrest rate, and the harsher sentences imposed on African Americans.

The Creation of Twentieth Century Slave Ships

Criminal justice statistics published by the U.S. Department of Justice provide documentation of the widespread perpetuation of discrimination in America. It is indeed not difficult to argue that the American system of criminal justice is giving birth to "Twentieth Century Slave Ships." Little Rock, Arkansas artist, Alice Ayers, provides, in her work entitled "20th Century Slave Ship" perceptual impetus of the phrase. The incarceration rate of African American males is alarming—such that a common expression in the African American community is that on any given day, more African American males of college age are in prisons and jails than in colleges or universities. Black males generally have been sentenced to long mandatory minimum sentences, including life without parole, for such offenses as drug possession, while white importers of drugs are seldom arrested or are able to negotiate a lessor charge and plea bargain a for lighter sentence.

Law Enforcement

The largest, and to some extent, the most imposing arm of the criminal justice system, police are the most visible criminal justice servants. As the first point of contact for persons entering the system, officers make discretionary, often quasi-judicial decisions to whether to arrest when an offense is alleged to have occurred. As implementors of local and national legal and political policy, police officers are agents of interest groups with power to effectuate their interest in our politically organized society. Law enforcers are organized and empowered to support the interest of those with means to shape law, a factor that may have significant bearing on why African Americans have had a particularly duplicitous relationship with the police.

Just like any other community, African Americans look to law enforcement for protection from an criminal elements present in their midst; the irony for most African Americans lies in the fact that those sworn to

Thurgood Marshall, 1958

protect have historically had little regard for the humanity of blacks, and have, in the exercise of their discretionary authority failed to enforce the law or to respond, when protection is sought by blacks. African Americans have for some time been perceived and treated as a race of people whose very existence threatens the dominant social group—the fact that the African American community has this duplicitous relationship with law enforcement is consistent with the purpose of law and law enforcement.

One way of mending the fences between law enforcement and minorities is to include them within the higher ranks of the organizations. In 1996, law enforcement executives included such big city police chiefs as Atlanta's Beverly Harvard, one of the first three women of any race and the first African American woman to head a major police force; Los Angeles's Willie L. Williams, that city's first black police chief; and Detroit's Isaiah "Ike" McKinnon.

Judicial and Legal Services and the Correctional System

Prosecutors have sole discretionary authority over the charges (if any) that are filed against offenders. Discrimination in charging occurs when African American offenders are subjected to multiple charges, including all possible lessor offenses, for one act, while an white offender is charged with lessor one offense for a similar criminal act. Plea bargaining, a process also coordinated by prosecutors, can be a source of discrimination as well.

The oppressive reality is that, like freed slaves, offenders released from prison, and or parole or probation, often are unable to pursue meaningful careers—rewarding work, and even menial work, is forever closed to them despite any possible genuine efforts to reform and to conform to the expectations of law abiding citizenship. To examine the statistical data demonstrating the likelihood that the criminal justice system is fostering twentieth century slave ships in the African American community, one need only examine the numerous statistical bases annually distributed by the U.S. Department of Justice. When viewing these statistics, it is important that the reader keep in mind that African Americans comprise 12 percent of the population of this country, approximately 30 million people.

In 1990, 3,224,060 African Americans were arrested compared to 7,712,339 whites (U.S. Department of Justice, Office of Justice Programs, Bureau of Justice Statistics. 1992. *Sourcebook of Criminal Justice Statistics—1991*, Washington, DC: U.S. Government Printing Office. p. 444). An examination of selected juvenile justice data shows that in 1990, whites and Hispanics under the age of 18 constituted 71.3 percent of the arrests made, while African Americans constituted 26.2 percent. Of adult offenders (those age eighteen and older), whites constitute 68.8 percent of persons arrested, while African Americans constitute only 29.4 percent (*Sourcebook of Justice Statistics—1991)*.

African American youth between the ages of 14 and 18, are being removed from the juvenile courts where rehabilitation and treatment is available, at least theoretically, and subjected at a young age to the harsh world of adult corrections. In 1989, 7,500 whites and Hispanics were transferred from the juvenile court to be tried as adults, while 8,500 African Americans were similarly transferred. In 1990, the number of whites and Hispanics in the system decreased to 7,400, while the number of African Americans increased to 9,200 (National Center for Juvenile Justice, National Institute of Justice, Juvenile Justice Clearing House). In addition, increased numbers of juvenile offenders are being subjected to life sentences without possibility of parole, and to the death penalty.

African Americans do not commit crimes in larger numbers. However, African Americans are treated more harshly by the criminal justice system. An examination of persons under correctional supervision is equally revealing. At public juvenile facilities in 1989, whites comprise 40 percent of the population, African Americans 42 percent, and Hispanics 16 percent (*Sourcebook of Criminal Justice Statistics)*. African Americans, in 1991 made up 43.4 percent of the jail population, whites 41.1 percent. In 1988, African Americans constituted 46.9 percent of the state prison population, whites 49.7 percent. In 1988 African Americans constituted 22.7 percent of the federal prison population, while whites constituted 75.2 percent. Significant is the fact that 53.8 percent of the African American male population and 68.4 percent of the female population of the federal prisons are incarcerated for drug offenses.

Because of the ravages of slavery, African Americans have long been placed "well outside of the pale" of American life (Arthur M. Schlesinger, Jr. 1992. *The Disuniting of America: Reflections on a Multicultural Society*, New York: W.W Norton & Company. p. 14). During slavery, and thereafter, African Americans were hung, castrated, raped, and otherwise physically and mentally devastated. Today, the same psychological and physical ravagement occurs at the hands of the criminal justice system, which affords them little or no protection from crime and removes them in large numbers from their communities to be barred upon return from reasonable opportunities in American life.

The "Trial of the Century"

On June 12, 1994, a brutal, double-murder led to one of the most pivotal criminal trials of the twentieth century. Nicole Brown Simpson, former wife of African American football legend O. J. Simpson, was brutally slain outside of her house; also killed was her friend Ron Goldman. Almost immediately, evidence pointed to O. J. Simpson as the primary suspect. The subsequent, year-long trial was aired on television, allowing viewers to witness the entire spectacle almost as if it were a soap opera. Many decried the circus atmosphere promoted by the entire media industry, not just television.

In one corner was the State of California, represented by prosecutors Marcia Clark and Christopher Darden, an African American. They portrayed Simpson as a jealous husband who had for years been locked in a pattern of domestic abuse. The murders would, therefore, be a case of spousal abuse taken to the extreme, the built-up result of the couple's breakup. In the other corner, Simpson's so-called "Dream Team" of defense attorneys focused on an alleged police-conspiracy theory based on race.

Simpson was found not guilty via jury verdict in October of 1995, a finding that divided the nation along color, class, and gender lines. *Broadcasting & Cable* reported that "the verdict ... broke all previous TV viewing records, with over 150 million people tuning in to watch the jury's decision."

Ultimately, the case had little to do with the actual murders. Rather than addressing the heinous crime that took place, the proceedings brought the ugly under belly of the country's prejudices, fears, and values to light. Polls showed that most whites thought Simpson was guilty, while most blacks thought him innocent. Many African Americans viewed Simpson as another black man caught trapped in a judicial system operated by bigots—a victim of racist law enforcement officials. Others lamented the black community's loss of a hero and accused the "white establishment" of systematic destruction of African American role models. Many sided against Simpson on the basis of his wealth, perceiving him as a rich man able to literally get away with murder because he could buy high-powered attorneys. Some women, certain that the murders were an extension of the physical abuse he had heaped on his wife, used the case as a way to turn public attention to the prevalence of domestic violence. Many black women were angry with Simpson for having divorced his first wife, a black woman, to marry a white woman, and determined him guilty in their own minds for that reason alone. Some of the public followed the case merely because it was one of the most prominent to rely on new forensic methodolgies, namely DNA testing. Whatever the attraction, most of those who believed in Simpson's innocence before the trial still believed he was innocent. Those who thought he was guilty remained against him. Following the verdict, the Brown and Goldman families filed a wrongful death civil suit against Simpson.

The Case of Mumia Abu-Jamal

Though not as big a newsmaker as "The Trial of the Century," the case of outspoken journalist and former Black Panther Mumia Abu-Jamal caused quite a ripple in the legal system during the mid-1990s. During an altercation between a Philadelphia police officer and Jamal's brother, Jamal claims to have entered the fracas in order to keep his brother from being beaten. Though details are sketchy and contested, the aftermath of the fray left Jamal wounded by a gunshot from the officer's gun and the officer dead. Arrested and convicted, Jamal received the death sentence in 1982 for that death.

Since then, a group of national and international supporters have advocated for Jamal's release, alleging that aspects of Jamal's case were improperly handled in regards to the U.S. Constitution and to correct legal procedure. Many believe Jamal was framed by the Philadelphia police who wanted to keep the blunt and forthright reporter from exposing evidence of corruption within the law enforcement agency.

On August 7, 1995, ten days before his execution was scheduled, Jamal was granted a one-year stay of execution, given the extension in order to complete his state court appeals. In July of 1996, that issue was still pending. Meanwhile, Jamal filed a suit against National Public Radio (NPR), who had hired him in 1994 as a news commentator. Jamal's commentaries about life on death row did not bode well in the conservative sector, however. In Jamal's suit, he claims that NPR gave in to pressure from U.S. Senator Bob Dole and others and refused to air his segments. Jamal hoped the court would force NPR to broadcast his prison recordings and then return them to him.

◆ AFRICAN AMERICANS IN THE FEDERAL COURTS

by Lorna M. Mabunda

When one considers that more than three-quarters of a century have passed since the first presidential appointment to a any judgeship—Theodore Roosevelt appointed Robert H. Terrell to a municipal jurisdiction in 1901—the specter of less than four percent of all judges being African American is daunting. Nonetheless, the amazing fact is that despite African Americans' complete lack of legal rights in the previous century—while in the midst of slavery—slaves, ironically, made the first in-roads into the courts. In separate incidents, escaped slave Elizabeth Freeman (c. 1775), New England slave Lucy Prince (1775), and Southern slave Dred Scott (1846) all blasted through racial barriers with unheralded courage and dignity.

Blacks did not enter the courts just as parties to actions; they also participated in the system in professional capacities. In 1844, Macon Allen became the first black admitted to a state bar; Charlotte Ray became the first black woman to gain the same distinction. Other pioneering woman followed, including Ellen Craft, Francis Watkins Harper, Laetitia Rowley, Maria Stewart, Mary Church Terrell, and Ida B. Wells. John S. Rock became the first African American lawyer to argue a case before the Supreme Court in 1865. In 1873, Mifflin Gibbs became the first black municipal judge. Though he only served a single term, his reputation for fairness was legendary, and he was named U.S. consul to Madagascar in 1897. Jonathan Jasper White was elected to the South Carolina State Supreme Court in 1870. In 1937, President Franklin D. Roosevelt appointed William H. Hastie to the Territorial Court of the Virgin Islands, making him the first black federal trial court judge. Hastie was succeeded by a black man, Herman E. Moore, in 1939, the same year Jane Matilda Bolin became the first black female judge, appointed by New York City Mayor Fiorello LaGuardia. In 1945, President Harry S. Truman appointed Irwin C. Mollison to what was then known as the U.S. Customs Court and is now the U.S. Court of International Trade, thus making him the first black lifetime appointee to a federal court. The 1996 swearing in of Joyce London Alexander as chief U.S. Magistrate judge for the District Court of Massachusetts made her the first African American female chief judge in the state and the first black chief U.S. magistrate judge in the United States.

The Federal System

The federal system is empowered to hear cases that present federal questions, i.e. questions about the Constitution or U.S. laws or treaties; actions involving more that $50,000; cases involving diverse citizenship, either between two or more states, between the United States and a state, by a state and citizens of other nations, or controversies involving ambassadors or other representatives of foreign states. As dictated by Article III, Section I of the U.S. Constitution, the Judicial Code statute outlines the specificities of a tiered federal court system, each level with its own exclusive legislative rights.

Each of the 94 districts, as drawn by Congress, has a U.S. District Court with original jurisdiction over matters under $10,000, landlord/tenant disputes, small claims, traffic matters, and arraignments/exams for certain felonies. 12 regional circuit courts and one "federal" circuit court possess original jurisdiction over matters greater than $10,000, divorces, and felony criminal trials. Furthermore, probate matters are handled by probate courts, which are a division of the circuit court system—literally a court system within a court system. The circuit courts also hear appeals from the district courts. Courts of Appeals hear appeals from the lower courts. The highest court in the land, the U.S. Supreme Court, examines case law and state laws/statutes. The Supreme Court also deals with appeals from circuit and appeals courts.

Nominated by the U.S. president and confirmed through Senate hearings, federal judgeships are lifetime appointments, usually crowning a distinguished legal career. Of the less than 1,000 active federal judges, in 1995, a scant 71 were African American, including 16 women. Still, blacks have steadily received appointments since the early 1960s, beginning with James B. Parsons, who was nominated by President John F. Kennedy to sit on the bench of the U.S. District Court for the Northern District of Illinois in 1961. At that time, the lack of federal black judges was glaring. Kennedy made great strides, successfully appointing Wade Hampton McCree, Jr., to the U.S. District Court for the Eastern Districts of Michigan in 1961, and Thurgood Marshall to the Second Circuit Court of Appeals in 1962. In five years, Marshall would go on to become the first African American appointed to the Supreme Court of the United States.

President Lyndon B. Johnson followed Kennedy's suit, nominating 11 blacks to federal benches. Among them were A. Leon Higginbotham, Jr.—Johnson's first appointee—and Constance Baker Motley. As a member of the U.S. District Court for the Southern District of New York, she became the first African American woman to hold a federal judgeship in 1966. The next female appointee did not come for 12 years, until Mary Johnson Lowe was seated in the same district court venue in 1978, by President Jimmy Carter. Carter also chose Amalya Lyle Kearse, who, in 1979, became the first black woman on the U.S. Court of Appeals. She was seated in the same venue in which Thurgood Marshall had started, the Second Circuit.

Interestingly, Republican presidents have had the poorest record of nominating blacks to the federal courts. For example, presidents Richard Nixon and Gerald R. Ford together only nominated 11 African American judges over an eight-year period. Democrat Lyndon Johnson nominated the same number in half the time, though it should be mentioned that Ford placed four black judges during his shortened, two-year term. Also of note is Nixon's appointment of Robert M. Duncan to the U.S. Court of Military Appeals in 1971, another notable black first. Republicans Ronald Reagan and George Bush had poor track records, particularly when compared with Democrat Bill Clinton. By 1995, Clinton had appointed 30 black federal judges, more than any other president with the exception of Carter.

◆ AFRICAN AMERICANS ON THE U.S. SUPREME COURT

Thurgood Marshall, a graduate of Lincoln University and Howard University Law School, was admitted to the Maryland Bar in 1933. He joined the National Association for the Advancement of Colored People staff as assistant to special counsel Charles Hamilton Houston. In 1938 Marshall succeeded Houston as special council, and in 1950 he became director of the NAACP Legal Defense and Education Fund. While working the NAACP and the NAACP Legal Defense and Education Fund, Marshall played a major role in some of the Supreme Court history's most important cases, including *Smith v. Allwright* (1944), *Morgan v. Virginia* (1946), *Shelley v. Kraemer* (1948), *Sweatt v. Painter* (1950), and *Brown v. Board of Education of Topeka*. Between 1938 and 1961, Marshall argued 32 cases before the U.S. Supreme Court, winning 29.

In 1961, Marshall became the second African American to serve on the U.S. Circuit Court of Appeal, when President John F. Kennedy named Marshall to fill a vacancy. In 1965, President Lnydon B. Johnson appointed Marshall to the post of U.S. Solicitor General. With the retirement of Associate Justice Tom Campbell Clark in 1967, Marshall was nominated to fill the vacancy. Marshall's nomination was met with objections from Southern Senators. Nevertheless, he was confirmed, becoming the first African American justice in Unites States history. While on the Court, Marshall served as a supporter of affirmative action, free speech, and the rights of workers. He wrote few famous decisions, but his dissenting opinions in such cases as *Milliken v. Bradley* (1974) and *Regents of the University v. Bakke* (1978).

On June 27, 1991, Justice Marshall announced his plan to retire, due to advancing age and poor health, after some 24 years on the nation's highest court. On July 1 President George Bush announced that he had chosen Clarence Thomas, a black, conservative appeals court judge, as his choice to fill the vacancy created by Marshall. In 1981, President Ronald Reagan appointed Clarence Thomas, a graduate of a Holy Cross College and Yale University Law School, to head the civil rights division of the Department of Education. A year later, Thomas was appointed to head the Equal Employment Opportunity Commission. In 1990 Thomas was appointed by President Bush to fill a vacancy on the U.S. Court of Appeals for the District of Columbia.

In a flurry of controversy, Clarence Thomas was appointed an associate justice of the U.S. Supreme Court in 1991, after being nominated by President George Bush. Besides Thomas's relative youth and judicial inexperience, his nomination hearings were marred by the accusations from Anita Hill that she had suffered from sexual harassment while under his employ at the Equal Employment Opportunity Commission (EEOC). The nomination committee chose to approve Thomas's nomination despite the serious accusations from Hill.

Anita Hill, a relatively unknown law professor at the University of Oklahoma, became a household name when she came forward with charges of sexual harassment against Judge Thomas, purportedly committed when both had worked for the EEOC. Hill claimed that Thomas repeatedly pressured her to date him, told her plots of pornographic movies, and bragged about his sexual exploits. When asked why she didn't quit her job or report Thomas when the incidents occurred during the early 1980s, Hill answered that she feared she would not be able to get another job.

The nation, as well as the Senate, seemed divided by the shocking testimony. Thomas denied the allegations and had many of his former coworkers testify for him. The case became highly politicized as conservatives and liberals fought for ground. Thomas, who was nominated by President George Bush, was supported by the conservatives in the Republican party because his appointment would mean an African American on the court who would uphold conservative policies. Therefore, Hill's case was taken up by many Democrats.

After the confirmation votes were counted, Thomas was nominated by the narrow margin of 52 to 48—one of the closest margins in Supreme Court history. Apparently, the American public mirrored the pro–Thomas view. In a poll taken soon after the hearings, 60 percent sided with Thomas and only 20 percent with Hill. One year later, however, only 38 percent of those Americans polled agreed with Thomas, while an equal number supported Hill's version.

◆ MAJOR FEDERAL LEGISLATION

Emancipation Act (April 1862)

ch.54, 12 state. 376

This act, abolishing slavery in the District of Columbia, was enacted April 16, 1862.

Clarence Thomas

Emancipation Act (June 1862)

ch. 111, 12 Stat. 432

This act, abolishing slavery in all other territories of the United States, was enacted June 19, 1862.

Amendment Thirteen to the U.S. Constitution (1865)

This Amendment, abolishing slavery and involuntary servitude in all of the United States, was ratified December 16, 1865.

Civil Rights Act (1866)

ch. 31, 14 Stat. 27

This act was enacted April 9, 1866, to provide all citizens, especially recently freed slaves, with basic civil rights, including the right to make and enforce contracts, to bring suits in court, to purchase and sell real and personal property, and to enjoy security of person and property.

Amendment Fourteen to the United States Constitution (1868)

This Amendment defined United States and state citizenship, and provided all citizens with the privileges and immunities of citizenship, the right to life, liberty and property, and equal protection under the law. It was ratified July 20, 1868.

Anita Hill testifies before the Senate Judiciary Committee.

Amendment Fifteen to the United States Constitution (1870)

This Amendment was designed to protect the right of all citizens to vote. It was ratified March 30, 1870.

Civil Rights Act (1870)
ch. 114, 16 Stat. 140

This act was enacted May 31, 1870, to carry–out the provision of the Fifteenth Amendment. It established penalties for violations of the provisions of the Amendment.

Civil Rights Act (1871)
ch. 99, 16 Stat. 433

This act was enacted February 28, 1871, to further define the protections established in the Fifteenth Amendment.

Civil Rights Act (April 1871)
ch. 22, 17 Stat. 13

This act was enacted April 20, 1871 to further outline the protections provided for by the Fourteenth Amendment. It provides for the vindication of crimes committed under the act in federal court.

Civil Rights Act (1875)
ch. 114, 18 Stat. 335

This act was designed to provide all citizens with equal access to public places. Ruling in 1883 in a set of cases, known as the *Civil Rights Cases*, the U.S. Supreme court invalidated the act.

Civil Rights Act of 1957
Pub.L. No. 85–315, 71 Stat. 634

This act created the Commission on Civil Rights and empowered it to investigate allegations of deprivation of a United States citizen's right to vote, and to appraise laws and policies of the federal government with respect to equal protection of the law, and to submit a report to the President and to the Congress within two years.

Civil Rights Act of 1960
Pub.L. No. 86–449, 74 Stat. 86

Guaranteed the provision of criminal penalties in the event a suspect crosses state lines to avoid legal process

Engraving depicting blacks celebrating the abolition of slavery in the District of Columbia.

for the actual or attempted bombing or burning of any vehicle or building, and provided penalties for persons who obstructed or interfered with any order of a federal court.

Civil Rights Act of 1964
Pub.L. No. 88–352, 78 Stat. 241

This act prohibited discrimination in the use of public accommodations whose operations involve interstate commerce, and provided enforcement measures to ensure equal access to public facilities. Also the Civil Rights Act of 1964 prohibited racial discrimination in any program receiving federal aid and prohibited discrimination in most areas of employment.

Voting Rights Act of 1965
Pub.L. No. 89–110, 79 Stat. 437

The Voting Rights Act of 1965 struck down requirements such as literacy and knowledge tests and poll tax payments which had been used to restrict black participation in voting, and provided for federal registrars to register voters should state registrars refuse to do so. It further stipulated that registered voters cannot be prohibited from voting.

Civil Rights Act of 1968
Pub.L. No. 90–284, 82 Stat. 73

This act provided for open housing by prohibiting discrimination based on race, color, religion, or national origin.

Equal Employment Opportunity Act of 1972
Pub.L. No. 92–261, 86 Stat. 103

This act provided the Equal Employment Opportunity Commission (which was established by the Civil Rights Act of 1964) with the authority to issue judicially enforceable cease and desist orders in cases involving discriminatory employment practices.

Public Works Employment Act of 1977
Pub.L. No. 95–28, 91 Stat. 116, Title I

The Public Works Employment Act of 1977 provided that ten percent of funds expended as a result of federal

Engraving depicting the trial of a freedman, Florida, 1867.

grants be earmarked for and paid to minority business enterprises.

Voting Rights Act of 1965 Amendment
Pub.L. No. 97–205, 96 Stat. 131 (1982)

This Amendment was a congressional response to the Supreme Court's ruling in *City of Mobile v. Bolden* that required proof of discriminatory intent in voting rights cases. Section 2 of the voting rights Act prohibits any voting practice or procedure "imposed or applied by any state or political subdivision in a manner which results in a denial or abridgement of the right of any citizen of the United States to vote on account of race or color"

Civil Rights Commission Act of 1983
Pub.L. No. 98–183, 87 Stat. 1301

This act created an eight–member bipartisan commission with four members appointed by the president, and two by the Senate and House, respectively. The Commissioners are appointed to four or six year terms and can be fired only for neglect of duty or malfeasance in office. The statute was enacted after President Reagan attempted to fire Commissioners who did not express his views on civil rights. The Act extended the life of the Civil Rights Commission Authorization Act of 1978, which was scheduled to expire in 1983.

Civil Rights Restoration Act of 1988
Pub.L. No. 100–259, 102 Stat. 31

Ruling in 1984 in the case *Grove City College v. Bell*, the U.S. Supreme Court ruled that not all programs and activities of an institution were covered by Title IX of the Education amendments of 1972 (Public Law 89–10, 79 Stat. 27) and that discrimination can be barred only in programs that directly receive federal funds. Section 6 of Public Law 100–259 amended portions of the Civil Rights Act of 1964, refined the definition of programs and activities which are covered by the Civil Rights Act and other legislation. Specifically the Amendment addressed Title IX of the Education amendments of 1972, which prohibits discrimination in educational programs receiving federal financial assistance.

Fair Housing amendments Act of 1988
Pub.L. No. 100–430, 102 Stat 1619

The Fair Housing amendments Act of 1988 strengthens laws that resulted from passage of the Fair Housing act of 1968. The Act of 1988 gives the Department of Housing and Urban Development (HUD) the authority to issue discrimination charges, allows administrative law justices the ability to review housing discrimination cases, and removed the $1000 limit on punitive damages that a victim of discrimination may receive.

Civil Rights Act of 1991
Pub.L. 102–166, 105 Stat. 1071

This act is designed to provide additional remedies to deter harassment and intentional discrimination in the workplace, to provide guidelines for the adjudication of cases arising under Title VII of the Civil Rights Act of 1964, and to expand the scope of civil rights legislation weakened by Supreme Court decisions, particularly the Court's ruling in *Wards Cove Packing Co. v. Antonio*, 490 US 642 (1989).

Glass Ceiling Act of 1991
Pub.L. 102–166, 105 Stat. 1081

Title II of the Civil Rights Act of 1991, designed to establish a means for studying and addressing the underrepresentation of women and minorities at management and decision making levels in the workforce.

◆ MAJOR U.S. SUPREME COURT DECISIONS

Access to the Polls

United States v. Reese
92 US 214 (1876)

Prior to the Fifteenth Amendment, states regulated all details of state and local elections; states prescribed the qualifications of voters, and the manner in which those desiring to vote at an election should make their qualifications known to the election officers. Thus, the Fifteenth Amendment interferes with the past sovereignly

Entrance to a segregated waiting room in Jackson, Mississippi.

practice and provides rules not prescribed by state law. However, this court restricted the scope of the Fifteenth Amendment and the ability of Congress to enforce it by not punishing election officials who unlawfully interfere and prevent the free exercise of the elective franchise.

The federal government indicted two Kentucky election inspectors for refusing to receive and count the vote of a black citizen. The Supreme Court held, that Congress had not yet provided "appropriate legislation'" for the punishment of the offense charged under any sections of the Fifteenth Amendment.

Guinn v. United States
238 US 347 (1915)

In 1910, an amendment to the constitution of Oklahoma, restricted the franchise according to a "grandfather clause" that provided that no illiterate person could be registered to vote. The clause, however, granted an exemption for persons who resided in a foreign country prior to January 1, 1866, and had been eligible to register prior to that date or had a lineal ancestor who was eligible to vote at that time. Since no blacks were eligible to vote in Oklahoma prior to 1866, the law disenfranchised all blacks.

The U.S. Supreme Court in *Guinn v. United States* ruled that the grandfather clause was invalid in Oklahoma or in any other state.

Nixon v. Herndon
273 US 536 (1927)

Dr. L. A. Nixon, an African American, was refused the right to vote in a primary election because of a state statute that prohibited blacks from participating in Democratic Party elections in Texas. Nixon filed suit against the election officials and his case ultimately reached the U.S. Supreme Court. In his opinion, on *Nixon v. Herndon* Justice Oliver Wendell Holmes wrote: "It is too clear for extended argument that color cannot be made the basis of a statutory classification affecting the right set up in this case." As a result of *Nixon v. Herndon* the Texas statute was declared unconstitutional.

Nixon v. Condon
286 US 73 (1932)

As a result of the U.S. Supreme Court ruling in *Nixon v. Herndon*, the Texas legislature passed a new statute. This statute empowered the state Democratic executive committee to set up its own rules regarding primary

President Lyndon B. Johnson

elections. The party promptly adopted a resolution stipulating that only white Democrats be allowed to participate in primaries. Dr. Nixon again filed suit, and his right to vote was again upheld by the U.S. Supreme Court.

Lane v. Wilson
307 US 268 (1939)

In an attempt to restrict voter registration, the Oklahoma legislature stated that all Oklahomans who were already registered would remain qualified voters, but that all others would have to register within 12 days (from April 30 to May 11, 1916) or be forever barred from the polls. In 1934, I. W. Lane, an African American, was refused registration on the basis of this statute. The U.S. Supreme Court declared that the statute was in conflict with the Fifteenth Amendment to the U.S. Constitution, and, therefore was unconstitutional.

Smith v. Allwright
321 US 649 (1944)

The Texas State Democratic party, during its convention in 1932, limited the right of membership to white electors. As a result, nonwhites were unable to participate in a Democratic party primary. In *Grovey v. Townsend* (295 U.S. Supreme Court Reports 45), the Supreme Court had upheld this limitation because it was made by the party in convention, not by a party executive committee. In *Smith v. Allwright*, the Supreme Court overruled *Grovey*, stating, "The United States is a constitutional democracy. Its organic law grants to all citizens a right to participate in the choice of elected officials without restriction by any state because of race." The Court noted that political party makes its selection of candidates as an agency of the state and, therefore, cannot exclude participation based on race and remain consistent with the Fifteenth Amendment.

Newspaper illustration depicting white opposition to black suffrage.

Gomillion v. Lightfoot
364 US 339

In this case African American citizens challenged an Alabama statute that redefined the boundaries of the City of Tuskegee. The statute altered the shape of Tuskegee and placed all but four of Tuskegee's 400 African American voters outside of the city limits, while not displacing a single white voter.

Baker v. Carr
369 US 186 (1962)

Baker v. Carr was brought to the Supreme Court by electors in several counties of Tennessee, who asserted that the 1901 legislative reapportionment statute was unconstitutional because the numbers of voters in the various districts had changed substantially since 1901. The plaintiffs requested that the Supreme Court either direct a reapportionment by mathematical application of the Tennessee constitutional formula to the 1960 Census, or instruct the state to hold direct at-large elections. The state district court had dismissed the case on the grounds that it was a political question and, as such, did not fall within the protection of the Fourteenth Amendment. The U.S. Supreme Court ruled that the case involved a basic constitutional right and thereby was within court jurisdiction, and remanded the case to the state district court.

South Carolina v. Kalzenback
383 US 301 (1966)

The Voting Rights Act of 1965 was designed to eliminate racial discrimination in voting, which had influenced the electoral process for nearly a century. The act abolished literacy tests, waived accumulated poll taxes, and alloted the U.S. Attorney General vast discretionary powers over regions suspect of discriminatory legislation and practices against black voters.

The Supreme Court dismissed South Carolina's petition asserting that the act violated the U.S. Constitution because it encroached on state sovereignty. The Constitution holds true under Section 1 of the Fifteenth Amendment, "... [t]he right of citizens of the United States to vote shall not be denied or abridged by the United States or by any state on account of race, color, or previous condition of servitude."

Allen v. State Board of Elections
393 US 110 (1969)

In *Allen v. State Board of Education*, the Supreme Court emphasized that subtle, as well as obvious state regulations, "which have the effect of denying citizens their right to vote because of their race" are prohibited. The court confirmed that Section 5 of the Voting Rights Act covered a variety of practices other than voter registration.

Georgia v. United States
411 US 526 (1973)

This case confirmed the propriety of the Voting Rights Act of 1965, which forbids states with a history of racial discrimination (Alabama, Georgia, Louisiana, Mississippi, North Carolina, South Carolina and Virginia) from implementing any change in voting practices and procedures without first submitting the proposed plan to the U.S. Attorney General for approval.

White v. Regester
412 US 755 (1973)

The Supreme Court in *White v. Regester*, struck down a Texas multi-member districting scheme that was used to prevent blacks from being elected to public office. The court upheld a finding that even though there was no evidence that blacks faced official obstacles to registration, voting or running for office, they had been excluded from effective participation in the political process in violation of the Equal Protection Clause of the Constitution.

City of Mobile, Alabama v. Wiley L. Bolden
446 US 55 (1980)

A class action suit was filed in the U.S. District Court for the Southern District of Alabama on behalf of black citizens in Mobile. The suit alleged that the city's practice of electing commissioners at large by a majority vote unfairly diluted the voting strength of blacks in violation of the Fourteenth Amendment and the Fifteenth Amendment. The District Court, ruled that the constitutional rights of Mobile's black citizens had been violated and entered a judgment in their favor. The court also ruled that Mobile's city commissioners be replaced by a municipal government consisting of a mayor and a city council composed of persons selected from single member districts.

Thornburg v. Gingles
478 US 30 (1986)

Thornburg v. Gingles was the Supreme Court's first decision interpreting the provisions of Section two of the Voting Rights Act, as amended in 1982. The amendments which prohibit voting schemes that result in a denial or abridgement of the right to vote due to race or color. In this landmark decision, the Court ruled that the redistricting plan adopted by the North Carolina legislature, which led to racially polarized voting by whites and diluted black voting strength is in violation of the Voting Rights Act. The Voting Rights Act prohibits voting requirements that have a discriminatory effect, as well as those that are intentionally discriminatory.

Martin v. Wilks
490 US 755 (1989)

In an attempt to remedy past racial discrimination in hiring and promotion practices, the City of Birmingham and its fire department consented to hiring blacks as firefighters as part of a settlement. White firefighters subsequently challenged the city, alleging that because of their race they were denied promotions in favor of less qualified blacks in violation of Title VII. Promotion decisions were made on the basis of race in reliance on the consent decree. The court held that a voluntary settlement between one group of employees and their employer cannot possibly settle voluntarily or otherwise, the conflicting claims of another group of employees who do not join in the agreement, on the basis that you can not deprive a person of legal rights in a proceeding to which he is not a party.

Education

Missouri ex rel. Lloyd Gaines v. Canada
305 US 339 (1938)

Gaines v. Canada was brought before the Supreme Court by Lloyd Lionel Gaines, an African American who had been refused admission to the School of Law of the State University of Missouri. Gaines contended that the University of Missouri's actions were a violation of his rights under the Fourteenth Amendment of the U.S. Constitution.

The University of Missouri defended its action by maintaining that Lincoln University, a predominantly black institution, would eventually establish its own law school. The Supreme Court of Missouri dismissed Gaines' petition and upheld the university's decision to reject his application. The U.S. Supreme Court, however, reversed this decision, maintaining that the State of Mis-

Lloyd Gaines

souri was obliged to provide equal facilities for blacks or, in the absence of such facilities, to admit them to the existing facility.

Sipuel v. Board of Regents of the University of Oklahoma
332 US 631 (1948)

Ada Lois Sipuel, an African American, was denied admission to the law school of the University of Oklahoma in 1948, Sipuel requested legal assistance from the National Association for the Advancement of Colored People (NAACP), which filed a petition in the Oklahoma courts requesting an order directing her admission. The petition was denied on the grounds that the *Gaines* decision did not require a state with segregation laws to admit a black student to its white schools. In addition, the Oklahoma court maintained that the state itself was not obligated to set up a separate school unless first requested to do so by blacks desiring a legal education. The Oklahoma court's decision was affirmed by the Supreme Court of Oklahoma. The U.S. Supreme Court, however, reversed this decision, and held that the state was required to provide African Americans with equal educational opportunities.

Sweatt v. Painter
339 US 629 (1950)

Herman Marion Sweatt, the African American petitioner in this case, was refused admission to the University of Texas Law School on the grounds that substantially equivalent facilities were already available in another Texas State law school open only to black students. The U.S. Supreme Court ruled that Sweatt be admitted to the University of Texas Law School. Chief Justice Fred M. Vinson wrote that "in terms of number of the faculty, variety of courses and opportunity for specialization, size of the student body, scope of the library, availability of law review and similar activities, the University of Texas Law School is superior" to those in the state law school for blacks. Therefore, the refusal to admit Sweatt to the University of Texas Law School was unconstitutional.

McLaurin v. Oklahoma State Regents for Higher Education
339 US 637 (1950)

After having been admitted to the University of Oklahoma, G. W. McLaurin, an African American, was required by school officials to occupy a special seat in each classroom and a segregated table in both the library and the cafeteria because of his race. The U.S. Supreme Court declared unanimously that the black student must receive the same treatment at the hands of the state as other students and could not be segregated.

Gray v. University of Tennessee
342 US 517 (1952)

This case resulted from the refusal of a U.S. District Court to force the University of Tennessee to admit black students. The lone judge to whom the matter was then referred ruled that the black students were entitled to admission, but did not order the university to enforce this ruling. The Supreme Court was asked to refer the case back to the District Court for further proceedings. Pending this appeal, however, one of the students seeking admission was enrolled at the University of Tennessee. Since the court found no suggestion that persons "similarly situated would not be afforded similar treatment," the case was dismissed as moot.

Brown v. Board of Education of Topeka
347 US 483 (1954)

This case involved the practice of denying black children equal access to state public schools due to state laws requiring or permitting racial segregation. The U.S. Supreme Court unanimously held that segregation deprived the children of equal protection under the Fourteenth Amendment to the U.S. Constitution. The "separate but equal" doctrine of *Plessy v. Ferguson* was overturned. After reargument a year later, the case was remanded (along with its four companion cases) to the

A black schoolroom in Missouri, c. 1930.

District Court, which was instructed to enter such orders as were necessary to ensure the admission of all parties to public schools on a racially nondiscriminatory basis.

Hawkins v. Board of Control
347 US 971 (1954)

This case resulted from a ruling of the Florida Supreme Court which denied an African American the right to enter the University of Florida Law School on the grounds that he had failed to show that a separate law school for blacks was not substantively equal to the University of Florida Law School. The U.S. Supreme Court vacated the judgment and remanded the case to the Florida Supreme Court for a decision in light of the ruling in *Brown* which overruled the separate but equal doctrine.

After two years, the Florida Supreme Court continued to deny Hawkins the right to enter the University of Florida. Also, it had appointed a commissioner to determine when in the future Hawkins could be admitted "without causing public mischief." However, the U.S. Supreme Court ruled that Hawkins should be admitted to the school promptly, since there was no palpable reason for further delay.

Turead v. Board of Supervisors
347 US 971 (1954)

This case was the result of a provisional injunction requiring the admittance of blacks to Louisiana State University. The state court of appeals reversed this action, declaring that it required the decision of a district court of three judges. The U.S. Supreme Court vacated this judgment and remanded the case for consideration, in light of *Brown v. Board of Education of Topeka.*

Frazier v. University of North Carolina
350 US 979 (1956)

The U.S. Supreme Court affirmed a District Court judgment that blacks may not be excluded from institutions of higher learning because of their race or color.

Cooper v. Aaron
358 US 1 (1958)

The impact of *Brown v. Board of Education of Topeka* was very slight until the Justice Department began to initiate its own desegregation lawsuits. Arkansas state officials passed state laws contrary to the Fourteenth Amendment holdings in *Brown I* and *Brown II* forbidding states to use their governmental powers to bar children on racial grounds from attending schools where there is state participation through any arrangement, management, funds or property; and to cease and desist from desegregation practices immediately.

In *Cooper*, the Attorney General of the United States filed a petition on behalf of the U.S. government to enjoin the governor of Arkansas and officers of the National Guard from preventing the admittance of nine black children into Central High School September 1957 in Little Rock. A law was passed relieving school children from compulsory attendance at racially mixed schools. The Supreme Court declared that the Fourteenth Amendment outlined in the *Brown* case is the supreme law of the land and cannot be nullified by state legislators, executive or judicial officers or evasive schemes for segregation.

Lee v. Macon County Board of Education
389 US 25 (1967)

The U.S. Supreme Court in *Lee v. Macon County Board of Education,* affirmed a lower court decision ordering the desegregation of Alabama's school districts and declared state school grants to white students attending segregated private schools unconstitutional.

Alexander v. Holmes County Board of Education
396 US 19 (1969)

The U.S. Supreme Court, in *Alexander v. Holmes County Board of Education,* ordered all thirty-three school districts in Mississippi to desegregate. The Department of Health, Education and Welfare (HEW) had asked that the districts be granted more time to desegregate. This was the first time HEW had sought a delay in integration, but the Court ordered that integration proceed immediately.

North Carolina State Board of Education v. Swann
402 US 43 (1971)

&

Swann v. Charlotte Mecklenburg Board of Education
402 US 1 (1971)

In these two cases the U.S. Supreme Court affirmed the use of busing and faculty transfers to overcome the effects of dual school systems-segregated school systems resulting from residential patterns. Writing the decision, Chief Justice Warren E. Burger noted that "bus transportation has long been a part of all public educational systems and it is unlikely that a truly effective remedy could be devised without continued reliance upon it." The court declared that segregation resulted from past misconduct and affirmed the lower court's order that the school board bus students to

Black students being bused.

achieve a racial mix at each school. The ruling, however, left local district judges the authority to decide whether a desegregation plan was constitutionally adequate.

Wright v. City of Emporia
402 US 43 (1971)

&

Cotton v. Scotland Neck Board of Education
407 US 485 (1972)

The Supreme Court held that two towns with heavy concentrations of white students could not secede from a largely black county school system and form its own school district in an attempt to frustrate integration.

Richmond, Virginia School Board v. State Board of Education
412 US 92 (1973)

By a four to four vote, the U.S. Supreme Court declined to order the integration of the predominantly black schools in Richmond with those of two white suburbs. Though the Court wrote no decision, integrationists expressed concern that permitting de facto segregation to stand in this manner would hinder corrective action in other metropolitan areas, perpetuate "neighborhood" one-race schools, and lessen the extent of integration in unitary school systems.

Runyon v. McCrary
427 US 160 (1976)

In an unanimous decision, it was held that the Constitution places no value on discrimination, and while invidious, private discrimination may be characterized as a form of exercising the freedom of association protected by the First Amendment. In the 1976 decision, two black children were denied admission to private schools in Virginia. The Civil Rights Act of 1866 prohibits racial discrimination in the making and enforcing of contracts. The children's parents sought to enter into a contractual relationship with the private schools on an equal basis to white and nonwhite students.

Regents of University of California v. Allan Bakke
438 US 265 (1978)

Allan Bakke, a white male who had been denied admission to the University of California Medical School at Davis for two consecutive years, charged that the university's minority quota system—under which only disadvantaged members of certain minority races were considered for 16 of the 100 places in each year's class—denied him equal protection.

The trial court declared that the school could not take race into account in making the admissions decision and held that the challenged admissions program violated the federal and state constitutions and Title VI of the 1964 Civil Rights Act. The university appealed. Upon hearing the case, the U.S. Supreme Court ruled that Bakke had been illegally discriminated against and that numerical quotas based on race were unconstitutional.

Bob Jones University v. IRS
461 US 574 (1983)

Contrary to long-standing IRS policy, the Reagan administration sought to extend tax-exempt status to schools that discriminate on the basis of race. The U.S. Supreme Court recognized the inability of the Justice Department to argue the case fairly, and requested former Secretary of Transportation William T. Coleman to present the argument. The Supreme Court rebuffed the Justice Department's arguments and unanimously agreed with Coleman's position that the denial of tax-exempt status to racially discriminatory schools is unconstitutional.

Allen v. Wright
488 US 737 (1984)

Parents of African American children instituted a nationwide lawsuit claiming that the Internal Revenue Service's failure to deny tax-exempt status to racially discriminating private schools constituted federal financial aid to racially segregated institutions and diminished the ability of their children to receive a racially an adequate education. The U.S. Supreme Court refused to hear the case on the grounds that the plaintiffs did not have "standing" because they failed to show that the injury suffered was "fairly traceable" or caused by the conduct of the IRS. In addition the Court maintained that the remedy was "speculative" since there was no evidence that the withdrawal of tax-exempt status would cause schools to end their racially discriminatory practices. The court's imposition of such an artificial and stringent standing requirement, which had not been used in other cases involving school desegregation, effectively denied the African American parents their day in court.

Employment

Griggs v. Duke Power Co.
401 US 424 (1971)

Black employees challenged their employer's requirement of a high school diploma or passing of intelligence tests as a condition of employment or transfer to jobs at the plant that were previously held solely by whites prior to the enactment of Title VII of the Civil Rights Act of 1964. Blacks were employed only in the Labor Department where the highest paying jobs paid less than the lowest jobs in the other departments. When the company abandoned its policy restricting blacks to Labor in 1965, completion of high school and median scores on two aptitude tests were required to transfer from Labor to another department.

The Supreme Court found the objective of Congress in Title III was to achieve equality of employment opportunities and remove barriers that have operated in the past to favor an identifiable group of whites over other employees. Under the Act, practices, procedures, or tests neutral on their face and even neutral in their intent cannot be maintained if they operate to "freeze" the status quo of prior discrimination. The employment practice must be related to job performance.

It was determined that neither the high school diploma nor the intelligence tests were shown to bear a demonstrable relationship to successful job performance. Good intent or absence of discriminatory intent does not redeem employment procedures and practices. The employment policies had a discriminatory effect toward black employees.

Albemarle Paper Co. v. Moody
422 US 405 (1975)

African American employees of a paper mill in Roanoke Rapids, North Carolina successfully challenged the company's use of written tests which allegedly measured numerical and verbal intelligence. Based upon the standards enunciated in *Griggs v. Duke Power Co.*, the U.S. Supreme Court determined that the tests were discriminatory because they were not job-related and did not predict success on the job. More importantly, the Supreme Court held that the plaintiffs were entitled to "complete justice" and necessary relief that would "make them whole." The court awarded the African American employees back pay and made it clear that back pay should rarely be denied once there has been a showing of discrimination. The court also stated that back pay cannot be denied simply because the employer acted in good faith or did not intend to discriminate.

Hazelwood School District v. United States
433 US 299 (1977)

In this case, several African American teachers seeking jobs in suburban St. Louis, Missouri offered statistical data indicating they had been denied employment opportunities. The plaintiffs attempted to prove their case by showing that the percentage of black students was greater than the percentage of black teachers in the school district.

Although the U.S. Supreme Court affirmed that "statistics can be an important source of proof in employment discrimination cases," it rejected the plaintiffs' statistical evidence calling it irrelevant. The court concluded that relevant statistical data would be the percentage of qualified black teachers in the relevant geographical area compared with the percentage of blacks in Hazelwood's teaching staff.

Teamsters v. United States
431 US 324 (1977)

In enforcing the Civil Rights Act of 1964, the U.S. Supreme Court held that victims of past union discrimination were entitled to retroactive seniority benefits. However, the Supreme Court required proof of "intent to discriminate," in order to establish that a given seniority system is illegal. Subsequent cases in lower federal courts during the late 1970s entitled discrimination victims to retroactive back pay in addition to retroactive seniority benefits.

Louis Swint and Willie Johnson v. Pullman Standard and the United Steelworkers of America
72 L.Ed 66 (1982)

African American employees of Pullman Standard brought a lawsuit into federal district court against Pullman Standard and the United Steelworkers of America. The lawsuit alleged that Title VII of the Civil Rights Act of 1964 was violated by a seniority system. In its decision, the District Court ruled "that the difference in terms, conditions or privileges of employment resulting from the seniority system are not the result of an intention to discriminate because of race or color" and held, therefore, that the system satisfied the requirements of Section 703(h) of the Civil Rights Act. This decision was later reversed by the Court of Appeals for the Fifth Circuit which stated that, "because we find the differences in the terms, conditions and standards of employment for black workers and white workers at Pullman Standard resulted from an intent to discriminate because of race, we hold that the system is not legally valid under Section 703(h) of Title VII U.S.C. 2000e-2(h)."

Meritor Savings Bank, FSB v. Vinson
106 S.Ct. 2399 (1985)

Michelle Vinson, an African American woman employed as a teller at a bank in Washington, DC, claimed that she had been sexually harassed for more than two months by her supervisor, Sidney Taylor, a white male. Vinson alleged that employment benefits were granted or denied based upon her performance of sexual favors.

In this first U.S. Supreme Court ruling on sexual harassment, the Court firmly condemned sexual harassment that creates an intimidating, hostile, and offensive working environment even when the harassment does not have economic ramifications. The unanimous ruling made it clear that Title VII of the Civil Rights Act prohibits sexual harassment that involves economic reprisals or harassment that creates a hostile, sexually charged atmosphere in the workplace.

Watson v. Fort Worth Bank and Trust
108 US 2777 (1987)

In the case of *Watson v. Fort Worth Bank and Trust* Clara Watson, an African American woman, alleged that she was repeatedly denied promotion to supervisory positions which were awarded to white employees with equivalent or lesser experience. The bank contended that its promotion decisions were based on various subjective criteria including experience, previous supervisory experience, and the ability to get along with others.

The U.S. Supreme Court held that Watson did not have to prove intentional discrimination. The court concluded that subjective facially neutral selection devices which disadvantage blacks in much the same way as objective criteria written tests are unlawful.

Lorance v. AT&T Technologies
490 US 900 (1989)

This case was brought by three women employed by ATT. A new seniority system was adopted and under the change the women were promoted from laborers to testers but lost some seniority in the process. The loss was intended to be temporary with full seniority restored in five years, but before that occurred the women were demoted. The women allege that their employer violated Title VII of the Civil Rights Act of 1964 by adopting the new seniority system with the purpose and effect of protecting incumbent testers—jobs traditionally dominated by men—from female employees who had greater plantwide seniority and who were becoming testers in increasing numbers. Unfortunately, the claims were brought too late. The court held that the charges had not been filed within the required period after the alleged unlawful employment practice occurred and therefore were thwarted.

Patterson v. McLean Credit Union
491 US 164 (1989)

A black female was employed as a teller and file coordinator for ten years until she was laid-off. She alleged that she had been harassed, denied promotion to accounting clerk, and later discharged because of her race. Petitioner filed suit asserting violations of Section 1981 of the Civil Rights Act.

Racial harassment relating to conditions of employment are not actionable under Section 1981 which provides, "... [a]ll persons ... shall have the same right to make and enforce contracts ... as any white citizen," because that provision does not apply to conduct which occurs after the formation of a contract including the breach of the contracts terms and enforcement thereof. Rather, the harassment asserted by the petitioner is past formation conduct of the employer which is actionable only under Title VII of the Civil Rights Act of 1964.

Wards Cove Packing Co. Inc. v. Antonio
490 US 642 (1989)

This case was brought by a class of nonwhite salmon cannery workers alleging that the employer's hiring and promotion practices were responsible for the workforces racial stratification and had denied them employment opportunities as noncannery workers on the basis of race. There were two types of jobs: unskilled cannery jobs, which were filled predominately by nonwhites; and noncannery jobs, mostly classified as skilled positions held by whites and virtually all paid more. Statistics were used to show a high percentage of nonwhites in cannery jobs and a low percentage in noncannery positions, in order to show a disparate impact caused by specific identifiable employment practices.

The U.S. Supreme Court found that the cannery workforce did not reflect the pool of qualified job applicants or the qualified labor force population. An employer's selection methods or employment practices cannot be said to have a disparate impact on nonwhites if the absence of minorities holding such skilled jobs reflects a dearth of qualified nonwhite applicants. A mere showing that nonwhites are underrepresented in the noncannery jobs will not suffice for a Title VII violation.

Jury Selection and Service

Neal v. Delaware
103 US 370 (1880)

The jury commissioner's conduct was found in violation of the U.S. Constitution where a black criminal defendant asserted that blacks were excluded from the jury based on their race. Every citizen is afforded the right to equal protection of the laws including that the selection of jurors to pass upon his life, liberty or property shall not be hindered by the exclusion of his race based on race.

Strauder v. West Virginia
100 US 303 (1880)

In this case, the Supreme Court granted immunity to a black criminal defendant from discrimination against him in the selection process of jurors based on their race. West Virginia's state law prohibited black men from eligibility to serve as a member of a grand jury or a petit jury in the state. Thereby, denying the equal protection of the laws to a citizen based solely on their race.

Virginia v. Rives
100 US 313 (1880)

The petitioners in *Rives* asserted that blacks had never been allowed to serve as jurors in their county in any case where a black man was interested. Virginia had no formalized or specific statute restricting black jurors from certain trials. It was held, that a mixed jury in a particular case is not essential to the equal protection of the laws, and that the right is not given by any state or federal statute.

Hollins v. Oklahoma
295 US 394 (1935)

The defendant in this case, an African American, was charged with rape and convicted on December 29, 1931 at a trial held in the basement of the jail in Sapula, Oklahoma. Three days before the scheduled execution, the National Association for the Advancement of Colored People secured a stay, and later, a reversal of his conviction by the Supreme Court of Oklahoma.

The U.S. Supreme Court—in a memorandum opinion—affirmed the principle that the conviction of an African American by a jury from which all blacks had been excluded was a denial of the equal protection clause of the Fourteenth Amendment to the U.S. Constitution.

Hale v. Commonwealth of Kentucky
303 US 613 (1938)

In 1936 Joe Hale, an African American, was charged with murder in McCracken County, Kentucky. Hale moved to set aside the indictment on the grounds that the jury commissioners had systematically excluded blacks from jury lists. Hale established that one out of every six residents of the county was black, and that at least 70 blacks out of a total of 6,700 persons qualified for jury duty. Still, there had not been a black on jury duty between 1906 and 1936. Hale's conviction and death sentence were upheld by the court of appeals of Kentucky, but both were struck down by the U.S. Supreme Court on the grounds that he had been denied equal protection of the law.

Patton v. Mississippi
332 US 463 (1947)

This case involved Eddie Patton, an African American who was indicted, tried, and convicted of the murder of a white man in Mississippi. At his trial and as part of his appeal, Patton alleged that all qualified blacks had been systematically excluded from jury service solely because of race. The state maintained that, since jury service was limited by statute to qualified voters and since few blacks were qualified to vote, such a procedure was valid in the eyes of the law. The U.S. Supreme Court, however, reversed Patton's conviction on the grounds that such a jury plan, resulting in the almost automatic elimination of blacks from jury service, constituted an infringement of Patton's rights under the Fourteenth Amendment.

Shepherd v. Florida
341 US 50 (1951)

The U.S. Supreme Court reversed the convictions of a Florida state court involving black defendants solely on the grounds that the method of selecting the grand jury discriminated against blacks.

Turner v. Fouche
396 US 346 (1970)

The U.S. Supreme Court, in *Turner v. Fouche*, affirmed the right of defendants to bring an action in federal court to end discrimination in jury selection.

Castanda v. Partida
430 US 482 (1977)

The U.S. Supreme Court in *Castanda v. Partida*, upheld the use of statistical evidence demonstrating that Mexican-Americans had been systematically excluded from jury selection, and that such discrimination on the basis of race or color violated the equal protection clause of the Constitution. The principle established in this case, that statistical evidence can be used to prove intentional discrimination, has been used in later cases involving employment, housing, voting and education.

Batson v. Kentucky
476 US 79 (1986)

In the U.S. Supreme Court ruling on *Batson v. Kentucky*, Justice Lewis F. Powell writing for the majority, held that the prosecution in a criminal case may not use its "preemptory challenge," those challenges to an individual juror for which no cause need be stated, to exclude black jurors in a case involving a black defendant.

Turner v. Murray
106 US 1683 (1986)

The U.S. Supreme Court in *Turner v. Murray*, expanded the right of black defendants in capital cases to question potential white jurors to uncover their racial prejudices and biases.

Public Accomodations

Hall v. DeCuir
95 US 485 (1878)

This case involved an unsuccessful attempt of the Louisiana legislature to prohibit racial desegregation in any form of transportation in the state. The statute was attacked as an interference with interstate commerce because it imposed a direct burden and control over common carriers when entering the state. The statute was declared unconstitutional and void because it required those engaged in the transportation of passengers among the states to carry black passengers in Louisiana in the same cabin with white passengers.

The congressional legislature will have to cure the defects in the existing laws, by refraining from action, Congress, in effect adopts the common or civil law; although, the State of Louisiana may see the need for adoption of new regulations for the public good concerning desegregation the enactments can only come from Congress where it effects interstate trade and influences business prospects.

Plessy v. Ferguson
163 US 537 (1896)

The *Plessy* case was a test of the constitutionality of an 1890 Louisiana statute providing for "separate but equal" railway carriages for whites and blacks. The information filed in the criminal District Court charged in substance that Homer Plessy, being a passenger between two stations within the state of Louisiana, was assigned by officers of the company to the coach used by the race to which he did not belong.

In the majority opinion of the U.S. Supreme Court, "separate but equal" accommodations for blacks constituted a "reasonable" use of state police power. Furthermore, it was said that the Fourteenth Amendment "could not have been intended to abolish distinctions based on color, or to enforce social ... equality or a co-mingling of the two races upon terms unsatisfactory to either."

Civil Rights Cases
332 US 46, 332 US 784, 333 US 831, 334 US 834, 378 US 226 (1883)

This group of civil rights cases was heard before the U.S. Supreme Court in an effort to determine the constitutionality of the Civil Rights Act of 1875, the first piece of national legislation which attempted to guarantee people of all races "full and equal enjoyment" of all public accommodations, including inns, public conveyances, theaters, and other places of amusement. The court ruled, however, that the 1875 Civil Rights Act was unconstitutional inasmuch as it did not spring directly from the Thirteenth and Fourteenth Amendment s to the Constitution. In the view of the Court, the Thirteenth Amendment was concerned exclusively with the narrow confines of slavery and involuntary servitude. The Fourteenth Amendment, by a comparable yardstick of interpretation, did not empower Congress to enact direct legislation to counteract the effect of state laws or policies. The effect of this ruling was to deprive blacks of the very protections which the three postwar Freedom amendments were designed to provide.

Morgan v. Commonwealth of Virginia
328 US 373 (1946)

Irene Morgan, an African American, refused to move to the rear seat of a Greyhound bus which was traveling from Virginia to Washington, D.C., and was subsequently convicted in the lower Virginia courts for violating a state statute requiring segregation of the races on all public vehicles.

National Association for the Advancement of Colored People (NAACP) attorneys then carried the case through the Virginia courts and on to the U.S. Supreme Court, where it was decided that the Virginia statute could not apply to interstate passengers or motor vehicles engaged in such traffic.

Bob-Lo v. Michigan
333 US 28 (1948)

In this case, the operator of a line of passenger ships used to transport patrons from Detroit to an island amusement park was convicted of violating the Michigan Civil Rights Act for refusing passage to an African American.The U.S. Supreme Court upheld the application of the Michigan Civil Rights Act.

Rice v. Arnold
340 US 848 (1950)

This case involved the successful attempt to abolish segregation on a Miami, Florida golf course owned and operated by the city. The U.S. Supreme Court granted a writ of certiorari and overturned the judgment of the Florida Supreme Court which authorized the segregated use of the course.

District of Columbia v. John R. Thompson
346 US 100 (1952)

The Supreme Court unanimously held that a restaurant owner had violated federal law by discriminating

Lunchcounter sit-in protesters.

against and refusing service to patrons on the basis of race.

Muir v. Louisville Park Theatrical Association
347 US 971 (1954)

In 1954, several African Americans were refused admission to an amphitheater located in a Louisville city park, leased and operated by a privately owned group not affiliated in any way with the city. The Kentucky court of appeals found no evidence of unlawful discrimination, but the U.S. Supreme Court overturned this judgment and remanded the case for consideration in the light of the prevailing legal climate as articulated in Brown v. Board of Education.

Mayor and City Council of Baltimore v. Dawson
350 US 377 (1955)

The U.S. Supreme Court affirmed a judgment that the enforcement of racial segregation in public beaches and bathhouses maintained by public authorities is unconstitutional.

Holmes v. Atlanta
350 US 859 (1955)

This case involved a suit brought by African Americans to integrate a city-owned and city-operated golf course in Atlanta, Georgia. The segregated arrangements were ordered sustained by a lower court, but that order was overturned by the U.S. Supreme Court and the case remanded to the District Court with directions to enter a decree for plaintiffs in conformity with Mayor and City Council of Baltimore v. Dawson.

Flemming v. South Carolina Electric
351 US 901 (1956)

This case involved a suit brought by an African-American passenger against a bus company for damages due to the bus driver's having required her to change seats in accordance with South Carolina's segregation law. The trial judge dismissed the case on the grounds that the statute in question was valid, but the court of appeals reversed this decision, holding that the "separate but equal" doctrine was no longer valid. The U.S. Supreme Court upheld the court of appeals.

A segregated bus station in Durham, North Carolina.

Black bus riders in Montgomery, Alabama.

Gayle v. Browder
352 US 114 (1956)

This case challenged the constitutionality of state statutes and ordinances in effect in the city of Montgomery, Alabama, which required the segregation of whites and blacks on public buses. These statutes were first declared unconstitutional by the decision of a three-judge federal district court. The U.S. Supreme Court then affirmed this judgment.

Katzenbach v. McClung
379 US 802 (1964)

&

Heart of Atlanta v. United States
379 US 803 (1964)

In the *Katzenbach* case, the Attorney General of the United States sued Ollie's Barbecue Restaurant in Birmingham, Alabama for its refusal to serve blacks in its dining accommodations, a direct violation of the anti-discriminatory public accommodations clause of the 1964 Civil Rights Act. The U.S. District Court, Northern District of Alabama, held that the Civil Rights Act could not be applied under the Fourteenth Amendment to the U.S. Constitution, inasmuch as there was no "demonstrable connection" between food purchased in interstate commerce and sold in a restaurant that would affect commerce. The U.S. Supreme Court, however, held that "the Civil Rights Act of 1964, as here applied, [is] plainly appropriate in the resolution of what. [Congress has]. found to be a national commercial problem of the first magnitude."

The *Heart of Atlanta* case dealt with a Georgia motel which solicited patronage in national advertising and had several out-of-state residents as guests from time to time. The motel had already instituted the practice of refusing to rent rooms to African Americans prior to the passage of the 1964 Civil Rights Act, and stated thereafter that it intended to continue this practice. The motel owner filed suit, maintaining that the 1964 Civil Rights Act violated both the Fifth Amendment and the Thirteenth Amendment. The United States countered with the argument that the refusal to accept blacks interfered with interstate travel, and that the Congress in voting to apply nondiscriminatory standards to interstate commerce was not violating either Amendment. The U.S. Supreme Court upheld the right of congressional regulation, stating that the power of Congress was not confined to the regulation of commerce among the states. "It extends to those activities intrastate which so affect interstate commerce, or the exercise of the power of Congress over it, as to make regulation of them appropriate means to the attainment of a legitimate end."

Bell v. Maryland
378 US 226 (1964)

The U.S. Supreme Court ordered a Maryland district court to reconsider its affirmation of a state court

Lunch counter protesters in Raleigh, North Carolina, 1960.

conviction of twelve African Americans for trespassing, when they refused to leave a restaurant that refused to serve them entirely on the basis of their color.

Evans v. Newton
382 US 296 (1966)

The U.S. Supreme Court ruled that transfer of a city park from municipal ownership to a board of private trustees does not remove its obligations under the Fourteenth Amendment.

Shuttlesworth v. Birmingham
394 US 147 (1969)

The U.S. Supreme Court invalidated Birmingham's Parade-Permit law which had been used in 1963 to harass participants in an Easter March organized by Dr. Martin Luther King, Jr. *New York State Club Association v. City of New York*

108 S.Ct. 2225 (1988)

In a unanimous decision, the U.S. Supreme Court upheld the constitutionality of a New York City ordinance that forbids so-called private clubs from discriminating against women and minorities.

Interacial Marriage

Loving v. Virginia
388 US 1 (1967)

This case virtually nullified the anti-miscegenation laws, many of which remain in southern state constitutions and legal codes. It concerned a white man and black woman, residents of Virginia, who married in Washington, D.C. The state of Virginia indicted and convicted them of violating its laws against racial intermarriage when the couple returned to Virginia and attempted to reside there, but released them when the couple agreed not to reside in the state for 25 years. The Lovings, however, decided to challenge the agreement and the law. Their appeal was rejected by the Virginia courts but upheld by the U.S. Supreme Court, which ruled the Virginia law unconstitutional. Soon thereafter, federal district courts in other states which forbade intermarriage were ordering local officials to issue marriage licenses to interracial couples applying for them.

Requirements for Legislative Membership

Powell v. McCormack
395 US 486 (1969)

According to the Constitution, only three basic factors govern eligibility to serve as a legislator in the U.S. House of Representatives: a minimum age requirement, the possession of U.S. citizenship, and the fulfillment of the state's residency requirement. When U.S. Representative Adam Clayton Powell, Jr. was excluded from the 90th Congress on the grounds that he had misused public funds and defied the courts of his home state, he filed suit in federal court in an attempt to force the House to review only the necessary credentials for membership.

The district court dismissed the first petition on the grounds that it lacked jurisdiction. By the time the case was finally heard before the U.S. Supreme Court, the

Plaintiffs Woodrow Lewis, Albert Dunn, and George Willis meet with attorneys William Alexander and D.L. Hollowell in a suit against an Atlanta restauranteur, 1965.

90th Congress had adjourned. Powell, however, was reelected and finally seated in the 91st Congress, a gesture which in the view of the court did not settle the case. The legal point on which the case hinged involved the distinction between "expulsion" and "exclusion." Despite the more than two-thirds majority required for expulsion, the Court ruled that the intent of the House was to "exclude," not to "expel." The court summation stated flatly that "the House was without power to exclude him from its membership."

Right of Sale and Restrictive Covenants

Buchanan v. Warley
245 US 60 (1917)

The plaintiff, Buchanan, brought an action in this case for the performance of a sale of certain real estate in Louisville, Kentucky. The purchaser, Warley an African American, maintained that he would be unable to occupy the land since it was located within what was defined by a Louisville ordinance as a white block. (The ordinance prohibited whites from living in black districts, and vice versa.) Buchanan alleged that the ordinance was in conflict with the Fourteenth Amendment to the U.S. Constitution. The U.S. Supreme Court maintained that the ordinance was unconstitutional.

Shelley v. Kraemer
334 US 1 (1948)

&

Hurd v. Hodge
334 US 26 (1948)

On August 11, 1945, an African American family, the Shelleys, received a warranty deed to a parcel of land which, unknown to them, was subject to a restrictive covenant barring its sale to blacks. A lawsuit was subsequently brought in the Circuit Court of St. Louis seeking to divest the Shelleys of the title to the land. The Supreme Court of Missouri directed the trial court to strip the petitioners of their warranty deed.

The U.S. Supreme Court reversed this decision, maintaining that restrictive covenants, though valid contracts, could not be enforced by state courts. In the *Hurd v. Hodge* case, involving a similar set of circumstances, federal courts were similarly prohibited from enforcing such restrictive covenants.

Adam Clayton Powell leaves the Capitol after the House voted to take away his Education and Labor Committee chairmanship.

Reitman v. Mulkey
387 US 369 (1967)

In 1964, the California electorate voted in favor of a referendum granting "absolute discretion" to real estate owners in the sale and rental of real property, in effect voiding the state's fair housing laws. Lincoln Mulkey filed suit against property owners in Orange County to challenge the validity of the referendum. Mulkey's position failed in the lower courts but was sustained five to two by the California Supreme Court on the grounds that the California referendum violated the Fourteenth Amendment of the U.S. Constitution. The U.S. Supreme Court upheld the decision.

Jones v. Alfred H. Mayer, Co.
392 US 409 (1968)

Joseph Lee Jones alleged that the sole reason a realtor refused to sell him a home was because he was black. The U.S. Supreme Court held that 42 U.S.C. 1982, a federal statute created during the Reconstruction era to eliminate the vestiges of slavery, prohibits all racial discrimination, public and private in the sale or rental of property.

Trafficante v. Metropolitan Life Insurance
409 US 205 (1972)

The U.S. Supreme Court ruled that a complaint of racial discrimination in housing may be brought by parties who have not themselves been refused accommodation but who, as members of the same housing unit, allege injury by discriminatory housing practices. The suit had been filed by a black and a white resident of a housing development in San Francisco, who contended that the owner of the development, in maintaining a "white ghetto," was depriving plaintiffs of the right to live in a racially integrated community.

Sentencing and Incarceration

McKlesky v. Kemp
481 US 279 (1987)

In April of 1987, the U.S. Supreme Court decided one of the most significant cases involving the imposition of the death penalty in America. Warren McKlesky, a 38-year-old African-American man accused of killing a police officer while robbing a furniture store, was sentenced to death by the State of Georgia. In support of his claim that the sentence violated his constitutional rights, McKlesky introduced a sophisticated statistical study that analyzed more than 2,000 murder cases in Georgia. The study demonstrated that there is a disparity in the imposition of the capital sentence based on the race of the victim, as well as the race of the defendant.

Defendants charged with killing white persons received the death penalty in eleven percent of the cases, but defendants charged with killing blacks received the death penalty in only one percent of the cases. The study further showed that prosecutors asked for the death penalty in seventy percent of the cases involving black defendants and white victims, and only nineteen percent of the cases involving white defendants and black victims. In sum, the analysis revealed that African Americans who kill whites are 4.3 times more likely to receive the death sentence.

In the five to four opinion, written by Justice Lewis F. Powell, the U.S. Supreme Court acknowledged that it had accepted statistics as proof of intent to discriminate in employment, housing and voting cases. However, despite the compelling statistical evidence the Court rejected McKlesky's claim that the death penalty in Georgia is applied in a racially discriminatory manner. The court's reasoning was that although McKlesky showed the existence of racial discrimination in sentencing, he failed to prove that "racial considerations played a part in his sentence." Finally, Justice Powell expressed concern that acceptance of McKlesky's argument would open the floodgates of litigation by black defendants seeking to introduce statistical evidence to demonstrate that race affected the outcome of their case.

Slavery

Prigg v. Pennsylvania
16 Peters 539

In violation of a 1826 Pennsylvania anti-kidnapping statute, Edward Prigg, a professional slave catcher, Maryland, took captive Margaret Morgan, a fugitive slave residing in Pennsylvania, and was tried and convicted for kidnapping. Hearing the case, the U.S. Supreme Court ruled that the Pennsylvania law was unconstitutional, on the grounds that the statute was an interference with Congress' power under Article 4, Section 2 of the Constitution.

Strader v. Graham
10 Howard 82 (1850)

In 1841, three slaves owned by Christopher Graham of Kentucky, boarded a steamboat owned by Jacob Strader and traveled to Cincinnati, from where they ultimately escaped to freedom in Canada. Graham sued Strader for the value of the slaves and the expenses incurred while trying to recover them. Graham won the case. However, Strader appealed, claiming that the slaves had become free under Ohio law and provisions of the Northwest Ordinance. The U.S. Supreme Court ruled unanimously that each state had the right to determine the status of slaves within its jurisdiction, that the status of these slaves was to be determined by the state of Kentucky, and that the Northwest Ordinance was no longer in force, since those territories had become states.

Dred Scott v. Sandford
19 Howard 393 (1857)

In 1835, Dred Scott, born a slave in Virginia, became the property of John Emerson, an Army doctor, in the slave state of Missouri. From there, he was taken into the free state of Illinois and later to the free territory of Minnesota.

In 1847, Scott instituted suit in the circuit court of the St. Louis County, Missouri, arguing that he should be given his freedom by virtue of his having resided on free soil. After nine years, his case was certified to the U.S. Supreme Court, where five of the nine justices, were Southerners.

In delivering his opinion, Chief Justice Roger Brooke Taney declared that, by virtue of both the Declaration of Independence and the Constitution, African Americans could not be regarded as citizens of the United States. Moreover, the Court could not deprive slaveholders of their right to take slaves into any part of the Union, North or South. In effect, therefore, the Missouri Compromise, as well as other antislavery legislation, was declared to be unconstitutional.

A newspaper depiction of a fugitive slave, 1837.

Ableman v. Booth
21 Howard 506 (1859)

The U.S. Supreme Court upheld Congress' fugitive slave law and all its provisions; but, more importantly upheld the supremacy of federal law over state law. Booth was held in a state jail for violating the federal fugitive slave laws. Booth secured a writ of habeas corpus from a state judge who declared the federal laws unconstitutional and the Wisconsin Supreme Court affirmed. The state court had stepped beyond its sphere of authority. The federal court held Booth guilty, although the State of Wisconsin is a sovereign within its territorial limits, it is limited and restricted by the U.S. Constitution.

State and Local Affirmative Action Requirements

United States Steelworkers of America v. Brian Weber
433 US 193 (1979)

The United Steelworkers of America and Kaiser Aluminum Company entered into a collective bargaining

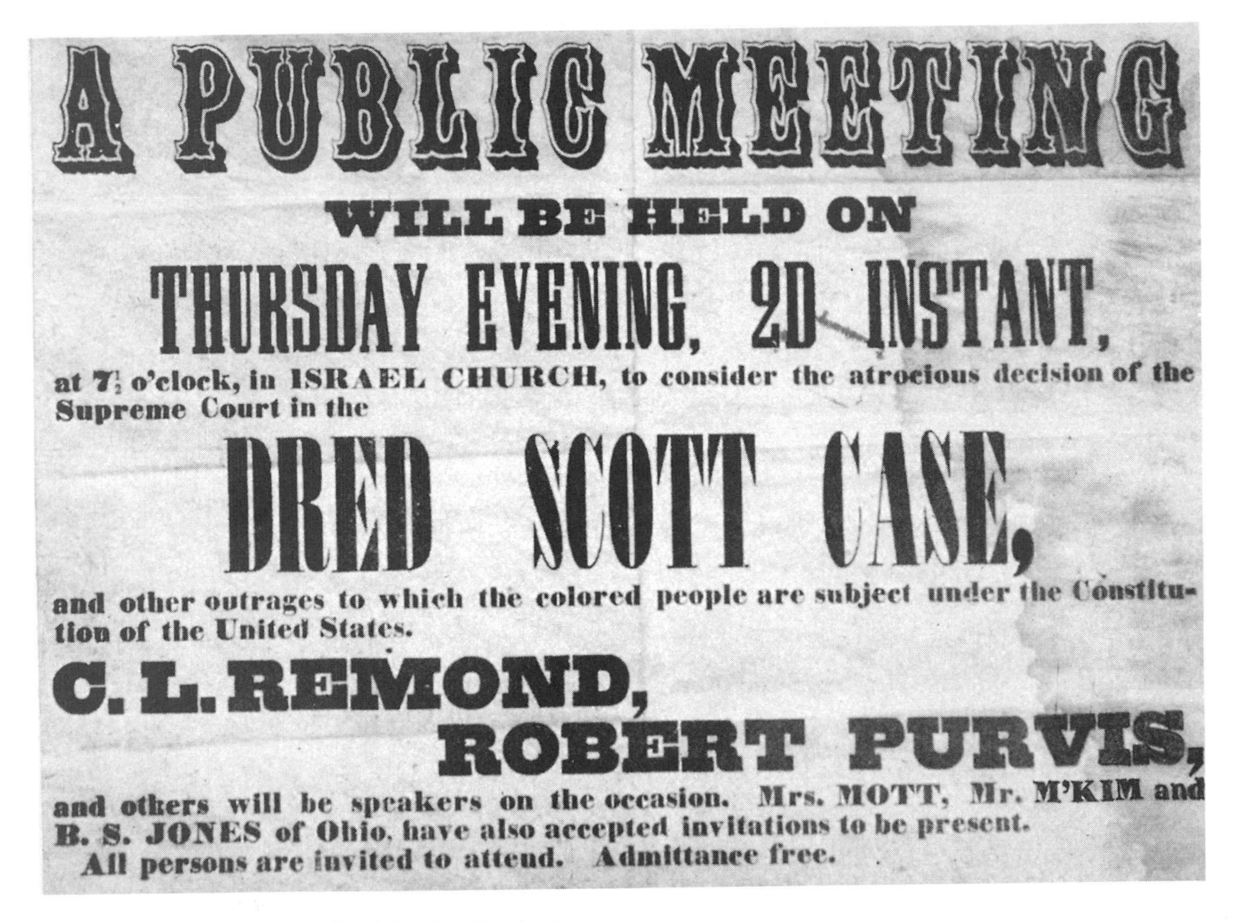

Poster advertising a public hearing on the *Dred Scott v. Sanford case.*

agreement including a voluntary affirmative action plan designed to eliminate conspicuous racial imbalances in Kaiser's almost exclusively white skilled workforce. The plant in Gramercy, Louisiana agreed to reserve 50 percent of the openings in the skilled job training programs for blacks until the percentage of African-American skilled workers was equal to the percentage of blacks in the local labor force. Brian Weber, a white production worker, who was turned down for the training program although he had more seniority than many accepted blacks, sued the United Steelworkers of America, claiming that the affirmative action program discriminated against whites.

The U.S. Supreme Court limited the issue to the narrow question of whether Title VII prohibited private employers and unions from establishing voluntary affirmative action plans. In a five to two decision, the Court upheld the affirmative action plan and established three factors to determine the validity of racial preference. The court approved the plan because it was designed to break down Kaiser's historic patterns of racial segregation; did not unnecessarily diminish the rights of white employees since it did not require the firing of white employees; and was a temporary measure not intended to maintain racial balance but simply to eliminate an imbalance. *Fullilove v. Klutznik*

448 US 448 (1980)

The U.S. Supreme Court upheld a provision of the Public Works Employment Act of 1977 that required a ten percent set-aside of federal funds for minority business enterprises on local public work projects. The provision had been challenged as violation of the equal protection clause of the Fifth Amendment.

Firefighters Local Union No. 1784 v. Stotts
467 US 561 (1984)

In May of 1981, for the first time in its history, the City of Memphis announced layoffs of city employees, due to a projected budget deficit. The layoffs, which included the fire department, were to be made on a "last hired, first fired" city-wide seniority system that had been adopted in 1973. Carl Stotts, an African American firefighter, sued to stop the layoffs, claiming that since African Americans had been hired pursuant to the affirmative action provisions of a 1980 court decree, they would be laid off in far greater numbers than their white coworkers. In a six to three decision the U.S. Supreme

Court held that since the 1980 court decree did not say that African Americans had special protection during a layoff, the layoffs had to be made according to the 1973 seniority system.

Wygant v. Jackson Board of Education
476 US 267 (1986)

The U.S. Supreme Court dealt a tremendous blow to affirmative action in this case involving a public school system's affirmative action plan. The record reflected that the first African American school teacher was not hired in Jackson, Michigan until 1953. By 1969, only 3.9 percent of the teachers were African American although 15.2 percent of the students were African American. In response, the school board developed an affirmative action plan that protected African American faculty members during layoffs.

Although the U.S. Supreme Court had approved affirmative action plans in prior cases, it rejected the Jackson plan. The court found that the goal of the plan, to remedy societal discrimination and afford positive role models to black students, was nebulous and not sufficiently compelling.

Local No. 93, International Association of Firefighters v. City of Cleveland
106 S.Ct. 3063 (1986)

The city of Cleveland, which had a long history of racial discrimination, negotiated a consent decree with African American firefighters who had filed a lawsuit alleging that they had been unlawfully denied jobs and promotions. The decree included an affirmative action plan with numerical goals for promotion of African Americans to the position of supervisor.

In response to the union's challenge on behalf of white firefighters, the U.S. Supreme Court ruled that the lower courts had broad discretion to approve decrees in which employers settle discrimination suits by agreeing to preferential promotions of African Americans, in spite of the objections of white employees.

Local 28, Sheet Metal Workers International Association v. EEOC
106 S.Ct. 3019 (1986)

After finding that the all-white union had discriminated against African Americans and Hispanics seeking to enter the sheet metal trades for more than a decade, the trial court ordered the union to establish a 29

African Americans are now represented on most city fire and police forces.

percent non-white membership goal. The court also ruled that the union would have to pay substantial fines if the union failed to meet the goals. After the union failed to reach the goal, the court found the union in contempt and established a new goal of 29.3 percent. The union challenged the court's order.

In a complex opinion, the U.S. Supreme Court upheld the affirmative action goal in light of the union's "persistent or egregious discrimination" and to eliminate "lingering effects of pervasive discrimination." This was the first time the Court expressly approved the use of race conscious relief to blacks and Hispanics who were not identified victims of discrimination.

United States v. Paradise
480 US 149 (1987)

This case originated in 1972 when the NAACP sued the Alabama Department of Highways because of its long-standing history of racially discriminating employment practices. More than 11 years later, after the Department had failed to hire or promote blacks, the trial court ordered the promotion of one black trooper for every white. The U.S. Attorney General challenged the constitutionality of the plan. The U.S. Supreme Court upheld the use of strict racial quotas and found that the plan was "narrowly tailored to serve a compelling government interest"—remedying "egregious" past discrimination against blacks.

Johnson v. Transportation Agency, Santa Clara County, California
480 US 616 (1987)

The U.S. Supreme Court held that the state transportation agency's voluntary affirmative action plan, under which a female had been promoted to the position of road dispatcher over a male whose score was slightly higher, was consistent with Title VII of the Civil Rights Act of 1964. The court held that an employer does not have to admit or prove that it has discriminated in order to justify efforts designed to achieve a more racially balanced workforce. The employer only needs to demonstrate that there is a "conspicuous ... imbalance in traditionally segregated job categories."

City of Richmond v. J. A. Croson Co.
109 S.Ct. 706 (1989)

Richmond adopted a Minority Business Utilization Plan that was not sufficiently narrowly tailored to remedy past discrimination in the construction industry. The Plan allowed minorities a fixed 30 percent quota of the public contracts based solely on their race. The policy provided no guidance for the city's legislating body to determine the precise scope of the injury it sought to remedy except racial balancing.

◆ LEGAL GATEKEEPERS

Clifford L. Jr. Alexander 1933-
Attorney, Federal Government Official

Born in New York City, September 21, 1933, Clifford Alexander went to Harvard and earned a bachelor's degree *cum laude* in 1955, and attended Yale Law School afterwards, earning a LL.B. in 1958. After attending these prestigious universities, he went on to become the assistant district attorney of New York County, working there from 1959 to 1961. Positions as the executive director of the Hamilton Grange Neighborhood Conservation district in Manhattanville from 1961 to 1962, and as executive program director of HARYOU from 1962 to 1963, followed. In 1963, he became a member of the National Security Council.

Alexander was hired by President Lyndon Johnson as his deputy special assistant in 1964, and quickly rose to become the President's deputy special counsel in 1967. He became chairman of the Equal Employment Opportunity Commission in 1967, where he was under constant pressure from Republican Senators like Everett Dirksen, who accused him of bullying reluctant employers into complying with federal guidelines for minority employment. He left that position in 1969.

In the years between 1969 and 1976, Alexander worked for several different law offices in private practice. He also became a Harvard overseer. At Harvard, he was involved in working out details with craft unions which were obliged to offer and implement concrete proposals for improving minority employment opportunities.

President Jimmy Carter appointed Alexander as the secretary of the Department of the Army, the first African American to serve in that position. Alexander won the Outstanding Civilian Service Award from the Department of the Army in 1980, after he finished his 1977–80 appointment to that position. Since 1981, Alexander has been president of Alexander Associates, Inc., and served as a consultant to Major League Baseball, working to improve minority hiring practices. In the early 1990s, Alexander served as Washington, DC's chief negotiator in hammering out a deal to build a new stadium for the National Football League's Washington Redskins.

In addition, Alexander has had his own television program, "Black on White," has been director of several Dreyfus money funds, has served on the board of directors for the Mexican–American Legal Defense and Education Fund, and has taught as a professor at Howard University.

Violette Anderson 1882-19??
Judge/Magistrate, Attorney

Violette Anderson was born July 16, 1882, in London, England, the daughter of Richard E. and Marie (Jordi) Neatley. When she was young, the family moved to the United States, where she attended North Division High School in Chicago, Illinois from 1895 to 1899; Chicago Athenaeum, 1903; the Chicago Seminar of Sciences from 1912 to 1915, and Chicago Law School from 1917 to 1920, earning her LL.B. in 1920. Soon after, she was wed to Albert E. Johnson. Anderson was a Republican and her church affiliation was Episcopalian.

Anderson worked as a court reporter from 1905 to 1920, a job which sparked her interest in law. She began a private practice in 1920, becoming the first African-American woman to practice law in the U.S. District Court Eastern Division. From 1922 to 1923, she served as the first female city prosecutor in Chicago.

After five years of practice before the high court of Illinois, by application of Judge James A. Cobb of Washington, DC, Anderson was admitted to practice for the Supreme Court of the United States, becoming the first African American woman to obtain this post. Her admission became a precedent that allowed other African American women to do the same.

Anderson also belonged to the Federal Colored Women's Clubs, was president of Friendly Big Sisters League of Chicago, First Vice-President of Cook County Bar

Association, and secretary of Idlewild Lot Owners Association. In addition, she was the member of the executive board of Chicago Council of Social Agencies.

Deborah A. Batts 1946?-
Judge/Magistrate

The first openly lesbian federal judge, Batts was confirmed to a Manhattan bench in 1994. A graduate of Radcliffe and Harvard Law School, Batts earned her credentials through hard work. A native Philadelphian, Batts clerked for a federal judge before joining Cravath, Swaine & Moore, where she worked as a litigator for six years. Next she served as assistant U.S. attorney in New York for five years before accepting a teaching post at Fordham University in 1994. There she taught property and family law.

A supporter of equal rights for gays and lesbians, Batts is known to be a an independent thinker unafraid to speak her mind. She was drawn to the legal field after experiencing the political turmoil of the 1960s, in particular, the bitter assassinations of Martin Luther King, Jr. and Bobby Kennedy. She was initially recommended for a federal judgeship during the Bush administration but did not receive a nomination. U.S. Senator Daniel Moynihan recommended her a second time when President Clinton assumed office. Clinton's nomination of Batts was confirmed by the Senate with no challenges.

Derrick Albert Bell 1930-
Attorney, Educator

Derrick Albert Bell, Jr. was born in Pittsburgh, Pennsylvania, November 6, 1930, the son of Derrick and Ada Bell. He attended Duquesne University and received his LL.B. from the University of Pittsburgh Law School. He married Jewel A. Hairston and the couple has three children. Bell is a member of the bar in Washington, DC, Pennsylvania, New York, California; the U.S. Supreme Court; the U.S. Courts of Appeals for fourth, fifth, sixth, eighth, and tenth circuits; and several federal district courts. Since 1969 he has been teaching law at Harvard Law School. Bell has written several important books on the law, including *Race, Racism and American Law*, second edition, 1980, and *And We Are Not Saved, The Elusive Quest for Racial Justice*, 1987. Bell also served as editor of *Desegregation Dialogue, Searching for Remedies Under Brown.*

After graduating from law school, Bell worked for the U.S. Department of Justice from 1957 to 1959, at the Pittsburgh Branch of the NAACP as executive secretary from 1959 to 1960, and for the NAACP Legal Defense and Education Fund as staff attorney from 1960 to 1966. In 1966 he was made deputy assistant to the secretary for civil rights for the Department of Health, Education and Welfare. He also served for a year as the director of the Western Center on Law and Poverty.

Bell began as a lecturer on law at Harvard Law School in 1969, became a professor in 1971, and left in 1980 to be dean of the University of Oregon Law School for five years. After spending one year teaching at Stanford University, he returned to Harvard Law School in 1986. Four years later, Bell took an unpaid extended leave from his teaching duties at Harvard in protest over the institution's lack of a tenured black woman professor. Student support for Bell's actions was immense, but Bell was formally removed from his position in 1992. Nonplussed, Bell went on to write two well-received books—1992's

Faces at the Bottom of the Well: The Permanence of Racism and 1994's *Confronting Authority: Reflections of an Ardent Protester.*

Jane Matilda Bolin 1908-
Judge/Magistrate, Attorney

At the relatively young age of 31, Jane Matilda Bolin was honored by being chosen to be the first African American woman judge in the United States. She presided over the Domestic Relations Court of the City of New York (subsequently called the Family Court of the State of New York) for forty years. Her first ten–year appointment came from Mayor Fiorello La Guardia in 1939. She was appointed to three more successive ten–year terms by mayors William O'Dwyer, John Lindsay, and Robert F. Wagner, Jr. After forty years of service, Bolin reached the mandatory retirement age and had to step down, but not before she became well known over the country for her work. Bolin was also known for her striking beauty. John Powers, head of a world–renowned modeling agency, named her one of the "Powers Girls" of 1949.

Born April 11, 1908 in Poughkeepsie, New York, her father was the first African American graduate of Williams College. Bolin attended Wellesley College and Yale University School of Law, where she received her LL.B. in 1931. She worked with her father, who was also a lawyer, until she passed the New York State Bar examination; she then practiced in Poughkeepsie before moving to New York City to practice law with her husband, Ralph E. Mizelle.

In 1937, Bolin was appointed assistant corporation counsel for New York City, a post which she held until she received her appointment to the Domestic Relations Court. Outside of her career, Bolin has taken an active role in the Wiltwyck School for Boys, the Child Welfare League of America, the Neighborhood Children's Center, and the local and national NAACP. She has also travelled extensively and met several heads of state in Africa. She counted among her friends Eleanor Roosevelt, educator Mary McLeod Bethune and Judge Waties Waring, who ruled in the first public school desegregation case. Bolin has received honorary degrees from Morgan State University, Western College for Women, Tuskegee Institute, Hampton University and Williams College.

After her retirement, Bolin became a volunteer reading teacher for the New York City public schools for a few years. She received an appointment to the Regents Review Committee of the New York State Board of Regents, which holds hearings involving professional discipline of more than 32 professions. Bolin was honored for her distinguished service by the corporation counsel's office on May 17, 1993.

Johnnie L. Cochran, Jr. 1937-
Attorney

Though he was born in Shreveport, Louisiana on October 2, 1937, Johnnie L. Cochran, Jr. grew up in Los Angeles. He received a bachelor's degree from the University of California in 1959. After finishing his law studies at the Loyola Marymount University School of Law, he passed the California bar exam in 1963. Cochran began his law career as prosecutor in the criminal division of the deputy city attorney's office in Los Angeles. In 1965, he left that post to join criminal lawyer Gerald Lenoir in private practice. Shortly thereafter, he created Cochran, Atkins & Evans, a three-partner law firm.

During his first stint in private practice, Cochran established himself with defending high-profile African American clients, such as Leonard Deadwyler's family, a young man shot to death by police while driving his pregnant wife to the hospital, and Geronimo Pratt, a former Black Panther charged with murder. Cochran lost both cases, but he demonstrated how such cases could garner media attention and foment the African American community into action.

Cochran returned to the Los Angeles County district attorney's office in 1978, in order to better his image as one of the best lawyers on the west coast. After five years as a prosecutor, he once again returned to private practice in 1983. Shortly thereafter, Cochran won a settlement for the family of Ron Settles, who had been strangled by police officers, though his death was originally identified as a suicide.

Cochran's victories increased from hundreds of thousands in settlements to millions, and he began representing celebrities such as pop-singer Michael Jackson actor Todd Bridges. Starting in the summer of 1994 and continuing through the summer of 1995, Cochran served as one of the team of defense lawyers for O. J. Simpson, accused of murdering his ex-wife Nicole Brown Simpson and her friend Ronald Goldman. Cochran wore down the prosecution by challenging evidence and concentrating on racially prejudiced officers. Cochran's closing arguments charged the jury to stop racism such as the kind that, as he claimed, framed O. J. Simpson for murder. In response, the jury acquitted Simpson on all counts.

Following the Simpson case—described in the media as "The Trial of the Century," Cochran became one of the best known lawyers in the country and was offered a million-dollar advance for his memoirs. Cochran has served as an adjunct professor at both the Los Angeles School of Law and the Loyola University School of Law. He served as chairman of the Rules Committee of the Democratic National Convention in 1984. In 1995, he was awarded the Trumpet Award by the Turner Broadcasting System.

George Crockett, Jr. 1909-
Attorney, Judge/Magistrate, Legislator, Civil Rights/ Human Rights Activist

Born in Jacksonville, Florida, on August 10, 1909, Crockett began working when he was only 12 and later graduated from Morehouse College. Traveling north to Michigan to pursue a law degree, Crockett then returned to his hometown and opened a law practice. In 1939, his accomplishments as a lawyer and community activist led him to be chosen as the first African American attorney in the U.S. Department of Justice.

While in Washington, DC, Crockett distinguished himself as counsel for cases that came before the Fair Labor Standards Act, and, in 1943, his work led to his appointment by President Franklin D. Roosevelt as an examiner with the Fair Employment Practices Committee. That same year, he was hired by the United Auto Workers headquarters in Detroit, to serve as director of their Fair Employment Practices office during a time of increased racial tensions in the city. In 1946, he went into private practice in Detroit with three other attorneys and for many years their firm took on significant civil rights cases. The passion with which Crockett once argued a case on behalf of accused Communists in a contentious courtroom battle landed him in prison for four months for a contempt of court violation.

Crockett became intensely involved in the civil rights struggle in the South during the 1960s, leaving Michigan for a time to direct the National Lawyers Guild civil rights efforts through an effort known as Project Mississippi. In 1966, he was elected to Detroit Recorder's Court, a bench that handled the city's criminal docket. During a 1969, incident in which members of a leftist group who were meeting at an African American church were brought en masse into police custody after a shooting outside the church, Crockett went down to the station in the middle of the night and set up his own impromptu court, letting most of the charged free on the basis of constitutional law. He was vilified by Detroit's white establishment for his application of the Bill of Rights in the fracas.

In 1980, two years after he had left the Recorder's Court bench, Crockett was elected as a Democratic Congressional representative for a Michigan district that included part of Detroit. He served in Washington for the next decade, continuing to distinguish himself by speaking out on civil rights issues and even serving another—albeit one-night—stint in jail for participating in a demonstration against apartheid in South Africa. The legislator was also a vocal opponent of Reagan Administration policies in Central America, especially during his tenure as chair of the Foreign Affairs Subcommittee on the Western Hemisphere. After his retirement from politics in 1990, Crockett, founder of the National Bar Association Judicial Council, continued to live in the Washington, DC area.

Drew S. Days III 1941-
Attorney, Educator

Days was born in Atlanta, Georgia on August 29, 1941. He received a bachelor's degree from Hamilton College in 1963 and continued his studies at the Yale Law School. During his free summer months, Days returned to Georgia to champion civil rights causes and represent the poor as an intern in a one-lawyer office. After graduating from law school near the top of his class in 1966, Days moved to Chicago to represent minorities in cases of housing discrimination in the city. Later Days quit practicing law to work in Honduras for the U.S. Peace Corps.

Upon his return to the United States one year later, Days worked in the Legal Defense and Educational Fund for the National Association for the Advancement of Colored People (NAACP). While working for NAACP, he served as an associate professor at Temple University in Philadelphia. In 1977, Days accepted a post as the first African American as the head of the civil rights division of the U.S. Department of Justice. In 1980, when the power in Washington shifted from Carter to Reagan, Days left the government to teach at Yale University.

In 1992, President Bill Clinton nominated Days to the position of solicitor general of the United States, the second leading position at the Justice Department. In this position, Days has criticized poorly conceived or poorly managed minority-assistance programs, and in 1995, he argued before the Supreme Court to keep in place "minority voting districts" in the Deep South. Early in 1996, Days resigned his position at the Justice Department to return to teaching law at Yale University.

Jerome Farris 1930-
Attorney, Judge/Magistrate

Jerome Farris was elected circuit judge of the U.S. Court of Appeals Ninth Circuit in 1979, and continues to serve in that capacity. Judge Farris was born on March 4, 1930, in Birmingham, Alabama. Willie Joe and Elizabeth Farris were his parents. He earned his B.S. degree from Morehouse College in 1951. In 1952, he joined the U.S. Army Signal Corps. He received a M.S.W. from Atlanta University in 1955, and received his J.D. from the University of Washington in 1958. Farris is married to Jean Shy and has two children.

Farris started out in private practice with Weyer, Schroeter and Sterne in 1958, becoming a partner in 1959. He stayed in private practice until he became a Washington State court of appeals judge in 1969. He was the chairman of the State Federal Judicial Council of Washington from 1983 to 1987. In addition, he has served as president on the Washington State Jr. Chamber of Commerce from 1965 to 1966; a trustee with the Pacific Northwest Ballet from 1978 to 1983; and as a regent of the University of Washington since 1985.

Farris has been honored with the Clayton Frost Award from the Jaycees in 1966, received an honorary LL.D. from Morehouse College in 1978, and the Order of the Coif from the University of Washington Law School.

Archibald H. Grimké 1849-1930
Attorney, Writer, Activist, Diplomat

Archibald Grimké was born on a plantation near Charleston, South Carolina, in 1849. His father was a successful lawyer who had given up his profession to become a planter. His mother had been a family slave and served as the nurse for Henry Grimké's first wife, Selena. Archibald was considered a slave due to South Carolina law at the time. He, along with his mother and siblings, were passed on to relatives after his father's death. Grimké attended a special school during his youth. He later fled his home. Grimké enrolled in a school directed by Frances Pillsbury and impressed the instructors there with his superior academic abilities. He completed undergraduate studies in only three years and obtained his master's degree from Lincoln University two years following that, in 1872.

Grimké moved to Boston and practiced law there from 1875 to 1883. Beginning in 1885, he presided over the Women's Suffrage Association of Massachusets. In the early 1890's, Grimké wrote for Boston-area publications, before being appointed the American consul for Santo Domingo (now the Dominican Republic) for four years. He then assumed the presidential role for the Washington chapter of the NAACP while writing, lecturing, and presiding over the American Negro Academy.

Grimké write several books, including biographies of William Lloyd Garrison in 1891 and Charles Sumner in 1892, and numerous essays and speeches.

William H. Hastie 1904-1976

Attorney, Judge/Magistrate, State Government Official/Executive

From 1949 to 1971, William H. Hastie served as a U.S. Court of Appeals Judge of the Third Circuit, the first African American man to hold a federal appeals judicial position. Hastie was born in Knoxville, Tennessee, November 17, 1904. He was the son of William Henry and Roberta Child Hastie. He received his A.B. from Amherst College in 1925, an LL.B. from Harvard University in 1930 and a S.J.D. from the same institution in 1933. He received honorary LL.D.s from many institutions, including Rutgers University, Howard University and Temple University. In 1943, he married Beryl Lockhart. The couple had three children.

Hastie was admitted to the bar in 1930 and was in private practice from 1930 to 1933. In 1933, he became assistant solicitor of the Department of the Interior, where he served until 1937. In 1937, he became a judge of the District Court of the Virgin Islands, leaving in 1939 to become dean of the Howard University School of Law. In 1942, he was the first civilian aide to the secretary of war. He was governor of the Virgin Islands between 1946 and 1949, before his subsequent position as U.S. Circuit Court of Appeals judge. Hastie was also a Trustee of the Amherst College and a Fellow of the American Academy of Arts and Sciences. Hastie died April 14, 1976, in Philadelphia, Pennsylvania.

Joseph W. Hatchett 1932-

Attorney, Judge/Magistrate, Author/Poet

Judge Joseph W. Hatchett was appointed a U.S. Circuit Judge of the U.S. Court of Appeals on October 1, 1981, and he currently retains that position. Judge Hatchett was the first black to be appointed to the highest court of a state since reconstruction, the first black to be elected to public office in a statewide election in the South, and first black to serve on a federal appellate court in the South.

Born in Clearwater, Florida, September 17, 1932, Hatchett received his A.B. from Florida A&M University in 1954 and his J.D. from Howard University in 1959. He also has certification in his specialties—a Naval Justice School Certificate in 1973, an Appellate Judge Course in 1977, and an American Academy of Judicial Education Appellate Judge Course in 1978.

Hatchett was in private practice in Florida from 1959 to 1966, and served as the contract consultant for the City of Daytona Beach for three years. He became an assistant U.S. attorney in Jacksonville, Florida in 1966, then served as the first assistant of the U.S. Attorney for the Middle District of Florida. In 1971, he became the U.S. magistrate for the Middle District of Florida, and was a Supreme Court justice for the state of Florida from 1975 to 1979. He was a U.S. Circuit judge for the U.S. Court of Appeals, Fifth Circuit from 1979 to 1981, before advancing to his current position.

Hatchett was honored with a Howard University Post Graduation Achievement Award in 1977, named Most Outstanding Citizen from the Broward County National Bar Association in 1976 received a Medallion for Human Relations from Bethune-Cookman in 1975, and has been awarded several honorary doctorates. He is the author of several publications in the field of law.

A. Leon Higginbotham, Jr. 1928-

Judge/Magistrate, Author

Leon Higginbotham, Jr. was appointed on October 13, 1977 by President Jimmy Carter to the U.S. Circuit Judge's position. Just prior to this appointment, he had served on the Federal Trade Commission—the first black and the youngest person ever to hold the post of commissioner. Born in Trenton, New Jersey, on February 25, 1928, Higginbotham began as an engineering student at Purdue University, but later went to Antioch College to study liberal arts. He received his LL.B. in 1952 from Yale School of Law. This was quite a step for a man who started out as a shoe store porter.

After graduation, he became an assistant district attorney in Philadelphia, and later moved into private practice. He was sought out by Pennsylvania Governor David Lawrence to become a member of the Pennsylvania Human Rights Commission. Elected president of the Philadelphia chapter of NAACP, Higginbotham later earned the honor of "One of the 10 Outstanding Young Men in America" by the U.S. Junior Chamber of Commerce. He was made district judge in 1964, where he served until his appointment as a federal appellate judge in 1977. Higginbotham was also a lecturer at Harvard Law School and an adjunct professor at the University of Pennsylvania. In 1993, he was nominated for a position on the New York Times Co. board of directors.

In 1995, a retired Higginbotham levied criticism at Supreme Court Justice Clarence Thomas, whose judicial philosophy differs greatly from his own. While Higginbotham advocated social engineering through legislation, Thomas vigorously held that law should be colorblind. Higginbotham was, in turn, criticized for what some saw as an unprovoked attack on a colleague.

Higginbotham is well known for his prolific writing. He has authored more than 100 articles as well as an acclaimed book, *In the Matter of Color: Race and the*

William Hastie, 1949

American Legal Process: The Colonial Period. He has also been praised for his unusual competency in logic and language; in his esteemed career, he has won more than 40 honorary degrees. Higginbotham was awarded the nation's highest medal in 1995, when the Presidential Medal of Freedom was bestowed upon him by President Clinton.

Anita Hill 1956-
Educator, Author, Lecturer

Born on July 30, 1956, in Morns, Oklahoma, Anita Hill was a relatively unknown law professor at the University of Oklahoma when her name became a household word virtually overnight. It was during the Senate confirmation hearings in October 1991, for U.S. Supreme Court Justice Clarence Thomas that Hill became famous. She came forward with sexual harassment charges against Judge Thomas that shocked the nation, and many watched as she poured out painful details of Thomas's alleged sexual harassment, purportedly committed when both had worked for the Equal Employment Opportunities Commission. Hill claimed that Thomas repeatedly pressured her to date him, told her plots of pornographic movies, and bragged about his sexual exploits. When asked why she didn't quit her job or report Thomas when the incidents occurred during the early 1980s, Hill answered that she feared she would not be able to get another job.

Following the hearings, Hill continued to be hounded by the press. Several books were written and a 76-minute documentary composed of testimony clips entitled *Sex and Justice: The Highlights of the Anita Hill/ Clarence Thomas Hearings* was released. Her experience with the hearings had changed her life, as well as her career direction. She had been a professor of commercial law. She decided to take a year–long sabbatical in order to look at the possibility of founding an institute with the purpose of researching racism and sexism. Hill also made many speeches around the country about her experience.

Controversy did not escape her on campus, either. Several lawmakers made news when they requested that Hill be fired. However, the University of Oklahoma dean and other members of the faculty supported her. In 1993, a university professorship to be established in Hill's name was proposed; though the suggestion met much opposition, the endowed chair was approved two years later.(The Anita Faye Hill Professorship provides

A. Leon Higginbotham, Jr., 1969

a salary and money for research and travel expenses incurred in the study of women's rights in the workplace.)

On March 9, 1995, Hill cited no reasons as she announced her resignation from the university, but after taking an unpaid leave during which she presumably intended to write, she resumed her teaching post in September of the same year. *Race, Gender, and Power in America,* co-edited by Hill and Emma Coleman Jordan, was published in 1995.

Anita Hill

Charles Hamilton Houston 1895-1950

Attorney, Educational Administrator

Charles Hamilton Houston was born in Washington, DC, on September 3, 1895. Finishing high school at the young age of fifteen, he went on to attend Amherst College and earned his A.B. from that institution in 1915, one of six valedictorians. He taught English briefly, then enlisted in the U.S. Army in 1917, and served in France and Germany until 1919. He attended Harvard Law School and became the first African American editor of the *Harvard Law Review*. He received his LL.B. in 1922, and was at the top five percent of his class. He also became the first African American to receive a S.J.D. from Harvard University in 1923. In 1923, he received a Sheldon Fellowship and studied civil law at the University of Madrid. He was admitted to the Washington, DC, bar in 1924.

Houston was in private practice with his father from 1924 to 1950. Between 1929 and 1935, he was vice dean of the school of law at Howard University. He was special counsel to the NAACP from 1935 to 1940, and a member of the national legal aid committee from 1940 to 1950. He served as the vice president for the American Council on Race Relations from 1944 to 1950, and was a member of the President's Commission on Fair Employment Practice in 1944.

While with the NAACP, Houston teamed with the American Fund for Public Service to direct a program of legal action and education aimed at the elimination of segregation. Former student Thurgood Marshall served under Houston for several years. While in this position, Houston argued several cases before the U.S. Supreme Court, including *Missouri ex rel. Gaines v. Canada.* The court ruled that Missouri could not keep an African American from attending the white state law school because no such school existed for African Americans. This ruling was a major blow to the separate but equal rule.

Historically, Houston's major impact was in his strengthening of Howard University's Law School, as well as his work in civil rights litigation. Much of the cases he argued were instrumental in setting precedents that were to be used in the historic *Brown v. Board of Education* and *Boling v. Sharpe* cases that were to outlaw racial segregation. In addition, he was a columnist for *The Afro-American.*

Houston died April 22, 1950, of a heart ailment and was buried in Lincoln Memorial Cemetery. Five Supreme Court justices attended his funeral. He received a great deal of recognition after his death, including the Springarn Medal, awarded by the NAACP.

Elaine R. Jones 1944-

Attorney, Organization Executive, Civil Rights/Human Rights Activist

Elaine Jones has maintained a very steady high profile throughout her career, holding the distinction of being "the first" in many of her life's experiences. Born on March 2, 1944, in Norfolk, Virginia, Jones always wanted to be a lawyer. Earning a bachelor's degree with honors in 1965 from Howard University, she became the first black female law student admitted to the University of Virginia School of Law.

Receiving her law degree in 1970, Jones was offered a job with a prestigious Wall Street firm. She eventually turned down the job on Wall Street and went to work instead for the NAACP Legal Defense and Educational Fund (LDF), following her conscience instead of her bank account. The LDF had argued more cases before the Supreme Court than any other organization except the U.S. Department of Justice.

In 1973, Jones became the managing attorney in the LDF's New York City office, the organization's largest. In the late 1970s, she helped set up and run the LDF's new Washington, DC, office. In 1988, Jones was promoted to deputy director-counsel of the LDF, making her second-in-command to the director, Julius Chambers. Jones used this higher profile position to challenge the administrations of Reagan and Bush on their federal judicial appointments. She was an outspoken opponent of both Robert Bork in 1987 and Clarence Thomas in 1991.

Julius Chambers resigned from the LDF directorship in 1993, and the organization's board unanimously chose Jones to succeed Chambers. As director, Jones has broadened the organization's agenda to include more cases of environmental and health care discrimination. In addition to litigation, she is concerned with the group's fundraising efforts.

Nathaniel R. Jones 1926-

Judge/Magistrate, Civil Rights/Human Rights Activist

Born in 1926, Nathaniel R. Jones is a distinguished judge, attorney and administrator. President Jimmy Carter appointed him to the Sixth Circuit Court of Appeals in Cincinnati, Ohio on October 15, 1979; Jones retired from the bench in 1995. Prior to that, he was general counsel for the NAACP from 1969 to 1979, executive director of the Fair Employment Practices Commission of the City of Youngstown, Ohio from 1966 to 1969, in private practice, and a U.S. Attorney for the Northern District of Ohio.

While with the NAACP, Judge Jones organized the attack against northern school segregation and also argued in the Supreme Court's Detroit school case *Bradley v. Milliken.* The Dayton and Columbus, Ohio school desegregation cases heard before the Supreme Court were also organized by Jones. He has headed a three–man team that investigated grievances of black servicemen in Germany and responded to the attacks against affirmative action. He was also a national liaison for the famous "Kalamazoo Case." He was made deputy general counsel to the President's Commission on Civil Disorders in 1967 and co–chairman of the Civilian Military Task Force on Military Justice in 1972.

Jones received a B.A. degree from Youngstown University in 1951, and his LL.B. in 1956. He has honorary degrees from Youngstown University and Syracuse University.

Star Jones 1962?-

Attorney

Star Jones was born Starlet Marie Jones in the early 1960s, and grew up in Trenton, New Jersey, the daughter of two city executives. Shortening her unusual moniker in 1979, upon entering American University, Jones took an active role in college and even served as a national officer of Alpha Kappa Alpha, the sorority to which she belonged. After earning a law degree from the University of Houston, Jones went to work for the Kings County District Attorney's office, whose jurisdiction included the crime-plagued New York City borough of Brooklyn. She served as a member of its prosecuting staff from 1986, until her promotion to senior assistant district attorney in 1991.

The year 1991 also landed Jones an invitation to appear on Court TV, a cable television network that broadcasts high-profile trials interjected with commentary from experts on the judicial system. The channel soon hired her to appear regularly in conjunction with the William Kennedy Smith rape trial in Florida, and Jones's eloquence before the camera and projection of intelligence and warmth soon had a major network knocking at her door.

NBC lured her away from her tough job at the Brooklyn D.A.'s office by offering her its legal correspondent slot. During the two years she appeared on the network, several notable trials attracted the attention of the

Nathaniel Jones, 1985

American viewing public, and Jones was there to provide commentary as well as explanation of some of the more complex legal points involved on both the *Today* show and *NBC Nightly News*. Those cases included the criminal trial of the Los Angeles police officers charged with beating motorist Rodney King and the rape trial of boxer Mike Tyson.

In 1994, Group W Communications offered Jones her own syndicated television show. Debuting that fall, *Jones & Jury* gave plaintiffs and defendants who had lawsuits pending in California's equivalent of small claims court a chance to resolve their disputes on television before a studio audience, who would then render the verdict. Jones was the moderator, an in-charge role that also showcased her deft explanations of the complexities of law. Unfortunately, the competitive world of syndicated television spelled cancellation for the show by the end of 1995.

Amalya Lyle Kearse 1937-
Judge/Magistrate

Judge Amalya Lyle Kearse was born June 11, 1937, in Vauxhall, New Jersey. She attended Wellesley College for her B.A. in 1959, and went to the University of Michigan for her J.D. in 1962. Kearse was in private practice from 1962 to 1969, also working as an adjunct lecturer for the New York University Law School from 1968 to 1969. She was then made U.S. Court of Appeals Circuit Judge.

Kearse has won the Jason L. Honigman Award for Outstanding Contribution to the Law Review Editorial Board. She has also served on the board of directors for the NAACP Legal Defense and Education Fund, as well as the National Urban League. She was appointed to the President's Commission for the Selection of Judges and served between 1977 and 1978. She served on the executive committee for Civil Rights Under Law for nine years, has been a member of the American Law Institute since 1977 and a fellow in the American College of Trial Lawyers since 1979.

Damon J. Keith 1922-
Judge/Magistrate, Attorney

Damon J. Keith was appointed to the U.S. District Court by President Lyndon Johnson and served there from 1967 to 1977. From 1977 to 1995, he served as judge for the U.S. Court of Appeals, Sixth Circuit Court in Cincinnati, Ohio. Born July 4, 1922 in Detroit, Keith attended West Virginia State College, where he received his A.B. in 1943. Following graduation, he served in the army for three years. He returned to school to earn his LL.B. from Howard University in 1949. In 1951 Keith took a job as an attorney for the Office of the Friend of the Court in Detroit, and held that position from 1951 to 1955. He received an LL.M. from Wayne State University in 1956.

Keith worked for the Wayne County Board of Supervisors from 1958 to 1963, then went into private practice from 1964 to 1967 before being appointed a judge. He has been active in the Michigan Civil Rights Commission, a trustee in the Medical Corporation of Detroit, a member of the Citizen's Advisory Committee on Equal Educational Opportunity, first vice president emeritus of the Detroit Chapter of the NAACP, a member of the management committee of the Detroit YMCA, a member of the Detroit Council of the Boy Scouts of America, a member of the Detroit Arts Commission, and vice president of the United Negro College Fund of Detroit. Keith is also a trustee of Interlochen Arts Academy and the Cranbrook School.

Judge Keith has been honored with many accolades, including being named one of one hundred Most Influential Black Americans by *Ebony* magazine, in 1971 and 1977; he received a citizen award from Michigan State University and became a Springarn Medalist in 1974. He has received honorary degrees from the University of

Damon Keith

Michigan, Howard University, Wayne State University, Michigan State University, and New York Law School.

Willie Lipscomb, Jr. 1944?-
Judge

Willie Lipscomb, Jr. grew up in Flint, Michigan with the intention of becoming a bus driver. He rose to higher aspirations, however, and after attending Wayne State University, he graduated with a law degree from the University of Notre Dame Law School in the early 1980s. For nearly 12 years he served as a prosecutor for Wayne County, Michigan, before being elected to serve as a jurist in the 36th District Court.

More than a judge, Lipscomb has differentiated himself through his community mentorship. He initiated an anti-gun violence seminar as part of the three-hour-long Handgun Intervention Program, mandatory for anyone arraigned in Detroit for a crime involving a gun. The Saturday morning seminar, a graphic slide presentation of gunshot victims from the morgue, is further punctuated by Lipscomb's vocal commentary, including snippets of civil rights history and personal anecdotes such as his struggle to give up sugar after he was diagnosed with diabetes. Part teacher and part preacher, Lipscomb tries to make his "students" realize that each person has choices in life. The program, one that Lipscomb runs on his own time, has been so successful that other cities have employed similar tactics. For his role, Lipscomb was named a Michiganian of the year in 1995.

Wade Hampton McCree, Jr. 1920-1987
Judge/Magistrate, Attorney

Wade Hampton McCree, Jr. was appointed to the post of solicitor general by President Jimmy Carter, where he served from 1977 to 1981. McCree had already led a distinguished career as a judge and lawyer by the time he reached that position. He died August 30, 1987. McCree was born in Des Moines, Iowa, on July 3, 1920. He attended Fisk University to earn his A.B. in 1941, and received his LL.B. from Harvard University in 1944. In 1948, he was admitted to the bar in Michigan.

McCree had a private law practice from 1948 to 1952. From 1952 to 1954 he was commissioner of the Michigan Workmen's Compensation Commission. He became a circuit judge for Wayne County, Michigan, in 1954 until 1961, then a judge for the U.S. District Court Eastern District in Michigan from 1961 to 1966. McCree had the honor of being the first African American judge in the state of Michigan. From 1966 to 1967 he presided over the U.S. Court of Appeals Sixth Circuit. From 1981 until his death in 1987, he was a member of the faculty at the University of Michigan Law School. Three years later, the Wade H. McCree, Jr. Professorship was established at the University of Michigan Law School, making it the first endowed chair at a major American law school to be named after an African American. McCree was honored with more than 30 honorary degrees in his lifetime, including LL.D. degrees from Howard University, Harvard University, Boston University, Brandeis University and Tuskegee Institute.

Theodore McMillian 1919-
Judge/Magistrate, Educator

Born January 28, 1919 in St. Louis, Missouri, Theodore McMillian attended Lincoln University, receiving his B.S. degree in 1941 and earned his LL.B. degree from St. Louis University Law School in 1949. He served in the Signal Corps from 1942 to 1946.

McMillian has been a lecturer at St. Louis University Law School as well as a faculty member of Webster College. He became a circuit judge for the state of Missouri and served as an assistant circuit attorney for the City of St. Louis from 1953 to 1956. From 1972 to

Wade McCree, Jr.

1978, he was a judge with the Missouri court of appeals. He became a U.S. Circuit Court of Appeals circuit judge for the eighth circuit in 1978. He continues to serve that capacity.

Judge McMillian has been a member of the board of trustees for Blue Cross, and a member of the Danforth Foundation Advisory Council. He served on the Presidential Council of St. Louis University, and as a board chairman for Human Development Corporation between 1964 and 1977. He has also been a member of the National Legal Aid Advisory Board. He has been honored with an Alumni Merit Award from St. Louis University, an Award of Honor from the Lawyers Association in 1970, and a Man of the Year Award in 1970.

Carmel Carrington Marr 1921-

Attorney, Diplomat, State Government Official/Executive

Carmel Carrington Marr was born in Brooklyn, New York, in 1921 and attended Hunter College for her B.A. (cum laude) in 1945, continuing education to earn her J.D. from Columbia University Law School in 1948. As an experienced lawyer in international law, she was appointed by President Harry Truman to the position of legal advisor to the U.S. Mission to the United Nations in 1953. She served that position until 1967, keeping in constant contact with missions from other parts of the world, and serving on a number of key committees of the United Nations General Assembly.

Marr began her career in private practice from 1949 to 1953. After her position as legal advisor to the United Nations, she became the senior legal officer of the United Nations Secretariat from 1967-68, and then left to become a member of the New York State Human Rights Appeal Board from 1968 to 1971. Between 1971 and 1986 she served as commissioner of the New York State Public Service Commission. She retired from that position, becoming an energy consultant from 1987 until 1990.

Marr was also the chairperson of the advisory council of the Gas Research Institute between 1979 and 1986, the chairperson of the U.S. Department of Transportation Technology Pipeline Safety Standards Commission from 1979 to 1985, and the chairperson of the National Association of Regulatory Utility Commissioners Gas Commission from 1984 to 1986. She became president of NARUC's Great Lakes Conference of Public Utility Commission, and was on the board of the National Arts Stabilization Fund.

Marr has been honored as an Outstanding Community Service by the Brooklyn Urban League, and has been honored by Gas Research Institute, NYS Public Service Commission, American Red Cross, National Council of Churches, and *Mademoiselle* magazine.

Thurgood Marshall 1908-1993

Judge/Magistrate, Federal Government Official, Attorney, Civil Rights/Human Rights Activist

Thurgood Marshall's long and illustrious career was capped by his 1967 nomination to the highest court in the land—the U.S. Supreme Court—where he became the first African-American to hold the coveted position of Supreme Court Justice. At fifty-nine, the son of a sleeping-car porter and the great-grandson of a slave became a sign of progress for many. He was viewed with the utmost respect for all of his years on the bench, retiring June 27, 1991. Marshall died at the age of eighty-four in 1993. He was laid in state in the Great Hall of the Supreme Court of the United States on the same bier where Abraham Lincoln once rested. More than 20,000 mourners paid their last respects to Justice Marshall.

Born in Baltimore, Maryland, on July 2, 1908, Marshall earned a B.A. degree from Lincoln University, hoping to become a dentist. He changed his mind, and instead went to Howard University's law school, gradu-

Carmel Carrington Marr, 1968

Thurgood Marshall

ating in 1933 at the top of his class. He immediately went into private practice in Baltimore, where he remained for five years. In 1936, Marshall entered into what was going to be a long and illustrious career with the NAACP, starting as an assistant special counsel, and eventually becoming director-counsel of the Legal Defense and Educational fund, a position he left in 1961. In 1938, as a national special counsel, he handled all cases involving the constitutional rights of African Americans. Then, in 1950, he was named director-counsel of the organization's 11-year-old Legal Defense and Education Fund.

In 1954, as part of an imposing team of lawyers, Marshall played a key role in the now-historic Supreme Court decision on school desegregation, *Brown v. Board of Education*, which overruled the "separate but equal" doctrine in public education. He also figured prominently in such important cases as *Sweatt v. Painter* (requiring the admission of a qualified black student to the law school of Texas University) and *Smith v. Allwright* (establishing the right of Texas blacks to vote in Democratic primaries). Of the 32 cases that he argued before the Supreme Court, Marshall won 29.

Marshall was also known for his lifelong support of rights for women. Constance Baker Motley commented that Marshall hired her for a NAACP counsel position when virtually every other employer had turned her down. He also encouraged her when he argued cases before the Supreme Court, and made certain he pointed out other African-American women role models.

In 1961, Marshall became a federal circuit judge for the second circuit. In 1946, he was awarded the prestigious Springarn Medal for his many achievements. He had over twenty honorary degrees to his credit, including LL.D. honors from the University of Liberia in 1960, the University of Michigan in 1964, and University of Otago, in Dunedin, New Zealand, in 1968. Marshall was also the representative for the White House Conference on Youth and Children, and a member of the National Bar Association. He was once sent by President John F. Kennedy to be a personal representative to the independence ceremonies of Sierra Leone.

Constance Baker Motley 1921-

Federal Government Official, Judge/Magistrate, Civil Rights/Human Rights Activist, Attorney

Born September 14, 1921, in New Haven, Connecticut, Constance Baker Motley became the first African American woman to become a federal judge. Born of West Indian parents, she was appointed in 1966 by President Johnson to the U.S. District Court for Southern New York. The appointment marked the high point of her long career in politics and civic affairs.

While still a law student at Columbia University, Motley began working with the NAACP Legal Defense

Constance Baker Motley

and Educational Fund, beginning an association that was to make her famous as a defender of civil rights. In 1946, she was awarded her LL.B., and began to work full–time with the NAACP, eventually becoming an associate counsel. During her 20–year career with the organization, Motley had argued nine successful NAACP cases before the U.S. Supreme Court, and had participated in almost every important civil rights case that had passed through the courts since 1954—from Autherine Lucy in Alabama to James Meredith in Mississippi.

In 1964, Motley decided to make a run for the New York State Senate, and was successful. She became the first African American woman to hold that position. After only a year in the Senate, Motley ran for the position of Manhattan Borough President, emerging the victor by the unanimous final vote of the city council. She thus became the first woman to serve as a city borough president, and, therefore, also the first woman on the Board of Estimate.

Motley was appointed to the U.S. District Court in 1966. In 1982, she was named chief judge of the federal district court that covers Manhattan, the Bronx, and six counties north of New York City. In 1986 she was named senior U.S. district judge.

During her career, Motley has received several awards for her contributions to the legal profession and for her role in the advancement of civil rights. She holds more than 20 honorary degrees from prestigious universities, including Princeton and Howard universities. In 1993, Motley was inducted into the National Women's Hall of Fame.

George Ruffin 1834-1886

Judge/Magistrate, Attorney, Civil Rights/Human Rights Activist

George Ruffin was born in Richmond, Virginia, in 1834, the first son of free African Americans. In 1853, the family moved to Boston and Ruffin graduated from Chapman Hall school and joined with the Republican party. He moved for a short while to Liverpool, England after becoming disillusioned by the *Dred Scott* decision. Returning to Boston, Ruffin worked as a barber. But he was busy with other works, writing a review for the *Anglo-African* in 1863, and attending the National Negro Convention in 1864.

As he continued his profession, Ruffin also began to read law with a local law firm. He was admitted to the Harvard Law School, which at that time did not require a bachelor's degree, and graduated in 1869. He became the first African American to earn the LL.B. from Harvard, and perhaps the first to graduate from a university law school in the United States He joined the firm of Harvey Jewell, and then won a seat on the Massachusetts legislature in 1869, becoming the second African American to serve in that body.

Ruffin became known as an exceptional speaker and debater as he focused his attention to the problems in the South. In 1876 and 1877, he won election to the Boston Common Council. He had the honor of presiding over the Negro convention of New Orleans in 1872. His law practice was also prospering at this time. Frederick Douglass was a friend of Ruffin's, and Ruffin was asked to contribute to the introduction to the 1881 revision of *The Life and Times of Frederick Douglass.* Ruffin was appointed in November of 1883 as judge of a municipal court in Charlestown. He became the first African American judge in Massachusetts, continuing his work on equality. He supported racial amalgamation, congratulating Douglass on his marriage to Helen Pitts, a white woman, despite the stormy controversy. In 1883, he was also made consul resident for the Dominican Republic in Boston. Ruffin's other activities included president of the Wendell Phillips Club of Boston, member and president of the Banneker Literary Club of Boston, and superintendent and officer of the Twelfth Baptist Church of Boston. Ruffin died of Bright's disease on November 20, 1886. Because of his generous giving to charities, he died a relatively poor man.

Clarence Thomas 1948-

Attorney, Judge/Magistrate

Thomas was born June 23, 1948, in Pin Point, Georgia. His parents were poor; when he was young, Thomas's father left the family. At the age of seven, the family's house burned down and his mother could no longer hold the family together. With his brother, Thomas went to live with his maternal grandparents in Savannah. While his grandfather had little education, he was determined that Thomas would go to school and make something of himself. Thomas's early atmosphere was one of strict discipline. He attended various all-black and mixed–race Catholic schools. He intended to enter the priesthood, but left when he encountered a racist seminarian.

Thomas transferred to Holy Cross College and earned his B.A. He was accepted into Yale Law School in 1971, after Yale had adopted an affirmative action program. Thomas was never certain whether he was admitted for his credentials or because of his race. This is perhaps one of the reasons he has remained staunchly against affirmative action. He earned his J.D. in 1974. After graduating, Thomas became an assistant attorney general for the state of Missouri, working there from 1974 to 1977. Thomas then worked briefly at Monsanto Company in St. Louis as an attorney, specializing in pesticide, fungicide, and rodenticide law. He also worked as a legal assistant for Senator John C. Danforth.

From 1981 to 1982, Thomas was an assistant secretary for civil rights with the Department of Education, then moved on to chair for the Equal Employment Opportunity Commission (EEOC), a position he held from until 1990. His time there was controversial, as he was not allied with either liberals or civil rights leaders, and he didn't feel comfortable with the white conservative hierarchy. It has been debated whether the status of African Americans was helped or hurt by the policies he set at the EEOC.

After Robert H. Bork resigned his Circuit Court position because he had been rejected for a place on the U.S. Supreme Court, Thomas was appointed to the post. He served there until he was made a justice on the Supreme Court in 1991, nominated by then-President George Bush. In flurry of controversy, Thomas's nomination hearings were marred by accusations of sexual harassment levied against him by former EEOC employee Anita Hill.

Then a relatively unknown law professor, Hill became a household name when she came forward with her allegations. The Senate was divided by Hill's shocking testimony. Though Thomas denied the charges and many of his former coworkers testified for him, the case became highly politicized as the nation's conservatives and liberals fought for ground. Thomas was nominated by a vote of 52 to 48, one of the closest margins in Supreme Court history. Results of a poll taken soon after the hearings suggested that the American public mirrored the pro-Thomas view, citing 60 percent buying

Clarence Thomas

with his account. However, one year later only 38 percent of those Americans polled believed Thomas, while the number of those supporting Hill's version of events rose by 18 percent to 38 percent.

Despite the "high-tech lynching," as Thomas has referred to the proceedings with Hill, Thomas has gone one to carve out a prominent role as one of the most conservative justices on the court. Together with Justice Scalia, a staunch conservative, Thomas forms the right-wing backbone of the court. In his tenure, Thomas has presented strong opinions against affirmative action and desegregation. He also supports limiting the fundamental powers of the federal government. In 1992, Thomas was one of ten people to receive the Horatio Alger Award.

Robert H. Terrell 1857-1915
Educator, Judge/Magistrate, Attorney

Robert H. Terrell was born in Charlottesville, Virginia, on November 27, 1857. He worked in a dining hall to pay for his classes at Harvard College, where he graduated in 1884, *magna cum laude*, the first African American to do so. He went to work in the Washington, DC public schools, and also attended Howard University Law School, earning his LL.B. in 1889 and his LL.M. in 1893. In 1889, he went to work as the chief clerk in the office of the auditor of the U.S. Treasury Department.

Terrell was involved in the private practice of law from 1892 to 1898, leaving to become a teacher again, and later became principal of the M Street High School. He was also elected to the Board of Trade in the 1890s. In 1901, he was appointed as a justice of the peace in Washington, DC, partially due to the influence of the conservative Booker T. Washington. Like many African Americans of his day, Terrell was torn between his strongly held civil rights beliefs and Washington's conservative ideas. Again, through Washington's influence, Terrell was nominated by President Taft for the position of judge of the Municipal Court of the District of Columbia in 1910. Despite racial protests in the Senate, Terrell signed the appointment, and held the position until his death on December 20, 1915. His tenure on the court was filled with Republican presidents. Terrell suffered from a stroke in 1911, and a second a year later. His health was also complicated with asthma.

Terrell taught at the Howard University Law School from 1910 to 1925. He was grand master of the Grand United Order of Odd Fellows of the District of Columbia. There was a Robert H. Terrell Law School in Washington, DC from August 12, 1931, to 1950, and an elementary school named after him.

Evelyn Williams 1922?-

Attorney

Born in the early 1920s, Williams grew up in Queens, New York, in a close-knit family. After graduating from Brooklyn College, she became a social worker for New York City, but was shaken by the poverty she encountered; hoping to take a more active role in helping her community, Williams became a juvenile probation officer, but that too offered little satisfaction.

In the late 1950s, Williams graduated from law school as one of two African Americans in her class. By 1960, she was active in defending those accused of crimes who had little means for expensive legal representation. She also helped raise her niece, who when grown became involved with the Black Liberation Army in the early 1970s. Williams's niece, Assata Shakur, was arrested in 1973, following a shoot-out with law enforcement officials.

For the next several years Williams—then working with the New York University Urban Affairs and Poverty Law Program—served as the attorney for Shakur and her co-defendants against a series of legal charges that seemed to demonstrate the zeal with which federal and state authorities were determined to obliterate the militant BLA. Often this zeal manifested itself in the suspension of the defendants' constitutional rights to a fair trial, but in several incidents Williams successfully battled and won small victories for Shakur and the others. The time-consuming case—which included the mysterious death of one of Williams's fellow attorneys—was chronicled in her 1993 autobiography *Inadmissable Evidence: The Story of the African-American Trial Lawyer Who Defended the Black Liberation Army.*

Williams's high-profile defense of Shakur—who escaped from federal prison in a surprising 1979 break and surfaced in Cuba a few years later—would cost her in more ways than she had imagined. During the 1980s, Williams again entered private practice, but became the target of an FBI sting operation whose ultimate aim was to disbar and discredit her, both of which proved unsuccessful. By 1989, she had joined the firm of Stevens, Hind and White in New York City, where she continued to work for social change.

African American Federal Judges

PRESIDENT FRANKLIN D. ROOSEVELT

1937	William H. Hastie*	District Court, Virgin Islands
1939	Harnian E. Moore*	District Court, Virgin Islands

PRESIDENT HARRY S. TRUMAN

1945	Irvin C. Mollison*	United States Customs Court
1949	William H. Hastie*	Court of Appeals, 3rd Circuit
1949	Hernian E. Moore (a)*	District Court, Virgin Islands

PRESIDENT DWIGHT D. EISENHOWER

1957	Scovel Richardson*	United States Customs Court
1958	Walter Gordon*	District Court, Virgin Islands

PRESIDENT JOHN F. KENNEDY

1961	James B. Parsons	Senior Judge, District Court, Illinois
1961	Wade M. McCree**	District Court, Michigan
1961	Thurgood Marshall**	Court of Appeals, 2nd Circuit

PRESIDENT LYDNON B. JOHNSON

1964	Spottswood Robinson**	District Court, District of Columbia
1964**	A. Leon Higginbotham	District Court, Pennsylvania
1965	William B. Bryant	Senior Judge, District Court, District of Columbia
1966	Wade H. McCree**/*	Court of Appeals, 6th Circuit
1966	James L. Watson	United States Customs Court
1966	Constance B. Motley	Senior Judge, District Court, New York
1966	Spottswood Robinson	Senior Judge, Court of Appeals for the Federal Circuit
1966	Aubrey E. Robinson	Chief Judge, District Court, District of Columbia
1967	Damon Keith	District Court, Michigan
1967	Thurgood Marshall	Associate Justice, Supreme Court
1967	Joseph C. Waddy*	District Court, District of Columbia

PRESIDENT RICHARD M. NIXON

1969	Almeric Christian**	District Court, Virgin Islands
1969	David W. Williams	Senior Judge, District Court, California
1969	Barrington D. Parker	Senior Judge, District Court, District of Columbia
1971	Lawrende W. Pierce**	District Court, New York
1971	Clifford Scott Green	District Court, Pennsylvania
1972	Robert L. Carter	Senior Judge, District Court, New York
1972	Rovert M. Duncan**	Military Court of Appeals
1974	Robert M. Duncan	District Court, Ohio

PRESIDENT GERALD R. FORD

1974	Henry Bramwell	Senior Judge, District Court, New York
1976	George N. Leighton	Senior Judge, District Court, Illinois
1976	Matthew Perry**	Military Court of Appeals
1976	Cecil F. Poole**	District Court, California

PRESIDENT JIMMY CARTER

1978	Almeric Christian (a)	Chief Judge, District Court, Virgin Islands
1979	U. W. Clemon	District Court, Alabama
1978	Robert F. Collins	District Court, Louisiana
1978	Julian A. Cook, Jr.	District Court, Michigan
1978	Damon J. Keith	Court of Appeals, 6th Circuit
1978	A. Leon Higginbotham	Court of Appeals, 3rd Circuit
1978	Mary Johnson Lowe	District Court, New York
1978	Theodore McMillian	Court of Appeals, 8th Circuit
1978	David S. Nelson	District Court, Massachusetts
1978	Paul A. Simmons	District Court, Pennsylvania
1978	Jack E. Tanner	District Court, Washington
1979	Harry T. Edwards	Court of Appeals for the Federal Circuit
1979	J. Jerome Farris	Court of Appeals, 9th Circuit
1979	Joseph W. Hatchett	Court of Appeals, 11th Circuit
1979	Terry J. Hatter	District Court, California
1979	Joseph C. Howard	District Court, Maryland
1979	Benjamin T. Gibson	District Court, Michigan
1979	James T. Giles	District Court, Pennsylvania
1979	Nathaniel R. Jones	Court of Appeals, 6th Circuit
1979	Amalya L. Kearse	Court of Appeals, 2nd Circuit
1979	Gabrielle Kirk McDonald**	District Court, Texas
1979	John Garrett Penn	District Court, District of Columbia
1979	Cecil F. Poole	Court of Appeals, 9th Circuit
1979	Matthew J. Perry	District Court, South Carolina
1979	Myron H. Thompson	District Court, Alabama
1979	Anne E. Thompson	District Court, New Jersey
1979	Odwll Horton	District Court, Tennessee
1979	Anna Digs Taylor	District Court, Michigan
1979	Horace T. Ward	District Court, Georgia
1979	Alcee L. Hastings****	District Court, Florida
1980	Clyde S. Cahill, Jr.	District Court, Missouri
1980	Richard C. Erwin	District Court, North Carolina
1980	Thelton E. Henderson	District Court, California
1980	George Howard, Jr.	District Court, Arkansas
1980	Earl B. Gilliam	District Court, California
1980	Norma Holloway Johnson	District Court, District of Columbia
1980	Consuela B. Marshall	District Court, California
1980	George White	District Court, Ohio

PRESIDENT RONALD REAGAN

1981	Lawrence W. Pierce	Court of Appeals, 2nd Circuit
1982	Reginald Gibson	United States Court of Claims
1984	John R. Hargrove	District Court, Maryland
1984	Henry Wingate	District Court, Mississippi
1985	Ann Williams	District Court, Illinois
1986	James Spencer	District Court, Virginia
1987	Kenneth Hoyt	District Court, Texas
1988	Herbert Hutton	District Court, Pennsylvania

PRESIDENT GEORGE BUSH

1990	Clarence Thomas	Court of Appeals for the Ferderal District
1990	James Ware	District Court, California
1991	Saundra Brown Armstrong	District Court, California
1991	Fernando J. Giatan	District Court, Missouri
1991	Donald L. Graham	District Court, Florida
1991	Sterling Johnson	District Court, New York
1991	J. Curtis Joyner	District Court, Pennsylvania
1991	Timothy K. Lewis	District Court, Pennsylvania
1991	Joe B. McDade	District Court, Illinois
1991	Clarence Thoma	Associate Justice, Supreme Court
1992	Garland E. Burrell, Jr.	District Court, California
1992	Carol Jackson	District Court, Missouri
1992	Timothy K. Lewis	Court of Appeals, 3rd Circuit

PRESIDENT BILL CLINTON

1993	Henry Lee Adams	District Court, Florida
1993	Wilkie Ferguson	District Court, Florida
1993	Raymond Jackson	District Court, Virginia
1993	Gary Lancaster	District Court, Pennsylvania
1993	Reginald Lindsay	District Court, Massachusetts
1993	Charles Shaw	District Court, Missouri
1994	Deborah Batts	District Court, New York
1994	Franklin Burgess	District Court, Washington
1994	James Beaty, Jr.	District Court, North Carolina
1994	David Coar	District Court, Illinois
1994	Audrey Collins	District Court, California
1994	Clarence Cooper	District Court, Georgia
1994	Michael Davis	District Court, Minnesota
1994	Raymond Finch	District Court, Virgin Islands
1994	Vanessa Gilmore	District Court, Texas
1994	A. Haggerty	District Court, Oregon
1994	Denise Page Hood	District Court, Michigan
1994	Napoleon Jones	District Court, California
1994	Blance Manning	District Court, Illinois
1994	Theodore McKee	Circuit Court, 3rd Circuit
1994	Vicki Miles-LaGrange	District Court, Oklahoma
1994	Solomon Oliver, Jr.	District Court, Ohio
1994	Barrington Parker, Jr.	District Court, New York
1994	Judith Rogers	Circuit Court, District of Columbia
1994	W. Louis Sands	District Court, Georgia
1994	Carl Stewart	Circuit Court, 5th Circuit
1994	Emmet Sullivan	Circuit Court, District of Columbia
1994	William Walls	District Court, New Jersey
1994	Alexander Williams	District Court, Maryland
1995	R. Guy Cole	Circuit Court, 6th Circuit
1995	Curtis Collier	District Court, Tennessee
1995	Wiley Daniel	District Court, Colorado
1995	Andre Davis	District Court, Maryland
1995	Bernice B. Donald	District Court, Tennessee

(a) Reappointment
* Deceased
** Resigned
*** Retired
**** Impeached

Appendix I

Appendix

◆ AFRICAN AMERICAN RECIPIENTS OF SELECTED AWARDS

ACADEMY AWARD OF MERIT (OSCAR)—ACADEMY OF MOTION PICTURE ARTS AND SCIENCES

Best Performance by an Actor in a Leading Role

1963 Sidney Poitier, in *Lilies of the Field*

Best Performance by an Actor in a Supporting Role

1982 Louis Gossett, Jr., in *An Officer and a Gentleman*

1989 Denzel Washington, in *Glory*

Best Performance by an Actress in a Supporting Role

1939 Hattie McDaniel, in *Gone with the Wind*

1990 Whoopi Goldberg, in *Ghost*

Best Original Score

1984 Prince, for *Purple Rain*

1986 Herbie Hancock, for *'Round Midnight*

AMERICAN ACADEMY AND INSTITUTE OF ARTS AND LETTERS AWARD

Art

1946 Richmond Barthe

1966 Romare Bearden

1971 Norman Lewis

Literature

1946 Gwendolyn Brooks; Langston Hughes

1956 James Baldwin

1961 John A. Williams

1970 James A. McPherson

1971 Charles Gordone

1972 Michael S. Harper

1974 Henry Van Dyke

1978 Lerone Bennett, Jr.; Toni Morrison

1985 John Williams

1987 Ernest J. Gaines

1992 August Wilson

Music

1974 Olly Wilson

1981 George Walker

1988 Hale Smith

1991 Tania J. Leon

EMMY AWARD—ACADEMY OF TELEVISION ARTS AND SCIENCES

Outstanding Supporting Actor in a Comedy, Variety, or Music Series

1985 Robert Guillaume, in "Benson" (ABC)

1979 Robert Guillaume, in "Soap" (ABC)

Outstanding Lead Actor in a Drama Series

1966 Bill Cosby as Alexander Scott, in "I Spy" (NBC)

1967 Bill Cosby as Alexander Scott, in "I Spy" (NBC)

1968 Bill Cosby as Alexander Scott, in "I Spy" (NBC)

1991 James Earl Jones, in "Gabriel's Fire" (ABC)

Outstanding Supporting Actor in a Miniseries or a Special

1991 James Earl Jones, in "Heatwave" (TNT)

Outstanding Lead Actress in a Comedy Series

1981 Isabel Sanford, in "The Jeffersons" (CBS)

Outstanding Supporting Actress in a Drama Series

1984 Alfre Woodard, in "Doris in Wonderland" episode of "Hill Street Blues" (NBC)

1991 Madge Sinclair, in "Gabriel's Fire" (ABC)

Outstanding Supporting Actress in a Miniseries or a Special

1991 Ruby Dee, in "Decoration Day" (NBC)

Outstanding Lead Actress in a Comedy or Drama Special

1974 Cicely Tyson, in "The Autobiography of Miss Jane Pittman" (CBS)

Outstanding Lead Actress in a Miniseries or a Special

1991 Lynn Whitfield, in "The Josephine Baker Story" (HBO)

Outstanding Achievement in Music Composition for a Series

1977 Quincy Jones and Gerald Fried, for "Roots" (ABC)

Outstanding Directing in a Drama Series

1986 Georg Stanford Brown, for "Parting Shots," episode of "Cagney & Lacey" (ABC)

1990 Thomas Carter, for "Equal Justice" episode of "Promises to Keep" (ABC)

1991 Thomas Carter, for "Equal Justice" episode of "In Confidence" (ABC)

1992 Eric Laneuville, for "I'll Fly Away" episode of "All God's Children" (NBC)

Outstanding Achievement in Music Composition

1971 Ray Charles, for "The First Nine Months Are the Hardest" (NBC)

1972 Ray Charles, for "The Funny Side of Marriage" (NBC)

GRAMMY AWARD—NATIONAL ACADEMY OF RECORDING ARTS AND SCIENCES

Record of the Year

1967 *Up, Up and Away*, by 5th Dimension

1969 *Aquarius/Let the Sun Shine In*, by 5th Dimension

1972 *The First Time Ever I Saw Your Face*, by Roberta Flack

1973 *Killing Me Softly with His Song*, by Roberta Flack

1976 *This Masquerade*, by George Benson

1983 *Beat It*, by Michael Jackson

1984 *What's Love Got To Do with It*, by Tina Turner

1985 *We Are the World*, by USA For Africa; produced by Quincy Jones

1988 *Don't Worry, Be Happy*, by Bobby McFerrin

1991 *Unforgettable*, by Natalie Cole with Nat "King" Cole

Album of the Year

1973 *Innervisions*, by Stevie Wonder; produced by Stevie Wonder

1974 *Fulfillingness' First Finale*, by Stevie Wonder; produced by Stevie Wonder

1976 *Songs in the Key of Life*, by Stevie Wonder; produced by Stevie Wonder

1983 *Thriller*, by Michael Jackson; produced by Quincy Jones

1984 *Can't Slow Down*, by Lionel Richie; produced by Lionel Richie and James Anthony Carmichael

1990 *Back on the Block*, by Quincy Jones; produced by Quincy Jones

1991 *Unforgettable*, by Natalie Cole

HEISMAN MEMORIAL TROPHY—DOWNTOWN ATHLETIC CLUB OF NEW YORK CITY, INC.

1961 Ernie Davis, Syracuse University, TB

1965 Michael Garrett, University of Southern California, TB

1968 O. J. Simpson, University of Southern California, TB

1971 Pat Sullilvan, Auburn University, QB

1972 Johnny Rodgers, University of Nebraska, FL

1974 Archie Griffin, University of Ohio State, HB

1975 Archie Griffin, University of Ohio State, HB

1976 Anthony Dorsett, University of Pittsburgh, HB

1977 Earl Campbell, University of Texas, FB

1978 Billy Sims, University of Oklahoma, HB

1979 Charles White, University of Southern California, TB

1980 George Rogers, University of South Carolina, HB

1981 Marcus Allen, University of Southern California, TB

1982 Herschel Walker, University of Georgia, HB

1983 Mike Rozier, University of Nebraska, TB

1985 Bo Jackson, Auburn University, TB

1987 Tim Brown, University of Notre Dame, FL

1988 Barry Sanders, Oklahoma State University, HB

1989 Andre Ware, University of Houston, QB

1991 Desmond Howard, University of Michigan, WR

CLARENCE L. HOLTE LITERARY PRIZE (BIANNUAL)—CO-SPONSORED BY THE PHELPS-STOKES FUND AND THE SCHOMBURG CENTER FOR RESEARCH IN BLACK CULTURE OF THE NEW YORK PUBLIC LIBRARY

1979 Dr. Chancellor Williams, for *The Destruction of Black Civililzation: Great Issues of a Race from 4500 B.C. to 2000 A.D.*

1981 Ivan Van Sertima, for *They Came Before Columbus*

1983 Vincent Harding, for *There Is a River: The Black Struggle for Freedom in America*

1985 No award

1986 John Hope Franklin, for *George Washington Williams: A Biography*

1988 Arnold Rampersad, for *The Life of Langston Hughes, Volume 1 (1902-1941): I, Too, Sing America*

1990 No award

1992 No award

KENNEDY CENTER HONORS—JOHN F. KENNEDY CENTER FOR THE PERFORMING ARTS

1978 Marian Anderson

1979 Ella Fitzgerald

1980 Leontyne Price

1981 William “Count” Basie

1983 Katherine Dunham

1984 Lena Horne

1986 Ray Charles

1987 Sammy Davis, Jr.

1988 Alvin Ailey

1989 Harry Belafonte

1990 Dizzy Gillespie

1991 Fayard and Harold Nicholas

1992 Lionel Hampton

MARTIN LUTHER KING, JR. NONVIOLENT PEACE PRIZE—MARTIN LUTHER KING, JR. CENTER FOR NONVIOLENT SOCIAL CHANGE, INC.

1973 Andrew Young

1974 Cesar Chavez

1975 John Lewis

1976 Randolph Blackwell

1977 Benjamin E. Mays

1978 Kenneth D. Kaunda; Stanley Levison

1979 Jimmy Carter

1980 Rosa Parks

1981 The Hon. Ivan Allen, Jr.

1982 Harry Belafonte

1983 Sir Richard Attenborough; Martin Luther King, Sr.

1984 No award

1985 No award

1986 Bishop Desmond Tutu

1987 Corazon Aquino

1988 No award

1989 No award

1990 Mikhail Gorbachev

1991 No award

1992 No award

1993 Jesse Jackson

MEDAL OF HONOR

Civil War

Army

William H. Barnes, Private, Company C, 38th United States Colored Troops.

Powhatan Beaty, First Sergeant, Company G, 5th United States Colored Troops.

James H. Bronson, First Sergeant, Company D, 5th United States Colored Troops.

William H. Carney, Sergeant, Company C, 54th Massachusetts Infantry, United States Colored Troops.

Decatur Dorsey, Sergeant, Company B, 39th United States Colored Troops.

Christian A. Fleetwood, Sergeant Major, 4th United States Colored Troops.

James Gardiner, Private, Company 1, 36th United States Colored Troops.

James H. Harris, Sergeant, Company B, 38th United States Colored Troops.

Thomas R. Hawkins, Sergeant Major, 6th United States Colored Troops.

Alfred B. Hilton, Sergeant, Company H, 4th United States Colored Troops.

Milton M. Holland, Sergeant, 5th United States Colored Troops.

Alexander Kelly, First Sergeant, Company F, 6th United States Colored Troops.

Robert Pinn, First Sergeant, Company I, 5th United States Colored Troops.

<n.LEdward Radcliff, First Sergeant, Company C, 38th United States Colored Troops.

Charles Veal, Private, Company D, 4th United States Colored Troops.

Navy

Aaron Anderson, Landsman, *USS Wyandank.*

Robert Blake, Powder Boy, *USS Marblehead.*

William H. Brown, Landsman, *USS Brooklyn.*

Wilson Brown, *USS Hartford.*

John Lawson, Landsman, *USS Hartford.*

James Mifflin, Engineer's Cook, *USS Brooklyn.*

Joachim Pease, Seaman, *USS Kearsarge.*

Interim Period

Navy

Daniel Atkins, Ship's Cook, First Class, *USS Cushing.*

John Davis, Seaman, *USS Trenton.*

Alphonse Girandy, Seaman, *USS Tetrel.*

John Johnson, Seaman, *USS Kansas.*

William Johnson, Cooper, *USS Adams.*

Joseph B. Noil, Seaman, *USS Powhatan.*

John Smith, Seaman, *USS Shenandoah.*

Robert Sweeney, Seaman, *USS Kearsage, USS Jamestown.*

Western Campaigns

Army

Thomas Boyne, Sergeant, Troop C, 9th United States Cavalry.

Benjamin Brown, Sergeant, Company C, 24th United States Infantry.

John Denny, Sergeant, Troop C, 9th United States Cavalry.

Pompey Factor, Seminole Negro Indian Scouts.

Clinton Greaves, Corporal, Troop C, 9th United States Cavalry.

Henry Johnson, Sergeant, Troop D, 9th United States Cavalry.

George Jordan, Sergeant, Troop K, 9th United States Cavalry.

William McBreyar, Sergeant, Troop K, 10th United States Cavalry.

Isaiah Mays, Corporal, Company B, 24th United States Infantry.

Issac Payne, Private (Trumpeteer) Seminole Negro Indian Scouts.

Thomas Shaw, Sergeant, Troop K, 9th United States Cavalry.

Emanuel Stance, Sergeant, Troop F, 9th United States Cavalry.

Augustus Walley, Private, Troop 1, 9th United States Cavalry.

John Ward, Sergeant, Seminole Negro Indian Scouts.

Moses Williams, First Sergeant, Troop 1, 9th United States Cavalry.

William O. Wilson, Corporal, Troop 1, 9th United States Cavalry.

Brent Woods, Sergeant, Troop B, 9th United States Cavalry.

Spanish-American War

Army

Edward L. Baker, Jr., Sergeant Major, 10th United States Cavalry.

Dennis Bell, Private, Troop H, 10th United States Cavalry.

Fitz Lee, Private, Troop M, 10th United States Cavalry.

William H. Thompkins, Private, Troop G, 10th United States Cavalry.

George H. Wanton, Sergeant, Troop M, 10th United States Cavalry.

Navy

Robert Penn, Fireman, First Class, *USS Iowa*.

World War I

Army

Freddie Stowers, Corporal, Company C, 371st Infantry Regiment, 93rd Infantry Division.

Korean Conflict

Army

Cornelius H. Charlton, Sergeant, 24th Infantry Regiment, 25th Division.

William Thompson, Private, 24th Infantry Regiment, 25th Division.

Vietnam Conflict

Army

Webster Anderson, Sergeant, Battery A, 2nd Battalion, 320th Artillery, 101st Airborne Division.

Eugene Ashley, Jr., Sergeant, Company C, 5th Special Forces Group (Airborne), 1st Special Forces.

William M. Bryant, Sergeant First Class, Company A, 5th Special Forces Group, 1st Special Forces.

Lawrence Joel, Specialist Sixth Class, Headquarters and Headquarters Company, 1st Battalion, 173d Airborne Brigade.

Dwight H. Johnson, Specialist Fifth Class, Company B, 1st Battalion, 69th Armor, 4th Infantry Division.

Garfield M. Langhorn, Private First Class, Troop C, 7th Squadron, 17th Cavalry, 1st Aviation Brigade.

Matthew Leonard, Platoon Sergeant, Company B, 1st Battalion, 16th Infantry, 1st Infantry Division.

Milton L. Olive III, Private First Class, Company B, 2nd Battalion 503d Infantry, 173d Airborne Brigade.

Charles C. Rogers, Lieutenant Colonel, 1st Battalion, 5th Infantry, 1st Infantry Division.

Donald R. Long, Sergeant, Troop C, 1st Squadron, 4th Cavalry, 1st Infantry Division.

Riley L. Pitts, Captain, Company C, 2nd Battalion, 27th Infantry, 25th Infantry Division.

Rupert L. Sargent, First Lieutenant, Company B, 4th Battalion, 9th Infantry, 25th Infantry Division.

Clarence E. Sasser, Specialist 5th Class, Headquarters Company, 3rd Battalion, 60th Infantry, 90th Infantry Division.

Clifford C. Sims, Staff Sergeant, Company D, 2nd Battalion, 501st Infantry, 101st Airborne Division.

John E. Warren, Jr., First Lieutenant, Company C, 2nd Battalion, 22d Infantry, 25th Infantry Division.

Marines

James A. Anderson, Jr. Private First Class, 2nd Platoon, Company F, 2nd Battalion, 3rd Marine Division.

Oscar P. Austin, Private First Class, Company E, 7th Marines, 1st Marine Division.

Rodney M. Davis, Sergeant, Company B, 1st Battalion, 5th Marines, 1st Marine Division.

Robert H. Jenkins, Jr., Private First Class, 3rd Reconnaissance Battalion, 3rd Marine Division.

Ralph H. Johnson, Private First Class, Company A, 1st Recon Battalion, 1st Marine Division.

MISS AMERICA—MISS AMERICA ORGANIZATION

1984 Vanessa Williams (New York); Suzette Charles (New Jersey)

1990 Debbye Turner (Missouri)

MISS BLACK AMERICA—J. MORRIS ANDERSON PRODUCTION COMPANY

1968 Sandy Willliams (Pennsylvania)

1969 G. O. Smith (New York)

1970 Stephanie Clark (District of Columbia)

1971 Joyce Warner (Florida)

1972 Linda Barney (New Jersey)

1973 Arnice Russell (New York)

1974 Von Gretchen Sheppard (California)

1975 Helen Ford (Mississippi)

1976 Twanna Kilgore (District of Columbia)

1977 Claire Ford (Tennessee)

1978 Lydia Jackson (New Jersey)

1979 Veretta Shankle (Mississippi)

1980 Sharon Wright (Illinois)

1981 Pamela Jenks (Massachusetts)

1982 Phyllis Tucker (Florida)

1983 Sonia Robinson (Wisconsin)

1984 Lydia Garrett (South Carolina)

1985 Amina Fakir (Michigan)

1986 Rachel Oliver (Massachusetts)

1987 Leila McBride (Colorado)

1989 Paula Swynn (District of Columbia)

1990 Rosie Jones (Connecticut)

1991 Sharmelle Sullivan (Indiana)

1992 Marilyn DeShields

1993 Pilar Ginger Fort

1994 Karen Wallace

1995 Asheera Ahmad

MISS USA—MADISON SQUARE GARDEN TELEVISION PRODUCTIONS

1990 Carole Gist (Michigan)

1992 Shannon Marketic

1993 Kenya Moore (Michigan)

1994 Frances Louise "Lu" Parker

1995 Chelsi Smith (Texas)

1996 Ali Landry

NATIONAL BASEBALL HALL OF FAME

1969 Roy Campanella

1962 Jackie Robinson

1971 Leroy R. "Satchel" Paige

1972 Josh Gibson; Walter "Buck" Leonard

1973 Roberto W. Clemente; Monford Irvin

1974 James T. "Cool Papa" Bell

1975 William "Judy" Johnson

1976 Oscar M. Charleston

1977 Ernest Banks; Martin Dihigo; John H. Lloyd

1979 Willie Mays

1981 Rube Foster; Robert T. Gibson

1982 Hank Aaron; Frank Robinson

1983 Jaun A. Marichal

1985 Lou Brock

1986 Willie L. "Stretch" McCovey

1987 Ray Dandridge; Billy Williams

1988 Willie Stargell

1990 Joe Morgan

1991 Rod Carew; Ferguson Jenkins

1993 Reggie Jackson

NATIONAL BOOK AWARD—NATIONAL BOOK FOUNDATION

1953 Ralph Ellison, for *Invisible Man*, Fiction

1969 Winthrop D. Jordan, for *White over Black: American Attitudes toward the Negro, 1550-1812*, History and Biography

1983 Gloria Naylor, for *The Women of Brewster Place*, First Novel; Joyce Carol Thomas, for *Marked By Fire*, Children's Literature; Alice Walker, for *The Color Purple*, Fiction

1990 Charles Johnson, for *Middle Passage*, Fiction

1991 Melissa Fay Green, for *Praying for Sheetrock*, Nonfiction

1992 Edward P. Jones, for *Lost in the City*, Fiction

NATIONAL MEDAL OF ARTS—NATIONAL ENDOWMENT FOR THE ARTS

1985 Ralph Ellison (writer); Leontyne Price (singer)

1986 Marian Anderson (singer)

1987 Romare Bearden (artist); Ella Fitzgerald (singer)

1988 Gordon Parks (photographer and film director)

1989 Katherine Dunham (choreographer); Dizzy Gillespie (musician)

1990 Riley "B. B." King (musician)

1991 James Earl Jones (actor); Billy Taylor (musician)

1994 Harry Belafonte (singer)

1995 Gwendolyn Brooks (poet); Ossie Davis (actor); Ruby Dee (actress)

NATIONAL SOCIETY OF ARTS AND LETTERS GOLD MEDAL OF MERIT AWARD

1982 Andre Watts (music)

NATIONAL TRACK AND FIELD HALL OF FAME—THE ATHLETICS CONGRESS OF THE USA

1974 Ralph Boston; Lee Calhoun; Harrison Dillard; Rafer Johnson; Jesse Owens; Wilma Rudolph; Malvin Whitfield

1975 Ralph Metcalfe

1976 Robert Hayes; Hayes Jones

1977 Robert Beamon; Andrew W. Stanfield

1978 Tommie Smith; John Woodruff

1979 Jim Hines; William DeHart Hubbard

1980 Wyomia Tyus

1981 Willye White

1982 Willie Davenport; Eddie Tolan

1983 Lee Evans

1984 Madeline Manning Mims

1986 Henry Barney Ewell

1988 Gregory Bell

1989 Milt Campbell; Edward Temple

1990 Charles Dumas

1994 Cornelius Johnson; Edwin Moses

NEW YORK DRAMA CRITICS' CIRCLE AWARD

Best American Play

1959 *A Raisin in the Sun*, by Lorraine Hansberry

1975 *The Taking of Miss Janie*, by Ed Bullins

1982 *A Soldier's Play*, by Charles Fuller

1996 *Seven Guitars*, by August Wilson

Best New Play

1985 *Ma Rainey's Black Bottom*, by August Wilson

1987 *Fences*, by August Wilson

1988 *Joe Turner's Come and Gone*, by August Wilson

1990 *The Piano Lesson*, by August Wilson

NOBEL PEACE PRIZE—NOBEL FOUNDATION

1950 Ralph J. Bunche

1964 Martin Luther King, Jr.

ANTOINETTE PERRY (TONY) AWARD—LEAGUE OF AMERICAN THEATRES AND PRODUCERS

Actor (Dramatic)

1969 James Earl Jones, for *The Great White Hope*

1975 John Kani, for *Sizwe Banzi*; Winston Ntshona, for *The Island*

1987 James Earl Jones, for *Fences*

Supporting or Featured Actor (Dramatic)

1982 Zakes Mokae, for *Master Harold ... and the Boys*

1992 Larry Fishburne, for *Two Trains Running*

Actor (Musical)

1970 Cleavon Litte, for *Purlie*

1973 Ben Vereen, for *Pippin*

1982 Ben Harvey, for *Dreamgirls*

1992 Gregory Hines, for *Jelly's Last Jam*

Supporting or Featured Actor (Musical)

1954 Harry Belafonte, for *John Murray Anderson's Almanac*

1975 Ted Rose, for *The Wiz*

1981 Hinton Battle, for *Sophisticated Ladies*

1982 Cleavant Derricks, for *Dreamgirls*

1983 Charles "Honi" Coles, for *My One and Only*

1984 Hinton Battle, for *The Tap Dance Kid*

1991 Hinton Battle, for *Miss Saigon*

Supporting or Featured Actress (Dramatic)

1977 Trazana Beverley, for *For Colored Girls Who Have Considered Suicide/When the Rainbow Is Enuf*

1987 Mary Alice, for *Fences*

1988 L. Scott Caldwell, for *Joe Turner's Come and Gone*

Actress (Musical)

1962 Diahann Carroll, for *No Strings*

1968 Leslie Uggams, for *Hallelujah, Baby*

1974 Virginia Capers, for *Raisin*

1982 Jennifer Holliday, for *Dreamgirls*

1989 Ruth Brown, for *Black and Blue*

Supporting or Featured Actress (Musical)

1950 Juanita Hall, for *South Pacific*

1968 Lillian Hayman, for *Halleluja, Baby*

1970 Melba Moore, for *Purlie*

1975 Dee Dee Bridgewater, for *The Wiz*

1977 Delores Hall, for *Your Arms's Too Short To Box with God*

1978 Nell Carter, for *Ain't Misbehavin*

1992 Tonya Pinkins, for *Jelly's Last Jam*

Play

1974 *The River Niger*, by Joseph A. Walker

1987 *Fences*, by August Wilson

PRESIDENTIAL MEDAL OF FREEDOM—UNITED STATES EXECUTIVE OFFICE OF THE PRESIDENT

1963 Marian Anderson; Ralph J. Bunche

1964 John L. Lewis; Leontyne Price; A. Philip Randolph

1969 Edward Kennedy "Duke" Ellington; Ralph Ellison; Roy Wilkins; Whitney M. Young, Jr.

1976 Jesse Owens

1977 Dr. Martin Luther King, Jr. (posthumously)

1981 James H. Eubie Blake; Andrew Young

1984 Jack Roosevelt Robinson (posthumously)

1985 William "Count" Basie (posthumously)

1988 Pearl Bailey

1991 General Colin L. Powell

1992 Ella Fitzgerald

1993 Colin L. Powell

1994 Dorothy Height; Barbara Jordan

1995 William T. Coleman, Jr.; John Hope Franklin; A. Leon Higginbotham, Jr.

PRO FOOTBALL HALL OF FAME

1967 Emlen Tunnell

1968 Marion Motley

1969 Fletcher "Joe" Perry

1971 Jim Brown

1972 Ollie Matson

1973 Jim Parker

1974 Richard "Night Train" Lane

1975 Roosevelt Brown; Leonard "Lenny" Moore

1976 Leonard "Len" Ford

1977 Gale Sayers; Bill Willis

1980 Herb Adderley; David "Deacon" Jones

1981 Willie Davis

1983 Bobby Bell; Bobby Mitchell; Paul Warfield

1984 Willie Brown; Charley Taylor

1985 O. J. Simpson

1986 Ken Houston; Willie Lanier

1987 Joe Greene; John Henry Johnson; Gene Upshaw

1988 Alan Page

1989 Mel Blount; Art Shell; Willie Wood

1990 Junious "Buck" Buchanan; Franco Harris

1991 Earl Campbell

1992 Lem Barney; John Mackey

1993 Larry Little; Walter Payton

1994 Tony Dorsett, Leroy Kelly

1995 Lee Roy Selmon

1996 Charlie Joiner, Mel Renfro

PULITZER PRIZE—COLUMBIA UNIVERSITY GRADUATE SCHOOL OF JOURNALISM

Journalism: Commentary

1996 E. R. Shipp

Letters: Drama

1970 *No Place To Be Somebody*, by Charles Gordone

1982 *A Soldier's Play*, by Charles Fuller

1987 *Fences*, by August Wilson

1990 *The Piano Lesson*, by August Wilson

Letters: Fiction

1978 *Elbow Room*, by James Alan McPherson

1983 *The Color Purple*, by Alice Walker

1988 *Beloved*, by Toni Morrison

Letters: Poetry

1950 *Annie Allen*, by Gwendolyn Brooks

1987 *Thomas and Beulah*, by Rita Dove

Letters: Special Awards and Citations

1977 Alexander Palmer Haley, for *Roots*

Music: Special Awards and Citations

1976 Scott Joplin

1996 George Walker

SPINGARN MEDAL—NATIONAL ASSOCIATION FOR THE ADVANCEMENT OF COLORED PEOPLE

1915 Prof. Ernest E. Just—head of the department of physiology at Howard University Medical School.

1916 Major Charles Young—United States Army.

1917 Harry T. Burleigh—composer, pianist, singer.

1918 William Stanley Braithwaite—poet, literary critic, editor.

1919 Archibald H. Grimke—former U.S. Consul in Santo Domingo, president of the American Negro Academy, author, president of the District of Columbia branch of the NAACP.

1920 William Edward Burghardt DuBois—author, editor, organizer of the first Pan-African Congress.

1921 Charles S. Gilpin—actor.

1922 Mary B. Talbert—former president of the National Association of Colored Women.

1923 George Washington Carver—head of research and director of the experiment station at Tuskegee Institute.

1924 Roland Hayes—singer.

1925 James Weldon Johnson—former United States Consul in Venezuela and Nicaragua, author, editor, poet; secretary of the NAACP.

1926 Carter G. Woodson—editor, historian; founder of the Association for the Study of Negro Life and History.

1927 Anthony Overton—businessman; president of the Victory Life Insurance Company (the first black organization permitted to do business under the rigid requirements of the State of New York).

1928 Charles W. Chestnutt—author.

1929 Mordecai Wyatt Johnson—the first black president of Howard University.

1930 Henry A. Hunt—principal of Fort Valley High and Industrial School, Fort Valley, Georgia.

1931 Richard Berry Harrison—actor.

1932 Robert Russa Moton—principal of Tuskegee Institute.

1933 Max Yergan—secretary of the YMCA in South Africa.

1934 William Taylor Burwell Williams—dean of Tuskegee Institute.

1935 Mary McLeod Bethune—founder and president of Bethune Cookman College.

1936 John Hope—president of Atlanta University.

1937 Walter White—executive secretary of the NAACP.

1939 Marian Anderson—singer.

1940 Louis T. Wright—surgeon.

1941 Richard Wright—author.

1942 A. Philip Randolph—labor leader, international president of the Brotherhood of Sleeping Car Porters.

1943 William H. Hastie—jurist, educator.

1944 Charles Drew—scientist.

1945 Paul Robeson—singer, actor.

1946 Thurgood Marshall—special counsel of the NAACP

1947 Dr. Percy Julian—research chemist.

1948 Channing H. Tobias—,minister, educator.

1949 Ralph J. Bunche—international civil servant, acting United Nations mediator in Palestine.

1950 Charles Hamilton Houston—chairman of the NAACP Legal Committee.

1951 Mabel Keaton Staupers—leader of the National Association of Colored Graduate Nurses.

1952 Harry T. Moore—state leader of the Florida NAACP.

1953 Paul R. Williams—architect.

1954 Theodore K. Lawless—physician, educator, philanthropist.

1955 Carl Murphy—editor, publisher, civic leader.

1956 Jack Roosevelt Robinson—athlete.

1957 Martin Luther King, Jr.—minister, civil rights leader.

1958 Daisy Bates and the Little Rock Nine—for their pioneer role in upholding the basic ideals of American democracy in the face of continuing harassment and constant threats of bodily injury.

1959 Edward Kennedy (Duke) Ellington—composer, musician, orchestra leader.

1960 Langston Hughes—poet, author, playwright.

1961 Kenneth B. Clark—professor of psychology at the City College of the City University of New York, founder and director of the Northside Center for Child Development, prime mobilizer of the resources of modern psychology in the attack upon racial segregation.

1962 Robert C. Weaver—administrator of the Housing and Home Finance Agency.

1963 Medgar Wiley Evers—NAACP field secretary for Mississippi, World War II veteran.

1964 Roy Wilkins executive director of the NAACP.

1965 Leontyne Price—singer.

1966 John H. Johnson—founder and president of the Johnson Publishing Company.

1967 Edward W. Brooke III—the first African-American to win popular election to the United States Senate.

1968 Sammy Davis, Jr.—performer, civil rights activist.

1969 Clarence M. Mitchell, Jr.—director of the Washington Bureau of the NAACP, civil rights activist.

1970 Jacob Lawrence—artist, teacher, humanitarian.

1971 Leon H. Sullivan—minister.

1972 Gordon Alexander Buchanan Parks—writer, photographer, filmmaker.

1973 Wilson C. Riles—educator.

1974 Damon Keith—jurist.

1975 Hank Aaron—athlete.

1976 Alvin Ailey—dancer, choreographer, artistic director.

1977 Alexander Palmer Haley—author, biographer, lecturer.

1978 Andrew Young—United States Ambassador to the United Nations, diplomat, cabinet member, civil rights activist, minister.

1979 Rosa Parks—community activist.

1980 Rayford W. Logan—educator, historian, author.

1981 Coleman A. Young—mayor of the City of Detroit, public servant, labor leader, civil rights activist.

1982 Benjamin E. Mays—educator, theologian, humanitarian).

1983 Lena Horn—performer, humanitarian.

1984 Tom Bradley—government executive, public servant, humanitarian.

1985 Dr. William H. Cosby—comedian, actor, educator, humanitarian.

1986 Benjamin Lawson Hooks—executive director of The NAACP.

1987 Percy Ellis Sutton—public servant, businessman, community leader.

1988 Frederick Douglass Patterson—doctor of veterinary medicine, educator, humanitarian, founder of the United Negro College Fund.

1989 Jesse Jackson—minister, political leader, civil rights activist.

1990 L. Douglas Wilder—governor of Virginia.

1991 General Colin L. Powell—chairman of the Joint Chiefs of Staff.

1992 Barbara C. Jordan—educator, former congresswoman.

1993 Dorothy I. Height—president of the National Council of Negro Woman

1994 Maya Angelou—poet, author, performing artist

1995 John Hope Franklin—historian

UNITED STATES POET LAUREATE

1993 Rita Dove

WIMBLEDON—ALL ENGLAND LAWN TENNIS AND CROQUET CLUB

Men's Singles

1975 Arthur Ashe

Ladies' Singles

1957 Althea Gibson

1958 Althea Gibson

1990 Zina Garrison, runner-up

Ladies' Doubles

1957 Althea Gibson, with Darlene Hard

1958 Althea Gibson, with Maria Bueno

Appendix II

Appendix II

◆ 1996 Olympic Games Medalists

* indicates African American athletes

Archery

MEN

Individual

GOLD—Justin Huish (Simi Valley, CA)
SILVER—Magnus Petersson (Sweden)
BRONZE—Oh Kyo-moon (South Korea)

Team

GOLD—United States: Justin Huish (Simi Valley, CA); Richard Johnson (Woodstock, CT); Rod White (Hermitage, PA)
SILVER—South Korea: Oh Kyo-moon; Kim Bo-ram; Jang Yong-ho
BRONZE—Italy: Matteo Bisiani; Michele Frangilli; Andrea Parenti

WOMEN

Individual

GOLD—Kim Kyung-wook (South Korea)
SILVER—He Ying (China)
BRONZE—Olena Sadovnycha (Ukraine)

Team

GOLD—South Korea: Kim Jo-sun; Yoon Hye-young; Kim Kyung-wook
SILVER—Germany: Barbara Mensing; Cornelia Pfohl; Sandra Wagner
BRONZE—Poland: Iwona Dzieciol; Katarzyna Klata; Joanna Nowicka

Track and Field

MEN

100 Meter

GOLD—Donovan Bailey (Canada)
SILVER—Frank Fredericks (Namibia)
BRONZE—Ato Boldon (Trinidad)

200 Meter

GOLD—*Michael Johnson (Rockwell, TX)
SILVER—Frank Fredericks (Namibia)
BRONZE—Ato Boldon (Trinidad)

400 Meter

GOLD—*Michael Johnson (Rockwell, TX)
SILVER—Roger Black (Britain)
BRONZE—Davis Kamoga (Uganda)

800 Meter

GOLD—Vebjoern Rodal (Norway)
SILVER—Hezekiel Sepeng (South Africa)
BRONZE—Fred Onyancha (Kenya)

1,500 Meter

GOLD—Noureddine Morceli (Algeria)
SILVER—Fermin Cacho (Spain)
BRONZE—Stephen Kipkorir (Kenya)

5,000 Meter

GOLD—Venuste Niyongabo (Burundi)
SILVER—Paul Bitok (Kenya)
BRONZE—Khalid Boulami (Morocco)

10,000 Meter

GOLD—Haile Gebrselassie (Ethiopia)
SILVER—Paul Tergat (Kenya)
BRONZE—Salah Hissou (Morocco)

110 Hurdles

GOLD—*Allen Johnson (Chapel Hill, NC)
SILVER—Mark Crear (Valencia, CA)
BRONZE—Florian Schwarthoff (Germany)

400 Hurdles

GOLD—*Derrick Adkins (Atlanta, GA)
SILVER—Samuel Matete (Zambia)
BRONZE—*Calvin Davis (Eutaw, AL)

3,000 Steeplechase

GOLD—Joseph Keter (Kenya)
SILVER—Moses Kiptanui (Kenya)
BRONZE—Alessandro Lamruschini (Italy)

20km Walk

GOLD—Jefferson Perez (Ecuador)
SILVER—Ilya Markov (Russia)
BRONZE—Bernardo Sugura (Mexico)

50km Walk

GOLD—Robert Korzeniowski (Poland)
SILVER—Mikhail Schennikov (Russia)
BRONZE—Valentin Massana (Spain)

Relay

GOLD—Canada: Donovan Bailey; Robert Esmie; Glenroy Gilbert; Bruny Surin; Carlton Chambers

SILVER—United States: *Tim Harden (Grandview, MT); *Jon Drummond (Culver City, CA); *Michael Marsh (Houston, TX); *Dennis Mitchell (Gainesville, FL); *Tim Montgomery (Gaffney, SC)

BRONZE—Brazil: Edson Ribeiro; Arnaldo Silva; Andre Silva; Robson da Silva

1,600 Relay

GOLD—United States: *LaMont Smith (Houston, TX); *Alvin Harrison (Salinas, CA); *Derek Mills (Marietta, GA); *Anthuan Maybank (Los Angeles, CA); *Jason Rouser (Norman, OK)

SILVER—Britain: Iwan Thomas; Jamie Baulch; Mark Richardson; Roger Black; Du'aine Ladejo

BRONZE—Jamaica: Michael McDonald; Roxbert Martin; Greg Haughton; Davian Clarke; Dennis Blake

Decathlon

GOLD—Dan O'Brien (Moscow, ID)
SILVER—Frank Busemann (Germany)
BRONZE—Tomas Dvorak (Czech Republic)

High Jump

GOLD—*Charles Austin (San Marcos, TX)
SILVER—Artur Partyka (Poland)
BRONZE—Steve Smith (Britain)

Long Jump

GOLD—*Carl Lewis (Houston, TX)
SILVER—James Beckford (Jamaica)
BRONZE—Joe Greene (Westerville, OH)

Triple Jump

GOLD—*Kenny Harrison (Bridgeton, MO)
SILVER—Jonathan Edwards (Britain)
BRONZE—Yoelbi Quesada (Cuba)

Discus

GOLD—Lars Riedel (Germany)
SILVER—Vladimir Dubrovshchik (Belarus)
BRONZE—Vasiliy Kaptyukh (Belarus)

Hammer

GOLD—Balazs Kiss (Hungary)
SILVER—Lance Deal (Eugene, OR)
BRONZE—Alexandr Krykun (Ukraine)

Javelin

GOLD—Jan Zelezny (Czech Republic)
SILVER—Steve Backley (Britain)
BRONZE—Seppo Raty (Finland)

Pole Vault

GOLD—Jean Galfione (France)
SILVER—Igor Trandenkov (Russia)
BRONZE—Andrei Tivontchik (Germany)

Shot Put

GOLD—Randy Barnes (South Charleston, WV)
SILVER—John Godina (Los Angeles, CA)
BRONZE—Oleksandr Bagach (Ukraine)

Marathon

GOLD—Josia Thugwane (South Africa)
SILVER—Lee Bong-ju (South Korea)
BRONZE—Eric Wainaina (Kenya)

WOMEN

100 Meter

GOLD—*Gail Devers (Bridgeton, MO)
SILVER—Merlene Ottey (Jamaica)
BRONZE—*Gwen Torrence (Lithonia, GA)

200 Meter

GOLD—Marie-Jose Perec (France)
SILVER—Merlene Ottey (Jamaica)
BRONZE—Mary Onyali (Nigeria)

400 Meter

GOLD—Marie-Jose Perec (France)
SILVER—Cathy Freeman (Australia)
BRONZE—Falilat Ogunkoya (Nigeria)

800 Meter

GOLD—Svetlana Masterkova (Russia)
SILVER—Ana Quirot (Cuba)
BRONZE—Maria Mutola (Mozambique)

1,500 Meter

GOLD—Svetlana Masterkova (Russia)
SILVER—Gabriela Szabo (Romania)
BRONZE—Theresia Kiesl (Austria)

5,000 Meter

GOLD—Wang Junxia (China)
SILVER—Pauline Konga (Kenya)
BRONZE—Roberta Bruney (Italy)

10,000 Meter

GOLD—Fernanda Ribeiro (Portugal)
SILVER—Wang Junxia (China)
BRONZE—Gete Wami (Ethiopia)

100 Hurdles

GOLD—Ludmila Enquist (Sweden)
SILVER—Brigita Bukovec (Slovenia)
BRONZE—Patricia Girard-Leno (France)

400 Hurdles

GOLD—Deon Hemmings (Jamaica)
SILVER—*Kim Batten (McRae, GA)
BRONZE—*Tonja Buford Bailey (Dayton, OH)

10km Walk

GOLD—Yelena Ninikolayeva (Russia)
SILVER—Elisabetta Perrone (Italy)
BRONZE—Wang Yan (China)

400 Relay

GOLD—United States: *Gail Devers (Bridgeton, MO); *Chryste Gaines (San Leandro, CA); *Gwen Torrence (Lithonia, GA); *Inger Miller (Altadena, CA); *Carlette Guidry (Austin, TX)

SILVER—Bahamas: Chandra Sturrup; Eldece Clarke; Sevatheda Fynes; Pauline Davis; Debbie Ferguson

BRONZE—Jamaica: Michelle Freeman; Juliet Cuthbert; Nikole Mitchell; Merlene Ottey; Gillian Russell; Andrea Lloyd

1,600 Relay

GOLD—United States: *Rochelle Stevens (Memphis, TN); *Maicel Malone (Gainesville, FL); *Kim Graham (Austin, TX); *Jearl Miles (Gainesville, FL); *Linetta Wilson (Hawthorne, CA)

SILVER—Nigeria: Bisi Afolabi; Fatima Yusuf; Charity Opara; Falilat Ogunkoya

BRONZE—Germany: Uta Rohlaender; Linda Kisabaka; Anja Ruecker; Grit Breuer

Heptathlon

GOLD—Ghada Shouaa (Syria)
SILVER—Natasha Sazanovich (Belarus)
BRONZE—Denise Lewis (Britain)

High Jump

GOLD—Stefka Kostadinova (Bulgaria)

SILVER—Niki Bakoyianni (Greece)
BRONZE—Inga Babakova (Ukraine)

Long Jump

GOLD—Chioma Ajunwa (Nigeria)
SILVER—Fiona May (Italy)
BRONZE—*Jackie Joyner-Kersee (Canoga Park, CA)

Triple Jump

GOLD—Inessa Kravets (Ukraine)
SILVER—Inna Lasovskaya (Russia)
BRONZE—Sarka Kasparkova (Czech Republic)

Discus

GOLD—Ilke Wyludda (Germany)
SILVER—Natalya Sadova (Russia)
BRONZE—Elya Zvereva (Belarus)

Javelin

GOLD—Heli Rantanen (Finland)
SILVER—Louise McPaul (Australia)
BRONZE—Trine Hattestad (Norway)

Shot Put

GOLD—Astrid Kumbernuss (Germany)
SILVER—Sui Xinmei (China)
BRONZE—Irina Khudorozhkina (Russia)

Marathon

GOLD—Fatuma Roba (Ethiopia)
SILVER—Valentina Yegorova (Russia)
BRONZE—Yuko Arimori (Japan)

Badminton

MEN

Singles

GOLD—Poul-Erik Hoyer-Larsen (Denmark)
SILVER—Dong Jiong (China)
BRONZE—Rashid Sidak (Malaysia)

Doubles

GOLD—Rexy Mainaky and Ricky Subagja (Indonesia)
SILVER—Cheah Soon Kit and Yap Kim Hock (Malaysia)
BRONZE—S Antonius and Denny Kantono (Indonesia)

WOMEN

Singles

GOLD—Bang Soo-hyun (South Korea)
SILVER—Mia Audina (Indonesia)
BRONZE—Susi Susanti (Indonesia)

Doubles

GOLD—Ge Fei and Gu Jun (China)
SILVER—Gil Young-ah and Jang Hye-ock (South Korea)
BRONZE—Qin Yiyuan and Tang Yongshu (China)

Mixed Doubles

GOLD—Gil Young-ah and Kim Dong-moon (South Korea)
SILVER—Ra Kyung-min and Park Joo-bong (South Korea)
BRONZE—Liu Jianjun and Sun Man (China)

Baseball

GOLD—Cuba: Omar Ajete, Miguel Caldes, Jose Ariel Contreras, Yobal Duenas, Jose Esrada, Jorge Fumero, Ernesto Guevara, Alberto Hernandez, Rey Isaac, Orestes Kindelan, Daniel Lazo, Pedro Luis Lazo, Omar Linares, Angel Lopez, Omar Luis, Juan Manrique, Eliecer Montes de Oca, Antonio Pacheco, Juan Padilla, Eduardo Paret, Osmany Romero, Antonio Scull, Luis Ulacia, Lazaro Vargas

SILVER—Japan: Naoto Adachi, Kosuke Fukudome, Tadahito Iguchi, Makoto Imaoka, Koichi Isobe, Takeo Kawamura, Jutaro Kimura, Takashi Kurosu, Takao Kuwamoto, Nobuhiko Matsunaka, Koichi Misawa, Masahiko Mori, Masao Morinaka, Daishin Nakamura, Kokoro Niida, Tomoaki Nishio, Masahiro Nojima, Hideaki Okubo, Hitoshi Ono, Yasuyuki Saigo, Tomoaki Sato, Masanori Sugiura, Takayuki Takabayashi, Yoshitomo Tani

BRONZE—United States: Chad Allen, Kris Benson, R.A. Dickey, Troy Glaus, Chad Green, Seth Greisinger, Kip Harkrider, A.J. Hingh, *Jacque Jones, Billy Koch, Mark Kotsay, Matt Lecroy, Travis Lee, Braden Looper, Brian Loyd, Warren Morris, Augie Ojeda, Jim Parque, Jeff Weaver, Jason Williams

Basketball

MEN

GOLD—United States: *Charles Barkley, *Anfernee Hardaway, *Grant Hill, *Karl Malone, *Reggie Miller, *Hakeem Olajuwon, *Shaquille O'Neal, *Gary Payton, *Scottie Pippen, *Mitch Richmond, *David Robinson, John Stockton

SILVER—Yugoslavia: Miroslav Beric, Dejan Bodiroga,

Nikola Bulatovic, Predrag Danilovic, Vlade Divac, Vladimir Djokic, Aleksandar Djordjevic, Predrag Drobnjak, Nikola Loncar, Sasa Obradovic, Zarko Paspalj, Zeljko Rebraca, Zoran Savic, Dejan Tomasevic, Zeljko Topalovic, Milenko Topic

BRONZE—Lithuania: Gintaras Einikis, Andrius Jurkunas, Arturas Karnisovas, Rimas Kurtinaitis, Darius Lukminas, Sarunas Marciulionis, Tomas Pacesas, Arvydas Sabonis, Saulius Stombergas, Rytis Vaisvila, Eurelijus Zukauskas, Mindaugas Zukauskas

WOMEN

GOLD—United States: Jennifer Azzi, *Ruthie Bolton, *Teresa Edwards, *Venus Lacey, *Lisa Leslie, Rebecca Lobo, *Katrina McClain, *Nikki McCray, *Carla McGhee, *Dawn Staley, Katy Steding, *Sheryl Swoopes

SILVER—Brazil: Maria Angelica, Janeth Arcain, Roseli Gustavo, Silvia Luz, Hortencia Marcari Oliva, Alessandra Oliveira, Claudia Maria Pastor, Adriana Santos, Cintia Santos, Maria Paula Silva, Leila Sobral, Mart de Sooza Sobral

BRONZE—Australia: Carla Boyd, Michelle Brogan, Sandy Brondello, Michelle Chandler, Allison Cook, Trisha Fallon, Joanne Hill, Robyn Maher, Fiona Robinson, Shelley Sandie, Rachael Sporn, Georgina Stevens, Michele Timms, Jennifer Whittle

Boxing

Light Flyweight (106 pounds)

GOLD—Daniel Petrov (Bulgaria)

SILVER—Mansueto Velasco (Philippines)

BRONZE—Oleg Kiryukhin (Ukraine); Rafael Lozano (Spain)

Flyweight (112 pounds)

GOLD—Maikro Romero (Cuba)

SILVER—Bolat Djumadilov (Kazakstan)

BRONZE—Albert Pakeev (Russia); Zoltan Lunka (Germany)

Bantamweight (119 pounds)

GOLD—Istvan Kovacs (Hungary)

SILVER—Arnaldo Mesa (Cuba)

BRONZE—Raimkul Malakhbekov (Russia); and Vichairachanon Khadpo (Thailand)

Featherweight (125 pounds)

GOLD—Somluck Kamsing (Thailand)

SILVER—Serafim Todorov (Bulgaria)

BRONZE—Pablo Chacon (Argentina); *Floyd Mayweather (Grand Rapids, MI)

Lightweight (132 pounds)

GOLD—Hocine Soltani (Algeria)

SILVER—Tontcho Tontchev (Bulgaria)

BRONZE—Terrance Cauthen (Philadelpha, PA); Leonard Doroftei (Romania)

Light Welterweight (139 pounds)

GOLD—Hector Vinent (Cuba)

SILVER—Oktay Urkal (Germany)

BRONZE—Bolat Niyazymbetov (Kazakstan); Fethi Missaoui (Tunisia)

Welterweight (147 pounds)

GOLD—Oleg Saitov (Russia)

SILVER—Juan Hernandez (Cuba)

BRONZE—Marian Simion (Romania); Daniel Santos (Puerto Rico)

Light Middleweight (156 pounds)

GOLD—David Reid (Philadelphia, PA)

SILVER—Alfredo Duvergel (Cuba)

BRONZE—Karim Tulaganov (Uzbekistan); Ermakhan Ibraimov (Kazakstan)

Middleweight (165 pounds)

GOLD—Ariel Hernandez (Cuba)

SILVER—Malik Beyleroglu (Turkey)

BRONZE—*Rhoshii Wells (Riverdale, GA); Mohamed Bahari (Algeria)

Light Heavyweight (178 pounds)

GOLD—Vassili Jirov (Kazakstan)

SILVER—Lee Seung-bao (South Korea)

BRONZE—Antonio Tarver (Orlando, FL); Thomas Ulrich (Germany)

Heavyweight (201 pounds)

GOLD—Felix Savon (Cuba)

SILVER—David Defiagbon (Canada)

BRONZE—Nate Jones (Chicago, IL); Luan Krasniqi (Germany)

Super Heavyweight (201-plus pounds)

GOLD—Vladimir Klitchko (Ukraine)
SILVER—Paea Wolfgramm (Tonga)
BRONZE—Alexei Lezin (Russia); Duncan Dokiwari (Nigeria)

Canoe-Kayak

MEN

Canoe Single 500

GOLD—Martin Doktor (Czech Republic)
SILVER—Slavomir Knazovicky (Slovakia)
BRONZE—Imre Pulai (Hungary)

Canoe Single 1000

GOLD—Martin Doktor (Czech Republic)
SILVER—Ivan Klementyev (Latvia)
BRONZE—Gyorgy Zala (Hungary)

Canoe Double 500

GOLD—Gyorgy Kolonics and Csaba Horvath (Hungary)
SILVER—Nikolai Juravschi and Victor Reneischi (Moldova)
BRONZE—Gheorghe Andriev and Grigore Obreja (Romania)

Canoe Double 1000

GOLD—Andreas Dittmer and Gunar Kirchbach (Germany)
SILVER—Marcel Glavan and Antonel Borsan (Romania)
BRONZE—Gyorgy Kolonics and Csaba Horvath (Hungary)

Kayak Single 500

GOLD—Antonio Rossi (Italy)
SILVER—Knut Holmann (Norway)
BRONZE—Piotr Markiewicz (Poland)

Kayak Single 1000

GOLD—Knut Holmann (Norway)
SILVER—Beniamino Bonomi (Italy)
BRONZE—Clint Robinson (Australia)

Kayak Double 500

GOLD—Kay Bluhm and Torsten Gutsche (Germany)
SILVER—Beniamino Bonomi and Daniele Scarpa (Italy)
BRONZE—Andrew Trim and Danny Collins (Australia)

Kayak Double 1000

GOLD—Antonio Rossi and Daniele Scarpa (Italy)
SILVER—Kay Bluhm and Torsten Gutsche (Germany)
BRONZE—Andrian Dushev and Milk Kazanov (Bulgaria)

Kayak Fours 1000

GOLD—Detlef Hofmann, Olaf Winter, Thomas Reineck, and Mark Zabel (Germany)
SILVER—Attila Adrovicz, Ferenc Csipes, Gabor Horvath, and Andras Rajna (Hungary)
BRONZE—Sergey Verlin, Oleg Gorobiy, Anatoliy Tishchenko, and Georgiy Tsybulnikov (Russia)

Women

Kayak Single 500

GOLD—Rita Koban (Hungary)
SILVER—Caroline Brunet (Canada)
BRONZE—Josefa Idem (Italy)

Kayak Double 500

GOLD—Agneta Andersson and Susanne Gunnarsson (Sweden)
SILVER—Birgit Fischer and Ramona Portwich (Germany)
BRONZE—Anna Wood and Katrin Borchert (Australia)

Kayak Fours 500

GOLD—Ramona Portwich, Manuela Mucke, Birgit Fischer, and Anett Schuck (Germany)
SILVER—Daniela Baumer, Sabine Eichenberger, Ingrid Haralamow, and Gabi Mueller (Switzerland)
BRONZE—Agneta Andersson, Ingela Ericsson, Anna Olsson, and Susanne Rosenqvist (Sweden)

MEN

Canoe Singles

GOLD—Michal Martikan (Slovakia)
SILVER—Lukas Pollert (Czech Republic)
BRONZE—Patrice Estanguet (France)

Canoe Doubles

GOLD—Frank Adisson and Wilfrid Forgues (France)
SILVER—Miroslav Simek and Jiri Rohan (Czech Republic)
BRONZE—Andre Ehrenberg and Michael Senft (Germany)

Kayak Singles

GOLD—Oliver Fix (Germany)

SILVER—Andraz Vehovar (Slovenia)
BRONZE—Thomas Becker (Germany)

WOMEN

Kayak Singles

GOLD—Stepanka Hilgertova (Czech Republic)
SILVER—Dana Chladek (Kensington, MD)
BRONZE—Myriam Fox–Jerusalmi (France)

Cycling

MEN

Sprint

GOLD—Jens Fiedler (Germany)
SILVER—Marty Nothstein (Trexlertown, PA)
BRONZE—Curt Harnett (Canada)

Points Race

GOLD—Silvio Martinello (Italy)
SILVER—Brian Walton (Canada)
BRONZE—Stuart O'Grady (Australia)

Individual Pursuit

GOLD—Andrea Collinelli (Italy)
SILVER—Philippe Ermenault (France)
BRONZE—Bradley McGee (Australia)

Road Race

GOLD—Pascal Richard (Switzerland)
SILVER—Rolf Sorensen (Denmark)
BRONZE—Maximilian Sciandri (Britain)

Individual Time Trial

GOLD—Miguel Indurain (Spain)
SILVER—Abraham Olano (Spain)
BRONZE—Chris Boardman (Britain)

Mountain Bike

GOLD—Bart Jan Brentjens (Netherlands)
SILVER—Thomas Frischknecht (Switzerland)
BRONZE—Miguel Martinez (France)

1km Time Trial

GOLD—Florian Rousseau (France)
SILVER—Erin Hartwell (Colorado Springs, CO)
BRONZE—Takanobu Jumonji (Japan)

Team Pursuit

GOLD—Christophe Capelle, Philippe Ermenault, Jean-Michel Monin, Francis Moreau, and Herve Thuet (France)
SILVER—Nikolay Kuznetsov, Aleksey Markov, Anton Chantyr, Eduard Gritsun, Yevgeniy Anashkin, Aleksandr Kirichenko, and Pavel Khamidulin (Russia)
BRONZE—Bradley McGee, Stuart O'Grady, Timothy O'Shannessey, and Dean Woods (Australia)

WOMEN

Sprint

GOLD—Felicia Ballanger (France)
SILVER—Michelle Ferris (Australia)
BRONZE—Ingrid Haringa (Netherlands)

Points Race

GOLD—Nathalie Lancien (France)
SILVER—Ingrid Haringa (Netherlands)
BRONZE—Lucy Tyler Sharman (Australia)

Individual Pursuit

GOLD—Antonella Bellutti (Italy)
SILVER—Marion Clignet (France)
BRONZE—Judith Arndt (Germany)

Road Race

GOLD—Jeannie Longo–Ciprelli (France)
SILVER—Imelda Chiappa (Italy)
BRONZE—Clara Hughes (Canada)

Individual Time Trial

GOLD—Zulfiya Zabirova (Russia)
SILVER—Jeannie Longo-Ciprelli (France)
BRONZE—Clara Hughes (Canada)

Mountain Bike

GOLD—Paola Pezzo (Italy)
SILVER—Alison Sydor (Canada)
BRONZE—Susan DeMattei (Gunnison, CO)

Diving

MEN

Platform

GOLD—Dmitry Sautin (Russia)
SILVER—Jan Hempel (Germany)
BRONZE—Xiao Hailiang (China)

Springboard

GOLD—Xiong Ni (China)
SILVER—Yu Zhuocheng (China)
BRONZE—Mark Lenzi (Bloomington, IN)

WOMEN

Platform

GOLD—Fu Mingxia (China)
SILVER—Annika Walter (Germany)
BRONZE—Mary Ellen Clark (Newtown Square, PA)

Springboard

GOLD—Fu Mingxia (China)
SILVER—Irina Lashko (Russia)
BRONZE—Annie Pelletier (Canada)

Equestrian

Individual Dressage

GOLD—Isabell Werth on *Gigolo* (Germany)
SILVER—Anky Van Grunsven on *Bonfire* (Netherlands)
BRONZE—Sven Rothenberger on *Weyden* (Netherlands)

Individual Jumping

GOLD—Ulrich Kirchhoff on *Jus de Pommes* (Germany)
SILVER—Willi Melliger on *Calvaro* (Switzerland)
BRONZE—Alexandra Ledermann on *Rochet M* (France)

Individual Three-Day Event

GOLD—Blyth Tait on *Ready Teddy* (New Zealand)
SILVER—Sally Clark on *Squirrel Hill* (New Zealand)
BRONZE—Kerry Millikin on *Out and About* (Westport,MA)

Team Dressage

GOLD—Germany: Isabell Werth on *Gigolo*; Monica Theodorescu on *Grunox*; Klaus Balkenhol on *Goldstern*; Martin Schuadt on *Durgo*

SILVER—Netherlands: Anky Van Grunsven on *Bonfire*; Sven Rothenberger on *Weyden*; Tineke Bartels-De Vries on *Olympic Barbria*; Gonnelien Rothenberger on *Dondolo*

BRONZE—United States: Robert Dover on *Metallic* (Wellington, FL); Steffen Peters on *Udon* (Escondido, CA); Michelle Gibson on *Peron* (Roswell, GA); Guenter Seidel on *Graf George* (Encinitas, CA)

Team Jumping

GOLD—Germany: Ulrich Kirchhoff on *Jus De Pommes*; Lars Nieberg on *For Pleasure*; Franke Sloothaak on *Joly*; Ludger Beerbaum on *Ratina*

SILVER—United States: Anne Kursinski on *Eros* (Flemington, NJ); Michael Matz on *Rhum* (Collegeville, PA); Peter Leone on *Legato* (Greenwich, CT); Leslie Burr-Howard on *Extreme* (Westport, CT)

BRONZE—Brazil: Rodrigo Pessoa on *Tomboy*; Andre Johannpeter on *Calei*; Luiz Azevedo Felipe on *Cassiana*; Alvaro Miranda Neto on *Aspen*

Team Three-Day Event

GOLD—Australia: Wendy Schaeffer; Phillip Dutton; Andrew Hoy, Darien Powers

SILVER—United States: David O'Connor (The Plains, VA); Bruce Davidson, (Unionville, PA); Karen O'Connor (The Plains, VA); Jill Henneberg, (Voorhees, NJ)

BRONZE—New Zealand: Blyth Tait; Vaughn Jefferis; Andrew Nicholson; Vicky Latta

Fencing

MEN

Individual Epee

GOLD—Aleksandr Beketov (Russia)
SILVER—Ivan Trevejo Perez (Cuba)
BRONZE—Geza Imre (Hungary)

Individual Foil

GOLD—Alessandro Puccini (Italy)
SILVER—Lionel Plumenail (France)
BRONZE—Franck Boidin (France)

Individual Sabre

GOLD—Stanislav Pozdnyakov (Russia)
SILVER—Sergey Sharikov (Russia)
BRONZE—Damien Touya (France)

Team Epee

GOLD—Italy: Sandro Cuomo; Angelo Mazzoni; Maurizio Randazzo

SILVER—Russia: Aleksandr Beketov; Pavel Kolobkov; Valeriy Zakharevich

BRONZE—France: Jean-Michel Henry; Robert Leroux; Eric Srecki

Team Foil

GOLD—Russia: Dmitriy Shevchenko; Ilgar Mamedov; Vladislav Pavlovich

SILVER—Poland: Piotr Kielpikowski; Adam Krzesinski; Ryszard Sobczak

BRONZE—Cuba: Elvis Gregory; Rolando Tucker Leon Samuel; Oscar Garcia Perez Manuel

Team Sabre

GOLD—Russia: Stanislav Pozdnyakov; Grigoriy Kiriyenko; Sergey Sharikov

SILVER—Hungary: Csaba Koves; Jozsef Navarrete; Bence Szabo

BRONZE—Italy: Raffaello Caserta; Luigi Tarantino; Tonhi Terenzi

WOMEN

Individual Epee

GOLD—Laura Flessel (France)

SILVER—Valerie Barlois (France)

BRONZE—Gyoengyi Szalay Horvathne (Hungary)

Individual Foil

GOLD—Laura Badea (Romania)

SILVER—Valentina Vezzali (Italy)

BRONZE—Giovanna Trillini (Italy)

Team Epee

GOLD—France: (Laura Flessel; Sophie Moresee-Pichot; Valerie Barlois

SILVER—Italy: Laura Chiesa; Elisa Uga; Margherita Zalaffi

BRONZE—Russia: Mariya Mazina; Yuliya Garayeva; Karina Aznavuryan

Team Foil

GOLD—Italy: Francesca Bortolozzi Borella; Giovanna Trillini; Valentina Vezzali

SILVER—Romania: Laura Badea; Reka Szabo; Roxana Scarlat

BRONZE—Germany: Anja Fichtel Mauritz; Sabine Bau; Monika Weber-Koszto

Field Hockey

MEN

GOLD—Netherlands: Floris Jan Bovelander, Danny Bree, Jacques Brinkman, Maurits Crucq, Teun de Nooijer, Marc Delissen, Jeroen Delmee, Ronald Jansen, Erik Jazet, Leo Klein Gebbink, Bram Lomans, Taco van den Honert, Rogier van der Wal, Tycho van Meer, Wouter van Pelt, Remco van Wijk, Stephan Veen, Guus Vogels

SILVER—Spain: Jaime Amat, Pablo Amat, Javier Arnau, Jordi Arnau, Oscar Barrena, Ignacio Cobos, Juan Dinares, Juan Escarre, Xavier Escude, Juantxo Garcia-Maruino, Antonio Gonzalez, Ramon Jufresa, Joaquin Malgosa, Victor Pujol, Ramon Sala, Pablo Usoz

BRONZE—Australia: Lee Bodimeade, Stuart Carruthers, Baeden Choppy, Stephen Davies, Damon Diletti, Lachlan Dreher, Darren Duff, Jason Duff, James Elmer, Lachlan Elmer, Brendan Garard, Paul Gaudoin, Mark Hager, Garry Jennison, Paul Lewis, Grant Smith, Matthew Smith, Daniel Sproule, Jay Stacy, Kenneth Wark, Michael York

WOMEN

GOLD—Australia: Katie Allen, Michelle Andrews, Alyson Annan, Louise Dobson, Renita Farrell, Juliet Haslam, Rechelle Hawkes, Clover Maitland, Karen Marsden, Claire Mitchell-Taverner, Jenny Morris, Nikki Mott, Alison Peek, Jackie Pereira, Nova Peris-Kneebone, Katrina Powell, Lisa Powell, Danni Roche, Justine Sowry, Kate Starre, Liane Tooth

SILVER—South Korea: Eun-Jung Chang, Eun-Jung Cho, Eun-Kyung Choi, Mi-Soon Choi, Young-Sun Jeon, Deok-San Jin, Myung-Ok Kim, Soo-Hyun Kown, Chang-Sook Kwon, Eun-Kyung Lee, Eun-Young Lee, Ji-Young Lee, Jeong-Sook Lim, Seung-Shin Oh, Hyun-Jung Woo, Jae-Sook You

BRONZE—Netherlands: Ageeth Boomgaardt, Stelle de Heij, Wietske de Ruiter, Wilhelmina Donners, Willemijn Duyster, Wendy Fortuin, Eleonoor Holsboer, Nicole Koolen, Ellen Kuipers, Jeannette Lewin, Suzanne Plesman, Florentine Steenberghe, Josepha Teeuwen, Carole Thate, Jacqueline Toxopeus, Fleur van de Kieft, Dillianne van den Boogaard

Gymnastics

MEN

All-Around

GOLD—Li Xiaoshuang (China)

SILVER—Alexei Nemov (Russia)

BRONZE—Vitaly Scherbo (Belarus)

Floor Exercise

GOLD—Ioannis Melissanidis (Greece)

SILVER—Li Xiaoshuang (China)

BRONZE—Alexei Nemov (Russia)

Horizontal Bar

GOLD—Andreas Wecker (Germany)

SILVER—Krasimir Dounev (Bulgaria)

BRONZE—Vitaly Scherbo (Belarus); Alexei Nemov (Russia); and Fan Bin (China)

Parallel Bars

GOLD—Rustam Sharipov (Ukraine)

SILVER—*Jair Lynch (Washington, D.C.)

BRONZE—Vitaly Scherbo (Belarus)

Pommel Horse

GOLD—Li Donghua (Switzerland)

SILVER—Marius Urzica (Romania)

BRONZE—Alexei Nemov (Russia)

Rings

GOLD—Yuri Chechi (Italy)

SILVER—Dan Burinca (Romania); and Szilveszter Csollany (Hungary)

BRONZE—None awarded

Vault

GOLD—Alexei Nemov (Russia)

SILVER—Yeo Hong-chul (South Korea)

BRONZE—Vitaly Scherbo (Belarus)

Team

GOLD—Russia: Eugeni Podgorni; Nikolay Krukov; Dmitriy Trush; Sergei Charkov; Alexei Voropaev; Alexei Nemov

SILVER—China: Zhang Jinjing; Fan Bin; Shen Jian; Fan Hongbin; Li Xiaoshuang; Huang Huadong

BRONZE—Ukraine: Vladimir Shamenko; Rustam Sharipov; Alexandre Svetlichnyi; Igchinski; Yuri Yermakov; Grigory Misutin

WOMEN

All-Around

GOLD—Lilia Podkopayeva (Ukraine)

SILVER—Gina Gogean (Romania)

BRONZE—Simona Amanar (Romania); and Lavinia Milosovici (Romania)

Balance Beam

GOLD—Shannon Miller (Edmond, OK)

SILVER—Lilia Podkopayeva (Ukraine)

BRONZE—Gina Gogean (Romania)

Floor Exercise

GOLD—Lilia Podkopayeva (Ukraine)

SILVER—Simona Amanar (Romania)

BRONZE—*Dominique Dawes (Silver Spring, MD)

Uneven Bars

GOLD—Svetlana Chorkina (Russia)

SILVER—Amy Chow (San Jose, CA); and Bi Wenjiing (China)

BRONZE-None awarded

Vault

GOLD—Simona Amanar (Romania)

SILVER—Mo Huilan (China)

BRONZE—Gina Gogean (Romania)

Team

GOLD—United States: Jaycie Phelps (Greenfield, IN); Amy Chow (San Jose, CA); Shannon Miller, (Edmond, OK); *Dominique Dawes (Silver Spring, MD); Dominique Moceanu (Hollywood, CA); Kerri Strug (Tucson, AZ)

SILVER—Russia: Oksana Liapina; Elena Grosheva; Svetlana Chorkina; Elena Dolgopolova; Dina Kochetkova; Rozalia Galiyeva

BRONZE—Romania: Ionela Loaies; Mirela Tugurlan; Gina Gogean; Alexandra Marinescu; Lavinia Milosovici; Simona Amanar

Judo

MEN

Extra Lightweight

GOLD—Tadahiro Nomura (Japan)

SILVER—Girolamo Giovinazzo (Italy)

BRONZE—Richard Trautmann (Germany); and Dorjpalam Narmandakh (Mongolia)

Half-Lightweight

GOLD—Udo Quellmalz (Germany)

SILVER—Yukimasa Nakamura (Japan)

BRONZE—Israel Hernandez (Cuba); and Henrique Guimares (Brazil)

Lightweight

GOLD—Kenzo Nakamura (Japan)

SILVER—Kwak Dae-sung (South Korea)

BRONZE—Jimmy Pedro (Danvers, MA); and Christophe Gagliano (France)

Half-Middleweight

GOLD—Djamel Bouras (France)

SILVER—Toshihiko Koga (Japan)

BRONZE—Soso Liparteliani (Georgia); and Cho In-chul (South Korea)

Middleweight

GOLD—Jeon Ki-young (South Korea)

SILVER—Armen Bagdasarov (Uzbekistan)

BRONZE—Marko Spittka (Germany); and Mark Huizinga (Netherlands)

Half-Heavyweight

GOLD—Pawel Nastula (Poland)

SILVER—Kim Min-soo (South Korea)

BRONZE—Stephane Traineau (France); and Miguel Fernandes (Brazil)

Heavyweight

GOLD—David Douillet (France)

SILVER—Ernesto Perez (Spain)

BRONZE—Harry van Barneveld (Belgium); and Frank Moeller (Germany)

WOMEN

Extra Lightweight

GOLD—Kye Sun (North Korea)

SILVER—Ryoko Tamura (Japan)

BRONZE—Yolanda Soler (Spain); and Amarilis Savon (Cuba)

Half-Lightweight

GOLD—Marie-Claire Restoux (France)

SILVER—Hyun Sook-hee (South Korea)

BRONZE—Noriko Sagawara (Japan); and Legna Verdecia (Cuba)

Lightweight

GOLD—Driulis Gonzalez (Cuba)

SILVER—Jung Sun-yong (South Korea)

BRONZE—Isabel Fernandez (Spain); and Marisbel Lomba (Belgium)

Half-Middleweight

GOLD—Yuko Emoto (Japan)

SILVER—Gella Van de Caveye (Belgium)

BRONZE—Jung Sung-sook (South Korea); and Jenny Gal (Netherlands)

Middleweight

GOLD—Cho Min-sun (South Korea)

SILVER—Aneta Szczepanska (Poland)

BRONZE—Wang Xianbo (China); and Claudia Zwiers (Netherlands)

Half-Heavyweight

GOLD—Ulla Werbrouck (Belgium)

SILVER—Yoko Tanabe (Japan)

BRONZE—Ylenia Scapin (Italy); and Diadenis Luna (Cuba)

Heavyweight

GOLD—Sun Fuming (China)

SILVER—Estela Rodriguez (Cuba)

BRONZE—Johanna Hagn (Germany); and Christine Cicot (France)

Modern Pentathlon

GOLD—Aleksandr Parygin (Kazakstan)

SILVER—Eduard Zenovka (Russia)

BRONZE—Janos Martinek (Hungary)

Rhythmic Gymnastics

Indvidual

GOLD—Yekaterina Serebryanskaya (Ukraine)

SILVER—Ianina Batyrchina (Russia)

BRONZE—Yelena Vitrichenko (Ukraine)

Team

GOLD—Spain: Marta Baldo; Nuria Cabanillas; Estela Gimenez; Lorena Gurendez; Tania Lamarca; Estibaliz Martinez

SILVER—Bulgaria: Ivelina Taleva; Valentina Kevlian; Ina Deltcheva; Maja Tabakova; Maria Koleva; Vjara Vatachka

BRONZE—Russia: Evguenia Botchkareva; Irina Dziouba; Angelina Iouchkova; Olga Chtyrenko; Elena Krivochei; Ioulia Ivanova

Rowing

MEN

Single Sculls

GOLD—Xeno Mueller (Switzerland)
SILVER—Derek Porter (Canada)
BRONZE—Thomas Lange (Germany)

Double Sculls

GOLD—Davide Tizzano and Agostino Abbagnale (Italy)
SILVER—Kjetil Undset and Steffen Stoerseth (Norway)
BRONZE—Frederic Kowal and Samuel Barathay (France)

Lightweight Double Sculls

GOLD—Michael Gier and Markus Gier (Switzerland)
SILVER—Maarten van der Linden and Pepjin Aardewijn (Netherlands)
BRONZE—Anthony Edwards and Bruce Hick (Australia)

Quadruple Sculls

GOLD—Germany: Andre Steiner; Andreas Hajek; Stephan Volkert; Andre Willms
SILVER—United States: Tim Young (Moorestown, NJ); Brian Jamieson (Livingston, NJ); Eric Mueller (Cedarburg, WI); Jason Gailes (Webster, MA)
BRONZE—Australia: Janusz Hooker; Duncan Free; Ronald Snook; Boden Hanson

Coxless Pair

GOLD—Steven Redgrave and Matthew Pinsent (Britain)
SILVER—David Weightman and Robert Scott (Australia)
BRONZE—Michel Andrieux and Jean-Christophe Rolland (France)

Coxless Four

GOLD—Australia: Drew Ginn; James Tomkins; Nicholas Green; Michael McKay
SILVER—France: Gilles Bosquet; Daniel Fauche; Bertrand Vecten; Olivier Moncelet
BRONZE—Britain: Rupert Obholzer; Jonny Searle; Gregory Searle; Timothy Foster

Lightweight Coxless Four

GOLD—Denmark: Niels Henriksen; Thomas Poulsen; Eskild Ebbesen; Victor Feddersen
SILVER—Canada: Jeffrey Lay; Dave Boyes; Gavin Hassett; Brian Peaker
BRONZE—United States: David Collins (Thousand Oaks, CA); Jeff Pfaendtner (Detroit, MI); Marcus Schneider (Everett, WA); William Carlucci (Rye Brook,NY)

Eights

GOLD—Netherlands: Henk-Jan Zwolle; Diederik Simon; Michiel Bartman; Koos Maasdyk; Niels van der Zwan; Niels van Steenis; Ronald Florijn; Nico Rienks; Jeroen Duyster
SILVER—Germany: Frank Richter; Mark Kleinschmidt; Wolfram Huhn; Marc Weber; Detlef Kirchhoff; Thorsten Streppelhoff; Ulrich Viefers; Roland Baar; Peter Thiede
BRONZE—Russia: Anton Chermashentsev; Andrey Glukhov; Dmitriy Rozinkevich; Vladimir Volodenkov; Nikolay Aksyonov; Roman Monchenko; Pavel Melnikov; Sergey Matveyev; Aleksandr Lukyanov

WOMEN

Single Sculls

GOLD—Yekaterina Khodotovich (Belarus)
SILVER—Silken Laumann (Canada)
BRONZE—Trine Hansen (Denmark)

Double Sculls

GOLD—Marnie McBean and Kathleen Heddle (Canada)
SILVER—Cao Mianying and Zhang Xiuyun (China)
BRONZE—Irene Eljs and Eeke van Nes (Netherlands)

Lightweight Double Sculls

GOLD—Constantina Burcica and Camelia Macoviciuc (Romania)
SILVER—Teresa Z. Bell (Washington Crossing, NJ) Lindsay Burns (Big Timber, MT)
BRONZE—Rebecca Joyce and Virginia Lee (Australia)

Quadruple Sculls

GOLD—Germany: Jana Sorgers; Katrin Rutschow; Kathrin Boron; Kerstin Koeppen
SILVER—Ukraine: Olena Ronzhina; Inna Frolova; Svitlana Maziy; Diana Miftakhutdinova
BRONZE—Canada: Laryssa Biesenthal; Marnie McBean; Diane O'Grady; Kathleen Heddle

Coxless Pair

GOLD—Megan Still and Kate Slatter (Australia)
SILVER—Missy Schwen (Bloomington, IN) and Karen Kraft (San Mateo, CA)

BRONZE—Christine Gosse and Helene Cortin (France)

Eights

GOLD—Romania: Anca Tanase; Vera Cochelea; Liliana Gafencu; Doina Spircu; Ioana Olteanu; Elisabeta Lipa; Marioara Popescu; Doina Ignat; Elena Georgescu

SILVER—Canada: Heather Mcdermid; Tosha Tsang; Maria Maunder; Alison Korn; Emma Robinson; Anna van der Kamp; Jessica Monroe; Theresa Luke; Lesley Thompson

BRONZE—Belarus: Natalya Lavrinenko; Aleksandra Pankina; Natalya Volchek; Tamara Davydenko; Valentina Skrabatun; Yelena Mikulich; Natalya Stasyuk; Marina Znak; Yaroslava Pavlovich

Shooting

MEN

Air Pistol

GOLD—Roberto Di Donna (Italy)
SILVER—Wang Yifu (China)
BRONZE—Tanu Kiriakov (Bulgaria)

Free Pistol

GOLD—Boris Kokorev (Russia)
SILVER—Igor Basinski (Belarus)
BRONZE—Roberto Di Donna (Italy)

Rapid Fire Pistol

GOLD—Ralf Schumann (Germany)
SILVER—Emil Milev (Bulgaria)
BRONZE—Vladimir Vokhmyanin (Kazakstan)

Running Target

GOLD—Yang Ling (China)
SILVER—Xiao Jun (China)
BRONZE—Miroslav Janus (Czech Republic)

Air Rifle

GOLD—Artem Khadzhibekov (Russia)
SILVER—Wolfram Waibel Jr. (Austria)
BRONZE—Jean-Pierre Amat (France)

Small-Bore Rifle Prone

GOLD—Christian Klees (Germany)
SILVER—Sergey Beliaev (Kazakstan)
BRONZE—Jozef Gonci (Slovakia)

Small-Bore Rifle 3-Position

GOLD—Jean-Pierre Amat (France)
SILVER—Sergey Beliaev (Kazakstan)
BRONZE—Wolfram Waibel Jr. (Austria)

Trap

GOLD—Michael Diamond (Australia)
SILVER—Josh Lakatos (Pasadena, CA)
BRONZE—Lance Bade (Ridgefield, WA)

Double Trap

GOLD—Russell Mark (Australia)
SILVER—Albano Pera (Italy)
BRONZE—Zhang Bing (China)

Skeet

GOLD—Ennio Falco (Italy)
SILVER—Miroslaw Rzepkowski (Poland)
BRONZE—Andrea Benelli (Italy)

WOMEN

Air Pistol

GOLD—Olga Klochneva (Russia)
SILVER—Marina Logvinenko (Russia)
BRONZE—Mariya Grozdeva (Bulgaria)

Air Rifle

GOLD—Renata Mauer (Poland)
SILVER—Petra Horneber (Germany)
BRONZE—Aleksandra Ivosev (Yugoslavia)

Sport Pistol

GOLD—Li Duihong (China)
SILVER—Diana Yorgova (Bulgaria)
BRONZE—Marina Logvinenko (Russia)

Small-Bore Rifle Three Position

GOLD—Aleksandra Ivosev (Yugoslavia)
SILVER—Irina Gerasimenok (Russia)
BRONZE—Renata Mauer (Poland)

Double Trap

GOLD—Kim Rhode (El Monte, CA)
SILVER—Susanne Kiermayer (Germany)
BRONZE—Deserie Huddleston (Australia)

Soccer

MEN

GOLD—Nigeria: Daniel Amokachi, Emmanuel Amunike, Jonathan Apoborie, Tijani Babangida, Celestine Babayaro, Emmanuel Babayaro, Abiodun Baruwa, Joseph Dosu, Teslim Fatusi, Victor Ikpeba, Nwankwo Kanu, Garba Lawal, Ndubuisi Ndah, Abiodon Obafemi, Mobi Obaraku, Kingsley Obiekwu, Augustine Okocha, Sunday Oliseh, Wilson Oruma, Patrick Pascal, Okechukwu Uche, Taribo West

SILVER—Argentina: Matias Almeyda, Roberto Ayala, Guillermo Barros Schelotto, Christian Bassedas, Carlos Bossio, Pablo Cavallero, Jose Antonio Chamot, Hernan Crespo, Marcelo Delgado, Marcelo Gallardo, Javier Lavallen, Claudio Lopez, Gustavo Lopez, Hugo Morales, Ariel Ortego, Pablo Paz, Hector Pineda, Roberto Sensini, Diego Simeone, Juan Pablo Sorin, Juan Veron, Javier Zanetti

BRONZE—Brazil: Aldair, Amaral, Andre Luiz, Bebeto, Danrlei, Dida, Flavio Conceicao, Juninho, Luizao, Marcelinho Paulista, Narciso, Rivaldo, Roberto Carlos, Ronaldinho, Ronaldo, Savio, Ze Elias, Ze Maria

WOMEN

GOLD—United States: Michelle Akers, Brandi Chastain, Amanda Cromwell, Joy Fawcett, Julie Foudy, Carin Gabarra, Mia Hamm, Mary Harvey, Kristine Lilly, Shannon MacMillan, Tiffeny Milbrett, Tracy Noonan, Carla Overback, Cindy Parlow, Tiffany Roberts, *Briànà Scurry, *Thori Staples, Jennifer Streiffer, Tisha Venturini, Saskia Webber, *Staci Wilson

SILVER—China: Yufeng Chen, Yunjie Fan, Hong Gao, Yating Li, Ailing Liu, Ying Liu, Lijie Niu, Guihong Shi, Qingxia Shui, Qingmei Sun, Wen Sun, Liping Wang, Haiying Wei, Lirong Wen, Huilin Xie, Hongqi Yu, Yan Zhang, Lihong Zhao, Yan Zhao, Honglian Zhong

BRONZE—Norway: Ann Kristin Aarones, Agnete Carlsen, Gro Espeseth, Tone Gunn Frustol, Tone Haugen, Linda Medalen, Merete Myklebust, Bente Nordby, Anne Nymark Andersen, Nina Nymark Anderson, Marianne Pettersen, Hege Riise, Brit Sandaune, Reidun Seth, Ingrid Sternhoff, Heidi Stoere, Tina Svensson, Trine Tangeraas, Kjersti Thun

Softball

GOLD—United States: Laura Berg; *Gillian Boxx; Sheila Cornell; Lisa Fernandez; Michele Granger; Lori Harrigan; Dionna Harris; Kim Maher; Leah O'Brien; Dot Richardson; Julie Smith; Michele Smith; Shelly Stokes; Dani Tyler; Christa Williams

SILVER—China: Chunfang Zhang; Fang Yan; Xuging Liu; Ying Wang; Hua Tao; Hong Chen; Jian Xu; Zhongxin An; Qiang Wei; LiLei; Yaju Liu; Lihong Wang; Li Ou

BRONZE—Australia: Kim Cooper; Jocalyn Lester; Joanne Brown; Kerry Dienelt; Sally Modermin; Natalie Ward; Tanya Harding; Hayles Petrie; Petra Ededone; Leslie McDermid; Jen McRae; Shelly Richardson; Eve Roche; Laura Wilkins; Penny Crudgington

Swimming

MEN

50 Freestyle

GOLD—Alexander Popov (Russia)
SILVER—Gary Hall Jr. (Phoenix, AZ)
BRONZE—Fernando Scherer (Brazil)

100 Freestyle

GOLD—Alexander Popov (Russia)
SILVER—Gary Hall Jr. (Phoenix,AZ)
BRONZE—Gustavo Borges (Brazil)

200 Freestyle

GOLD—Danyon Loader (New Zealand)
SILVER—Gustavo Borges (Brazil)
BRONZE—Daniel Kowalski (Australia)

400 Freestyle

GOLD—Danyon Loader (New Zealand)
SILVER—Paul Palmer (Britain)
BRONZE—Daniel Kowalski (Australia)

1500 Freestyle

GOLD—Kieren Perkins (Australia)
SILVER—Daniel Kowalski (Australia)
BRONZE—Graeme Smith (Britain)

100 Backstroke

GOLD—Jeff Rouse (Fredericksburg, VA)
SILVER—Rodolfo Falcon (Cuba)
BRONZE—Neisser Bent (Cuba)

200 Backstroke

GOLD—Brad Bridgewater (Dallas, TX)
SILVER—Tripp Schwenk (Sarasota, FL)
BRONZE—Emanuele Merisi (Italy)

100 Breaststroke

GOLD—Fred Deburghgraeve (Belgium)

SILVER—Jeremy Linn (Harrisburg, PA)

BRONZE—Mark Warnecke (Germany)

200 Breaststroke

GOLD—Norbert Rozsa (Hungary)

SILVER—Karoly Guttler (Hungary)

BRONZE—Andrey Korneyev (Russia)

100 Butterfly

GOLD—Denis Pankratov (Russia)

SILVER—Scott Miller (Australia)

BRONZE—Vladislav Kulikov (Russia)

200 Butterfly

GOLD—Denis Pankratov (Russia)

SILVER—Tom Malchow (St. Paul, MN)

BRONZE—Scott Goodman (Australia)

200 Individual Medley

GOLD—Attila Czene (Hungary)

SILVER—Jani Sievinen (Finland)

BRONZE—Curtis Myden (Canada)

400 Individual Medley

GOLD—Tom Dolan (Arlington, VA)

SILVER—Eric Namesnik (Butler, PA)

BRONZE—Curtis Myden (Canada)

400 Medley Relay

GOLD—United States: Tripp Schwenk (Sarasota, FL); Kurt Grote (San Diego, CA); John Hargis (Clinton, AR); Josh Davis (San Antonio, TX); Gary Hall Jr. (Paradise Valley, AZ); Mark Henderson (Fort Washington, MD); Jeremy Linn (Harrisburg, PA); Jeff Rouse (Fredericksburg, VA)

SILVER—Russia: Vladimir Selkov; Stanislav Lopukhov; Denis Pankratov; Aleksandr Popov; Roman Ivanovskiy; Vladislav Kulikov; Roman Yegorov

BRONZE—Australia: Steven Dewick; Philip Rogers; Scott Miller; Michael Klim; Toby Haenen

400 Freestyle Relay

GOLD—United States: Jon Olsen (Jonseboro, AR); Josh Davis (San Antonio, TX); Bradley Schumacher (Bowie, MD); Gary Hall Jr. (Phoenix, AZ); Scott Tucker (Birmingham, AL); David Fox, Raleigh, NC)

SILVER—Russia: Roman Yegorov; Aleksandr Popov; Vladimir Predkin; Denis Pimankov; Vladimir Pyshnenko; Konstantin Ushkov

BRONZE—Germany: Christian Troger; Bengt Zikarsky; Bjorn Zikarsky; Mark Pinger; Alexander Luderitz

800 Freestyle Relay

GOLD—United States: Josh Davis (San Antonio, TX); Joe Hudepohl (Cincinnati, OH); Ryan Berube (Tequesta, FL); Bradley Schumacher (Bowie, MD); Jon Olsen (Jonesboro, AR)

SILVER—Sweden: Chriter Wallin; Anders Holmertz; Lars Frolander; Andre Lyrbring; Christer Walle

BRONZE—Germany: Aimo Heilmann; Christian Keller; Christian Troger; Steffen Zesner; Konstantin Dubrovin; Oliver Lampe

WOMEN

50 Freestyle

GOLD—Amy Van Dyken (Englewood, CO)

SILVER—Le Jingyi (China)

BRONZE—Sandra Volker (Germany)

100 Freestyle

GOLD—Le Jingyi (China)

SILVER—Sandra Volker (Germany)

BRONZE—Angel Martino (Americus, GA)

200 Freestyle

GOLD—Claudia Poll (Costa Rica)

SILVER—Franziska van Almsick (Germany)

BRONZE—Dagmar Hase (Germany)

400 Freestyle

GOLD—Michelle Smith (Ireland)

SILVER—Dagmar Hase (Germany)

BRONZE—Kirsten Vlieghuis (Netherlands)

800 Freestyle

GOLD—Brooke Bennett (Plant City, FL)

SILVER—Dagmar Hase (Germany)

BRONZE—Kirsten Vlieghuis (Netherlands)

100 Backstroke

GOLD—Beth Botsford (Baltimore, MD)

SILVER—Whitney Hedgepeth (Rocky Mount, NC)

BRONZE—Marianne Kriel (South Africa)

200 Backstroke

GOLD—Krisztina Egerszegi (Hungary)

SILVER—Whitney Hedgepeth (Rocky Mount, NC)
BRONZE—Cathleen Rund (Germany)

100 Breaststroke

GOLD—Penny Heyns (South Africa)
SILVER—Amanda Beard (Irvine, CA)
BRONZE—Samantha Riley (Australia)

200 Breaststroke

GOLD—Penny Heyns (South Africa)
SILVER—Amanda Beard (Irvine, CA)
BRONZE—Agnes Kovacs (Hungary)

100 Butterfly

GOLD—Amy van Dyken (Englewood, CO)
SILVER—Liu Limin (China)
BRONZE—Angel Martino (Americus, GA)

200 Butterfly

GOLD—Susan O'Neill (Australia)
SILVER—Petria Thomas (Australia)
BRONZE—Michelle Smith (Ireland)

200 Individual Medley

GOLD—Michelle Smith (Ireland)
SILVER—Marianne Limpert (Canada)
BRONZE—Lin Li (China)

400 Individual Medley

GOLD—Michelle Smith (Ireland)
SILVER—Allison Wagner (Gainesville, FL)
BRONZE—Krisztina Egerszegi (Hungary)

400 Freestyle Relay

GOLD—United States: Jenny Thompson (Dover, NH); Catherine Fox (Shawnee Mission, KS); Angel Martino (Americus, GA); Amy Van Dyken (Englewood, CO); Lisa Jacob (Mission Viejo, CA); Melanie Valerio (Campbell, OH)

SILVER—China: Le Jingyi; Chao Na; Nian Yun; Shan Ying

BRONZE—Germany: Sandra Volker; Simone Osygus; Antje Buschschulte; Franziska van Almsick; Meike Freitag

400 Medley Relay

GOLD—United States: Beth Botsford (Baltimore, MD); Amanda Beard (Irvine, CA); Angel Martino (Americus, GA); Amy Van Dyken (Englewood, CO); Whitney Hedgepeth (Rocky Mount, NC); Kristine Quance (Northridge, CA); Jenny Thompson (Dover, NH); Catherine Fox (Shawnee Mission, KS)

SILVER—Australia: Nicole Stevenson; Samantha Riley; Susan O'Neill; Helen Denman; Angela Kennedy; Sarah Ryan

BRONZE—China: Chen Yan; Han Xue; Cai Huijue; Shan Ying

800 Freestyle Relay

GOLD—United States: Trina Jackson (Jacksonville, FL); Sheila Taormina (Livonia, MI); Cristina Teuscher (New Rochelle, NY); Jenny Thompson (Dover, NH); Lisa Jacob (Mission Viejo, CA); Ashley Whitney (Nashville, TN); Annette Salmeen (Ann Arbor, MI)

SILVER—Germany: Franziska van Almsick, Kerstin Kielgass, Anke Scholz, Dagmar Hase, Simone Osygus, Meike Freitag

BRONZE—Australia: Julia Greville, Nicole Stevenson, Emma Johnson, Susan O'Neill, Lise Mackie

Synchronized Swimming

GOLD—United States: Tammy Cleland (Walnut Creek, CA); Becky Dyroen-Lancer (Campbell, CA); Heather Pease (Lafayette, C); Jill Savery (Concord, CA); Nathalie Schneyder (Walnut Creek, CA); Jill Sudduth (Morgan Hill, CA); Emily Lesueur (Mesa, AZ); Margot Thien (Berkeley, CA); Heather Simmons-Carrasco (Santa Clara, CA); Suzannah Bianco (Saratoga, CA)

SILVER—Canada: Karen Clark; Christine Larsen; Janice Bremner; Sylvie Frechette; Valerie Hould-Marchand; Karen Fonteyne; Kasia Kulesza; Cari Read; Erin Woodley; Lisa Alexander

BRONZE—Japan: Akiko Kawase; Miya Tachibana; Kaori Takahashi; Miho Takeda; Rei Jimbo; Raika Fujii; Miho Kawabe; Riho Nakajima; Junko Tanaka; Mayuko Fujiki

Table Tennis

MEN

Singles

GOLD—Liu Guoliang (China)
SILVER—Wang Tao (China)
BRONZE—Joerg Rosskopf (Germany)

Doubles

GOLD—Kong Linghui and Liu Guoliang (China)
SILVER—Lu Lin and Wang Tao (China)

BRONZE—Lee Chul-seung and Yoo Nam-kyu (South Korea)

WOMEN

Singles

GOLD—Deng Yaping (China)

SILVER—Chen Jing (Taiwan)

BRONZE—Qiao Hong (China)

Doubles

GOLD—Deng Yaping and Qiao Hong (China)

SILVER—Liu Wei and Qiao Yunping (China)

BRONZE—Park Hae-jung and Ryu Ji-hae (South Korea)

Team Handball

MEN

GOLD—Croatia: Patrik Cavar, Valner Frankovic, Slavko Goluza, Bruno Gudelj, Vladimir Jelcic, Bozidar Jovic, Nenad Kljavic, Venio Losert, Valter Matosevic, Zoran Mikulic, Alvaro Nacinovic, Goran Perkovac, Iztok Puc, Zlatko Saracevic, Irfan Smajlagic, Vladimir Sujster

SILVER—Sweden: Magnus Andersson, Robert Andersson, Anders Backegren, Per Carlen, Martin Frandesjo, Peter Gentzel, Erik Hajas, Robert Hedin, Andreas Larsson, Ola Lindgren, Stafan Lofgren, Nicklas Martinsson, Mats Olsson, Staffan Olsson, Johan Pettersson, Thomas Sivertsson, Jan Stankiewicz, Thomas Svensson, Pierre Thorsson, Magnus Wislander

BRONZE—Spain: Talant Dujshebaev, Salvador Esquer, Aitor Etxaburu, Jesus Fernandez, Jaume Fort, Mateo Garralda, Raul Gonzalez, Rafael Guijosa, Fernando Hernandez, Jose Hombrados, Demetrio Lozano, Jordi Nunez, Jesus Olalla, Juan Perez, Inaki Urdangarin, Alberto Urdiales

WOMEN

GOLD—Denmark: Anja Jul Andersen, Camilla Andersen, Kristine Anderson, Heidi Astrup, Tina Bottzau, Marianne Florman, Conny Hamann, Anja Hansen, Anette Hoffman, Tonje Kjaergaard, Janne Kolling, Susanne Lauritsen, Gitte Madsen, Lene Rantala, Rikke Solberg, Gitte Sunesen, Dorthe Tanderup

SILVER—South Korea: Eun-Hee Cho, Sun-Hee Han, Jeong-Ho Hong, Soon-Young Huh, Cheong-Shim Kim, Eun-Mi Kim, Jeong-Mi Kim, Mi-Sim Kim, Rang Kim, Hye-Jeong Kwag, Sang-Eun Lee, O-Kyeong Lim, Hyang-Ja Moon, Seong-Ok Oh, Yong-Ran Oh, Jeong-Rim Park

BRONZE—Hungary: Eva Erdos, Andrea Farkas, Rita Hochrajter, Beata Hoffmann, Aniko Kantor, Erzsebet Kocsis, Beatrix Kokeny, Eszter Matefi, Auguszta Matyas, Aniko Meksz, Aniko Nagy, Helga Nemeth, Ildiko Padar, Beata Siti, Anna Szanto, Katalin Szilagyi, Beatrix Toth, Melinda Tothne Szabo, Annamaria Vas, Zsuzsanna Viglasi

Tennis

MEN

Singles

GOLD—Andre Agassi (Las Vegas, NV)

SILVER—Sergi Bruguera (Spain)

BRONZE—Leander Paes (India)

Doubles

GOLD—Todd Woodbridge and Mark Woodforde (Australia)

SILVER—Neil Broad and Tim Henman (Great Britain)

BRONZE—Marc-Kevin Goellner and David Prinosil (Germany)

WOMEN

Singles

GOLD—Lindsay Davenport (Newport Beach, CA)

SILVER—Arantxa Sanchez Vicario (Spain)

BRONZE—Jana Novota (Czech Republic)

Doubles

GOLD—Gigi Fernandez (Aspen, CO) and Mary Joe Fernandez (Miami, FL)

SILVER—Jana Novotna and Helena Sukova (Czech Republic)

BRONZE—Arantxa Sanchez Vicario and Conchita Martinez (Spain)

Volleyball

MEN

GOLD—Netherlands: Peter Blange, Markus Broere, Frank Denkers, Guido Gortzen, Rob Grabert, Henk-Jan Held, Misha Latuhihin, Reinder Nummerdor, Jan Posthuma, Brecht Rodenburg, Richard Schuil, Johannes van der Horst, Robert van Es, Bas van de Goor, Mike van de Goor, Olaf van der Meulen, Ron Zwerver

SILVER—Italy: Lorenzo Bernardi, Vigor Bovolenta, Marco Bracci, Luca Cantagalli, Andrea Gardini, Andrea Giani, Pasquale Gravina, Marco Meoni, Samuele Papi, Andrea Sartoretti, Paolo Tofoli, Andrea Zorzi

BRONZE—Yugoslavia: Vladimir Batez, Slobodan Boskan, Dejan Brdovic, Dorde Duric, Andrija Geric, Nikola Grbic,

Vladimir Grbic, Rajko Jokanovic, Slobodan Kovac, Strahinja Kozic, Dula Mester, Zarko Petrovic, Vanja Prtenjaca, Edin Skoric, Zeljko Tanaskovic, Goran Vujevic, Igor Vusurovic

WOMEN

GOLD—Cuba: Taismari Aguero, Regla Bell, Magalys Carvajal, Marleny Costa, Ana Ibis Fernandez, Mirka Francia, Idalmis Gato, Lilia Izquierdo, Mireya Luis, Raiza O'Farrill, Yumilka Ruiz, Regla Torres

SILVER—China: Yongmei Cui, Qi He, Yawan Lai, Yan Li, Xiaoning Liu, Wenli Pan, Yue Sun, Lina Wang, Yi Wang, Ziling Wang, Yongmei Wu, Yunying Zhu

BRONZE—Brazil: Ana Ida Alivares, Leila Barros, Ericleia Filo Bodziak, Hilma Calderia, Ana Paula Connelly, Marcia Fu Cunha, Virna Dias, Ana Moser, Ana Flavia Sanglard, Heila Fofao Souza, Sandra Suruagy, Fernanda Venturini

Beach Volleyball

MEN

GOLD—Karch Kiraly (San Clemente, CA) and Kent Steffes (Pacific Palisades, CA)

SILVER—Mike Dodd (Manhattan Beach, CA) and Mike Whitmarsh (San Diego, CA)

BRONZE—John Child and Mark Heese (Canada)

WOMEN

GOLD—Jackie Silva and Sandra Pires (Brazil)

SILVER—Monica Rodrigues and Adriana Samuel (Brazil)

BRONZE—Natalie Cook and Kerri Pottharst Ann (Australia)

Water Polo

GOLD—Spain: Jose Maria Abarca, Angel Andreo, Daniel Ballart, Manuel Estiarte, Pedro Garcia, Salvador Gomez, Ivan Moro, Miguel Oca, Jorge Paya, Sergi Pedrerol, Jesus Rollan, Jordi Sans, Carlos Sanz

SILVER—Croatia: Maro Balic, Perica Bukic, Damir Glavan, Igor Hinic, Vjekoslav Kobescak, Josko Krěkovic, Ognjen Krzic, Dubravko Simenc, Sinisa Skolnekovic, Ratko Stritof, Tino Vegar, Renato Vrbicic, Zdeslav Vrdoljak

BRONZE—Italy: Alberto Angelini, Francesco Attolico, Fabio Bencivenga, Alessandro Bovo, Alessandro Calcaterra, Roberto Calcaterra, Marco Gerini, Alberto Ghibellini, Luca Giustolisi, Amedeo Pomilio, Francesco Postiglione, Carlo Silipo, Leonardo Sottani

Weightlifting

54kg (119 pounds)

GOLD—Halil Mutlu (Turkey)

SILVER—Zhang Xiangsen (China)

BRONZE—Sevdalin Minchev (Bulgaria)

59kg (130 pounds)

GOLD—Tang Ningsheng (China)

SILVER—Leonidas Sabanis (Greece)

BRONZE—Nikolay Pechalov (Bulgaria)

64kg (141 pounds)

GOLD—Naim Suleymanoglu (Turkey)

SILVER—Valerios Leonidis (Greece)

BRONZE—Xiao Jiangang (China)

70kg (154 pounds)

GOLD—Zhan Xugang (China)

SILVER—Kim Myong-nam (North Korea)

BRONZE—Attila Feri (Hungary)

76kg (167.5 pounds)

GOLD—Pablo Lara (Cuba)

SILVER—Yoto Yotov (Bulgaria)

BRONZE—Jon Chol (North Korea)

83kg (183 pounds)

GOLD—Pyrros Dimas (Greece)

SILVER—Marc Huster (Germany)

BRONZE—Anderzej Cofalik (Poland)

91kg (200.5 pounds)

GOLD—Aleksey Petrov (Russia)

SILVER—Leonidas Kokas (Greece)

BRONZE—Oliver Caruso (Germany)

99kg (218 pounds)

GOLD—Akakide Kakhiashvilis (Greece)

SILVER—Anatoli Khrapaty (Kazakstan)

BRONZE—Denis Gotfrid (Ukraine)

108 kg (238 pounds)

GOLD—Timur Taimazov (Ukraine)

SILVER—Sergey Syrtsov (Russia)

BRONZE—Nicu Vlad (Romania)

108kg-plus (238-plus pounds)

GOLD—Andrey Chemerkin (Russia)

SILVER—Ronny Weller (Germany)
BRONZE—Stefan Botev (Australia)

Wrestling

48kg (105.5 pounds) Freestyle

GOLD—Kim Il (North Korea)
SILVER—Armen Mkrttchian (Armenia)
BRONZE—Alexis Vila (Cuba)

52kg (114.5 pounds) Freestyle

GOLD—Valentin Jordanov (Bulgaria)
SILVER—Namik Abdullaev (Azerbaijan)
BRONZE—Maulen Mamirov (Kazakstan)

57kg (125.5 pounds) Freestyle

GOLD—Kendall Cross (Raleigh, NC)
SILVER—Giya Sissauori (Canada)
BRONZE—Ri Yong Sam (North Korea)

62kg (136.5 pounds) Freestyle

GOLD—Tom Brands (Iowa City, IA)
SILVER—Jang Jae-sung (South Korea)
BRONZE—Elbrus Tedeev (Ukraine)

68kg (149.5 pounds) Freestyle

GOLD—Vadim Bogiev (Russia)
SILVER—Townsend Saunders (Phoenix, AZ)
BRONZE—Zaza Zazirov (Ukraine)

74kg (163 pounds) Freestyle

GOLD—Bouvaisa Satiev (Russia)
SILVER—Park Jang-soon (South Korea)
BRONZE—Takuya Ota (Japan)

82kg (180.5 pounds) Freestyle

GOLD—Khadzhimurad Magomedov (Russia)
SILVER—Yang Hyun-Mo (South Korea)
BRONZE—Amir Reza Khadem (Iran)

90kg (198 pounds) Freestyle

GOLD—Rasul Khadem (Iran)
SILVER—Makharbek Khadartsev (Russia)
BRONZE—Eldari Kurtanidze (Georgia)

100kg (220 pounds) Freestyle

GOLD—Kurt Angle (Pittsburgh, PA)
SILVER—Abbas Jadidi (Iran)
BRONZE—Arawat Sabejew (Germany)

130kg (286 pounds) Freestyle

GOLD—Mahmut Demir (Turkey)
SILVER—Alexei Medvedev (Belarus)
BRONZE—Bruce Baumgartner (Cambridge Springs, PA)

48kg (105.5 pounds) Greco-Roman

GOLD—Sim Kwon-Ho (South Korea)
SILVER—Alexander Pavlov (Belarus)
BRONZE—Zafar Gulyov (Russia)

52kg (114.5 pounds) Greco-Roman

GOLD—Armen Nazaryan (Armenia)
SILVER—Brandon Paulson (Anoka, MN)
BRONZE—Andriy Kalashnikov (Ukraine)

57kg (125.5 pounds) Greco-Roman

GOLD—Yuri Melnichenko (Kazakhstan)
SILVER—Dennis Hall (Stevens Point, WI)
BRONZE—Sheng Zetian (China)

62kg (136.5 pounds) Greco-Roman

GOLD—Wlodzimierz Zawadzki (Poland)
SILVER—Juan Luis Maren (Cuba)
BRONZE—Mahmet Pirim (Turkey)

68kg (149.5 pounds) Greco-Roman

GOLD—Ryszard Wolny (Poland)
SILVER—Ghani Yolouz (France)
BRONZE—Alexander Tretyakov (Russia)

74kg (163 pounds) Greco-Roman

GOLD—Feliberto Ascuy (Cuba)
SILVER—Marko Asell (Finland)
BRONZE—Josef Tracz (Poland)

82kg (180.5 pounds) Greco-Roman

GOLD—Hamza Yerlikaya (Turkey)
SILVER—Thomas Zander (Germany)
BRONZE—Valery Tsilent (Belarus)

90kg (198 pounds) Greco–Roman

GOLD—Vyacheslav Oleynyk (Ukraine)
SILVER—Jacek Fafinski (Poland)
BRONZE—Maik Bullman (Germany)

100kg (220 pounds) Greco–Roman

GOLD—Andrzej Wronski (Poland)
SILVER—Sergei Lishtvan (Belarus)
BRONZE—Mikael Ljungberg (Sweden)

130kg (286 pounds) Greco–Roman

GOLD—Alexander Karelin (Russia)
SILVER—Matt Ghaffari (Colorado Springs, CO)
BRONZE—Sergei Moureiko (Moldova)

Yachting

MEN

Finn

GOLD—Mateusz Kusznierewicz (Poland)
SILVER—Sebastien Godefroid (Belgium)
BRONZE—Roy Heiner (Netherlands)

Mistral

GOLD—Nikolaos Kaklamanakis (Greece)
SILVER—Carlos Espinola (Argentina)
BRONZE—Gal Fridman (Israel)

470

GOLD—Yevhen Braslavets and Ihor Matviyenko (Ukraine)
SILVER—John Merricks and Ian Walker (Great Britain)
BRONZE—Vitor Rocha and Nuno Barreto (Portugal)

WOMEN

Europe

GOLD—Kristine Roug (Denmark)
SILVER—Margriet Matthijsse (Netherlands)
BRONZE—Courtenay Becker-Dey (The Dalles, OR)

Mistral

GOLD—Lee Lai-shan (Hong Kong)
SILVER—Barbara Kendall (New Zealand)
BRONZE—Alessandra Sensini (Italy)

470

GOLD—Theresa Zabell and Begona Via Dufresne (Spain)
SILVER—Yumiko Shige and Alicia Kinoshita (Japan)
BRONZE—Rusiana Taran and Olena Pakholchik (Ukraine)

OPEN

Laser

GOLD—Robert Scheidt (Brazil)
SILVER—Ben Ainslie (Great Britain)
BRONZE—Peer Moberg (Norway)

Soling

GOLD—Germany: Jochen Schuemann; Thomas Flach; and Bernd Jaekel
SILVER—Russia: Georgiy Shayduko; Dmitriy Shabanov; and Igor Skalin
BRONZE—United States: Jeff Madrigali (San Anselmo, CA); Jim Barton (Fairfax, CA); and Kent Massey (Santa Barbara, CA)

Star

GOLD—Torben Grael and Marcello Ferreira (Brazil)
SILVER—Hans Wallen and Bobby Lohse (Sweden)
BRONZE—Colin Beashel and David Giles (Australia)

Tornado

GOLD—Fernando Leon and Jose Luis Ballester (Spain)
SILVER—Mitch Booth and Andrew Landenberger (Australia)
BRONZE—Lars Grael and Kiko Pellicano (Brazil)

Appendix III

Appendix III

♦ Selecting A Historically Black College (by Deborah Jones)

So you're ready to apply to the school of your choice—or are you? Applying to a college or university can be a costly and time-consuming venture—but it does not have to be. If you do enough digging, you can eliminate illogical choices, and spend your time and money wisely.

The key is to honestly evaluate your interests, strengths, and needs. The best person to do this is yourself; nobody knows you better.

ASK YOURSELF THE TOUGH QUESTIONS

The first thing you'll want to do is ask yourself the following questions to pinpoint exactly which schools are in the running:

- Do I want a 2-year or a 4-year degree?

A 2-year—or associate's—degree is often a stepping stone to a 4-year—or bachelor's—degree. It's a good place to start if the field you plan to enter requires only an associate's degree or if you plan to earn a four-year degree, but need a firmer academic foundation before you are accepted into a four-year school. While a four-year bachelor's degree may be a bit more competitive in the job market, it requires more academic stamina and will cost you more money. Consider this when deciding whether you will attend a 2-year or 4-year school.

Talk with people who work in the professions you are interested in. Find out what kinds of people they want to hire, and what the academic requirements are for that field. Once you determine whether you will pursue a 2-year or 4-year degree, you will have eliminated a considerable number of schools from your search.

- Do I want to attend a school that is in-state or out-of-state?

Although this seems simple, it is a critical piece of information. Attending school in-state is often much less expensive than going out-of-state because schools tend to charge higher tuition to nonresidents. You'll also want to factor in the travel expenses you will incur going between home and school for breaks. If money is tight, you might want to limit your list of potential schools to in-state institutions. On the other hand, if your budget isn't so limited, then you might as well consider out-of-state institutions as well.

- Do I want to attend a small (2,500 or less), medium (2,500–8,000), large (8,000–15,000), or very large (more than 15,000) school?

If you don't mind the prospect of being in a class with more than 150 other people and perhaps never getting a chance to really have a chat with the instructor; if choosing from a wider range of course offerings and getting lost in a larger crowd is appealing, perhaps the larger institution is for you. On the other hand, if you feel you would thrive in an environment that would afford you more one-on-one attention, then a smaller school may be right for you.

- If I am attending school within-state, will I live at home and commute to school, or live on campus, away from home.

Again, if you are trying to go to college on the tightest budget, you should seriously consider commuting to a local college, if there is one that meets your needs. You could save yourself costly room and board expenses.

However, if you plan to commute from home, you need some mode of transportation in order to do so. Find out if you can reach your school of choice by public transportation or if you will need a car. Be sure to factor in the various expenses of running a car, including insurance, maintenance, and parking fees on campus.

THE TOUGHEST QUESTION: WHO AM I?

- What kind of degree am I interested in?

Once you have answered the broadest practical questions, listed above, and have targeted your search accordingly, ask yourself who you are. What do you hope to accomplish with your degree? Although you probably won't know exactly what you want to do with your life just yet, you should have a fair understanding of what you enjoy and what you do well, or at least what you want to do well. Focus your energy there and explore the careers related to your interests and talents.

Your high school counselor should be able to help you with this decision. Now is the time to take inventory of your extracurricular activities, and your special skills and talents. Ask for evidence of your strengths from sources such as standardized tests, academic records, and other data in your school's counseling office, such as the Holland Self-Directed Search or the World of Work section on the ACT.

- What special needs do I have?

If there are specific features that you require in a school, such as excellent handicapped services, a large fraternity/sorority network, a sprawling green campus, or an excellent pre-veterinary medicine program, eliminate the schools that do not qualify immediately. Ask yourself if there is a special need that you have, and decide if it is important enough to drive your decision.

Once you know which schools you are interested in, you need to know how to apply. Below are requirements and some tips for freshmen, transfer students, and international students on the application process.

PAPERWORK: PULLING THE PIECES TOGETHER

Freshman Students

What you need:

- graduation from an accredited high school or a passing grade on the General Education Diploma examination (GED)
- completed applications to the schools of your choice. You can get blank applications from your high school counselor or contact the prospective schools' admissions department.
- the nonrefundable application fees
- scores for either the Scholastic Aptitude Test (SAT) or the American College Testing Program (ACT)

Tips for Freshman Applicants

- You can begin applying to schools as early as the latter part of your junior year in high school. Sometimes, applying early will allow you a better chance at being admitted.
- Your high school academic preparation should be balanced, and should emphasize the five major academic areas, including English, history, mathematics, science, and foreign language.
- SAT or ACT scores are used both for admission and for placement counseling. Let these tests work for you.
- Once you're admitted, you might also need to submit the following: housing forms, physical examination forms, and proof of immunization.

Transfer Students

What You Need:

- potentially, all of the above items listed under "Freshman Students: What You Need"
- transcripts of all credit earned
- often, if student has attended another institution for less than one year, she or he must submit a high school transcript along with a college transcript

Tip for Transfers

- Upon acceptance, a transfer evaluator will assess previous college credits to be transferred. If you are dissatisfied with the evaluation, you may often request a review

International Students

What You Need:

- completed application
- proof that you have received 12 years of elementary and secondary education
- an English Proficiency Report, which should be completed by a person who can verify that you have the ability to speak English
- Teaching of English as a Foreign Language (TOEFL) scores (only if your native language is not English)
- nonrefundable application fee
- foreign student financial aid statements

LEVEL OF SELECTIVITY: EXACTLY HOW CHOOSY ARE THEY?

One of the most important pieces of information in making your decision is a college's level of selectivity. Be realistic about your qualifications and know which schools you are qualified for. To help you with this, *Black American Colleges and Universities* ranks the degree of competitiveness in the admissions' policy for each school profiled. Each school is ranked according to the number of requirements needed for admission which may include: minimum SAT or ACT scores, GED score or GPA; class rank; college preparatory units; high school recommendations; personal essay and statement of intent; and completion of 18 or more units. Competitive schools request four to six of the above requirements; moderately competitive schools require three to four; slightly competitive schools require two to three; and non-competitive schools ask for only one or two of the above requirements. Look for a handy breakdown of each school's level of selectivity and other key pieces of information, such as coed vs. single sex school and two-year vs. four-year, in the **Schools-at-a-Glance** section in this book. The chart will help you quickly identify key facts about schools of interest to you, and help you to narrow your search.

At some schools, conditional admissions are sometimes available to students who do not meet regular admission requirements. In this case, students are placed on probation for the first year while completing developmental courses to make up for deficiencies. Other admission policies include early admissions, early decision, advanced placement, and deferred entrance

A WORD ABOUT THE PERSONAL ESSAY

The best advice you can get when you are preparing to write an essay for college entry is this: know what the assignment is. Read the instructions on your applications and ask yourself the question "what are they asking me to do here?" Then, do it. And do it well. In some cases reviewing your instructions will leave more questions than answers for you. For example, you might be instructed to write a 1,000-word personal essay. If that is all the guidance you are given, then it is your job to fill in the details of your discussion. Review your acheivements, your academic and professional goals, and seize this opportunity to reveal to an admissions officer what is not evident on a college application, just what makes you unique, an asset to his or her school. You might start with what you discovered about yourself when you asked "the tough questions" in deciding what kind of a degree you were looking for.

Start by writing a quick draft of whatever first comes to mind, if only to have something to rewrite. Write several drafts, and try setting your complete draft aside for a day, then go back and refine it. Once you have all of your thoughts down, reread your essay to ensure that it flows from beginning, to middle, to end.

Technology is Your Friend

No matter what people tell you to the contrary, neatness counts. Unless the application stipulates that you handwrite it, type your essay, preferably on a word processor or computer so you can spell check it. Then proofread it again for those errors that only the human eye can detect. (Most software packages don't know enough to choose between to, too, and two for you.)

Lastly, ask someone—a professional writer, editor, or English teacher— to proofread it and give you their comments. It's better to know at this point—while it's still in your hands—if you have made some ugly grammatical snafu. While it is acceptable to get this type of technical advice on your essay, remember that this is your essay, and must be your work.

And while we're on the subject of outside help, a word of advice when you ask an adult to complete a teacher recommendation form or write a letter of recommendation: GIVE THEM AT LEAST TWO WEEKS' NOTICE. Even if the people you are asking to recommend you are not terribly busy, they will certainly appreciate your respect for their schedule. If they agree to write a letter on your behalf, send them a note of thanks after about a week. This will also serve as a tactful reminder to them of their commitment to you. And, if you want better letters of recommendation, do your letter-writers a favor by supplying them with a brief list of your achievements, special projects or activities, or anything that might help them write a more specific letter for you.

Finally, apply to more than one school; give yourself options. And, if you possibly can, make an effort to visit your prospective schools. If you call in advance you can even sit in on some relevant classes. Really explore the campus, and see if it feels like you.

♦ Funding Your College Education

You've lived through four years of high school, you've taken your SATs, you're about to embark on that great adventure called "college." So, again, you do your homework: you graze through college catalogs and you finally find "the one"—the perfect school for you. But how do you make it happen? Pursuing an education is a major investment of time, energy—and money.

According to a recent *Fortune* article, tuitions increased 9% annually during the 1980s and are expected to grow at an annual rate of 7% throughout the 1990s. What does this mean in real numbers? Well, according to national averages, a student entering college in the fall of 1993 will pay $77,000 for four years of tuition, room, and board at a private college; $36,000 for four years at a public university. Traditionally, tuitions at black colleges and universities are about half the national average, yet they are not immune to the average tuition hikes. For example, at Stillman—a private four-year college—tuition, room, and board for 1990–91 was $5,404. For 1993–94, college costs rose to $7,214, an increase of 33%.

Don't panic! These figures aren't meant to discourage you, they are only offered to make you aware of the reality of college costs. Although the primary obligation for college expenses lies with the family, keep in mind that at most schools almost all students receive some sort of financial aid. In addition, a number of other options exist to make your financial road a little less rocky. The following chapter is designed to let you know of viable alternatives and to help you devise a feasible financial aid plan.

WHAT IS FINANCIAL AID?

You may be eligible to receive three types of financial aid:

- grants or scholarships (outright gifts that do not have to be repaid)
- loans (money that must be repaid at low interest after graduation or after leaving school)
- work-study programs/internships (employment opportunities that help defray tuition costs)

FINANCIAL NEED: AM I ELIGIBLE?

The majority of colleges receive financial aid from the federal and state government. The various grants, loans, and work opportunity funds are provided to assist those students demonstrating the greatest need. For financial aid, need is defined as the difference between the amount of money a family may be expected to contribute and the total cost of education. Financial need is expressed as an equation:

Cost of Education
– Expected Family Contribution
= Financial Need

While cost may vary from school to school, the expected family contribution generally does not, since it is derived through a national formula. (*See* the Estimated Family Contribution chart located at the end of this section.)

COST OF EDUCATION

The cost of education includes expenses that are reasonably related to education:

- Tuition and fees
- Room
- Board
- Books
- Supplies
- Transportation
- Personal Expenses

Cost may also include other expenses such as childcare for dependents; disability expenses not covered by other agencies; or participation in a program of study abroad. If you believe that you will incur extra expenses in order to attend college, write a letter explaining your circumstances to your college's financial aid officer.

HOW DO I APPLY?— IT ALL STARTS WITH THE CORRECT FORM!

First, contact your high school guidance counselor or the financial aid director of the college that you are interested in attending. He/she will make sure that you know exactly which forms to complete, and the dates by which these forms must be returned. Do not wait for an admissions decision to apply for financial aid. Start your search early.

To apply for federal aid, all students must complete the Free Application for Federal Student Aid (FAFSA). No fee is charged in accordance with filling out the FAFSA (see example on page 11).

To be considered for non-federal aid, you may be required to fill out the following, all of which require a fee for each college that you list on the application:

- Financial Aid Form of the College Scholarship Service (FAF) (see example on page 10)
- Family Financial Statement of the American College Testing Service (FFS)
- Application form of the Pennsylvania Higher Education Assistance Agency (PHEAA)

In addition to the above, you may be required to complete individual state scholarship or grant program applications. Some colleges may require a campus application as well.

Complete the forms as soon as possible after January 1. (You will be required to file financial aid forms for each year of college that you attend.) You may file your applications using estimated income figures in order to meet the application deadlines. The records that you will need from the previous year to complete your FAFSA are:

- W-2 forms; income tax forms for you, your parents, and your spouse, if married
- records of social security benefits, veteran benefits, and other nontaxable income
- bank statements
- business/farm records
- statements of trust funds, money market funds, stocks, bonds, certificates of deposit, and similar assets

Save all your records after you have completed the applications in case you have to prove that the information is correct. Keep a copy of the applications you are filing for your records. For additional information about federal student financial aid, call the Federal Student Aid Information Center at 800-4 FED AID.

Dependency Status

Income and asset information is used to determine eligibility for financial aid. The information you will be asked to provide is contingent on whether you are dependent or independent. If you are considered dependent, you must report your parent's income and assets, as well as your own. If you're independent, only your income and asset information (and that of your spouse) is needed. The definition of an independent student has changed.

You will be considered independent if you meet one of the following:

- you turn 24 by December 31 of the school year for which you are applying for financial aid (e.g., applying for aid for 1994–95, you must be born before January 1, 1970)
- veteran of U.S. Armed Forces
- graduate/professional student
- married
- orphan or ward of court
- have dependents other than a spouse

If you think you have some unusual circumstances that should be taken into consideration regarding your dependency status, contact your financial aid officer. Be prepared to document your case.

FEDERAL FINANCIAL AID PROGRAMS: WHAT IS AVAILABLE?

Federal Pell Grant

Depending on financial circumstances, undergraduate students from families with annual incomes of up to about $40,000 may qualify for a Pell Grant. For 1993-94, Pell Grants range from $400 to $2,300. Eligibility is based on financial need as determined by a national formula that takes into account total income; net assets, such as savings/checking accounts and real estate investments (not including your home); family size; and number of family members in college. Grant payments may be made for the period of time required to complete the first bachelor's degree.

FEDERAL CAMPUS-BASED PROGRAMS

The three programs listed below are called "campus-based" programs because they are administered by individual colleges. Availability of funding is different at each institution.

Federal Supplemental Educational Opportunity Grant (FSEOG)

The FSEOG is available for undergraduates with exceptional financial need. Priority is given to Pell Grant (*See* Federal Pell Grant above) recipients. The college determines award amounts based on the funds available at that college. Awards range from $100 to $4,000 and do not have to be repaid.

Federal Perkins Loan Program

Under the guidelines of the Perkins Loan Program, undergraduate students may borrow up to $3,000 per year for a total of no more than $15,000 for undergraduate programs; up to $4,000 per year for graduate study; and up to $30,000 total for all years of study. This loan is interest-free while the student is enrolled at least half-time. Eligibility is based on exceptional financial need and availability of funds at each college. Repayment of interest and principal begins six to nine months after the student is no longer enrolled at least half-time. The interest rate is fixed at 5%.

Federal Work-Study Program (FWS)

The FWS program provides job opportunities for undergraduate and graduate students to earn minimum wage or more. Eligibility is based on student's financial need. Students usually work 10 to 20 hours per week.

FEDERAL FAMILY EDUCATION LOAN PROGRAMS

Some banks, credit unions, or savings and loan associations offer low-interest education loans that are insured by the federal government. Forms may be obtained from your lender, your college, or your state guaranty agency. For a list of lenders in your state, contact your state guaranty agency.

Federal Stafford Student Loan (Subsidized)

As of July 1, 1993, the subsidized Stafford Student Loan limit for a new undergraduate student is $2,625 for the first year, $3,500 for the second, and $5,500 per academic year for the third through fifth years. Graduate students can borrow up to $8,500 a year. The total loan amount for undergraduate studies is $23,000. The total debt for graduate or professional study is $65,000, including any Federal Stafford Loans received as an undergraduate. The college certifies enrollment and loan eligibility on the loan application. Loans are subject to a origination fee and an insurance fee. The interest rate is variable and will change each year on July 1, but is capped at 9%. Repayment of interest and principal begins six months after the student is no longer enrolled at least half-time. Eligibility is based on need by completing the FAFSA.

Federal Stafford Student Loan (Unsubsidized)

The terms and conditions of the unsubsidized loan are the same as for the subsidized loan (above), except that: 1) interest on the loan is due while the student is in school or the interest can be deferred, and 2) loan limits cover the cost of education minus any aid received up to the limits of the subsidized Stafford Loan. Accrued interest may be paid against or added to the loan (capitalized) as agreed by the borrower and the lender.

Federal Supplemental Loans for Students (SLS)

Independent undergraduate students as of July 1, 1993, may borrow $4,000 per academic year for the first two years and $5,000 per academic year for the third through fifth years. The total loan amount for undergraduate studies is $23,000; for graduate students it is $10,000 per year with the total debt for graduate or professional study not to exceed $65,500 including Federal SLS loans made at the undergraduate level. An insurance fee of up to 3% and an origination fee of 5% are deducted from the amount borrowed. The interest rate on SLS loans is variable and will change each year on July 1—but is capped at 11%. Repayment begins within 60 days of receipt of the loan. Full-time undergraduate students may defer the principal but are responsible for the payment of interest while in school.

Federal Parent Loans for Undergraduate Students (PLUS)

Parents may borrow up to the cost of education, minus any other aid received, per academic year on behalf of each dependent student. Eligibility is not based on need. PLUS loans can be used to meet all or part of the calculated family contribution. For new borrowers, the interest rate is variable, with a 10% cap. The interest rate is recalculated on July 1 of each year. An insurance fee of up to 3% on the amount borrowed and an origination fee of 5% are deducted from the amount borrowed. Repayment begins within 60 days of receipt of the loan. A credit check is required for loans disbursed after July 1, 1993.

OTHER FEDERAL PROGRAMS

Military Service Scholarships

The Army, Air Force, and Navy offer Reserve Officer Training Corps (ROTC) Scholarships and Armed Forces Health Professions Scholarships. Contact the appropriate military service recruiting office for specific information and a directory of participating colleges.

National Science Scholars Program (NSSP)

This program awards funds to graduating high school seniors (or those who will obtain the equivalent of a certificate of graduation), who have demonstrated excellence and achievement in the physical, life, or computer sciences; mathematics; or engineering. The award is $5,000 per year for undergraduate study, or the cost of education, whichever is less, and is awarded to two students from each congressional district. For 1993-94, funding is expected to be $3,300. To obtain an application and additional information, contact your high school guidance counselor or your college's financial aid officer.

Office of Vocational and Educational Services for Individuals with Disabilities (VESID)

Disabled students pursuing higher education may be eligible for assistance through the State Office of Vocational and Educational Services for Individuals with Disabilities (VESID). Criteria and funding vary. Applications and eligibility requirements may be obtained at the local VESID office.

Paul Douglas Teacher Scholarship Program

This scholarship awards up to $5,000 per year for up to four years of full-time undergraduate study. To be eligible, students must be in the top 10% of their high school class or have high GED scores, and be matriculated in a degree program leading to certification in teaching. Students must teach two years for each year of aid received. To obtain an application and additional information contact your high school guidance counselor or your college's financial aid officer.

Robert C. Byrd Honors Scholarship Program

The Byrd Program was established to recognize students with outstanding academic achievement who show promise of continued excellence. Students may receive $1,500 a year for up to four years at a college. At least 10 scholarships are available per state. To obtain an application and additional information, contact your high school guidance counselor or your college's financial aid officer.

SAMPLE FREE APPLICATION FOR FEDERAL STUDENT AID

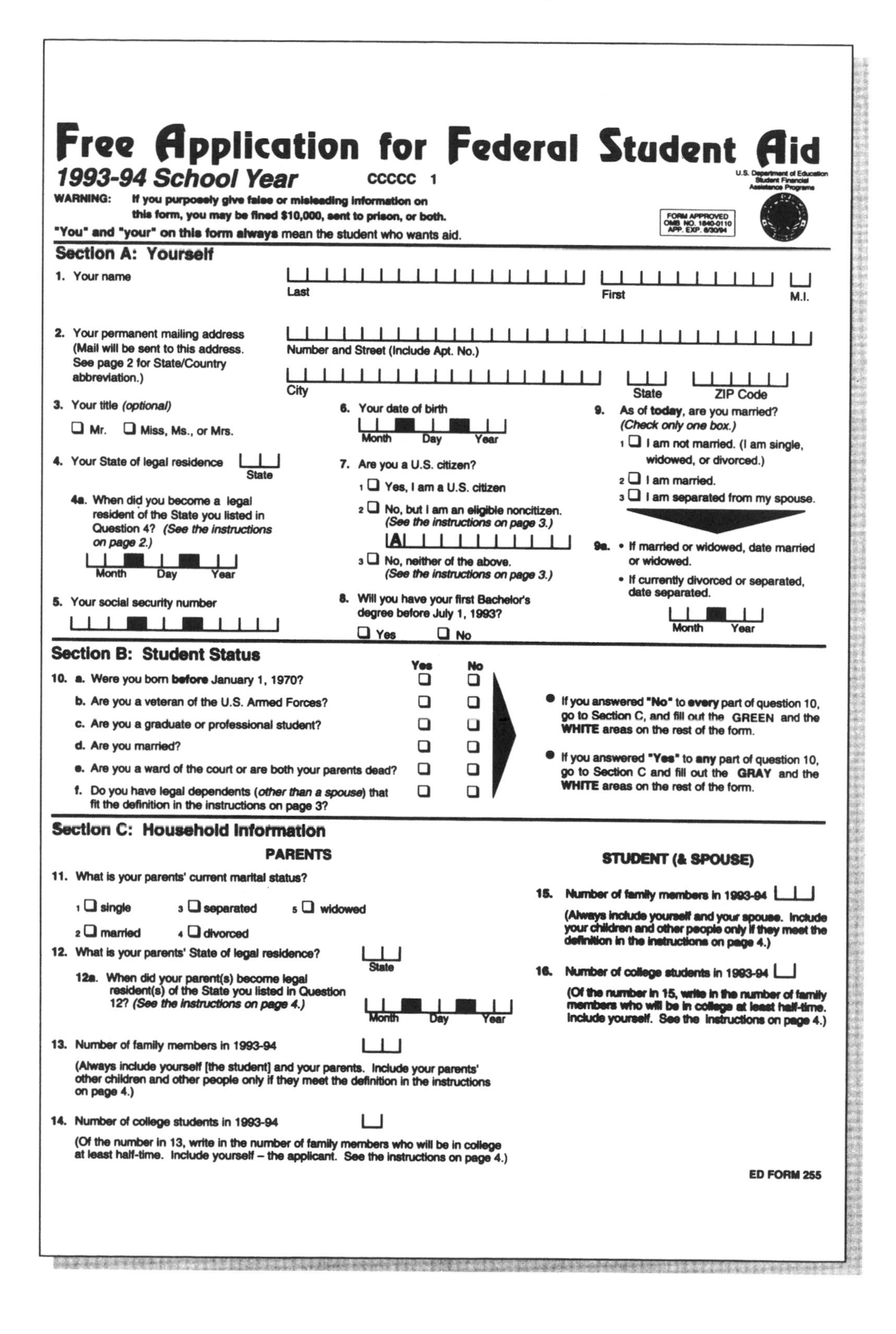

Free Application for Federal Student Aid

1993-94 School Year CCCCC 1

U.S. Department of Education Student Financial Assistance Programs

FORM APPROVED OMB NO. 1840-0110 APP. EXP. 6/30/94

WARNING: **If you purposely give false or misleading information on this form, you may be fined $10,000, sent to prison, or both.**

"You" and "your" on this form always mean the student who wants aid.

Section A: Yourself

1. Your name — Last / First / M.I.
2. Your permanent mailing address (Mail will be sent to this address. See page 2 for State/Country abbreviation.) — Number and Street (Include Apt. No.) / City / State / ZIP Code
3. Your title *(optional)* — ❑ Mr. ❑ Miss, Ms., or Mrs.
4. Your State of legal residence — State

4a. When did you become a legal resident of the State you listed in Question 4? *(See the instructions on page 2.)* — Month / Day / Year

5. Your social security number
6. Your date of birth — Month / Day / Year
7. Are you a U.S. citizen?
   1 ❑ Yes, I am a U.S. citizen
   2 ❑ No, but I am an eligible noncitizen. *(See the instructions on page 3.)* A
   3 ❑ No, neither of the above. *(See the instructions on page 3.)*
8. Will you have your first Bachelor's degree before July 1, 1993? ❑ Yes ❑ No
9. As of **today**, are you married? *(Check only one box.)*
   1 ❑ I am not married. (I am single, widowed, or divorced.)
   2 ❑ I am married.
   3 ❑ I am separated from my spouse.

9a. • If married or widowed, date married or widowed.
• If currently divorced or separated, date separated. — Month / Year

Section B: Student Status

	Yes	No
10. a. Were you born **before** January 1, 1970?	❑	❑
b. Are you a veteran of the U.S. Armed Forces?	❑	❑
c. Are you a graduate or professional student?	❑	❑
d. Are you married?	❑	❑
e. Are you a ward of the court or are both your parents dead?	❑	❑
f. Do you have legal dependents (*other than a spouse*) that fit the definition in the instructions on page 3?	❑	❑

• If you answered **"No"** to **every** part of question 10, go to Section C, and fill out the **GREEN** and the **WHITE** areas on the rest of the form.

• If you answered **"Yes"** to **any** part of question 10, go to Section C and fill out the **GRAY** and the **WHITE** areas on the rest of the form.

Section C: Household Information

PARENTS

11. What is your parents' current marital status?
   1 ❑ single 3 ❑ separated 5 ❑ widowed
   2 ❑ married 4 ❑ divorced
12. What is your parents' State of legal residence? — State

12a. When did your parent(s) become legal resident(s) of the State you listed in Question 12? *(See the instructions on page 4.)* — Month / Day / Year

13. Number of family members in 1993-94
   (Always include yourself [the student] and your parents. Include your parents' other children and other people only if they meet the definition in the instructions on page 4.)
14. Number of college students in 1993-94
   (Of the number in 13, write in the number of family members who will be in college at least half-time. Include yourself – the applicant. See the instructions on page 4.)

STUDENT (& SPOUSE)

15. **Number of family members in 1993-94**
   (Always include yourself and your spouse. Include your children and other people only if they meet the definition in the instructions on page 4.)
16. **Number of college students in 1993-94**
   (Of the number in 15, write in the number of family members who will be in college at least half-time. Include yourself. See the instructions on page 4.)

ED FORM 255

SAMPLE FAF

FAF® Financial Aid Form — 1993-94

This form is not required to apply for Title IV federal student aid. However, information from the FAF is used by some colleges and private organizations to award their own financial aid funds. CSS charges students a fee to collect and report this information. By filling out this form, you are agreeing to pay the fee, which is calculated in question 44.

Section A — Student's Identification Information — Be sure to complete this section. Answer the questions the same way you answered them in Section A of the Free Application for Federal Student Aid (FAFSA).

1. **Your name** Last First M.I.
2. **Your permanent mailing address** (Mail will be sent to this address.) **Number, street, and apartment number** City State Zip Code
3. **Title** (optional) 1 ☐ Mr. 2 ☐ Miss, Ms., or Mrs.
4. **Your date of birth** Month Day Year
5. **Your social security number**

Section B — Student's Other Information

6. **If you are now in high school, give your high school 6-digit code number.**
7. **What year will you be in college in 1993-94?** (Mark only one box.)
   - 1 ☐ 1st (never previously attended college)
   - 2 ☐ 1st (previously attended college)
   - 3 ☐ 2nd
   - 4 ☐ 3rd
   - 5 ☐ 4th
   - 6 ☐ 5th or more undergraduate
   - 7 ☐ first-year graduate/professional (beyond a bachelor's degree)
   - 8 ☐ second-year graduate/professional
   - 9 ☐ third-year graduate/professional
   - 0 ☐ fourth-year or more graduate/ professional
8. a. **If you have previously attended any college or other postsecondary school, write in the total number of colleges and schools you have attended.**

   b. **List below the colleges (up to five) that you have attended. Begin with the college you attended most recently. Use the CSS code numbers from the list in the FAF instruction booklet. If more space is needed, use Section M.**

Name, city, and state of college	Period of attendance From (mo./yr.)	To (mo./yr.)	CSS Code Number

9. **During the 1993-94 school year, you want institutional financial aid** from Month Year through Month Year
10. **Mark your preference for institutional work and/or loan assistance.**
    - 1 ☐ Part-time job only
    - 2 ☐ Loan only
    - 3 ☐ Will accept both, but prefer loan
    - 4 ☐ Will accept both, but prefer job
    - 5 ☐ No preference
11. **If it is necessary to borrow money to pay for educational expenses, do you want to be considered for a Stafford Loan? (optional)** Yes ☐ 1 No ☐ 2

    (If you mark "Yes," your information may be sent to the loan agency within your state.)
12. a. **Your employer/occupation** ______

    b. **Employer's address** ______

    c. **Will you continue to work for this employer during the 1993-94 school year?** Yes ☐ 1 No ☐ 2
13. **If you have dependents other than a spouse, how many will be in each of the following age groups during 1993-94?** Ages 0-5 ☐ Ages 6-12 ☐ Ages 13+ ☐
14. **1992 child support paid by you** $ ______ .00

Section C — Student's Expected Summer/School-Year Income

	Summer 1993 3 months	School Year 1993-94 9 months
15. **Income earned from work by you**	$ ______ .00	$ ______ .00
16. **Income earned from work by spouse**	$ ______ .00	$ ______ .00
17. **Other taxable income**	$ ______ .00	$ ______ .00
18. **Nontaxable income and benefits**	$ ______ .00	$ ______ .00

Page 1

State Student Incentive Grant (SSIG)

These federal funds are allocated to states to encourage scholarship/grant assistance to college students who demonstrate need. Further information may be obtained from your high school guidance counselor or your college financial aid officer.

Veterans Educational Benefits

Eligible veterans and children or spouses of eligible deceased or service-connected disabled veterans may be able to receive aid for approved college study. Information and application forms are available at all Veterans Administration Offices.

INSTITUTIONAL GRANTS AND SCHOLARSHIPS

Thurgood Marshall Scholarship

The Thurgood Marshall Scholarship fund provides a four-year scholarship to one entering freshman at each of the 37 historically black public college and universities including the University of the District of Columbia and the University of the Virgin Islands. To qualify, students need a high school GPA of 3.0, and a SAT score of 1000 or a ACT score of 24 or more. Students must be recommended by their high school counselor as exceptional or exemplary in the creative or performing arts. Students should contact the Thurgood Marshall Coordinators at each of the 37 historically black public colleges and universities listed in Appendix IX of *BACU*.

United Negro College Fund (UNCF)

The United Negro College Fund program awards 300 scholarships through its 41 member schools. To be eligible students must attend one of the 41 UNCF schools listed in Appendix IV of *BACU* and must demonstrate financial need. UNCF scholarships range from $500 to $7,500 per year.

COVERING THE BASES

Don't limit your search for financial aid to the federal and state levels. Explore all your options. Many grants and scholarships are available through individual colleges and universities. Some are based on academic achievement; others could be based on creative talent or athletic ability. Contact the financial aid office at the colleges where you are applying to find out:

1. What institutional grants and scholarships are available?
2. What are the eligibility requirements?
3. What is the criteria for selection?
4. What are the range of awards?
5. How and when can I apply?

Not-So-Obvious Sources

- Companies that you or your parents are associated with may provide some type of assistance for pursuing post-secondary education.
- Contact local clubs, fraternal organizations (such as Elks, Kiwanas, etc.), and civic leagues. Community-based associations often have scholarships available.
- The local library or bookstore has myriad sourcebooks that provide information on locating funds for college.

Many private sector resources often go untapped because prospective students are simply not aware of them. All sources cited in the bibliography following this chapter are readily available at your local library.

FINAL NOTE

It is important to note that it is never too early to begin your search for financial aid. In fact, it is not uncommon to begin two years prior to entering your freshman year in college. The search for financial aid should be an aggressive one, and although it may be an arduous journey, it is one that definitely pays off in the long run.

ESTIMATED FAMILY CONTRIBUTION CHART

The following estimated family contribution chart provides an idea of what colleges expect families to contribute at various income levels. This is an estimate based on averages. The chart is also based on the following assumptions:

- Two-parent family
- Assets estimated at $20,000
- One family member in college

ESTIMATED FAMILY CONTRIBUTION FOR A DEPENDENT STUDENT FROM A TWO-PARENT FAMILY 1993-94

Total 1992 Family Income	Number of Family Members 3	4	5	6
$15,000	0	0	0	0
20,000	483	0	0	0
25,000	1,203	651	172	0
30,000	2,045	1,419	905	315
40,000	4,065	3,173	2,525	1,803
50,000	7,015	5,863	4,799	3,501
60,000	9,858	8,628	7,292	6,049
70,000	12,000	11,747	10,545	9,358
80,000	15,615	14,458	13,116	12,039
100,000	21,630	20,193	19,070	18,145

SCHOOLS-AT-A-GLANCE

UNIVERSITY OR COLLEGE NAME	TOTAL ENROLLMENT	4-YEAR, 2-YEAR OR PROFESSIONAL	COED OR SINGLE SEX
ALABAMA			
Alabama Agricultural & Mechanical University	5,215	four-year	coed
Alabama State University	5,490	four-year	coed
Bishop State Community College	2,144	two-year	coed
Concordia College	383	two-year	coed
J. F. Drake State Technical College	979	two-year	coed
Lawson State Community College	1,738	two-year	coed
Lomax-Hannon Junior College	60	two-year	coed
Miles College	751	four-year	coed
Oakwood College	1,334	four-year	coed
Selma University	287	four-year	coed
Stillman College	822	four-year	coed
Talladega College	615	four-year	coed
Trenholm State Technical College	704	two-year	coed
Tuskegee University	3,598	four-year	coed
ARKANSAS			
Arkansas Baptist College	291	four-year	coed
Philander Smith College	640	four-year	coed
Shorter College	120	two-year	coed
University of Arkansas at Pine Bluff	3,709	four-year	coed
CALIFORNIA			
Charles R. Drew University of Medicine & Science	140	four-year	coed
Compton Community College	5,700	two-year	coed
DELAWARE			
Delaware State University	2,882	four-year	coed
FLORIDA			
Bethune-Cookman College	2,301	four-year	coed

ESTIMATED TOTAL COST PER YEAR	INCOMING FRESHMAN AVERAGE GPA	STUDENT/ TEACHER RATIO	LEVEL OF SELECTIVITY
$4,675	2.41	19:1	slightly competitive
$4,333	2.49	21:1	noncompetitive
$1,730	n/a	15:1	noncompetitive
$6,362	n/a	28:1	noncompetitive
$1,825	n/a	n/a	noncompetitive
$1,550	n/a	20:1	noncompetitive
$3,974	n/a	18:1	noncompetitive
$7,150	n/a	18:1	noncompetitive
$10,940	2.81	12:1	noncompetitive
$6,265	n/a	11:1	noncompetitive
$8,064	n/a	15:1	noncompetitive
$7,444	n/a	13:1	slightly competitive
$2,029	n/a	16:1	noncompetitive
$10,655	2.7	13:1	slightly competitive
$4,715	n/a	14:1	noncompetitive
$5,660	n/a	16:1	noncompetitive
$4,081	n/a	5:1	noncompetitive
$3,885	n/a	19:1	slightly competitive
$15,739	n/a	20:1	competitive
$645	n/a	24:1	noncompetitive
$5,696	2.49	15:1	moderately competitive
$9,145	2.45	16:1	slightly competitive

SCHOOLS-AT-A-GLANCE

UNIVERSITY OR COLLEGE NAME	TOTAL ENROLLMENT	4-YEAR, 2-YEAR OR PROFESSIONAL	COED OR SINGLE SEX
FLORIDA			
Edward Waters College	634	four-year	coed
Florida Agricultural & Mechanical University	9,200	four-year	coed
Florida Memorial College	2,172	four-year	coed
GEORGIA			
Albany State College	3,106	four-year	coed
Clark Atlanta University	3,507	four-year	coed
Fort Valley State College	2,368	four-year	coed
Interdenominational Theological Center	383	three-year	coed
Morehouse College	2,992	three-year	all-male
Morehouse School of Medicine	140	four-year	coed
Morris Brown College	2,030	four-year	coed
Paine College	790	four-year	coed
Savannah State College	2,656	four-year	coed
Spelman College	1,906	four-year	all-female
ILLINOIS			
Chicago State University	8,648	four-year	coed
Kennedy-King College	3,137	two-year	coed
KENTUCKY			
Kentucky State University	2,500	four-year	coed
Simmons University Bible College	103	four-year	coed
LOUISIANA			
Dillard University	1,700	four-year	coed
Grambling State University	6,485	four-year	coed
Southern University and Agricultural & Mechanical University at Baton Rouge	8,941	four-year	coed
Southern University (New Orleans)	3,734	four-year	coed

ESTIMATED TOTAL COST PER YEAR	INCOMING FRESHMAN AVERAGE GPA	STUDENT/ TEACHER RATIO	LEVEL OF SELECTIVITY
$7,466	n/a	12:1	noncompetitive
$4,874	2.5	24:1	moderately competitive
$7,900	2.5	17:1	slightly competitive
$4,020	n/a	16:1	slightly competitive
$11,252	n/a	19:1	slightly competitive
$4,657	n/a	14:1	slightly competitive
$6,695	n/a	13:1	moderately competitive
$12,910	n/a	17:1	slightly competitive
$25,962	n/a	4:1	competitive
$11,298	2.5	13:1	slightly competitive
$8,707	2.66	12.8:1	noncompetitive
$4,375	n/a	22:1	slightly competitive
$12,571	3.0	16:1	moderately competitive
$1,528	2.39	30:1	slightly competitive
$1,653	n/a	19:1	noncompetitive
$4,702	n/a	13:1	slightly competitive
$1,345	n/a	n/a	noncompetitive
$9,815	2.5	15:1	slightly competitive
$5,037	n/a	21:1	noncompetitive
$4,747	n/a	17:1	noncompetitive
$2,090	n/a	19:1	noncompetitive

SCHOOLS-AT-A-GLANCE

UNIVERSITY OR COLLEGE NAME	TOTAL ENROLLMENT	4-YEAR, 2-YEAR OR PROFESSIONAL	COED OR SINGLE SEX
LOUISIANA			
Southern University (Shreveport)	1,067	two-year	coed
Xavier University of Louisiana	3,330	four-year	coed
MARYLAND			
Bowie State University	4,437	four-year	coed
Coppin State College	2,816	four-year	coed
Morgan State University	5,034	four-year	coed
Sojourner-Douglass College	441	four-year	coed
University of Maryland, Eastern Shore	2,100	four-year	coed
MASSACHUSETTS			
Roxbury Community College	1,800	two-year	coed
MICHIGAN			
Highland Park Community College	2,335	two-year	coed
Lewis College of Business	346	two-year	coed
Wayne County Community College	11,123	two-year	coed
MISSISSIPPI			
Alcorn State University	3,526	four-year	coed
Coahoma Community College	1,373	two-year	coed
Hinds Community College	934	two-year	coed
Jackson State University	6,203	four-year	coed
Mary Holmes Community College	745	two-year	coed
Mississippi Valley State University	1,691	four-year	coed
Rust College	1,129	four-year	coed
Tougaloo College	1,003	four-year	coed
MISSOURI			
Harris-Stowe State College	1,881	four-year	coed

ESTIMATED TOTAL COST PER YEAR	INCOMING FRESHMAN AVERAGE GPA	STUDENT/ TEACHER RATIO	LEVEL OF SELECTIVITY
$1,455	2.0	17:1	noncompetitive
$10,950	2.78	16:1	moderately competitive
$4,595	2.49	20:1	slightly competitive
$5,483	n/a	25:1	moderately competitive
$8,280	n/a	18:1	moderately competitive
$3,930	n/a	10:1	noncompetitive
$6,731	2.4	19:1	slightly competitive
$2,080	n/a	25:1	noncompetitive
$1,620	n/a	21:1	noncompetitive
$2,875	n/a	13:1	noncompetitive
$1,639	n/a	25:1	noncompetitive
$2,762	2.495	20:1	slightly competitive
$2,962	n/a	22:1	noncompetitive
$3,367	n/a	19:1	noncompetitive
$5,621	n/a	16:1	slightly competitive
$8,300	2.495	20:1	noncompetitive
$4,814	n/a	18:1	slightly competitive
$6,100	2.5	18:1	slightly competitive
$6,810	2.50	19:1	slightly competitive
$2,253	n/a	18:1	slightly competitive

SCHOOLS-AT-A-GLANCE

UNIVERSITY OR COLLEGE NAME	TOTAL ENROLLMENT	4-YEAR, 2-YEAR OR PROFESSIONAL	COED OR SINGLE SEX
MISSOURI			
Lincoln University (MO)	4,101	four-year	coed
NEW YORK			
LaGuardia Community College	9,000	two-year	coed
Medgar Evers College	4,400	four-year	coed
New York City Technical College	10,426	two-year	coed
NORTH CAROLINA			
Barber-Scotia College	708	four-year	coed
Bennett College	568	four-year	all-female
Elizabeth City State University	1,762	four-year	coed
Fayetteville State University	3,903	four-year	coed
Johnson C. Smith University	1,256	four-year	coed
Livingstone College	654	four-year	coed
North Carolina Agricultural & Technical State University	7,119	four-year	coed
North Carolina Central University	5,385	four-year	coed
Saint Augustine's College	1,900	four-year	coed
Shaw University	2,149	four-year	coed
Winston-Salem State University	2,655	four-year	coed
OHIO			
Central State University	3,913	four-year	coed
Cuyahoga Community College	6,200	two-year	coed
Wilberforce University	758	four-year	coed
OKLAHOMA			
Langston University	3,323	four-year	coed
PENNSYLVANIA			
Cheyney University of Pennsylvania	1,607	four-year	coed

ESTIMATED TOTAL COST PER YEAR	INCOMING FRESHMAN AVERAGE GPA	STUDENT/ TEACHER RATIO	LEVEL OF SELECTIVITY
$4,885	n/a	18:1	noncompetitive
$2,704	n/a	18:1	noncompetitive
$1,960	n/a	19:1	noncompetitive
$1,600	n/a	10:1	slightly competitive
$7,212	2.5	12:1	noncompetitive
$8,924	n/a	10:1	slightly competitive
$4,172	2.68	15:1	noncompetitive
$4,125	2.85	18:1	slightly competitive
$8,922	n/a	15:1	slightly competitive
$9,100	n/a	15:1	slightly competitive
$4,560	n/a	14:1	moderately competitive
$5,119	n/a	13.5:1	slightly competitive
$8,200	n/a	16:1	slightly competitive
$9,146	n/a	16:1	slightly competitive
$4,641	2.56	15:1	slightly competitive
$7,493	n/a	21:1	noncompetitive
$1,782	n/a	14:1	noncompetitive
$10,838	2.5	20:1	slightly competitive
$3,850	n/a	24:1	noncompetitive
$6,813	n/a	16:1	slightly competitive

SCHOOLS-AT-A-GLANCE

UNIVERSITY OR COLLEGE NAME	TOTAL ENROLLMENT	4-YEAR, 2-YEAR OR PROFESSIONAL	COED OR SINGLE SEX
PENNSYLVANIA			
Lincoln University of Pennsylvania	1,458	four-year	coed
SOUTH CAROLINA			
Allen University	223	four-year	coed
Benedict College	1,469	four-year	coed
Claflin College	900	four-year	coed
Clinton Junior College	200	two-year	coed
Denmark Technical College	725	two-year	coed
Morris College	792	four-year	coed
South Carolina State University	5,145	four-year	coed
Voorhees College	600	four-year	coed
TENNESSEE			
Fisk University	867	four-year	coed
Knoxville College	1,200	four-year	coed
Lane College	562	four-year	coed
LeMoyne-Owen College	1,297	four-year	coed
Meharry Medical College	867	professional	coed
Tennessee State University	7,500	four-year	coed
TEXAS			
Huston-Tillotson College	536	four-year	coed
Jarvis Christian College	592	four-year	coed
Paul Quinn College	517	four-year	coed
Prairie View Agricultural & Mechanical University	5,590	four-year	coed
Southwestern Christian College	244	four-year	coed
Texas College	400	four-year	coed
Texas Southern University	10,777	four-year	coed
Wiley College	406	four-year	coed

ESTIMATED TOTAL COST PER YEAR	INCOMING FRESHMAN AVERAGE GPA	STUDENT/ TEACHER RATIO	LEVEL OF SELECTIVITY
$6,702	2.50	15:1	moderately competitive
$8,902	n/a	12:1	noncompetitive
$7,776	n/a	17:1	slightly competitive
$7,260	n/a	14:1	moderately competitive
$3,710	n/a	17:1	noncompetitive
$3,914	n/a	16:1	noncompetitive
$7,170	n/a	14:1	noncompetitive
$5,411	2.50	19:1	slightly competitive
$6,628	n/a	15:1	moderately competitive
$9,415	n/a	14:1	slightly competitive
$8,595	n/a	n/a	noncompetitive
$7,460	n/a	14:1	slightly competitive
$6,825	n/a	18:1	noncompetitive
$15,906	n/a	6:1	competitive
$4,633	2.50	25:1	moderately competitive
$8,639	2.50	13:1	slightly competitive
$7,395	2.85	14:1	noncompetitive
$6,275	n/a	12:1	noncompetitive
$2,626	2.50	20:1	slightly competitive
$6,093	n/a	10:1	noncompetitive
$7,225	n/a	16:1	noncompetitive
$4,985	2.50	18:1	slightly competitive
$6,494	2.49	15:1	noncompetitive

SCHOOLS-AT-A-GLANCE

UNIVERSITY OR COLLEGE NAME	TOTAL ENROLLMENT	4-YEAR, 2-YEAR OR PROFESSIONAL	COED OR SINGLE SEX
VIRGIN ISLANDS			
University of the Virgin Islands	2,176	four-year	coed
VIRGINIA			
Hampton University	5,161	four-year	coed
Norfolk State University	8,624	four-year	coed
Saint Paul's College	750	four-year	coed
Virginia Seminary	40	four-year	coed
Virginia State University	4,585	four-year	coed
Virginia Union University	1,511	four-year	coed
WASHINGTON, DISTRICT OF COLUMBIA			
Howard University	11,222	four-year	coed
Howard University School of Law	380	three-year	coed
University of the District of Columbia	11,153	four-year	coed
WEST VIRGINIA			
Bluefield State College	2,907	four-year	coed
West Virginia State College	4,986	four-year	coed

ESTIMATED TOTAL COST PER YEAR	INCOMING FRESHMAN AVERAGE GPA	STUDENT/ TEACHER RATIO	LEVEL OF SELECTIVITY
$6,415	n/a	15:1	slightly competitive
$10,626	2.3	18:1	competitive
$6,655	n/a	22:1	noncompetitive
$9,218	n/a	17:1	slightly competitive
$5,145	n/a	n/a	noncompetitive
$8,749	n/a	18:1	noncompetitive
$10,152	2.3	16:1	slightly competitive
$11,300	n/a	15:1	competitive
$12,730	n/a	8:1	competitive
$1,589	n/a	10:1	noncompetitive
$2,351	2.5	25:1	noncompetitive
$2,906	2.0	21:1	slightly competitive

Bibliography

Compiled by Donald Franklin Joyce

Included in this selected bibliography are titles which were published between 1990 and 1992, reviewed favorably in the reviewing media, and judged to be significant contributions to the study of black history and culture in the United States and in Africa. The titles are arranged under two major divisions: "Africana" and "African Americana." Within these two divisions titles are arranged alphabetically by author under categories indicative of their subject matter.

◆ AFRICANA

Agriculture

Barnett, Tony, and Abbas Abdelkarim. *Sudan: The Gezira Scheme and Agricultural Transition.* London: Frank Cass, 1991.

Freeman, Donald B. *A City of Farmers: Informal Urban Agriculture in the Open Spaces of Nairobi, Kenya.* Montreal: McGill-Queen's University Press, 1991.

Gyllstrom, Bjorn. *State Administrative Rural Change: Agricultural Cooperatives in Rural Kenya.* New York: Routledge, 1991.

Kidane, Mengisteab. *Ethiopia: Failure of Land Reform and Agricultural Crisis.* Westport, CT: Greenwood Press, 1990.

Apartheid

Burman, Sandra, and Pamela Reynolds, eds. *Growing Up In a Divided Society.* With forewords by Archbishop Desmond Tutu and Robert Coles. Evanston, IL: Northwestern University Press, 1992.

Cohen, Robin, Yvonne G. Muthien, and Abebe Zegeye, eds. *Repression and Resistance: Inside Accounts of Apartheid.* London; New York: Hans Zell Publishers, 1990.

Davis, R. Hunt, ed. *Apartheid Unravels.* Gainesville, FL: University of Florida Presses, 1991.

Dumor, E.K. *Ghana, OAU and Southern Africa: An African Response to Apartheid.* Accra: Ghana University Press, 1991.

Ellis, Stephen. *Comrades Against Apartheid: The ANC and the South African Communist Party in Exile.* London: James Currey/Indiana University Press, 1992.

Ellman, Stephen. *In a Time of Trouble: Law and Liberty in South Africa's State of Emergency.* New York: Oxford University Press, 1992.

Giliomee, Herman, and Laurence Schlemmer. *From Apartheid to Nation-Building.* Capetown, S.A.: Oxford University Press, 1990.

Grundy, Kenneth. *South Africa: Domestic Crisis and Global Challenge.* Boulder, CO: Westview Press, 1991.

Heard, Anthony Hazlett. *The Cape of Storms: A Personal History of the Crisis in South Africa.* Fayetteville: University of Arkansas Press, 1990.

Holland, Heidi. *The Struggle: A History of the African National Congress.* New York: Braziller, 1990.

Hull, Richard W. *American Enterprise in South Africa: Historical Dimensions of Engagement and Disengagement.* New York: New York University Press, 1990.

Human Rights Watch. *The Killings of South Africa: The Role of the Security Forces and the Response of the State.* New York: Human Rights Watch, 1991.

Johns, Sheridan, and R. Hunt Davis, eds. *Mandela, Tambo and the African National Congress: The Struggle Against Apartheid, 1948-1990: A Documentary Survey.* New York: Oxford University Press, 1991.

Kalley, Jacqueline A. *South Africa Road to Change, 1987-1990.* Westport, CT: Greenwood Press, 1991.

Lemon, Anthony, ed. *Homes Apart: South Africa's Segregated Cities.* Bloomington: Indiana University Press, 1991.

Maasdorp, Gavin, and Alan Whiteside, eds. *Towards a Post-Apartheid Future: Political and Economic Relations in South Africa.* New York: St. Martin's Press, 1992.

Mallaby, Sebastian. *After Apartheid: The Future of South Africa.* New York: Times Books, 1992.

Moss, Rose. *Shouting at the Crocodile: Popo Molefe, Patrick Lekota, and the Freeing of South Africa.* Boston: Beacon Press, 1990. (Dist. by Farrar, Strauss, Giroux)

Price, Robert M. *The Apartheid State in Crisis: Political*

Transformation in South Africa, 1975-1990. New York: Oxford University Press, 1991.

Segal, Ronald. *The Black Diaspora: Five Centuries of the Black Experience Outside Africa.* New York: Farrar, Straus and Giroux, 1995.

Shepherd, George W., ed. *Effective Sanctions on South Africa: The Cutting Edge of Economic Intervention.* Westport, CT: Greenwood Press, 1991.

Sparks, Allister. *The Mind of South Africa.* New York: Knopf, 1990.

Spink, Kathryn. *Black Sash: The Beginning of a Bridge in South Africa.* With a foreword by Archbishop Desmond Tutu.

London: Methuen, 1991.

Art

Courtney-Clarke, Margaret. *African Canvas: The Art of West African Women.* New York: Rizzoli, 1990.

Okediji, Mayo, ed. *Principles of "Traditional" African Art.* Ile Ife: Bard Book, 1992 (Dist. by Avon).

Smithsonian Institution. Libraries. National Museum of African Art Branch. *Catalog of the Library of the National Museum of African Art Branch of the Smithsonian Library.* Boston: G.K. Hall, 1991.

Vogel, Susan. *Africa Explores: Twentieth Century African Art.* New York: The Center for African Art, 1991.

Williams College Museum of Art. *Assuming the Guise: African*

Masks Considered and Reconsidered. Williamstown, MA: Williams College Museum of Art, 1991.

Williamson, Sue. *Resistance Art in South Africa.* New York: St. Martin's Press, 1990.

Autobiography and Biography

Appiah, Joseph. *Joe Appiah: The Autobiography of an African Patriot.* New York: Praeger, 1990.

Bunche, Ralph Johnson. *An African American in South Africa: The Travel Notes of Ralph J. Bunche, 28 September 1937 - 1 January 1938.* Edited by Roger R. Edgar. Athens: Ohio University Press, 1992.

Gastrow, Shelagh, ed., *Who's Who in South African Politics.* 3rd ed., London: Hans Zell Publishers, 1990.

Glickman, Harvey, ed., *Political Leaders of Contemporary Africa South of the Sahara: A Biographical Dictionary.* Westport, CT: Greenwood Press, 1992.

Harris, Eddy L. *Native Stranger: A Black American's*

Journey into the Heart of Africa. New York: Simon & Schuster, 1992.

Isert, Paul Erdmann. *Letters on West Africa: Paul Erdmann Isert's Journey to Guinea and the Caribbean Islands in Columbia (1788).* Translated by Selena Axelrod Winsnes. New York: Oxford University Press, 1992.

Lockot, Hans Wilhelm. *The Mission: The Life, Reign and Character of Haile Selassie I.* New York: St. Martin's Press, 1990.

Mashinini, Emma. *Strikes Have Followed Me All My Life: A South African Autobiography.* New York: Routledge, 1991.

Meer, Fatima. *Higher Than Hope: The Authorized Biography of Nelson Mandela.* New York: Harper & Row, 1990.

Mendelsohn, Richard. *Sammy Marks: the Uncrowned King of the Transvaal.* Athens: Ohio University Press, 1991.

Modisan, Blake. *Blame Me on History.* New York: Simon & Schuster, 1990.

Nkrumah, Kwame. *Kwame Nkrumah: The Conakry Years: His Life and Letters.* Compiled by June Milne. New York: Zed Books, 1991. (Dist. by Humanities Press)

Rake, Alan. *Who's Who in Africa: Leaders for the 1990s.* Metuchen, NJ: Scarecrow, 1992.

Rodney, Walter. *Walter Rodney Speaks: The Making of an African Intellectual.* With introduction by Robert Hill. Foreword by Howard Dodson. Trenton, NJ: Africa World Press, 1990.

Vaillant, Janet G. *Black, French and African: A Life of Leopold Sedar Senghor.* Cambridge: Harvard University Press, 1990.

Vige, Randolph, ed. *A Gesture of Belong: Letters from Bessie Head, 1965-1979.* Portsmouth, NH: Heinemann, 1991.

Wiseman, John A. *Political Leaders in Black Africa: A Biographical Dictionary of the Major Politicians Since Independence.* Brookfield, VT: Gower Publishing Co., 1991.

Economics

Blumenfield, Jesmond. *Economic Interdependence in Southern Africa: From Conflict to Cooperation.* New York: Printer/St. Martin's Press, 1991.

Chole, Eschetu, ed. *Food Crisis in Africa: Policy and Management Issues.* New Delhi: Vikas Publishing House, 1990. (Dist. by Advent House)

Claessen, Henri J.M., and Pieter van de Velde, eds. *Early State Economies.* New Brunswick, NJ: Transaction Publishers, 1991.

Cock, Jacklyn, ed. *Going Green: People, Politics and the Environment in South Africa.* New York: Oxford University Press, 1991.

Crockcroft, Laurence. *Africa's Way: A Journey from the Past.* UK: Tauris, 1990. (Dist. by St. Martin's Press)

Crush, Jonathan, Alan Jeeves, and Donald Yudelman *Africa's Labor Empire: A History of Black Migrancy to the Gold Mines.* Boulder, CO: Westview Press/D. Philip, 1991.

Edington, J.A.S. *Rubber in West Africa.* Anaheim, CA: Collings, 1991.

Henige, David, and T.C. McCaskie, eds. *West African Economic and Social History: Studies in Memory of Marion Johnson.* Madison: African Studies Program, University of Wisconsin, 1990.

Hodd, Michael. *The Economies of Africa: Geography, Population, History, Stability, Performance, Forecasts.* Boston: G. K. Hall, 1991.

Mahjoub, Azzam, ed. *Adjustment or Delinking? The African Experience.* London: Zed Press, 1990. (Dist. by Humanities Press)

Martin, Matthew. *The Crumbling Facade of African Debt Negotiations: No Winners.* New York: St. Martin's Press, 1991.

Mingst, Karen A. *Politics and the African Development Bank.* Lexington: University of Kentucky Press, 1990.

Nyango'oro, Julius, and Timothy Shaw, eds. *Beyond Structural Adjustment in Africa: The Political Economy of Sustainable and Democratic Development.* New York: Praeger, 1992.

Okolo, Julius Emeka, and Stephen Wright, eds. *West African Regional Cooperation and Development.* Boulder, CO: Westview Press, 1990.

Peckett, James, and Hans Singer, eds. *Towards Economic Recovery in Sub-Saharan Africa: Essays in Honor of Robert Gardner.* New York: Routledge, 1991.

Pradervand, Pierre. *Listening to Africa: Developing Africa from the Grassroots.* New York: Praeger, 1990.

Pryor, Frederic L. *The Political Economy of Poverty, Equity and Growth: Malawi and Madagascar.* New York: Oxford University for the World Bank, 1990.

Rau, Bill. *From Feast to Famine: Official Cures and Grassroots Remedies to Africa's Food Crisis.* New York: Zed Books, 1991 (Dist. by Humanities Press).

Riddell, Roger C. *Manufacturing Africa: Performance and Prospects of Seven Countries in Sub-Saharan Africa.* Portsmouth, NH: Heinemann, 1990.

Sarhof, Joseph A. *Hydropower Development in West Africa: A Study in Resource Development.* New York: P. Lang, 1990.

Siddle, David, and Ken Swindell. *Rural Change in Tropical Africa: From Colonies to Nation-States.* Cambridge, MA: Basil Blackwell, 1990.

Stewart, Frances, ed. *Alternative Development Strategies in Sub-Saharan Africa.* New York: St. Martin's Press, 1992.

Education

King, Kenneth, ed., *Botswana: Education, Culture and Politics.* Edinburgh: University of Edinburgh Press, 1990.

Mungazi, Dickson A. *Colonial Education for Africana: George Starks in Zimbabwe.* Westport, CT: Praeger, 1991.

Njobe, M.W. *Education for Liberation.* Johannesburg: Skotaville, 1990.

Okeem, E.O., ed. *Education in Africa: Search for Realistic Alternatives.* London: Institute for African Alternatives, 1990.

Okunor, Shiame. *Politics, Misunderstandings, Misconceptions: The History of Colonial Universities.* New York: P. Lang, 1991.

Folklore and Folk Culture

Berry, Jack, comp. and trans. *West African Folktales.* Edited with introduction by Richard Spears. Evanston, IL: Northwestern University Press, 1991.

Gunter, Liz, and Mafika Gwala, eds. and trans., *Mushal: Zula*

Popular Praises. East Lansing: Michigan State University Press, 1991.

McDermott, Gerald. *Zomo the Rabbit: A Trickster Tale from West Africa.* San Diego: Harcourt Brace Jovanovich, 1992.

Mohindra, Kamlesh. *Folk Tales of West Africa.* New Delhi: Sterling Pubs., 1991. (Dist. by APT Books)

Njoku, John E. Eberegbulaum. *The Igbos of Nigeria: Ancient Rites, Changes and Survival.* Lewiston, NY: Edwin Mellen Press, 1990.

Schipper, Mineke. *Source of All Evil: African Proverbs and Sayings on Women.* Chicago: Ivan R. Dee, 1991.

Smith, Alexander McCall. *Children of Wax: African Folk Tales.* New York: Interlink Books, 1991.

Ugorji, Okechukwu K. *The Adventures of Torti: Tales from West Africa.* Trenton, NJ: Africa World Press, 1991.

General Reference

Asante, Molafi Keto *The Book of African Names.* Trenton, NJ: Africa World Press, 1991.

Blackhurst, Hector, comp. *Africa Bibliography 1989.* Manchester, UK: Manchester University Press,

1991. (Dist. by St. Martin's Press, Inc.)

Fredland, Richard. *A Guide to African International Organizations.* New York: Hans Sell Publishers, 1991.

Morrison, Donald George, Robert Cameron Mitchell, and John Naber Paden. *Black Africa: A Comparative Handbook.* 2nd ed., New York: Paragon House/Irvington, 1990.

Moss, Joyce, and George Wilson. *Peoples of the World: Africans South of the Sahara.* Detroit: Gale Research Inc., 1991.

Sarfoh, Joseph A. *Energy in the Development of West Africa: A Selected Annotated Bibliography.* New York: Greenwood Press, 1991.

Thurston, Anne. *Guide to Archives and Manuscripts Relating to Kenya and East Africa in the United Kingdom.* New York: Hans Zell Publishers, 1991.

Zell, Hans M. *The African Studies Companion: A Resources Guide and Directory.* Providence, NJ: Hans Zell Publishers, 1990.

Government and Politics

Bowman, Larry W. *Mauritius: Democracy and Development in the Indian Ocean.* Boulder, CO: Westview Press, 1991.

Charlick, Robert B. *Niger: Personal Rule and Survival in the Sahel.* Boulder, CO: Westview Press, 1991.

Clingman, Stephen, ed. *Regions and Repertoires: Topics in South African Politics and Culture.* Johannesburg: Raven Press, 1991. (Dist. by Ohio University Press.)

Clough, Marshall S. *Fighting Two Sides: Kenyan Chiefs and Politicians, 1918-1940.* Niwot, CO: University Press of Colorado, 1990.

Cowell, Alan. *Killing the Wizards: Wars of Power and Freedom from Zaire to South Africa.* New York: Simon & Schuster, 1992.

Deng, Frances M., and I. William Zartman, eds. *Conflict Resolution in Africa.* Washington: Brookings Institution, 1991.

Forrest, Joshua B. *Guinea-Bissau: Power, Conflict and Renewal in a West African Nation.* Boulder, CO: Westview Press, 1992.

Gambari, I.A. *Political and Comparative Dimensions of Regional Integration: The Case of ECOWAS.* New York: The Humanities Press, 1991.

Hanlon, Joseph. *Mozambique: Who Calls the Shots.* Bloomington: Indiana University Press, 1991.

Hansen, Holger Bernt, ed. *Changing Uganda: The Dilemmas of Structural Adjustment and Revolutionary Change.* Athens: Ohio University Press, 1991.

Henze, Paul B. *The Horn of Africa: From War to Peace.* New York: St. Martin's Press, 1991.

Herbst, Jeffrey. *State Politics in Zimbabwe.* Berkeley: University of California, 1990.

Hughes, Arnold, ed. *The Gambia: Studies in Society and Politics.* Birmingham, UK: University of Birmingham, Centre for African Studies, 1991.

Ingham, Kenneth. *Politics in Modern Africa: The Uneven Tribal Dimension.* New York: Routledge, 1990.

Johnson, Willard R. *West African Governments and Volunteer Development Organizations: Priorities for Partnerships.* Lanham, MD: University Press of America, 1990.

Khalid, Mansour. *The Government They Deserve: The Role of the Elite in Sudan's Political Evolution.* New York: Kegan Paul International, 1990.

Kriger, Norma J. *Zimbabwe's Guerrilla War: Peasant Voices.* New York: Cambridge University Press, 1991.

Machobane, L.B.B.J. *Government and Change in Lesotho, 1800-1966: A Study of Political Institutions.* New York: Macmillan, 1990.

Moss, Glenn, and Ingrid Obery, eds. and comps. *South Africa Contemporary Analysis.* London: Hans Zell Publishers, 1990.

Nyang'oro, Julius E., and Timothy M. Shaw, eds. *Beyond Structural Adjustment in Africa: The Political*

Economy of Sustainable and Democratic Development. New York: Praeger, 1992.

O'Brien, Donal B. Cruise, John Dunn, and Richard Rathbone, eds. *Contemporary West African States.* New York: Cambridge University Press, 1990.

Ogunsanwo, Alaba. *The Transformation of Nigeria: Scenarios and Metaphors.* Lagos: University of Lagos Press, 1991.

Reyna, Stephen P. *Wars Without End: The Political Economy of a Precolonial African State.* Hanover, NH: University Press of New England, 1990.

Riley, Eileen. *Major Political Events in South Africa, 1948-1990.* New York: Facts on File, 1991.

Schlosser, Dirk Berg, and Rainer Siegler. *Political Stability and Development: A Comparative Analysis of Kenya, Tanzania and Uganda.* Boulder, CO: Lynne Rienner, 1990.

Sklar, Richard L., and C. S. Whitaker. *African Politics and Problems in Development.* Boulder, CO: Lynne Rienner, 1991.

Tareke, Gebru. *Ethiopia, Power and Protest: Peasant Revolts in the Twentieth Century.* New York: Cambridge University Press, 1991.

Vines, Alex. *Renamo: Terrorism in Mozambique.* Bloomington: Indiana University Press, 1991.

Wunsch, James S., and Dele Olowu, eds. *The Failure of the Centralized State: Institutions and Self-Governance in Africa.* Boulder, CO: Westview Press, 1990.

Wylie, Diana. *A Little God: The Twilight of Patriarchy in a Southern Africa Chiefdom.* Hanover, NH: University Press of New England, 1990.

Health

Baron, Vida C. *African Power: Secrets of the Ancient Ibo Tribe.* San Diego, Barez Publishing Co., 1992.

Falala, Toyin, ed. *The Political Economy of Health in Africa.* Athens: Ohio University for International Studies/Ohio University Press, 1992.

King, Richard D. *African Origin of Biological Psychiatry.* Germantown, TN: Seymour-Smith, Inc., 1990.

Turner, Edith L.B., et al. *Experiencing Ritual: A New Interpretation of African Healing.* Philadelphia: University of Pennsylvania Press, 1992.

Williams, A. Olufemi. *AIDS: An African Perspective.* Boca Rotan, FL: CRC Press, 1992.

Wolff, James, et. al. *Beyond Clinic Walls, Case Studies in Community-Based Distribution.* West Hartford, CT: Kumarian Press, 1990.

History

Ayittey, George B.N. *Indigenous African Institutions.* Ardsley-on-Hudson, NY: Transnational Publishers, 1991.

Banbera, Tayiru. *A State of Intrigue: The Epic of Bamana Segu According to Tayiru Banbera.* Edited by David Conrad; transcribed and translated with the assistance of Soumaila Diakit'e. Oxford, UK: Oxford University Press, 1990.

Cammack, Diana. *The Rand at War, 1899-1902: The Witwatersrand and the Anglo-Boer War.* Berkeley: University of California Press, 1990.

Collelo, Thomas. *Angola: A Country Study* 3rd ed., Washington, DC: Government Printing Office, 1991.

Collins, Robert O. *Western African History.* New York: W. Wiener, 1990.

Crais, Clifton C. *White Supremacy and Black Resistance in Pre-Industrial South Africa: The Making of the Colonial Order in the Eastern Cape, 1770-1865.* Cambridge, UK: Cambridge University Press, 1992.

Digre, Brian. *Imperialism's New Clothes: The Repartition of Tropical Africa, 1914-1919.* New York: P. Lang, 1990.

Diop, Cheikh Anta. *Civilization or Barbarism: An Authentic Anthropology.* Translated by Yaa-Lengi Meema Ngemi; edited by Harold J. Salemson and Marjolijn de Jager. Brooklyn: Lawrence Hill Books, 1991.

Echenberg, Myron J. *Colonial Conscripts: The Tirailleurs S'en'egalais in French West Africa, 1857-1960.* Portsmouth, NH: Heinemann, 1991.

Friedman, Kajsa Ekholm. *Catastrophe and Creation: The Transformation of an African Culture.* Philadelphia: Hardwood Academic Publishers, 1991.

Gann, L.H., and Pete Duignan. *Hope for Africa.* Stanford, CA: Stanford University Press, 1991.

Gordon, April, ed. *Understanding Contemporary Africa.* Boulder, CO: Lynne Reinner Publishers, 1992.

Hair, P.E.H. *Black Africa in Time Perspective: Four Talks on Wide Historical Themes.* Liverpool, UK: Liverpool University Press, 1990. (Dist. by University of Pennsylvania Press).

Hair, P.E.H. *English Seamen and Traders in Guinea, 1553-1565: The New Evidence of their Wills.* Lewiston, NY: E. Mellen Press, 1992.

Hansen, Emmanuel. *Ghana Under Rawlings: Early Years.* Lagos: Malthouse Press, 1991.

Hassen, Mohammed. *The Oromo of Ethiopia: A History.* New York: Cambridge University Press, 1990.

Hudson, Peter. *Two Rivers: In the Footsteps of Mungo Park.* London: Chapmans Publishers, 1991.

Human Rights Watch. *Evil Days: Thirty Years of War and Famine in Ethiopia.* New York: Human Rights Watch, 1990.

Ki-Zerbo, J., ed.UNESCO General History of Africa, Vol. 1: Methodology and African Prehistory. Berkeley: University of California Press, 1990.

Lamphear, John. *The Scattering Time: Turkans Responses to Colonial Time.* New York: Oxford University Press, 1992.

Law, Robin. *The Slave Coast of West Africa, 1550-1750: The Impact of the Atlantic Slave Trade on African Society.* New York: Oxford University Press, 1991.

Manning, Patrick. *Slavery and African Life: Occidental, Oriental and African Slave Trades.* New York: Cambridge University Press, 1990.

Metaferia, Getchew. *The Ethiopian Revolution of 1974 and the Exodus of Ethiopia's Trained Human Resources.* Lewiston, NY: Edwin Mellen Press, 1991.

Mokhtar, G., ed. *UNESCO General History of Africa, Vol. II: Ancient History of Africa.* Berkeley: University of California Press, 1990.

Mooncraft, Paul L. *African Nemesis: War and Revolution in Southern Africa (1945-2010).* Riverside, NJ: Pergamon Press, 1990.

Morton, Fred. *Children of Ham: Freed Slaves and Fugitive Slaves on the Kenya Coast, 1873-1907.* Boulder, CO: Westview, 1990.

Mostert, Noel. *Frontiers: The Epic of South Africa's Creation and the Tragedy of the Xhosa People.* New York: Knopf, 1992.

Munford, Clarence J. *The Black Ordeal of Slavery and Slave Trading in the French West Indies, 1625-1715.* Lewiston, NY: Edwin Mellen Press, 1991.

Nasson, Bill. *Abraham Esau's War: A Black South African War in the Cape, 1899-1902.* New York: Cambridge University Press, 1991.

Obasanjo, Olusegun, and Hans d'Orville, eds. *The Impact of Europe in 1992 on West Africa.* New York: C. Russak, 1990.

Ochieng, William, ed. *Themes in Kenyan History.* Nairobi: Heinmann Kenya, 1990.

Ogot, B.A., ed. *Africa from the Sixteenth to the Eighteenth Century.* Berkeley: University of California Press, 1992.

Remmer, Douglas, ed. *Africa Thirty Years Ago.* Portsmouth, NH: Heinemann, 1991.

Shillington, Kevin. *History of Africa.* New York: St. Martin's Press, 1990.

Solow, Barbara L., ed. *Slavery and the Rise of the Atlantic System.* Cambridge, UK; New York: Cambridge University Press, 1991.

Stauton, Irene, comp. and ed. *Mothers of the Revolution: The War Experiences of Thirty Zimbabwean Women.* Bloomington: Indiana University Press, 1991.

Stedman, Stephen John. *Peacemaking in the Civil War: International Mediation in Zimbabwe, 1974-1980.* Boulder, CO: Lynne Rienner, 1991.

Temperley, Howard. *White Dreams, Black Africa: The Anti-Slavery Expedition to the River Niger, 1841-42.* New Haven: Yale University Press, 1991.

Thompson, Leonard. *A History of South Africa.* New Haven: Yale University Press, 1990.

Wyse, Akintola J.G., and H.C. Bankhole-Bight. *Politics in Colonial Sierra Leone, 1919-1958.* New York:Cambridge University Press, 1991.

Yarak, Larry W. *Asante and the Dutch, 1744-1873.* New York: Oxford University Press, 1990.

Young, John. *They Fell Like Stones: Battles and Casualties of the Zulu War, 1879.* Novato, CA: Presidio Press, 1991.

International Relations

Kent, John. *The Internationalization of Colonialism: Britain, France and Black Africa.* New York: Oxford University Press, 1992.

Russell, Sharon Stanton, Karen Jacobsen, and William Deane Stanley. *International Migration and Development in Sub-Sahara Africa.* Washington, DC: The World Bank, 1991.

Thompson, Joseph E. *American Policy and African Famine: The Nigeria-Biafra War, 1966-1970.* New York: Greenwood Press, 1970.

Winros, Gareth M. *The Foreign Policy of GDR in Africa.* Cambridge, UK: Cambridge University Press, 1991.

Language and Literature

Abraham, Cecils ed. *The Tragic Life: Bessie Head and Literature in South Africa.* Trenton, NJ: Africa World Press, 1990.

Achebe, Chinua. *Hopes and Impediments: Selected Essays.* New York: Doubleday, 1990.

Bjornson, Richard. *The African Quest for Freedom and Identity: Cameroonian Writing and the National Experience.* Bloomington: Indiana University Press, 1991.

Dram'e, Kandioura. *The Novel as Transformation Myth: A Study of the Novels of Mongo Beti and Ngugi wa Thiongo.* Syracuse, NY: Syracuse University, 1990.

Dunton, Chris. *Make Man Talk True: Nigerian Drama in English Since 1970.* New York: Hans Zell Publishers, 1992.

Elimimian, Isaac Iraber. *Theme and Style in African Poetry.* Lewiston, NY: E. Mellen, 1991.

February, V.A. *Mind Your Colour: The Coloured Stereotype in South African Literature.* London and New York: Kegan Paul International, 1991. (Dist. by Routledge, Chapman & Hall, Inc.).

Gikandi, Simon. *Reading Chinua Achebe: Language and Ideology in Fiction.* Portsmouth, NH: Heinemann, 1991.

Gunner, Liz, ed., and trans. *Musho!: Zulu Popular Praises.* East Lansing: Michigan State University Press, 1991.

Hale, Thomas A. *Scribe, Griot and Novelist: Narrative Interpreters of the Songhay Empire Followed by the Epic of Askia Mohammed Recounted,* Gainesville, FL: University of Florida Press/Center for African Studies, 1990.

Harrow, Kenneth, ed., *Faces of Islam in African Literature.* Portsmouth, NH: Heinemann, 1991.

Harrow, Kenneth, Jonathan Ngate, and Clarissa Zimra, eds. *Crisscrossing Boundaries in African Literatures, 1986.* Washington, DC: Three Continents Press/African Literature

Association, 1991.

Ikonne, Chidi, Emelia Oko, and Peter Onwudinjo, eds. *African Literature and African Historical Experience.* New York: Heinemann, 1991.

Innes, Catherine Lynette. *Chinua Achebe.* New York: Cambridge University Press, 1990.

Innes, Catherine Lynette. *The Devil's Own Mirror: The Irishman and the African Modern Literature.* Washington, DC: Three Continents Press, 1990.

James, Adeola, ed., *In Their Own Voices: African Women Writers Talk.* Portsmouth, NH: Heinemann, 1990.

Jones, Eldred Durosimi, ed. *The Question of Language in African Literature Today: Borrowing and Carrying: A Review.* Trenton, NJ: Africa World Press, 1991.

Julien, Eileen. *African Novels and the Question of Orality.* Bloomington: Indiana University Press, 1992.

Lazarus, Neil. *Resistance in Postcolonial African Fiction.* New Haven, CT: Yale University Press, 1991.

Lindfors, Bernth. *Popular Literature in Africa.* Trenton, NJ: Africa World Press, 1991.

Liyong, Taban Lo. *Another Last Word.* New York: Heinemann, 1990.

Miller, Christopher L. *Theories of Africans: Franco-Phone Literature and Anthropology in Africa.* Chicago: University of Chicago Press, 1990.

Mortimer, Mildred. *Journey Through the French African Novel.* Portsmouth, NH: Heinemann, 1990.

Nethersole, Reingard, ed. *Emerging Literature.* New York: P. Lang, 1990.

Ngara, Emmanuel. *Ideology and Form in African Poetry: Implications for Communication.* Portsmouth, NH: Heinemann, 1990.

Obiechina, Emmanuel N. *Language and Theme: Essays on African Literature.* Washington, DC: Howard University Press, 1990.

Orisawayi, Dele, et. al., eds. *Literature and Black Aesthetics.* New York: Heinemann, 1990.

Owomoyela, Onjekan. *Visions and Revisions: Essays on African Literatures and Criticisms.* New York: P. Lang, 1991.

Research in African Literatures: Critical Theory and African Literature. Bloomington: Indiana University Press, 1990.

Research in African Literature: Dictatorship and Oppression. Bloomington: Indiana University Press, 1990.

Roscoe, Adrian A., and Hangson Msika. *The Quiet Chameleon: Modern Poetry from Central Africa.* New York: Hans Zell Publishers, 1992.

Scheub, Harold. *The African Storyteller: Stories from African Oral Traditions.* Dubuque, IA: Kendell/Hunt, 1991.

Schipper, Mineke. *Beyond the Boundaries: Text and Context in African Literature.* Chicago: Ivan R. Dee, 1990.

Sicherman, Carol. *Ngugi wa Thiong: A Source Book on Kenyan Literature and Resistance.* New York: Hans Zell Publishers, 1990.

Soyinka, Wole. *Myth, Literature, and the African World.* New York: Cambridge University Press, 1990.

Trump, Martin, ed. *Rendering Things Visible: Essays on South African Literary Culture.* Athens: Ohio University Press, 1991.

Wilentz, Gay Alden. *Binding Cultures: Black Women Writers in Africa and the Diaspora.* Bloomington: Indiana University Press, 1992.

Wylie, Hal, Dennis Brutus, and Juris Silenieks, eds. *African Literature, 1988: New Masks.* Washington, DC: Three Continents Press/The African Literature Association, 1990.

Law, Law Enforcement, Civil and Human Rights

Ahire, Philip Terdo. *Imperial Policing: The Emergence and Role of the Police in Nigeria, 1860-1960.* Philadelphia: Open University Press, 1991.

Bazille, Susan, ed. *Putting Women on the Agenda.* Johannesburg, S.A.: Raven Press, 1991. (Dist. by Ohio University Press).

Braham, Peter, ed. *Racism and Antiracism: Inequalities in Opportunities and Policies.* Philadelphia: Sage/ Open University Press, 1992.

Hansson, Desiree, and Dirk van Zyl Smit, eds. *Toward Justice? Crime and State Control in South Africa.* New York: Oxford University Press, 1990.

Mann, Kristin, ed. *Law in Colonial Africa.* Portsmouth, NH: Heinemann, 1991.

Shepherd, George W., and Mark O.G. Anikpo, eds. *Emerging Human Rights: The African Political Economy Concept.* Westport, CT: Greenwood Press, 1990.

Media

Faringer, Gunilla L. *Press Freedom in Africa.* Westport, CT: Praeger, 1991.

Harden, Blaine. *Africa: Dispatches from a Fragile Continent.* London: Harper Collins, 1990.

Hawk, Beverly G., ed. *Africa's Media Image.* New York: Praeger, 1992.

Sturges, Paul, and Richard Neill. *The Quiet Struggle: Libraries and Information for Africa.* New York: Mansell, 1990.

Music

Arom, Simha. *African Polyphony and Polyrhythm: Musical Structure and Methodology.* Translated by Martin Thom and Barbara Tucker. New York: Cambridge University Press, 1991.

Bender, Wolfgang. *Sweet Mother: Modern African Music.* Translated by Wolfgang Freis. Chicago: University of Chicago Press, 1991.

Collins, John. *West African Pop Roots.* Philadelphia: Temple University Press, 1992.

Gray, John. *African Music: A Bibliographic Guide to the Traditional Popular Art and Liturgical Music of Sub-Saharan Africa.* Westport, CT: Greenwood Press, 1991.

Lems-Dworkin, Carol. *African Music: A Pan-African Annotated Bibliography.* New York: Hans Zell Publishers, 1991.

Stewart, Gary. *Breakout: Profiles in African Rhythm.* Chicago: University of Chicago Press, 1992.

Waterman, Christopher Alan. *Juju: A Social History and Ethnography of an African Popular Music.* Chicago: University of Chicago Press, 1990.

Pan-Africanism

Agyeman, Opoku. *Nkrumah's Ghana and Esat Africa: Pan-Africanism and African Interstate Relations.* Cranbury, NJ: Fairleigh Dickinson University Press, 1992.

Clarke, John H. *Africans at the Crossroads: Notes for an African World Revolution.* Trenton, NJ: Africa World Press, 1992.

Staniland, Martin. *American Intellectuals and African Nationalists, 1950-1970.* New Haven: Yale University Press, 1991.

Performing Arts

Diawara, Manthia. *African Cinema: Politics and Culture.* Bloomington: Indiana University Press, 1992.

Erlman, Veit. *African Stars: Studies in Black South African Performance.* Chicago: University of Chicago Press, 1991.

Lee, Jacques K. *Sega: The Mauritius Folk Dance.* London: Nautilus Publishing Co., 1990.

Orkin, Martin. *Drama and the South African State.* Manchester, UK: Manchester University Press, 1991. (Dist. by St. Martin's Press)

Religion and Philosophy

Dankwa, Nano O., III. *Christianity and African Traditional Beliefs.* Edited by John W. Branch. New York: Power of the World Publishing Co., 1990.

Felder, Cain Hope, ed. *Stony the Road We Trod: African American Biblical Interpretation.* Minneapolis: Fortress Press, 1991.

Gbadegesin, Segun. *African Philosophy: Traditional Yoruba Philosophy and Contemporary African Realities.* New York: Lang, 1991.

Gifford, Paul. *The New Crusaders: Christianity and the New Right in Southern Africa.* London: Pluto, 1991.

Gray, Richard. *Black Christians and White Missionaries.* New Haven: Yale University Press, 1991.

Oldfield, J.R. *Alexander Crummell (1819-1898) and the Creation of an African-American Church in Africa.* Lewiston, NY: Edwin Mellin Press, 1990.

Olupona, Jacob K. *African Traditional Religions in Contemporary Society.* New York: Paragon, 1991.

Oruka, H. O. *Trends in Contemporary African Philosophy.* Nairobi, Kenya: Shirikon Publishers, 1990.

Peek, Philip M., ed. *African Divination Systems: Ways of Knowing.* Bloomington: Indiana University Press, 1991.

Prozesky, Martin, ed. *Christianity Amidst Apartheid* New York: London, Macmillan, 1990.

Soyinka, Wole. *The Credo of Being and Nothingness.* Ibadan: Spectrum Books, 1990.

Vanderaa, Larry A. *A Survey of Christian Reformed World Missions and Churches in West Africa.* Grand Rapids, MI: Christian Reformed World Missions, 1991.

Sociology and Psychology

Barnes, James Franklin. *Gabon: Beyond the Colonial Legacy.* Boulder, CO: Westview Press, 1992.

Bell, Leland V. *Mental and Social Disorder in Sub-Saharan Africa: The Case of Sierra Leone, 1787-1990.* Westport, CT: Greenwood Press, 1991.

Carr-Hill, Roy A. *Social Conditions in Sub-Saharan Africa.* London; New York: Macmillan, 1991.

Cleaver, Tessa, and Marion Wallace. *Namibia: Women in War.* Foreword by Glenys Kinnock. Atlantic Highlands, NJ: Zed Books, 1990.

Cobley, Alan Gregord. *Class and Consciousness: The Black Petty Bourgeoisie in South Africa, 1924-1950.* Westport, CT: Greenwood Press, 1990.

Coles, Catherine, and Beverly Mack, eds. *Hausa Women in the Twentieth Century.* Madison: University of Wisconsin Press, 1991.

Gordon, Robert J. *The Bushman Myth: The Making of a Nambian Underclass.* Boulder, CO: Westview Press, 1992.

Hill, Martin J.D., ed. *The Harambee Movement in Kenya: Self-Help Development and Education Among the Kamba of Chat District.* Atlantic Highlands, NJ: Athlone Press, 1991.

Kilbride, Philip Leroy. *Changing Family Life in East Africa: Women and Children at Risk,* Philadelphia: Pennsylvania State University Press, 1990.

Mohammad, Duri, ed., *Social Development in Africa: Strategies, Policies and Programmes After the Lagos Plan.* Providence, NJ: H. Zell Publishers, 1991.

Moran, Mary. *Civilized Women: Gender and Prestige in Southeastern Liberia.* Ithaca, NY: Cornell University Press, 1991.

Nsamenang, A. Bame. *Human Development in Cultural Conflict.* Foreword by Michael Lamb. Newbury Park, CA: Sage Publications, 1992.

Ominde, S. H., ed. *Kenya' s Population Growth and Development to the Year 2000.* Columbus: Ohio University Press, 1990.

Reynolds, Pamela. *Dance Cat: Child Labour in the Zambezi Valley.* London: Hans Zell Books, 1991.

Riseman, Paul. *First Find Your Child A Good Mother: The Construction of Self in Two African Communities.* New Brunswick, NJ: Rutgers University Press, 1992.

Robertson, Struan. *The Cold Choice: Pictures of a South African Reality.* Grand Rapids, MI: Wm. B. Erdmans Publishing Co., 1992.

◆ AFRICAN AMERICANA

Art, Architecture, and Photography

Bearden, Romare. *Memory and Metaphor: The Art of Romare Bearden, 1940-1987.* New York: Studio Museum of Harlem/Oxford University Press, 1991.

Durham, Michael S. *Powerful Days: The Civil Rights Photography of Charles Moore.* Introduction by Andrew Young. New York: Stewart, Tabori & Chang, 1991.

Easter, Eric, D. Michael Cheers, and Dudley M. Brooks, eds. *Songs of My People: African Americans: A Self-Portrait.* Introduction by Gordon Parks. Essays by Sylvester Monroe. Boston: Little, Brown, 1992.

Gumbo Ya Ya: Anthology of Contemporary African-American Women Artists, New York: Mid-March Arts Press, 1995.

McElroy, Guy C. *Facing History: The Black Image in American Art, 1710-1940.* Edited by Christopher C. French. Washington, DC: Bedford Arts/Corcoran Gallery, 1990.

Powell, Richard J. *Homecoming: The Art and Life of William H. Johnson.* New York: National Museum of American Art/Rizzoli, 1991.

Rozelle, Robert V., et. al. eds. *Black Art: Ancestral Legacy: The African-American Impulse in African-American Art.* New York: Abrams, 1990.

Thomison, Dennis, comp. *The Black Artist in America: An Index to Reproductions.* Metuchen, NJ: Scarecrow Press, 1991.

Travis, Jack, ed. *African-American Architects in Current Practice.* New York: Princeton Architecture Press, 1991.

Autobiography and Biography

Baker, Donald P. *Wilder: Hold Fast to Dreams: A Biography of L. Douglas Wilder.* Cabin John, MD: Seven Locks, 1990.

Baldwin, Lewis V. *There Is a Balm in Gilead: The Cultural Roots of Martin Luther King, Jr.* Minneapolis: Fortress Press, 1991.

Bigelow, Barbara Carlisle, ed. *Contemporary Black Biography.* Detroit: Gale Research Inc., 1992.

Bjarkman, Peter C. *Ernie Banks.* Introduction by Jim Murray. New York: Chelsea House, 1992.

Brown, Drew T., III. *You Gotta Believe!: Education + Hard Work - Drugs = The American Dream.* New York: Morrow, 1991.

Brown, James, and Bruce Tucker. *James Brown: The Godfather of Soul.* New York: Thunder's Mouth Press, 1990.

Buchmann-Moller, Frank. *You Just Fight for Your Life: The Story of Lester Young.* New York: Praeger, 1990.

Campbell, James. *Talking at the Gate: A Life of James Baldwin.* New York: Viking, 1991.

Carson, Clayborne. *Malcolm X; The FBI File.* Introduction by Spike Lee. Edited by David Gallen. New York: Carroll & Graf Publishers, Inc., 1991.

Carson, Clayborne, ed. *The Papers of Martin Luther King, Jr.* Berkeley: University of California Press, 1991.

Chilton, John. *The Song of the Hawk: The Life and Recordings of Coleman Hawkins.* New York: St. Martin's Press, 1990.

Davis, Benjamin O., Jr. *Benjamin O. Davis, Jr., American: An Autobiography.* Washington, DC: Smithsonian Institution, 1991.

Davis, Miles, and Quincy Troupe. *Miles, The Autobiography.* New York: Simon & Schuster, 1990.

Deane, Bill. *Bob Gibson.* Introduction by Jim Murray. New York: Chelsea House, 1992.

Dees, Morris. *A Season for Justice: The Life and Times of Civil Rights Lawyer Morris Dees.* New York: Scribner, 1991.

Faser, Jane. *Walter White.* New York: Chelsea House, 1991.

Goldman, Roger, and David Gallen. *Thurgood Marshall: Justice for All.* New York: Carroll & Graf, 1992.

Hamilton, Charles V. *Adam Clayton Powell, Jr.: The Political Biography of an American Dilemma.* New York: Atheneum, 1991.

Hawkins, Walter L. *African American Biographies: Profiles of 558 Current Men and Women.* Jefferson, NC: McFarland & Co., 1992.

Hayes, Bob. *Run, Bullet, Run.* New York: Harper Collins, 1990.

Kranz, Rachel C. *The Biographical Dictionary of Black Americans.* New York: Facts on File, 1992.

Kremer, Gary R. *James Milton Turner and the Promise of America: The Public Life of a Post-Civil War Black Leader.* Columbia: University of Missouri Press, 1991.

Levi, Darrell E. *Michael Manley: The Making of a Leader.* Athens: University of Georgia Press, 1990.

McFeely, William S. *Frederick Douglass.* New York: Norton, 1990.

Mosby, Dewey F., and Darrel Sewell. *Henry Ossawa Tanner.* New York: Rizzoli, 1991.

Naughton, Jim. *Taking to the Air: The Rise of Michael Jordan.* New York: Warner Books, 1992.

Pallister, Janis L. *Aime Cesaire.* New York: Twayne, 1991.

Perry, Bruce. *Malcolm: The Life of a Man Who Changed Black America.* Barrytown, NY: Station Hill, 1991.

Pfieffer, Paula F. *A. Philip Randolph, Pioneer of the Civil Rights Movement.* Baton Rouge: Louisiana State University Press, 1990.

Phelps, J. Alfred. *Chappie: America's First Black Four-Star General.* Novato, CA: Presidio Press, 1991.

Phelps, Shirelle, ed. *Who's Who Among Black Americans, 1993-94.* 7th ed., William C. Matney, Jr., Consulting Editor.

Detroit: Gale Research Inc., 1993.

Pickens, William. *Bursting Bonds: Enlarged edition (of) The Heir of Slaves: The Autobiography of a "New Negro".* Edited by William L. Andrews. Bloomington: Indiana University Press, 1991.

Rattenbury, Ken. *Duke Ellington, Jazz Composer.* New Haven: Yale University Press, 1991.

Rivlin, Benjamin, ed. *Ralph Bunche, The Man and His Times.* Foreword by Donald F. Henry. New York: Holmes & Meier, 1990.

Rose, Cynthia. *Living in America: The Soul Saga of James Brown.* London: Serpent Tale, 1990 (Dist. by Consortium Book Sales Distribution.)

Rout, Kathleen. *Eldridge Cleaver.* Boston: Twayne/G.K. Hall, 1991.

Schwartzman, Myron. *Romare Bearden: His Life and Art.* New York: Abrams, 1990.

Shapiro, Leonard. *Big Man on Campus: John Thompson and the Georgetown Hoyas.* New York: Holt, 1991.

Shapiro, Miles. *Bill Russell.* Introductory essay by Coretta Scott King. New York: Chelsea House, 1991.

Sifford, Charlie. *Just Let Me Play: The Story of Charlie Sifford: The First Black PGA Golfer.* Latham, NY: British American Publishers, 1992.

Smith, Eric Ledell. *Bert Williams: A Biography of the Pioneer Black Comedian.* Jefferson, NC: McFarland, 1992.

Stewart, James Brewer. *William Lloyd Garrison and the Challenge of Emancipation.* Arlington Heights, IL: Harlan Davidson, 1992.

Strode, Woody, and Sam Young. *Goal Dust: An Autobiography.* Lantham, MD: Madison Books, 1990.

Tucker, Ken. *Ellington: The Early Years.* Champaign: University of Illinois Press, 1991.

Urban, Wayne J. *Black Scholar: Horace Mann Bond, 1904-1972.* Athens: University of Georgia Press, 1992.

Vache, Warren W. *Crazy Fingers: Claude Hopkins' Life in Jazz.* Washington, DC: Smithsonian Institution Press, 1992.

Watts, Jill. *God, Harlem U.S.A.: The Father Divine Story.* Berkeley: University of California Press, 1992.

Weland, Gerald. *Of Vision and Valor: General O. O. Howard, A Biography.* Canton, OH: Daring Publishing Group, 1991.

Wells, Dicky. *The Night People: The Jazz Life of Dicky Wells.* As told to Stanley Dance. rev. ed., Washington, DC: Smithsonian Institution Press, 1991.

Wills, Maury, and Mike Celizic. *On the Run: The Never Dull and Often Shocking Life of Maury Wills.* New York: Carroll & Graf, 1991.

Black Nationalism and Pan-Africanism in the United States

Crosby, Edward W., and Linus A. Hoskins, eds. *Africa for the Africans: Selected Speeches of Marcus Mosiah Garvey; Malcolm X; and Nelson Kolihlahla Mandela.* Kent, OH: The Institute for African American Affairs, Department of Pan-African Studies, Kent State University, 1991.

Crummell, Alexander. *Destiny and Race: Selected Writings, 1840-1898.* Edited with introduction by Wilson J. Moses. Amherst: University of Massachusetts Press, 1992.

Drake, St. Clair. *Black Folks Here and There: An Essay in History and Anthropology.* 2 vols. Los Angeles: University of California, Los Angeles, Center for Afro-American Studies, 1991.

Harris, Robert, et. al. *Carlos Cooks: And Black Nationalism from Garvey to Malcolm.* Dover, MA: Majority Press, 1992.

Jacques, Geoffrey. *The African-American Movement Today.* New York: Watts, 1992.

Lemelle, Sid. *Pan-Africanism for Beginners.* New York: Writers and Readers Publishing, Inc., 1992.

Lewis, Rupert, ed. *Garvey: His Work and Impact.* Trenton, NJ: Africa World Press, 1991.

Martin, Tony, comp. and ed. *African Fundamentalism: A Literary and Cultural Anthropology of Garvey's Harlem Renaissance.* Dover, MA: Majority Press, 1991.

Moses, Wilson J. *Alexander Crummell: A Study of Civilization and Discontent.* Amherst: University of Massachusetts Press, 1992.

Civil Rights, Law, and Civil Protests

Administrative History of the Civil Rights Division of the Department of Justice During the Johnson Administration. 2 vol., New York: Garland Publishing Co., 1991.

Aguirre, Adalberto, Jr., and David V. Baker. *Race, Racism and the Death Penalty in the United States.* Barrien Springs, MI: Vande Vere Publishers, 1992.

Belknap, Michal. *Racial Violence and Law Enforcement in the South.* New York: Garland Publishing Co., 1991.

Belknap, Michal. *Securing the Enactment of Civil Rights Legislation, 1965-1968.* New York: Garland Publishing Co., 1991.

Belknap, Michal. *Urban Race Riots.* New York: Garland Publishing Co., 1991.

Belknap, Michal. *Voting Rights.* New York: Garland Publishing Co., 1991.

Belz, Herman. *Equality Transformed: A Quarter-Century of Affirmative Action.* New Brunswick, NJ: Transaction, 1991.

Blumberg, Rhoda L. *Civil Rights, the Freedom Struggle.* rev. ed., Boston: Twayne G.K. Hall, 1991.

Bolick, Clint. *Unfinished Business: A Civil Rights Strategy for America's Third Century.* San Francisco: Research Institute of Public Policy, 1990.

Cagin, Seth, and Philip Dray. *We Are Not Afraid: The Story of Goodman, Schwerner and Chaney and the Civil Rights Campaign for Mississippi.* New York: Bantam Books, 1991.

Capeci, Dominic, and Martha Wilkerson. *Layered Violence: the Detroit Rioters of 1943.* Jackson: University Press of Mississippi, 1991.

Carson, Clayborne, et. al. eds. *"The Eyes on the Prize" Civil Rights Reader: Documents, Speeches, and First-hand Accounts from the Black Freedom Struggle, 1954-1990.* New York: Viking, 1991.

Cashman, Sean Dennis. *African-Americans and the Quest for Civil Rights, 1900-1990.* New York: New York University Press, 1991.

Cashmore, Ellis, and Eugene McLaughlin, eds. *Out of Order?: Policing Black People.* New York: Routledge, 1991.

Cone, James H. *Martin and Malcolm and America: A Dream or a Nightmare.* New York: Orbis Books, 1991.

Cook, Anthony. *Law, Race and Social Theory.* Boston: New England School of Law, 1991.

Detefsen, Robert R. *Civil Rights Under Reagan.* San Francisco: ICS Press, 1991.

Encyclopedia of African American Civil Rights: From Emancipation to the Present. Westport, CT: Greenwood Press, 1992.

Epstein, Richard Allen. *Forbidden Grounds: The Case Against Employment Discrimination Laws.* Cambridge: Harvard University Press, 1992.

Ezorsky, Gertrude. *Racism and Justice: The Case for Affirmative Action.* Ithaca, NY: Cornell University Press, 1991.

Fendrich, James Max. *Ideal Citizens: The Legacy of the Civil Rights Movement.* Albany: State University of New York Press, 1993.

Finkelman, Paul, ed. *African Americans and the Law.* New York: Garland Publishing Co., 1991 (*Race, Law and American History, 1700-1900. The African American Experience.*)

Finkelman, Paul, ed. *African-Americans and the Legal Profession in Historical Perspective.* New York: Garland Publishing Co., 1991 (*Race, Law, and American History, 1700-1990. The African American Experience.* vol. 10).

Finkelman, Paul, ed. *African-Americans and the Right to Vote.* Edited by Paul Finkelman. New York: Garland Publishing Co., 1992. (*Race, Law, and American History, 1700-1900. The African-American Experience.* vol. 6).

Finkelman, Paul, ed. *Lynching, Racial Violence, and Law.* New York: Garland Publishing Co., 1992. (*Race, Law, and American History, 1700-1990. The African-American*

Experience, vol. 9.)

Finkelman, Paul, ed. *Race and Criminal Justice.* New York: Garland Publishing Co., 1992. (*Race, Law, and American History, 1700-1900. The American Experience*, vol. 8.)

Finkelman, Paul, ed. *Race and Law Before Emancipation.* New York: Garland Publishing Co., 1992. (*Race, Law and American History, 1700-1990. The African American Experience*, vol. 2.)

Finkelman, Paul, ed. *The Era of Integration and Civil Rights, 1930-1990.* New York: Garland Publishing Co., 1992. (*Race, Law, and American History, 1700-1990. The African American Experience* vol. 5).

Fiscus, Ronald Jerry. *The Constitutional Logic of Affirmative Action.* Edited by Stephen Wasby. Durham, NC: Duke University Press, 1992.

Fisher, Sethard. *From Margin to Mainstream: The Social Progress of Black Americans.* 2nd ed., Savage, MD: Rowman & Littlefield, 1992.

Goings, Kenneth W. *The NAACP Comes of Age: The Defeat of Judge Parker.* Bloomington: Indiana University Press, 1990.

Goldwin, Robert A. *Why Blacks, Women and Jews Are Not Mentioned in the Constitution, and Other Unorthodox Views.* Washington, DC: American Enterprise Institute, 1990.

Graetz, Robert S. *Montgomery, A White Preachers Memoir.* Minneapolis: Fortress Press, 1991.

Grafman, Bernard, ed. *Controversies in Minority Voting: The Voting Rights Act in Perspective.* Washington, DC: Brookings Institute, 1992.

Graham, Hugh Davis. *The Civil Rights Era: Race, Gender and National Policy, 1960-1972.* New York: Oxford University Press, 1990.

Hampton, Henry, and Steve Fayer, comps. *Voices of Freedom: An Oral History of the Civil Rights Movement from the 1950s Through the 1980s.* New York: Bantam Books, 1990.

Harding, Vincent. *Hope and History: Why We Must Share the Story of the Movement.* Maryknoll, NY: Orbis Books, 1990.

Harris, Jacqueline. *A History of the NAACP.* New York: Watts, 1992.

Jackson, James E. *The Bold Bad '60s: Pushing the Point for Equality Down South and Out Yonder.* New York: International Publishers, 1992.

James, Hunter. *They Didn't Put That on the Huntley-Brinkley Report!: A Vagabound Reporter Encounters the New South.* Athens: University of Georgia, 1993.

Justice Department Briefs in Crucial Civil Rights Cases. 2 vols., New York: Garland, 1991.

Kapur, Sudarshan. *Raising Up a Prophet: The African-American Encounter with Gandhi.* Boston: Beacon, 1992.

King, Richard. *Civil Rights and the Idea of Freedom.* New York: Oxford University Press, 1992.

Kull, Andrew. *The Color-Blind Constitution.* Cambridge: Harvard University Press, 1992.

Levy, Peter B., ed. *Dictionary History of the Modern Civil Rights Movement.* New York: Greenwood Press, 1992.

Levy, Peter B., ed. *Let Freedom Ring: A Documentary History of the Modern Civil Rights Movement.* New York: Praeger, 1992.

Lyon, Danny. *Memories of the Civil Rights Movement.* Text and photographs by Danny Lyon; foreword by Julian Bond. Chapel Hill: University of North Carolina Press, 1992.

Meier, August, et. al. eds. *Black Protest in the Sixties.* New York: M. Wiener, 1991.

Meier, August. *A White Scholar and the Black Community, 1945-1965: Essays and Reflections.* Afterword by John H. Bracey, Jr. Amherst: University of Massachusetts Press, 1992.

Mills, Nicolaus. *Like a Holy Crusade: Mississippi, 1964—The Turning of the Civil Rights Movement in America.* Chicago: I.R. Dee, 1992.

Nieli, Russell, ed. *Racial Preference and Racial Justice: The New Affirmative Action Controversy.* Washington, DC: Ethics and Public Policy Center, 1991 (Dist. by National Book Network.)

Nieman, Donald G. *Promises to Keep: African Americans and the Constitutional Order, 1776 to the Present.* New York: Oxford University Press, 1991.

O'Reilly, Kenneth. *Racial Matters: The FBI's Secret File on Black America, 1960-1972.* New York: Free Press, 1991.

Powledge, Fred. *Free At Last?: The Civil Rights Movement and the People Who Made It.* Boston: Little, Brown, 1990.

Reed, Merl E. *Seedtime for the Modern Civil Rights Movement: The President's Committee on Fair Employment Practice, 1941-1946.* Baton Rouge: Louisiana State University Press, 1991.

Robinson, Amelia Boynton. *Bridge Across Jordan.* rev. ed., Washington, DC: Schiller Institute, 1991.

Robinson, Armistead L., and Patricia Sullivan, eds. *New Directions in Civil Rights Studies.* Charlottesville: University Press of Virginia, 1991.

Sigelman, Lee, and Susan Welch. *Black Americans' Views of Racial Inequality: The Dream Deferred.* New York: Cambridge University Press, 1991.

Sikora, Frank. *Until Justice Rolls Down: The Birmingham*

Church Bombing Case Tuscaloosa: University of Alabama Press, 1991.

Stern, Mark. *Calculating Visions: Kennedy, Johnson and Civil Rights.* New Brunswick, NJ: Rutger University Press, 1992.

Swift, Jeanne, ed. *Dream and Reality: The Modern Black Struggle for Freedom and Equality.* New York: Greenwood Press, 1991.

Thomas, Clarence. *Clarence Thomas: Confronting the Future: Selections from the Senate Confirmation Hearing and Prior Speeches.* Washington, DC: Regnery Gateway, 1992.

Urofsky, Melvin I. *A Conflict of Rights: The Supreme Court and Affirmative Action.* New York: Scribners, 1991.

Watson, Denton L. *Lion in the Lobby: Clarence Mitchell, Jr.'s Struggle for the Passage of Civil Rights Laws.* New York: Morrow, 1990.

Wright, Roberta Hughes. *The Birth of the Montgomery Bus Boycott.* Southfield, MI: Charro Book Co., 1991.

Economics, Entrepreneurship, and Labor

Broadnax, Derek. *The Black Entrepreneurs Guide to Million Dollar Business Opportunities.* Austin, TX: Black Entrepreneurs Press, 1990.

Broadnax, Derek. *The Black Entrepreneurs Guide to Money Sources: How to Get Your Share.* Austin, TX: Black Entrepreneurs Press, 1990.

Butler, John Sibley. *Entrepreneurship and Self-Help Among Black Americans: A Reconsideration of Race and Economics.* Albany: State University of New York Press, 1991.

Dewart, Janet, ed. *The State of Black America, 1991.* New York: National Urban League, 1991.

Duncan, Mike. *Reach Your Goals In Spite of the Old Boy Network: A Guide for African American Employees.* Edgewood, MD:

M.E. Duncan and Co., 1990.

Grant, Nancy L. *TVA and Black Americans: Planning for the Status Quo.* Philadelphia: Temple University Press, 1990.

Green, Shelley, and Paul Pryde. *Black Entrepreneurship in America.* Brunswick, NJ: Transactions Publishers, 1990.

Greenberg, Jonathan D. *Staking a Claim: Jake Simmons and the Making of an African-American Oil Dynasty.* New York: Atheneum, 1991.

Reed, Wornie, ed. *Social, Political and Economic Issues in Black America.* Amherst: University of Massachusetts, William Monroe Trotter Institute, 1990.

Rosen, George H. *Black Money.* Chelsea, MI: Scaraborough House, 1990.

Education

Allen, Walter R., Edgar Epps, and Nesha Z. Haniff, eds. *College in Black and White: African American Students in Predominately White and Historically Black Public Universities.* Albany: State University of New York Press, 1991.

Altbach, Philip G., and Kofi Lomotey, eds. *The Racial Crisis in American Higher Education.* Albany: State University of New York Press, 1991.

Bowman, J. Wilson. *America's Black Colleges.* South

Pasadena, CA: Sandcastle Publishing Co., 1992.

Fife, Brian L. *Desegregation in American Schools: Comparative Intervention Strategies.* New York: Praeger, 1992.

Finkelman, Paul, ed. *The Struggle for Equal Education.* New York: Garland Publishing Co., 1992. (*Race, Law, and American History, 1700-1990. African-American Experience*, vol. 7.)

Formisano, Ronald P. *Boston Against Busing: Race, Class, and Ethnicity in the 1960s and 1970s.* Chapel Hill: University of North Carolina Press, 1991.

Harmon, Marylen E. *The Infusion of African and African American Studies into the Curriculum.* Roanoke, VA: Absolute Writings Ltd., 1991.

Irvine, Jacqueline Jordan. *Black Students and School Failure: Policies, Practices, and Prescriptions.* Westport, CT: Greenwood Press, 1990.

Lomotey, Kofi, ed. *Going to School: The African-American Experience.* Albany: State University of New York Press, 1990.

Lusane, Clarence. *The Struggle for Equal Education.* New York: F. Watts, 1992.

Margo, Robert A. *Race and Schooling in the South, 1880-1950.* Chicago: University of Chicago Press, 1991.

National Afro-American Museum and Cultural Center. *From Victory to Freedom: The African American Experience: Curriculum Guide, Secondary School Course of Study.* Wilberforce, OH: National Afro-American Museum and Cultural Center, 1991.

Neufeldt, Harvey G., and Leo McGee, eds. *Education of the African American Adult: An Historical Overview.* Westport, CT: Greenwood, 1990.

Pratt, Robert A. *The Color of Their Skin: Education and Race in Richmond, Virginia, 1954-89.* Charlottesville: University of Virginia Press, 1992.

Sachar, Emily. *Shut Up and Let the Lady Teach: A Teacher's Year in a Public School.* New York: Poseidon Press, 1991.

Thompkins, Susie Powers. *Cotton-Patch Schoolhouse.*

Tuscaloosa: University of Alabama Press, 1992.

Willie, Charles V., Anatoine M. Garibaldi, and Wornie L. Reed, eds. *The Education of African Americans.* Westport, CT: Auburn House/Greenwood Publishing Group, 1991.

Folklore and Folk Culture

Abrahams, Roger D. *Singing the Master: The Emergence of African American Culture in the Plantation South.* New York: Pantheon Books, 1992.

Hall, Gwendolyn Midlo. *Africans in Colonial Louisiana: The Development of Afro-Creole Culture.* Baton Rouge: Louisiana State University Press, 1992.

Hazzard-Gordon, Katrina. *Jookin': The Rise of Social Dance Formation in African-American Culture.* Philadelphia: Temple University Press, 1990.

Hill, James L., ed. *Studies in African and African American Culture.* New York: P. Lang, 1990.

Holloway, Joseph E., ed. *Africanisms in American Culture.* Bloomington: Indiana University Press, 1990.

Njeri, Itabari. *Every Good-Bye Ain't Gone: Family Portraits and Personal Escapades.* New York: Times Books, 1990.

Roberts, John W. *From Trickster to Badman: The Black Folk Hero in Slavery and Freedom.* Philadelphia: University of Pennsylvania Press, 1990.

Spalding, Henry D., comp. and ed. *Encyclopedia of Black Folklore and Humor.* Introduction by J. Mason Brewer. Middle Village, NY: Jonathan David Publishers, 1990.

Sundquist, Eric J. *The Hammers of Creation: Folk Culture in Modern African-American Culture.* Athens: University of Georgia Press, 1992.

Twining, Mary A., and Keith E. Baird, eds. *Sea Island Roots: African Presence in Carolina and Georgia.* Trenton, NJ: Africa World Press, 1991.

General Reference

Asante, Molefi K. *The Historical and Cultural Atlas of African Americans.* New York: Macmillan, 1991.

The Black Resource Guide, 1990-1991 Edition. Washington, DC: Black Resource Guide, Inc., 1991.

Bogle, Donald, ed. *Black Arts Annual, 1988/89.* New York: Garland, 1990.

Donovan, Richard X. *Black Scientists of America.* Portland, OR: National Book Co., 1990.

Fitzpatrick, Sandra, and Maria Godwin. *The Guide to Black Washington: Places and Events of Historical and Cultural Significance in the Nation's Capital.* New York: Hippocrene, 1990.

Furtaw, Julia C., ed. *Black American Information Directory.* 2nd ed., Detroit: Gale Research Inc., 1992.

Hancock, Sybil. *Famous Firsts of Black Americans.* Gretna, LA: Pelican Publishing Co., 1991.

Horton, Carrell Peterson, and Jessie Carney Smith, comps. and eds. *Statistical Record of Black America.* 2nd ed., Detroit: Gale Research Inc., 1991.

Smithsonian Institution. *African and African American Resources at the Smithsonian.* Washington, DC: Smithsonian Institution, 1991.

Southern, Eileen, and Josephine Wright, comps. *African American Traditions in Song, Sermon, Tale, and Dance, 1600s-1920: An Annotated Bibliography of Literature, Collections, and Artworks.* Westport, CT: Greenwood Press, 1990.

Thum, Marcella. *Hippocrene U.S.A. Guide to Black America: A Directory of Historic and Cultural Sites Relating to Black America.* New York: Hippocrene Books, 1992.

Health

Bailey, A. Peter. *The Harlem Hospital Story: 100 Years of Struggle Against Illness.* Richmond, VA: Native Sun Publishers, 1991.

Bailey, Eric J. *Urban African American Health Care.*

Lantham, MD: University Press of America, 1991.

The Black Women's Health Book: Speaking for Ourselves. Seattle: Seal Press, 1990.

Dixon, Barbara M., with Josleen Wilson, *Good Health for African-American Kids,*, Crown Trade Paperbacks, 1995.

Duh, Samuel V. *Blacks and AIDS: Genetic or Environmental Causes.* Newbury Park, CA: Sage Publications, 1991.

Health of Black Americans from Post Reconstruction to Integration, 1871-1960: An Annotated Bibliography of Contemporary Sources. Westport, CT: Greenwood Press, 1990.

McBride, David. *From TB to AIDS: Epidemics Among Urban Blacks Since 1900.* Albany: State University of New York Press, 1991.

National Black Health Leadership Directory, 1990-91. Washington, DC: NRW Associates, 1991.

Villarosa, Linda, ed. *Body & Soul: The Black Woman's Guide to Physical Health and Mental Well-Being.* HarperCollins, 1994.

History

The African American Experience: A History. Sharon Harley, Stephen Middleton, and Charlotte Stokes, Consultants. Englewood Cliffs, NJ: Prentice-Hall, 1992.

America, Richard, ed. *The Wealth of Races: The Present Value of Benefits from Past Injustices.* Westport, CT: Greenwood Press, 1991.

Anderson, Eric, and Alfred Moss, Jr., eds. *The Facts of Reconstruction: Essays in Honor of John Hope Franklin.* Baton Rouge: Louisiana State University Press, 1991.

Andrews, George Reid. *Blacks and Whites in Sao Paulo Brazil, 1888-1988.* Madison: University of Wisconsin Press, 1992.

Aptheker, Herbert. *Anti-Racism in U.S. History: The First Hundred Years.* New York: Greenwood Press, 1992.

Aptheker, Herbert. *To Be Free: Pioneering Studies in Afro-American History.* Introduction by John Hope Franklin. New York: Citadel Press, 1991.

Bailey, Richard. *Neither Carpetbaggers Nor Scalawags: Black Officeholders During the Reconstruction in Alabama.* Montgomery, AL: R. Bailey Publishers, 1991.

Beeth, Howard, and Cary E. Wintz, eds. *Black Dixie: Afro-Texan History and Culture in Houston.* College Station, TX: Texas A&M University Press, 1992.

Berlin, Irs, and Philip D. Morgan, eds. *The Slaves' Economy: Independent Production by Slaves in the Americas.* London: F. Cass, 1991.

Berlin, Irs, et. al., eds. *Slaves No More: Three Essays on Emancipation and the Civil War.* New York: Cambridge University Press, 1992.

The Black Abolitionist Papers, Vol. 3: The United States, 1830-1846. Chapel Hill: University of North Carolina Press, 1991.

Boney, F.N., Richard L. Hume, and Rafia Zafar. *God Made Man, Man Made the Slave.* Macon, GA: Mercer University Press, 1990.

Bryan, Patrick. *The Jamaican People, 1880-1902: Race and Social Control.* New York: Macmillan, 1991.

Bush, Barbara. *Slave Women in Caribbean Society, 1650-1838.* Bloomington: University of Indiana Press, 1990.

Campbell, Randolph B. *An Empire for Slavery: The Peculiar Institution in Texas, 1821-1865.* Baton Rouge: Louisiana State University Press, 1991.

Cantor, George. *Historic Landmarks of Black America.* Detroit: Gale Research Inc., 1991.

Cohen, William. *At Freedom Edge: Black Mobility at the Southern Quest for Racial Control, 1861-1915.* Baton Rouge: Louisiana State University Press, 1991.

Cornelius, Janet Duitsman. *"When I Can Read My Title Clear": Literacy, Slavery, and Religion in the Antebellum South.* Columbia: University of South Carolina Press, 1991.

Counter, S. Allen. *North Pole Legacy: Black, White and Eskimo.* Amherst: University of Massachusetts Press, 1991.

Crouch, Berry A. *The Freedmen's Bureau and Black Texans.* Austin: University of Texas Press, 1992.

Davis, Lenwood G. *A Travel Guide to Black Historical Sites and Landmarks in North Carolina.* Winston-Salem, NC: Bandit Books, 1991.

Deromantizing Black History: Critical Essays and Reappraisals. Knoxville: University of Tennessee Press, 1991.

Dillon, Merton L. *Slavery Attacked: Southern Slaves and Their Allies, 1619-1865.* Baton Rouge: Louisiana State University Press, 1990.

Downey, Dennis B., and Raymond M. Hyser. *No Crooked Death: Coatsville, Pennsylvania, and the Lynching of Zachariah Walker.* Champaign: University of Illinois Press, 1991.

Drago, Edmund L., ed. *Broke by the War: Letters of a Slave Trader.* Columbia: University of South Carolina Press, 1991.

Dykstra, Robert. *Bright Radical Star: Black Freedom and White Supremacy on the Hawkeye Frontier.* Cambridge: Harvard University Press, 1993.

Fede, Andrew. *People Without Rights: An Interpretation of the Fundamentals of the Law of Slavery in the U.S. South.* New York: Garland Publishing Co., 1992.

Ferguson, Leland G. *Uncommon Ground: Archaeology and Early African America, 1650-1800.* Washington, DC: Smithsonian Institution Press, 1992.

Finkelman, Paul, ed. *The Age of Jim Crow: Segregation from the End of Reconstruction to the Great Depression.* New York: Garland Publishing Co., 1992. (*Race, Law, and American History, 1760-1990. The African American Experience*, vol. 4.)

Finkelman, Paul, ed. *Emancipation and Reconstruction.* New York: Garland Publishing Co., 1992. (*Race, Law and American History, 1700-1990. The African American Experience.* vol. 3.)

Franklin, Vincent P. *Black Self-Determinism: A Cultural History of African-American Resistance.* 2nd ed., Brooklyn, NY: Lawrence Hill Books, 1992.

Frey, Sylvia. *Water from the Rock: Black Resistance in a Revolutionary Age.* Princeton, NJ: Princeton University Press, 1992.

Gatewood, Willard B. *Aristocrats of Color: The Black Elite, 1880-1920.* Bloomington: Indiana University Press, 1990.

Genovese, Eugene D. *The Slaveholders' Dilemma: Freedom and Progress in Southern Conservative Thought, 1820-1860.* Columbia: University of South Carolina Press, 1992.

Greenberg, Cheryl Lynn. *"Or Does It Explode?": Black Harlem in the Great Depression.* New York: Oxford University Press, 1991.

Hamilton, Kenneth Marvin. *Black Towns and Profit, Promotion and Development in the Trans-Appalachian West, 1877-1915.* Champaign: University of Illinois Press, 1991.

Harley, Sharon. *The African American Experience: A History.* Englewood Cliffs, NJ: Globe, 1992.

Harris, Richard S. *Politics & Prejudice: A History of Chester, Pennsylvania Negroes.* Apache Junction, AZ: Relmo Pubs., 1991.

Harrison, Alfredteen, ed. *Black Exodus: The Great Migration from the American South.* Oxford: University Press of Mississippi, 1991.

Henry, Paget, and Paul Buhle, eds. *C.L.R. James' Caribbean.* Durham, NC: Duke University Press, 1992.

Hornsby, Jr., Alton. *Chronology of African-American History: Significant Events and People from 1619 to the Present.* Detroit: Gale Research Inc., 1991.

Horton, James Oliver. *Free People of Color: Inside the African American Community.* Washington, DC: Smithsonian Institution, 1993.

Inikoroi, Joseph E., and Stanley L. Engerman, eds. *The Atlantic Slave Trade: Effects on Economic Societies, and Peoples in Africa, the Americas and Europe.* Durham, NC: Duke University Press, 1992.

Jackson, Terrance. *Putting It All Together: World Conquest, Global Genocide and African Liberation.* Bronx, NY: AKASA, 1991.

Jones, Howard. *The Red Diary: A Chronological History of Black Americans in Houston and Some Neighboring Harris County Communities-122 Years Later.* Austin, TX: Nortex Press, 1992.

Jones, Norrece T. *Born a Child of Freedom, Yet A Slave: Mechanisms of Control and Strategies of Resistance in Antebellum South Carolina.* Middletown, CT: Wesleyan University Press, 1990.

Jordan, Winthrop. *Tumult and Silence at Second Creek: An Inquiry into a Civil War Slave Conspiracy.* Baton Rouge: Louisiana State University Press, 1993.

Katz, William Loren. *Breaking the Chains: African American Slave Resistance.* New York: Atheneum, 1990.

Lane, Roger. *William Dorsey's Philadelphia and Ours: On the Origins and Future Prospects of Urban Black America.* New York: Oxford University Press, 1991.

Lesko, Kathleen M., ed. *Black Georgetown Remembered: A History of Its Black Community from the Founding of "The Town of George" in 1751 to the Present Day.* Washington, DC: Georgetown University Press, 1991.

Malone, Ann Patton. *Sweet Chariot: Slave Family and Household Structure in Nineteenth Century Louisiana.* Chapel Hill: University of North Carolina Press, 1992.

McLaurin, Melton A. *Celia, a Slave.* Athens: University of Georgia Press, 1991.

McMillen, Sally Gregory. *Southern Women: Black and White in the Old South.* Arlington Heights, IL: Harlan Davidson, 1992.

Meillassaux, Claude. *The Anthropology of Slavery: The Womb of Iron and Gold.* Translated by Alide Dasnois. Chicago: University of Chicago Press, 1991.

Meyer, Mary K. *Free Blacks in Hartford, Somerset, and Talbort Counties, Maryland.* Mt. Airy, MD: Pipe Creek Publications, 1991.

Middleton, Stephen. *The Black Laws in the Old Northwest: A Documentary History.* New York: Greenwood Press, 1992.

Munford, Clarence J. *The Black Ordeal of Slavery and Slave Trading in the French West Indies, 1625-1715.* Lewiston, ME: Edwin Mellen, 1991.

Nash, Gary B. *Freedom by Degrees: Emancipation in Pennsylvania and Its Aftermath.* New York: Oxford University Press, 1991.

Nash, Gary B. *Race and Revolution.* Madison, WI: Madison House, 1990.

Oakes, James. *Slavery and Freedom: An Interpretation of the Old South.* New York: Knopf, 1990.

Pearson, Edward. *Slave Work and Culture in Town and Country.* Williamsburg, VA: Institute of Early American History and Culture, 1991.

Perdue, Charles L., ed. *Weevils in the Wheat: Interviews with Virginia Ex-Slaves.* Charlottesville: University Press of Virginia, 1992.

Reidy, Joseph. *From Slavery to Agrarian Capitalism in the Cotton Plantation South: Central Georgia, 1800-1880.* Chapel Hill: University of North Carolina Press, 1992.

Richardson, Bonham C. *The Caribbean in the Wide World, 1492-1922.* New York: Cambridge University Press, 1992.

Richter, William L. *Overreached on All Sides: The Freedmen's Bureau Administrators in Texas, 1865-1868.* College Station: Texas A&M University Press, 1991.

Schwartz, Stuart B. *Slaves, Peasants, and Rebels: Reconsidering Brazilian Slavery.* Champaign: University of Illinois Press, 1992.

Schweninger, Loren. *Black Property Owners in the South, 1790-1915.* Champaign: University of Illinois Press, 1990.

Slaughter, Thomas P. *Bloody Dawn: The Christiania Riot and Racial Violence in Antebellum North.* New York: Oxford University Press, 1991.

Solow, Barbara L., ed. *Slavery and the Rise of the Atlantic System.* New York: Cambridge University Press/ W.E.B. DuBois Institute for Afro-American Research, 1991.

Stanisland, Martin. *American Intellectuals and African Nationalists; 1955-1970.* New Haven, CT: Yale University Press, 1991.

Stevenson, Lisbeth Gant. *African-American History: Heroes in Hardship.* Cambridge, MA: Cambridgeport Press, 1992.

Stone, Albert E. *The Return of Nat Turner: History, Literature, and Cultural Politics in Sixties America.* Athens: University of Georgia, 1992.

Stone, Frank Andrews. *African American Connecticut: African Origins, New England Roots.* Storrs, CT: Isaac N. Thut World Education Center, 1991.

Terry, Ted. *American Black History: Reference Manual.* Tulsa, OK: Myles Publishing Co., 1991.

Thomas, Richard W. *Life for Us: Building Black Community in Detroit, 1915-1945.* Bloomington: Indiana University Press, 1992.

Thornton, John. *Africa and Africans in the Making of the Atlantic World, 1400-1680.* New York: Cambridge University Press, 1992.

White, Shane. *Somewhat More Independent: The End of Slavery in New York City 1770-1870.* Athens: University of Georgia Press, 1991.

Williams, Jacob C. *Lillie: Black Life in Martins Ferry, Ohio During the 1920s and 1930s.* Ann Arbor, MI: Braun-Brumfield, 1991.

Williams, Lee E. *Post-War Riots in America, 1919 and 1946: How the Pressures of War Exacerbated American Urban Tensions to the Breaking Points.* Lewiston, NY: E. Mellen, 1991.

Language, Literature, and Drama

Babb, Valerie Melissa. *Ernest Gaines.* Boston: Twayne/G.K. Hall, 1991.

Bailey, Guy, Natalie Maynor, and Patricia Cukor-Avila, eds. *The Emergence of Black English: Text and Commentary.* Philadelphia: J. Benjamins Publishing Co., 1991.

Baker, Houston A., and Patricia Redmond, eds. *Afro-American Literary Study in the 1990s.* Chicago: University of Chicago Press, 1990.

Baraka, Imamu Amiri. *The Leroi Jones/Amiri Baraka Reader.* Edited William J. Harris. New York: Thunder's Mouth Press, 1991.

Barksdale, Richard K. *Praisesong of Survival: Lectures and Essays, 1957-1989.* Introduction by R. Baxter Miller. Urbana: University of Illinois, 1992.

Bassett, John E. *Harlem in Review: Critical Reactions to Black American Writers, 1917-1939.* Selinsgrove, PA: Susquehanna University Press, 1992.

Benitoz-Rojo, Antonio. *The Repeating Island: The Caribbean and the Postmodern Perspective.* Durham, NC: Duke University Press, 1992.

Blackshire-Belay, Carol Aisha, ed. *Language and Literature in the African American Imagination.* Westport, CT: Greenwood Press, 1992.

Bloom, Harold, ed. *Bigger Thomas.* New York: Chelsea House, 1990.

Brown, Stewart, ed. *The Art of Derek Walcott.* UK: Seren Books, 1992. (Dist. by Dufour Editions, Inc.)

Busby, Mark. *Ralph Ellison.* Boston: Twayne/G.K. Hall, 1991.

Butler, Robert. *Native Son: The Emergence of a New Black Hero.* Boston: Twayne/G.K. Hall, 1991.

Cartey, Wilfred. *Whispers form the Caribbean: I Going Away, I Going Home.* Los Angeles: University of California, Los Angeles, Center for Afro-American Studies, 1991.

DeJongh, James. *Vicious Modernism: Black Harlem and the Literary Imagination.* New York: Cambridge University Press, 1990.

Dieke, Ikenna. *The Primordial Image: African, Afro-American, and Caribbean Mythopoetic Text.* New York: P. Lang, 1991.

Draper, James P., ed. *Black Literature Criticism: Excerpts from Criticism of the Most Significant Works of Black Authors over the Past 200 Years.* 3 vols., Detroit: Gale Research Inc., 1992.

Edwards, Walter F., and Donald Winford, eds. *Verb Phrase Patterns in Black English and Creole.* Detroit: Wayne State University Press, 1991.

Fabre, Michel. *Richard Wright: Books and Writers.* Oxford: University Press of Mississippi, 1990.

Gates, Henry Louis, Jr. *Loose Canons: Notes on the Culture Wars.* New York: Oxford University Press, 1992.

Hamalian, Leo, and James V. Hatch, eds. *The Roots of African American Drama: An Anthology of Early Plays, 1858-1938.* Detroit: Wayne State University Press, 1991.

Hord, Fred L. *Reconstructing Memory: Black Literary Criticism.* Chicago: Third World Press, 1991.

Johnson, Dianne. *Telling Tales: The Pedagogy and Power of African American Literature for Youth.* New York: Greenwood Press, 1990.

Jones, Gayl. *Liberating Voices: Oral Tradition in African American Literature.* Cambridge, MA: Harvard University Press, 1991.

Joseph, Margaret Paul. *Caliban in Exile: The Outsider in Caribbean Fiction.* New York: Greenwood Press, 1992.

Kinnamon, Kenneth, ed. *New Essays on Native Son.* New York: Cambridge University Press, 1990.

Metzger, Linda, Hal May, Deborah A. Straub, and Susan M. Trotsky, eds. *Black Writers.* Detroit: Gale Research Inc., 1989.

Mikolyzk, Thomas A. comp. *Langston Hughes: A Bio-Bibliography.* Westport, CT: Greenwood Press, 1990.

Miller, R. Baxter. *The Art and Imagination of Langston Hughes.* Lexington: University of Kentucky Press, 1990.

Morrison, Toni. *Playing in the Dark: Whiteness and the Literary Imagination.* Cambridge, MA: Harvard University Press, 1992.

Newby, James Edwards. *Black Authors: A Selected Annotated Bibliography.* New York: Garland, 1990.

Ntire, Daphne Williams, ed., and comp. *Roots and Blossoms; African American Plays for Today.* Troy, MI: Bedford Publishers, 1991.

Peterson, Bernard L. *Early Black American Playwrights and Dramatic Writers: A Biographical Dictionary and Catalog of Plays, Films and Broadcasting Scripts.* Westport, CT: Greenwood Press, 1990.

Rajiv, Sudhi. *Forms of Black Consciousness.* New York: Advent Books, 1992.

Rollock, Barbara. *Black Authors and Illustrators of Children's Books: A Biographical Dictionary.* 2nd ed., New York: Garland, 1992.

Smith, Valerie. *Self-Discovery and Authority in Afro-American Narrative.* Cambridge, MA; Harvard University Press, 1991.

Stepto, Robert B. *From Behind the Veil: A Study of Afro-American Narrative.* 2nd ed., Urbana: University of Illinois Press, 1991.

Thurman, Wallace. *Infants of the Spring.* With foreword by Amritjit Singh. Boston: Northeastern University Press, 1992.

Toomer, Jean. *Essentials.* Edited by Rudolph P. Bird.

Athens: University of Georgia Press, 1991.

Washington, Mary Helen, ed. *Memory of Kin: Stories About Family by Black Writers.* New York: Doubleday, 1991.

Wilson, August. *Two Trains Running.* New York: Dutton, 1992.

Media, Publishing, and Book Collecting

Chester, Thomas Morris. *Thomas Morris Chester, Black Civil War Correspondent: His Dispatches from the Virginia Front.* With Biographical Essay and Notes by R.J.M. Blackett. New York: DeCapo Press, 1991.

Dates, Jannette L., and William Barlow. *Split Image: African Americans in the Mass Media.* Washington, DC: Howard University Press, 1990.

Hill, George. *Black Women in Television: An Illustrated History and Bibliography.* New York: Garland Publishing Co., 1990.

Joyce, Donald Franklin. *Black Book Publishers in the United States: A Historical Dictionary of the Press, 1817-1990.* Westport, CT: Greenwood Press, 1991.

Schuyler, George S. *Black Empire: George S. Schuyler Writing As Samuel I. Brooks.* Edited by Robert A. Hill and R. Kent Rasmussen. Boston: Northeastern University, 1991.

Silk, Catherine, and John Silk. *Racism and Anti-Racism in American Popular Culture: Portrayals of African-Americans in Fiction and Film.* Manchester, UK: Manchester University Press, 1990. (Dist. by St. Martin's Press)

Sinnette, Elinor Des Verney, W. Paul Coates, and Thomas C. Battle, eds. *Black Bibliophiles and Collectors: Preservers of Black History.* Washington, DC: Howard University Press, 1990.

Military Participation

Collum, Danny Duncan, ed. *African Americans in the Spanish Civil War: "This Ain't Ethiopia, but It'll Do".* New York: G.K.Hall, 1992.

Cox, Clinton. *Undying Glory: The Story of the Massachusetts 54th Regiment.* New York: Scholastic, Inc., 1991.

Donaldson, Gary. *The History of African-Americans in the Military: Double V.* Malabar, FL: Krieger Publishing Co., 1991.

Gooding, James Henry. *On the Alter of Freedom: A Black Soldier's Civil War Letters from the Front.* Edited by Virginia Matzke Adams. Amherst: University of Massachusetts Press, 1991.

Johnson, Charles. *African American Soldiers in the National Guard: Recruitment and Deployment During Peacetime and War.* New York: Greenwood Press, 1992.

Redkey, Edwin S., ed. *A Grand Army of Black Men: Letters from African-American Soldiers in the Union Army.* New York: Cambridge University Press, 1992.

Music

Allen, Ray. *Singing in the Spirit: African-American Sacred Quartets in New York City.* Philadelphia: University of Pennsylvania Press, 1991.

Boggs, Vernon W. *Salsiology: Afro-Cuban Music and the Evolution of Salsa in New York City.* Westport, CT: Greenwood Press, 1992.

Booth, Stanley. *Rhythm Oil: A Journey Through the Music of the American South.* New York: Pantheon, 1991.

Cantor, Louis. *Wheelin' on Beale.* Foreword by B.B. King. New York: Pharos, 1992.

Costello, Mark, and David Foster Wallace. *Signifying Rappers: Rap and Race in the Urban Present.* New York: Ecco Press, 1990.

Donovan, Richard X. *Black Musicians of America.* Portland, OR: National Book Co., 1991.

Finn, Julio. *The Bluesman: The Musical Heritage of Black Men and Women in the Americas.* New York: Interlink Books, 1991.

Floyd, Samuel A., ed. *Black Music in the Harlem Renaissance: A Collection of Essays.* Westport, CT: Greenwood Press, 1990.

Friedwall, Will. *Jazz Singing: America's Great Voices from Bessie Smith to Bebop and Beyond.* New York: Scribner's, 1990.

Harris, Michael W. *The Rise of Gospel Blues: The Music of Thomas Andrew Dorsey in the Urban Church.* New York: Oxford University Press, 1992.

Horne, Aaron, comp. *Keyboard Music of Black Composers: A Bibliography.* Westport, CT: Greenwood Press, 1992.

Horne, Aaron, comp. *String Music of Black Composers: A Bibliography.* Westport, CT: Greenwood Press, 1991.

Horne, Aaron. comp. *Woodwind Music of Black Composers* Westport, CT: Greenwood Press, 1990.

Jackson, John A. *Big Beat Heat: Alan Freed and the Early Years of Rock & Roll.* New York: Schirmer/Macmillan, 1991.

Merrill, Hugh. *The Blues Route.* New York: Morrow, 1990.

Morgan, Thomas L. *From Cakewalk to Concert Hall: An Illustrated History of African American Popular Music from 1895 to 1930.* Washington, DC: Elliott & Clark Publishers, 1992.

Morton, David C. and Charles K. Wolfe. *DeFord Bailey: A Black Star in Early Country Music.* Knoxville: University of Tennessee Press, 1991.

Peretti, Burton W. *The Creation of Jazz: Music, Race and Culture in Urban America.* Urbana: University of Illinois Press, 1992.

Perry, Frank. *Afro-American Vocal Music: A Select Guide to Fifteen Composers.* Berrien Springs, MD: Vande Verde Publishers, 1991.

Porter, Lewis, ed. *A Lester Young Reader.* Washington, DC: Smithsonian Institution Press, 1991.

Price, Sammy. *What Do They Want: A Jazz Autobiography.* Edited by Caroline Richmond. Chronological discography compiled by Bob Weir. Urbana: University of Illinois Press, 1990.

Roach, Hildred. *Black American Music Past and Present: Pan-African Composers.* 2nd ed., Malabar, FL: Kruger, 1992.

Rosenthal, David H. *Hard Bop: Jazz and Black Music, 1955-1965.* New York: Oxford University Press, 1992.

Scott, Frank. *The Down Home Guide to the Blues.* Pennington, NJ: A Capella Books, 1990.

Spencer, Jon Michael, ed. *The Emergency Black and the Emergence of Rap.* Durham: Duke University Press, 1991.

Spencer, Jon Michael, ed. *Sacred Music of the Secular City: From Blues to Rap.* Durham: Duke University Press, 1992.

Story, Rosalyn. *And So I Sing: African American Divas of Opera and Concert.* New York: Warner Books, 1990.

Tate, Greg. *Flyboy in the Buttermilk: Essays on Contemporary America.* New York: Simon and Schuster, 1992.

Turner, Patricia. *Dictionary of Afro-American Performers: 78 RPM and Cylinder Recordings of Opera, Choral Music and Song, ca. 1900-1949.* New York: Garland, 1990.

Walker-Hill, Helen. *Piano-Music by Black Women Composers: A*

Catalogue of Solo and Ensemble Works. New York: Greenwood Press, 1992.

Wright, Josephine, and Samuel A. Floyd, Jr., eds. *New Perspectives on Music: Essays in Honor of Eileen Southern.* Warren, MI: Harmonie Park Press, 1992.

Performing Arts

Adamczke, Alice J. *Black Dance: An Annotated Bibliography.* New York: Garland Publishing Co., 1990.

Ely, Melvin Patrick. *The Adventures of Amos 'n' Andy: A Social History of an American Phenomenon.* New York: Free Press, 1991.

Gray, John, comp. *Black Theatre and Performance: A PanAfrican Bibliography.* Westport, CT: Greenwood Press, 1990.

Gray, John, comp. *Blacks in Film and Television: A Pan-African Bibliography of Films, Filmmakers, and Performers.* Westport, CT: Greenwood Press, 1990.

Hansberry, Lorraine. *A Raisin in the Sun: The Unfilmed Original Screenplay.* Edited by Robert Nemiroff. Foreword by Jewell Gres. Afterword by Spike Lee. New York: Dutton, 1992.

Hughes, Langston, and Zora Neale Hurston. *Mule Bone: A Comedy of Negro Life.* Edited by George H. Bass and Henry L. Gates. New York: Harper Collins, 1991.

Jhally, Sut, and Justin Lewis. *Enlightened Racism: The Cosby Show, Audiences, and the Myth of the American Dream.* Boulder, CO: Westview Press, 1992.

Jones, G. William. *Black Cinema Treasurey: Lost and Found.* Denton, TX: University of North Texas Press, 1991.

Klotman, Phyllis Rauch, ed. *Screenplays of the African American Experience.* Bloomington: Indiana University Press, 1991.

Mapp, Edward. *Directory of Blacks in the Performing Arts.* 2nd ed., Metuchen, NJ: Scarecrow Press, 1990.

Politics

Barker, Lucius J., ed. *Ethnic Politics and Civil Liberties.* New Brunswick, NJ: Transaction Books, 1992.

Clavel, Pierre, and Wim Wiewel, eds. *Harold Washington and the Neighborhoods: Progressive City Government in Chicago, 1983-1987.* New Brunswick, NJ: Rutgers University Press, 1991.

Gomes, Ralph C., and Linda Faye Williams eds. *From Exclusion to Inclusion: The Long Struggle for African American Political Power.* Westport, CT: Greenwood Press, 1992.

Henry, Charles P. *Culture and African American Politics.* Bloomington: Indiana University Press, 1990.

Henry, Charles P. *Jesse Jackson: The Search for Common Ground.* Oakland, CA: Black Scholar Press, 1990.

Jennings, James. *The Politics of Black Empowerment: The Transformation of Black Activism in Urban America.* Detroit: Wayne State University Press, 1992.

Joint Center for Political and Economic Studies. *Black Elected Officials: A National Roster.* Washington, DC: Joint Center for Political and Economic Studies Press, 19–.

Kimball, Penn. *Keep Hope Alive: Super Tuesday and Jesse Jackson's 1988 Campaign for the Presidency.* Washington, DC: Joint Center for Political and Economic Studies, 1992.

Lawson, Steven. *Running for Freedom: Civil Rights and Black Politics in America Since 1941.* Philadelphia: Temple University Press, 1990.

Marable, Manning. *The Crisis of Color and Democracy: Essays on Race, Class and Power.* Monroe, ME: Common Courage Press, 1992.

McCartney, John T. *Black Power Ideologies: An Essay in African American Political Thought.* Philadelphia: Temple University Press, 1992.

Natanson, Nicholas. *The Black Image in the New Deal: The Politics of FSA.* Knoxville: University of Tennessee Press, 1992.

Orfield, Gar, and Carole Ashkinaze. *The Closing Door: Conservative Policy and Black Opportunity.* Chicago: University of Chicago Press, 1991.

Parker, Frank R. *Black Votes Count: Political Empowerment in Mississippi After 1965.* Chapel Hill: University of North Carolina Press, 1990.

Rees, Matthew. *From the Deck to the Sea: Blacks and the Republican Party.* Wakefield, NH: Longwood Press, 1991.

Rivlin, Gar. *Fire on the Prairie: Chicago's Harold Washington and the Politics of Race.* New York: Holt, 1992.

Van DeBurg, William L. *New Day in Babylon: The Black Power Movement and American Culture.* Chicago: University of Chicago Press, 1992.

Race Relations

Brady, Paul L. *A Certain Blindness: A Black Family's Quest for the Promise of America.* Atlanta: ALP Publishers, 1990.

Brooks, Roy L. *Rethinking the American Race Problem.* Berkeley: University of California, 1991.

Collier, Peter, ed. *Second Thoughts About Race in America.* Lanham, MD: Madison Books, 1991.

Crouch, Stanley. *Notes of a Hanging Judge: Essays and Reviews.* New York: Oxford University Press, 1990.

Davis, F. James. *Who Is Black: One Nation's Definition.* University Park: Pennsylvania State University Press, 1991.

DeSantis, John. *For the Color of His Skin: The Murder of Yusuf Hawkins and the Trial of the Bensonhurst.* Introduction by Alan M. Dershowitz. New York: Pharos Books, 1991.

Essed, Philomena. *Understanding Racism: An Interdisciplinary Theory.* Newbury Park, CA: Sage, 1991.

Hacker, Andrew. *Two Nations: Black and White, Separate, Hostile, Unequal.* New York: Scribner's, 1992.

Horowitz, Irving Louis. *Daydreams and Nightmares: Reflections on a Harlem Childhood.* Jackson: University Press of Mississippi, 1990.

Hynes, Charles J., and Bob Drury. *Incident at Howard Beach: The Case for Murder.* New York: Putnam, 1990.

Leiman, Melvin M. *Racism in the U.S.A.: History and Political Economy.* Concord, MA: Paul & Co., 1992.

Lewis, Earl. *In Their own Interests: Race, Class, and Power in Twentieth-Century Nolf, Virginia.* Berkeley: University of California Press, 1991.

McFadden, Robert, et. al. *Outrage: The Story Behind the Tawana Brawley Hoax.* New York: Bantam, 1990.

Pemberton, Gayle. *The Hottest Water in Chicago: One Family, Race, Time and American Culture.* Winchester, MA: Faber & Faber, 1992.

Perlmutter, Philip. *Divided We Fall: A History of Ethnic, Religious, and Racial Prejudice in America.* Ames: Iowa State University Press, 1992.

Rasberry, William. *Looking Backward at Us.* Jackson: University Press of Mississippi, 1991.

Salzman, Jack, ed. *Bridges and Boundaries: African Americans and American Jews.* New York: Braziller, 1992.

Steele, Shelby. *The Contest of Our Character: A New Vision of Race in America.* New York: St. Martin's Press, 1990.

Stepan, Nancy Leys. *The Hour of Eugenics: Race, Gender, and Nation.* Ithaca, NY: Cornell University Press, 1991.

Terkel, Studs. *Race: How Blacks and Whites Think and Feel About the American Obsession.* New York: New Press/Norton, 1992.

Welch, Susan, and Lee Sigelman. *Black America's Views of Racial Equality: The Dream Deferred., New York: Cambridge University Press, 1991.*

Zegeye, Abebe, ed. Exploitation and Exclusion: Race and Class in Contemporary U.S. Society. London: Hans Zell Publishers, 1991.

Zweigenhaft, Richard L., and G. William Domhoff. *Blacks in the White Establishment: A Study of Race and Class in America.* New Haven, CT: Yale University Press, 1991.

Religion and Philosophy

Baer, Hans, and Merrill Singer. *African-American Religion in the Twentieth Century: Varieties of Protest and Accommodation.* Knoxville: University of Tennessee, 1992.

Davis, Lenwood G. *Daddy Grace: An Annotated Bibliography.* New York: Greenwood Press, 1992.

Dvorak, Katherine L. *An African-American Exodus: the Segregation of Southern Churches.* With preface by Jerald C. Brauer. Brooklyn, NY: Carlson Publishing Co., 1991.

Harris, Leonard, ed. *The Philosophy of Alain Locke.* Philadelphia: Temple University Press, 1990.

Haynes, Lemuel. *Black Preacher to White America: the Collected Writings of Lemuel Haynes, 1774-1833.* Edited by Richard Newman. New York: Carlson Publishing Co., 1990.

Hopkins, Dwight N., and George C.L. Cummings, eds. *Cut Loose*

Your Stammering Tongue: Black Theology in the Slave Narratives. Maryknoll, NY: Orbis Books, 1991.

Howard, Victor B. *Conscience and Slavery: the Evangelistic Calvinistic Domestic Missions, 1837-1861.* Kent, OH: Kent State University Press, 1990.

Irvin, Dona L. *The Unsung Heart of Black America: A Middle-Class Church at Midcentury.* Columbia: University of Missouri Press, 1992.

Jacobs, Claude F., and Andrew J. Kaslow. *The Spiritual Churches of New Orleans: Origins, Beliefs and Rituals of an African-American Religion.* Knoxville: University of Tennessee Press, 1991.

Johnson, John L. *Black Biblical Heritage.* Nashville: Winston-Derek Publishers, 1990.

Lincoln, C. Eric, and Lawrence H. Mamiya. *The Black Church in the American Experience.* Durham: Duke University Press, 1990.

Martin, Sandy D. *Black Baptists and African Missions: the Origins of a Movement, 1880-1915.* Macon: Mercer University Press, 1990.

Ochs, Stephen J. *Desegregating the Alter: The Josephites and the Struggle for Black Priests, 1871-1960.* Baton Rouge: Louisiana State University Press, 1990.

Payne, Wardell J., ed. *Directory of African American Religious Bodies: A Compendium by the Howard University School of Divinity.* Prepared under the auspices of the Research Center on Black Religious Bodies, Howard University School of Divinity. Washington, DC: Howard University Press, 1991.

Seymour, Robert E. *Whites Only: A Pastor's Retrospective on Signs of a New South.* Valley Forge, PA: Judson Press, 1991.

Spencer, Jon Michael. *Black Hymnody: A Hymnological History of the African-American Church.* Knoxville: University of Tennessee Press, 1992.

Spencer, Jon Michael. *Protest and Praise: Sacred Music of Black Religion.* Minneapolis: Augsburg Fortress Publishers, 1990.

Walker, Theodore, Jr. *Empower the People: Social Ethics for the African-American Church.* Maryknoll, NY: Orbis Books, 1991.

Walker, Wyatt Tee. *Spirits That Dwell in Deep Woods III: The Prayer and Praise Hymns of the Black Religious Experience.* New York: Martin Luther King Press, 1991.

Wood, Forrest G. *The Arrogance of Faith: Christianity and Race in America from the Colonial Era to the Twentieth Century.* New York: Knopf, 1990.

Sociology and Psychology

Andersen, Margaret L. *Race, Class and Gender: An Anthology.* Belmont, CA: Wadsworth Publishing Co., 1992.

Anderson, Elijah. *Streetwise: Race, Class and Social Change in an Urban Community.* Chicago: University of Chicago Press, 1990.

Baer, Hans, and Yvonne Jones, eds. *African Americans in the South: Issues of Race, Class and Gender.* Athens: University of Georgia Press, 1992.

Benjamin, Lois. *The Black Elite: Facing the Color Line in the Twentieth Century.* Chicago: Nelson-Hall, 1991.

Billingsley, Andrew. *Climbing Jacob's Ladder: The Future of*

the African-American Family New York: Simon and Schuster, 1991.

Blackwell, James Edward. *The Black Community: Diversity and Unity.* 3rd ed., New York: Harper Collins, 1991.

Bowser, Benjamin, ed. *Black Male Adolescents: Parenting and Education in Community Context.* Latham, MD: University Press of America, 1991.

Consortium for Research on Black Adolescence Staff and Patricia Bell-Scott. *Black Adolescence: Current Issues and Annotated Bibliography.* Boston: G.K. Hall, 1990.

Edelman, Marian Wright. *The Measure of Our Success: A Letter to My Children and Yours.* Boston: Beacon Press, 1992.

Hay, Fred J. *African-American Community Studies from North America. A Classified, Annotated Bibliography.* New York: Garland, 1991.

Hopson, Darlene, and Derek Hopson. *Different and Wonderful: Raising Black Children in a Race Conscious Society.* New York: Simon and Schuster, 1992.

Jones, Howard, and Wanda Jones. *Heritage and Hope: The Legacy and Future of the Black Family in America.* Wheaton, IL: Victor Books, 1992.

Kunjufu, Jawanza. *Countering the Conspiracy to Destroy Black Boys.* Chicago: African American Images, 1990.

Leigh, Wilhemina A., ed. *The Housing Status of Black Americans.* New Brunswick, NJ: Transaction Books, 1992.

Lemann, Nicholas. *The Promised Land: The Great Black Migration and How It Changed America.* New York: Knopf, 1991.

Platat, Anthony M. *E. Franklin Frazier Reconsidered.* New Brunswick, NJ: Rutgers University Press, 1991.

Trotter, Joe William, ed. *The Great Migration in Historical Perspective: New Dimensions of Race, Class and Gender.* Bloomington: Indiana University Press, 1991.

Sports

Cooper, Michael L. *Playing America's Game: The Story of Negro League Baseball.* New York: Lodestar Books, 1993.

Page, James A. *Black Olympian Medalists.* Englewood, CO: Libraries Unlimited, 1991.

Women

Alexander, Adele Logan. *Free Women of Color in Rural Georgia, 1789-1879.* Fayetteville: University of Arkansas Press, 1991.

Baker, Houston A. *Working of the Spirit: The Poetics of Afro-American Women's Writings.* Chicago: University of Chicago Press, 1991.

The Black Women Oral History Project. *Guide to the Transcripts.* Edited by Ruth E. Hill. Westport, CT: Meckler, 1991.

Braxton, Joanne M. *Black Women Writing Autobiography: A Tradition Within a Tradition.* Philadelphia: Temple University Press, 1990.

Braxton, Joanne M., and Andree Nicola McLaughlin, eds. *Wild Women in the Whirlwind: Afro-American Culture and the Contemporary Literary Renaissance.* New Brunswick, NJ: Rutgers University Press, 1990.

Brown, Karen McCarthy. *Mama Lola: A Voodoo Priestess in Brooklyn.* Berkeley, University of California Press, 1991.

Brown-Guillory, Elizabeth, ed., and comp. *Wines in the Wilderness: Plays by African American Women from the Harlem Renaissance to the Present.* Westport, CT: Greenwood Press, 1990.

Bundles, A'Lelia Perry. *Madam C. J. Walker.* New York: Chelsea House, 1991.

Busby, Margaret, ed. *Daughters of Africa: An International Anthology of Words and Writings by Women of African Descent; From the Ancient World to Present.* New York: Pantheon, 1992.

Butler-Evans, Elliott. *Race, Gender, and Desire: Narrative Strategies in the Fiction of Toni Cade Bambara, Toni Morrison, and Alice Walker.* Philadelphia: Temple University Press, 1990.

Caraway, Nancie. *Segregated Sisterhood: Racism and the Politics of American Feminism.* Knoxville: University of Tennessee Press, 1991.

Celsi, Teresa N. *Rosa Parks and the Montgomery Bus Boycott.* Brookfield, CT: Millbrook Press, 1991.

Crawford, Vicki L. Crawford, Jacqueline Anne Reese, and Barbara Woods, eds. *Women in the Civil Rights Movement: Trailblazers and Torchbears, 1941-1965.* Brooklyn, NY: Carlson Publishing Co., 1990. (*Black Women in United States History*, vol. 16.)

Davis, Michael D. *Black American Women in Olympic Track and Field: A Complete Illustrated Reference.* Jefferson, NC: McFarland, 1992.

Gates, Henry Louis, Jr. *Reading Black, Reading Feminist.* New York: Meridan, 1991.

Glassman, Steve, and Kathryn Lee Seidel, eds. *Zora in Florida.* Gainesville: University Presses of Florida, 1991.

Guy-Sheftall, Beverly. *Daughters of Sorrow: Attitudes Toward Black Women.* New York: Carlson Publishing Co., 1990. (*Black Women in United States History*, vol. II.)

Guy, Sheftall, Beverly. *Words of Fire: An Anthology of African American Feminist Thought.* New Press, 1995.

Harris, Trudier. *Fiction and Folklore: The Novels of Toni Morrison.* Knoxville: University of Tennessee Press, 1991.

Hine, Darlene Clark, ed. *Black Women in American History, From Colonial Times Through the Nineteenth Century.* Brooklyn, NY: Carlson Publishing Co., 1990.

Hooks, Bell. *Black Looks: Race and Representation.* Boston: South End Press, 1992.

Ihle, Elizabeth L., ed. *Black Women in Higher Education: An Anthology of Essays, Studies and Documents.* New York: Garland Publishing Co., 1992.

Jackson, Carlton. *Hattie: The Life of Hattie McDaniel.* Lantham, MD: Madison Books, 1990.

Jones, Adrienne Lash. *Jane Edna Hunter: A Case Study of Black Leadership.* Brooklyn, NY: Carlson Publishing Co., 1990.

(*Black Women in United States History*, vol. 12)

Jones, Beverly Washington. *Quest for Equality: The Life and Writing of Mary Eliza Church Terrell, 1863-1954.* Brooklyn, NY: Carlson Publishing Co., 1990. (*Black Women in United States History*, vol. 13.)

Kent, George E. *A Life of Gwendolyn Brooks.* Lexington: University of Kentucky Press, 1990.

King, Joyce Elaine, and Carolyn Ann Mitchell. *Black Mothers to Sons: Juxtaposing African American Literature and the Social Practice.* New York: Peter Lang, 1990.

Kubitschek, Missy Dehn. *Claiming the Heritage: African-American Women Novelists and History.* Oxford: University Press of Mississippi, 1991.

Mabalia, Dorethea Drummond, *Toni Morrison's Developing Class*

Consciousness. Cranbury, NJ: Susquehanna University

Press/Associated University Presses, 1991.

Morton, Patricia. *Disfigured Images: The Historical Assault on Afro-American Women.* Westport, CT: Greenwood Press, 1991.

Nathiri, N.Y., ed. *Zora! Zora Neale Hurston: A Woman and Her Community.* Orlando, FL: Sentinel Books, 1991.

Neverdon-Morton, Cynthia. *Afro-American Women of the South and the Advancement of the Race, 1895-1925.* Knoxville:. University of Tennessee Press, 1990.

Otfinoski, Steven. *Marian Wright Edelman—Defender of Children's Rights.* New York: Rosen Publishing Group, 1991.

Reckley, Ralph. *Twentieth Century Black Women in Print: Essays.* Acton, MA: Copley Publishers, 1991.

Roses, Lorraine Elena, and Ruth Elizabeth Randolph. *Harlem Renaissance and Beyond: Literary Biographies of 100 Black Women Writers, 1900-1945.* Boston: G.K. Hall, 1990.

Salem, Dorothy. *To Better Our World: Black Women in Organized Reform.* Brooklyn, NY: Carlson Publishing Co., 1990. (*Black Women in United States History*, vol. 14.)

Samuels, Wilfred D., and Clenora Hudson-Weems. *Toni Morrison.* Boston: G.K. Hall, 1990.

Scott, Kesho Yvonne. *The Habit of Surviving: Black Women's Strategies for Life.* New Brunswick, NJ: Rutgers University Press, 1991.

Smith, Jesse Carney, ed. *Notable Black American Women.* Detroit: Gale Research Inc., 1991.

Smith, Rita Webb, and Tony Chapelle. *The Woman Who Took Back Her Streets: One Woman Fights the Drug*

Wars and Rebuilds Her Community. Far Hill, NJ: New Horizon, 1991.

Thompson, Mildred I. *Ida B. Wells-Barnett: An Exploratory Study of An American Black Woman, 1893-1930.* Brooklyn, NY: Carlson Publishing Co., 1990. (*Black Women in United States History*, vol. 15)

Walker, Melissa. *Down From the Mountaintop: Black Women's Novels in the Wake of the Civil Rights Movement, 1966-1989.* New Haven, CT: Yale University Press, 1991.

Walker, Robbie Jean, ed. *The Rhetoric of Struggle: Public Addresses by African American Women.* New York: Garland Publishing Co., 1992.

Werner, Craig. *Black American Women Novelists: An Annotated Bibliography.* Englewood Cliffs, NJ: Salem Press, 1990.

Williams, Constance Willard. *Black Teenage Mothers: Pregnancy and Child Rearing from Their Perspective.* Lexington, MA: Lexington Books, 1991.

Woody, Bette. *Black Women in the Workplace: Impacts of Structural Change in the Economy.* Westport, CT: Greenwood Press, 1992.

Yee, Shirley J. *Black Women Abolitionists: A Study in Activism, 1828-1860.* Knoxville: University of Tennessee Press, 1992.

Picture and Text Credits

Photo and Text Credits

Photographs

Courtesy of ABC Records/Ron Rogers, used with permission: p. 931 (King, B. B., performing). **Courtesy of ABC-TV:** p. 739 (Goode, Mal, photograph). **A. Phillip Randolph Institute,** used with permission: p. 375 (African Americans in front of Voter Registration Headquarters, photograph). **AP/Wide World Photos,** reproduced by permission: pp. 29 (Randolph, Asa Philip, photograph); 33 (Segregation sign "White Waiting Room", photograph); 36 (Parks, Rosa, being fingerprinted, photograph); 39 (Student sit-in , Atlanta, GA, photograph); 49 (1967 Detroit Riots, aerial view, photograph); 51 (King, Martin Luther, Jr., King's funeral, photograph); 57 (J. Bruce Llewellyn); 58 (Chisholm, Shirley, photograph); 61 (Bakke Decision March, photograph); 67 (Hooks, Benjamin L., photograph); 67 (Wilson, Margaret Bush, speaking, photograph); 70 (Black leaders urging sanctions against South Africa, photograph); 75 (Wilder, Lawrence Douglas, photograph); 78 (Powell, Colin, visiting troops during Gulf War, photograph); 82 (Brown, Jesse L., Clinton, Bill, photograph); 95 (*U.S.S. Harmon,* photograph); 96 (Campanella, Roy, photograph); 102 (Alexander, Clifford, photograph); 102 (Harris, Patricia Roberts, photograph); 103 (Dinkins, David, photograph); 103 (Wilder, Lawrence, photograph); 104 (Mosely-Braun, Carol, at Democratic Convention, photograph); 125 (Frederick Douglass); 136 (Ku Klux Klan, cross burning, photograph); 141 (Segregation sign, man placing segregation sign, photograph; 152 (Federal troops escorting four black students, photograph); 160 (Johnson, Lyndon B., photograph); 175 (Tuskegee Institute, view of chapel, photograph); 176 (Central High School, Little Rock, AR, photograph); 183 (Ebenezer Baptist Church, photograph); 188 (Attucks, Crispus, photograph); 193 (Lincoln University, photograph); 196 (Abysinnian Baptist Church, photograph); 197 (Apollo Theater, photograph); 207 (Harper's Ferry National Park, photograph); 302 (Douglass, Frederick, photograph); 316 (Civil Rights Protest in Birmingham, AL, photograph); 317 (Rustin, Bayard, photograph); 318 (Rights Protest in Birmingham, AL, photograph); 321 (King, Martin Luther, Jr., riding on bus, photograph); 322 (Bates, Daisy, photograph); 322 (Carmichael, Stokley, photograph); 325 (Evers, Medgar, photograph); 326 (Hamer, Fannie Lou, photograph); 328 (Coretta Scott King); 330 (King, Martin Luther, Jr., with group of people, photograph); 334 (Sharpton, Al, photograph); 349 (Farrakhan, Louis, photograph); 361 (King, Martin Luther, Jr., facing microphone, photograph); 362 (Chavis, Benjamin Franklin, Jr., photograph); 363 (Carmichael, Stokley, photograph); 364 (Seale, Bobby, photograph); 365 (Robinson, Randall, with Nelson Mandela, photograph); 366 (Chavis, Benjamin Franklin, Jr., photograph); 367 (Farmer, James, photograph); 369 (Hooks, Benjamin L., photograph); 370 (Innis, Roy, photograph); 371 (Jacob, John E., photograph); 372 (Jordan, Vernon E., Jr., photograph); 373 (Lowery, Joseph E., photograph); 376 (Robinson, Randall, photograph); 421 (Thomas, Clarence, photograph); 437 (Busing Protests/ Segregation Ends, photograph); 438 (Lunch counter sit-in, photograph); 439 (Lewis, Woodrow T., with Albert L. Dunn, photograph); 425 (Segregation sign at Rail-

Michael, photograph); 978 (Jones, Quincy, photograph); 981 (Knight, Gladys, with Pips, photograph); 983 (Little Richard, clapping and singing, photograph); 984 (Pride, Charley, photograph); 985 (Prince, photograph); 988 (Ross, Diana, with the Supremes, photograph); 989 (Turner, Tina, photograph); 990 (Wilson, Jackie, photograph); 993 (Wonder, Stevie, photograph); 1010 (Barthe, Richmond, photograph); 1014 (Blackburn, Robert, photograph); 1017 (DeCarava, Roy); 1030 (Perkins, Marion, photograph); 1037 (Van der Zee, James, photograph); 1058 (Percy, Julian, holding beaker, photograph); 1062 (Bluford, Guion, photograph); 1065 (Bolden, Charles, Frank, Jr., photograph); 1074 (Lawrence, Robert H., Jr., photograph); 1076 (McNair, Ronald, photograph); 1076 (Morgan, Garrett A., photograph); 1087 (Dickerson, Eric, photograph); 1088 (Frazier, Joe, photograph); 1089 (Hagler, Marvin, photograph); 1090 (Abdul-Jabbar, Kareem, shooting basketball, photograph); 1090 (Jordan, Michael, photograph); 1092 (Joyner, Florence Griffith, in Olympic uniform, photograph); 1093 (Gibson, Althea, photograph); 1094 (Aaron, Hank, photograph); 1095 (Abdul-Jabbar, Kareem, ceremony with Governor, photograph); 1096 (Armstrong, Henry, photograph); 1100 (Chamberlain, Wilt, photograph); 1100 (Elder, Lee, photograph); 1102 (Gibson, Althea, photograph); 1104 (Jackson, Reggie, photograph); 1106 (Jordan, Michael, photograph); 1106 (Joyner, Florence Griffith, photograph); 1111 (Owens, Jesse, photograph); 1114 (Joyner, Florence Griffith, and Wilma Rudolph, photograph); 1115 (Russell, Bill, photograph); 1116 (Simpson, O. J., photograph); 1117 (White, Bill, photograph); 1118 (Stargell, Willie, photograph); 1119 (Joiner, Charlie, photograph); 1119 (Owens, Jesse, broad jumping, photograph); 1136 (Anderson, James, Jr., parents of, photograph); 1152 (Davison, F.-Brig. General, photograph); 1153 (Powell, Colin at Vietnam War Memorial, photograph); 1158 (James, Daniel "Chappie", photograph); 1159 (Johnson, Hazel, photograph); 1161 (Powell, Colin, with Kristen Baker, photograph). **Archive Photos, Inc.,** used with permission: pp. 305 (Truth, Sojourner, photograph); 343 (Delaney, Martin R., photograph); 345 (Malcolm X at black Muslim gathering, photograph); 352 (Muhammad, Elijah, photograph); 353 (Henry McNeal Turner); 489 (Dinkins, David, photograph); 663 (Baptism on the Potomac, photograph); 845 (McQueen, Butterfly); 850 (Roundtree, Richard, photograph); 856 (Washington, Denzel, kneeling in Mosque); 883 (Kay, Ulysses); 893 (Still, William Grant, photograph). **Archive Photos/Frank Driggs Collection,** reproduced by permission: p. 953 (Jordan, Louis, photograph). **Archive Photos/Lass,** used with permission: p. 11 (Blacks weighing cotton, photograph). **Courtesy of Molefi Kete Asante:** p. 630 (Molefi Kete Asante). **Courtesy of Associated Publishers:** p. 757 (Murphy, John Henry, photograph). **Bahama News Bureau:** p. 261 (Nassau Police Band, photograph). **Bettmann,** used with permission: pp. 5 (African slaves arrive on the shores of America); 44 (Selma to Montgomery march, photograph); 45 (Marshall, Thurgood, with Javits and Kennedy, photograph); 46 (Watts Riot, 1965, photograph); 50 (Johnson, Lyndon B., photograph); 80 (National Guards in front of grafitti covered building, photograph); 100 (Motley, Constance Baker, photograph); 124 (Slave Auction, photograph); 324 (DuBois, W. E. B., photograph); 329 (McKissick, Floyd B., photograph); 417 (Marshall, Thurgood, photograph); 479 (Brown, Ron, photograph); 571 (Beckwourth, Jim); 627 (Busing-Woodville, Mississippi, photograph); 666 (Worshipers of the Pentacostal denomination); 676 (Muhammad, Elijah, speaking into microphone, photograph); 685 (Marino, Eugene, photograph); 883 (Joplin, Scott, photograph); 925 (Handy, W. C., photograph);1057 (Carver, George Washington, photograph); 1026 (Lawarence, Jacob, photograph); 1079 (Williams, Daniel Hale, photograph); 1108 (Louis, Joe, photograph). **The Bettmann Archive,** reproduced with permission: pp. 38 (Federal troops escorting black students, photograph); 40 (Freedom Riders, photograph); 41 (Shabazz, Betty, photograph); 52 (Resurrection City, Washington, DC, photograph); 66 (Washington, Harold, in office, photograph); 81 (Brown, Ron, photograph); 138 (Washington, Booker T., photograph); 167 (Height, Dorothy, with George Bush, photograph); 298 (Lincoln, Abraham, photograph); 315 (DuBois, W. E. B., photograph); 320 (Abernathy, Ralph, Rev., photograph); 323 (Davis, Angela, press conference, photograph); 333 (King, Martin Luther, Jr., crowd of people at funeral); 344 (Garvey, Marcus, photograph); 365 (Brown, H. Rap, photograph); 369 (Height, Dorothy, photograph); 374 (Newton, Huey P., photograph); 377 (Seale, Bobby, photograph); 429 (Black school room in Missouri, c. 1930, photograph); 450 (Higginbotham, A. Leon, photograph); 466 (Waters, Maxine, speaking at conference, photograph); 474 (Bradley, Thomas, photograph); 475 (Moseley-Braun, Carol, photograph); 478 (Bond, Julian, photograph); 490 (Dixon, Sharon Pratt, photograph); 549 (Female firefighter, photograph); 687 (Powell, Adam Clayton, Sr., at pulpit, photograph); 755 (Johnson, John H., photograph); 817 (Hines, Gregory, with brother Maurice, photograph); 840 (Ingram, Rex, photograph); 858 (Williams, Bert, photograph); 873 (Coleridge, Samuel Taylor, photograph); 903 (Henderson, Fletcher, portrait standing); 904 (Eldridge, Roy, with Ella Fitzgerald, photograph); 926 (Henderson, Fletcher, photograph); 944 (Waller, Thomas "Fats", photograph); 986 (Redding, Otis, photograph); 1029 (Motley, Archibald, photograph); 1030 (Parks, Gordon, photograph); 1035 (Smith, Willi, photograph); 1085 (Gibson, Josh, photograph); 1091 (Ashe, Arthur, photograph); 1160 (Petersen, Frank E., photograph); 1114 (Robinson, Jackie, photograph). **The Bettmann Archive/Newsphotos, Inc.,** used with permission: pp. 20 (Lincoln, Abraham, with Mathew

Brady, photograph); 43 (Malcolm X, at microphone, photograph); 48 (National Guard arrest three men, photograph); 55 (Protest against forced busing, Montgomery, AL, photograph); 64 (Pierce, Samuel R., photograph); 99 (Brooks, Gwendolyn, photograph); 101 (Marshall, Thurgood, photograph); 351 (Malcolm X, with hat and scarf, photograph); 430 (Busing-group of students, photograph); 455 (Marshall, Thurgood, in robes, photograph); 480 (Brown, Ron); 500 (Mitchell, Arthur W., seated, photograph); 542 (Assembly Line Worker, photograph); 886 (Mitchell, Leona, photograph); 935 (Mingus, Charles, photograph); 936 (Morton, Ferdinand "Jelly Roll", photograph). **Bettmann Newsphotos,** used with permission: pp. 443 (Firefighter in Miami, Florida, photograph); 578 (Sims, Naomi, photograph); 1105 (Johnson, Earvin "Magic," photograph). **(c) Bill Sparrow/*Encore Magazine:*** p. 378 (Wilkins, Roy, photograph). **Courtesy of Dave Bing:** p. 572 (Dave Bing). ***Black Enterprise Magazine,*** courtesy of: p. 754 (Graves, Earl G., photograph). **Black Entertainment Television,** p. 745 (Johnson, Robert L., photograph). **Burton Historical Collection/Detroit Public Library,** used with permission: p. 191 (Second Baptist Church, Detroit, MI, photograph). **Clement-Petrocik Company,** p. 268 (Guadeloupe, open air market, photograph). **Courtesy of Columbia Records:** p. 928 (Holiday, Billie, photograph). **Consulate General of Jamaica:** p. 145 (Garvey, Marcus, photograph). **(c) Darlene Hammond/Archive Photos,** used with permission: p. 860 (Winfrey, Oprah, photograph). **Courtesy of Denver Public Library:** p. 203 (Love, Nat, photograph). **Denver Public Library-Wester Collection:** p. 524 (Nicodemus, Kansas). **Ken Estell,** reproduced by permission: pp. 522 (Downtown Detroit, photograph); 523 (Men playing chess, photograph); 528 (Children playing with water hydrant, photograph); 529 (African American children with woman, photograph); 546 (Black family, photograph); 549 (Blue collar workers); 570 (Spight, Benita, photograph); 591 (African American boy with glasses, photograph). **Fairchild Publications:** p. 1009 (Burrows, Stephen). **Fisk University Library:** p. 580. **Courtesy of General Motors Public Relations,** used with permission: p. 1038 (1993 Oldsmobile Achieva SC, photograph). **Geoffrey Clements Photography,** used with permission: p. 1005 (Bearden, Romare "Eastern Barn,"). **Courtesy of Geoffrey Clements Photgraphy/Whitney Museum:** pp. 1004 (Jacob Lawrence's "Depression"); 1025 (Jacob Lawrence's "Tombstones"). **(c) Bruce Giffin,** used with permission: p. 629 (Malcolm X Academy school, photograph). **Courtesy of Hurok Attractions:** p. 869 (Anderson, Marian, photograph). **Courtesy of The John F. Kennedy Library:** p. 639 (Mays, Benjamin E., photograph). **Brian V. Jones:** pp. 585 (African American family); 586 (Extended family); 588 (Father with daughters). **(c) Faustine Jones-Wilson,** used with permission: pp. 584 (Black family-turn of the century-wedding, photograph. **Courtesy of The Library of Congress:** pp. 6 (Advertisement for a slave auction); 8 (Typical slave life, photograph); 11 (Jefferson, Thomas, photograph); 16 (Typical slave family, photograph); 17 (Scott, Dred, photograph); 34 (Lynching victim, man hanging in tree, photograph); 37 (Faubus, Orval, photograph); 41 (Wallace, George, photograph); 90 (Langston, John Mercer, photograph); 112 (Delegates meet to draft a national Constitution); 114 (Franklin, Benjamin, photograph); 116 (Slave Cell, photograph); 120 (*Liberator Newspaper, The,* photograph); 122 (Escaped slaves being returned, photograph); 125 (Douglass, Frederick, photograph); 130 (Lincoln, Abraham, seated with other men, photograph); 284 (Slaves and slave ships, photograph); 285 (Slave ship diagram); 286 (Slave catching apparatus, photograph); 287 (Attucks, Crispus, photograph); 289 (Slaves standing outside of slave quarters, photograph); 290 (Slave women sitting in pile of cotton, photograph); 292 (Slave catcher poster, photograph); 296 (Escaped slaves on the Underground Railway, photograph); 298 (Freed slaves leaving the South, photograph); 300 (Freed Man's Bureau poster, photograph); 301 (Typical rural residence, people outside of cabin, photograph); 305 (Tubman, Harriet, photograph); 312 (Douglass, Frederick); 314 (Colored Drinking Fountain, photograph); 331 (Martin Luther King, Jr.); 347 (Black Muslims, photograph); 347 (Blyden, Edward Wilmot, photograph.); 358 (DuBois, W. E .B., profile); 360 (Women laundry workers, photograph); 424 (Freed man being sold to pay his fine, photograph); 437 ("Colored Waiting Room," photograph); 508 (Smalls, Robert, photograph); 564 (Slaves picking cotton, photograph); 615 (Black segregated school, photograph); 617 (Black school children c. 1865, photograph); 618 (Freedman's school); 619 (Snow Hill Institute, photograph); 622 (Tuskegee Institute, photograph); 623 (Fisk University); 1067 (Carver, George Washington, photograph); 807 (Minstrel show poster, photograph); 1135 (Rifle company); 1138 (Troop H, 10th Cavalry, photograph). **Courtesy of The Library of Congress, Prints and Photographs Division:** pp. 31 (Klu Klux Klan, front view of march, photograph). **Courtesy of Helen Marcus:** p. 721 (Morrison, Toni, photograph). **Martha Swope Associates/Carol Rosegg:** p. 839 (Hyman, Earle, photograph). **Courtesy of National Archives:** pp. 919 (Europe, James Reese, photograph); 1156 (Flipper, Henry O., photograph). **NAACP,** used with permission: pp. 359 (NAACP office, 1945, photograph); 428 (Gaines, Lloyd, photograph). **National Museum of African Art:** p. 214 (Tuareg peoples, woman pounding grain, photograph); 221 (Kongo peoples, photograph); 227 (Koranic school in Chad, photograph); 245 (Laoye I, John Adetoyese, photograph); 258 (Mbuti people of Ituri Forest, Zaire, photograph); 260 (Man and oxcart, photograph). **National Museum of American Art/Art Resource:** p. 1000 (Edward Mitchell Bannister's

"Newspaper Boy"); 1023 (William H. Johnson's "Going to Chruch"); 1033 (Augusta Savage's "Gamin"). **National Park Service, Department of the Interior:** p. 180 (Douglass, Frederick, two story house, photograph). **National Portrait Gallery/Smithsonian,** used with permission: pp. 293 (Pennsylvania Abolition Society, photograph); 312 (Allen, Richard, photograph). **National Urban League:** p. 378 (Young, Whitney M., Jr., photograph). **NBC-TV,** used with permission: p. 1108 (Lewis, Carl, photograph). **Carl Nesfield,** courtesy of: p. 1096 (Clay, Cassius, photograph). ***New York Amsterdam News,*** used with permission: pp. 164 (Black Panthers demonstrating outside of courthouse, photograph); 332 (King, Martin Luther, Jr.); 362 (McKissick, Floyd B., photograph). ***New York Daily News,*** used with permission: p. 674 (Black Rabbi, photograph). **New York Historical Society:** p. 725 (Vassa, Gustavus, photograph). **New York Public Library Picture Collection,** reproduced by permission: pp. 312 (Allen, Richard, photograph); 662 (Allen, Richard, photograph); 941 (Smith, Bessie, photograph). **Andy Roy:** p. 565 (Freedom National Bank). **Courtesy of Ron Scherl:** p. 812 (Jones, James Earl, cast of "Fences," photograph). **Schomburg Center for Black Culture,** reproduced by permission: pp. 204 (Haley's boyhood home); 616 (New York African Free School No. 2, photograph); 696 (Fauset, Jessie, photograph); 837 (Horne, Lena, photograph); 863 (Jones, Matilda Sisieretta). **Stanley B. Burns, M.D. and the Burns Archive,** used with permission: pp. 524 (Rural black family in Savannah, GA, photograph); 664 (A.M.E. Church Reunion, photograph); 923 (Hampton, Lionel, photograph). **Susan Stetler:** pp. 545 (White collar worker); 551 (Woman using computer). **Tony Brown Productions, Inc.:** p. 744 (Brown, Tony, photograph). **Turner Broadcasting System Management:** p. 751. **United Nations:** pp. 212 (Pan-African Movement leaders); 220 (Angolans celebrating independence); 224 (Woman husking corn, photograph); 225 (Central Africa family, photograph); 226 (Rural farmers in Chad, photograph); 230 (Children in Equitorial Guinea, photograph); 231 (Selassie, Haile, photograph); 232 (Ethiopia, market, photograph); 233 (Cattleherders in rural Gambia, photograph); 234 (Jawara, Prime Minister, photograph); 236 (Masai tribesman, Kajiado, Kenya, photograph); 242 (Morocccan dancers, photograph); 245 (Minaret in Agadez, Niger, photograph); 249 (South African youths, photograph); 250 (South African children, photograph); 252 (South African village of Cross Roads, photograph); 253 (Swazi woman, South Africa, photograph); 256 (Togolese woman, photograph); 266 (Santo Domingo, Dominican Republic, photograph); 267 (Stevedores carrying bananas, photograph); 270 (Workers on banana plantation, photograph); 271 (Jamaican children, Hope Gardens, photograph); 273 (Nicaragua, open air market, photograph); 507 (Sampson, Edith, photograph). **UPI/Bettmann,** used with permission: pp. 29 (Scottsboro Boys, photograph); 32 (Marian Anderson); 206 (Washington, Booker T., boyhood home, photograph); 436 (Lunch counter sit-in, photograph); 711 (Haley, Alex, photograph); 845 (McDonald, Hattie); 1072 (Jemison, Mae C., photograph). **Courtesy of the U.S. Air Force:** p. 1155 (Davis, Benjamin O., Jr., photograph). **Courtesy of the U.S. Army:** p. 1143 (Davis, Benjamin O., Sr., photograph); 1144 (Davis, Benjamin O., Sr. pins medal on his son, photograph); 1146 (Soldiers from the 92nd Division, 1944, photograph); 1150 (Korean Conflict, photograph); 1156 (Davis, Benjamin O., Sr., portrait). **Courtesy of the U.S. Marine Corps:** p. 1151 (Cooper, Capt. Jerome, photograph); 1152 (Military officers). **Courtesy of the U.S. National Aeronautics and Space Administration:** pp. 550 (Caw, Lawrence, photograph). **Courtesy of the U.S. Navy:** p. 1153 (Winstead, John T., photograph); 1160 (Miller, Dorie, photograph). **Courtesy of the U.S. Senate Historical Office:** pp. 480 (Bruce, Blanche K., photograph); 506 (Revels, Hiram Rhodes, photograph). **U.S. Signal Corps-National Archives:** p. 23 (Freed slaves waiting for work opportunities, photograph); 1137 (Ninth U.S. Calvalry, 1889, photograph). **Walker Collection of A'Lelia Perry Bundles:** p. 567 (Madame C. J. Walker). **Courtesy of the U.S. War Department General Staff National Archives:** pp. 27 (Black soldiers leaving for war, photograph); 1140 (Black sailors, photograph). **The Washington Post Writers Group,** used with permission: p. 759 (Raspberry, William, photograph). **Alix B. Williamson:** p. 895 (Watts, Andre, photograph). **William Morris Agency:** p. 917 (Davis, Miles). **Edwin L. Wilson, Sr.:** p. 601 (Children playing basketball).

Text

Edward B. Marks Music Company, used by permission: "Lift Every Voice and Sing." **Reprinted by arrangement with The Heirs to the Estate of Martin Luther King, Jr., c/o Joan Daves Agency as agent for the proprietor; copyright 1963 by Martin Luther King, Jr., copyright renewed 1991 by Coretta Scott King:** "I Have a Dream." Copyright 1995 by University of Sankore Press: "Million Man March/Day of Absence Mission Statement."

Index

Index

A

B

C

D

E

F

G

H

I

J

K

L

M

N

O

P

Q

R

S

T

V

W

X

Y

Z